LIVING IN AMERICA

LIVING IN AMERICA
A Popular Culture Reader

Patricia Y. Murray
California State University, Northridge

Scott F. Covell
Antelope Valley College

Mayfield Publishing Company
Mountain View, California
London • Toronto

Copyright © 1998 by Mayfield Publishing Company

Library of Congress Cataloging-in-Publication Data

Murray, Patricia Y.
    Living in America : a popular culture reader / Patricia Y. Murray,
    Scott F. Covell.
       p.   cm.
    Includes index.
    ISBN 1-55934-977-8
    1. Minorities—United States—Social life and customs.   2. Popular
culture—United States—History—20th century.   3. Pluralism (Social
sciences—United States—History—20th century.   4. United States—
Social life and customs—1971–   5. American literature—Minority
authors.   I. Covell, Scott F.   II. Title.
E184.A1M894 1997
305.8'00973—DC21   97-29734
                                                    CIP

Manufactured in the United States of America

10   9   8   7   6   5   4   3   2   1

Mayfield Publishing Company
1280 Villa Street
Mountain View, CA 94041

Sponsoring editor, Renée Deljon; production editor, Julianna Scott Fein; manuscript editor, Shari Hatch; design manager, Jean Mailander; text and cover designer, Linda M. Robertson; cover art, Melissa Grimes; art manager, Amy Folden; manufacturing manager, Randy Hurst. The text was set in 10/12.5 Sabon by Archetype Book Composition and printed on acid-free 45# PennTech Penn Plus by R. R. Donnelley & Sons Company.

Acknowledgments and copyrights continue at the back of the book on pages 569–574, which constitute an extension of the copyright page.

 Printed on recycled paper.

CONTENTS

PREFACE

Living in America: A Popular Culture Reader offers short, manageable readings on topics that students are familiar with and interested in—and that have proven suitable for and effective in college and university writing courses. This text was conceived as an effort to fulfill at least two needs: first, that students need access to a reader that intrigues them with its interesting, even provocative, selections and that prompts them to investigate ideas further; and, second, that students need reading and writing instruction that motivates them to improve their language skills and exercise higher-level thinking. We therefore provide engaging, and often humorous, readings that will lead, along with their accompanying questions, to stimulating discussions and meaningful reading and writing assignments.

By focusing on the theme of life in America, students can consider America's history, its formative principles and critical issues, and its many problems, along with possible solutions to those problems. Within this context we attempt to provide as many perspectives as possible, so that students will experience the profound diversity that defines our country, and the effects our actions can have on society.

Living in America is a two-dimensional reader, focusing both on popular American culture and on the issues that divide and unite Americans. Each dimension draws upon this country's rich multiculturalism and the contributions of America's diverse population, as well as complements the text's other dimension. By offering selections depicting ethnic experiences of writers such as Alice Walker, Amy Tan, and N. Scott Momaday, and selections on popular topics such as violence in films and rock lyrics, media icons who establish models of behavior for young Americans, and popular but dangerous sports that invite public participation, we point students to the places where these readings intersect thematically—and that are areas for exciting academic discovery and debate.

ORGANIZATION

To highlight its dual dimensions, the text is divided into two parts: popular culture in America and issues in America. Because the parts inform each other, they are best used in combination. The focus of the first part is on cultural similarities and differences, including *ethnic* similarities and differences. The second part expands that focus to consider the arguments that arise from different opinions and interpretations that either separate or unite Americans on important and controversial topics such as affirmative action, ecology, and censorship. The result of this flexible organization is that *Living in America* invites experimentation. Each chapter can be used as a discrete unit of study, as is; or the chapters' readings can be recombined into units of the instructor's choosing.

Our focus on American popular culture and issues complements *Living in America*'s decidedly rhetorical thrust. Following each selection, we ask students to consider the intention or motive of the writer, the expectations and background of the intended audience, the context out of which the selection arose, the writer's style, and the selection's overall effect as a conscious, crafted act of communication. All questions in the discussions following each selection and in the end-of-chapter "Making Connections" sections emphasize several of these rhetorical matters. Our goal in the end is to help student writers appreciate the power all writers can wield as users of language.

SUMMARY LIST OF FEATURES

- 90 short contemporary selections, representing a variety of genres
- Focus on the theme of popular culture in America
- Substantial and consistent attention paid to issues of cultural diversity within American popular culture, including representation of many writers of diverse backgrounds
- A refreshing number of humorous selections
- An emphasis on potential solutions, not just problems
- Abundant optional apparatus that encourages pre-reading and post-reading analysis
- Activities and follow-up exercises that promote critical thinking, research, and writing
- Selections that, within each unit, progress from very accessible to more complex and academic
- Attention to rhetorical situation
- A sample of readings written by students
- The benefits of a thoroughly class-tested text

ACKNOWLEDGMENTS

We are indebted to contemporary studies of rhetoric, especially those of Kenneth Burke, that inform this text's primary emphasis on written communication that is purposeful and effective. We also want to acknowledge the theories of our predecessors, our mentors, and our teachers (many of whom are individually named below) for the education they've given us that enabled us to produce this text. In particular, the theories of James L. Kinneavy and James Moffett are basic to the pedagogical framework that complements every selection, and W. Ross Winterowd has influenced our concept of rhetoric and the application of composition theory to teaching. We are also grateful to our colleagues in secondary schools, community colleges, state and private universities, and businesses who have helped us formulate our ideas and our materials, in many cases by providing classes for testing this text's content.

Thanks are also due to the many people who have helped and inspired us with the creation and writing of *Living in America*. Our thanks in particular to Mark Hoffer, for his assistance in brainstorming ideas, editing, and reviewing, and for his unwavering support. To our colleagues and mentors Pam Bourgeois, Robert Chianese, Ben Saltman, Jack Solomon, Sonia Maasik, Kate Haake, Bryan Cooper, Debra Ballard, Joan Takayama-Ogawa, for your encouragement and help: our gratitude. To all of the students at California State University, Northridge; Otis College of Art and Design; East Los Angeles College; Antelope Valley College; and Los Angeles Valley College, who willingly and good-naturedly helped us try out the readings and many of the writing assignments: thanks again.

We especially want to recognize Tom Broadbent of Mayfield Publishing Company for his insight into the potential of *Living in America* and his wise guidance in the early stages of its development. His enthusiasm for our project gave us the incentive necessary to carry it through. We are indebted to several others at Mayfield who brought our book to completion: Julianna Scott Fein, our production editor; Susan Shook, developmental editor for the instructor's guide; and Renée Deljon, sponsoring editor, who took over for Tom Broadbent at a crucial stage in our book's development. Thanks also to Shari Hatch, our copyeditor, who taught us much about being careful readers and succinct writers.

Finally, our deepest thanks to our families for their sustained, and sustaining, involvment: John (Jack) Murray, whose steady support and infinite patience have been felt before; and to Lori Turner Covell and Chase McLaughlin Covell for their love, understanding, faith, and patience, without which this book would not have been possible.

INTRODUCTION

Living in America takes you on a journey into the heart of the American cultural experience. In these pages, you will encounter many of the ways life unfolds in America: the rites, myths, histories, ideologies, critical issues, major happenings, and everyday events that make up this amazing nation of diverse peoples.

One of the first aspects of life in America you will examine is the retelling of experience: narratives by people of various ages and ethnicities writing about important events of their lives. Perhaps there is nothing so American as a good story, as you will see in Chapter 1, "Personal Narratives: The Good, the Rad, and the Humorous." Chapter 2, "Generation Clash and the Family Experience," focuses on older citizens and grandparents. In the stories and lives of our parents and grandparents, there often exists important insight into our individual and distinctly American heritages. Chapter 3, "America at Play: Vegas, Football, Bungee Jumping, and More," offers a selection of readings on typically American cultural events and experiences, from Las Vegas to rock concerts, baseball to shopping sprees. Chapter 4, "Media Madness: Sex, Violence, and Rock and Roll," continues with essays and articles on America's popular media and entertainment, including TV, movies, music videos, and more. Chapter 5, " 'Generation X': Cybernauts Hungering for More," concludes the first half of *Living in America*. These readings reveal Americans' ingrained attitude that wanting and having more is justified. This chapter focuses on Generation X, cybernauts, cyberspace, and the Information Superhighway.

Chapters 6 through 10 explore important issues in American life, including multiculturalism, women's and minorities' rights, controversial music and the regulation of art, and environmental concerns. Among the selections in these chapters are writings that demonstrate attempts at resolving conflicts, redressing wrongs, understanding each other's cultures, and building community.

Living in America provides a variety of selections—some you will find more interesting and pertinent to your life than others, but all of them will challenge you to read actively and think about what you've read. The "Suggestions for Further Study" section following each selection (except the student essays) asks you to clarify the meanings of some words to ensure

CARTOONS IN AMERICA

©1993 Washington Post Writers Group. Reprinted with permission.

that you understand how these words are used in specific contexts. An occasional feature, "Language and Style," asks you to focus on *how* writers write and on the many ways language can affect readers. Other questions ask you to *interpret, discuss, write about,* and *think* about the purpose, audience, style, content, and effect of the selection.

"Activities for Discussion and Writing: Making Connections," the section ending each chapter, leads you directly to writing with the aforementioned concepts in mind. As a writer, you will start with a *purpose* and will want to create an *effect* that will cause a reaction in readers. This implies that you have an *audience* of readers in mind, for you will choose your writing *style* to appeal to that audience and to present the *content* of your message in an appropriate *form.*

Take a look ahead at some of the selections in this book, and notice how flexible a written form can be. Notice, for example, that William Least Heat Moon inserts a list of things he observed in the desert into the middle of his descriptive essay about West Texas. Notice, too, that Alice Walker illustrates her idea of "our mothers' gardens" by using bits and pieces quoted from other writers. Note also that Hunter S. Thompson interweaves two voices in narrating the events of a motorcycle race, the Mint 400: his own first-person voice and his third-person reporter's voice.

In *Living in America*, the various writings, their forms, and the activities that follow them—while by no means exhausting the incredible array of American stories, images, issues, conflicts, and attempts at resolution, or of every means of written expression—provide numerous ways to encounter, respond to, and express your own views about the American experience.

Enjoy!

POPULAR CULTURE I
Personal Narratives: The Good, the Rad, and the Humorous

We begin our journey into the heart of the American experience by focusing on the stories of people who reflect the diversity of that experience. Through these personal narratives, humble stories, and shared private experiences, we can gain tools and ideas for improving our own writing; we can discover different people and places; and we can learn about American ideology and what it is to be an American. To foster understanding among all people in America, as the musician Quincy Jones says, "it is important for us to learn to sing each other's songs." We, the editors, echo this concept, maintaining that we must learn each other's *stories* as well.

Native American William Least Heat Moon begins the personal narratives of Chapter 1 with "West Texas," a story that shows there is more to the desert—and to America—than meets the eye. In "Our Parents Had More," Douglas Coupland humorously recounts the adventures of five members of "Generation X" as they drive out to Palm Springs. Maya Angelou's "Graduation" recounts both inspirational and noninspirational moments from her high school graduation. Alice Walker, in "Beauty: When the Other Dancer Is the Self," relates a disastrous experience she endured as a child and the resultant trauma that she had to overcome as an adult. In "The Library Card," Richard Wright depicts his struggle to get books from a library in the deep South when he was a child. His moving account includes not only the frustrations of racism but also the inspiration that came from reading. Lois-Ann Yamanaka, in "The Last Dance Is Always a Slow Dance," humorously describes a young woman's internal conflict during a high school prom. In "Mauve Desert," Nicole Brossard offers a stylish and lyrical portrait of a young woman escaping from her family life as she drives headlong into the desert. Student writer Hethur Suval relates her alienation as a high school student in "High School Psyche-Out." And finally, student writer Glen McCoy graphically recounts his horrifying experience of war in "The Vietnam War: Not Very Pretty."

West Texas

William Least Heat Moon

William Least Heat Moon (born in 1939) is Native American. His best-selling book Blue Highways: A Journey into America, *published in 1982, chronicles his journeys around America. In the following selection from* Blue Highways, *Moon stops in the supposed "nowhereland" of southwest Texas and records everything he sees and hears before moving on to a small town up the road.*

Straight as a chief's countenance, the road lay ahead, curves so long and gradual as to be imperceptible except on the map. For nearly a hundred miles due west of Eldorado, not a single town. It was the Texas some people see as barren waste when they cross it, the part they later describe at the motel bar as "nothing." They say, "There's nothing out there." 1

Driving through the miles of nothing, I decided to test the hypothesis and stopped somewhere in western Crockett County on the top of a broad mesa, just off Texas 29. At a distance, the land looked so rocky and dry, a religious man could believe that the First Hand never got around to the creation in here. Still, somebody had decided to string barbed wire around it.

No plant grew higher than my head. For a while, I heard only miles of wind against the Ghost; but after the ringing in my ears stopped, I heard myself breathing, then a bird note, an answering call, another kind of birdsong, and another: mockingbird, mourning dove, an enigma. I heard the high *zizz* of flies the color of gray flannel and the deep buzz of a blue bumblebee. I made a list of nothing in particular:

1. mockingbird
2. mourning dove
3. enigma bird (heard not saw)
4. gray flies
5. blue bumblebee
6. two circling buzzards (not yet, boys)
7. orange ants
8. black ants
9. orange-black ants (what's been going on?)

10. three species of spiders

11. opossum skull

12. jackrabbit (chewed on cactus)

13. deer (left scat)

14. coyote (left tracks)

15. small rodent (den full of seed hulls under rock)

16. snake (skin hooked on cactus spine)

17. prickly pear cactus (yellow blossoms)

18. hedgehog cactus (orange blossoms)

19. barrel cactus (red blossoms)

20. devil's pincushion (no blossoms)

21. catclaw (no better name)

22. two species of grass (neither green, both alive)

23. yellow flowers (blossoms smaller than peppercorns)

24. sage (indicates alkali-free soil)

25. mesquite (three-foot plants with eighty-foot roots to reach water that fell as rain two thousand years ago)

26. greasewood (oh, yes)

27. joint fir (steeped stems make Brigham Young tea)

28. earth

29. sky

30. wind (always)

That was all the nothing I could identify then, but had I waited until dark when the desert really comes to life, I could have done better. To say nothing is out here is incorrect; to say the desert is stingy with everything except space and light, stone and earth is closer to the truth.

I drove on. The low sun turned the mesa rimrock to silhouettes, angular and weird and unearthly; had someone said the far side of Saturn looked just like this, I would have believed him. The road dropped to the Pecos River, now dammed to such docility I couldn't imagine it formerly demarking the western edge of a rudimentary white civilization. Even the old wagonmen felt the unease of isolation when they crossed the Pecos, a small but once serious river that has had many names: Rio de las Vacas (River of Cows—perhaps a reference to bison), Rio Salado (Salty River), Rio Puerco (Dirty River).

West of the Pecos, a strangely truncated cone rose from the valley. In the oblique evening light, its silhouette looked like a Mayan temple, so perfect was its symmetry. I stopped again, started climbing, stirring a panic of lizards on the way up. From the top, the rubbled land below—veined with the highway and arroyos, topographical relief absorbed in the dusk—looked like a roadmap.

The desert, more than any other terrain, shows its age, shows time because so little vegetation covers the ancient erosions of wind and storm. What appears is tawny grit once stone and stone crumbling to grit. Everywhere rock, earth's oldest thing. Even desert creatures come from a time older than the woodland animals, and they, in answer to the arduousness, have retained prehistoric coverings of chitin and lapped scale and primitive defenses of spine and stinger, fang and poison, shell and claw.

The night, taking up the shadows and details, wiped the face of the desert into a simple, uncluttered blackness until there were only three things: land, wind, stars. I was there too, but my presence I felt more than saw. It was as if I had been reduced to mind, to an edge of consciousness. Men, ascetics, in all eras have gone into deserts to lose themselves—Jesus, Saint Anthony, Saint Basil, and numberless medicine men—maybe because such a losing happens almost as a matter of course here if you avail yourself. The Sioux once chanted, "All over the sky a sacred voice is calling."

Back to the highway, on with the headlamps, down Six Shooter Draw. In the darkness, deer, just shadows in the lights, began moving toward the desert willows in the wet bottoms. Stephen Vincent Benét:

When Daniel Boone goes by, at night,
The phantom deer arise
And all lost, wild America
Is burning in their eyes.

From the top of another high mesa: twelve miles west in the flat valley floor, the lights of Fort Stockton blinked white, blue, red, and yellow in the heat like a mirage. How is it that desert towns look so fine and big at night? It must be that little is hidden. The glistening ahead could have been a golden city of Cibola. But the reality of Fort Stockton was plywood and concrete block and the plastic signs of Holiday Inn and Mobil Oil.

The desert had given me an appetite that would have made carrion crow stuffed with saltbush taste good. I found a Mexican cafe of adobe, with a whitewashed log ceiling, creekstone fireplace, and jukebox pumping out mariachi music. It was like a bunkhouse. I ate burritos, chile rellenos, and pinto beans, all ladled over with a fine, incendiary sauce the color of sludge from an old steel drum. At the next table sat three big, round men: an Indian wearing a silver headband, a Chicano in a droopy Pancho Villa mustache, and a Negro in faded overalls. I thought what a litany of grievances that table could recite. But the more I looked, the more I believed they were someone's vision of the West, maybe someone making ads for Levy's bread, the ads that used to begin "You don't have to be Jewish."

10

SUGGESTIONS FOR FURTHER STUDY

Key Words

The author uses language with which you may not be familiar. Find the following words in the paragraphs indicated, and explain their meanings in the context of the sentences in which the words appear. Consult a dictionary, as needed.

countenance (par. 1)
enigma (par. 3)
docility (par. 4)
rudimentary (par. 4)
truncated (par. 5)
arduousness (par. 6)
ascetics (par. 7)

Language and Style

The author makes extensive use of figurative or metaphorical language to make his description of West Texas vivid. Discuss with other readers what makes these passages effective:

"Straight as a Chief's countenance. . . ." (par. 1)

"I heard the *zizz* of flies. . . ." (par. 3)

"Even desert creatures come from a time older than the woodland animals . . . [and] have retained prehistoric coverings of chitin and lapped scale and primitive defenses of spine and stinger, fang and poison, shell and claw." (par. 6)

"The night . . . wiped the face of the desert into a simple, uncluttered blackness. . . ." (par. 7)

". . .'All over the sky a sacred voice is calling.' " (par. 7)

"The desert had given me an appetite that would have made carrion crow stuffed with saltbush taste good." (par. 10)

Topics for Discussion and Writing

1. After establishing that he is "[d]riving through the miles of nothing," the author then makes a list "of nothing in particular." Look again at his list of things and actions. Which ones do you think most contribute to his change of mind so that later he can write "To say nothing is out here is incorrect; to say the desert is stingy with everything except space and light, stone and earth is closer to the truth"?

2. Look up the area described on a topographical map of Texas and notice the close fit between the author's description of West Texas and the topography indicated on the map. In addition, the author mentions place names. How many of them are indicated on the map?

3. The author refers to historical people, places, and things such as Pancho Villa, Fort Stockton, the golden city of Cibola, and Levy's bread. Identify such references and discuss what they add to the effectiveness of the description in "West Texas."

4. What is the point of the author's comments about ads for Levy's bread? How do his comments reflect the place, the people, and the situation described in the last paragraph?

5. Write about a geographical area that has made a lasting impression on you. It may be a place close to home or one you visited on a trip. Use as many vivid details and words or phrases that appeal to the reader's senses as you can. The purpose of your description is to help your readers "see" and experience the place almost as vividly and deeply as you did.

Our Parents Had More

Douglas Coupland

Douglas Coupland is from British Columbia, Canada. Generation X, his first novel, was published in 1991 and is considered the prototypical work enunciating the "Gen-X" phenomenon. The novel revolves around the exploits of the characters Andy, Dag, and Claire, who exist in a world influenced by the media, with no social or political ideals to fight for, no fixed beliefs to anchor them, and little direction in their lives.

Strip." ¶ "Talk to yourself." ¶ "Look at the view." ¶ "Masturbate." ¶ It's [1] a day later (well, actually not even twelve hours later) and the five of us are rattling down Indian Avenue, headed for our afternoon picnic up in the mountains. We're in Dag's syphilitic old Saab, an endearingly tinny ancient red model of the sort driven up the sides of buildings in Disney cartoons and held together by Popsicle sticks, chewing gum and Scotch tape. And in the car we're playing a quick game—answering Claire's open command to "name all of the activities people do when they're by themselves out in the desert." ¶ "Take nude Polaroids." ¶ "Hoard little pieces of junk and debris." ¶ "Shoot those little pieces of junk to bits with a shotgun." ¶ "Hey," roars Dag, "it's kind of like life, isn't it?" ¶ The car rolls along. ¶ "Sometimes," says Claire, as we drive past the I. Magnin where she works, "I develop this weird feeling when I watch these endless waves of gray hair gobbling up the jewels and perfumes at work. I feel like I'm watching this enormous dinner table surrounded by hundreds of greedy little children who are so spoiled, and so impatient, that they can't even wait for food to be prepared. They have to reach for live animals placed on the table and suck the food right out of them."

Okay, okay. This is a cruel, lopsided judgment of what Palm Springs really is—a small town where old people are trying to buy back their youth and a few rungs on the social ladder. As the expression goes, we spend our youth attaining wealth, and our wealth attaining youth. It's really not a bad place here, and it's undeniably lovely—hey, I *do* live here, after all.

But the place makes me worry.

There is no weather in Palm Springs—just like TV. There is also no middle class, and in that sense the place is medieval. Dag says that every time someone on the planet uses a paper clip, fabric softens their laundry, or watches a rerun of "Hee Haw" on TV, a resident somewhere here in the Coachella Valley collects a penny. He's probably right.

Claire notices that the rich people here pay the poor people to cut the thorns from their cactuses. "I've also noticed that they tend to throw out their houseplants rather than maintain them. God. Imagine what their *kids* are like."

Nonetheless, the three of us chose to live here, for the town is undoubtedly a quiet sanctuary from the bulk of middle-class life. And we certainly don't live in one of the dishier neighborhoods the town has to offer. No way. There are neighborhoods here, where, if you see a glint in a patch of crew-cut Bermuda grass, you can assume there's a silver dollar lying there. Where *we* live, in our little bungalows that share a courtyard and a kidney-shaped swimming pool, a twinkle in the grass means a broken scotch bottle or a colostomy bag that has avoided the trashman's gloved clutch.

The car heads out on a long stretch that heads toward the highway and Claire hugs one of the dogs that has edged its face in between the two front seats. It is a face that now grovels politely but insistently for attention. She lectures into the dog's two obsidian eyes: "*You*, you cute little creature. *You* don't have to worry about having snowmobiles or cocaine or a third house in Orlando, *Flor*ida. That's right. No *you* don't. You just want a nice little pat on the head."

The dog meanwhile wears the cheerful, helpful look of a bellboy in a foreign country who doesn't understand a word you're saying but who still wants a tip.

"That's right. You wouldn't want to worry yourself with so many *things*. And do you know *why*?" (The dog raises its ears at the inflection, giving the illusion of understanding. Dag insists that all dogs secretly speak the English language and subscribe to the morals and beliefs of the Unitarian church, but Claire objected to this because she said she knew for a *fact*, that when she was in France, the dogs spoke French.) "Because all of those objects would only mutiny and slap you in the face. They'd only remind you that all you're doing with your life is collecting objects. And nothing else."

We live small lives on the periphery; we are marginalized and there's a great deal in which we choose not to participate. We wanted silence and we have that silence now. We arrived here speckled in sores and zits, our colons so tied in knots that we never thought we'd have a bowel movement again. Our systems had stopped working, jammed with the odor of copy machines, Wite-Out, the smell of bond paper, and the endless stress of pointless jobs done grudgingly to little applause. We had compulsions that made us confuse shopping with creativity, to take downers and assume that merely renting a video on a Saturday night was enough. But now that we live here in the desert, things are much, *much* better.

SUGGESTIONS FOR FURTHER STUDY

Key Words

The author uses language with which you may not be familiar. Find the following words in the paragraphs indicated, and explain their meanings in the context of the sentences in which the words appear. Consult a dictionary, as needed.

colostomy (par. 6)
obsidian (par. 7)
periphery (par. 10)

Topics for Discussion and Writing

1. These sketches from the novel *Generation X* provide "snapshots" of people traveling through an area populated by their parents' generation. What impressions do these sketches give of the characters' attitude? Locate specific language that expresses that attitude.
2. What audience of readers do you think these sketches are intended to reach? What audiences of readers might agree or disagree with the attitude expressed in them?
3. The writer points out in some detail the materialism and commercialism he sees in a place like Palm Springs, California. What specific items or actions does he criticize?
4. Write a journal entry that expresses your attitude about this comment: "As the expression goes, we spend our youth attaining wealth, and our wealth attaining youth." (par. 3) To what extent do you see evidence of this claim?

Graduation

Maya Angelou

Maya Angelou (born in 1933) is the author of five collections of poetry and four autobiographical novels: Wouldn't Take Nothing for My Journey Now, Gather Together in My Name, Heart of a Woman, *and* I Know Why the Caged Bird Sings, *from which the following selection is taken. She has received numerous honorary degrees, has worked in theater and television, and most recently wrote and read her classic inaugural poem for President Clinton's inauguration in 1993. Angelou is currently Reynolds Professor at Wake Forest University, Winston-Salem, North Carolina.*

The children in Stamps trembled visibly with anticipation. Some adults were excited too, but to be certain the whole young population had come down with graduation epidemic. Large classes were graduating from both the grammar school and the high school. Even those who were years removed from their own day of glorious release were anxious to help with preparations as a kind of dry run. The junior students who were moving into the vacating classes' chairs were tradition-bound to show their talents for leadership and management. They strutted through the school and around the campus exerting pressure on the lower grades. Their authority was so new that occasionally if they pressed a little too hard it had to be overlooked. After all, next term was coming, and it never hurt a sixth grader to have a play sister in the eighth grade, or a tenth-year student to be able to call a twelfth grader Bubba. So all was endured in a spirit of shared understanding. But the graduating classes themselves were the nobility. Like travelers with exotic destinations on their minds, the graduates were remarkably forgetful. They came to school without their books, or tablets or even pencils. Volunteers fell over themselves to secure replacements for the missing equipment. When accepted, the willing workers might or might not be thanked, and it was of no importance to the pregraduation rites. Even teachers were respectful of the now quiet and aging seniors, and tended to speak to them, if not as equals, as beings only slightly lower than themselves. After tests were returned and grades given, the student body, which acted like an extended family, knew who did well, who excelled, and what piteous ones had failed.

Unlike the white high school, Lafayette County Training School distinguished itself by having neither lawn, nor hedges, nor tennis court, nor climbing ivy. Its two buildings (main classrooms, the grade school and home economics) were set on a dirt hill with no fence to limit either its boundaries or those of bordering farms. There was a large expanse to the left of the school which was used alternately as a baseball diamond or a basketball court. Rusty hoops on the swaying poles represented the permanent recreational equipment, although bats and balls could be borrowed from the P. E. teacher if the borrower was qualified and if the diamond wasn't occupied.

Over this rocky area relieved by a few shady tall persimmon trees the graduating class walked. The girls often held hands and no longer bothered to speak to the lower students. There was a sadness about them, as if this old world was not their home and they were bound for higher ground. The boys, on the other hand, had become more friendly, more outgoing. A decided change from the closed attitude they projected while studying for finals. Now they seemed not ready to give up the old school, the familiar paths and classrooms. Only a small percentage would be continuing on to college—one of the South's A & M (agricultural and mechanical) schools, which trained Negro youths to be carpenters, farmers, handymen, masons, maids, cooks and baby nurses. Their future rode heavily on their shoulders, and blinded them to the collective joy that had pervaded the lives of the boys and girls in the grammar school graduating class.

Parents who could afford it had ordered new shoes and ready-made clothes for themselves from Sears and Roebuck or Montgomery Ward. They also engaged the best seamstresses to make the floating graduating dresses and to cut down secondhand pants which would be pressed to a military slickness for the important event.

Oh, it was important, all right. Whitefolks would attend the ceremony, and two or three would speak of God and home, and the Southern way of life, and Mrs. Parsons, the principal's wife, would play the graduation march while the lower-grade graduates paraded down the aisles and took their seats below the platform. The high school seniors would wait in empty classrooms to make their dramatic entrance.

In the Store I was the person of the moment. The birthday girl. The center. Bailey had graduated the year before, although to do so he had had to forfeit all pleasures to make up for his time lost in Baton Rouge.

My class was wearing butter-yellow piqué dresses, and Momma launched out on mine. She smocked the yoke into tiny crisscrossing puckers, then shirred the rest of the bodice. Her dark fingers ducked in and out of lemony cloth as she embroidered raised daisies around the hem. Before she considered herself finished she had added a crocheted cuff on the puff sleeves, and a pointy crocheted collar.

I was going to be lovely. A walking model of all the various styles of fine hand sewing and it didn't worry me that I was only twelve years old and merely graduating from the eighth grade. Besides, many teachers in Arkansas Negro schools had only that diploma and were licensed to impart wisdom.

The days had become longer and more noticeable. The faded beige of former times had been replaced with strong and sure colors. I began to see my classmates' clothes, their skin tones, and the dust that waved off pussy willows. Clouds that lazed across the sky were objects of great concern to me. Their shiftier shapes might have held a message that in my new happiness and with a little bit of time I'd soon decipher. During that period I looked at the arch of heaven so religiously my neck kept a steady ache. I had taken to smiling more often, and my jaws hurt from the unaccustomed activity. Between the two physical sore spots, I suppose I could have been uncomfortable, but that was not the case. As a member of the winning team (the graduating class of 1940) I had outdistanced unpleasant sensations by miles. I was headed for the freedom of open fields.

Youth and social approval allied themselves with me and we trammeled   10
memories of slights and insults. The wind of our swift passage remodeled my features. Lost tears were pounded to mud and then to dust. Years of withdrawal were brushed aside and left behind, as hanging ropes of parasitic moss.

My work alone had awarded me a top place and I was going to be one of the first called in the graduating ceremonies. On the classroom blackboard, as well as on the bulletin board in the auditorium, there were blue stars and white stars and red stars. No absences, no tardinesses, and my academic work was among the best of the year. I could say the preamble to the Constitution even faster than Bailey. We timed ourselves often: "WethepeopleoftheUnitedStatesinordertoformamoreperfectunion . . ." I had memorized the Presidents of the United States from Washington to Roosevelt in chronological as well as alphabetical order.

My hair pleased me too. Gradually the black mass had lengthened and thickened, so that it kept at last to its braided pattern, and I didn't have to yank my scalp off when I tried to comb it.

Louise and I had rehearsed the exercises until we tired out ourselves. Henry Reed was class valedictorian. He was a small, very black boy with hooded eyes, a long, broad nose and an oddly shaped head. I had admired him for years because each term he and I vied for the best grades in our class. Most often he bested me, but instead of being disappointed I was pleased that we shared top places between us. Like many Southern Black children, he lived with his grandmother, who was as strict as Momma and as kind as she knew how to be. He was courteous, respectful and soft-spoken to elders, but on the playground he chose to play the roughest games. I admired him. Anyone, I reckoned, sufficiently afraid or sufficiently dull could be polite. But to be able to operate at a top level with both adults and children was admirable.

His valedictory speech was entitled "To Be or Not to Be." The rigid tenth-grade teacher had helped him write it. He'd been working on the dramatic stresses for months.

The weeks until graduation were filled with heady activities. A group of small children were to be presented in a play about buttercups and daisies and bunny rabbits. They could be heard throughout the building practicing their hops and their little songs that sounded like silver bells. The older girls (non-graduates, of course) were assigned the task of making refreshments for the night's festivities. A tangy scent of ginger, cinnamon, nutmeg and chocolate wafted around the home economics building as the budding cooks made samples for themselves and their teachers.

In every corner of the workshop, axes and saws split fresh timber as the woodshop boys made sets and stage scenery. Only the graduates were left out of the general bustle. We were free to sit in the library at the back of the building or look in quite detachedly, naturally, on the measures being taken for our event.

Even the minister preached on graduation the Sunday before. His subject was, "Let your light so shine that men will see your good works and praise your Father, Who is in Heaven." Although the sermon was purported to be addressed to us, he used the occasion to speak to backsliders, gamblers and general ne'er-do-wells. But since he had called our names at the beginning of the service we were mollified.

Among Negroes the tradition was to give presents to children going only from one grade to another. How much more important this was when the person was graduating at the top of the class. Uncle Willie and Momma had sent away for a Mickey Mouse watch like Bailey's. Louise gave me four embroidered handkerchiefs. (I gave her three crocheted doilies.) Mrs. Sneed, the minister's wife, made me an underskirt to wear for graduation, and nearly every customer gave me a nickel or maybe even a dime with the instruction "Keep on moving to higher ground," or some such encouragement.

Amazingly the great day finally dawned and I was out of bed before I knew it. I threw open the back door to see it more clearly, but Momma said, "Sister, come away from that door and put your robe on."

I hoped the memory of that morning would never leave me. Sunlight was itself still young, and the day had none of the insistence maturity would bring it in a few hours. In my robe and barefoot in the backyard, under cover of going to see about my new beans, I gave myself up to the gentle warmth and thanked God that no matter what evil I had done in my life He had allowed me to live to see this day. Somewhere in my fatalism I had expected to die, accidentally, and never have the chance to walk up the stairs in the auditorium and gracefully receive my hard-earned diploma. Out of God's merciful bosom I had won reprieve.

Bailey came out in his robe and gave me a box wrapped in Christmas paper. He said he had saved his money for months to pay for it. It felt like a box of chocolates, but I knew Bailey wouldn't save money to buy candy when we had all we could want under our noses.

He was as proud of the gift as I. It was a soft-leather-bound copy of a collection of poems by Edgar Allan Poe, or, as Bailey and I called him, "Eap." I turned to "Annabel Lee" and we walked up and down the garden rows, the cool dirt between our toes, reciting the beautifully sad lines.

Momma made a Sunday breakfast although it was only Friday. After we finished the blessing, I opened my eyes to find the watch on my plate. It was a dream of a day. Everything went smoothly and to my credit. I didn't have to be reminded or scolded for anything. Near evening I was too jittery to attend to chores, so Bailey volunteered to do all before his bath.

Days before, we had made a sign for the Store, and as we turned out the lights Momma hung the cardboard over the doorknob. It read clearly: CLOSED: GRADUATION.

My dress fitted perfectly and everyone said that I looked like a sunbeam   25 in it. On the hill, going toward the school, Bailey walked behind with Uncle Willie, who muttered, "Go on, Ju." He wanted him to walk ahead with us because it embarrassed him to have to walk so slowly. Bailey said he'd let the ladies walk together, and the men would bring up the rear. We all laughed, nicely.

Little children dashed by out of the dark like fireflies. Their crepe-paper dresses and butterfly wings were not made for running and we heard more than one rip, dryly, and the regretful "uh uh" that followed.

The school blazed without gaiety. The windows seemed cold and unfriendly from the lower hill. A sense of ill-fated timing crept over me, and if Momma hadn't reached for my hand I would have drifted back to Bailey and Uncle Willie, and possibly beyond. She made a few slow jokes about my feet getting cold, and tugged me along to the now-strange building.

Around the front steps, assurance came back. There were my fellow "greats," the graduating class. Hair brushed back, legs oiled, new dresses and pressed pleats, fresh pocket handkerchiefs and little handbags, all homesewn. Oh, we were up to snuff, all right. I joined my comrades and didn't even see my family go in to find seats in the crowded auditorium.

The school band struck up a march and all classes filed in as had been rehearsed. We stood in front of our seats, as assigned, and on a signal from the choir director, we sat. No sooner had this been accomplished than the band started to play the national anthem. We rose again and sang the song, after which we recited the pledge of allegiance. We remained standing for a brief minute before the choir director and the principal signaled to us, rather desperately I thought, to take our seats. The command was so unusual that our carefully rehearsed and smooth-running machine was thrown off. For a full minute we fumbled for our chairs and bumped into each other awkwardly. Habits change or solidify under pressure, so in our state of nervous tension we had been ready to follow our usual assembly pattern: the American national anthem, then the pledge of allegiance, then the song every Black person I knew called the Negro National Anthem. All done in the same key, with the same passion and most often standing on the same foot.

Finding my seat at last, I was overcome with a presentiment of worse things to come. Something unrehearsed, unplanned, was going to happen, and we were going to be made to look bad. I distinctly remember being explicit in the choice of pronoun. It was "we," the graduating class, the unit, that concerned me then. 30

The principal welcomed "parents and friends" and asked the Baptist minister to lead us in prayer. His invocation was brief and punchy, and for a second I thought we were getting back on the high road to right action. When the principal came back to the dais, however, his voice had changed. Sounds always affected me profoundly and the principal's voice was one of my favorites. During assembly it melted and lowed weakly into the audience. It had not been in my plan to listen to him, but my curiosity was piqued and I straightened up to give him my attention.

He was talking about Booker T. Washington, our "late great leader," who said we can be as close as the fingers on the hand, etc. . . . Then he said a few vague things about friendship and the friendship of kindly people to those less fortunate than themselves. With that his voice nearly faded, thin, away. Like a river diminishing to a stream and then to a trickle. But he cleared his throat and said, "Our speaker tonight, who is also our friend, came from Texarkana to deliver the commencement address, but due to the irregularity of the train schedule, he's going to, as they say, 'speak and run.' " He said that we understood and wanted the man to know that we were most grateful for the time he was able to give us and then something about how we were willing always to adjust to another's program, and without more ado—"I give you Mr. Edward Donleavy."

Not one but two white men came through the door offstage. The shorter one walked to the speaker's platform, and the tall one moved over to the center seat and sat down. But that was our principal's seat, and already occupied. The dislodged gentleman bounced around for a long breath or two before the Baptist minister gave him his chair, then with more dignity than the situation deserved, the minister walked off the stage.

Donleavy looked at the audience once (on reflection, I'm sure that he wanted only to reassure himself that we were really there), adjusted his glasses and began to read from a sheaf of papers.

He was glad "to be here and to see the work going on just as it was in the other schools." 35

At the first "Amen" from the audience I willed the offender to immediate death by choking on the word. But Amens and Yes, sir's began to fall around the room like rain through a ragged umbrella.

He told us of the wonderful changes we children in Stamps had in store. The Central School (naturally, the white school was Central) had already been granted improvements that would be in use in the fall. A well-known artist was coming from Little Rock to teach art to them. They were going to have the newest microscopes and chemistry equipment for their laboratory. Mr. Donleavy didn't leave us long in the dark over who made these improvements available to Central High. Nor were we to be ignored in the general betterment scheme he had in mind.

He said that he had pointed out to people at a very high level that one of the first-line football tacklers at Arkansas Agricultural and Mechanical College had graduated from good old Lafayette County Training School. Here fewer Amen's were heard. Those few that did break through lay dully in the air with the heaviness of habit.

He went on to praise us. He went on to say how he had bragged that "one of the best basketball players at Fisk sank his first ball right here at Lafayette County Training School."

The white kids were going to have a chance to become Galileos and   40
Madame Curies and Edisons and Gauguins, and our boys (the girls weren't even in on it) would try to be Jesse Owenses and Joe Louises.

Owens and the Brown Bomber were great heroes in our world, but what school official in the white-goddom of Little Rock had the right to decide that those two men must be our only heroes? Who decided that for Henry Reed to become a scientist he had to work like George Washington Carver, as a bootblack, to buy a lousy microscope? Bailey was obviously always going to be too small to be an athlete, so which concrete angel glued to what county seat had decided that if my brother wanted to become a lawyer he had to first pay penance for his skin by picking cotton and hoeing corn and studying correspondence books at night for twenty years?

The man's dead words fell like bricks around the auditorium and too many settled in my belly. Constrained by hard-learned manners I couldn't look behind me, but to my left and right the proud graduating class of 1940 had dropped their heads. Every girl in my row had found something new to do with her handkerchief. Some folded the tiny squares into love knots, some into triangles, but most were wadding them, then pressing them flat on their yellow laps.

On the dais, the ancient tragedy was being replayed. Professor Parsons sat, a sculptor's reject, rigid. His large, heavy body seemed devoid of will or willingness, and his eyes said he was no longer with us. The other teachers examined the flag (which was draped stage right) or their notes, or the windows which opened on our now-famous playing diamond.

Graduation, the hush-hush magic time of frills and gifts and congratulations and diplomas, was finished for me before my name was called. The accomplishment was nothing. The meticulous maps, drawn in three colors of ink, learning and spelling decasyllabic words, memorizing the whole of *The Rape of Lucrece*—it was for nothing. Donleavy had exposed us.

We were maids and farmers, handymen and washerwomen, and anything higher that we aspired to was farcical and presumptuous.   45

Then I wished that Gabriel Prosser and Nat Turner had killed all whitefolks in their beds and that Abraham Lincoln had been assassinated before the signing of the Emancipation Proclamation, and that Harriet Tubman had been killed by that blow on her head and Christopher Columbus had drowned in the *Santa María*.

It was awful to be Negro and have no control over my life. It was brutal to be young and already trained to sit quietly and listen to charges brought against my color with no chance of defense. We should all be dead. I thought I should like to see us all dead, one on top of the other. A pyramid of flesh with the whitefolks on the bottom, as the broad base, then the Indians with their silly tomahawks and teepees and wigwams and treaties, the Negroes with their mops and recipes and cotton sacks and spirituals sticking out of their mouths. The Dutch children should all stumble in their wooden shoes and break their necks. The French should choke to death on the Louisiana Purchase (1803) while silkworms ate all the Chinese with their stupid pigtails. As a species, we were an abomination. All of us.

Donleavy was running for election, and assured our parents that if he won we could count on having the only colored paved playing field in that part of Arkansas. Also—he never looked up to acknowledge the grunts of acceptance—also, we were bound to get some new equipment for the home economics building and the workshop.

He finished, and since there was no need to give any more than the most perfunctory thank-you's, he nodded to the men on the stage, and the tall white man who was never introduced joined him at the door. They left with the attitude that now they were off to something really important. (The graduation ceremonies at Lafayette County Training School had been a mere preliminary.)

The ugliness they left was palpable. An uninvited guest who wouldn't   50
leave. The choir was summoned and sang a modern arrangement of "Onward, Christian Soldiers," with new words pertaining to graduates seeking their place in the world. But it didn't work. Elouise, the daughter of the Baptist minister, recited "Invictus," and I could have cried at the impertinence of "I am the master of my fate, I am the captain of my soul."

My name had lost its ring of familiarity and I had to be nudged to go and receive my diploma. All my preparations had fled. I neither marched up to the stage like a conquering Amazon, nor did I look in the audience for

Bailey's nod of approval. Marguerite Johnson, I heard the name again, my honors were read, there were noises in the audience of appreciation, and I took my place on the stage as rehearsed.

I thought about colors I hated: ecru, puce, lavender, beige and black.

There was shuffling and rustling around me, then Henry Reed was giving his valedictory address, "To Be or Not to Be." Hadn't he heard the whitefolks? We couldn't *be,* so the question was a waste of time. Henry's voice came out clear and strong. I feared to look at him. Hadn't he got the message? There was no "nobler in the mind" for Negroes because the world didn't think we had minds, and they let us know it. "Outrageous fortune"? Now, that was a joke. When the ceremony was over I had to tell Henry Reed some things. That is, if I still cared. Not "rub," Henry, "erase." "Ah, there's the erase." Us.

Henry had been a good student in elocution. His voice rose on tides of promise and fell on waves of warnings. The English teacher had helped him to create a sermon winging through Hamlet's soliloquy. To be a man, a doer, a builder, a leader, or to be a tool, an unfunny joke, a crusher of funky toadstools. I marveled that Henry could go through with the speech as if we had a choice.

I had been listening and silently rebutting each sentence with my eyes   55
closed; then there was a hush, which in an audience warns that something unplanned is happening. I looked up and saw Henry Reed, the conservative, the proper, the A student, turn his back to the audience and turn to us (the proud graduating class of 1940) and sing, nearly speaking,

> "Lift ev'ry voice and sing
> Till earth and heaven ring
> Ring with the harmonies of Liberty . . ."

It was the poem written by James Weldon Johnson. It was the music composed by J. Rosamond Johnson. It was the Negro national anthem. Out of habit we were singing it.

Our mothers and fathers stood in the dark hall and joined the hymn of encouragement. A kindergarten teacher led the small children onto the stage and the buttercups and daisies and bunny rabbits marked time and tried to follow:

> "Stony the road we trod
> Bitter the chastening rod
> Felt in the days when hope, unborn, had died.

"Lift Ev'ry Voice and Sing"—words by James Weldon Johnson and music by J. Rosamond Johnson. Copyright by Edward B. Marks Music Corporation. Used by permission.

> Yet with a steady beat
> Have not our weary feet
> Come to the place for which our fathers sighed?"

Every child I knew had learned that song with his ABC's and along with "Jesus Loves Me This I Know." But I personally had never heard it before. Never heard the words, despite the thousands of times I had sung them. Never thought they had anything to do with me.

On the other hand, the words of Patrick Henry had made such an impression on me that I had been able to stretch myself tall and trembling and say, "I know not what course others may take, but as for me, give me liberty or give me death."

And now I heard, really for the first time:

> "We have come over a way that with tears
> has been watered,
> We have come, treading our path through
> the blood of the slaughtered."

While echoes of the song shivered in the air, Henry Reed bowed his head, said "Thank you," and returned to his place in line. The tears that slipped down many faces were not wiped away in shame.

We were on top again. As always, again. We survived. The depths had been icy and dark, but now a bright sun spoke to our souls. I was no longer simply a member of the proud graduating class of 1940; I was a proud member of the wonderful, beautiful Negro race.

Oh, Black known and unknown poets, how often have your auctioned pains sustained us? Who will compute the lonely nights made less lonely by your songs, or by the empty pots made less tragic by your tales?

If we were a people much given to revealing secrets, we might raise monuments and sacrifice to the memories of our poets, but slavery cured us of that weakness. It may be enough, however, to have it said that we survive in exact relationship to the dedication of our poets (include preachers, musicians and blues singers).

SUGGESTIONS FOR FURTHER STUDY

Key Words

The author uses language with which you may not be familiar. Find the following words in the paragraphs indicated, and explain their meanings in the context of the sentences in which the words appear. Consult a dictionary, as needed.

exotic (par. 1)
pique (par. 7)
trammeled (par. 10)
parasitic (par.10)
vied (par. 13)
backsliders (par. 17)
presentiment (par. 30)
devoid (par. 43)
decasyllabic (par. 44)
presumptuous (par. 45)
soliloquy (par. 54)

Topics for Discussion and Writing

1. The author, in telling about her own experience, reveals the excitement and anticipation that surrounded the preparations for graduation day. Find several vivid passages that describe the preparations she and her family and fellow students made, and discuss the feelings that these passages reveal.

2. In "Graduation," the long-anticipated event turns from an occasion of celebration to one of disillusionment. How does the speaker, Edward Donleavy, cause this disillusionment? What does he say and do that creates a negative effect? How does the writer react to his words? Find specific phrases or longer passages that describe the ugliness that Donleavy left.

3. How does Henry Reed's valedictory address revitalize the dejected students at the ceremony so that the writer can say "We were on top again"?

4. Think about your own graduation day experience, and write a short essay or journal entry describing it. Tell your readers what you and your companions felt about the event, how you and they reacted to it, and what lasting memories you have of it. Or choose a comparable event such as a wedding or awards ceremony that made a lasting impression on you, and describe it as vividly as you can.

Beauty: When the Other Dancer Is the Self

Alice Walker

Alice Walker (born in Eatonville, Georgia, in 1944) currently resides in northern California. Her novels include The Secret Life of Grange Copeland, Meridian, The Temple of My Familiar, *and* The Color Purple. The Color Purple *received the Pulitzer Prize in 1982; in 1985, it was made into a popular film directed by Steven Spielberg, starring Danny Glover and Whoopi Goldberg, and featuring Oprah Winfrey in her screen debut. Walker has also published two books of short stories, four books of poetry, and two collections of essays. The following selection comes from Walker's book of essays* In Search of Our Mothers' Gardens.

It is a bright summer day in 1947. My father, a fat, funny man with beautiful eyes and a subversive wit, is trying to decide which of his eight children he will take with him to the county fair. My mother, of course, will not go. She is knocked out from getting most of us ready: I hold my neck stiff against the pressure of her knuckles as she hastily completes the braiding and then beribboning of my hair.

My father is the driver for the rich old white lady up the road. Her name is Miss Mey. She owns all the land for miles around, as well as the house in which we live. All I remember about her is that she once offered to pay my mother thirty-five cents for cleaning her house, raking up piles of her magnolia leaves, and washing her family's clothes, and that my mother—she of no money, eight children, and a chronic earache—refused it. But I do not think of this in 1947. I am two and a half years old. I want to go everywhere my daddy goes. I am excited at the prospect of riding in a car. Someone has told me fairs are fun. That there is room in the car for only three of us doesn't faze me at all. Whirling happily in my starchy frock, showing off my biscuit-polished patent-leather shoes and lavender socks, tossing my head in a way that makes my ribbons bounce, I stand, hands on hips, before my father. "Take me, Daddy," I say with assurance; "I'm the prettiest!"

Later, it does not surprise me to find myself in Miss Mey's shiny black car, sharing the back seat with the other lucky ones. Does not surprise me that I thoroughly enjoy the fair. At home that night I tell the unlucky ones all I can remember about the merry-go-round, the man who eats live chickens, and the teddy bears, until they say: that's enough, baby Alice. Shut up now, and go to sleep.

It is Easter Sunday, 1950. I am dressed in a green, flocked, scalloped-hem dress (handmade by my adoring sister, Ruth) that has its own smooth satin petticoat and tiny hot-pink roses tucked into each scallop. My shoes, new T-strap patent leather, again highly biscuit-polished. I am six years old and have learned one of the longest Easter speeches to be heard that day, totally unlike the speech I said when I was two: "Easter lilies / pure and white / blossom in / the morning light." When I rise to give my speech I do so on a great wave of love and pride and expectation. People in the church stop rustling their new crinolines. They seem to hold their breath. I can tell they admire my dress, but it is my spirit, bordering on sassiness (womanishness), they secretly applaud.

"That girl's a little *mess,*" they whisper to each other, pleased.   5

Naturally I say my speech without stammer or pause, unlike those who stutter, stammer, or, worst of all, forget. This is before the word "beautiful" exists in people's vocabulary, but "Oh, isn't she the *cutest* thing!" frequently floats my way. "And got so much sense!" they gratefully add . . . for which thoughtful addition I thank them to this day.

It was great fun being cute. But then, one day, it ended.

I am eight years old and a tomboy. I have a cowboy hat, cowboy boots, checkered shirt and pants, all red. My playmates are my brothers, two and four years older than I. Their colors are black and green, the only difference in the way we are dressed. On Saturday nights we all go to the picture show, even my mother; Westerns are her favorite kind of movie. Back home, "on the ranch," we pretend we are Tom Mix, Hopalong Cassidy, Lash LaRue (we've even named one of our dogs Lash LaRue); we chase each other for hours rustling cattle, being outlaws, delivering damsels from distress. Then my parents decide to buy my brothers guns. These are not "real" guns. They shoot "BBs," copper pellets my brothers say will kill birds. Because I am a girl, I do not get a gun. Instantly I am relegated to the position of Indian. Now there appears a great distance between us. They shoot and shoot at everything with their new guns. I try to keep up with my bow and arrows.

One day while I am standing on top of our makeshift "garage"—pieces of tin nailed across some poles—holding my bow and arrow and looking out toward the fields, I feel an incredible blow in my right eye. I look down just in time to see my brother lower his gun.

Both brothers rush to my side. My eye stings, and I cover it with my hand. "If you tell," they say, "we will get a whipping. You don't want that to happen, do you?" I do not. "Here is a piece of wire," says the older brother, picking it up from the roof; "say you stepped on one end of it and the other flew up and hit you." The pain is beginning to start. "Yes," I say. "Yes, I will say that is what happened." If I do not say this is what happened, I know my brothers will find ways to make me wish I had. But now I will say anything that gets me to my mother.

Confronted by our parents we stick to the lie agreed upon. They place   10
me on a bench on the porch and I close my left eye while they examine the right. There is a tree growing from underneath the porch that climbs past the railing to the roof. It is the last thing my right eye sees. I watch as its trunk, its branches, and then its leaves are blotted out by the rising blood.

I am in shock. First there is intense fever, which my father tries to break using lily leaves bound around my head. Then there are chills: my mother tries to get me to eat soup. Eventually, I do not know how, my parents learn what has happened. A week after the "accident" they take me to see a doctor. "Why did you wait so long to come?" he asks, looking into my eye and shaking his head. "Eyes are sympathetic," he says. "If one is blind, the other will likely become blind too."

This comment of the doctor's terrifies me. But it is really how I look that bothers me most. Where the BB pellet struck there is a glob of whitish scar tissue, a hideous cataract, on my eye. Now when I stare at people—a favorite pastime, up to now—they will stare back. Not at the "cute" little girl, but at her scar. For six years I do not stare at anyone, because I do not raise my head.

Years later, in the throes of a mid-life crisis, I ask my mother and sister whether I changed after the "accident." "No," they say, puzzled. "What do you mean?"

What do I mean?

I am eight, and, for the first time, doing poorly in school, where I have   15
been something of a whiz since I was four. We have just moved to the place where the "accident" occurred. We do not know any of the people around us because this is a different county. The only time I see the friends I knew is when we go back to our old church. The new school is the former state penitentiary. It is a large stone building, cold and drafty, crammed to overflowing with boisterous, ill-disciplined children. On the third floor there is a huge circular imprint of some partition that has been torn out.

"What used to be here?" I ask a sullen girl next to me on our way past it to lunch.

"The electric chair," says she.

At night I have nightmares about the electric chair, and about all the people reputedly "fried" in it. I am afraid of the school, where all the students seem to be budding criminals.

"What's the matter with your eye?" they ask, critically.

When I don't answer (I cannot decide whether it was an "accident" or   20
not), they shove me, insist on a fight.

My brother, the one who created the story about the wire, comes to my rescue. But then brags so much about "protecting" me, I become sick.

After months of torture at the school, my parents decide to send me back to our old community, to my old school. I live with my grandparents and the teacher they board. But there is no room for Phoebe, my cat. By the time my grandparents decide there *is* room, and I ask for my cat, she cannot be found. Miss Yarborough, the boarding teacher, takes me under her wing, and begins to teach me to play the piano. But soon she marries an African— a "prince," she says—and is whisked away to his continent.

At my old school there is at least one teacher who loves me. She is the teacher who "knew me before I was born" and bought my first baby clothes. It is she who makes life bearable. It is her presence that finally helps me turn on the one child at the school who continually calls me "one-eyed bitch." One day I simply grab him by his coat and beat him until I am satisfied. It is my teacher who tells me my mother is ill.

My mother is lying in bed in the middle of the day, something I have never seen. She is in too much pain to speak. She has an abscess in her ear. I stand looking down on her, knowing that if she dies, I cannot live. She is being treated with warm oils and hot bricks held against her cheek. Finally a doctor comes. But I must go back to my grandparents' house. The weeks pass but I am hardly aware of it. All I know is that my mother might die, my father is not so jolly, my brothers still have their guns, and I am the one sent away from home.

"You did not change," they say.   25

Did I imagine the anguish of never looking up?

I am twelve. When relatives come to visit I hide in my room. My cousin Brenda, just my age, whose father works in the post office and whose mother is a nurse, comes to find me. "Hello," she says. And then she asks, looking at my recent school picture, which I did not want taken, and on which the "glob," as I think of it, is clearly visible, "You still can't see out of that eye?"

"No," I say, and flop back on the bed over my book.

That night, as I do almost every night, I abuse my eye. I rant and rave at it, in front of the mirror. I plead with it to clear up before morning. I tell it I hate and despise it. I do not pray for sight. I pray for beauty.

"You did not change," they say.

I am fourteen and baby-sitting for my brother Bill, who lives in Bos-   30 ton. He is my favorite brother and there is a strong bond between us. Understanding my feelings of shame and ugliness he and his wife take me to a local hospital, where the "glob" is removed by a doctor named O. Henry. There is still a small bluish crater where the scar tissue was, but the ugly white stuff is gone. Almost immediately I become a different person from the girl who does not raise her head. Or so I think. Now that I've raised my head I win the boyfriend of my dreams. Now that I've raised my head I have plenty of friends. Now that I've raised my head classwork comes from my lips as faultlessly as Easter speeches did, and I leave high school as valedictorian, most popular student, and *queen*, hardly believing my luck. Ironically, the girl who was voted most beautiful in our class (and was) was later shot twice through the chest by a male companion, using a "real" gun, while she was pregnant. But that's another story in itself. Or is it?

"You did not change," they say.

It is now thirty years since the "accident." A beautiful journalist comes to visit and to interview me. She is going to write a cover story for her magazine that focuses on my latest book. "Decide how you want to look on the cover," she says. "Glamorous, or whatever."

Never mind "glamorous," it is the "whatever" that I hear. Suddenly all I can think of is whether I will get enough sleep the night before the photography session: if I don't, my eye will be tired and wander, as blind eyes will.

At night in bed with my lover I think up reasons why I should not appear on the cover of a magazine. "My meanest critics will say I've sold out," I say. "My family will now realize I write scandalous books."

"But what's the real reason you don't want to do this?" he asks.

"Because in all probability," I say in a rush, "my eye won't be straight."

"It will be straight enough," he says. Then, "Besides, I thought you'd made your peace with that."

And I suddenly remember that I have.

I remember:

I am talking to my brother Jimmy, asking if he remembers anything unusual about the day I was shot. He does not know I consider that day the last time my father, with his sweet home remedy of cool lily leaves, chose me, and that I suffered and raged inside because of this. "Well," he says, "all I remember is standing by the side of the highway with Daddy, trying to flag down a car. A white man stopped, but when Daddy said he needed somebody to take his little girl to the doctor, he drove off."

I remember:

I am in the desert for the first time. I fall totally in love with it. I am so overwhelmed by its beauty, I confront for the first time, consciously, the meaning of the doctor's words years ago: "Eyes are sympathetic. If one is blind, the other will likely become blind too." I realize I have dashed about the world madly, looking at this, looking at that, storing up images against the fading of the light. *But I might have missed seeing the desert!* The shock of that possibility—and gratitude for over twenty-five years of sight—sends me literally to my knees. Poem after poem comes—which is perhaps how poets pray.

On Sight

I am so thankful I have seen
The Desert
And the creatures in the desert
And the desert Itself.

The desert has its own moon
Which I have seen
With my own eye.
There is no flag on it.

Trees of the desert have arms
All of which are always up
That is because the moon is up
The sun is up
Also the sky
The stars
Clouds
None with flags.

If there *were* flags, I doubt
the trees would point.
Would you?

But mostly, I remember this:

I am twenty-seven, and my baby daughter is almost three. Since her birth I have worried about her discovery that her mother's eyes are different from other people's. Will she be embarrassed? I think. What will she say? Every day she watches a television program called "Big Blue Marble." It begins with a picture of the earth as it appears from the moon. It is bluish, a little battered-looking, but full of light, with whitish clouds swirling around it. Every time I see it I weep with love, as if it is a picture of Grandma's house. One day when I am putting Rebecca down for her nap, she suddenly focuses on my eye. Something inside me cringes, gets ready to try to protect myself. All children are cruel about physical differences, I know from experience, and that they don't always mean to be is another matter. I assume Rebecca will be the same.

But no-o-o-o. She studies my face intently as we stand, her inside and   45
me outside her crib. She even holds my face maternally between her dimpled little hands. Then, looking every bit as serious and lawyerlike as her father, she says, as if it may just possibly have slipped my attention: "Mommy, there's a *world* in your eye." (As in, "Don't be alarmed, or do anything crazy.") And then, gently, but with great interest: "Mommy, where did you *get* that world in your eye?"

For the most part, the pain left then. (So what, if my brothers grew up to buy even more powerful pellet guns for their sons and to carry real guns themselves. So what, if a young "Morehouse man" once nearly fell off the steps of Trevor Arnett Library because he thought my eyes were blue.) Crying and laughing I ran to the bathroom, while Rebecca mumbled and sang herself off to sleep. Yes indeed, I realized, looking into the mirror. There *was* a world in my eye. And I saw that it was possible to love it: that in fact, for all it had taught me of shame and anger and inner vision, I *did* love it. Even to see it drifting out of orbit in boredom, or rolling up out of fatigue, not to mention floating back at attention in excitement (bearing witness, a friend has called it), deeply suitable to my personality, and even characteristic of me.

That night I dream I am dancing to Stevie Wonder's song "Always" (the name of the song is really "As," but I hear it as "Always"). As I dance, whirling and joyous, happier than I've ever been in my life, another bright-faced dancer joins me. We dance and kiss each other and hold each other through the night. The other dancer has obviously come through all right, as I have done. She is beautiful, whole and free. And she is also me.

SUGGESTIONS FOR FURTHER STUDY

Key Words

The author uses language with which you may not be familiar. Find the following words in the paragraphs indicated, and explain their meanings in the context of the sentences in which the words appear. Consult a dictionary, as needed.

subversive (par. 1)
beribboning (par. 1)
crinolines (par. 4)
cataract (par. 13)

Topics for Discussion and Writing

1. The "accident" is, for Walker, the central incident in this selection. But she also talks about other incidents in her life, from childhood to adulthood. How do the other incidents relate to the central "accident"?

2. How are the separate incidents at different times during Walker's life tied together to create an integrated story? Look for repeated phrases, visual division of parts, and other techniques that help to integrate individual anecdotes. What effect does Walker achieve by these techniques?

3. Walker frequently uses first person "I" and present tense verbs in telling her story although it is about past events and past emotions.

Discuss with others the effect such a technique has on different readers. Try this experiment to see how different ways of telling stories convey different effects: rewrite one of the short anecdotes in third person and past tense. You will discover other changes that must be made as you rewrite.

4. Write about a significant event in your childhood or adolescence, one that has contributed greatly to the person you have become. Present the event to your readers as vividly as you can. Show them how that event has continued to be important in your life.

The Library Card

Richard Wright

Richard Wright was born in 1908 at Rucker's Plantation near Roxie, Mississippi. All four of his grandparents were born into slavery. In the 1930s he lived, worked, and wrote in New York City, but in 1947 he and his family moved to Paris, France, permanently to escape the racism in New York. He died in Paris in 1960. His works include Uncle Tom's Children *(1938); his classic,* Native Son *(1940); and* Black Boy *(1945), his autobiography.* Native Son *was filmed twice: once in 1950 by Pierre Chenal and again in 1986 by Jerold Freedman. Wright himself starred in the former, playing the tragic hero Bigger Thomas. The following selection from* Black Boy *symbolizes Wright's lifelong battle against racial oppression and prejudice.*

One morning I arrived early at work and went into the bank lobby where the Negro porter was mopping. I stood at a counter and picked up the Memphis *Commercial Appeal* and began my free reading of the press. I came finally to the editorial page and saw an article dealing with one H. L. Mencken. I knew by hearsay that he was the editor of the *American Mercury,* but aside from that I knew nothing about him. The article was a furious denunciation of Mencken, concluding with one hot, short sentence: Mencken is a fool.

I wondered what on earth this Mencken had done to call down upon him the scorn of the South. The only people I had ever heard denounced in the South were Negroes, and this man was not a Negro. Then what ideas did Mencken hold that made a newspaper like the *Commercial Appeal* castigate him publicly? Undoubtedly he must be advocating ideas that the South did not like. Were there, then, people other than Negroes who criticized the South? I knew that during the Civil War the South had hated northern whites, but I had not encountered such hate during my life. Knowing no more of Mencken than I did at that moment, I felt a vague sympathy for him. Had not the South, which had assigned me the role of a non-man, cast at him its hardest words?

Now, how could I find out about this Mencken? There was a huge library near the riverfront, but I knew that Negroes were not allowed to patronize its shelves any more than they were the parks and playgrounds of the city. I had gone into the library several times to get books for the white men on the job. Which of them would now help me to get books? And how could I read them without causing concern to the white men with whom I worked? I had so far been successful in hiding my thoughts and feelings from them, but I knew that I would create hostility if I went about this business of reading in a clumsy way.

I weighed the personalities of the men on the job. There was Don, a Jew; but I distrusted him. His position was not much better than mine and I knew that he was uneasy and insecure; he had always treated me in an off-hand, bantering way that barely concealed his contempt. I was afraid to ask him to help me to get books; his frantic desire to demonstrate a racial solidarity with the whites against Negroes might make him betray me.

Then how about the boss? No, he was a Baptist and I had the suspicion 5 that he would not be quite able to comprehend why a black boy would want to read Mencken. There were other white men on the job whose attitudes showed clearly that they were Kluxers or sympathizers, and they were out of the question.

There remained only one man whose attitude did not fit into an anti-Negro category, for I had heard the white men refer to him as a "Pope lover." He was an Irish Catholic and was hated by the white Southerners. I knew that he read books, because I had got him volumes from the library several times. Since he, too, was an object of hatred, I felt that he might refuse me but would hardly betray me. I hesitated, weighing and balancing the imponderable realities.

One morning I paused before the Catholic fellow's desk.

"I want to ask you a favor," I whispered to him.

"What is it?"

"I want to read. I can't get books from the library. I wonder if you'd let 10 me use your card?"

He looked at me suspiciously.

"My card is full most of the time," he said.

"I see," I said and waited, posing my question silently.

"You're not trying to get me into trouble, are you, boy?" he asked, staring at me.

"Oh, no, sir." 15

"What book do you want?"

"A book by H. L. Mencken."

"Which one?"

"I don't know. Has he written more than one?"

"He has written several." 20

"I didn't know that."

"What makes you want to read Mencken?"

"Oh, I just saw his name in the newspaper," I said.

"It's good of you to want to read," he said. "But you ought to read the right things."

I said nothing. Would he want to supervise my reading?   25

"Let me think," he said. "I'll figure out something."

I turned from him and he called me back. He stared at me quizzically.

"Richard, don't mention this to the other white men," he said.

"I understand," I said. "I won't say a word."

A few days later he called me to him.   30

"I've got a card in my wife's name," he said. "Here's mine."

"Thank you, sir."

"Do you think you can manage it?"

"I'll manage fine," I said.

"If they suspect you, you'll get in trouble," he said.   35

"I'll write the same kind of notes to the library that you wrote when you sent me for books," I told him. "I'll sign your name."

He laughed.

"Go ahead. Let me see what you get," he said.

That afternoon I addressed myself to forging a note. Now, what were the names of books written by H. L. Mencken? I did not know any of them. I finally wrote what I thought would be a foolproof note: *Dear Madam: Will you please let this nigger boy*—I used the word "nigger" to make the librarian feel that I could not possibly be the author of the note—*have some books by H. L. Mencken?* I forged the white man's name.

I entered the library as I had always done when on errands for whites,   40
but I felt that I would somehow slip up and betray myself. I doffed my hat, stood a respectful distance from the desk, looked as unbookish as possible, and waited for the white patrons to be taken care of. When the desk was clear of people, I still waited. The white librarian looked at me.

"What do you want, boy?"

As though I did not possess the power of speech, I stepped forward and simply handed her the forged note, not parting my lips.

"What books by Mencken does he want?" she asked.

"I don't know, ma'am," I said, avoiding her eyes.

"Who gave you this card?"   45

"Mr. Falk," I said.

"Where is he?"

"He's at work, at the M— Optical Company," I said. "I've been in here for him before."

"I remember," the woman said. "But he never wrote notes like this."

Oh, God, she's suspicious. Perhaps she would not let me have the   50
books? If she had turned her back at that moment, I would have ducked out the door and never gone back. Then I thought of a bold idea.

"You can call him up, ma'am," I said, my heart pounding.

"You're not using these books, are you?" she asked pointedly.

"Oh, no, ma'am. I can't read."

"I don't know what he wants by Mencken," she said under her breath.

I knew now that I had won; she was thinking of other things and the   55
race question had gone out of her mind. She went to the shelves. Once or
twice she looked over her shoulder at me, as though she was still doubtful.
Finally she came forward with two books in her hand.

"I'm sending him two books," she said. "But tell Mr. Falk to come in
next time, or send me the names of the books he wants. I don't know what
he wants to read."

I said nothing. She stamped the card and handed me the books. Not daring to glance at them, I went out of the library, fearing that the woman would
call me back for further questioning. A block away from the library I opened
one of the books and read a title: *A Book of Prefaces*. I was nearing my nineteenth birthday and I did not know how to pronounce the word "preface." I
thumbed the pages and saw strange words and strange names. I shook my
head, disappointed. I looked at the other book; it was called *Prejudices*. I
knew what that word meant; I had heard it all my life. And right off I was on
guard against Mencken's books. Why would a man want to call a book
Prejudices? The word was so stained with all my memories of racial hate that
I could not conceive of anybody using it for a title. Perhaps I had made a mistake about Mencken? A man who had prejudices must be wrong.

When I showed the books to Mr. Falk, he looked at me and frowned.

"That librarian might telephone you," I warned him.

"That's all right," he said. "But when you're through reading those   60
books, I want you to tell me what you get out of them."

That night in my rented room, while letting the hot water run over my
can of pork and beans in the sink, I opened *A Book of Prefaces* and began
to read. I was jarred and shocked by the style, the clear, clean, sweeping sentences. Why did he write like that? And how did one write like that? I pictured the man as a raging demon, slashing with his pen, consumed with
hate, denouncing everything American, extolling everything European or
German, laughing at the weaknesses of people, mocking God, authority.
What was this? I stood up, trying to realize what reality lay behind the
meaning of the words. . . . Yes, this man was fighting, fighting with words.
He was using words as a weapon, using them as one would use a club.
Could words be weapons? Well, yes, for here they were. Then, maybe, perhaps, I could use them as a weapon? No. It frightened me. I read on and
what amazed me was not what he said, but how on earth anybody had the
courage to say it.

Occasionally I glanced up to reassure myself that I was alone in the
room. Who were these men about whom Mencken was talking so passionately? Who was Anatole France? Joseph Conrad? Sinclair Lewis, Sherwood

Anderson, Dostoevski, George Moore, Gustave Flaubert, Maupassant, Tolstoy, Frank Harris, Mark Twain, Thomas Hardy, Arnold Bennett, Stephen Crane, Zola, Norris, Gorky, Bergson, Ibsen, Balzac, Bernard Shaw, Dumas, Poe, Thomas Mann, O. Henry, Dreiser, H. G. Wells, Gogol, T. S. Eliot, Gide, Baudelaire, Edgar Lee Masters, Stendhal, Turgenev, Huneker, Nietzsche, and scores of others? Were these men real? Did they exist or had they existed? And how did one pronounce their names?

I ran across many words whose meanings I did not know, and I either looked them up in a dictionary or, before I had a chance to do that, encountered the word in a context that made its meaning clear. But what strange world was this? I concluded the book with the conviction that I had somehow overlooked something terribly important in life. I had once tried to write, had once reveled in feeling, had let my crude imagination roam, but the impulse to dream had been slowly beaten out of me by experience. Now it surged up again and I hungered for books, new ways of looking and seeing. It was not a matter of believing or disbelieving what I read, but of feeling something new, of being affected by something that made the look of the world different.

As dawn broke I ate my pork and beans, feeling dopey, sleepy. I went to work, but the mood of the book would not die; it lingered, coloring everything I saw, heard, did. I now felt that I knew what the white men were feeling. Merely because I had read a book that had spoken of how they lived and thought, I identified myself with that book. I felt vaguely guilty. Would I, filled with bookish notions, act in a manner that would make the whites dislike me?

I forged more notes and my trips to the library became frequent.   65 Reading grew into a passion. My first serious novel was Sinclair Lewis's *Main Street*. It made me see my boss, Mr. Gerald, and identify him as an American type. I would smile when I saw him lugging his golf bags into the office. I had always felt a vast distance separating me from the boss, and now I felt closer to him, though still distant. I felt now that I knew him, that I could feel the very limits of his narrow life. And this had happened because I had read a novel about a mythical man called George F. Babbitt.

The plots and stories in the novels did not interest me so much as the point of view revealed. I gave myself over to each novel without reserve, without trying to criticize it; it was enough for me to see and feel something different. And for me, everything was something different. Reading was like a drug, a dope. The novels created moods in which I lived for days. But I could not conquer my sense of guilt, my feeling that the white men around me knew that I was changing, that I had begun to regard them differently.

Whenever I brought a book to the job, I wrapped it in newspaper—a habit that was to persist for years in other cities and under other circumstances. But some of the white men pried into my packages when I was absent and they questioned me.

"Boy, what are you reading those books for?"

"Oh, I don't know, sir."

"That's deep stuff you're reading, boy."

"I'm just killing time, sir."

"You'll addle your brains if you don't watch out."

I read Dreiser's *Jennie Gerhardt* and *Sister Carrie* and they revived in me a vivid sense of my mother's suffering; I was overwhelmed. I grew silent, wondering about the life around me. It would have been impossible for me to have told anyone what I derived from these novels, for it was nothing less than a sense of life itself. All my life had shaped me for the realism, the naturalism of the modern novel, and I could not read enough of them.

Steeped in new moods and ideas, I bought a ream of paper and tried to write; but nothing would come, or what did come was flat beyond telling. I discovered that more than desire and feeling were necessary to write and I dropped the idea. Yet I still wondered how it was possible to know people sufficiently to write about them? Could I ever learn about life and people? To me, with my vast ignorance, my Jim Crow station in life, it seemed a task impossible of achievement. I now knew what being a Negro meant. I could endure the hunger. I had learned to live with hate. But to feel that there were feelings denied me, that the very breath of life itself was beyond my reach, that more than anything else hurt, wounded me. I had a new hunger.

In buoying me up, reading also cast me down, made me see what was   75 possible, what I had missed. My tension returned, new, terrible, bitter, surging, almost too great to be contained. I no longer *felt* that the world about me was hostile, killing; I *knew* it. A million times I asked myself what I could do to save myself, and there were no answers. I seemed forever condemned, ringed by walls.

I did not discuss my reading with Mr. Falk, who had lent me his library card; it would have meant talking about myself and that would have been too painful. I smiled each day, fighting desperately to maintain my old behavior, to keep my disposition seemingly sunny. But some of the white men discerned that I had begun to brood.

"Wake up there, boy!" Mr. Olin said one day.

"Sir!" I answered for the lack of a better word.

"You act like you've stolen something," he said.

I laughed in the way I knew he expected me to laugh, but I resolved to   80 be more conscious of myself, to watch my every act, to guard and hide the new knowledge that was dawning within me.

If I went north, would it be possible for me to build a new life then? But how could a man build a life upon vague, unformed yearnings? I wanted to write and I did not even know the English language. I bought English grammars and found them dull. I felt that I was getting a better sense of the language from novels than from grammars. I read hard, discarding a writer as soon as I felt that I had grasped his point of view. At night the printed page stood before my eyes in sleep.

Mrs. Moss, my landlady, asked me one Sunday morning: "Son, what is this you keep on reading?"

"Oh, nothing. Just novels."

"What you get out of 'em?"

"I'm just killing time," I said.

85

"I hope you know your own mind," she said in a tone which implied that she doubted if I had a mind.

I knew of no Negroes who read the books I liked and I wondered if any Negroes ever thought of them. I knew that there were Negro doctors, lawyers, newspapermen, but I never saw any of them. When I read a Negro newspaper I never caught the faintest echo of my preoccupation in its pages. I felt trapped and occasionally, for a few days, I would stop reading. But a vague hunger would come over me for books, books that opened up new avenues of feeling and seeing, and again I would forge another note to the white librarian. Again I would read and wonder as only the naive and unlettered can read and wonder, feeling that I carried a secret, criminal burden about with me each day.

That winter my mother and brother came and we set up housekeeping, buying furniture on the installment plan, being cheated and yet knowing no way to avoid it. I began to eat warm food and to my surprise found that regular meals enabled me to read faster. I may have lived through many illnesses and survived them, never suspecting that I was ill. My brother obtained a job and we began to save toward the trip north, plotting our time, setting tentative dates for departure. I told none of the white men on the job that I was planning to go north; I knew that the moment they felt I was thinking of the North they would change toward me. It would have made them feel that I did not like the life I was living, and because my life was completely conditioned by what they said or did, it would have been tantamount to challenging them.

I could calculate my chances for life in the South as a Negro fairly clearly now.

I could fight the southern whites by organizing with other Negroes, as   90 my grandfather had done. But I knew that I could never win that way; there were many whites and there were but few blacks. They were strong and we were weak. Outright black rebellion could never win. If I fought openly I would die and I did not want to die. News of lynchings were frequent.

I could submit and live the life of a genial slave, but that was impossible. All of my life had shaped me to live by my own feelings and thoughts. I could make up to Bess and marry her and inherit the house. But that, too, would be the life of a slave; if I did that, I would crush to death something within me, and I would hate myself as much as I knew the whites already hated those who had submitted. Neither could I ever willingly present myself to be kicked, as Shorty had done. I would rather have died than do that.

I could drain off my restlessness by fighting with Shorty or Harrison. I had seen many Negroes solve the problem of being black by transferring their hatred of themselves to others with a black skin and fighting them. I would have to be cold to do that, and I was not cold and I could never be.

I could, of course, forget what I had read, thrust the whites out of my mind, forget them; and find release from anxiety and longing in sex and alcohol. But the memory of how my father had conducted himself made that course repugnant. If I did not want others to violate my life, how could I voluntarily violate it myself?

I had no hope whatever of being a professional man. Not only had I been so conditioned that I did not desire it, but the fulfillment of such an ambition was beyond my capabilities. Well-to-do Negroes lived in a world that was almost as alien to me as the world inhabited by whites.

What, then, was there? I held my life in my mind, in my consciousness each day, feeling at times that I would stumble and drop it, spill it forever. My reading had created a vast sense of distance between me and the world in which I lived and tried to make a living, and that sense of distance was increasing each day. My days and nights were one long, quiet, continuously contained dream of terror, tension, and anxiety. I wondered how long I could bear it. 95

SUGGESTIONS FOR FURTHER STUDY

Key Words

The author uses language with which you may not be familiar. Find the following words in the paragraphs indicated, and explain their meanings in the context of the sentences in which the words appear. Consult a dictionary, as needed.

castigate (par. 2)
bantering (par. 4)
doffed (par. 40)
preface (par. 57)
extolling (par. 61)
reveled (par. 63)
naive (par. 87)
tantamount (par. 88)
repugnant (par. 93)

Topics for Discussion and Writing

1. Research the life and career of Richard Wright. Then indicate what descriptions of the setting and actions in this chapter of his auto-

biography reflect the times in which Wright lived. Note particularly his need to be deceptive about checking out books from the library, his manners in relating to other people, and his choice of reading materials.

2. Wright talks about his reaction to reading Mencken's *A Book of Prefaces*. What does he mean by "using words as weapons"? Explain how reading Mencken's book changed his life as a reader. What does Wright say about how reading the works of H. L. Mencken, Sinclair Lewis, Theodore Dreiser, and other authors influenced his insight into "life and people"?

3. Wright says that reading stirred a "vague hunger . . . for books, books that opened up new avenues of feeling and seeing . . ." (par. 87) Later he writes "I held my life in my mind, in my consciousness each day" and "[m]y reading had created a vast sense of distance between me and the world in which I lived and tried to make a living . . ." (par. 95). If you have ever experienced a similar reaction to or feeling about reading, write a journal entry or brief essay explaining that experience and indicating its impact on you. You may want to focus on a single book or author rather than many books or authors in general.

The Last Dance Is
Always a Slow Dance

Lois-Ann Yamanaka

Lois-Ann Yamanaka, a Japanese American native of Hawaii, currently is living in Honolulu. She is the author of the award-winning short-story collection Saturday Night at the Pahala Theater, *and she appears on PBS's* United States of Poetry *series. The following section appears in Yamanaka's first novel,* Wild Meat and the Bully Burgers (1996). *The narrator, young Lovey Nariyoshi, tells her story in Hawaiian Creole (the local spoken dialect) which adds to the distinctiveness of her narrative.*

From the window, we can see Jenks by the bathroom. He can see us too. Lucky if we get a head jerk by the end of recess. One by the end of the year. One that we can count.

At school, it's always Jerry and me in the typing teacher's class 'cause he's our next period after lunch recess and has a phonograph he lets us use to play our Carly Simon records.

At school, Jenks stays with Levi Nalani, Kenneth Spencer, Thomas Lorenzo, and Baron Ahuna, who's still going with Ginger Geiger. They hang by the courts or by B-building bathroom.

On the weekends, Jenks and me still work down at the Lei Stand for his mother, Aunty Shige. When we have nothing better to do on our lunch breaks and Jerry comes down to the Lei Stand with his mother on Saturdays, we count.

The fishing boats out past the break. The haole tourists with matching clothes. All the shells on the leis from the Philippines. Sand crabs. The stones in the moss rock wall across the street.

Jerry and me got our own count going at school. We figure by the end of the year Jenks will top five times that he actually made like he knew us at school. Count the time he sat with us at the bus stop. Count the time he sat on the bench with us at recess. By the caf.

We know that Jenks and us are good friends on the weekends, even though at school all we get is a head jerk, "howzit," but never when Lori Shigemura and her friends are around us or Patti Paet, Kawehi Wells,

Natalie Leialoha, or Marlene Spencer around the corner. So we can count about five of those times too by the end of the year.

I guess God knows what kind of friends we are. That's what counts. That Lori, Gina, Traci, and Jodie don't know doesn't matter. God counts the times we all sat on the beach and ended the day leaning on each other talking story.

We read aloud too. Old *Watchtower* magazines from Mrs. Gomes down the beach road. "Masturbation: Why It's Evil and Against God."

Jenks got all tall and handsome this year. Part Hawaiian and Japanese with some haole blood. And after that dope-stealing thing passed and Jenks said it wasn't his anyways, we started work together at the beach on the weekends.   10

Mostly if Larry and Dwayne aren't there, we play Hawaiian music cassettes and harmonize so nice in our booth that the tourists buy lots more from us. Make our own lunch and trade sandwiches. Sew the ugliest lei contest and then who can sell it before the day's up. Wear matching T-shirts from the gift shop in the hotel. Just like Jerry and me but better.

Jenks told me last Sunday, "With you and Jerry, I can be who I like, 'cause you guys no care. With Baron and Thomas them, gotta ack, eh. But they the braddas, right?"

I should've said something right there about ignoring Jerry and me in school and how one or several love or friendship type moves from him would instantly make us popular. But I don't.

In our school, if part Hawaiian goes with pure Jap, that's the ultimate. Everybody wants a hapa girlfriend or boyfriend. Everybody wants a part Hawaiian person. The Cosmopolitan May Day Prince and Princess, to our school, that's the Most Handsome and Most Pretty in the Hoss Elections. And Jenks was Cosmopolitan Prince and Most Handsome this year. Plus Valentine's Court King and Nicest Smile.

Jerry says, "For sure Jenks going ask you for dance so plenny times at   15
the Grad Dance. Just like he going ask you for *go with him*. The way he ack when you guys at the Lei Stand—" Jerry says this at least all the time nowadays.

"Then why he ignore us in school?" I ask him.

" 'Cause, okay, Lovey, I your best friend so I going be honest, okay? He popular, right? He all handsome since Aunty Shige took him dermatologist, right? I mean, he going be on the JV volleyball team next year and all the girls kinda nuts over him, right? But he like *you*. But you *unpopular*.

"But I promise, I know his tricks 'cause I one boy too. See, on the night of the Grad Dance, he going ask you for dance with him fast songs for warm-up, then plenny slow songs to get the courage for whisper in your ear, 'I like go with you.'

"Then after that, going be summer and you guys going go together and next year, you guys already going be going strong and then, Lovey, and then, you going go from unpopular to popular over the summer. Promise."

"How you know this, Jerome?" I ask him. Then Jerry shrugs his shoulders and makes like he has the biggest secret he cannot tell.   20

"Believe me, Lovey. *I know.* And what I know, I know for a fact. Plus, I seen you guys holding hands by the ponds last Saturday. He going ask you for dance so many times, you going melt. Count on it."

From the window of Mr. Otake's typing class, we can see Jenks by the bathroom. He can see us too. Lucky if we get a head jerk by the end of recess. One by the end of the year. One that we can count.

Grad Dance. Semiformal Attire. Cafeteria. 7:00 p.m. to 10:00 p.m. Featuring the Sounds of Pegasus DJs and Company. Theme: *Seasons in the Sun.*

All the teachers say, "Wear like Sunday best, no miniature high school prom. Nobody better wear gloves or gowns or you going straight home. And, boys, no three-piece suits or tux or we'll call your father from the cafeteria manager's phone and send you straight home too. No bouquets or corsage. No be silly or we'll cancel the Grad Dance, you wait. Damn kids act like this one prom and all the damn mothers calling the school asking why they gotta spend one hundred dollars for gown, hair appointment, flowers, heels, makeup, and limo too. Get a grip on yourselves. Please."

Jerry got himself on the Grad Dance Committee. He worked all year on   25
getting kind of popular so that he could make me kind of popular and on committees too. All he could do for now was put me on the Grad Dance Cleanup Committee. Not Refreshments even or, best of all, the Decorations Committee.

Seasons in the Sun—cardboard letters covered first with tinfoil, then blue cellophane, blue being everybody's favorite color these days, and the members of the Grad Dance Committee get to take the letters home. Usually the initials of someone they like or their own initials to masking-tape to their bedroom wall. But no J's or L's, so big deal.

When Jenks dances with me, and I know he will, all the Rays of the Rising Dawn and Chantilly and Lace Emeralds will wonder why this tall, athletic, and part Hawaiian chose me. And all those girls who thought I was making all this Jenks stuff up will finally see for sure who was telling the truth. And all those suicide notes I wrote for all the times Gina, Laura, Traci, and Lori humiliated me, I can rip them all up, after Jenks asks me to dance.

Grad Dance Committee members have to start off the first dance, so Jerry says he'll dance with me. Take that long walk across the cafeteria concrete floor to dance with me, the shiny mirrored disco ball spinning lights all around us.

6:30. My mother acts like it's a prom. Takes Polaroids of Jerry and me by the front door. Me with the Yvonne Elliman lip mole eyebrow pencil job my mother put on my upper lip. False eyelashes too and jade-colored Revlon eye shadow. Eyebrows plucked for the first time and penciled in with an arch. Mother painted my fingernails and toenails Peachy-Keen Cutex to match my dress and makes a fake Press-on with Scotch tape for the baby finger only, the nail I bit off to the meat in nervousness over the Grad Dance.

When Jerry's mother drops us off, we act cool and walk toward the main door of the cafeteria. It smells stink in there. All closed up to make it real dark, the smell of sour milk, dry yeast, bare feet on damp cement, and stale heat. It's hot inside and the disco lights spin red and yellow like the lights on City and County cars, the Pegasus DJs and Company high on the stage borrowed from Mr. Hokama, the band teacher.

Everybody's here.

Everybody who's anybody served on the Grad Dance Committee and arrived an hour early.

Lori Shigemura dressed in black chiffon all the way to the floor. Baby's breath and red baby roses with leather fern in her bouffant hairdo. A matching wrist corsage that she probably ordered for herself. Grad Dance Committee chairperson can dress formal attire and not be sent home, I guess.

Gina Oshiro. Tiara in hair and long white gloves.

Laura Murayama. Home-sewn, shiny quiana lavender, off-the-shoulder, with lots of gathers by the waist, to-the-floor gown, looking pretty prom-ish to me and two tons of baby's breath in her hair.

I don't see anybody being sent home.

And all the Rays of the Rising Dawn and Chantilly Lace and Emeralds members taking pictures with their Instamatic cameras and throwing the used flashcubes behind the hibiscus hedge. While dorks like Jerry stand around waiting to be asked to be in a picture or two with the great and popular ones.

The cafeteria doors close like institution doors. Clink shut.

Jerry dances the first dance with me like he said he would and all the time looking around the dance floor for who he can dance with next and who's dancing with who.

I go back and sit with Nancy Miyamoto holding hands with Craig Kunishige on the folded cafeteria tables. And whenever they go up for a dance, Nancy says, "Watch my bag, eh." All night long, "Watch my bag, eh, Lovey. Hea, watch this for me." Shove the shiny sequins black clutch bag across the linoleum tabletop. Like what she got in there? Only her damn lip gloss and a brush. Big deal.

Every dance I go to makes me think of every other dance I've been to—sitting there on the side, watching all the boys, and waiting as every crowd of boys comes over to the girls' side of the caf, waiting for someone's eyes to meet mine, waiting for the head jerk to the dance floor as I point to my chest: Who me?

Anybody.

And as the crowd leaves for the dance floor and the leftovers sit on the cafeteria chairs, Jerry's in the back of the crowd waiting to see if I need someone to dance with and it's him and me. Jerry and me.

But tonight, he wants to dance with Lori Shigemura. He makes like I'm jealous and maybe I am jealous but maybe it's because I'm always left sitting on the side with Ruby Hagimura, who weighs two hundred pounds, chews her bubble gum like it's always in the juicy stage, has pimples on pimples and gums swelling over her silver braces. Maybe I'm jealous because he acts like I should be jealous, so I pretend to be. Jerry dances lots of dances with Lori Shigemura. Black chiffon gibbon chocho lips monkey.

I dance once with Dennis Kawano. Short. Japanese. Side comb. Oily, slicked-back hair. Dances like an elf. I watch everything that Jenks does with side eye and he sees me, looks at me for a long time like he's about ready to come over, but always turns away. When my mother and Jerry's mother ask if Jenks danced with me, what will I say? No, but he looked long and hard at me. It's so humiliating. Looks, turns away, and talks to Thomas Lorenzo and Baron Ahuna, who has his hands on Ginger Geiger's ass. All night so far.

Jenks dances every dance with a popular cosmopolitan girl. Tonight, he didn't even say hi to me and he was here early because Lori put him on the Decorations Committee though he didn't do nothing but put up the letters 'cause he's tall. Not one hi. Not outside. Not in the cookie-and-punch break. Not on the cafeteria dance floor. Not once.

So far, Jenks danced with Wilma Kahale, Pop Warner cheerleader for the Homestead Chargers with thick thighs and one line of hair for eyebrows.

Kawehi Wells. Rich with haole father, who sends her to tennis lessons at the hotel with a real pro and never the Parks and Recreation League with the rest of us.

Natalie Leialoha. May Day Queen, Valentine's Court attendant, small waist and big ass but who can tell in a gown, right?

Marlene Spencer. Younger sister of the co-captain of the Hilo High School Viking boys varsity volleyball team and cousin of Kenneth and Melvin Spencer.

Patty Paet. Sworn Jap hater, spent the whole year smoking cigarettes and swearing in the B-building girls' bathroom with fresh purple hickeys all over her neck every day.

Slow-dance twice with Jamielyn Trevino surfer style with his face in her hair, hold her hand onto the floor, then off the floor. Jenks's ex, Jamielyn.

"Lovey, dance with me this slow one, please."

"Feeling sorry for me, Jerry? Fuck off."

"Fuck you too then. C'mon, Lori." And all the Rays laugh. Then they   55
all get the let's-dance head jerk one by one and I watch all the bags again.
Tell you the truth, if Dennis Kawano asked, I would dance with him. I mean
even if I would be dancing with an elf, better than sitting here behind the
huge pile of bags and lace shawls.

Shame, I tell you, sitting here by myself with only Ruby Hagimura and
Melody Maldonado on the other end of the cafeteria table and they so
shame, they don't even talk to each other and they're friends.

"I go ask Jenks for dance with you already, Lovey. At least one time,
that fucka."

"Aw fuck him too. Why, Jerry? What I did wrong?"

"Maybe that *was his dope* we stole long time ago to buy all that Barbie
stuff but he holding out the truth."

"I doubt it."   60

"Maybe," Jerry says and pulls me to the dance floor.

"Frankenstein." "Pick Up the Pieces." "Chinagrove."

But the last dance is always a slow dance.

Jerry walks me off the floor. We're dripping.

"Nightbird" by Kalapana.   65

"*Oh God.*" The whole class sighs at once.

"I going dance with Lori," Jerry tells me as he runs to get her. Trying to
make sure he's for real popular next year.

I sly-eye try to look for Jenks. Like I care already. I hate him too, the
coward. Cannot even make like he knows us Japs. Well, I don't know him
too. Not even one fast dance. My nostrils start flaring. So I don't even know
who taps me on the shoulder.

Him. It's really him. It sounds made up but it's for real. Feet don't feel
the ground. Put my arms around his neck. He's so tall. And handsome.

"*Soar onto the night wind. Take a star to her for me.*"   70

See Lori and Jerry and wave like I was meant to be there. Lori staring.
Dot the *i* with hearts Traci and Jodie too—a popular Hawaiian and a Jap.

Jenks pulling me close. He smells like everyone else's perfume and
sweat. Breathing heavy. My face on his chest, his mouth by my ear. My
hands in his hair. *Oh God.*

Flute solo at the end of the song.

I want the song to go on and on, of course. It doesn't. When the dance
ends and the lights immediately go on, Jerry and me sit together on the cafeteria chairs. Jenks goes back to Thomas, Baron, and Levi, who hoot and
tease him about dancing all out on the last dance with a dork.

The teachers yak at the door, the disco ball comes down, and Jerry and   75
me and a few other dorks start sweeping. The Cleanup Committee of five.

"Lovey, Your Yvonne Elliman lip mole. Stay gone. And one eyebrow
too. Musta smeared off."

"You mean I danced the last dance with Jenks with one eyebrow and no lip mole?"

"He waiting outside for us 'cause his mother and father playing poker at your house tonight. Tonight poker night, remember? He told me he catching ride home with us."

"Oh shit."

Jerry leans on his broom and peeks out of the dusty cafeteria window. "Omigod, Lovey. Jenks get your eyebrow mark on his cheek, look. The lip mole too, on his neck, oh no." 80

"Omigod, Jerry, my Press-on Scotch tape fingernail gone too."

"Holy shit, Lovey, where you was touching. I seen you touching all over the place. Ho, when we get close, I go look fo' um. Maybe stay on his ass. Nah."

I grab a broom and start to sweep. Jerry and me laugh and laugh until my false eyelashes peel off. Jerry peels them off and sticks them to his balls, says, "Fuzz." Then sticks them to his knuckles, says, "Uncle Ed. Hairy knuckles."

He holds the dustpan for me and by the time the five of us on the Cleanup Committee finish, even the yellow bug lights outside the cafeteria go off.

In the dark, Jenks, Jerry, and me wait for our ride home and nobody 85 says very much. So that when my mother pulls up in front of us in the Land Rover missing one headlight, it's kind of a relief.

Then I see Jenks up close with the eyebrow on his cheek and lip mole on his neck. Jerry's scanning Jenks's ass for the fingernail. And Jenks, he looks so serious like he just made the greatest sacrifice of his life, the hero of the story, the happy ending, so that when we get home and Aunty Shige asks in front of all the adults, "So, Jenks, did you dance with Lovey?" he can say, "Yes, Mommy."

Jenks opens the backseat door of the Land Rover for me, and then the *after-you* gesture for me to get in the car before him so we can sit close together in the back.

But when Jerry climbs in the backseat after me, instead of Jenks, puts his arm around my neck, and kisses me, the two of us punching each other's arms and singing "Nightbird" in harmony, we look long into each other's eyes, Jerry and me. I rest my head on his shoulders and laugh on our way home.

SUGGESTIONS FOR FURTHER STUDY

Language and Style

The uniqueness of this narrative is its use of local dialect, in this case the dialect of Hawaiian Creole (what nonspecialists have called "pidgin

English") spoken by Hawaiian teenagers. Find out how *Creole* or *pidgin* are defined by linguists and others who study language formation, and discuss these terms. Then do the following:

1. Make a list of several examples of words and phrases in this selection that you think represent that dialect. What do they mean?

2. How would you say the same things in your dialect, the variety of English you speak? Translate several of the examples you chose from Yamanaka's story into your own dialect.

Topics for Discussion and Writing

1. Although the characters in this story may speak a dialect different from yours, the situation and events described in it may seem quite familiar—at least recognizable. Discuss with other readers what characters, situations, and attitudes in the story seem familiar and realistic to you. What seems most similar to or dissimilar from your experience in a comparable situation?

2. How does the writer achieve the effect of actual people talking in their natural manner? How do you characterize that "talk"? Select several examples of "talk" in this selection, and discuss their effect on you as a reader.

3. Select a recent experience and write a narrative account of it in the dialect you ordinarily use in speaking to your friends. When you have finished, ask a friend to read your story and comment on whether or not your language in the story "sounds" the way you usually talk.

Mauve Desert

Nicole Brossard

*Nicole Brossard, poet, novelist, and essayist, was born in Montreal
in 1943. Her work has influenced thinking about feminism, postmod-
ernism, and lesbianism. Her books, translated into English, include*
Mauve Desert *(1987) and* Picture Theory *(1990). She has twice been
awarded Canada's most prestigious literary prize, Governor General's
Award for poetry in 1974 and 1984. The following selection features
the beginning of her novel* Mauve Desert.

The desert is indescribable. Reality rushes into it, rapid light. The gaze   1
melts. Yet this morning. Very young, I was already crying over humanity.
With every new year I could see it dissolving in hope and in violence. Very
young, I would take my mother's Meteor and drive into the desert. There I
spent entire days, nights, dawns. Driving fast and then slowly, spinning out
the light in its mauve and small lines which like veins mapped a great tree of
life in my eyes.

I was wide awake in the questioning but inside me was a desire which
free of obstacles frightened me like a certitude. Then would come the pink,
the rust, and the grey among the stones, the mauve and the light of dawn. In
the distance, the flashing wings of a tourist helicopter.

Very young I had no future like the shack on the corner which one day
was set on fire by some guys who 'came from far away,' said my mother
who had served them drinks. Only one of them was armed, she had sworn
to me. Only one among them. All the others were blonde. My mother
always talked about men as if they had seen the day in a book. She would
say no more and go back to her television set. I could see her profile and the
reflection of the little silver comb she always wore in her hair and to which I
attributed magical powers. Her apron was yellow with little flowers. I never
saw her wearing a dress.

I was moving forward in life, wild-eyed with arrogance. I was fifteen.
This was a delight like the power of dying or of driving into the night with
circles under my eyes, absolutely delirious spaces edging the gaze.

I was well acquainted with the desert and the roads running through it.   5
Lorna, this friend of my mother's, had introduced me to erosion, to all the
ghosts living in the stone and the dust. She had described landscapes, some

familiar, some absolutely incompatible with the vegetation and barren soil of my childhood. Lorna was inventing. I knew she was because even I knew how to distinguish between a Western diamondback and a rattlesnake, between a troglodyte and a mourning turtledove. Lorna was inventing. Sometimes she seemed to be barking, so rough and unthinkable were her words. Lorna had not known childhood, only young girls after school whom she would ostentatiously arrange to meet at noon. The girls loved kissing her on the mouth. She loved girls who let themselves be kissed on the mouth.

The first time I saw Lorna I found her beautiful and said the word 'bitch.' I was five years old. At supper my mother was smiling at her. They would look at each other and when they spoke their voices were full of intonations. I obstinately observed their mouths. Whenever they pronounced words starting with *m*, their lips would disappear for a moment then, swollen, reanimate with incredible speed. Lorna said she liked moly and salmon mousse. I spilled my glass of milk and the tablecloth changed into America with Florida seeping under the saltshaker. My mother mopped up America. My mother always pretended not to notice when things were dirtied.

I often took to the road. Long before I got my driver's license. At high noon, at dusk, even at night, I would leave with my mother yelling sharp words at me which would get lost in the parking lot dust. I always headed for the desert because very young I wanted to know why in books they forget to mention the desert. I knew my mother would be alone like a woman can be but I was fleeing the magical reflection of the comb in her hair, seeking the burning reflections of the blinding sun, seeking the night in the dazzled eyes of hares, a ray of life. 'Let me confront aridity,' and I would floor the accelerator, wild with the damned energy of my fifteen years. Some day I would reach the right age and time as necessary as a birth date to get life over with. Some day I would be fast, so fast, sharp so sharp, some day, faced with the necessity of dawn, I would have forgotten the civilization of men who came to the desert to watch their equations explode like a humanity. I was driving fast, alone like a character cut out of history. Saying 'so many times I have sunk into the future.'

At night there was the desert, the shining eyes of antelope jack rabbits, *senita* flowers that bloom only in the night. Lying under the Meteor's headlights was the body of a humanity that did not know Arizona. Humanity was fragile because it did not suspect Arizona's existence. So fragile. I was fifteen and hungered for everything to be as in my body's fragility, that impatient tolerance making the body necessary. I was an expert driver, wild-eyed in mid-night, capable of going forward in the dark. I knew all that like a despair capable of setting me free of everything. Eternity was a shadow cast in music, a fever of the brain making it topple over into the tracings of highways. Humanity was fragile, a gigantic hope suspended over cities. Everything was fragile, I knew it, I had always known it. At fifteen I pretended that I had forgotten mediocrity. Like my mother, I pretended that nothing was dirtied.

Shadows on the road devour hope. There are no shadows at night, at noon, there is only certitude traversing reality. But reality is a little trap, little shadow grave welcoming desire. Reality is a little passion fire that pretexts. I was fifteen and with every ounce of my strength I was leaning into my thoughts to make them slant reality toward the light.

SUGGESTIONS FOR FURTHER STUDY

Key Words

The author uses language with which you may not be familiar. Find the following words in the paragraphs indicated, and explain their meanings in the context of the sentences in which the words appear. Consult a dictionary, as needed.

arrogance (par. 4)
troglodyte (par. 5)
ostentatiously (par. 5)
intonations (par. 6)
reanimate (par. 6)
certitude (par. 9)
traversing (par. 9)
pretexts (par. 9)

Language and Style

Part of the vividness of description in "Mauve Desert" lies in the writer's frequent use of figurative language. Locate the following expressions and discuss the ways in which they are effective in describing the desert or the writer's observations:

". . . its mauve and small lines which like veins mapped a great tree of life in my eyes." (par. 1)

"My mother always talked about men as if they had seen the day in a book." (par. 3)

"My mother mopped up America." (par. 6)

"But reality is a little trap, little shadow grave welcoming desire. Reality is a little passion fire that pretexts." (par. 9)

What other features of the writer's style do you notice in this essay? Look especially at sentence length and sentence structure. Make a brief list of the most interesting and effective features of this writer's style. In your journal, try imitating those style features in a description of your own.

Topics for Discussion and Writing

1. Read Saltman's poem "The Bungee Jumpers" on p. 112, and compare his description of an experience with Brossard's description of her experience driving in the mauve desert. What in their writing can you compare and contrast?

2. "The Bungee Jumpers" is written in the form of a poem. What in Brossard's prose can be characterized as "poetic"?

3. Discuss Lorna's role in this essay. What does her character add to the description?

4. Discuss the role of the mother in this essay. How does her presence affect the writer's actions?

5. Write about a drive or journey you have taken that meant something important to you in understanding your environment or yourself. Be clear about what that journey signifies to you and what caused it to take place.

High School Psyche-Out

Hethur Suval

In her narrative essay, student writer Hethur Suval relates her uncomfortable experience of going to a new high school and looking and seemingly being different from everybody else. Notice Suval's use of description and sardonic humor.

The pungent odor of ammonia hung heavy on the brisk morning air.   1
Whispers hissing through the hallways and eyes screaming with discontent filled my head with the awful racket of closed-minded teenagers. My first day at public high school was going to be hell; I knew it and so did they. As I walked across the dewy grass, I could feel the stares searing through my Thrill Kill Cult t-shirt and long flowing black skirt. Though my head remained tilted down, my gaze shifted from my combat boots to the halls crawling with acne-infested teens. I gently brushed a jet black lock away from my eye and sighed longingly for the liberal campus of 200 that I attended the previous year. I trudged hopelessly to my first class. "How bad could it be?" I thought. Little did I know that I had made immediate enemies somehow. I hadn't even uttered a word and yet it appeared that they hated me already, all 1400 of them. First and second period came and went, students staring all the while."

"Did you see the way that bitch looked at me?"

"Ya, I heard she's a Satan-worshiping Nazi. And what's up with that stupid collar?"

"I don't know, but she ain't gonna last long, ya know?"

"Ya, ya. Jasmine and Nikeisha said they're down to beat that bigot ass,   5
'cuz."

Did they think that I couldn't hear them? I mean they were walking directly behind me, but I pretended to be entranced by my new surroundings.

"Betelgeuse, Betelgeuse, Betelgeuse! Hey, aren't you supposed to disappear or something, freak?"

I rolled my eyes, "How could this day get any worse?—and it's only 10 o'clock in the morning." I wandered into the bathroom and stood in front of the mirror, sulking next to all the pretty cheerleaders; I could hardly tell them apart. Shrouded in green and gold, they stood before me, a menacing obstacle of a false self-worth and societal ideals of how a "good" teenage girl should behave. I wonder if they knew that I could see them beneath their fake tans, Claire's Boutique crown jewels, and the perfect color of iridescent pink lip gloss. The bathroom reeked of cheap Impostor's perfume, Aquanet hair spray, and the rancid stench of popularity . . . all of which were beginning to make me nauseous. The bell rang and the girls skipped off giggling and gossiping, tossing their curly golden ponytails behind them. And so I headed off to my third class of the day.

I watched the cracks in the cement wind away into the grass as I walked.

"Oh my god, I'm so sorry." I had walked right into somebody. "I'm   10 really sorry, it's my first day here and . . ." I looked up to see a smiling face. He was gorgeous: big doe eyes, spiky blue hair, Sex-Pistols t-shirt, ragged blue pants, and black steel-toed Docs. Surprisingly enough he didn't laugh at me, make fun of me, or give me a dead cold stare. He grinned slyly, squinting his eyes a bit, and asked with head cocked slightly to the left, "Freshman?"

"No, I'm a sophomore," I muttered shyly.

"Ya . . . right. So, you headin' to class or what?"

"Ya," I said rolling my eyes.

"Well, let's go, you're late, chic." He grabbed my collar and yanked it lightly, dragging me close behind him. Normally I wouldn't stand for being called "chic" or anything of the sort; but since this was the first friendly gesture from anyone all day, I ignored it and followed willingly.

"My name's Nick."   15

"I'm Hethur, nice to meet you . . . or anyone for that matter."

"Rough day?"

"Ya. So what's up with this school anyway? So far I've been called a bitch, a bigot, a freak, and Betelgeuse and I haven't even looked anyone in the eyes yet."

"I don't know where you went to school before, chic, but most people at this school are kind of closed-minded, ya know?" He stopped suddenly and turned to look at me, "Hey, did that hurt?" He pointed to my eyebrow ring and pushed it back and forth a little.

"No, not really," I replied.   20

"Right on," he turned back and walked on. I dragged my feet a bit as we wandered up the steps. When we reached the top step, Nick jumped up and grabbed a branch from the nearest tree and handed me a leaf, his chain still jingling.

"Thanks . . . I guess." Our boots scraped against the linoleum floor as Nick and I made our way to the classroom. The halls echoed with the deafening sound of emptiness.

"Room 77, right?"

"Uh huh."

"Okay here it is, see ya around, Silly Girl." He smiled and ran down the   25
hallway, jumping at the end to hit the top of the doorway.

"Ya." I said under my breath as I wandered into class.

The hustle and bustle of public high school in the "real world" was
beginning to sink in to my somewhat naive mindset regarding everyday life.
I had come upon a world of misconceptions and horrifically misunderstood
stereotypes from a "fantasy land institution" (more commonly known as an
exclusive private school). I sat through my classes paying little attention to
the droning "getting to know you" lectures and the jeerings of bitter students. All I could do was embrace the solitude of individuality and be
thankful for a little bit of company, namely that of Nick. Could he possibly
understand the breathless stares and unforgiving eyes? Was he also given a
good "once over" as he returned from the restroom so that the teachers
might catch a bit of cocaine on the nose or paraphernalia hanging from a
pocket to confirm their suspicions? There seemed to be no doubt in everyone's mind that, like him, I was a definite bad seed. It was amazing that all
anyone could see was my morbid style of dress or the hairstyles of a budding artist that I was so fond of creating. These people, caught up in their
own personal suburban nightmares and sadistic dreams, had no idea who I
was. "So, this is life, the life that I'm striving so hard to penetrate with my
words and ideas. What a letdown." It's amazing how time flies when you're
deeply analyzing the abstract structure of the society that you're being
trained to enter (or is it 'time flies when you're having fun'?).

Lunch could not have arrived at a more perfect time. "What are you
doing for lunch?" I heard a familiar voice from behind me. It was
Nick . . . thank god, I wouldn't be left as a sideshow for all the kids who
forgot to brown-bag-it to school and had nothing better to do than to stare
at me and think up mundane commentary about my clothes.

"Hanging out with you, it looks like. So, what are we doing?"

"Well, I thought we'd talk about politics, hair care products, and why   30
more politicians aren't avid users of hair care products." He smiled as
though he was quite possibly the most amusing person he had ever had the
pleasure of knowing. I smirked in his general direction but was not nearly
as proud of his suggestion as he. "Do you smoke?"

"Unfortunately," I replied with a shrug and a look of utter exaspera-
tion. No one likes being controlled by a substance.

"Follow me." I followed this little punk-rock boy to a spot that looked
like it would have been fairly secretive except for the fact that there were
about twenty other students hanging around smoking. It was like one monstrous fire hazard. We had come upon a clearing, not unlike a crop circle
regarding the patterned depressions of the grass, the place where all the
"losers" hung out. It was obvious that no one cared enough about them to
bother them here. "So, what do you think of your new high school? Just a

little piece of heaven, don't ya think? Your posh little private school probably doesn't compare to the magnificence and splendor that is M— High
School." He had a sort of charm to him though his sarcasm was so thick
that you would need a Cutco knife to slice through it.

"I'm not used to this incredibly bitter reception. They're so afraid of
me, it's like I'm some sort of vicious jungle beast or fatal airborne
virus . . . but what am I? I'm a fifteen-year-old girl having a severe first day
of school. Now does that seem so scary to you?"

"No . . . but I'm not your average high-school attendee and neither are
you. You're just going to have to get used to the fact that you're not like
everybody else, ya know? And this is the way things are . . . people are
afraid of unfamiliar things, you know that. You just have to wait it out and
maybe one day in your acceptance speech for the Nobel Prize you can thank
them all for ostracizing you." We both laughed at the mention of the award
and I pushed him lightly away from me. He smiled the most incredible smile
that I had ever seen and the topic switched to an upcoming concert. He was
great. . . . I guess it wasn't too difficult to find a real friend in a sea of
unfriendly faces.

It takes time to discover yourself and understand your surroundings.   35
I'm very well aware of that. As always, time is irrelevant to this discovery.
Someone is always "different" or "special." At age 15, I figured out just
how different I am.

The Vietnam War: Not Very Pretty

Glen McCoy

In this narrative selection, student writer Glen McCoy recounts his horrifying experience during the Vietnam War in the early 1970s. Notice how McCoy's essay begins with basic matter-of-fact information and then builds in intensity as he acquaints the reader with the atrocities that he witnessed and experienced.

The Vietnam War: the mention of it brings memories flooding into my mind—most of them not very pretty. I'll never forget the hot, balmy July evening in 1971 when the U.S. Army C-140 landed in Saigon (now called Ho Chi Minh City), and rolled to a stop on the tarmac. As we got off the plane, a sergeant yelled, "bag and baggage"—everything you owned was in your duffel bag. Next, we were separated into groups according to assignments. I was assigned to USA STRAT COM (United States Army Strategic Communication). After being assigned to our units we were taken to the mess hall, where we ate a pretty good meal. After the meal we were issued bedding, then assigned bunks where we were to sleep, or at least rest. I don't remember sleeping at all; I was scared, or at least restless. All through the night I could hear planes landing and taking off. I could hear helicopters coming and going, shuttling men in and out.

The next morning we were loaded into a Bell Huie UH3 helicopter and transported to a firebase well outside of Saigon. Ours was Firebase A or Alpha. Before going to the firebase we were issued our gear: a steel pot, helmet liner, all-web gear, canteen, ammo pouch, and of course, an M16 with six clips or magazines. Ammo in a combat zone is issued to the units, not individuals; however, you could have all the ammo you could carry. Most people take five hundred rounds. While in the air we checked our weapons and our equipment and prepared to land.

At the landing pad at Firebase A we were met by a sergeant who showed us our quarters, which was a Quonset hut. A Quonset hut is a pre-fabricated shelter made out of corrugated metal shaped like a cylinder cut vertically in two and resting on the flat side. There were sandbags piled up on the outside walls to absorb shrapnel and incoming rounds. We were assigned bunks, stowed our gear, then went back outside and got into formation. The sergeant said: "Troops! Welcome to Southeast Asia." We were briefed, then assigned to our duty stations.

I was assigned to be a gunner on a helicopter. I was assigned to the left-side gun, an M60 mounted on a stand about 38 inches high behind the left-side door that had been removed. When the gunners mounted up, we sat in a canvas seat strapped in with a shoulder harness and a safety strap. Each gunner usually carried three 1000-round ammo belts and two extra barrels for the M60. If the barrel gets hot, the M60 will pop or not stop firing and you have to break the ammo belt and then replace the barrel. This is no easy task when you are under fire.

I flew as a gunner on many missions in Vietnam. I was only 19 when I first arrived, and I saw many things that a young man should not see. I did many things that a young man should not have to do. Many of those things I try to forget; many I cannot. Even today when I hear the sound of blades on a helicopter change pitch, it makes me nervous and edgy. Sounds like that from Vietnam are imprinted in my mind; like the chatter of an AK47; like the roar of a mini-gun as it fires faster than a person can comprehend.

Many times it rained so hard that the helicopters could not take off and we would sit and guard the perimeter for who-knows-why, shooting on sight the enemy—whoever or whatever that was supposed to be. Why were we there? I have no idea. Why did we kill each other? I do not know. The United States lost over fifty thousand troops in the Vietnam War. The Vietnamese people lost three million during the conflict, both military and civilian. I do know that anybody who thinks combat is exciting or glorious is badly mistaken. The horrors were too many to name. It was a terrible experience where I constantly encountered atrocities. But I think it was the sickening smells that haunt me the most to this day: the sweet but rank stench of bodies drenched in diesel fuel being burned, the smell of human waste mixed with animal waste on the rice paddies, the pungent foul odor of drying fish and animal entrails, the awful smell and sight of human scalps and ears worn on the belts of the special forces troops whom we would pick up and fly back to base camp after five or six days in the jungle.

The conflict in Vietnam was not glorious or exciting as war is often portrayed on TV or in the movies. War is a horror that is a hell on earth. Anything and everything happened in the dense foliage of the jungle's triple canopy. We watched as the Cobra squads would strafe a village of Viet Cong (the North Vietnamese communists). The V.C. called the Cobras "flying death." The Cobra helicopter gunships could strafe a village and destroy everything in a matter of minutes. The F15 Tomcats could jump from a carrier, drop fire and destruction, and be gone in seconds. Often, the military would conduct combat operations known as "Extreme Prejudice," in which F15's would lay down walls of firebombs or the artillery would pound the target with "Willy Peater" rounds. When a Willy Peater explodes, it burns everything. This action would be followed by a squad of Cobra gunships finishing off whatever was left. Sometimes, from our spotter helicopter we could see people and animals being burned alive as they ran, the flesh falling from them as they died. Finally, bulldozers were brought in to dig a big trench and push all the remains in. The bodies of men, women, children, and animals—all were indiscriminately pushed into the trench and covered up. After the trench or ditch was covered with dirt, all the equipment and troops were moved as soon as possible; there remained no evidence of a village ever having been in that location.

Another thing I hated about my tour in Vietnam was the fear factor: fear when our "ship" was taking fire from the ground, fear when landing to pick up wounded or other troops for evacuation, fear of being shot or being hit by shrapnel, fear of being blinded or crippled for life, fear of being killed or dying alone on a battlefield, and the fear that your life could end without meaning or anyone caring.

I remember sitting in the rain and the dark when it was my turn as a perimeter guard, eating cold C-rations out of a can. I can still see the smoke lingering from the gun barrels and the flares eerily illuminating the night and turning it into day, the smell of human waste burning, the chatter of the radio to the constant call of "Iron Man"—the call sign of the artillery that covered our positions.

I remember my good friend John, who, like me, spent most of his time   10
in the air as a gunner on board a Cobra. John was a good guy and a great friend, but he would often say that because of their "slant eyes," the "gooks (Vietnamese) couldn't see straight." So John would always—against procedure—dismount to aid ground troops. One day, while making a pick-up of ground troops who were under fire, John's ship, Python One, dropped down to make the pick-up while we circled to supply cover fire. As Python One landed and the elephant grass was blown back and pushed down, our troops came out of the bush taking small arms fire. I tried to lay down cover with my 60, and I could see that John—as usual—had left the ship with his 60 in hand. Suddenly I saw Python One raising up and I yelled, "The motherf . . . . . s are going to leave him!" At that moment, on the ground I saw a puff of smoke, then a trailer, and then an RPG (rocket-propelled grenade) hit Python One. After the first grenade hit, I saw another, and then another. Python One exploded into a ball of fire. The mortar fire began coming in. RPG's were whizzing by our copter, and we had to pull back and call for air support from the planes. The planes came in, laid down fire, and obliterated everything. By the time we had refueled and returned, all we found were body parts entwined with scraps of metal. John was listed as missing-in-action. According to the body count, we lost a helicopter, five crew members, and four ground troops; the Vietnamese lost seventy troops. On paper we won; but I lost a good friend.

The time I spent in Vietnam was very hard to deal with. The Vietnam conflict was a tragedy to both the United States and the Vietnamese. I believe that war should be avoided at all costs. I hope that the next generations will not have to endure the horrors of war. As a reporter in WWII once said, "How can anyone who has been in combat ever harm another person?" Combat changes your life forever.

The Vietnam War was not very pretty.

CHAPTER 1: ACTIVITIES FOR DISCUSSION AND WRITING
Making Connections

1. Write a personal narrative recounting a particular time or period of your life, as did the writers in this chapter. Be sure to add specific detail (including physical description and dialogue) to help make your characters and experiences "come alive" for your readers.

    Before you begin, you may want to do the following:
    a. Brainstorm several ideas for your narrative topic.
    b. Once you have selected good potential topics, create clusters and/or lists to help generate material for your story.
    c. Make an informal outline to help you create the order of events in your story.
    d. Try freewriting one or several parts of your story to generate as much story material as you can quickly.

    Decide what style you might use for your story, since personal narratives are often highly stylized (see "Our Parents Had More," "The Last Dance Is Always a Slow Dance," and "Mauve Desert" for examples). You might choose a colorful, creative approach; or you might choose to write in a more traditional manner, as in "The Library Card" and "Graduation."

2. Compare Walker's "Beauty: When the Other Dancer Is the Self" with Angelou's "Graduation" and Richard Wright's "The Library Card." How does racism factor into these three stories? Discuss this question, citing specific examples and language from the texts.

3. "West Texas" and "Mauve Desert" both provide an encounter with and impressions of a desert landscape. How do the two encounters with the desert compare or contrast? In discussing this question, take into consideration the kinds of things either writer chooses to focus on and his or her attitude about the desert landscape and inhabitants.

4. Discuss the different ways Lois-Ann Yamanaka and Hethur Suval work out their social relations problems in high school. What about their experiences are alike or different?

5. Write a reply to Hethur Suval who wrote "High School Psyche-Out." To what extent can you sympathize or criticize the "outsider" experience she writes about? How do your high school experiences in social relations compare to hers?

6. Glen McCoy's "The Vietnam War: Not Very Pretty" is a disturbing piece about his experiences and observations while assigned to duty in Vietnam. To investigate comparable experiences further, try one of the following:
   a. Find other essays or books that discuss the Vietnam War (fictional or nonfictional). How do the depictions of that war in these texts differ from or substantiate McCoy's experience?
   b. Watch one of the many films about Vietnam such as *Apocalypse Now, Born on the Fourth of July, Platoon,* or *The Deerhunter.* How do impressions of the war in the movie you have chosen differ from or parallel McCoy's experiences and observations? If you have viewed more than one film focusing on the Vietnam War experience, how have they differed from or paralleled each other?

POPULAR CULTURE II

Generation Clash and the Family Experience

Siblings, parents, aunts and uncles, grandparents, and other family members are powerful influential forces in our lives. As writer Robin Abcarian states, "You can't make sense of how you live without making some kind of sense of how your parents lived." Yet generation gaps often result in a breakdown in communication. People can try to resolve their differences by building a bridge of empathy and understanding. One effective way to build that bridge is to write about such differences and their resolutions.

Writing and research can be powerful tools to help us understand our past, our own ethnic heritage. In the lives, blood, and memories of our grandparents lies the key to "mak[ing] sense of how [we] live." In this chapter, we explore how writers build bridges between generations. The following selections not only show other Americans' attempts at understanding family relations, but also will help and encourage you to pursue your own solutions through writing. In large part, this chapter focuses on grandparents in order to highlight generational differences and illustrate chronicled attempts at reconciliation and understanding.

Dan Kwong's "Grandpa Story" probes a Chinese American man's love/hate relationship with his grandfather. In "Gramps," Scott F. Covell writes about the two different worlds he experienced with his grandfather in New York City and the interesting truth he learned from him. In "I Ask Myself, Should I Cry? Or Laugh?" Jimmy Santiago Baca fondly remembers his grandmother and the exemplary role she played in his life. Louise Erdrich's "Grandpa Nector and the Story of June's Hanging" illustrates the importance of family stories in conveying heritage. In the lighthearted story "My Mother Stands on Her Head," Toshio Mori highlights the interaction between a family and an outcast in their community. In "The Last of the Kiowas," N. Scott Momaday comes to an understanding of his Native American grandmother and her intense connection to the land. Alice Walker's classic, "In Search of Our Mothers' Gardens," eulogizes all of the African American women who have come before her. Finally, in "Nana," student Diane Rubio describes her grandmother's simple everyday experiences and comes to appreciate their shared family history.

Grandpa Story

Dan Kwong

*Dan Kwong is an award-winning Los Angeles performance artist
whose solo performances are based on autobiographical material,
combining monologues with movement, martial arts, and multimedia.
Kwong's keen sense of social commentary and gently twisted humor
work well in personal stories that examine larger issues of social conditioning. He is founder and curator of "Treasure in the House," Los
Angeles's, first Asian-Pacific American performance and visual art
series presented both in L.A. and on tour.*

PREFACE

The Grandpa Story monologue is from a performance entitled *Monkhood in 3 Easy Lessons,* a solo multimedia work dealing with male identity
from an Asian American perspective. This monologue marks the culmination of the performance, which includes personal stories from my life, the
life of my Chinese grandfather, and images from popular culture and mass
media. Along with storytelling, *Monkhood in 3 Easy Lessons* also incorporates poetry, athletics, dance, puppetry, Japanese sword technique, video,
and slide projection.

I have chosen here to minimize stage direction notes indicating my location or movements onstage, even though they are an integral part of the performance. Also, the evolving emotional journey through this monologue
may or may not be apparent in the writing alone, as much is communicated
through tone of voice and manner of delivery. I often use irony and sarcasm, which can be difficult to interpret from the printed word.

GRANDPA STORY

The following monologue is the conclusion of Monkhood in 3 Easy
Lessons.

(The stage is dark. We hear a voice.)

In my last semester of high school, I discovered marijuana. 1

(A pool of red light comes up, center stage. We see Dan lying flat on his back, buried under a pile of phone books. He slowly sits up.)

And I got stoned after school on a regular basis. *(staggers to feet)* I was looking for escape from the miserable loneliness of my petrified social life, and there was no alternative I could see. As with many Asians, for me alcohol produced a mild allergic reaction, turning my face bright crimson and filling me with a strong desire to sleep. So I got stoned. . . .

(Stumbles offstage with phone books. Returns briskly, overall lighting comes up.)

Later on I remember hearing a story about my Chinese grandfather, Kwong Kwok Hing. Born and raised in Los Angeles, just like me. Seems he had the same after-school routine as me. Except, he got stoned in the biblical sense—white boys pelting him with rocks as he ran home to Chinatown. No student of martial arts, he! Could've used Bruce Lee. Even Brandon would've been nice to have around. . . .

He was a lonely one too, my Grandpa. I must've been about five years old when he came to live with us. He was the kind of man who could sit in his room all day long reading newspapers or autobiographies of famous people. Scarcely a sound ever came out of that room except for maybe an occasional soft belch.

"*Ah Danny-ah, you go brush yo teeth an' come eat yo oatmeal!*" This did not make sense to me: I brush my teeth now and *then* I eat the oatmeal??? 5

"*DANNY YOU GO BRUSH YO TEETH RIGHT NOW!!!*"

Grandpa could get in your face. Used to drive me nuts that he pronounced "margarine" with a hard "g":

"*Naw Danny, you pass the marGarine to Maria.*"

He was a classic "Chinaman." A thin, wiry, round-shouldered man wearing cardigan sweaters, round horn-rimmed glasses, and a wispy goatee. Kinda looked like Mahatma Gandhi waking up from a bad dream.

What kind of man was he? Growing up in Los Angeles, Grandpa's 10 English was actually quite well formed. He was sent back to China for an arranged marriage, fathered seven children, came right back to America, almost never lived with his family. Alone for most of his adult life. Believed everything he read.

What was it that lay deepest in this man's heart? Nobody knew. And nobody asked. There was an emptiness in his life that I could sense, even as a child. Not the kind of emptiness that brings enlightened peace or freedom from worldly concerns, but an emptiness borne of dislocation of the spirit, of bent mental framework—and too many rocks upside the head. . . .

Grandpa was a twentieth century man, but his life followed a pattern first set in the mid-1800's by the earliest Chinese immigrants, over 90% of them male because America was trying to avoid having them breed over here. From the beginning, Chinese men in this country led invisible lives, voiceless, veritable monks. Crammed into all-male Chinatowns, their miserable monastery-ghettoes, families ten thousand li to the west, no hope to return, *there's gotta be a gold nugget around here somewhere.* . . .

Resigned to an empty lifetime doing laundry, waiting tables, cooking chop suey or, for the "lucky" ones, serving as domestic houseboys. America's favorite cartoon of what an Oriental man is and does! There were no laundrymen in China—the women wound up doing that work. . . . Chinese men found jobs here which avoided direct competition with white working-class men, because that kind of situation seemed to produce—dead Chinamen. *Velly bad for business!*

They lived isolated from American society by language, by law, by a cultural chasm as vast as the great Pacific, and by a peculiar strain of white Christian supremacy which lumped the Chinese at the bottom of the evolutionary ladder—along with redskins and colored folk. Over time, various other Asian Pacific cultures shared the position of "primary heathen" in America. Men from Japan, the Philippines, India, each had their turn in history to be viewed as the lowest scum on the block. But the Chinese were the first Asian men to taste it. And like so many other immigrants before and after, they came as workers dreaming of a better life.

Work. That's all that life was about. Because somewhere back there is a legacy of starvation by the hundreds of thousands. *Work*—because across that ocean, people are counting on you to save them from misery worse than your own. *Work*—because desperation has been planted in the soil of your heart and if you dig deep enough you'll find China, find home, maybe a grave. *Work*—because then maybe your face and skin will transform into that of a human being in the eyes of this country. *Work*—because you have been castrated by enough Hop Sings and Charlie Chans to fill a slop bucket full of testicles, and all that's left to prove your American manhood is "a job well done. . . ." Prove it! You can try—but the bucket just keeps on getting deeper. It's a trick! *(pointing to an audience member)*—and *your* balls are next. *Confucious say: "Industriousness merely another form of co-dependency!"*

We used to laugh at my Chinese grandfather. My three sisters and I. We found him genuinely amusing. He would sing for us. Yeah, Grandpa used to sing the white pages of the phone book. He would sing The Golden Book Encyclopedia—especially Volume Six, "Erosion to Geysers." This is the one my two younger sisters would specifically request because it contained "Fruits," "Flowers," and "Flags"—lots of pretty, colorful illustrations.

"Grandpa! Grandpa! Sing the encyclopedia!" Didi and Poppy would parade into Grandpa's bedroom brandishing Volume Six, in preparation for The Sacred Ritual of the Tome of Knowledge. . . .

"Ahh! Awright now, Grandpa sing for you!" Before he even uttered a note, we'd be giddy with anticipation because Grandpa was gonna get weeiirrrd! He'd open his mouth and suddenly that wheezy, tentative voice of his transformed into a rich, resonant sound (heavy on vibrato) filling the room:

"Watermelon! Pineapple! Pomegranate! Cherry, Apple, Coconut!" Then he'd turn to the page of flowers.

"Dandelion! Goldenrod! Poppy, Tulip, Daffodil." Then on to the national flags!   20

"Denmark! Sweden! France! Canada, Peru!"

And no matter what he sang, it always came out like Chinese music. . . .

"Grandpa, Grandpa! Sing the phone book, sing the phone book!"

"Smith, Mariann! Smith, Martin R.! Smith, Max & Judy! Smith, Monica . . ."

And we laughed. HAAAAAAAA! We laughed so hard we'd be rolling   25
around on the floor, we practically peed in our pants it was so funny to us. *He thinks he's actually singing!* Grandpa would laugh too from the contagion of our hysteria but he sang on unperturbed, even though I wasn't laughing *with* him, I was laughing *at* him! Because that's what Grandpa was. Something to be laughed at. A kooky old man. An oddball eccentric. The "yellow sheep" of the family. Lost in some sorry-ass world of sensational tabloid delusion, he was a Chinese version of Don Knotts! Grandpa . . .

I believe, no matter how contradictory outward appearances may seem, everyone has something of the heroic inside them. Somewhere in everyone, there is courage. There is spirit. A voice that says, "I *am* somebody, I am alive and my life has meaning." And looking back I wanted so much to find that something in my Grandpa, my oldest personal link to Kwong men. To find that in us, my family, because his life looked so pathetically empty through and through, and I thought surely this must reflect on the rest of us Kwong men: my father, my uncles, my cousins and I. . . .

"Please—give me something manly *to be proud of! Isn't there anything, anywhere in my Chinese blood? Somewhere? Give me something. Father of my father: be a man; be a hero; be a stud. Be something, anything, but don't be some wimpy CHINK!"*

Grandpa, what was it like for you when those rocks were bouncing off your head? Sorry I couldn't be there to stand by your side, Grandpa. I was a helluva good rock thrower, arm like a bazooka. I would've fired on those punks so hard and fast they'd never know what hit 'em. We would've fought 'em off, Grandpa! We woulda kicked ass and stood tall, and I would've told you how proud of you I was! I would've helped you find your courage and keep your self-respect! I would've helped you. I would've held you in my arms when you felt scared and alone, let you shake and cry, I would've told you how brave and strong you were—and *no one* would laugh at you, Grandpa! No one would laugh at us. They would treat us right. They would see our humanity. And they would respect us. 'Cause we got nothing to prove to anyone, and we don't take any shit."

Nahhhhh . . .

My Grandpa lived a strange and lonely life, and he died a strange and lonely man. I couldn't find any hero in him. No "right stuff" to make him more studly.

(Dan slowly walks upstage, picks up a phone book. Turns around to face audience.)

I finished high school. Went to college, art school, got a degree, got a job. Traveled to Asia. Hong Kong, China, and Japan, every year for five years. Started to explore the unknown, the forgotten, the ignored. Listening to unheard voices of culture, family, "self." Around that time I finally decided to try and deal with my "feelings." And I quit getting stoned. . . .

And I remembered my Grandpa's singing. Now, I remember a man who delighted in the sound of his own spirited voice, completely uninhibited. A man who, though he knew we were laughing at him, allowed himself to sing out loud. Who said "*Yes!*" to a song—songs that had never been sung before and would never again be repeated.

And I thought—how many could do that very same thing? How many of us willing to sing *our* song, even in the face of ridicule? Because the simple delight of singing is too great to be denied. Because the moment calls for a song. Because your life is a song.

And what a rich and wise lesson from a funny old man.

(He slowly looks up to the heavens. Sings.)

Watermelon! Pineapple! Pomegranate. Cherry, apple, coconut . . .

(Fade to black with singing.)

SUGGESTIONS FOR FURTHER STUDY

Key Words

The author uses language with which you may not be familiar. Find the following words in the paragraphs indicated, and explain their meanings in the context of the sentences in which the words appear. Consult a dictionary, as needed.

resonant (par. 19)
vibrato (par. 19)
unperturbed (par. 25)
eccentric (par. 25)

Topics for Discussion and Writing

1. List some of the physical characteristics of Kwong's Chinese grand-father. What is the author's perception of those characteristics?

2. Why does Kwong originally dislike his grandfather? Locate several passages that convey this dislike.

3. What does Kwong ultimately learn about his grandfather? How does what he learns affect his feelings about his grandfather?

4. Kwong expresses strong feelings about the social–political treatment of Chinese male immigrants. For example, Kwong points out that there were no laundrymen in China, yet a stereotype exists that classifies early Chinese male immigrants as cooks and laundrymen. Find several other passages that illustrate Kwong's feelings about Americans' perceptions of Chinese immigrants, and discuss their relevance today.

5. As Kwong's preface indicates, this essay was originally an oral per-formance. Several markers of spoken discourse remain in the writ-ten text. For example, Kwong describes his grandfather "singing" selections from the encyclopedia and the phone book that "always came out like Chinese music." Try to imagine how that passage might sound if it were spoken aloud. Find several other markers of oral storytelling, and discuss their effectiveness in this essay.

6. To help in understanding the experiences of immigrants from Asia to the United States, research the historical background of one group of Asian Americans in the twentieth century and write about their efforts to become a part of mainstream American life.

Gramps

Scott F. Covell

Scott F. Covell is the co-editor of Living in America. *"I wrote this piece in response to a creative writing class I had as a senior in college. Eventually I pieced two separate writings about my grandfather together, both illustrating different facets of his character and the environment in which he lived."*

I

7E, 151 East 83rd Street, New York City. That's where he lived. We 1
called him Gramps.

In a three-room flat on the seventh floor of an eleventh story 1920's brownstone apartment house, he lived with his wife—whom we called Nana—for over fifty years. With its well-known yet relentlessly evolving musty smells, Gramps' apartment seemed like an old potted plant, an ancient life that existed, hovered, dissipated somewhere within the space between the high peeling walls and the sullen relics and antiquities.

When you stepped into that 83rd Street apartment you felt like you had literally stepped into "the Past." The living room—Gramps' stage, as it were—was hot, dry, and cramped; the radiator by the window hissed. Here was the main refuge for Gramps' treasured "antique" furniture, paintings, vases, lamps, mirrors, bizarrities—all unbelievably old and decrepit. Most of the pieces were actually only held together by layers of glue and tiny nails that constituted the essential aspect of Gramps' inexplicable "Kentucky Antique-repair process." What was really fun was that we had to sit on this stuff.

The living room was really more like a museum, or a library, with the historian, Gramps, always on call. Shuffling about his three-room kingdom—the way old folks do without actually ever lifting their feet off the floor—with his brown English slippers, his custom-tailored Kolman Marcus gray slacks and simple open-collared print shirt, his stark gray full head of hair jetting back like it was caught in a permanent typhoon, his horn-rimmed glasses, and the expectant smile, he was always optimistic when company arrived. Now he had some poor sucker to tell his stories to.

Gramps would immediately sit you down in the large teal-blue damask couch in the living room upon your arrival and you would sink back into its perfect luxurious depths; and as he began recounting the story, topic, or event of the day, you would exert your best effort to remain alert and attentive. But it never worked. The dry heat, the hissing of the radiator, the voice rambling on in the chair in the corner, the dark solemn antiquities and early American faces surrounding you in the tiny apartment, and it would only be moments before you surrendered to the spell of this aged, hoary vault and drifted off into your own private world. Most people simply passed out.

The recurrence of his audience "drifting off," however, never seemed to deter Gramps from his relentless recountings. Or maybe, somehow, incredibly, he just didn't *know* that people faded out. Mom said that it didn't matter if you were "there" or not—he would just keep talking. Dad said that when Gramps left our house you had to open up the windows and let all the words out. His glasses reflecting the feeble light from one of the incredible cloisonne-dragon Chinese lamps, his mouth parted slightly showcasing a fine set of white upper dentures, he would struggle to remember some little-known detail as you struggled to remain with the "Gramps program."

"I was just repairing the Italian mirror," he would say, pointing to the gigantic mirror on the north wall with the gold rococo leaves surrounding it, "and you know what, Scott? . . ." (he would make a "snick" sound with his tongue and teeth), "I had to marvel at the mastery of the workmanship of it once again." There would follow a pause that seemed to last for an eternity. We would both remain seated, staring at the gold Italian rococo mirror. Finally, he would continue. "Scott (snick), my father, God bless his soul, used to tell me that . . . a thing is valuable by how it's made, not how much it costs! (eternal pause) He used to take me . . . this was, of course, many years ago . . . (snick), to this . . . fine establishment in Louisville. Called McGuffin's. Used to be called Johnson's. Before that it was a livery station (eternal pause). A man named . . . Benington . . . no—Burlington, that's right, Albert Benington . . . or Burlington . . . well, whatever, he was the proprietor . . . a wonderful man . . . (snick) always glad to see my father. . . .'Ah, Mr. Chase!' he would say, and rush over to shake his hand. . . . People loved my father. . . . He was one of the most well-known and respected men in Louisville" (eternal pause).

And so it would go. Start talking about a mirror and end up back in Louisville. Every time. And the heat, and the musty perfumed womb-like sofa, the man sitting in the upright chair talking, thinking back, sermonizing on his antiquities, his gray jetting head cocked back and upper teeth showing as he struggled with dim pictures of the past while you drifted off. . . .

II

Fortunately, Gramps and I would often venture out into the wilds of New York City, breaking out of the venerable apartment, clothed in Nana's last-minute apparel alterations, and often headed for Yankee stadium. If baseball, in the words of Philip Roth, was my "literature" as a kid, then Gramps was my Poet Laureate. And together we spent many an afternoon camped out in Yankee Stadium watching the late-60's and 70's version of the once mighty New York Yankees.

Gramps and I would usually take the subway from Lexington and 81st and travel through the eerie squealing underground darkness up to the Bronx. We'd walk briskly into one of the giant front vestibules of Yankee Stadium and I would instantly feel the rush of adrenaline and excitement from the massed energies of 50,000 sports enthusiasts who were virtually all, like myself and Gramps, staunch Yankee fanatics.

Gramps and I would usually sit in the grandstand above first base or third base, and I would bring my glove in case a long fly ball would spin out of the sky toward me for a free souvenir. One time I actually had a chance at a pop fly and went dashing down an aisle, flipped over a seat, and the ball popped out of the web of my glove into the hands of a beer-bellied guy who dropped his Schaefer ale to grab it. "Two hands, pal," said Gramps upon my return, "but good try. . . ." Later we went over the *correct* way to make that catch outside his apartment on 83rd Street.

While at the stadium, Gramps would frequently regale me with "Tales of Yankee Lore," which were fortunately a lot more interesting than the "Antiques in the Apartment" tales, but still undoubtedly, ineluctably, finaled in "Kentucky Days" stories. "See that '500 Foot' sign?" Gramps would say, pointing to the giant white figures on the centerfield wall. "That's where Mickey Mantle hit one of his greatest World Series home runs! No one's ever hit it out that far. No one! Ach! (eternal pause) Although, now that I think about it, there was a guy back in Louisville, name of Billy Bob Banderslagen. . . . This fellow could really pound the tar off the ball—Now wait a minute . . . wasn't his name . . . ?" And so it would go.

When the Yankees took the field, Gramps would gasp as we watched the currently hobbled version of the mighty Mickey Mantle trundle out onto the field. My first year as a Yankee fan in 1968 was Mickey's last—his knees had blown-out from too many diving catches and crashing slides into the plate. But at one game, even as I prayed him to park one, he blasted one of his last home runs way up into the right field bleachers. Everyone went nuts, but no one was more effusive than Gramps. "*That's* the ticket, Mickey!" He hollered, standing up and clapping like a madman. "*Oh!* What a guy!" This was immediately followed by the obligatory dissertation on the early days of the "Mickey Mantle Legend": his 54 homers in '61, his spectacular catches in the late '50's, his clutch hitting throughout many a World Series, and, of course, somehow, incredibly, how it all linked back to Louisville. Gramps then sighed and motioned beleagueredly to the current Yankees: "They're gonna be nothin' without 'im, pal . . . just you watch . . . nothin'!"

And he was right; for the next eleven years the Yankees sank right to the cellar, as did my hopes. All I was left with was Gramps' endless stories of the "glory days" and the great Yankee teams of the past: Babe Ruth, who hit 714 home runs; Roger Maris, who hit 61 home runs in a season; Lou Gehrig, the "Ironman," who played in over 2000 games straight; Joe DiMaggio, the "Yankee Clipper," who hit safely in 56 straight games; the fiery Billy Martin, the electrifying Casey Stengel, the towering Elston Howard—against these formidable, haunting giants of the past, how could my pitiful no-name Yankees ever measure up?

Well . . . they couldn't. There was Horace Clark, who always got   15
thrown out trying to steal second base; Dooley Womack, who gave up one towering home run after another; Gene Michael, who couldn't hit his way out of a paper bag and whom Gramps always called "a bum." "Aach . . ." he would periodically utter, turning away in disgust and blaming it all on the owners—CBS Broadcasting: "If they don't spend any money on talent they'll always be a bunch of bums," he would say. And he was right.

Every now and then we'd be watching a good game and some guy on the other team would make a "grandstand" play and rob one of the pitiful late-60's Yankees of a hit. Gramps would immediately leap to his feet and applaud in exuberant appreciation, totally oblivious to the massed silence. "Oh! What a play! (applauding furiously) Now that's the ticket! What a catch!" He'd carry on while I attempted to shrink, and I'd look up into the gigantic angered throng glaring down at us: virtually thousands of crimsoning faces venting rage, bottle caps, and shredded bits of hot dog bun at this insignificant little man applauding the other team. And Gramps would just stand there with his jetted-back gray hair, the horn-rimmed glasses caught in the sun, the fine set of upper dentures showing brightly: oblivious to it all. There, alone, in the cluster of dim humanity, applauding.

Eventually, it became apparent to me that Gramps was on to something. Emerging out of the vast impenetrable midst of his meandering stories was a great truth: A great performance is a great performance no matter what side it occurs on. "That's how you win ball games, pal. You have to throw caution to the wind! You have to have a little 'chutzpa!' . . . Now, there was this guy back in Louisville . . ."

That was why Roy White—my favorite player as a kid—was the one no-name Yankee even Gramps liked. He only hit in the .290's, but could this guy play some mean outfield! Unbelievable "circus catches" were his forte. Catapulting over the fence to snag a sure home run; leaping, diving, sprawling catches in the dirt to take away yet another extra base hit. "That's the ticket!" Gramps would yell, as White sprinted deftly into the left field corner and robbed Killebrew of a sure base-clearing "double" with an impossible gliding backhanded stab. And we'd both leap up together, clapping, whooping, exulting together in one of the true moments of inspired derring-do achieved by one of the men in pinstripes during those frustrating years.

That's the thing Gramps loved about the Roy Whites, the Willy Mayses, the Mickey Mantles of the world. While others are content to play it safe, let the ball bounce, avoid injury, these guys risk it all by diving head-long into the air like ballpark Baryshnikovs—every fiber, muscle, shred of flesh, bone, and blood straining, stretching, hurtling, reaching out to—YES! Make the catch! Hit the dirt and come up throwing! The crowd on its feet roaring, the man who hit the ball standing by the plate and gasping incredulously, the world and time neatly staked to the bright green turf for a moment, caught in that one instant of "go-for-broke" physical excellence. For Gramps, it didn't matter what team the player was on, or what the people around him thought; he would be on his feet applauding, cheering, and gearing up to begin yet another story.

III

Meanwhile, I endured eleven losing seasons in a row and few Roy 20
Whites.

Gramps started going to Shea Stadium and watching the Mets.

I moved out to California.

However (fanfare!), all of a sudden came 1977, when the Yankees finally won a World Series again! (George Steinbrenner had bought the team and bought good players—as Gramps suggested.) Reggie Jackson hit three out in the last World Series game in 1977 to officially pulverize the Dodgers—a night I'll never forget—and I finally had my moment of ecstatic deliverance. And while my formerly east coast friends and I danced and celebrated in a West L.A. bar, I knew that Gramps, back in his cluttered apartment on 83rd Street, was rising up out of his armchair amongst the fragile relics, fading paintings, and endless Louisville memories, and hollering: "Now *that's* the ticket!"

Hopefully, there was someone there to tell a story to.

SUGGESTIONS FOR FURTHER STUDY

Key Words

The author uses language with which you may not be familiar. Find the following words in the paragraphs indicated, and explain their meanings in

the context of the sentences in which the words appear. Consult a dictionary, as needed.

recount (par. 5)
cloisonne (par. 6)
regale (par. 12)
ineluctably (par. 12)
derring-do (par. 18)

Topics for Discussion and Writing

1. What artifacts in Covell's grandparents' apartment clearly convey the atmosphere of the room?

2. List some of Gramps' personal characteristics. How are these characteristics related to his physical environment?

3. Notice that the essay is divided into three sections. What is the central idea in each of the three sections? How do the three sections relate to each other?

4. What is the lesson that Covell learns from Gramps? How did Gramps convey this lesson? How does the story of Roy White function in this lesson?

5. Gramps makes an indelible impression on the author both as a young boy and as a mature man remembering his grandfather. Find several passages that create a strong impression and explain how they are effective. For example, in paragraph nine the author uses the word "snick" to describe Gramps' manner of speaking. What effect does "snick" create? Find other vivid examples that convey Gramps' character.

6. Write a short essay about a lesson you learned from an older member of your immediate or extended family. Try using dialogue to convey the personalities of the characters you write about.

I Ask Myself, Should I Cry?
Or Laugh?

Jimmy Santiago Baca

Jimmy Santiago Baca is the author of several books of poetry, including Martin and Meditations on the South Valley *and* Black Mesa Poems. *The following selection is from his collection* Immigrants in Our Own Land, *which focuses on his experiences while in prison, where he taught himself to read and write.*

I am like a glossy green leaf, sticking out   1
in midnight moon, waxy drum-skin the moon pounds with wind. . . .
    Guilt itches my heart, as though a grasshopper,
chewing half, or a thick lazy caterpillar spinning silk nets,
hanging blue raindrops, baskets that carry invisible rocks,
that crack their stomachs, making wings of my eyelids.
    Should I cry or laugh, thinking of you,
you?

    An old woman on bent legs and burning green eyes,
what did you do on Saturday afternoons, in your small trailer? 10
Like a whitening sandbar, as the days took more and more
of your dark healthy grains, pressing against the current
of age, your tongue printed in sand washed over silently
by water, malevolent water, a ripple washing your
thunder-jeweled life, under, under, sweet pearl of mine.

    Mother of my mother, after being moved away,
a small child clutching pennies you gave me from a purse
hidden and hooked with a pin, next to your breasts. . . .
    You showed me a picture of my mother, said
she was a good woman, and pictures of my uncles, killed 20
in wars, their airplanes hut-hut-hut-hutting out,
hurtling down the blue gray sky in a crying fire.

    I saw their pictures, all of them,
but when you showed the one of my mother, a white flare of love
exploded in me, cascading down my naked soul,
as though a waterfall, in which I bathed.

But you? Your trailer in a weedy lot,
crocheting tableclothes rich as butterfly wings, pillowcases
designed as sun spreading on dawn-colored silk,
thick-fingered frontiering heart in your wild loneliness,   30
bad-mouthing my father's drunkenness softly,

in your little trailer, with a toaster, cloth
potholder, tiny-windowed low-ceilinged box, a jewel case
to you, where your memories sang from each night. . . .
I wanted to stay with you forever! To find
the truth, to ask and ask and ask, an orphan boy! Swirling
with stallion storms in me!

I could not ride, set free into your wood-wind
throat, that sang me calm in your great box-canyon, dripping
water, and silence that shone in our eyes;   40
our love, our confusion, our fears, tumbled
like massive boulders down our red-veined hearts,
thousand and thousand of years old,
covering the shards and death skulls of your life,
holding the ocean of my future, my prehistoric hunger
for gods and demons unleashed, satiated by you, weaver woman.
You died while I was in prison,
This poem is for you, my one.

SUGGESTIONS FOR FURTHER STUDY

Key Words

The author uses language with which you may not be familiar. Find these words in the lines indicated, and explain their meanings, in the context in which they appear. Consult a dictionary if necessary.

malevolent (line 14)
shards (line 43)
satiated (line 45)

Language and Style

The effectiveness of this poem depends largely on figurative language.

1. Explain the use and effect of the following words and phrases:
   "I am like a glossy green leaf . . ." (line 1)
   "Guilt itches my heart . . ." (line 2)
   ". . . malevolent water . . ." (line 14)
   ". . . thunder-jeweled life . . ." (line 15)

"... airplanes hut-hut-hut-hutting out ..." (line 21)

"... your wood-wind throat," (lines 38–39)

2. Find and discuss other images that offer strong or vivid descriptions of people, events, and emotions.

Topics for Discussion and Writing

1. Baca describes his grandmother both directly and indirectly. Find and discuss examples of each method of description.
2. What "things" did Baca's grandmother teach him?
3. What is the significance of the title of this poem?
4. Find several instances of comparisons in this poem. What is being compared, and what effect does the comparison have?
5. The poet speaks directly to his grandmother. Characterize his tone of voice, and point to words or phrases that convey this tone.
6. Write a short description of someone, perhaps a member of your family, who helped you understand your own heritage. Try to include words and phrases that make either direct or indirect comparisons as Baca does in his poem.

Grandpa Nector and the Story of June's Hanging

Louise Erdrich

Louise Erdrich (born in 1954) grew up in Wahpeton, North Dakota. She is of German and Chippewa descent, belonging to the Turtle Mountain Band of Chippewa. Her novels include The Beet Queen, Tracks, *and* The Bingo Palace. *Her first novel,* Love Medicine *(1984), from which the following selection has been taken, won the National Book Critics Circle Award.* Love Medicine *begins by depicting the tragic death of June Kashpaw, the narrator's aunt, who wandered out into a snowstorm and died. The following selection continues the Kashpaw story and the attempts of various family members to cope with the aunt's inexplicable death.*

Grandma Kashpaw's rolled-down nylons and brown support shoes   1
appeared first, then her head in its iron-gray pageboy. Last of all the entire rest of her squeezed through the door, swathed in acres of tiny black sprigged flowers. When I was very young, she always seemed the same size to me as the rock cairns commemorating Indian defeats around here. But every time I saw her now I realized that she wasn't so large, it was just that her figure was weathered and massive as a statue roughed out in rock. She never changed much, at least not so much as Grandpa. Since I'd left home, gone to school, he'd turned into an old man. Age had come upon him suddenly, like a storm in fall, shaking yellow leaves down overnight, and now his winter, deep and quiet, was on him. As Grandma shook out her dress and pulled bundles through the back window, Grandpa sat quietly in the car. He hadn't noticed that it had stopped. "Why don't you tell him it stopped," Grandma called to Lynette.

Lynette was changing King Junior's diaper in the front seat. She generally used paper diapers with stick-'em tabs at her home in the Cities, but since she'd been here my mother had shamed her into using washable cloth diapers and sharp pins. The baby wiggled and fought her hands.

"You hear?" King, already out of the car and nervously examining his tires, stuck his head back in the driver's side window and barked at Lynette. "She was calling you. My father's mother. She just told you to do something."

Lynette's face, stained and swollen, bloomed over the wheel. She was a dirty blond, with little patches of hair that were bleached and torn. "Yes I heard," she hissed through the safety pins in her teeth. "You tell him."

Jerking the baby up, ankles pinned in the forks of her fingers, she repositioned the triangle of cloth under his bottom.

"Grandma told you to tell him." King leaned farther in. He had his mother's long slim legs, and I remembered all at once, seeing him bend all the way into the car, June bending that way too. Me behind her. She had pushed a rowboat off the gravel beach of some lake we'd all gone to visit together. I had jumped into the rowboat with her. She had one son at the time and didn't think that she would ever have another child. So she spoiled me and told me everything, believing I did not understand. She told me things you'd only tell another woman, full grown, and I had adored her wildly for these adult confidences, for her wreaths of blue smoke, for the figure she cut. I had adored her into telling me everything she needed to tell, and it was true, I hadn't understood the words at the time. But she hadn't counted on my memory. Those words stayed with me.

And even now, King was saying something to Lynette that had such an odd dreaming ring to it I almost heard it spoken out in June's voice.

June had said, "He used the flat of his hand. He hit me good." And now I heard her son say, ". . . flat of my hand . . . but good . . ."

Lynette rolled out the door, shedding cloth and pins, packing the bare-bottomed child on her hip, and I couldn't tell what had happened.

Grandpa hadn't noticed, whatever it was. He turned to the open door and stared at his house.

"This reminds me of something," he said.

"Well, it should. It's your house!" Mama barreled out the door, grabbed both of his hands, and pulled him out of the little backseat.

"You have your granddaughter here, Daddy!" Zelda shrieked carefully into Grandpa's face. "Zelda's daughter. She came all the way up here to visit from school."

"Zelda . . . born September fourteenth, nineteen forty-one . . ."

"No, Daddy. This here is my daughter, Albertine. Your granddaughter."
I took his hand.

Dates, numbers, figures stuck with Grandpa since he strayed, and not the tiring collection of his spawn, proliferating beyond those numbers into nowhere. He took my hand and went along, trusting me whoever I was.

Whenever he came out to the home place now, Grandpa had to get reacquainted with the yard of stunted oaks, marigold beds, the rusted car that had been his children's playhouse and mine, the few hills of potatoes and stalks of rhubarb that Aurelia still grew. She worked nights, managing a bar called the So Long, and couldn't keep the place as nicely as Grandpa always had. Walking him slowly across the lawn, I sidestepped prickers. The hollyhocks were choked with pigweed, and the stones that lined the driveway, always painted white or blue, were flaking back to gray. So was the flat boulder under the clothesline—once my favorite cool place to sit doing nothing while the clothes dried, hiding me.

This land had been allotted to Grandpa's mother, old Rushes Bear, who had married the original Kashpaw. When allotments were handed out all of her eighteen children except the youngest—twins, Nector and Eli— had been old enough to register for their own. But because there was no room for them in the North Dakota wheatlands, most were deeded less-desirable parcels far off, in Montana, and had to move there or sell. The older children left, but the twin brothers still lived on opposite ends of Rushes Bear's land.

She had let the government put Nector in school, but hidden Eli, the   20 one she couldn't part with, in the root cellar dug beneath her floor. In that way she gained a son on either side of the line. Nector came home from boarding school knowing white reading and writing, while Eli knew the woods. Now, these many years later, hard to tell why or how, my Great-uncle Eli was still sharp, while Grandpa's mind had left us, gone wary and wild. When I walked with him I could feel how strange it was. His thoughts swam between us, hidden under rocks, disappearing in weeds, and I was fishing for them, dangling my own words like baits and lures.

I wanted him to tell me about things that happened before my time, things I'd been too young to understand. The politics for instance. What had gone on? He'd been an astute political dealer, people said, horse-trading with the government for bits and shreds. Somehow he'd gotten a school built, a factory too, and he'd kept the land from losing its special Indian status under that policy called termination. I wanted to know it all. I kept asking questions as we walked along, as if he'd take the hook by mira-cle and blurt the memory out right there.

"Remember how you testified . . . What was it like . . . the old schools . . . Washington . . . ?

Elusive, pregnant with history, his thoughts finned off and vanished. The same color as water. Grandpa shook his head, remembering dates with no events to go with them, names without faces, things that happened out of place and time. Or at least it seemed that way to me. Grandma and the others were always hushing up the wild things he said or talking loudly over them. Maybe they were bored with his craziness, and then again maybe his mind blurted secrets from the past. If the last was true, sometimes I thought I understood.

Perhaps his loss of memory was a protection from the past, absolving him of whatever had happened. He had lived hard in his time. But he smiled into the air and lived calmly now, without guilt or desolation. When he thought of June, for instance, she was a young girl who fed him black plums. That was the way she would always be for him. His great-grandson,

King Junior, was happy because he hadn't yet acquired a memory, while perhaps Grandpa's happiness was in losing his.

We walked back down the driveway, along the flaking rocks. "He likes 25 that busted lawn chair," Grandma hollered now, leaning out the door. "Set him there awhile."

"Want me to get you a plate from the kitchen?" I asked Grandpa. "Some bread and butter?"

But he was looking at the collapsed heap anxiously and did not answer.

I pulled the frayed, woven plastic and aluminum into the shape of a chair, he settled into it, and I left him counting something under his breath. Clouds. Trees. All the blades of grass.

I went inside. Grandma was unlocking her expensive canned ham. She patted it before putting it in the oven and closed the door carefully.

"She's not used to buying this much meat," Zelda said. "Remember we 30 used to trade for it?"

"Or slaughter our own." Aurelia blew a round gray cloud of Winston smoke across the table.

"Pew," said Zelda. "Put the top on the butter." She flapped her hand in front of her nose. "You know, Mama, I bet this makes you wish it was like it used to be. All us kids in the kitchen again."

"Oh, I never had no trouble with kids," Grandma wiped each finger on a dishrag. "Except for once in a while."

"Except for when?" asked Aurelia.

"Well now . . ." Grandma lowered herself onto a long-legged stool, 35 waving Zelda's more substantial chair away. Grandma liked to balance on that stool like an oracle on her tripod. "There was that time someone tried to hang their little cousin," she declared, and then stopped short.

The two aunts gave her quick, unbelieving looks. Then they were both uneasily silent, neither of them willing to take up the slack and tell the story I knew was about June. I'd heard Aurelia and my mother laughing and accusing each other of the hanging in times past, when it had been only a family story and not the private trigger of special guilts. They looked at me, wondering if I knew about the hanging, but neither would open her lips to ask. So I said I'd heard June herself tell it.

"That's right," Aurelia jumped in. "June told it herself. If she minded being hung, well she never let on!"

"Ha," Zelda said. "If she minded! You were playing cowboys. You and Gordie had her up on a box, the rope looped over a branch, tied on her neck, very accurate. If she minded! I had to rescue her myself!"

"Oh, I know," Aurelia admitted. "But we saw it in the movies. Kids imitate them, you know. We got notorious after that, me and Gordie. Remember Zelda? How you came screaming in the house for Mama?"

"Mama! Mama!" Grandma yodeled an imitation of her daughter.   40
"They're hanging June!"

"You came running out there, Mama!" Zelda was swept into the story.
"I didn't know you could run so fast."

"We had that rope around her neck and looped over the tree, and poor
June was shaking, she was so scared. But we *never* would have done it."

"Yes!" asserted Zelda. "You meant to!"

"Oh, I licked you two good," Grandma remembered. "Aurelia, you
and Gordie both."

"And then you took little June in the house. . . ." Zelda broke down   45
suddenly.

Aurelia put her hands to her face. Then, behind her fingers, she made a
harsh sound in her throat. "Oh Mama, we could have killed her. . . ."

Zelda crushed her mouth behind a fist.

"But then she came in the house. You wiped her face off," Aurelia
remembered. "That June. She yelled at me. 'I wasn't scared! You damn
chicken!'"

And then Aurelia started giggling behind her hands. Zelda put her fist
down on the table with surprising force.

"Damn chicken!" said Zelda.   50

"You had to lick her too." Aurelia laughed, wiping her eyes.

"For saying hell and damn . . ." Grandma nearly lost her balance.

"Then she got madder yet. . . ." I said.

"That's right!" Now Grandma's chin was pulled up to hold her laughter
back. "She called me a damn old chicken. Right there! A damn old hen!"

Then they were laughing out loud in brays and whoops, sopping tears   55
in their aprons and sleeves, waving their hands helplessly.

SUGGESTIONS FOR FURTHER STUDY

Key Words

The author uses language with which you may not be familiar. Find the
following words in the paragraphs indicated, and explain their meanings in
the context of the sentences in which the words appear. Consult a dictionary, as needed.

swathed (par. 1)
cairns (par. 1)
spawn (par. 17)
proliferating (par. 17)
finned (par. 23)

absolving (par. 24)
oracle (par. 35)

Topics for Discussion and Writing

1. The storyteller often describes characters and events metaphorically. What is the effect of the following expressions:

   "When I was very young, she [Grandma] always seemed the same size to me as *the rock cairns* commemorating Indian defeats around here." (par. 1)

   "In that way she gained a son on *either side of the line*." (par. 20)

   "Elusive, pregnant with history, his thoughts *finned off and vanished*." (par. 23)

   Locate other uses of metaphor in the story.

2. What have Grandpa's accomplishments been?

3. How does his current physical and mental condition affect the way we see him in the story?

4. Compare what Grandpa Kashpaw and the baby, King Junior, have in common.

5. Describe the differing emotions Grandma, Zelda, and Aurelia experience in retelling the story of June's hanging.

6. How does dialogue help our understanding of the story and its characters?

7. To help you understand Native American history, research the U.S. government's relocation policies in the nineteenth and twentieth centuries. Focus on one group of Native Americans such as the Navajo, the Lakota, or the Seminoles. Write an informative description of what happened to that group as a result of U.S. government relocation policies and treaties.

My Mother Stands
on Her Head

Toshio Mori

*Toshio Mori was born in Oakland, California, in 1910 and lived
in San Leandro, California, until he died in 1980. During World War
II, Mori was camp historian at the Topaz Relocation Center in Utah.
Mori, like most Japanese Americans, was forcibly imprisoned in
internment camps during the war. The following short story was
taken from* Yokohama, California *(1949), the first published collection of short stories by a Japanese American.*

This was the thirty-ninth time it happened. Our family sat at the   1
kitchen table and did nothing but talk. In the morning Ishimoto-san, the
food peddler, had come and left a bill of statement. "What's the matter with
that man?" my father kept saying. Then his face became red. "Mama, don't
buy from him again! Don't buy, that's all!"

"Eleven dollars and eighty-five cents! For what?" my brother said.
"This is funny. Who does he think he is? What did we buy from him?"

"How do we know? He doesn't leave the sales tag when we buy," I
said. "And when does he put down what we buy? I haven't seen him with a
sales book."

"Don't buy anything from him. That'll settle it," my father said.

"He's got a fine memory. He goes home in the evening and writes down   5
what we bought that day," my brother said.

We laughed although we were sore. Every time we bought half a dozen
articles he'd forget to leave one or two things. If it wasn't the matches it was
the eggs. If it wasn't the eggs it was the butter.

"Look here," my mother angrily said, showing us the latest statement.
"Look at the seventeenth. That was last Wednesday. He forgot to leave the
eggs that day. I clearly remember it because I needed them, and he's got
eighty cents down here. I told him to leave a pound of butter, two soybean cakes, and one dozen eggs. When he forgets the eggs how could it be
eighty cents?"

"Don't buy from him," my father said. "He couldn't charge us anything on that."

"Let's see," my brother said. "A pound of butter from him must cost about forty cents, and the two soybean cakes is ten cents. That's fifty cents, and the eggs must be thirty cents to make it eighty cents altogether."

"That's the way it goes every time," my mother said, furiously. "What fools we are."

"Tell him to knock off the thirty cents," my brother said.

"Let's see you convince him he forgot the eggs," I said. "He'll swear that he left the eggs last Wednesday. He'll clearly remember that he gave us the box with the two brown eggs."

"You can't beat his memory," my father said.

Every Monday, Wednesday, and Friday Ishimoto-san came around in his 1928 Model-A Ford. He brought vegetables and groceries and peddled them within the radius of fifty miles. My mother pitied him, remembering the old days when he had a prosperous grocery store on Seventh Street. She saw him go down the ladder of success until he had only the old route left for a living. Even the route wasn't on a paying basis. The customers suffered for it, and we paid outlandish prices for things which we could have bought cheaply at the neighborhood stores. My father always squawked when he saw the bill.

"Today at the Safeway we could have bought the number one grade salad oil for a dollar and a quarter," he moaned to Mother. "That's cheap. Look at Ishimoto-san's price. A dollar and seventy."

"He sells a bit high," my mother admitted. "You know, he must bring it out here. And he must live."

"And we must live," my father said. "Don't buy from him, Mama. Buy at the Safeway and save."

Mother shook her head. "I couldn't do that," she said. "He's been coming here for twenty years, and I couldn't do a thing like that as if it's nothing."

Father was now on the defensive. "When I used to go to the Oakland Free Market for groceries I always used to see him there. You know what that market is—a retail market. He buys his stuff there and brings it out here and sells at a profit. How do you like that?"

Mother shook her head with finality. She knew all about it. It was an old story. Our neighbors quit buying from Ishimoto-san long ago. They learned from a competitive grocer that Ishimoto-san often came into his store and bought articles at retail price to peddle in the out-of-town district. The news wrecked Ishimoto-san's business in our district. One by one the customers dropped him.

"We won't drop him," my mother said. "We'll continue buying from him, even if it's a little amount."

"At the Safeway," my father observed, "you could buy Salinas lettuce three for a nickel. And you buy an apple-size lettuce from him for a nickel apiece."

"They're bigger than an apple," Mother defended herself and Ishimoto-san.

Ishimoto-san came regularly to the house. He pestered my mother. If she didn't want carrots would she care for dry onions. If she didn't want a can of bamboo sprouts would she need a package of shredded shrimp. Some days he would stop on the way home and look up my mother. When he found her he'd look anxiously at her.

"Would you lend me a dollar, Mama?" he'd ask. "I had a flat, and I   25 must get a tire patch and fix my spare."

"Business is bad," my mother would say. "My boy goes collecting on the old bills and nothing comes in. This is a bad year for nurseries."

She would then drop her work and go in the house for the money. "Put two dollars credit on the bill," she'd tell Ishimoto-san. And he would go away happy, his problem solved.

Then this thing happened. We were putting Ishimoto-san on trial for one month. The month was July, and every time we bought something we mentally noted it down.

"I think our July bill will be around six dollars. Anyway it won't be over seven dollars," Mother calculated. She added, looking wisely at Father, "If Ishimoto-san's figures matches ours, Papa, you'll have no kick coming."

"Don't buy from him and you'll have no worry like this," Father said.   30 He looked up brightly. "If he overcharges us this time we'll quit buying from him."

"In that case we'll stop buying from him," Mother agreed.

We didn't have to wait long. Punctually Ishimoto-san left the statement on the first. At noon we pounced on the statement as if it was an important pronouncement. My brother glanced at the total amount and whistled. My mother became furious for the first time on Ishimoto-san's account. My father laughed.

"Eleven eighty-five!" my brother echoed, and whistled again.

"The brainless fool! What does he use his head for?" Mother fumed. Father continued to laugh.   35

My brother looked up from Ishimoto-san's statement as if he had suddenly smelled a rotten odor. He looked at us and then turned again to the paper.

"What's the matter?" I asked. "Anything wrong?"

"'Wait a minute," he said importantly. He kept adding the figures. Then he looked up, convinced. "Add those figures, Papa. See if the total is right."

"Is his addition wrong too?" I asked my brother.

"Wrong?" he said, half-chuckling. "That guy's added a dollar and   40 forty-nine on the total, that's all."

"What!" Mother cried. "This is the end. We'll never buy from him again."

Father added again and again. My brother went to the corner where the old bills were kept.

"What's happened to him lately?" Mother wanted to know. "Is he loose in the head?"

From the corner my brother exclaimed, "Here's some more profit for Ishimoto-san on last month's bill.

Mother moaned.   45

"He made a dollar on nothing," my brother continued. "It should have been seven thirty-three and he's got it down eight thirty-three."

My father finished adding at last. "Don't buy any more!" he shouted. "Don't buy any more."

We all agreed.

"No more," Mother said solemnly.

On his next round we watched Ishimoto-san from the house while   50
Mother went out to meet him with the bill. We watched him add several times. Finally he scratched his head. He burst out, "Ho-ho-ho-ho-ho." His sweat-stained derby went up and down with vibration.

When Mother came in the house she had with her two bean cakes and a big head of cabbage.

"Did you buy those, Mama?" Father demanded.

"No. He gave these to me," she said somewhat sadly.

"Remember, don't buy any more," Father warned us.

"We won't buy again," we said.   55

For several weeks we didn't buy a thing. Sometimes Mother waved him away. Sometimes I did it. Then one day Mother lost her fury, and the old habit overtook her. Ishimoto-san began coming as before.

SUGGESTIONS FOR FURTHER STUDY

Language and Style

1. This story is told more through dialogue than narration. Examine the following passage and discuss the questions that follow:

    Ishimoto-san came regularly to the house. He pestered my mother. If she didn't want carrots would she care for dry onions. If she didn't want a can of bamboo sprouts would she need a package of shredded shrimp. Some days he would stop on the way home and look up my mother. When he found her he'd look anxiously at her.

"Would you lend me a dollar, Mama?" he'd ask. "I had a flat, and I must get a tire patch and fix my spare.

'Business is bad,' my mother would say."

    a. Which sentences in this passage represent the author narrating the meeting between his mother and the peddler?

    b. Which sentences represent Ishimoto-san speaking? Is his speech direct or indirect? When does he ask a question directly? Indirectly? When does he make a statement?

    c. Which sentences represent the mother speaking directly to the peddlar? How does she answer the peddlar's question, "Would you lend me a dollar, Mama?"

2. Rewrite this passage in direct conversation only. Omit the author's narration and create a dialogue between the peddlar and the mother only. Notice how the tone and language change in order to create a direct conversation.

Topics for Discussion and Writing

1. Mori begins his story by stating: "This was the thirty-ninth time it happened." What does he mean by *this*?

2. How does the author describe the old peddlar and his life?

3. Why do you think mother changes her mind at the end of the story?

4. How does the title reflect what happens in the story?

5. What makes this story humorous? How would you describe the kind of humor in this story? Pick out instances of humor and show how they work to create the character of the mother and her relationship with the peddlar.

6. Most families tell stories about someone who has annoyed or amused them in some way. If you know of such a story in your family, retell it in writing, using dialogue where it is appropriate. Or create an amusing story that reflects an interesting character like Ishimoto-san in "My Mother Stands on Her Head."

The Last of the Kiowas

N. Scott Momaday

*N. Scott Momaday (born in 1934) is a Native American, a Kiowa
who grew up on a reservation in New Mexico and now teaches at the
University of Arizona. He is a poet, novelist, and nonfiction writer
who won the Pulitzer Prize for his novel* House Made of Dawn. *He is
also an artist and a Kiowa tribal dancer. Momaday's work chronicles
the experience of Native Americans and their identity as part of the
natural world. The following selection, from* The Way to Rainy
Mountain, *describes his Kiowa grandmother and her relationship
to the land.*

A single knoll rises out of the plain in Oklahoma, north and west of the   1
Wichita Range. For my people, the Kiowas, it is an old landmark, and they
gave it the name Rainy Mountain. The hardest weather in the world is
there. Winter brings blizzards, hot tornadic winds arise in the spring, and in
summer the prairie is an anvil's edge. The grass turns brittle and brown, and
it cracks beneath your feet. There are green belts along the rivers and
creeks, linear groves of hickory and pecan, willow and witch hazel. At a distance in July or August the steaming foliage seems almost to writhe in fire.
Great green and yellow grasshoppers are everywhere in the tall grass, popping up like corn to sting the flesh, and tortoises crawl about on the red
earth, going nowhere in the plenty of time. Loneliness is an aspect of the
land. All things in the plain are isolate; there is no confusion of objects in
the eye, but *one* hill or *one* tree or *one* man. To look upon that landscape in
the early morning, with the sun at your back, is to lose the sense of proportion. Your imagination comes to life, and this, you think, is where Creation
was begun.

I returned to Rainy Mountain in July. My grandmother had died in the
spring, and I wanted to be at her grave. She had lived to be very old and at
last infirm. Her only living daughter was with her when she died, and I was
told that in death her face was that of a child.

I like to think of her as a child. When she was born, the Kiowas were
living the last great moment of their history. For more than a hundred years
they had controlled the open range from the Smoky Hill River to the Red,
from the headwaters of the Canadian to the fork of the Arkansas and
Cimarron. In alliance with the Comanches, they had ruled the whole of the

southern Plains. War was their sacred business, and they were among the finest horsemen the world has ever known. But warfare for the Kiowas was preeminently a matter of disposition rather than of survival, and they never understood the grim, unrelenting advance of the U.S. Cavalry. When at last, divided and ill-provisioned, they were driven onto the Staked Plains in the cold rains of autumn, they fell into panic. In Palo Duro Canyon they abandoned their crucial stores to pillage and had nothing then but their lives. In order to save themselves, they surrendered to the soldiers at Fort Sill and were imprisoned in the old stone corral that now stands as a military museum. My grandmother was spared the humiliation of those high gray walls by eight or ten years, but she must have known from birth the affliction of defeat, the dark brooding of old warriors.

Her name was Aho, and she belonged to the last culture to evolve in North America. Her forebears came down from the high country in western Montana nearly three centuries ago. They were a mountain people, a mysterious tribe of hunters whose language has never been positively classified in any major group. In the late seventeenth century they began a long migration to the south and east. It was a journey toward the dawn, and it led to a golden age. Along the way the Kiowas were befriended by the Crows, who gave them the culture and religion of the Plains. They acquired horses, and their ancient nomadic spirit was suddenly free of the ground. They acquired Tai-me, the sacred Sun Dance doll, from that moment the object and symbol of their worship, and so shared in the divinity of the sun. Not least, they acquired the sense of destiny, therefore courage and pride. When they entered upon the southern Plains they had been transformed. No longer were they slaves to the simple necessity of survival; they were a lordly and dangerous society of fighters and thieves, hunters and priests of the sun. According to their origin myth, they entered the world through a hollow log. From one point of view, their migration was the fruit of an old prophecy, for indeed they emerged from a sunless world.

Although my grandmother lived out her long life in the shadow of   5
Rainy Mountain, the immense landscape of the continental interior lay like memory in her blood. She could tell of the Crows, whom she had never seen, and of the Black Hills, where she had never been. I wanted to see in reality what she had seen more perfectly in the mind's eye, and traveled fifteen hundred miles to begin my pilgrimage.

Yellowstone, it seemed to me, was the top of the world, a region of deep lakes and dark timber, canyons and waterfalls. But, beautiful as it is, one might have the sense of confinement there. The skyline in all directions is close at hand, the high wall of the woods and deep cleavages of shade. There is a perfect freedom in the mountains, but it belongs to the eagle and the elk, the badger and the bear. The Kiowas reckoned their stature by the distance they could see, and they were bent and blind in the wilderness.

Descending eastward, the highland meadows are a stairway to the plain. In July the inland slope of the Rockies is luxuriant with flax and buckwheat, stonecrop and larkspur. The earth unfolds and the limit of the land recedes. Clusters of trees, and animals grazing far in the distance, cause the vision to reach away and wonder to build upon the mind. The sun follows a longer course in the day, and the sky is immense beyond all comparison. The great billowing clouds that sail upon it are shadows that move upon the grain like water, dividing light. Farther down, in the land of the Crows and Blackfeet, the plain is yellow. Sweet clover takes hold of the hills and bends upon itself to cover and seal the soil. There the Kiowas paused on their way; they had come to the place where they must change their lives. The sun is at home on the plains. Precisely there does it have the certain character of a god. When the Kiowas came to the land of the Crows, they could see the dark lees of the hills at dawn across the Bighorn River, the profusion of light on the grain shelves, the oldest deity ranging after the solstices. Not yet would they veer southward to the caldron of the land that lay below; they must wean their blood from the northern winter and hold the mountains a while longer in their view. They bore Tai-me in procession to the east.

A dark mist lay over the Black Hills, and the land was like iron. At the top of a ridge I caught sight of Devil's Tower upthrust against the gray sky as if in the birth of time the core of the earth had broken through its crust and the motion of the world was begun. There are things in nature that engender an awful quiet in the heart of man; Devil's Tower is one of them. Two centuries ago, because they could not do otherwise, the Kiowas made a legend at the base of the rock. My grandmother said:

> Eight children were there at play, seven sisters and their brother.
> Suddenly the boy was struck dumb; he trembled and began to run
> upon his hands and feet. His fingers became claws, and his body was
> covered with fur. Directly there was a bear where the boy had been.
> The sisters were terrified; they ran, and the bear after them. They
> came to the stump of a great tree, and the tree spoke to them. It bade
> them climb upon it, and as they did so it began to rise into the air.
> The bear came to kill them, but they were just beyond its reach. It
> reared against the tree and scored the bark all around with its claws.
> The seven sisters were borne into the sky, and they became the stars
> of the Big Dipper.

From that moment, and so long as the legend lives, the Kiowas have kinsmen in the night sky. Whatever they were in the mountains, they could be no more. However tenuous their well-being, however much they had suffered and would suffer again, they had found a way out of the wilderness.

My grandmother had a reverence for the sun, a holy regard that now is all but gone out of mankind. There was a wariness in her, and an ancient awe. She was a Christian in her later years, but she had come a long way about, and she never forgot her birthright. As a child she had been to the Sun Dances; she had taken part in those annual rites, and by them she had learned the restoration of her people in the presence of Tai-me. She was about seven when the last Kiowa Sun Dance was held in 1887 on the Washita River above Rainy Mountain Creek. The buffalo were gone. In order to consummate the ancient sacrifice—to impale the head of a buffalo bull upon the medicine tree—a delegation of old men journeyed into Texas, there to beg and barter for an animal from the Goodnight herd. She was ten when the Kiowas came together for the last time as a living Sun Dance culture. They could find no buffalo; they had to hang an old hide from the sacred tree. Before the dance could begin, a company of soldiers rode out from Fort Sill under orders to disperse the tribe. Forbidden without cause the essential act of their faith, having seen the wild herds slaughtered and left to rot upon the ground, the Kiowas backed away forever from the medicine tree. That was July 20, 1890, at the great bend of the Washita. My grandmother was there. Without bitterness, and for as long as she lived, she bore a vision of deicide.

Now that I can have her only in memory, I see my grandmother in the   10 several postures that were peculiar to her: standing at the wood stove on a winter morning and turning meat in a great iron skillet; sitting at the south window, bent above her beadwork, and afterwards, when her vision failed, looking down for a long time into the fold of her hands; going out upon a cane, very slowly as she did when the weight of age came upon her; praying. I remember her most often at prayer. She made long, rambling prayers out of suffering and hope, having seen many things. I was never sure that I had the right to hear, so exclusive were they of all mere custom and company. The last time I saw her she prayed standing by the side of her bed at night, naked to the waist, the light of a kerosene lamp moving upon her dark skin. Her long, black hair, always drawn and braided in the day, lay upon her shoulders and against her breasts like a shawl. I do not speak Kiowa, and I never understood her prayers, but there was something inherently sad in the sound, some merest hesitation upon the syllables of sorrow. She began in a high and descending pitch, exhausting her breath to silence; then again and again—and always the same intensity of effort, of something that is, and is not, like urgency in the human voice. Transported so in the dancing light among the shadows of her room, she seemed beyond the reach of time. But that was illusion; I think I knew then that I should not see her again.

Houses are like sentinels in the plain, old keepers of the weather watch. There, in a very little while, wood takes on the appearance of great age. All colors wear soon away in the wind and rain, and then the wood is burned gray and the grain appears and the nails turn red with rust. The window-panes are black and opaque; you imagine there is nothing within, and indeed there are many ghosts, bones given up to the land. They stand here and there against the sky, and you approach them for a longer time than you expect. They belong in the distance; it is their domain.

Once there was a lot of sound in my grandmother's house, a lot of coming and going, feasting and talk. The summers there were full of excitement and reunion. The Kiowas are a summer people; they abide the cold and keep to themselves, but when the season turns and the land becomes warm and vital they cannot hold still; an old love of going returns upon them. The aged visitors who came to my grandmother's house when I was a child were made of lean and leather, and they bore themselves upright. They wore great black hats and bright ample shirts that shook in the wind. They rubbed fat upon their hair and wound their braids with strips of colored cloth. Some of them painted their faces and carried the scars of old and cherished enmities. They were an old council of warlords, come to remind and be reminded of who they were. Their wives and daughters served them well. The women might indulge themselves; gossip was at once the mark and compensation of their servitude. They made loud and elaborate talk among themselves, full of jest and gesture, fright and false alarm. They went abroad in fringed and flowered shawls, bright beadwork and German silver. They were at home in the kitchen, and they prepared meals that were banquets.

There were frequent prayer meetings, and great nocturnal feasts. When I was a child I played with my cousins outside, where the lamplight fell upon the ground and the singing of the old people rose up around us and carried away into the darkness. There were a lot of good things to eat, a lot of laughter and surprise. And afterwards, when the quiet returned, I lay down with my grandmother and could hear the frogs away by the river and feel the motion of the air.

Now there is funeral silence in the rooms, the endless wake of some final word. The walls have closed in upon my grandmother's house. When I returned to it in mourning, I saw for the first time in my life how small it was. It was late at night, and there was a white moon, nearly full. I sat for a long time on the stone steps by the kitchen door. From there I could see out across the land; I could see the long row of trees by the creek, the low light upon the rolling plains, and the stars of the Big Dipper. Once I looked at the moon and caught sight of a strange thing. A cricket had perched upon the handrail, only a few inches away from me. My line of vision was such that the creature filled the moon like a fossil. It had gone there, I thought, to live and die, for there, of all places, was its small definition made whole and eternal. A warm wind rose up and purled like the longing within me.

The next morning I awoke at dawn and went out on the dirt road to Rainy Mountain. It was already hot, and the grasshoppers began to fill the air. Still, it was early in the morning, and the birds sang out of the shadows. The long yellow grass on the mountain shone in the bright light, and a

"Grandmother" by Noah Buchanan, artist and book illustrator whose work has been displayed in the Hall of Congress, Washington, D.C.

scissortail hied above the land. There, where it ought to be, at the end of a long and legendary way, was my grandmother's grave. Here and there on the dark stones were ancestral names. Looking back once, I saw the mountain and came away.

SUGGESTIONS FOR FURTHER STUDY

Key Words

The author uses language with which you may not be familiar. Find the following words in the paragraphs indicated, and explain their meanings in

the context of the sentences in which the words appear. Consult a dictionary, as needed.

preeminently (par. 3)
pillage (par. 3)
profusion (par. 7)
solstices (par. 7)
consummate (par. 9)
deicide (par. 9)
purled (par. 14)
hied (par. 15)

Make a list of other words you are not familiar with, and look up their meanings in a standard dictionary. Try using them in a sentence of your own.

Topics for Discussion and Writing

1. In paragraph 1, Momaday says, "Loneliness is an aspect of the land." What images help explain that comment?

2. How does Momaday describe the Rainy Mountain area?

3. What is the significance of Rainy Mountain to the Kiowa? To Momaday?

4. What is the role of the buffalo in the Kiowa culture?

5. Momaday remembers his grandmother praying. What other kinds of things does he remember most clearly about his grandmother?

6. Momaday's descriptions are often metaphoric, as in "The prairie is an anvil's edge." Find other metaphors and similes in the text and describe their effectiveness.

7. Research a Native American tribe and, in a brief essay, describe some of their cultural characteristics. Or review a film such as *Dances with Wolves* or a TV presentation such as *How the West Was Lost,* featuring Native Americans, and comment on how the media portray them historically or in the present.

In Search of Our Mothers' Gardens

Alice Walker

Alice Walker is known for her many novels, short stories, and essays, among them The Color Purple, *which won a Pulitzer Prize in 1982 and was subsequently made into a popular movie. One of her short stories, "To Hell with Dying," has been published also as an illustrated children's book, and she has edited a Zora Neale Hurston reader. She writes personally, with a voice that is forceful yet beguiling, about relationships among black women, their families, and their culture. In* In Search of Our Mothers' Gardens, *Walker tells us how she found her own "garden," guided by her heritage of "love of beauty and a respect for strength."*

When the poet Jean Toomer walked through the South in the early   1
twenties, he discovered a curious thing: black women whose spirituality was so intense, so deep, so *unconscious,* that they were themselves unaware of the richness they held. They stumbled blindly through their lives: creatures so abused and mutilated in body, so dimmed and confused by pain, that they considered themselves unworthy even of hope. In the selfless abstractions their bodies became to the men who used them, they became more than "sexual objects," more even than mere women: they became "Saints." Instead of being perceived as whole persons, their bodies became shrines: what was thought to be their minds became temples suitable for worship. These crazy Saints stared out at the world, wildly, like lunatics—or quietly, like suicides; and the "God" that was in their gaze was as mute as a great stone.

Who were these Saints? These crazy, loony, pitiful women?

Some of them, without a doubt, were our mothers and grandmothers.

In the still heat of the post-Reconstruction South, this is how they seemed to Jean Toomer: exquisite butterflies trapped in an evil honey, toiling away their lives in an era, a century, that did not acknowledge them, except as "the *mule* of the world." They dreamed dreams that no one knew, not even themselves, in any coherent fashion, and saw visions no one could understand. They wandered or sat about the countryside crooning lullabies to ghosts, and drawing the mother of Christ in charcoal on courthouse walls.

They forced their minds to desert their bodies and their striving spirits   5
sought to rise, like frail whirlwinds from the hard red clay. And when those
frail whirlwinds fell, in scattered particles, upon the ground, no one
mourned. Instead, men lit candles to celebrate the emptiness that remained,
as people do who enter a beautiful but vacant space to resurrect a God.

Our mothers and grandmothers, some of them: moving to music not
yet written. And they waited.

They waited for a day when the unknown thing that was in them would
be made known; but guessed, somehow in their darkness, that on the day of
their revelation they would be long dead. Therefore to Toomer they walked,
and even ran, in slow motion. For they were going nowhere immediate, and
the future was not yet within their grasp. And men took our mothers and
grandmothers, "but got no pleasure from it." So complex was their passion
and their calm.

To Toomer, they lay vacant and fallow as autumn fields, with harvest
time never in sight: and he saw them enter loveless marriages, without joy;
and become prostitutes, without resistance; and become mothers of children, without fulfillment.

For these grandmothers and mothers of ours were not Saints, but
Artists; driven to a numb and bleeding madness by the springs of creativity
in them for which there was no release. They were Creators, who lived lives
of spiritual waste, because they were so rich in spirituality—which is the
basis of Art—that the strain of enduring their unused and unwanted talent
drove them insane. Throwing away this spirituality was their pathetic
attempt to lighten the soul to a weight their work-worn, sexually abused
bodies could bear.

What did it mean for a black woman to be an artist in our grandmoth-   10
ers' time? In our great-grandmothers' day? It is a question with an answer
cruel enough to stop the blood.

Did you have a genius of a great-great-grandmother who died under
some ignorant and depraved white overseer's lash? Or was she required to
bake biscuits for a lazy backwater tramp, when she cried out in her soul to
paint watercolors of sunsets, or the rain falling on the green and peaceful
pasturelands? Or was her body broken and forced to bear children (who
were more often than not sold away from her)—eight, ten, fifteen, twenty
children—when her one joy was the thought of modeling heroic figures of
rebellion, in stone or clay?

How was the creativity of the black woman kept alive, year after year
and century after century, when for most of the years black people have
been in America, it was a punishable crime for a black person to read or
write? And the freedom to paint, to sculpt, to expand the mind with action
did not exist. Consider, if you can bear to imagine it, what might have been
the result if singing, too, had been forbidden by law. Listen to the voices of

Bessie Smith, Billie Holiday, Nina Simone, Roberta Flack, and Aretha Franklin, among others, and imagine those voices muzzled for life. Then you may begin to comprehend the lives of our "crazy," "Sainted" mothers and grandmothers. The agony of the lives of women who might have been Poets, Novelists, Essayists, and Short-Story Writers (over a period of centuries), who died with their real gifts stifled within them.

And, if this were the end of the story, we would have cause to cry out in my paraphrase of Okot p'Bitek's great poem:

O, my clanswomen
Let us all cry together!
Come,
Let us mourn the death of our mother,
The death of a Queen
The ash that was produced
By a great fire!
O, this homestead is utterly dead
Close the gates
With *lacari* thorns,
For our mother
The creator of the Stool is lost!
And all the young women
Have perished in the wilderness!

But this is not the end of the story, for all the young women—our mothers and grandmothers, *ourselves*—have not perished in the wilderness. And if we ask ourselves why, and search for and find the answer, we will know beyond all efforts to erase it from our minds, just exactly who, and of what, we black American women are.

One example, perhaps the most pathetic, most misunderstood one, can   15
provide a backdrop for our mothers' work: Phillis Wheatley a slave in the 1700s.

Virginia Woolf, in her book *A Room of One's Own,* wrote that in order for a woman to write fiction she must have two things, certainly: a room of her own (with key and lock) and enough money to support herself.

What then are we to make of Phillis Wheatley, a slave, who owned not even herself? This sickly, frail black girl who required a servant of her own at times—her health was so precarious—and who, had she been white, would have been easily considered the intellectual superior of all the women and most of the men in the society of her day.

Virginia Woolf wrote further, speaking of course not of our Phillis, that "any woman born with a great gift in the sixteenth century [insert "eighteenth century," insert "black woman," insert "born or made a slave"] would certainly have gone crazed, shot herself, or ended her days in some lonely cottage outside the village, half witch, half wizard [insert "Saint"], feared and mocked at. For it needs little skill and psychology to be sure that a highly gifted girl who had tried to use her gift for poetry would have been so thwarted and hindered by contrary instincts [add "chains, guns, the lash, the ownership of one's body by someone else, submission to an alien religion"], that she must have lost her health and sanity to a certainty."

The key words, as they relate to Phillis, are "contrary instincts." For when we read the poetry of Phillis Wheatley—and when we read the novels of Nella Larsen or the oddly false-sounding autobiography of that freest of all black women writers, Zora Hurston—evidence of "contrary instincts" is everywhere. Her loyalties were completely divided, as was, without question, her mind.

But how could this be otherwise? Captured at seven, a slave of wealthy, doting whites who instilled in her the "savagery" of the Africa they "rescued" her from . . . one wonders if she was even able to remember her homeland as she had known it, or as it really was.   20

Yet, because she did try to use her gift for poetry in a world that made her a slave, she was "so thwarted and hindered by . . . contrary instincts, that she . . . lost her health. . . ." In the last years of brief life, burdened not only with the need to express her gift but also with a penniless, friendless "freedom" and several small children for whom she was forced to do strenuous work to feed, she lost her health, certainly. Suffering from malnutrition and neglect and who knows what mental agonies, Phillis Wheatley died.

So torn by "contrary instincts" was black, kidnapped, enslaved Phillis that her description of "the Goddess"—as she poetically called the Liberty she did not have—is ironically, cruelly humorous. And, in fact, has held Phillis up to ridicule for more than a century. It is usually read prior to hanging Phillis's memory as that of a fool. She wrote:

> The Goddess comes, she moves divinely fair,
> Olive and laurel binds her *golden* hair.
> Wherever shines this native of the skies,
> Unnumber'd charms and recent graces rise. [My italics]

It is obvious that Phillis, the slave, combed the "Goddess's" hair every morning; prior, perhaps, to bringing in the milk, or fixing her mistress's lunch. She took her imagery from the one thing she saw elevated above all others.

With the benefit of hindsight we ask, "How could she?"

But at last, Phillis, we understand. No more snickering when your stiff,   25 struggling, ambivalent lines are forced on us. We know now that you were not an idiot or a traitor; only a sickly little black girl, snatched from your home and country and made a slave; a woman who still struggled to sing the song that was your gift, although in a land of barbarians who praised you for your bewildered tongue. It is not so much what you sang, as that you kept alive, in so many of our ancestors, *the notion of song.*

Black women are called, in the folklore that so aptly identifies one's status in society, "the *mule* of the world," because we have been handed the burdens that everyone else—*everyone* else—refused to carry. We have also been called "Matriarchs," "Superwomen," and "Mean and Evil Bitches." Not to mention "Castraters" and "Sapphire's Mama." When we have pleaded for understanding, our character has been distorted; when we have asked for simple caring, we have been handed empty inspirational appellations, then stuck in the farthest corner. When we have asked for love, we have been given children. In short, even our plainer gifts, our labors of fidelity and love, have been knocked down our throats. To be an artist and a black woman, even today, lowers our status in many respects, rather than raises it: and yet, artists we will be.

Therefore we must fearlessly pull out of ourselves and look at and identify with our lives the living creativity some of our great-grandmothers were not allowed to know. I stress *some* of them because it is well known that the majority of our great-grandmothers knew, even without "knowing" it, the reality of their spirituality, even if they didn't recognize it beyond what happened in the singing at church—and they never had any intention of giving it up.

How they did it—those millions of black women who were not Phillis Wheatley, or Lucy Terry or Frances Harper or Zora Hurston or Nella Larsen or Bessie Smith; or Elizabeth Catlett, or Katherine Dunham, either—brings me to the title of this essay, "In Search of Our Mothers' Gardens," which is a personal account that is yet shared, in its theme and its meaning, by all of us. I found, while thinking about the far-reaching world of the creative black woman, that often the truest answer to a question that really matters can be found very close.

In the late 1920s my mother ran away from home to marry my father. Marriage, if not running away, was expected of seventeen-year-old girls. By the time she was twenty, she had two children and was pregnant with a third. Five children later, I was born. And this is how I came to know my mother: she seemed a large, soft, loving-eyed woman who was rarely impatient in our home. Her quick, violent temper was on view only a few times a year, when she battled with the white landlord who had the misfortune to suggest to her that her children did not need to go to school.

She made all the clothes we wore, even my brothers' overalls. She made 30 all the towels and sheets we used. She spent the summers canning vegetables and fruits. She spent the winter evenings making quilts enough to cover all our beds.

During the "working" day, she labored beside—not behind—my father in the fields. Her day began before sunup, and did not end until late at night. There was never a moment for her to sit down, undisturbed, to unravel her own private thoughts; never a time free from interruption—by work or the noisy inquiries of her many children. And yet, it is to my mother—and all our mothers who were not famous—that I went in search of the secret of what has fed that muzzled and often mutilated, but vibrant, creative spirit that the black woman has inherited, and that pops out in wild and unlikely places to this day.

But when, you will ask, did my overworked mother have time to know or care about feeding the creative spirit?

The answer is so simple that many of us have spent years discovering it. We have constantly looked high, when we should have looked high—and low.

For example: in the Smithsonian Institution in Washington, D.C., there hangs a quilt unlike any other in the world. In fanciful, inspired, and yet simple and identifiable figures, it portrays the story of the Crucifixion. It is considered rare, beyond price. Though it follows no known pattern of quilt-making, and though it is made of bits and pieces of worthless rags, it is obviously the work of a person of powerful imagination and deep spiritual feeling. Below this quilt I saw a note that says it was made by "an anonymous Black woman in Alabama, a hundred years ago."

If we could locate this "anonymous" black woman from Alabama, she would turn out to be one of our grandmothers—an artist who left her mark in the only materials she could afford, and in the only medium her position in society allowed her to use.

As Virginia Woolf wrote further, in *A Room of One's Own*:

> Yet genius of a sort must have existed among women as it must have existed among the working class. [Change this to "slaves" and "the wives and daughters of sharecroppers."] Now and again an Emily Brontë or a Robert Burns [change this to "a Zora Hurston or a Richard Wright"] blazes out and proves its presence. But certainly it never got itself on to paper. When, however, one reads of a witch being ducked, of a woman possessed by devils [or "Sainthood"], of a wise woman selling herbs [our root workers], or even a very remarkable man who had a mother, then I think we are on the track of a lost novelist, a suppressed poet, of some mute and inglorious Jane Austen. . . . Indeed, I would venture to guess that Anon, who wrote so many poems without signing them, was often a woman. . . .

And so our mothers and grandmothers have, more often than not anonymously, handed on the creative spark, the seed of the flower they themselves never hoped to see: or like a sealed letter they could not plainly read.

And so it is, certainly, with my own mother. Unlike "Ma" Rainey's songs, which retained their creator's name even while blasting forth from

Bessie Smith's mouth, no song or poem will bear my mother's name. Yet so many of the stories that I write, that we all write, are my mother's stories. Only recently did I fully realize this: that through years of listening to my mother's stories of her life, I have absorbed not only the stories themselves, but something of the manner in which she spoke, something of the urgency that involves the knowledge that her stories—like her life—must be recorded. It is probably for this reason that so much of what I have written is about characters whose counterparts in real life are so much older than I am.

But the telling of these stories, which came from my mother's lips as naturally as breathing, was not the only way my mother showed herself as an artist. For stories, too, were subject to being distracted, to dying without conclusion. Dinners must be started, and cotton must be gathered before the big rains. The artist that was and is my mother showed itself to me only after many years. This is what I finally noticed:

Like Mem, a character in *The Third Life of Grange Copeland*, my   40
mother adorned with flowers whatever shabby house we were forced to live in. And not just your typical straggly country stand of zinnias, either. She planted ambitious gardens—and still does—with over fifty different varieties of plants that bloom profusely from early March until late November. Before she left home for the fields, she watered her flowers, chopped up the grass, and laid out new beds. When she returned from the fields she might divide clumps of bulbs, dig a cold pit, uproot and replant roses, or prune branches from her taller bushes or trees—until night came and it was too dark to see.

Whatever she planted grew as if by magic, and her fame as a grower of flowers spread over three counties. Because of her creativity with her flowers, even my memories of poverty are seen through a screen of blooms—sunflowers, petunias, roses, dahlias, forsythia, spirea, delphiniums, verbena . . . and on and on.

And I remember people coming to my mother's yard to be given cuttings from her flowers; I hear again the praise showered on her because whatever rocky soil she landed on, she turned into a garden. A garden so brilliant with colors, so original in its design, so magnificent with life and creativity, that to this day people drive by our house in Georgia—perfect strangers and imperfect strangers—and ask to stand or walk among my mother's art.

I notice that it is only when my mother is working in her flowers that she is radiant, almost to the point of being invisible—except as Creator: hand and eye. She is involved in work her soul must have. Ordering the universe in the image of her personal conception of Beauty.

Her face, as she prepares the Art that is her gift, is a legacy of respect she leaves to me, for all that illuminates and cherishes life. She has handed down respect for the possibilities—and the will to grasp them.

For her, so hindered and intruded upon in so many ways, being an artist   45
has still been a daily part of her life. This ability to hold on, even in very simple ways, is work black women have done for a very long time.

This poem is not enough, but it is something, for the woman who literally covered the holes in our walls with sunflowers:

They were women then
My mama's generation
Husky of voice—Stout of
Step
With fists as well as
Hands
How they battered down
Doors
And ironed
Starched white
Shirts
How they led
Armies
Headragged Generals
Across mined
Fields
Booby-trapped
Kitchens
To discover books
Desks
A place for us
How they knew what we
Must know
Without knowing a page
Of it
Themselves.

Guided by my heritage of a love of beauty and a respect for strength—in search of my mother's garden, I found my own.

And perhaps in Africa over two hundred years ago, there was just such a mother; perhaps she painted vivid and daring decorations in oranges and yellows and greens on the walls of her hut; perhaps she sang—in a voice like Roberta Flack's—*sweetly* over the compounds of her village; perhaps she wove the most stunning mats or told the most ingenious stories of all the village storytellers. Perhaps she was herself a poet—though only her daughter's name is signed to the poems that we know.

Perhaps Phillis Wheatley's mother was also an artist.

Perhaps in more than Phillis Wheatley's biological life is her mother's signature made clear.   50

SUGGESTIONS FOR FURTHER STUDY

Key Words

The author uses language with which you may not be familiar. Find the following words in the paragraphs indicated, and explain their meanings in the context of the sentences in which the words appear. Consult a dictionary, as needed.

spirituality (par. 1)
fallow (par. 8)
precarious (par. 17)
thwarted (par. 18)
ambivalent (par. 25)
appellations (par. 26)
counterparts (par. 38)
profusely (par. 40)
headragged (par. 46)

Language and Style

1. The author employs several effective unconventional strategies in her essay. Among them are single-sentence paragraphs, frequent questions, poems intermixed with prose, incomplete sentences, and division of the whole essay into separate sections. Locate instances of these and other strategies in the essay you think are particularly interesting and perhaps surprising.
2. Walker frequently refers to black women artists to show that "grandmothers and mothers of ours were not Saints, but Artists. . . ." You may recognize the names of several of these women, such as Roberta Flack or Aretha Franklin, but be unfamiliar with others. Make a list of those unfamiliar references and find out about their professions and their artistic accomplishments. Discuss how their achievements may have contributed to those of contemporary black women artists such as Walker herself.

Topics for Discussion and Writing

1. According to Walker, who are the "Saints"?
2. How did black women keep alive their creativity through various kinds of oppression? Cite passages in the essay that demonstrate different kinds of creativity and spirituality.
3. How is Virginia Woolf's *A Room of One's Own* significant for Walker, the author of this essay? How does she rewrite Woolf's text and integrate her own into it? Give some examples.

4. At the end of paragraph 25, the author says of Phillis Wheatley, "It is not so much what you sang, as that you kept alive, in so many of our ancestors, *the notion of song*." What is the significance of the last phrase?

5. In what ways does Walker's mother demonstrate her creativity?

6. What conclusion does the author draw from her examination of her mother and other black women before her?

7. Respond to Walker's essay in one or more of these written forms:

   A letter asking for more information or explanation regarding a topic that interested you in this essay

   A commentary agreeing or disagreeing (or both) with an issue Walker raises in her essay

   A journal entry commenting on an idea from Walker's essay that interested or puzzled you

Nana

Diane Rubio

In this selection, student writer Diane Rubio writes an autobiographical/biographical essay about her "Nana" as well as the many diverse experiences Rubio has shared with her grandmother. Notice the use of specific details and the sense of humor Rubio uses to describe her grandmother and their times together.

"Quien tiene lodo en los zapatos?" (Who has mud on their shoes?)   1
Nana yelled. "Levantan los pies, dejame ver!" (Lift your feet; let me see!)
My cousins and I lifted our feet as we were asked because we knew we were
not the culprits of the mud tracked through Nana's house. "It wasn't me,
Nana!" I exclaimed, as she looked over my shoes for a trace of mud that
just wasn't there. My cousins, Mark and David, and I had been playing
Monopoly all morning as we did many days during our youthful summers.
We hadn't yet ventured outside, so we knew we were clean. Nana started to
clean the mud from the floor when I noticed Nana had mud all over her
slippers. My cousins and I snickered uncontrollably. "Que risa?" (What's so
funny?) Nana asked. "Nana," we laughed, "you are the one that stepped in
the mud!"

Dolores Ledesma was born in Albuquerque, New Mexico, and when
her mother passed on—she was very young—she moved to Michoacan,
Mexico. There in Mexico she lived with her grandmother and learned the
proper ways of a young señorita. Nana had a very strict childhood and had
to grow up fast. She was burdened with many chores and cooking and was
not to speak unless spoken to. Nana was twelve years old when her grandmother passed away and her father, who lived in Los Angeles, sent his new
wife to Mexico to bring Nana to her new home. Not too many years later,
Dolores Ledesma became Dolores Flores. With grandfather, Juan Flores,
they raised nine children—seven girls and two boys.

A short, plump woman, Nana dresses mostly in housecoats unless she
ventures into public. When she goes out, which isn't too often, she dresses
in dark colors, for she thinks she is too old for bright colors. Her mannerisms are still quite like her upbringing, as she is very quiet while in public
and sits with her hands folded properly on her lap and doesn't say a word
unless she is spoken to. Currently, Nana lives in Downey, California, and

has since she was about thirteen years old. Her home is immaculate and feels like the home of a grandparent. The furniture is wrapped in plastic, so one can't enjoy it too much, and the house always smells of Pledge or Pine-Sol. But the house is cozy and whenever I visit I find myself wanting to catch twenty winks.

Nana's social calendar involves attending church (she is very Catholic), paying her utility bills in person, and going to the bank and the grocery store. She doesn't like to go to church on Sunday because it is too crowded, so she goes on Saturday evenings. She also has to pay all of her bills in person because she doesn't have a checking account; if she does have to send a bill through the mail, she has to get a money order—thus her trip to the bank. Going to the grocery store is Nana's most masterful accomplishment. First, she scours the newspapers for the best prices in town and then scurries around to all the different grocery stores for the best bargains. On any given day, she might shop at three different stores and still go all the way across town to another because there cat food is 29 cents a can.

I'll always remember the summers I spent with Nana. She spoiled me   5
rotten. She was always awake early, carefully sneaking around the house as I slept in. I drifted in and out of slumber as I heard her occasionally take a peek at me to see if I were awake.

As soon as the sun shone, Nana was outside and full of life, puttering in her garden. She would rant and rave about the weeds and how the dog had urinated on her roses. But the God-honest truth was that she loved her garden and still does. The garden consists of a giant king bed of grass that is forever green, and in the center of the grass is an etched-out square of red brick surrounded by its entourage of flowers. The endless grass is bordered on one side with roses of every color, and scattered about and throughout are trees bearing fruit: peaches, lemons, apricots, avocados, figs, and guavas.

She always knew when someone had been near any of her flowers. "Quien estuvo aqui?" (Who's been here?) pointing at a broken stem. That question was usually directed at me or my cousins. We knew who had been in her garden or what had broken the precious stem of the rose in full bloom. We would shrug our shoulders and say, "It was Blackie, Nana." We couldn't risk telling her the truth because our 69-cent rubber ball had popped against the tender stem of the pinkish roses as it hit them, and she might never have bought us another ball. Poor old Blackie, a good dog, was always taking the heat for us.

When I finally awoke from the morning hours of slumber, Nana would hurry in from the garden to make me breakfast. Nana is quite possibly the best cook of all time. Well, maybe I'm exaggerating a little, but everything she makes is just incredible. Sometimes she was too busy, so I just had cereal. But most of the time she went full steam ahead and cooked enough to feed an army. My favorite breakfast was chorizo con heuvos. Chorizo, a spicy Mexican sausage, is often cooked with eggs to make a Mexican scrambled egg dish that can be enjoyed with tortillas. You can eat it burrito style or in the real Mexican way, using the tortilla as a scoop for each spoonful. Nana is such a great cook, and has such a special touch, that even her peanut butter and jelly sandwich is the best around. She is so proud of her culinary status that a plaque on her wall reads "No matter where I serve my guests, they seem to like my kitchen best." Every year at Easter and Christmas she makes tamales from scratch that are out-of-this-world. Sometimes, if there are tamales around, she cooks them up for breakfast with eggs over easy. I know *I* like her kitchen best!

Every year Nana planned a trip to Disneyland and my cousins and I looked forward to it. We would get up early for our annual visit to the Magic Kingdom so we could race down Main Street when the gates opened to be the first ones on Thunder Mountain. Before we left for Disneyland, I remember Nana braiding my hair so tightly it hurt, and I would squirm and moan until she said, "Silencia!" and I would sit while my eyes became slanted from the pulling of my hair. As soon as she turned her back, I tried to loosen my braids. But she always caught me and scolded, "Deja los trenzas; vas a ver grenuda!" (Leave your braids alone; you're going to look messy!) So I let them be because the title "grenuda" was totally shameful. Grenuda means shock-headed, and I always pictured a scary little witch with messy hair when Nana said the word.

After the hair encounter, we began our travels toward Disneyland   10
where we spent the whole day from nine o'clock to six, leaving there totally exhausted. Nana lived in Downey, so Disneyland wasn't far to travel, but she didn't drive on freeways. She never gave any particular reason for this; it just came to be an understanding. Nana also didn't like to ride the wild rides in the Magic Kingdom, rides such as Space Mountain and the Matterhorn. But she loved the slow rides like It's a Small World and the Pirates of the Caribbean. I remember that once she rode Thunder Mountain; I can't remember how we coaxed her to do it, but what a sight! She never once yelled or screamed, and I think out of politeness she smiled and said she'd liked it. But we could see the terror in her face and she never rode it again. During the day, we always met for lunch at the same place: the only Mexican restaurant in Disneyland. We never ate anywhere else and we never asked why.

Ever since I can recall, Nana has always spent her evenings the same way. It's really kind of funny, but she watches Mexican soap operas called novelas. She sits in her rocking chair, sometimes with her cat on her lap, and watches novelas on channel 34 from early evening until the local news hour. She doesn't like to miss her novelas either, so if you show up for a visit or call on the phone during this precious time she may very well ignore you. Her favorite novela is "Pura Sangre," which means "Pure Blood." Nana can tell you who all the heroes are, who is having whose baby, and so on. I guess the novelas are the Spanish versions of *Melrose Place* or *Beverly Hills 90210*.

Nana is also a very superstitious person. She has an old map-type paper that she lays out on the table, then you ask a question and drop a needle to see where your answer lies. The needle lands on a symbol which Nana looks up in an almost ragged book that accompanies her map. It seems silly, and Nana laughs every time we ask her to get it out. But when the questions start flying, she means serious business. "Tira la agujaa!" (Drop the needle!) she says excitedly, and I drop the needle. I like to ask questions about my love life, and she is more than pleased to accommodate me because she thinks I should be married with children by now. I'm 30 years old and Nana thinks I should give up the marriage part and just have children. You can see how the 90s have corrupted her, or perhaps she has been watching too many novelas. Although this little game we play with the map of symbols and the needle is quite fun, she never asks any questions of herself. I've always been curious about the kinds of questions she might ask, but she only gives the answers from the ragged little book. Answers to my questions always indicate that I will be involved with a hard-working man whose love for me is very true, and so far that has been true. My mother used to ask questions about her love life, and her answers came true as well. Maybe there is some truth to this old Mexican fortune-telling system.

I spent most of my years growing up with Nana and I can pretty much speak her language and she mine. But when I go to visit her, the strangest thing happens. She'll say, "Como estas?" (How are you?) and I'll answer "Fine, how are you?" Our conversation goes on like this; she speaks to me in Spanish and I respond in English. When my mother is with us it gets even better, because my mother speaks in a combination of both languages. None of us thinks it's odd either; I guess that is how we bonded all these years. I do, of course, owe my Spanish-speaking skills to Nana.

I still love to visit Nana, although I have different reasons now. It's not because she spoils me, but because we have a history that no one can take from us. We sit for hours, talking and laughing, and sometimes I even confess that it was my cousins and I who broke her roses way back when. The yard and her garden seem much smaller now, and Blackie has passed on. But as I sit with her, some things have never changed. Sometimes she still braids my hair except that now she makes only one braid instead of two. If I decline her offer to braid my hair, she never hesitates to call me grenuda. The roses are still there, and if I'm lucky she cuts a bouquet for me to take home along with a couple of chorizo burritos or even some tamales. I always feel sad when I leave Nana's house; I give her a kiss and tell her I love her, and she starts to cry. She stands on the front porch softly saying, "Via con Dios"—"Go with God."

CHAPTER 2: ACTIVITIES FOR DISCUSSION AND WRITING
Making Connections

1. Brainstorm the personal characteristics of one or more older members of your family.

2. Interview your grandparents or older family members and research their history.

3. Write an essay about one of your family members modeled after one of the essays in this chapter. Use the material you compiled in your family research and additional material as you need it.

4. How is understanding family history important in understanding ourselves? Relate to one or more of the selections you read in this chapter in considering this question.

5. Compare and contrast Dan Kwong's "Grandpa Story" and Scott F. Covell's "Gramps." What elements does Kwong's piece have that Covell's doesn't? In what ways are the two stories similar?

6. Select three essays in this chapter and discuss the individual conclusions their authors draw in regard to their perceptions of their grandparents (or parents). In what ways are these conclusions similar? In what ways are they different?

7. In "Nana," written by a student, humor and dialogue are two means of developing the grandmother's character. How effective is humor in introducing this essay? How does the use of Spanish dialogue in the story enhance the grandmother's character? Compare "Nana" with other essays in this chapter that portray vivid characters through humor and dialogue.

8. In your opinion, what story or essay in this chapter was most effective in conveying the author's experience with a family member? Explain why. Be specific in pointing to details and language that convey experience vividly.

POPULAR CULTURE III
America at Play: Vegas, Football, Bungee Jumping, and More

The American experience is diverse beyond imagination. This chapter focuses on the range of human experiences illustrated in the many recreational and lifestyle activities in which Americans participate. In the heart of the American experience lies a passion for boundless fun, danger, and violence; an enthusiasm for sporting activities; a thirst for the ultimate concert experience; a propensity for madcap shopping; and an unceasing interest in new and better ways of having fun.

We begin the chapter with Benjamin Saltman's interpretation of an increasingly popular and dangerous sport in "The Bungee Jumpers." Hunter Thompson offers his perspective on a gaudy Las Vegas casino and a desert motorcycle race in two selections from *Fear and Loathing in Las Vegas*. In "Death in the Mosh Pit," Eric Boehlert describes some out-of-control fans at a Smashing Pumpkins concert. Jerry Adler's "America 2000: Fast and Furious Fun" illustrates the explosive growth of recreational activities in America—particularly the rise of virtual-reality bars—as Americans clamor for state-of-the-art entertainment. In "Rules of the Game: Rodeo," Gretel Ehrlich chronicles the events at a rodeo and surprisingly equates the experience to a good marriage. Philip Roth, in "My Baseball Years," explores his continuing passion for baseball and describes how it led him to an appreciation of literature. John McMurtry's "Kill 'Em! Crush 'Em! Eat 'Em Raw!" exposes the "warrior ethos" inherent in America's favorite spectator sport, football. In "Graceland," Albert Goldman takes us on a tour of Elvis Presley's Graceland mansion, with a surprising twist at the end. Maxine Hong Kingston, in "Wittman Ah Sing's Halloween Play," creates a fantastic theatrical event showcasing Chinese American multiculturalism. In "Shopping," a selection from his novel *White Noise*, Don DeLillo's narrator Jack Gladney eagerly participates in the great American experience of shopping—to his family's unbounded delight. Finally, in "Waiting in Line All Night for Cure Tickets," student writer Chris Hernandez describes what it was like to stay up all night waiting in line for tickets to see his favorite band.

The Bungee Jumpers

Benjamin Saltman

For many years, Benjamin Saltman (born in Pittsburgh, Pennsylvania, in 1927) taught literature, writing, and poetry to university students at California State University, Northridge, and elsewhere. An award-winning poet, Saltman has published six books of poetry, including Elegies of Place, Deck, The Book of Moss, *and his latest,* The Sun Takes Us Away. *"The Bungee Jumpers" is from his collection* The Book of Moss.

The number of calls I get from people wanting to jump is overwhelming.

—Rico Nel, President
California Bungee

The jumping became a rising   1
and the world turned upside down
it was a leap into cancer
it was the jump of a surrogate star.
The rocks below boulders yellow
of lion beneath the bridge
repeated suicide suicide and drove emotion
roared through ribs and pelvis
with the sudden heaviness of a shook thermometer
The jump: first abandoning the eyes of others   10
and then soaring to applause and new friends
tingling skin eyes become jewels
"I couldn't even scream," she said. "All
the way down I thought 'What am I doing?'"

From the ledge she leaped with all the fear
for sale in California then she knew
how well the beer would wash her tongue
how clear bright threads of her plaid shirt
would braid in the sun. She saw the threads
alive with molecules she saw what she could do   20
now reeled up no longer flopping
but standing like the winning fish
in a crew of friends trophy at last she
was not one among many she was the only one

with jumpers who knew death
as fizzing of the blood tightening
memory. "That was terrific!" she cried
it was a cry, her friends would understand
hugging one another in delight and she
the hugged one still shaking in a pile of cord   30
on a bridge on a back road of the Angeles Forest
remembered how she held for a moment at the crest
eyes wide moving neither up nor down
astounded by the smooth curves of the bridge
from underside like a church ceiling

Geoff Todosiev of San Pedro said
"I kept inhaling all the way down"
the air controlled his blood he needed everyone
and when he bounced to the sky
it was no better going up immersed in flight   40
broken free enslaved by air free
in the green view of the forest and its goodbye

he was practicing the right goodbye
like an actor over and over
the dive toward stone knowing he loved the sun
both right side up and upside down
when he had cried "This is insane!" and said
he'd be the first to go toward luck
and swept aside the future dropped into air
and flew again in the wind's flapping canvas rush   50
like all good stories

SUGGESTIONS FOR FURTHER STUDY

Language and Style

The poet employs colorful, vivid language to express the experience of bungee jumping and his feelings about it. Explain in your own words what the following images and figures of language mean, as they are used in the poem. Find other expressions that convey vivid images, as well.

"a leap into cancer" (line 3)

"the jump of a surrogate star" (line 4)

"sudden heaviness of a shook thermometer" (line 9)

"smooth curves of the bridge / from underside like a church ceiling" (lines 34–35)

Topics for Discussion and Writing

1. In what sense does this poem explain why people want to jump into space dangling from a harness meant to protect them from actually crashing onto earth or water?

2. Notice the blandness of the woman jumper's language (she could say only "That was terrific!") in describing her experience, as compared with the richness of the poet's figurative words and phrases throughout the poem. Discuss the effectiveness of the poet's descriptions of scene, event, and feeling through figurative language.

3. Chapter 3 contains selections that explore the thrill of adventure, alongside the presence of irrationality and violence in our lives. Write a short essay or journal entry that explores how "The Bungee Jumpers" reflects that theme.

Selections from *Fear and Loathing in Las Vegas*

Hunter S. Thompson

Hunter S. Thompson is a proponent of the New Journalism mode of writing. His publications include The Great White Shark Hunt, Hell's Angels, *and* Fear and Loathing in Las Vegas *(1971), from which the following selections have been taken. According to Lucian K. Truscott IV of the* Village Voice, Fear and Loathing *"is the final word, a brilliant vision, a terrible magnificently funny telling of what happened to this country in the 1960s." In the following selections, the author narrates two experiences he encounters in the Las Vegas area while working on assignment for* Rolling Stone Magazine: *going to the Circus-Circus casino and viewing the Mint 400 motorcycle race in the desert.*

CIRCUS-CIRCUS

The Circus-Circus is what the whole hep world would be doing on Saturday night if the Nazis had won the war. This is the Sixth Reich. The ground floor is full of gambling tables, like all the other casinos . . . but the place is about four stories high, in the style of a circus tent, and all manner of strange County-Fair/Polish Carnival madness is going on up in this space. Right above the gambling tables the Forty Flying Carazito Brothers are doing a high-wire trapeze act, along with four muzzled Wolverines and the Six Nymphet Sisters from San Diego . . . so you're down on the main floor playing blackjack, and the stakes are getting high when suddenly you chance to look up, and there, right smack above your head is a half-naked fourteen-year-old girl being chased through the air by a snarling wolverine, which is suddenly locked in a death battle with two silver-painted Polacks who come swinging down from opposite balconies and meet in mid-air on the wolverine's neck . . . both Polacks seize the animal as they fall straight down towards the crap tables—but they bounce off the net; they separate and spring back up towards the roof in three different directions, and just as they're about to fall again they are grabbed out of the air by three Korean Kittens and trapezed off to one of the balconies.

This madness goes on and on, but nobody seems to notice. The gambling action runs twenty-four hours a day on the main floor, and the circus never ends. Meanwhile, on all the upstairs balconies, the customers are being hustled by every conceivable kind of bizarre shuck. All kinds of funhouse-type booths. Shoot the pasties off the nipples of a ten-foot bull dyke and win a cotton-candy goat. Stand in front of this fantastic machine, my friend, and for just 99¢ your likeness will appear, two hundred feet tall, on a screen above downtown Las Vegas. Ninety-nine cents more for a voice message. "Say whatever you want, fella. They'll hear you, don't worry about that. Remember you'll be two hundred feet tall."

Jesus Christ. I could see myself lying in bed in the Mint Hotel, half-asleep and staring idly out the window, when suddenly a vicious nazi drunkard appears two hundred feet tall in the midnight sky, screaming gibberish at the world: "*Woodstock Über Alles!*"

We will close the drapes tonight.

THE MINT 400

What were we doing here? What was the meaning of this trip? Did I   5
actually have a big convertible out there on the street? . . . My immediate task was to get back to the room . . . and then hopefully get straight enough to cope with whatever might happen at dawn.

Now off to the elevator and into the casino, big crowds still tight around the crap tables. Who *are* these people? These faces? Where do they come from? They look like caricatures of used-car dealers from Dallas. But they're *real*. And, sweet Jesus, there are a *lot* of them—still screaming around those desert city crap tables at four-thirty on a Sunday morning. Still humping the American Dream, that vision of the Big Winner somehow emerging from the last-minute pre-dawn chaos of a stale Vegas casino.

Big Strike in Silver City. Beat the dealer and go home rich. Why not? I stopped at the Money Wheel and dropped a dollar on Thomas Jefferson—a $2 bill, the straight freak ticket, thinking as always that some idle instinct might carry the whole thing off.

But no. Just another two bucks down the tube. You bastards!

No. Calm down. Learn to enjoy losing. The important thing is to cover this story. . . .

Moments after we picked up the car my attorney went into a drug   10
coma and ran a red light on Main Street before I could bring us under control. I propped him up in the passenger seat and took the wheel myself . . . feeling fine, extremely sharp. All around me in traffic I could see people talking and I wanted to hear what they were saying. All of them. But the shotgun mike was in the trunk and I decided to leave it there. Las Vegas is not the kind of town where you want to drive down Main Street aiming a black bazooka-looking instrument at people.

Turn up the radio. Turn up the tape machine. Look into the sunset up ahead. Roll the windows down for a better taste of the cool desert wind. Ah yes. This is what it's all about. Total control now. Tooling along the main drag on a Saturday night in Las Vegas, two good old boys in a fireapple-red convertible . . . stoned, ripped, twisted . . . Good People.

Great God! What is this terrible music?
"The Battle Hymn of Lieutenant Calley":

"*. . . as we go marching on . . .*
When I reach my final campground, in that land
   beyond the sun,
and the Great Commander asks me . . ."

(What did he ask you, Rusty?)

"*. . . Did you fight or did you run?*"

(and what did you tell him, Rusty?)

"*. . . We responded to their rifle fire with everything*
we had . . ."

No! I *can't* be hearing this! . . . I glanced over at my attorney, but he was staring up at the sky, and I could see that his brain had gone off to that campground beyond the sun. Thank christ he can't hear this music, I thought. It would drive him into a racist frenzy.

Mercifully, the song ended. But my mood was already shattered . . . plunging me into a sub-human funk as we suddenly came up on the turnoff to the Mint Gun Club. "One mile," the sign said. But even a mile away I could hear the crackling scream of two-stroke bike engines winding out . . . and then, coming closer, I heard another sound.

Shotguns! No mistaking that flat hollow boom.

I stopped the car. What the hell is going on down there? I rolled up all the windows and eased down the gravel road, hunched low on the wheel . . . until I saw about a dozen figures pointing shotguns into the air, firing at regular intervals.

Standing on a slab of concrete out here in the mesquite-desert, this scraggly little oasis in a wasteland north of Vegas . . . They were clustered, with their shotguns, about fifty yards away from a one-story concrete/block-house, half-shaded by ten or twelve trees and surrounded by cop-cars, bike-trailers and motorcycles.

Of course. The Mint *Gun Club!* These lunatics weren't letting *anything* interfere with their target practice. Here were about a hundred bikers, mechanics and assorted motorsport types milling around in the pit area, signing in for tomorrow's race, idly sipping beers and appraising each other's machinery—and right in the middle of all this, oblivious to everything but the clay pigeons flipping out of the traps every five seconds or so, the shotgun people never missed a beat.

15

Well, why not? I thought. The shooting provided a certain rhythm— 20
sort of a steady bass-line—to the high-pitched chaos of the bike scene. I
parked the car and wandered into the crowd, leaving my attorney in his
coma.

I bought a beer and watched the bikes checking in. Many 405
Husquavarnas, high-tuned Swedish fireballs . . . also many Yamahas, Ka-
wasakis, a few 500 Triumphs, Maicos, here & there a CZ, a Pursang . . .
all very fast, super-light dirt bikes. No Hogs in this league, not even a
Sportster . . . that would be like entering our Great Red Shark in the dune
buggy competition.

Maybe I should *do* that, I thought. Sign my attorney up as the driver,
then send him out to the starting line with a head full of ether and acid.
How would they handle it? . . .

The racers were ready at dawn. Fine sunrise over the desert. Very tense.
But the race didn't start until nine, so we had to kill about three long hours
in the casino next to the pits, and that's where the trouble started.

The bar opened at seven. There was also a "koffee & donut canteen" in
the bunker, but those of us who had been up all night in places like the
Circus-Circus were in no mood for coffee & donuts. We wanted strong
drink. Our tempers were ugly and there were at least two hundred of us, so
they opened the bar early. By eight-thirty there were big crowds around the
crap-tables. The place was full of noise and drunken shouting.

A boney, middle-aged hoodlum wearing a Harley-Davidson T-shirt   25
boomed up to the bar and yelled: "God damn! What day is this—Saturday?"

"More like Sunday," somebody replied.

"Hah! That's a *bitch*, ain't it?" the H-D boomer shouted to nobody in
particular. "Last night I was out home in Long Beach and somebody said
they were runnin' the Mint 400 today, so I says to my old lady, 'Man, I'm
goin'.'" He laughed. "So she gives me a lot of crap about it, you
know . . . so I started slappin' her around and the next thing I knew two
guys I never even seen before got me out on the sidewalk workin' me over.
Jesus! They beat me stupid."

He laughed again, talking into the crowd and not seeming to care who
listened. "Hell yes!" he continued. "Then one of 'em says, 'Where you
going?' And I says, 'Las Vegas, to the Mint 400.' So they gave me ten bucks
and drove me down to the bus station. . . . " He paused. "At least I *think* it
was them. . . .

"Well, anyway, here I am. And I tell you that was one *hell* of a long
night, man! Seven hours on that goddamn bus! But when I woke up it was
dawn and here I was in downtown Vegas and for a minute I didn't know
what the hell I was *doin'* here. All I could think was, 'O Jesus, here we go
again: Who's divorced me this time?'"

He accepted a cigarette from somebody in the crowd, still grinning as 30 he lit up. "But then I remembered, by God! I was here for the Mint 400 . . . and, man, that's all I needed to know. I tell you it's wonderful to be here, man. I don't give a damn who wins or loses. It's just wonderful to be here with you people . . . ."

Nobody argued with him. We all understood. In some circles, the "Mint 400" is a far, far better thing than the Super Bowl, the Kentucky Derby and the Lower Oakland Roller Derby Finals all rolled into one. This race attracts a very special breed, and our man in the Harley T-shirt was clearly one of them . . . .

I turned away. It was too horrible. We were, after all, the absolute cream of the national sporting press. And we were gathered here in Las Vegas for a very special assignment: to cover the Fourth Annual "Mint 400" . . . and when it comes to things like this, you don't fool around.

But now—even before the spectacle got under way—there were signs that we might be losing control of the situation. Here we were on this fine Nevada morning, this cool bright dawn on the desert, hunkered down at some greasy bar in a concrete blockhouse & gambling casino called the "Mint Gun Club" about ten miles out of Vegas . . . and with the race about to start, we were dangerously disorganized.

Outside, the lunatics were playing with their motorcycles, taping the headlights, topping off oil in the forks, last minute bolt-tightening (carburetor screws, manifold nuts, etc.) . . . and the first ten bikes blasted off on the stroke of nine. It was extremely exciting and we all went outside to watch. The flag went down and these ten poor buggers popped their clutches and zoomed into the first turn, all together, then somebody grabbed the lead (a 405 Husquavarna, as I recall), and a cheer went up as the rider screwed it on and disappeared in a cloud of dust.

"Well, that's that," somebody said. "They'll be back around in an hour 35 or so. Let's go back to the bar."

But not yet. No. There were something like a hundred and ninety more bikes waiting to start. They went off ten at a time, every two minutes. At first it was possible to watch them out to a distance of some two hundred yards from the starting line. But this visibility didn't last long. The third brace of ten disappeared into the dust about a hundred yards from where we stood . . . and by the time they'd sent off the first hundred (with still *another* hundred to go), our visibility was down to something like fifty feet. We could see as far as the hay-bales at the end of the pits. . . .

Beyond that point the incredible dustcloud that would hang over this part of the desert for the next two days was already formed up solid. None of us realized, at the time, that this was the last we would see of the "Fabulous Mint 400"—

SUGGESTIONS FOR FURTHER STUDY

Language and Style

Hunter Thompson is credited with being one of the New Journalism stylists. In these selections, look at the features of journalism reporting that depart from the usual, straightforward objective reporting style still used by many newspapers and magazines. Discuss these and other examples of Thompson's style:

Metaphorical language (e.g., "The Circus-Circus is what the whole hep world would be doing on Saturday night if the Nazis had won the war. This is the Sixth Reich." [par. 1])

Personal voice and commentary (e.g., "What are we doing here? What was the meaning of this trip? Did I actually have a big convertible out there on the street?" [par. 5])

Dialogue (e.g., "Well, anyway, here I am. And I tell you that was one *hell* of a long night, man!" [par. 29])

Personal impression (e.g., "I turned away. It was too horrible. We were, after all, the absolute cream of the national sporting press. And we were gathered here in Las Vegas for a very special assignment . . . and when it comes to things like this, you don't fool around." [par. 32])

Topics for Discussion and Writing

1. What impression of Las Vegas and its visitors and inhabitants do you get from these selections by Hunter Thompson? Does he give you anything to admire or anything to criticize in what he describes?

2. What purpose do you think is achieved by Thompson's description of the Mint 400? How does this description affect you as a reader?

3. If you have visited Las Vegas, Atlantic City, 7 Flags Texas, Disney World, a state fair, or any other major U.S. entertainment center, write about your experience and impressions of your visit there. Try to capture the culture of the place, as Thompson does in describing Circus-Circus, or paint a picture in words of an event such as the Mint 400 motorcycle race. Use any of the techniques discussed in the preceding "Language and Style" section.

Death in the Mosh Pit

Eric Boehlert

Eric Boehlert, currently an associate editor and writer for Rolling
Stone Magazine *and formerly a senior writer for* Billboard *maga-
zine, has written for* Inside Media, The New York Times, Vibe, *and*
Musician. *Boehlert, a graduate of the University of Massachusetts in
Amherst, currently resides in New York City. "Death in the Mosh Pit"
appeared in* Rolling Stone *in the July 11–25, 1996, issue.*

When the lights dimmed at Dublin's Point Theatre at 9:30 p.m. on May 1
11, 7,000 Irish fans, crammed hip to hip on the floor, erupted as Smashing
Pumpkins hit the stage. With the night's first note, swirling mosh pits sprang
up, and 110 security guards scrambled behind the barricades to control the
flow of the crowd.

The adrenalin-pumping ritual was the same one that has greeted the
Pumpkins at every stop of their *Infinite Sadness* world tour. Yet almost
immediately, band leader Billy Corgan sensed that something was wrong.
Five minutes into the show, he stopped, admonished the crowd and
demanded that everyone take a step back. The crowd did not relent, and
at 10 p.m., Corgan said that the show would be halted if the moshing
didn't stop.

It was already too late for Bernadette O'Brien, a 17-year-old high
school student from the small coastal village of Shanagarry, in County
Cork. Camped out near the front of the stage with a hometown friend and
two cousins from Dublin, O'Brien was overpowered by a surge of the
crowd and crushed by the masses.

Informed of O'Brien's injuries, Corgan addressed the crowd. "I'm sorry
we can't play on," he said. "The gig's over. There's a girl out there who's
nearly dying. We as human beings cannot continue to play up here while
people are getting seriously hurt down there." The next day, doctors at
Dublin's Mater Hospital disconnected O'Brien's life-support system and
announced that she had died from massive internal injuries. The Pumpkins
sent flowers to the funeral and released a statement extending their con-
dolences to O'Brien's family and friends. (The group and its managers
declined further comment.)

No doubt, American rock promoters read the news from Dublin and 5
flinched. The concert industry already faces three major mosh-pit lawsuits:

One involves the only moshing-related death in the United States to date, while the other two involve young fans who were left paralyzed. There is no hard data on the number of moshing-related injuries suffered in this country, and insurance companies refuse to say how many lawsuits have been pursued by fans. But hundreds of concert claims have been filed recently. And promoters, facing rising insurance premiums, may be forced to abandon some alternative tours deemed too costly to insure.

When moshing, or slam dancing, originated at hardcore punk shows in the early '80s, there was a strict but unspoken code that called for mutual respect among participants. Now, moshing is *de rigueur* at every alternative-rock show—fans slam and bodysurf to acoustic ballads—and the good Samaritan mentality is a distant memory. "It's not as simple as moshers say it is," says Ken MacDonald, who manages three rock venues for Cellar Door Entertainment, one of the nation's largest concert promoters. "They talk about this whole lifestyle and how everybody knows each other and watches out for each other, but noses are getting broken."

Many promoters are reluctant to advocate the outright ban of moshing or bodysurfing because they don't want to lose concert business. Most alternative-rock bands, feeding off the crowd's energy, insist that promoters allow the activity. Ironically, Smashing Pumpkins have been one of the most outspoken groups in criticizing reckless violence in the pit.

One promoter privately concedes that the industry "has just been lucky" that there have not been more life-threatening injuries in the pit. "In the past, most concerts didn't have debilitating, long-term injuries occurring with the frequency they are now," says Dean Grose, medical coordinator for Event Medical Services, which provides support for 200 concerts each year. Grose points specifically to body surfing as the primary cause of injuries. "We need to eliminate it," he says.

"Every year there are needless deaths and needless injuries," adds Paul Wertheimer, a self-employed concert-safety consultant who tracks concert injuries. (He estimates that Woodstock '94 alone resulted in hundreds of mosh-pit injuries.) Wertheimer began his crusade when he wrote a report for the city of Cincinnati after 11 fans were trampled to death before a Who concert at Riverfront Coliseum in 1979. That incident resulted in widespread condemnation of general-admission seating, but the policy is once again widely accepted at most alternative-rock concerts. The difference is that arena general admission, or party in the pit, tickets are sold in advance; ticket holders are usually identified with a wristband; general-admission barricades and floors are often padded; and doors are open hours before show time.

"Moshing is a dangerous activity," says Cory Meredith, president of   10
Staff Pro, the largest provider of event security on the West Coast. "But because this type of music is what's selling right now, the industry is candy-coating it. They don't want to talk about it."

Claims for injuries sustained in the pit have gone up sixfold over the last five years, according to Walter Howell, owner of Entertainment Insurance Agency, a Florida-based company that insures 50 concert promoters. Like many other insurers, Howell refuses to talk exact numbers, but he says that 80 to 90 percent of the concert lawsuits he's involved in today are pit related. Insurance premiums have nearly doubled for the concert industry in the last five years. For a major rock promoter whose concerts draw half a million fans a year, annual insurance premiums have jumped from $100,00 to $175,000. And insurance executives speculate that if the mosh pit is not controlled, alternative-rock promoters will have problems purchasing liability coverage, just as their rap-industry peers do.

To protect themselves in lawsuits, many promoters have taken to videotaping mosh pits to persuade angry parents against filing suit by showing them the dangerous but voluntary behavior in which their children were involved. Promoters are also closely watching three major moshing-related suits, all of them from injuries sustained at 1994 concerts.

On June 29, 1994, 23-year-old auto-parts worker Brian Cross bodysurfed his way up to the stage during a Pantera concert at the Merriweather Post Pavilion, in Columbia, Md. He claims that while being hauled over the railing by security guards, his neck was broken. Now a quadriplegic, Cross sued the venue for $100 million and later settled for an undisclosed amount.

On Aug. 3, 1994, at a Lollapalooza date in Rhode Island, 15-year-old Jeremy Libby was bodysurfing above the crowd when a hole opened up and he crashed to the ground, breaking his neck. He is now confined to a wheelchair, and his family is suing Lollapalooza's promoters. Libby's lawyer, Ken Hovermale, argues that crowd surfing should have been banned by posting signs and making announcements from the stage. Hovermale concedes that nobody forced Libby to bodysurf but says that Libby was a minor who did not "have the inherent ability to weigh risks and benefits." (Lollapalooza officials refused to comment.) A source close to the case suggests that it may be settled soon for $3.5 million.

On Dec. 17, 1994, the first American moshing death occurred when 18-year-old Christopher Mitchell dived from the stage at the now-defunct Brooklyn club L'Amour, in New York. He landed on his head, fractured his skull and died the next day from a brain hemorrhage. A friend of Mitchell claims that James Gheida, one of the club's bouncers, pushed the fan from the stage. Gheida, who denies he was near the stage at the time, is set to stand trial this August.

In the wake of Mitchell's death, a New York state senator has introduced the nation's first statewide moshing legislation, which would hold promoters and club owners liable for any injuries. (Currently, injured fans must prove negligence on the part of promoters.)

MacDonald of Cellar Door says the proposal shows an "absurd lack of understanding" about the problem and says that it will simply force promoters to abandon alternative-rock shows. Now, however, the specter of O'Brien's death and the sound of Corgan beseeching the crowd linger over the debate. "It's only a concert," the anxious singer pleaded from the stage in Dublin. "It's not worth dying for."

SUGGESTIONS FOR FURTHER STUDY

Key Words

The author uses language with which you may not be familiar. Find the following words in the paragraphs indicated, and explain their meanings in the context of the sentences in which the words appear. Consult a dictionary, as needed.

de rigueur (par. 6)
debilitating (par. 8)
now-defunct (par. 15)

Topics for Discussion and Writing

1. Identify in this article the *attitudes* of participants, promoters, and others involved in or responsible for mosh-pit or other concert-related injuries. In what ways do these attitudes differ? In what ways are they alike?

2. In your opinion, who or what is responsible for the tragedies that have and still may result from moshing or similar forms of entertainment? Discuss your opinion with others, and compare your ideas.

3. Write an opinion paper or a letter to the editor of your campus newspaper or of a trade magazine such as *Rolling Stone*, expressing your views about entertainment that may potentially involve violence and injury.

4. Research other real incidents of violence at concerts or sports events where participants or fans were endangered. What were the causes of endangerment or violence? Write a brief essay describing such an incident. Express and defend your opinion about whether potentially dangerous entertainment should be allowed.

America 2000:
Fast and Furious Fun

Jerry Adler

Jerry Adler was promoted to senior editor in January 1995, after serv-
ing as a Newsweek *senior writer since January 1981. He has written*
cover stories on such varied topics as political correctness, America's
infatuation with self-esteem, the men's movement, and NASA. Adler
has also worked for the New York Daily News *and* The Journal of
Commerce, *and he has won numerous awards since joining* Newsweek *in 1973. A graduate of Yale University, Adler currently resides in*
Brooklyn, New York, with his wife and two sons. "America 2000: Fast
and Furious Fun" (with Corie Brown, John McCormick, and Susan
Miller) appeared in the January 27, 1997, edition of Newsweek.

It is the promise of America, fulfilled, a nation of limitless, unbounded   1
fun, of mountain majesties iridescent with Gore-Tex-backed rock climbers
and skies filled to the vast horizon with direct-satellite broadcasts of minor-
league hockey games. It is a vision that dates from the very dawn of
America, when John Adams wrote of studying war and diplomacy so that
succeeding generations could be schooled in agriculture, industry, music, art
and poetry—never imagining that casino gambling, Snowboarding, golf and
gourmet dining would join that roster as indispensable amenities in the
nation he helped found. It was for this that Lewis and Clark trudged relentlessly through the finest backpacking terrain in the world, and generations of
comics risked dying night after night on the spotlit floors of Las Vegas—a
city where, if the number of hotel rooms (now about 100,000) continues to
increase at 10 percent a year, sometime around the year 2074 the entire population of the United States will be able to take a vacation at the same time.

If you had fun in the 20th century, or even if you didn't, you will find it
almost impossible to avoid in the 21st. Working ever harder to keep your
place in the world economy, you will seek out fun in compensatory doses.
Fun in the next century will be of much higher quality, because there will be
so many more playoff games in comparison to the regular season, a trend
clearly in evidence in last year's baseball schedule. And outdoor fun will be
better than ever. There won't be any new mountains, but the ones already in
place will be exploited even more imaginatively by people climbing up them,
and sliding, rolling, rappelling or hang-gliding down. Try to escape fun and

it will seek you out anyway, at your hotel or restaurant, where eating will increasingly be impossible without the accompaniment of 32 bedsheet-size TV screens showing highlights from the World Cup quarterfinals.

What Hollywood represented to the 20th century, Las Vegas will be to the 21st, the embodiment of American entertainment in all its irresponsible, greedy exuberance. While the studios spend $100,000 a second on computer simulations of explosions, Las Vegas actually blew up a real hotel on New Year's Eve in front of 200,000 tourists, just for the fun of it. In its place will rise a 4,000-room, $800 million resort whose theme is described as "an ancient forbidden city discovered on a lush, wave-tossed tropical island." The project includes manmade surf, a swim-up shark exhibit and a microbrewery themed as a sugar refinery, with regularly scheduled rain showers. Las Vegas has a childlike fascination with ancient cities, like Rome, Venice, Luxor and New York, whose architecture can be gleefully parodied in billion-dollar hotels ringed with roller coasters. "There's no evidence that Las Vegas is even close to topping out," says Mark Manson, who follows the entertainment industries for Donaldson, Lufkin and Jenrette. No wonder Hollywood, which last year released more movies than ever into a domestic market that's been stagnant for years, looks forward to the turn of the century with none of Vegas's brash self-confidence. "People will still want to go out," predicts John Calley, chairman of Sony Pictures Entertainment. "The places they go, however, will be more exotic. People will be actualizing fantasies in new ways. I envision entertainment malls with a striking array of things to see. Including movies. Look at Vegas."

To feel the breeze of the onrushing 21st century, says architect Louis Hedgecock of the New York firm of Brennan Beer Gorman, step out into the 100-mile-an-hour updraft of a sky-diving simulator, an attraction you can find near the Las Vegas Hilton. Spread-eagled, suspended in midair, you float and bob, exploring unsuspected aerodynamic features of your body. Hedgecock knows about this because his firm has made a sky-diving simulator the centerpiece of a new restaurant/health club—which will also have the inevitable barrage of television monitors, a glass-walled basketball court and a rock-climbing wall, without which no meal will feel complete in the 21st century. What makes this remarkable is that it is planned to be built right at the sidewalk on a busy corner of midtown Manhattan, on the ground floor of the New York Sheraton, until now the very model of the staid, bland businessman's hotel. "We used to be just in the Feed 'Em and Bed 'Em business," says Paul O'Neil, president of Sheraton Hotels of New York. "Now we're thinking, in the next century we're going to have to entertain 'em, too." Even Michael Whiteman, a consultant who has helped create some of New York's most sophisticated restaurants, sees the continued integration of dining and spectacle as inevitable, boldly predicting that the new millennium will see a return of the dinner theater—perhaps in some new format that will bring Neil Simon into the world of multimedia. On the bright side, he says, life in the next century will be made greatly more bearable as themed restaurants, exploiting ever thinner slices of the imaginative spectrum (The Motor Scooter Cafe? Planet Soap Opera?), begin to kill each other off.

O'Neil, from the most elemental of commercial motives, has hit on a   5
deep trend shaping American society, the interpenetration of fun with the rest of life. The revolution in communications technology has made the office inescapable for many people who hold what once were considered 9-to-5 jobs. If they want to float in midair for a few minutes between appointments, who could blame them? At the same time, Americans harbor a popular mythology of escape—to the wilderness, the open road, the farmhouse in Vermont or the ranch in Montana—dreams that have little or no relation to the way most people actually live their lives. "You want to go backpacking with your friends," says John Sharpless, a professor of modern American history at the University of Wisconsin, "so you spend six months on the phone arranging your work schedules so you can get one week together. Then you drive like mad to the Rockies, climb up and down and up and down and drive like mad back to your jobs so you won't get fired." Nostalgia for the endless summers of youth drives people to all sorts of extreme behavior—like investing in mutual funds, hoping to miraculously transform a middle-class salary into independent wealth. If the stock market somehow continues on its present course and reaches 10,000 by the millennium, it will call the bluff of an awful lot of middle-aged professionals.

Another way to blunt the existential pain of middle-class life is to estheticize it, so that tasks earlier generations were happy to escape—like cooking or painting the house—are redefined as fun, an intellectual and imaginative challenge. "People buy an old Victorian and spend every Saturday scraping the walls," Sharpless says. "They claim it's agonizing work, but nobody made them do it. It's middle-class sport." This explains why social critics unanimously agree that the most important American cultural figure of the 21st century will be Martha Stewart, who gives this trend a necessary patina of uppercrust cachet.

Of course, it's not to everyone's taste. People under the age of 30 don't seem particularly riveted by the romance of home improvement. In the next century, they'll be too busy at Sega Gameworks, a chain of 21st-century arcades backed by Sega, Universal Studios and DreamWorks SKG. President Michael Montgomery describes it as "an alternative to discos for the young adult," which can be loosely translated as "save your quarters, bring a credit card." When the first branch opens in Seattle in March—there are 40 planned by the year 2000—its centerpiece will be Vertical Reality, an interactive game designed by Steven Spielberg in which the player's chair rises with each new skill level to a maximum height of 24 feet . . . and then drops in free fall if he loses. Is it just coincidence that DreamWorks, intended to represent the future of Hollywood, is producing an arcade game before it has a movie in the theaters?

When not playing futuristic videogames, the sub-boomers can wile away their idle weekends jouncing down hills on a MountainBoard, an all-terrain oversize skateboard equipped with a suspension and balloon tires. "It's the closest thing to Snowboarding without snow, way more fun than skating and much saner than road luge," raves Steve Casimiro, editor of the hip ski magazine Powder. It's part of a trend toward "hybrids and mutations" in sports, according to Joanne DeLuca, a partner in Sputnik, a youth-oriented marketing-research firm. Snowboarding, a cross between surfing and skiing, grew out of this trend and gave rise to wakeboarding, in which a short board takes the place of water skis. Ice hockey's offspring, in-line skating, gave rise in turn to in-line basketball, a very hip-hop thing to do in Manhattan's East Village. Youthful energy, when channeled into golf, has produced radical golf, a sport in which players strap one or two clubs to a backpack and set off on a quest to see who can finish a course in the fewest number of strokes *and the shortest time,* running from stroke to stroke and dodging their opponents' balls as they go. It's already been played a couple of times in Palo Alto, and it could be very hot sometime in the next century.

Which is about as far into the unknown as the imagination of man can extend, although it's certainly possible to conceive of a microbrewery featuring radical-golf virtual-reality simulators and 65 giant video-walls showing an interactive version of "The Prisoner of Second Avenue." In fact, someone's probably planning one right now, as part of a $12 billion, 10,000-room resort that will re-create the entire topography of Dante's Divine Comedy and feature daily re-creations of the Normandy landings and a simulated solar eclipse every hour.

And you can guess where it will be built.   10

> —*With* CORIE BROWN *in Los Angeles,*
> JOHN McCORMICK *in Chicago and*
> SUSAN MILLER *in New York*

SUGGESTIONS FOR FURTHER STUDY

Key Words

The author uses language with which you may not be familiar. Find the following words in the paragraphs indicated, and explain their meanings in the context of the sentences in which the words appear. Consult a dictionary, as needed.

amenities (par. 1)
compensatory (par. 2)

exuberance (par. 3)
parodied (par. 3)
barrage (par. 4)
estheticize (par. 6)
patina (par. 6)
cachet (par. 6)

Topics for Discussion and Writing

1. The writers of "Fast and Furious Fun" not only describe the entertainment currently projected by promoters in Las Vegas and elsewhere, but also predict the kind of entertainment that will be available in the next century. Do you agree or disagree with the claim that American entertainment in the twenty-first century will be characterized by "irresponsible, greedy exuberance"? Explain.

2. Entertainment such as radical golf, skydiving simulators, and interactive video games are either already in existence or planned for the near future. In what ways do such futuristic sports and games appeal to people? If you are familiar with any of the entertainments described in this article, what appeal do they have for you? Explain your answer.

3. What is the dominant tone of voice in this article? Look at such comments as the following in describing that tone:

   "It was for this that Lewis and Clark trudged relentlessly through the finest backpacking terrain in the world, and generations of comics risked dying night after night on the spotlit floors of Las Vegas. . . . " (par. 1)

   "Try to escape fun and it will seek you out anyway, at your hotel or restaurant, where eating will increasingly be impossible without the accompaniment of 32 bedsheet-size TV screens showing highlights from the World Cup quarterfinals." (par. 2)

   "Nostalgia for the endless summers of youth drives people to all sorts of extreme behavior—like investing in mutual funds, hoping to miraculously transform a middle-class salary into independent wealth." (par. 5)

   Find other passages that reflect the dominant tone, and comment on their effectiveness.

4. Write a short essay describing a futuristic entertainment you would like to experience. It might be one mentioned in this article, or it might be one you create. Explain how this entertainment will work and what its appeal might be.

Rules of the Game: Rodeo

Gretel Ehrlich

Gretel Ehrlich (born in California) went to school at Bennington (in Vermont) and attended the UCLA Film School. She went to Wyoming in 1976, as part of a documentary film crew, and stayed there to work and write. Her publications include Heart Mountain *(1988),* The Solace of Open Spaces, *two volumes of poetry, and numerous essays.*

Instead of honeymooning in Paris, Patagonia, or the Sahara as we had 1 planned, my new husband and I drove through a series of blizzards to Oklahoma City. Each December the National Finals Rodeo is held in a modern, multistoried colosseum next to buildings that house banks and petroleum companies in a state whose flatness resembles a swimming pool filled not with water but with oil.

The National Finals is the "World Series of Professional Rodeo," where not only the best cowboys but also the most athletic horses and bucking stock compete. All year, rodeo cowboys have been vying for the honor to ride here. They've been to Houston, Las Vegas, Pendleton, Tucson, Cheyenne, San Francisco, Calgary; to as many as eighty rodeos in one season, sometimes making two or three on a day like the Fourth of July, and when the results are tallied up (in money won, not points) the top fifteen riders in each event are invited to Oklahoma City.

We climbed to our peanut gallery seats just as Miss Rodeo America, a lanky brunette swaddled in a lavender pantsuit, gloves, and cowboy hat, loped across the arena. There was a hush in the audience; all the hats swimming down in front of us, like buoys, steadied and turned toward the chutes. "Out of chute number three, Pat Linger, a young cowboy from Miles City, Montana, making his first appearance here on a little horse named Dillinger." And as fast as these words sailed across the colosseum, the first bareback horse bumped into the lights.

There's a traditional order to the four timed and three rough stock events that make up a rodeo program. Bareback riders are first, then steer wrestlers, team ropers, saddle bronc riders, barrel racers, and finally, the bull riders.

After Pat Linger came Steve Dunham, J. C. Trujillo, Mickey Young, and 5 the defending champ, Bruce Ford on a horse named Denver. Bareback riders do just that: they ride a horse with no saddle, no halter, no rein, clutching only a handhold riveted into a girth that goes around the horse's belly. A bareback rider's loose style suggests a drunken, comic bout of lovemaking: he lies back on the horse and, with each jump and jolt, flops delightfully, like a libidinous Raggedy Andy, toes turned out, knees flexed, legs spread and pumping, back arched, the back of his hat bumping the horse's rump as if nodding, "Yes, let's do 'er again." My husband, who rode saddle broncs in amateur rodeos, explains it differently: "It's like riding a runaway bicycle down a steep hill and lying on your back; you can't see where you're going or what's going to happen next."

Now the steer wrestlers shoot out of the box on their own well-trained horses: there is a hazer on the right to keep the steer running straight, the wrestler on the left, and the steer between them. When the wrestler is neck and neck with the animal, he slides sideways out of his saddle as if he'd been stabbed in the ribs and reaches for the horns. He's airborne for a second; then his heels swing into the dirt, and with his arms around the horns, he skids to a stop, twisting the steer's head to one side so the animal loses his balance and falls to the ground. It's a fast-paced game of catch with a thousand-pound ball of horned flesh.

The team ropers are next. Most of them hail from the hilly, oak-strewn valleys of California where dally roping originated.[1] Ropers are the graceful technicians, performing their pas de deux (plus steer) with a precision that begins to resemble a larger clarity—an erudition. Header and heeler come out of the box at the same time, steer between them, but the header acts first: he ropes the horns of the steer, dallies up, turns off, and tries to position the steer for the heeler who's been tagging behind this duo, loop clasped in his armpit as if it were a hen. Then the heeler sets his generous, unsweeping loop free and double-hocks the steer. It's a complicated act which takes about six seconds. Concomitant with this speed and skill is a feminine grace: they don't clutch their stiff loop or throw it at the steer like a bag of dirty laundry the way I do, but hold it gently, delicately, as if it were a hoop of silk. One or two cranks and both arm and loop vault forward, one becoming an appendage of the other, as if the tendons and pulse that travel through the wrist had lengthened and spun forward like fishing line until the loop sails down on the twin horns, then up under the hocks like a repeated embrace that tightens at the end before it releases.

The classic event at rodeo is saddle bronc riding. The young men look as serious as academicians: they perch spryly on their high-kicking mounts, their legs flicking forward and back, "charging the point," "going back to the cantle" in a rapid, staccato rhythm. When the horse is at the high point of his buck and the cowboy is stretched out, legs spurring above the horse's shoulder, rein-holding arm straight as a board in front, and free hand lifted

---

[1]The word *dally* is a corruption of the Spanish *da la vuelta,* meaning to take a turn, as with rope around the saddle horn.

behind, horse and man look like a propeller. Even their dismounts can look aeronautical: springing off the back of the horse, they land on their feet with a flourish—hat still on—as if they had been ejected mechanically from a burning plane long before the crash.

Barrel racing is the one women's event. Where the men are tender in their movements, as elegant as if Balanchine had been their coach, the women are prodigies of Wayne Gretsky, all speed, bully, and grit. When they charge into the arena, their hats fly off; they ride brazenly, elbows, knees, feet fluttering, and by the time they've careened around the second of three barrels, the whip they've had clenched between their teeth is passed to a hand, and on the home stretch they urge the horse to the finish line.

Calf ropers are the whiz kids of rodeo: they're expert on the horse and   10 on the ground, and their horses are as quick-witted. The cowboy emerges from the box with a loop in his hand, a piggin' string in his mouth, coils and reins in the other, and a network of slack line strewn so thickly over horse and rider, they look as if they'd run through a tangle of kudzu before arriving in the arena. After roping the calf and jerking the slack in the rope, he jumps off the horse, sprints down the length of nylon, which the horse keeps taut, throws the calf down, and ties three legs together with the piggin' string. It's said of Roy Cooper, the defending calf-roping champion, that "even with pins and metal plates in his arm, he's known for the fastest groundwork in the business; when he springs down his rope to flank the calf, the resulting action is pure rodeo poetry." The six or seven separate movements he makes are so fluid they look like one continual unfolding.

Bull riding is last, and of all the events it's the only one truly dangerous. Bulls are difficult to ride: they're broad-backed, loose-skinned, and powerful. They don't jump balletically the way a horse does; they jerk and spin, and if you fall off, they'll try to gore you with a horn, kick, or trample you. Bull riders are built like the animals they ride: low to the ground and hefty. They're the tough men on the rodeo circuit, and the flirts. Two of the current champs are city men: Charlie Samson is a small, shy black from Watts, and Bobby Del Vecchio, a brash Italian from the Bronx who always throws the audience a kiss after a ride with a Catskill-like showmanship not usually seen here. What a bull rider lacks in technical virtuosity—you won't see the fast spurring action of a saddle bronc rider in this event—he makes up for in personal flamboyance, and because it's a deadlier game they're playing, you can see the belligerence rise up their necks and settle into their faces as the bull starts his first spin. Besides the bull and the cowboy, there are three other men in the ring—the rodeo clowns—who aren't there to make children laugh but to divert the bull from some of his deadlier tricks, and, when the rider bucks off, jump between the two—like secret service men—to save the cowboy's life. . . .

The National Finals run ten nights. Every contestant rides every night, so it is easy to follow their progress and setbacks. One evening we abandoned our rooftop seats and sat behind the chutes to watch the saddle broncs ride. Behind the chutes two cowboys are rubbing rosin—part of their staying power—behind the saddle swells and on their Easter-egg-colored chaps which are pink, blue, and light green with white fringe. Up above, standing on the chute rungs, the stock contractors direct horse traffic: "Velvet Drums" in chute #3, "Angel Sings" in #5, "Rusty" in #1. Rick Smith, Monty Henson, Bobby Berger, Brad Gjermudson, Mel Coleman, and friends climb the chutes. From where I'm sitting, it looks like a field hospital with five separate operating theaters, the cowboys, like surgeons, bent over their patients with sweaty brows and looks of concern. Horses are being haltered; cowboys are measuring out the long, braided reins, saddles are set: one cowboy pulls up on the swells again and again, repositioning his horn-less saddle until it sits just right. When the chute boss nods to him and says, "Pull 'em up, boys," the ground crew tightens front and back cinches on the first horse to go, but very slowly so he won't panic in the chute as the cow-boy eases himself down over the saddle, not sitting on it, just hovering there. "Okay, you're on." The chute boss nods to him again. Now he sits on the saddle, taking the rein in one hand, holding the top of the chute with the other. He flips the loose bottoms of his chaps over his shins, puts a foot in each stirrup, takes a breath, and nods. The chute gate swings open releasing a flood—not of water, but of flesh, groans, legs kicking. The horse lunges up and out in the first big jump like a wave breaking whose crest the cowboy rides, "marking out the horse," spurs well above the bronc's shoulders. In that first second under the lights, he finds what will be the rhythm of the ride. Once again he "charges the point," his legs pumping forward, then so far back his heels touch behind the cantle. For a moment he looks as though he were kneeling on air, then he's stretched out again, his whole body taut but released, free hand waving in back of his head like a palm frond, rein-holding hand thrust forward: "*En garde!*" he seems to be saying, but he's airborne; he looks like a wing that has sprouted suddenly from the horse's broad back. Eight seconds. The whistle blows. He's covered the horse. Now two gentlemen dressed in white chaps and satin shirts gallop beside the bucking horse. The cowboy hands the rein to one and grabs the waist of the other—the flank strap on the bronc has been undone, so all three horses move at a run—and the pickup man from whom the cowboy is now dangling slows almost to a stop, letting him slide to his feet on the ground.

Rick Smith from Wyoming rides, looking pale and nervous in his white shirt. He's bucked off and so are the brash Monty "Hawkeye" Henson, and Butch Knowles, and Bud Pauley, but with such grace and aplomb, there is no shame. Bobby Berger, an Oklahoma cowboy, wins the go-round with a score of 83.

By the end of the evening we're tired, but in no way as exhausted as these young men who have ridden night after night. "I've never been so sore and had so much fun in my life," one first-time bull rider exclaims breathlessly. When the performance is over we walk across the street to the chic lobby of a hotel chock full of cowboys. Wives hurry through the crowd with freshly ironed shirts for tomorrow's ride, ropers carry their rope bags with them into the coffee shop, which is now filled with contestants, eating mild midnight suppers of scrambled eggs, their numbers hanging crookedly on their backs, their faces powdered with dust, and looking at this late hour prematurely old.

We drive back to the motel, where, the first night, they'd "never heard   15
of us" even though we'd had reservations for a month. "Hey, it's our honeymoon," I told the night clerk and showed him the white ribbons my mother had tied around our duffel bag. He looked embarrassed, then surrendered another latecomer's room.

The rodeo finals in Oklahoma may be a better place to honeymoon than Paris. All week, we've observed some important rules of the game. A good rodeo, like a good marriage, or a musical instrument when played to the pitch of perfection, becomes more than what it started out to be. It is effort transformed into effortlessness; a balance becomes grace, the way love goes deep into friendship.

In the rough stock events such as the one we watched tonight, there is no victory over the horse or bull. The point of the match is not conquest but communion: the rhythm of two beings becoming one. Rodeo is not a sport of opposition; there is no scrimmage line here. No one bears malice—neither the animals, the stock contractors, nor the contestants; no one wants to get hurt. In this match of equal talents, it is only acceptance, surrender, respect, and spiritedness that make for the midair union of cowboy and horse. Not a bad thought when starting out fresh in a marriage.

SUGGESTIONS FOR FURTHER STUDY

Key Words

The author uses language with which you may not be familiar. Find the following words in the paragraphs indicated, and explain their meanings in the context of the sentences in which the words appear. Consult a dictionary, as needed.

libidinous (par. 5)
pas de deux (par. 7)
erudition (par. 7)
concomitant (par. 7)
careened (par. 9)
kudzu (par. 10)
flamboyance (par. 11)

Language and Style

In describing the action and setting of a rodeo, the author uses the colorful jargon of the sport. If you are not familiar with that jargon, find out what the following words or phrases specifically refer to. You may need either to use a dictionary or to ask someone who is familiar with the language of rodeos.

hazer (par. 6)
wrestler (par. 6)
double-hocks (par. 7)
saddle bronc (par. 8)
charging the point (par. 8)
going back to the cantle (par. 8)
piggin' string (par. 10)
wins the go-round (par. 13)

Notice that the author uses the first person, "I," in opening and closing her essay, but the rest is reported in third person. What effect does this dual point of view have on you as a reader? How does it help to organize the essay?

Topics for Discussion and Writing

1. Discuss the organization of this essay. Note the methods the author uses in developing her description of a typical rodeo. For instance, she outlines the sequence of her description by listing the sequence of events in a rodeo program in paragraph 4. Locate the paragraphs that focus on that sequence. Find other methods of developing topics, such as classification and narration.

2. Notice the author's use of imagery and figurative language to highlight the action in a rodeo. For example, the author's husband says that bareback riding is "like riding a runaway bicycle down a steep hill and lying on your back. . . ." Find and discuss the effective use of other figurative language in this essay.

3. How would you describe the tone of this essay? Does the author admire those who take part in rodeos? How does she use humor in describing the action? Is she a careful observer of people and events? Summarize in your own words the tone of this essay.

4. What is the effect of the author's comparing a rodeo with the start of a marriage?

5. Write about an event involving several participants. Group and classify those participants, then describe them and their activities in the event in some detail. Finally, reflect and comment on the event's meaning to you.

My Baseball Years

Philip Roth

Philip Roth (born in Newark, New Jersey, in 1933) has written criti-cally acclaimed novels, short stories, and essays. His novels include Portnoy's Complaint, Letting Go, The Great American Novel *and his latest best-seller,* American Pastoral. *His collection of short stories,* Goodbye, Columbus, *is a classic of Jewish American fiction. "My Baseball Years" is taken from his collection of essays,* Reading Myself and Others.

In one of his essays George Orwell writes that, though he was not very good at the game, he had a long, hopeless love affair with cricket until he was sixteen. My relations with baseball were similar. Between the ages of nine and thirteen, I must have put in a forty-hour week during the snowless months over at the neighborhood playfield—softball, hardball, and stickball pick-up games—while simultaneously holding down a full-time job as a pupil at the local grammar school. As I remember it, news of two of the most cataclysmic public events of my childhood—the death of President Roosevelt and the bombing of Hiroshima—reached me while I was out playing ball. My performance was uniformly erratic; generally okay for those easygoing pick-up games, but invariably lacking the calm and the expertise that the naturals displayed in stiff competition. My taste, and my talent, such as it was, was for the flashy, whiz-bang catch rather than the towering fly; running and leaping I loved, all the do-or-die stuff—somehow I lost confidence waiting and waiting for the ball lofted right at me to descend. I could never make the high school team, yet I remember that, in one of the two years I vainly (in both senses of the word) tried out, I did a good enough imitation of a baseball player's *style* to be able to fool (or amuse) the coach right down to the day he cut the last of the dreamers from the squad and gave out the uniforms.

Though my disappointment was keen, my misfortune did not necessitate a change in plans for the future. Playing baseball was not what the Jewish boys of our lower-middle-class neighborhood were expected to do in later life for a living. Had I been cut from the high school itself, *then* there would have been hell to pay in my house, and much confusion and shame in me. As it was, my family took my chagrin in stride and lost no more faith in me than I actually did in myself. They probably would have been shocked if I had made the team.

Maybe I would have been too. Surely it would have put me on a somewhat different footing with this game that I loved with all my heart, not simply for the fun of playing it (fun was secondary, really), but for the mythic and aesthetic dimension that it gave to an American boy's life—particularly to one whose grandparents could hardly speak English. For someone whose roots in America were strong but only inches deep, and who had no experience, such as a Catholic child might, of an awesome hierarchy that was real and felt, baseball was a kind of secular church that reached into every class and region of the nation and bound millions upon millions of us together in common concerns, loyalties, rituals, enthusiasms, and antagonisms. Baseball made me understand what patriotism was about, at its best.

Not that Hitler, the Bataan Death March, the battle for the Solomons, and the Normandy invasion didn't make of me and my contemporaries what may well have been the most patriotic generation of schoolchildren in American history (and the most willingly and successfully propagandized). But the war we entered when I was eight had thrust the country into what seemed to a child—and not only to a child—a struggle to the death between Good and Evil. Fraught with perilous, unthinkable possibilities, it inevitably nourished a patriotism grounded in moral virtue and bloody-minded hate, the patriotism that fixes a bayonet to a Bible. It seems to me that through baseball I was put in touch with a more humane and tender brand of patriotism, lyrical rather than martial or righteous in spirit, and without the reek of saintly zeal, a patriotism that could not so easily be sloganized, or contained in a high-sounding formula to which you had to pledge something vague but all-encompassing called your "allegiance."

To sing the National Anthem in the school auditorium every week, even 5 during the worst of the war years, generally left me cold. The enthusiastic lady teacher waved her arms in the air and we obliged with the words. "See! Light! Proof! Night! There!" But nothing stirred within, strident as we might be—in the end, just another school exercise. It was different, however, on Sundays out at Ruppert Stadium, a green wedge of pasture miraculously walled in among the factories, warehouses, and truck depots of industrial Newark. It would, in fact, have seemed to me an emotional thrill forsaken if, before the Newark Bears took on the hated enemy from across the marshes, the Jersey City Giants, we hadn't first to rise to our feet (my father, my brother, and I—along with our inimical countrymen, the city's Germans, Italians, Irish, Poles, and, out in the Africa of the bleachers, Newark's Negroes) to celebrate the America that had given to this unharmonious mob a game so grand and beautiful.

Just as I first learned the names of the great institutions of higher learning by trafficking in football pools for a neighborhood bookmaker rather than from our high school's college adviser, so my feel for the American landscape came less from what I learned in the classroom about Lewis and Clark than from following the major-league clubs on their road trips and reading about the minor leagues in the back pages of *The Sporting News*. The size of the continent got through to you finally when you had to stay up to 10:30 p.m. in New Jersey to hear via radio "ticker-tape" Cardinal pitcher Mort Cooper throw the first strike of the night to Brooklyn shortstop Pee Wee Reese out in "steamy" Sportsmen's Park in St. Louis, Missouri. And however much we might be told by teacher about the stockyards and the Haymarket riot, Chicago only began to exist for me as a real place, and to matter in American history, when I became fearful (as a Dodger fan) of the bat of Phil Cavarretta, first baseman for the Chicago Cubs.

Not until I got to college and was introduced to literature did I find anything with a comparable emotional atmosphere and aesthetic appeal. I don't mean to suggest that it was a simple exchange, one passion for another. Between first discovering the Newark Bears and the Brooklyn Dodgers at seven or eight and first looking into Conrad's *Lord Jim* at age eighteen, I had done some growing up. I am only saying that my discovery of literature, and fiction particularly, and the "love affair"—to some degree hopeless, but still earnest—that has ensued, derives in part from this childhood infatuation with baseball. Or, more accurately perhaps, baseball—with its lore and legends, its cultural power, its seasonal associations, its native authenticity, its simple rules and transparent strategies, its longueurs and thrills, its spaciousness, its suspensefulness, its heroics, its nuances, its lingo, its "characters," its peculiarly hypnotic tedium, its mythic transformation of the immediate—was the literature of my boyhood.

Baseball, as played in the big leagues, was something completely outside my own life that could nonetheless move me to ecstasy and to tears; like fiction it could excite the imagination and hold the attention as much with minutiae as with high drama. Mel Ott's cocked leg striding into the ball, Jackie Robinson's pigeon-toed shuffle as he moved out to second base, each was to be as deeply affecting over the years as that night—"inconceivable," "inscrutable," as any night Conrad's Marlow might struggle to comprehend—the night that Roger Wildman, Rex Barney (who never lived up to our expectations, who should have been "our" Koufax), not only went the distance without walking in half a dozen runs, but, of all things, threw a no-hitter. A thrilling mystery, marvelously enriched by the fact that a light rain had fallen during the early evening, and Barney, figuring the game was going to be postponed, had eaten a hot dog just before being told to take the mound.

This detail was passed on to us by Red Barber, the Dodger radio sportscaster of the forties, a respectful, mild Southerner with a subtle rural tanginess to his vocabulary and a soft country-parson tone to his voice. For the adventures of "dem bums" of Brooklyn—a region then the very symbol of urban wackiness and tumult—to be narrated from Red Barber's highly alien but loving perspective constituted a genuine triumph of what my English professors would later teach me to call "point of view." James himself might have admired the implicit cultural ironies and the splendid possibilities for oblique moral and social commentary. And as for the detail about Rex Barney eating his hot dog, it was irresistible, joining as it did the spectacular to the mundane, and furnishing an adolescent boy with a glimpse of an unexpectedly ordinary, even humdrum, side to male heroism.

Of course, in time, neither the flavor and suggestiveness of Red Barber's 10 narration nor "epiphanies" as resonant with meaning as Rex Barney's pregame hot dog could continue to satisfy a developing literary appetite; nonetheless, it was just this that helped to sustain me until I was ready to begin to respond to the great inventors of narrative detail and masters of narrative voice and perspective like James, Conrad, Dostoevsky, and Bellow.

SUGGESTIONS FOR FURTHER STUDY

Key Words

The author uses language with which you may not be familiar. Find the following words in the paragraphs indicated, and explain their meanings in the context of the sentences in which the words appear. Consult a dictionary, as needed.

cataclysmic (par. 1)
inimical (par. 5)
inscrutable (par. 8)
epiphanies (par. 10)

Topics for Discussion and Writing

1. Roth claims that baseball provided a "mythic and aesthetic dimension . . . to an American boy's life." First, explain what you think he means by "mythic and aesthetic," then explain how he develops this claim in terms of his own life. Cite specific examples from the essay itself.

2. To what extent do you think Roth's feelings about baseball extend to other young Americans? Can other sports or hobbies provide the same depth of experience? Explain your answers.

3. What connections does Roth make between his love for and understanding of baseball and his comparable feeling for and appreciation of literature? For example, he says that "baseball . . . was the literature of my boyhood." In what ways does he make that connection?

4. Compare Roth's essay to Covell's essay on a similar topic ("Gramps"). How are their attachments to baseball alike or different?

5. Write about a sport or other activity in which you or someone you know was deeply involved as a young woman or man. Make clear the *significance* of the activity to the person involved.

Kill 'Em! Crush 'Em! Eat 'Em Raw!

John McMurtry

John McMurtry earned a BA at the University of Toronto and a PhD at the University of London. He is a professor of philosophy at the University of Guelph in Canada and has written numerous books and scholarly articles. His latest book is Unequal Freedoms *(Toronto: Garamond Press). McMurtry played varsity football and, during his MA studies, he played professionally as a starting cornerback with the Calgary Stampeders of the Canadian Football League. "Kill 'Em! Crush 'Em! Eat 'Em Raw!" first appeared in the Canadian news-magazine* Maclean's *in 1971.*

A few months ago my neck got a hard crick in it. I couldn't turn my head; to look left or right I'd have to turn my whole body. But I'd had cricks in my neck since I started playing grade-school football and hockey, so I just ignored it. Then I began to notice that when I reached for any sort of large book (which I do pretty often as a philosophy teacher at the University of Guelph) I had trouble lifting it with one hand. I was losing the strength in my left arm, and I had such a steady pain in my back I often had to stretch out on the floor of the room I was in to relieve the pressure.

A few weeks later I mentioned to my brother, an orthopedic surgeon, that I'd lost the power in my arm since my neck began to hurt. Twenty-four hours later I was in a Toronto hospital not sure whether I might end up with a wasted upper limb. Apparently the steady pounding I had received play-ing college and professional football in the late Fifties and early Sixties had driven my head into my backbone so that the discs had crumpled together at the neck—"acute herniation"—and had cut the nerves to my left arm like a pinched telephone wire (without nerve stimulation, of course, the muscles atrophy, leaving the arm crippled). So I spent my Christmas holidays in the hospital in heavy traction and much of the next three months with my neck in a brace. Today most of the pain has gone, and I've recovered most of the strength in my arm. But from time to time I still have to don the brace, and surgery remains a possibility.

Not much of this will surprise anyone who knows football. It is a sport in which body wreckage is one of the leading conventions. A few days after I went into hospital for that crick in my neck, another brother, an outstanding football player in college, was undergoing spinal surgery in the same hospital two floors above me. In his case it was a lower, more massive herniation, which every now and again buckled him so that he was unable to lift himself off his back for days at a time. By the time he entered the hospital for surgery he had already spent several months in bed. The operation was successful, but, as in all such cases, it will take him a year to recover fully.

These aren't isolated experiences. Just about anybody who has ever played football for any length of time, in high school, college or one of the professional leagues, has suffered for it later physically.

Indeed, it is arguable that body shattering is the very *point* of football, as killing and maiming are of war. (In the United States, for example, the game results in 15 to 20 deaths a year and about 50,000 major operations on knees alone.) To grasp some of the more conspicuous similarities between football and war, it is instructive to listen to the imperatives most frequently issued to the players by their coaches, teammates and fans. "Hurt 'em!" "Level 'em!" "Kill 'em!" "Take 'em apart!" Or watch for the plays that are most enthusiastically applauded by the fans. Where someone is "smeared," "knocked silly," "creamed," "nailed," "broken in two," or even "crucified." (One of my coaches when I played corner linebacker with the Calgary Stampeders in 1961 elaborated, often very inventively, on this language of destruction: admonishing us to "unjoin" the opponent, "make 'im remember you" and "stomp 'im like a bug.") Just as in hockey, where a fight will bring fans to their feet more often than a skillful play, so in football the mouth waters most of all for the really crippling block or tackle. For the kill. Thus the good teams are "hungry," the best players are "mean," and "casualties" are as much a part of the game as they are of a war.

The family resemblance between football and war is, indeed, striking. Their languages are similar: "field general," "long bomb," "blitz," "take a shot," "front line," "pursuit," "good hit," "the draft" and so on. Their principles and practices are alike: mass hysteria, the art of intimidation, absolute command and total obedience, territorial aggression, censorship, inflated insignia and propaganda, blackboard maneuvers and strategies, drills, uniforms, formations, marching bands and training camps. And the virtues they celebrate are almost identical: hyper-aggressiveness, coolness under fire and suicidal bravery. All this has been implicitly recognized by such jock-loving Americans as media stars General Patton and President Nixon, who have talked about war as a football game. Patton wanted to make his Second World War tank men look like football players. And Nixon, as we know, was fond of comparing attacks on Vietnam to football plays and drawing coachly diagrams on a blackboard for TV war fans.

One difference between war and football, though, is that there is little or no protest against football. Perhaps the most extraordinary thing about the game is that the systematic infliction of injuries excites in people not concern, as would be the case if they were sustained at, say, a rock festival, but a collective rejoicing and euphoria. Players and fans alike revel in the spectacle of a combatant felled into semiconsciousness, "blindsided," "clotheslined" or "decapitated." I can remember, in fact, being chided by a coach in pro ball for not "getting my hat" injuriously into a player who was already lying helpless on the ground. (On another occasion, after the Stampeders had traded the celebrated Joe Kapp to BC, we were playing the Lions in Vancouver and Kapp was forced on one play to run with the ball. He was coming "down the chute," his bad knee wobbling uncertainly, so I simply dropped on him like a blanket. After I returned to the bench I was reproved for not exploiting the opportunity to unhinge his bad knee.)

After every game, of course, the papers are full of reports on the day's injuries, a sort of post-battle "body count," and the respective teams go to work with doctors and trainers, tape, whirlpool baths, cortisone and morphine to patch and deaden the wounds before the next game. Then the whole drama is reenacted—injured athletes held together by adhesive, braces and drugs—and the days following it are filled with even more feverish activity to put on the show yet again at the end of the next week. (I remember being so taped up in college that I earned the nickname "mummy.") The team that survives this merry-go-round spectacle of skilled masochism with the fewest incapacitating injuries usually wins. It is a sort of victory by ordeal: "We hurt them more than they hurt us."

My own initiation into this brutal circus was typical. I loved the game from the moment I could run with a ball. Played shoeless on a green open field with no one keeping score and in a spirit of reckless abandon and laughter, it's a very different sport. Almost no one gets hurt and it's rugged, open and exciting (it still is for me). But then, like everything else, it starts to be regulated and institutionalized by adult authorities. And the fun is over.

So it was as I began the long march through organized football. Now   10 there was a coach and elders to make it clear by their behavior that beating other people was the only thing to celebrate and that trying to shake someone up every play was the only thing to be really proud of. Now there were severe rule enforcers, audiences, formally recorded victors and losers, and heavy equipment to permit crippling bodily moves and collisions (according to one American survey, more than 80% of all football injuries occur to fully equipped players). And now there was the official "given" that the only way to keep playing was to wear suffocating armor, to play to defeat, to follow orders silently and to renounce spontaneity for joyless drill. The game had been, in short, ruined. But because I loved to play and play skillfully, I stayed. And progressively and inexorably, as I moved through high school, college and pro leagues, my body was dismantled. Piece by piece.

I started off with torn ligaments in my knee at 13. Then, as the organization and the competition increased, the injuries came faster and harder.

Broken nose (three times), broken jaw (fractured in the first half and dismissed as a "bad wisdom tooth," so I played with it for the rest of the game), ripped knee ligaments again. Torn ligaments in one ankle and a fracture in the other (which I remember feeling relieved about because it meant I could honorably stop drill-blocking a 270-pound defensive end). Repeated rib fractures and cartilage tears (usually carried, again, through the remainder of the game). More dislocations of the left shoulder than I can remember (the last one I played with because, as the Calgary Stampeder doctor said, it "couldn't be damaged any more"). Occasional broken or dislocated fingers and toes. Chronically hurt lower back (I still can't lift with it or change a tire without worrying about folding). Separated right shoulder (as with many other injuries, like badly bruised hips and legs, needled with morphine for the games). And so on. The last pro game I played—against Winnipeg Blue Bombers in the Western finals in 1961—I had a recently dislocated left shoulder, a more recently wrenched right shoulder and a chronic pain centre in one leg. I was so tied up with soreness I couldn't drive my car to the airport. But it never occurred to me or anyone else that I miss a play as a corner linebacker.

By the end of my football career, I had learned that physical injury—giving it and taking it—is the real currency of the sport. And that in the final analysis the "winner" is the man who can hit to kill even if only half his limbs are working. In brief, a warrior game with a warrior ethos into which (like almost everyone else I played with) my original boyish enthusiasm had been relentlessly taunted and conditioned.

In thinking back on how all this happened, though, I can pick out no villains. As with the social system as a whole, the game has a life of its own. Everyone grows up inside it, accepts it and fulfills its dictates as obediently as helots. Far from ever questioning the principles of the activity, people simply concentrate on executing these principles more aggressively than anybody around them. The result is a group of people who, as the leagues become of a higher and higher class, are progressively insensitive to the possibility that things could be otherwise. Thus, in football, anyone who might question the wisdom or enjoyment of putting on heavy equipment on a hot day and running full speed at someone else with the intention of knocking him senseless would be regarded simply as not really a devoted athlete and probably "chicken." The choice is made straightforward. Either you, too, do your very utmost to efficiently smash and be smashed, or you admit incompetence or cowardice and quit. Since neither of these admissions is very pleasant, people generally keep any doubts they have to themselves and carry on.

Of course, it would be a mistake to suppose that there is more blind acceptance of brutal practices in organized football than elsewhere. On the contrary, a recent Harvard study has approvingly argued that football's characteristics of "impersonal acceptance of inflicted injury," an overriding "organization goal," the "ability to turn oneself on and off" and being, above all, "out to win" are of "inestimable value" to big corporations. Clearly, our sort of football is no sicker than the rest of our society. Even its organized destruction of physical well-being is not anomalous. A very large part of our wealth, work and time is, after all, spent in systematically destroying and harming human life. Manufacturing, selling and using weapons that tear opponents to pieces. Making ever bigger and faster predator-named cars with which to kill and injure one another by the million every year. And devoting our very lives to outgunning one another for power in an ever more destructive rat race. Yet all these practices are accepted without question by most people, even zealously defended and honored. Competitive, organized injuring is integral to our way of life, and football is simply one of the more intelligible mirrors of the whole process: a sort of colorful morality play showing us how exciting and rewarding it is to Smash Thy Neighbor.

Now it is fashionable to rationalize our collaboration in all this by 15 arguing that, well, man *likes* to fight and injure his fellows and such games as football should be encouraged to discharge this original-sin urge into less harmful channels than, say, war. Public-show football, this line goes, plays the same sort of cathartic role as Aristotle said stage tragedy does: without real blood (or not much), it releases players and audience from unhealthy feelings stored up inside them.

As an ex-player in this seasonal coast-to-coast drama, I see little to recommend such a view. What organized football did to me was make me *suppress* my natural urges and re-express them in an alienating, vicious form. Spontaneous desires for free bodily exuberance and fraternization with competitors were shamed and forced under ("If it ain't hurtin' it ain't helpin'") and in their place were demanded armored mechanical moves and cool hatred of all opposition. Endless authoritarian drill and dressing-room harangues (ever wonder why competing teams can't prepare for a game in the same dressing room?) were the kinds of mechanisms employed to reconstruct joyful energies into mean and alien shapes. I am quite certain that everyone else around me was being similarly forced into this heavily equipped military precision and angry antagonism, because there was always a mutinous attitude about full-dress practices, and everybody (the pros included) had to concentrate incredibly hard for days to whip themselves into just one hour's hostility a week against another club. The players never speak of these things, of course, because everyone is so anxious to appear tough.

The claim that men like seriously to battle one another to some sort of finish is a myth. It only endures because it wears one of the oldest and most propagandized of masks—the romantic combatant. I sometimes wonder whether the violence all around us doesn't depend for its survival on the existence and preservation of this tough-guy disguise.

SUGGESTIONS FOR FURTHER STUDY

Key Words

The author uses language with which you may not be familiar. Find the following words in the paragraphs indicated, and explain their meanings in the context of the sentences in which the words appear. Consult a dictionary, as needed.

orthopedic (par. 2)
herniation (par. 2)
masochism (par. 8)
inexorably (par. 10)
harangues (par. 16)

Topics for Discussion and Writing

1. Notice that the author alternates in telling his story between first-person ("I") narration and third-person exposition. Locate several places in the essay that use either first or third person. Discuss the effects created by the alternation of first and third person.

2. The author develops his discussion of football in several ways. Find instances where the author uses anecdote, analogy, and comparison. Identify other methods of development, and indicate where they appear in the essay. Which methods do you find most effective? Why?

3. In this essay, the author projects his point of view in such expressions as "warrior game with a warrior ethos" (par. 12), "I can pick out no villains" (par. 13), and "the romantic combatant" (par. 17). How do these and other expressions of point of view contribute to the author's analogy between football and war? In your opinion, how relevant is the author's analogy?

4. Write about another sport or physical activity that might be likened to war, or draw a different analogy (e.g., between fencing and dancing, or chess and mathematics), and develop it in an essay.

Graceland

Albert Goldman

Albert Goldman attended both Carnegie–Mellon University and the University of Chicago and then earned a PhD at Columbia University, where he taught English. A former pop-music critic for Life *magazine, Goldman has written several non-fiction books, including* Wagner on Music and Drama, Ladies and Gentlemen—Lenny Bruce!!, The Lives of John Lennon *(1988), and* Elvis *(1981), from which this selection was taken.*

Though the holidays are long past, Graceland looks still like a picture on a Christmas card. The classic colonial façade, with its towering white columns and pilasters, is aglow with jewel lights, rose, amethyst and emerald. The templelike pediment is outlined in pale blue fire. This same eerie electric aura runs like St. Elmo's fire along the eaves, zigzags up and down the gables and shimmies down the drainpipes to the ground. Here it pales beside the brilliance of a rank of Christmas trees that have been transformed into cones of ruby, topaz, carnelian and aquamarine incandescence.

Prominently displayed on the front lawn is an elaborate crèche. The stable is a full-scale adobe house strewn with straw. Life-sized are the figures of Joseph and Mary, the kneeling shepherds and Magi, the lambs and ewes, as well as the winged annunciatory angel hovering over the roof beam. Real, too, is the cradle in which the infant Jesus sleeps.

When you step through the ten-foot oak door and enter the house, you stop and stare in amazement. Having just come from the contemplation of the tenderest scene in the Holy Bible, imagine the shock of finding yourself in a *whorehouse!* Yet there is no other way to describe the drawing room of Graceland except to say that it appears to have been lifted from some turn-of-the-century bordello down in the French Quarter of New Orleans. Lulu White or the Countess Willie Piazza might have contrived this plushy parlor for the entertainment of Gyp the Blood. The room is a gaudy mélange of red velour and gilded tassels, Louis XV furniture and porcelain bric-a-brac, all informed by the kind of taste that delights in a ceramic temple d'amour housing a miniature Venus de Milo with an electrically simulated waterfall cascading over her naked shoulders.

Looking a little closer, you realize that the old madams of the French Quarter would have been horrified at the quality of the hangings and furniture at Graceland. They decorated their sporting houses with magnificent pieces crafted in Europe, upholstered them in the finest reps and damasks, laid costly Persian carpets on their floors and hung imposing oil paintings on their walls. Though it cost a lot of money to fill up Graceland with the things that appealed to Elvis Presley, nothing in the house is worth a dime.

Take that fake fireplace that blocks with its companion bookcases   5 (filled with phony leather bindings) the two big windows that should offer a commanding view of the front lawn. This hokey facsimile looks like it was bought at the auction of some bankrupt road company of *East Lynne*. Or consider the Louis Quinze furniture strewn about the parlor. Every piece is elaborately carved and gilded, escutcheoned and cabrioled; but it's not only fake (Louis XV's upholsterers didn't go in for sectional sofas), it's that dreadful fake antique that Italian gangsters dote on: garish, preposterous, uncomfortable and cheating wherever it can, as in the substitution of velour for velvet. Or look at the real fireplace of white marble that stands against the back wall of the room, obviously innocent of use. It, too, has been flanked not with bookcases but with a great spread of smoked-glass mirror threaded with gold seams. The whole ensemble is crowned with an electric clock inside a three-foot sunburst that looks like someone took an ostrich egg and smashed it against the glass.

The entrance to the adjoining music room is flanked by two tall, broad windows adorned with painted peacocks. Marvelously campy as are these bits of stained glass, they can't hold a candle to the bizarre chamber they frame. In this mad room, King Elvis's obsession with royal red reaches an intensity that makes you gag. Not so much a room as a crimson cocoon, every inch of it is swathed in red satin drapes, portieres, valences and braided ropes. As weird as anything in Edgar Allan Poe, the effect is that of stepping into the auricle of an immense heart. At the center of this king-sized valentine is the crowning touch: a concert grand piano that appears to have been dipped in liquid gold.

The entrance to the next room is blocked by a tall folding screen covered with mirrored glass. Screens and other masking devices abound at Graceland because Gladys and Vernon, Elvis's parents, imbued him with the old hillbilly superstition: Never close up windows or doors. Through this folding looking glass lies one of Elvis's favorite spots, the trophy room. A pop archeologist would find the excavation of this site a satisfying occupation. No part of Graceland was subject to more visions and revisions.

Originally, this room was a patio adjoining the dressing rooms for the outdoor pool. On hot Nilotic nights, Elvis and the Guys (known to the media as the "Memphis Mafia") would sit here cutting the ripe red hearts out of iced watermelons and vying to see who could eat the most. As they consumed this sweet satisfying pap, they would spit the pits out on the ground as Sweetpea, Gladys's Pomeranian, pranced about in the black hail.

In the late sixties, Elvis decided to build a forty-foot room over the patio to house his slot car racecourse. On a huge raised platform, a figure-eight track was laid out, in whose grooves could be fitted expensive scale-model replicas of Ferraris, Maseratis, Lotuses and Porsches. By means of an electric drive system, you could race these little cars around the tracks and up and down inclines at great speeds, which Elvis sought constantly to increase by means of continual improvements in the cars' motors. Manipulating the pistol-grip controls, you could make the cars skid, spin out and crash. It was a grand if costly game, and the Guys enjoyed it enormously.

Like all of Elvis's toys, the slot cars soon lost their charm. One day the track was banished to the attic, where it was stored alongside cartons of old teddy bears, discarded guitars and gilt lamps from the house on Audubon Avenue. Elvis never allowed anything to be cast out of Graceland except human beings. Once an object, no matter how trivial, came into his possession, it remained with him for the rest of his life.

Commencing in the Royal Period, the slot car room became the trophy room. Elvis pushed back the end wall twenty feet to make a chamber fit for a pharaoh's tomb. Then he filled it with gold. He ranked his fifty-three gold records along one wall, like patents of nobility. Against the opposite wall, he piled up, like the offerings before a shrine, a great heap of gold loving cups, gold statuettes and gold tablets. The effect is less that of a trophy case than of the display case of a trophy manufacturer.

The showcase effect is even more pronounced in the center of the room, which is occupied by a set of old-fashioned department store counters, under whose glass tops or stuffed inside storage drawers and cupboards lie an immense profusion of plaques, medals, certificates and scrapbooks received from professional organizations, charities and fan clubs. Like any true sovereign, King Elvis never forgets that all his wealth and power are derived from his subjects. No matter what they offer him, whether it be a huge stuffed animal or a little crocheted doily, he not only keeps the gift but puts it on display.

The oddest feature of the trophy room is the soda fountain that stands in one corner, one of two at Graceland, the other one being downstairs in the poolroom. Soda fountains and jukeboxes are symbolic objects for fifties rock heroes, no more to be wondered at than the old binnacle in the den of a steamship captain or the pair of crossed sabers on the wall of a retired general. What is disconcerting about this domestic altar is its formica meanness. Yet it would be out of character for Elvis to own a handsome old green marble counter with mottled glass lamps and quaint seltzer pulls because Elvis detests everything antique with the heartfelt disgust of a real forward-looking American of his generation. Like so many of his kind, he gloats over the spectacle of the wrecking ball bashing down the walls of historic Memphis. In fact, he likes to get into the driver's seat of a bulldozer and smash down old buildings himself. . . .

On the left-hand side of the entrance hall is the dining room. In the center of the crimson carpet is a large quadrangle of black marble tiles on

10

which is set the table: an eight-foot oval of mirrored glass on an ebonized and fluted wooden pedestal. Round the table in great state stand ten tall, ladder-backed Louis XIV chairs with tufted velour seats. They appear to have been drawn up for King Elvis and the Nine Worthies. (When Elvis dines with the Guys, he often jokes about Jesus breaking bread with his disciples. They respond by singing the old hymn, "What a Friend We Have in Jesus," substituting "Elvis" for "Jesus.") Above the table hangs a brass Louis XIV chandelier with two tiers of scrolled candlearms fitted with glass lusters. At each corner of the room, like bumpers on a game board, are tall diagonal bric-a-brac cabinets or chrome-plated étagères crammed with statuettes, vases, jars, boxes, plaques, goblets, ewers, compotes, porringers, shells, cloches, etc., *viz:*

> ceramic statuette of a grey poodle
> ceramic statuette of a nude girl with perched bird
> pair of Portuguese glazed pottery drug jars
> five specimens of butterflies in plastic cases
> artificial floral bouquet under a glass cloche
> two glass bowls with bouquet of black and white feathers
> model of 1932 antique radio
> ceramic statuette of a trumpeting elephant

Wherever Elvis goes in his travels, he indulges his middle-aged woman's passion for knickknacks, curios and chatzkahs. A domestic appraiser once remarked that Elvis appeared to have furnished Graceland largely from roadside stands.

A familiar feature of a number of the world's greatest palaces is a room   15
decorated in an exotic style, inspired, perhaps, by the culture of one of the ruler's most remote or colorful provinces. Graceland possesses such a room; indeed, of all the public rooms in the mansion, it is the King's favorite. The den is an addition to the original building, created by enlarging and enclosing a back porch that ran along the entire rear wall. The room looks like Elvis scooped up the setting for one of his Hawaiian movies and brought it home inside a sixty-foot walnut hope chest. You reach the den by going through the kitchen, which is all white formica, walnut paneling and Kitchen-Aid stainless steel, with a couple of oddly feminine touches, like the calico carpeting and the hanging lampshades painted with fruits and vegetables. Entering the den, the first thing that strikes you is a towering statue of the god Tiki, confronting the visitor with outstretched arms holding an empty bowl. Obviously not an ashtray nor an hors d'oeuvre tray nor a place to drop your calling card, this empty basin is a puzzler. In any case, the statue serves to proclaim the room's provenance.

The style of the den could be characterized as Polynesian Primitive or Ugh! The decorator divided its sixty-foot length with another of those hinged screens that one finds all over Graceland. This one is composed of huge panels of stressed, stained pine perforated in long spermatozoid scrolls cut in the wood with a chain saw. On the side of the screen opposite that dominated by the figure of Tiki is a seating area focused upon an early-model Advent video projector.

Here, as Elvis watches his favorite football teams or boxing matches with the Guys, he enjoys the full flavor of the Polynesian Primitive. The huge sofa and the pair of oversized armchairs are carved out of the same dark coarse pine as the room divider and upholstered with thick, dark artificial fur. As the chairs have huge pawlike armrests, the impression created by this curious suite is rather like the Three Bears watching TV. This animalistic sofa is also Elvis's favorite downstairs dining spot. Like so many boy-men, he dislikes the formality of table service. Whenever possible, he has his meals served to him here on the cocktail table, a huge slab of boldly grained wood cut out of the crotch of a cypress tree and surfaced with what appears to be about a quarter-inch layer of lustrous polyurethane.

The most impressive feature of the den is the wall behind the TV, which is straight out of the lobby of a Waikiki Beach resort hotel. Constructed of layers of roughcut fieldstone, it has been arranged artfully like a natural cataract and equipped with pipes and a pumping system so that a constant stream of soothing water flows down over the jutting rocks, catching as it falls the colors cast by the lamps concealed in the ceiling. What more perfect object of contemplation could be imagined for a man who is perpetually stoned?

The King's bedchamber is the most bizarre room in the hillbilly palace. The walls are padded and tufted with button-studded strips of black artificial suede. The crimson carpet covers not only the floor but rises at the foot of the bed like a red wave, atop which rides an enormous color TV set. Confronting the bed are two big windows that overlook the front lawn. Sealed with the same black upholstery that covers the walls, they are crowned with gold valences and hung with floor-length crimson drapes, producing a somberly surrealistic image, like a painting by Magritte. The space between the windows is filled with a mirror, which reflects the bed.

What a bed! An immense slab, nine by nine, a double king size, it has a [20] mortuary headboard of black quilted Naugahyde, with a built-in plastic back angle and retractable armrests of speckled metal, like the skeletons of those padded "husbands" beloved of suburban matrons. To one side is an easel supporting a large photograph of Elvis's mother; on the other a sepia-toned portrait of Jesus Christ. Back in the corners of the room crouch big round seats covered with white fake fur like enormous bunnies.

As in a funeral parlor, the light in this inner sanctum is always dim, supplied by cove lamps that illuminate the ceiling but produce below only a murky subaqueous gloaming. The air is chilled, the temperature being driven down during the hot Memphis summer by powerful refrigeration units that groan night and day to keep the King from sweating. The odor of the room is sometimes fetid, the stink of a Bowery flophouse full of dirty old men incontinent of their urine and feces. The most grotesque object in this Cave of Morphia, this black and crimson womb, this padded cell, is the King.

SUGGESTIONS FOR FURTHER STUDY

Key Words

The author uses language with which you may not be familiar. Find the following words in the paragraphs indicated, and explain their meanings in the context of the sentences in which the words appear. Consult a dictionary, as needed.

pediment (par. 1)
mélange (par. 3)
escutcheoned (par. 5)
cabrioleted (par. 5)
portieres (par. 6)
valences (par. 6)
spermatozoid (par. 16)

Topics for Discussion and Writing

1. How would you describe the author's point of view concerning Graceland and Elvis's taste? For example, he says such things as "nothing in the house is worth a dime," and "What is disconcerting about this domestic altar is its formica meanness." Find other expressions of the author's opinion about Graceland, and explain how they reflect his point of view.

2. Cite instances of the author's satire of Graceland and of Elvis's taste. Look at such expressions as "Elvis detests everything antique with the heartfelt disgust of a real forward-looking American of his generation," or "The style of the den could be characterized as Polynesian Primitive or Ugh!"

3. The author makes references to Elvis and his surroundings in Graceland through figures of speech such as allusion, hyperbole, and metaphor. What is the effect of the following references in the overall impression of the man and his home? Find other like references, and add them to the following list.

   "Graceland . . . appears to have been lifted from some turn-of-the-century bordello down in the French Quarter of New Orleans." (par. 3) "the effect is that of stepping into the auricle of an immense heart." (par. 6)

"Elvis appeared to have furnished Graceland largely from roadside stands." (par. 14)

"Like so many boy-men, he dislikes the formality of table service." (par. 17)

"The odor of the room is sometimes fetid, the stink of a Bowery flophouse." (par. 21)

4. In addition to using figures of speech to characterize Elvis and Graceland, the author employs contrasts in the level of language and vocabulary, from formal to informal. For example, he names many items in Graceland with their French terms (étagères, cloches), and he describes each room at length and in elaborate detail. In contrast, he characterizes some people and objects in more commonplace terms to emphasize the artificiality and pretension to culture found in Graceland. Following a detailed description of Graceland's electric clock, the author concludes that it "looks like someone took an ostrich egg and smashed it against the glass" (par. 5). Look for other contrasts in the level of language and vocabulary, and discuss how this technique contributes to the satire.

5. Write a brief essay describing a place in such a way as to reflect the taste and personality of a person who lives or lived there. Try using figures of speech to characterize the place, its furnishings or surroundings, and its inhabitants.

Wittman Ah Sing's Halloween Play

Maxine Hong Kingston

Maxine Hong Kingston is the author of two earlier books: The Woman Warrior—Memoirs of a Girlhood Among Ghosts, *winner of the National Book Critics Circle Award for nonfiction, and* China Men, *winner of the National Book Award for nonfiction. She lives in Oakland, California, and is married to Earl Kingston, an actor; they have a son, Joseph Kingston, a musician.*

The following selection is exerpted from her most recent novel, Tripmaster Monkey—His Fake Book. *In the novel, Wittman Ah Sing, Chinese American poet–dramatist from San Francisco, dreams of staging a gala multicultural communal dramatic event to celebrate the art, history, and culture of Chinese Americans—both in China and America. His dreams become fulfilled, and the following excerpts describe the third night of his mammoth Halloween extravaganza.*

All hell broke loose on the third night of [Wittman's] play, for which the audience kept growing. The public, including white strangers, came and made the show important. The theater went beyond cracking up family, friends and neighbors come to see one another be different from everyday. The take at the box office paid for the explosives for the climactic blowout. The audience sat on the staircase and windowsills; there was no longer an aisle.

We are in a snow palace on the frontier. . . . When the sun is farthest from the Earth, Lantern Festival lights up the five days of deepest winter. Curves of scaffolding form a white dragon; the white lanterns are its scales. Each holding a lantern, children file singing through the ice tunnels. Dragons are playing with flames englobed in ice—the pearl that is the universe or Earth. A thousand lanterns—phoenixes in paper cages—hang from the blue cloud tower, the most famous restaurant ever, with over a hundred dining rooms. . . . This is Tai Ming Fu, the Great Bright City, and to this city of big lights on the clear silver-and-gold night of the full moon will come the one hundred and eight bandits. Or so warns the poem on the gate, scrolls of poetry unfurling on walls and posts . . . warning that the bandits are about to attack. But the innocent shall not be harmed; the imprisoned shall be free. Teams of husband-and-wife knights enter the city from different

1

routes. It's the Dwarf Tiger and the Tigress, played by Zeppelin and Rudy; the Vegetarian and the Night Ogress, played by Charles Bogart Shaw and Nanci Lee; the Dry Land Water Beast and Devil Face, played by Lance and Sunny Kamiyama; the pursuing God of Death and the Lively Woman, played by Mr. Lincoln Fong and PoPo. They're wearing party clothes to account for glamour. They shop and eat until time to reveal themselves as the toughest fighters of all . . . .

As in real life, things were happening all over the place. The audience looks left, right, up and down, in and about the round, everywhere, the flies, the wings, all the while hearing reports from offstage. Too much goings-on, they miss some, okay, like life.

Inside a grocery store, some bad Caucasians plant dope among the mayjing and the black-bean sauce, then call the cops. A lynch mob raids the store, where the grocers both work and live. They jerk the Chinamen down the streets by their long hair. Ropes hang from lampposts and fire escapes. Nooses are lowered over heads. The accusation and the sentence are read: To be hung by the neck until he dies for dealing opium, which debauches white girls for the slave trade. The kung fu gang leaps to the rescue. Everybody dukes it out. The opium war in the West. John Wayne rides into town, asking, "Where's the Chinaman? Gotta see the Chinaman about some opium." The police break up the riot, and arrest the grocers for assaulting officers. So Chinese-Americans founded the Joang Wah for the purpose of filing legal complaints with the city of New York against lynchings, illegal arrests, opium, slavery, and grocery store licensing. A tong is not a crime syndicate and not a burial society. It is organization of community, for which Chinese-Americans have genius . . . .

At the climactic free-for-all—everybody fights everybody everywhere at once. The hundred and eight bandits and their enemies (played by twenty-five actors) knock one another in and out all entrances and exits, sword-fighting up and down the stairs and out amongst the audience, take that and *that,* kicking the mandarin duck kick, swinging the jeweled-ring swing, drums and cymbals backing up the punches. The intellectuals grasp their five-pronged penholders, and make of their hands claw-fists. Everybody chased one another outside and battled on 22nd Avenue among the cars. Audience hung out the window. . . . Bullets and arrows zing from the false fronts of the sharpshooter roofs. Gunslingers and archers jump from balconies into the saddle. Rain barrels explode. Puppets cudgel and pummel and wack-wack. Tenderfoot drinkers of lemonade and sarsaparilla and milk bust out from swinging doors and over hitching posts into water troughs and rain barrels and Ali Baba wine jars. Through the smoke, a juggernaut, an iron roller with spikes, thunders across a hollow floor. The audience got to its feet in participation. The sheriff will surely come soon to stop the show with a cease-and-desist-disturbing-the-peace order. Jail us for performing without a permit, like our brave theatrical ancestors, who were

5

violators of zoning ordinances; they put on shows, they paraded, they raised chickens within city limits. . . .

In chain reactions, thousand-firecracker strands climbed poles to the microphones and blasted out the loudspeakers. Blow it all up. Set the theater on fire. The playwright goes down with his play like the historians who were killed at the end of their eras, their books burning at their feet. No asbestos-and-metal guillotine curtain here. The Globe and the Garrick had many fires, then holocaust. It's a theater tradition. Chinese hold all the Guinness records—1,670 audience members and actors killed in Canton in 1845 at the Theater, which was enclosed by a high wall. The fire in the Theater at Kamli killed two thousand in 1893. The Fu Chow playhouse burned down in 1884 under bombardment by the French fleet. Every theater you've ever been to or heard of has had its fire. The Bowery Theater in Vauxhall Gardens, New York—burned and rebuilt six times. Eleven hundred theater fires all over the world in the last hundred years. . . . Floors caught fire when winter stoves underneath the stage heated up the boards too hot. The candles in the luster pooled and became a bowl of sheet-flame. The gasman at the Baltimore Front Street Theater held his pole-torch up to a jet, and a gust of fire shot out through the stage, which is a wind tunnel. The hay bales for dragging the floors clean caught sparks and smoldered. For the sake of verisimilitude, the actor-soldiers at the court theater in Oldenburg set fire to a stage fortress, midnight, 1891, and the rest of the building went with it. On Bastille Day, 1873, cannons were shot off indoors, which destroyed the Grand Opera House and the bibliotheque. The last act of *Faust*, the masked ball, caused many theaters to burn, including the holocausts of the Leghorn and the Teatro degli Acquidotti. There was a cinematographe fire in Paris in 1897; and in 1908, at the Rhodes Opera House, Boyerton, Pennsylvania, a motion-picture machine exploded and killed a hundred people. And just this past spring in Saigon, three hundred children were killed at a waterfront theater. We'll do anything for lighting, die for it, kill for it. . . .

In tradition of theater fires, in remembrance of the burnings of Chinatowns, and of the great earthquake and fire, and of the Honolulu plague fire at the New Year and the new century, and in protest of the school fact that the Chinese invented gunpowder but were too dumb to use it in warfare, and in honor of artists who were arrested for incendiarism, Wittman Ah Sing—"Gotta match?" he asked. "Not since Superman died," answered a chorus of kids in the audience—lit every last explosive. Go up in flames and down in history. Fireworks whiz-banged over and into the neighborhood. Percussion caps, powders, and instruments banged and boomed. . . .

The neighbors turned in four alarums. Fire engines were coming, wailing louder than Chinese opera. On cue—the S.F.F.D was bringing the red-ness and the wailing. Sirens. Bells. A hook-and-ladder truck. The audience ran out into the street. More audience came. And the actors were out from backstage and the green room, breaking rules of reality-and-illusion. Their armor and swords were mirrored in fenders, bumpers, and the long sides of the fire trucks. The clear clean red metal with the silver chrome glorified all that was shining. The emergency lights reddened faces and buildings. "Fire!" "Fire!" The *Chron*'s banner tomorrow: Chinese Fire!

"Where's the fire?"

"No fire. Chinese custom."   10

"Do you have a fireworks permit?"

"Permit?" Only three flashpowder technicians in the State of California had a Class C license for setting off theatrical explosives. Wittman Ah Sing wasn't one of them.

"You don't plan to keep this racket up all night long, do you?"

"The noisy part of our ritual is done. Would you like some tickets to the quiet part? You're invited to come in and see it." And to the crowd of neighbors. "We invite you too," papering the house. "I promise to be quiet."

The next part of Wittman's night could have him caged and taken   15
through the city in a paddywagon. He might have seen the streets through grillwork and between the heads of a pair of cops.

Instead, he was given a chance; Chinese are allowed more fireworks than other people. He went back inside, and continued the play. . . .

Of course Wittman Ah Sing didn't really burn down the Association house and the theater. It was an illusion of fire. Good monkey. He kept control of the explosives, and of his arsonist's delight in flames. He wasn't crazy; he was a monkey. What's crazy is the idea that revolutionaries must shoot and bomb and kill, that revolution is the same as war. We keep losing our way on the short cut—killing for freedom and liberty and community and a better economy. Wittman could have torched the curtains and the dry flowers; he could have downpoured the oil lamps onto the chairs and fruit crates. He'd been envying that Japanese-American guy that got shot allegedly helping to set the Watts fires, yelling, "Burn, baby, burn." But, no, Wittman would not have tried to burn the City. It's all too beautiful to burn.

The world was splitting up. Tolstoy had noted the surprising gaiety of war. During his time, picnickers and fighters took to the same field. We'd gotten more schizzy. The dying was on the Asian side of the planet while the playing—the love-ins and the be-ins—were on the other, American side. Whatever there is when there isn't war has to be invented. What do people do in peace? Peace has barely been thought.

Our monkey, master of change, staged a fake war, which might be very well displacing some real war. Wittman was learning that one big bang-up show has to be followed-up by a second show, a third show, shows until something takes hold. He was defining a community, which will meet every night for a season. Community is not built once-and-for-all; people have to imagine, practice, and re-create it. His community surrounding him, then, we're going to reward and bless Wittman with our listening.

SUGGESTIONS FOR FURTHER STUDY

Language and Style

1. How would you characterize the author's style of writing in this selection? How does she create a sense of both excitement and confusion in her description of the Halloween play? Locate several sentences or longer passages that you think represent the author's style of writing, and discuss their effect on you and other readers.

2. Notice that much of the action is reported from the first-person point of view, in present tense (e.g., "We are in a snow palace on the frontier . . ."). At times, however, the description of the Halloween play and its aftermath changes to third person and past tense (e.g., "The next part of Wittman's night could have him caged and taken through the city in a paddywagon"). In what ways are these changes in point of view effective?

Topics for Discussion and Writing

1. How does Wittman Ah Sing's play reflect the art, history, and culture of Chinese Americans? Point to specific actions in the play itself and to the setting in which it takes place.

2. How does the author create a humorous effect in telling about the Halloween play? Cite several passages that you find humorous to greater or lesser degree.

3. Discuss with other readers how Wittman Ah Sing was, in the author's view, "defining a community." Do you agree or disagree with her conclusion that "community is not built once-and-for-all; people have to imagine, practice, and re-create it"? Explain why.

4. Write an essay, a journal entry, or a letter to someone unfamiliar with your cultural background, describing a celebration in your family or community that reflects your cultural history. You might focus on a festival, a religious holiday, a legend, or any other occasion for celebration. Create as vivid a picture of the occasion as you can for your readers.

Shopping

Don DeLillo

*Don DeLillo has authored many acclaimed contemporary novels,
including* Libra, Ratner's Star, Running Dog, *and* Mao II. *He received
the 1984 Award in Literature from the American Academy and Institute of Arts and Letters, and in 1985, he received the American Book
Award for fiction for* White Noise, *from which this selection is taken.*

In a huge hardware store at the mall I saw Eric Massingale, a former   1
microchip sales engineer who changed his life by coming out here to join the
teaching staff of the computer center at the [College on the] Hill. He was
slim and pale with a dangerous grin.

"You're not wearing dark glasses, Jack."

"I only wear them on campus."

"I get it."

We went our separate ways into the store's deep interior. A great echo-   5
ing din, as of the extinction of a species of beast, filled the vast space. People
bought twenty-two-foot ladders, six kinds of sandpaper, power saws that
could fell trees. The aisles were long and bright, filled with oversized
brooms, massive sacks of peat and dung, huge Rubbermaid garbage cans.
Rope hung like tropical fruit, beautifully braided strands, thick, brown,
strong. What a great thing a coil of rope is to look at and feel. I bought
fifty feet of Manila hemp just to have it around, show it to my son, talk
about where it comes from, how it's made. People spoke English, Hindi,
Vietnamese, related tongues.

I ran into Massingale again at the cash terminals.

"I've never seen you off campus, Jack. You look different without your
glasses and gown. Where did you get that sweater? Is that a Turkish army
sweater? Mail order, right?"

He looked me over, felt the material of the water-repellent jacket I was
carrying draped across my arm. Then he backed up, altering his perspective,
nodding a little, his grin beginning to take on a self-satisfied look, reflecting
some inner calculation.

"I think I know those shoes," he said.

What did he mean, he knew these shoes?   10

"You're a different person altogether."

"Different in what way, Eric?"

"You won't take offense?" he said, the grin turning lascivious, rich with secret meaning.

"Of course not? Why should I?"

"Promise you won't take offense." 15

"I won't take offense."

"You look so harmless, Jack. A big, harmless, aging, indistinct sort of guy."

"Why would I take offense?" I said, paying for my rope and hurrying out the door.

The encounter put me in the mood to shop. I found the others and we walked across two parking lots to the main structure in the mid-Village Mall, a ten-story building arranged around a center court of waterfalls, promenades and gardens. Babette and the kids followed me into the elevator, into the shops set up along the tiers, through the emporiums and the department stores, puzzled and excited by my desire to buy. When I could not decide between two shirts, they encouraged me to buy both. When I said I was hungry, they fed me pretzels, beer, souvlaki. The two girls scouted ahead, spotting things they thought I might want or need, running back to get me, to clutch my arms, plead with me to follow. They were my guides to endless well-being. People swarmed through the boutiques and gourmet shops. Organ music rose from the great court. We smelled chocolate, popcorn, cologne; we smelled rugs and furs, hanging salamis and deathly vinyl. My family gloried in the event. I was one of them, shopping, at last. They gave me advice, badgered clerks on my behalf. I kept seeing myself unexpectedly in some reflecting surface. We moved from store to store, rejecting not only items in certain departments, not only entire departments but whole stores, mammoth corporations that did not strike our fancy for one reason or another. There was always another store, three floors, eight floors, basement full of cheese graters and paring knives. I shopped with reckless abandon. I shopped for immediate needs and distant contingencies. I shopped for its own sake, looking and touching, inspecting merchandise I had no intention of buying, then buying it. I sent clerks into their fabric books and pattern books to search for elusive designs. I began to grow in value and self-regard. I filled myself out, found new aspects of myself, located a person I forgot existed. Brightness settled around me. We crossed from furniture to men's wear, walking through cosmetics. Our images appeared on mirrored columns, in glassware and chrome, on TV monitors in security rooms. I traded money for goods. The more money I spent, the less important it seemed. I was bigger than these sums. These sums poured off my skin like so much rain. These sums, in fact, came back to me in the form of existential credit. I felt expansive, inclined to be sweepingly generous, and told the kids to pick out their Christmas gifts here and now. I gestured in what I felt was an expansive manner. I could tell they were impressed. They fanned out across the area, each of them suddenly inclined to be private, shadowy, even secretive. Periodically one of them would return to register the name of a product with Babette, careful not to let the others know what it was. I myself was not to be bothered with tedious details. I was the benefactor, the one who dispenses gifts, bonuses, bribes, "baksheesh." The children knew it was the technical nature of such things that I could not be expected to engage in technical discussions about the gifts themselves. We ate another meal. A band played live Muzak. Voices rose ten stories from the gardens and the promenades, a roar that echoed and swirled through the vast gallery, mixing with noises from the tiers, with shuffling feet and chiming bells, the hum of escalators, the sound of people eating, the human buzz of some vivid and happy transaction.

We drove home in silence. We went to our respective rooms, wishing to   20
be alone.

SUGGESTIONS FOR FURTHER STUDY

Key Words

The author uses language with which you may not be familiar. Find the following words in the paragraphs indicated, and explain their meanings in the context of the sentences in which the words appear. Consult a dictionary, as needed.

hemp (par. 5)
souvlaki (par. 19)
boutiques (par. 19)
contingencies (par. 19)
existential (par. 19)
baksheesh (par. 19)

Topics for Discussion and Writing

1. The author tells readers a first-person narrative about his shopping experience. What is the overall impression of that experience? To support your answer, point to several words, phrases, or longer passages that help you define that impression.

2. As mentioned, "Shopping" is a narrative piece told in first person. Choose a similar event in which you took part, and write a narrative account of it from your point of view. Try to leave an overall impression on your readers, such as humor, dislike, excitement, or appreciation.

Waiting in Line All Night for Cure Tickets

Chris Hernandez

In this selection, student writer Chris Hernandez examines a favorite pastime of America's music lovers: waiting in line to get concert tickets. He also discusses his love of the English rock band The Cure, and the fanaticism that prompted him to wait up all night for tickets to one of the band's concerts.

Five years, five years I had to wait for this night to happen, and it's finally here, The Cure is actually coming to California and I'm waiting in line to buy a ticket. It's about 9 o'clock on a warm Friday night; I'm patiently sitting in front of a Blockbuster Music store waiting for thirteen hours 'til 11 o'clock the next morning. I know this is going to be an extremely long night, but with my girlfriend by my side, and other hopeless Cure fans surrounding me, I couldn't wish to be in a happier place.

But before I explain to you what a thrill this night was for me, I must first take you back to the very first time I ever heard The Cure's music. This was five years ago, and I was only a mere freshman in high school. My brother was playing a tape of The Cure on his stereo when I ventured by and heard my very first song. The song was titled "Why can't I be you?" and let me tell you I was immediately taken aback by this song that was so unlike anything else I have ever heard. And being so unfamiliar with something I didn't quite understand, I naturally made fun of it.

Like a young child watching two teenagers indulge in a long passionate kiss, I was absolutely appalled at the idea of anything so mysterious and obscure. But the more I noticed . . . , the more curious I would become, eventually giving in and experiencing firsthand exactly what it was I was missing out on. In this case, it was the perfect form of music that seemed to actually breathe into me the power to move me, excite me, depress me, and even love.

The Cure's amazingly original blend of music contained not only rich and colorful melodies but also painfully dark and emotional lyrics that could sometimes leave me feeling emotionally vulnerable as the music overpowered my own senses. Their music can capture any emotion I have ever felt, and accurately play a song that would enhance that feeling several times over. I could fall in love twelve times in a row just by listening to a single album.

Now that I had my first taste of The Cure, I wanted it all. So the next   5
step was to try to buy a few more Cure albums. Well, it wasn't really a few
albums I bought, it was some T-shirts, and some postcards, a few books,
posters, buttons, patches, stickers, and eventually even a comic book.

Now that I owned just about everything with the name "Cure" on it, I
was slowly realizing that I was on my way to being a fanatic. Ahhh! Now I
don't know about you, but when I bear the word "fanatic" I automatically
think of an overweight woman kneeling down inside her run-down trailer
worshipping a bottle of Elvis sweat. This was definitely not where I wanted
to end up, so with a quick halt on my minor obsession with Robert Smith I
was in the clear.

After a few months (or was it years?) of being a semi-fanatic, I realized
I should focus my attention on what really got me started as a fan in the first
place, and that was the music. Coming full circle from music lover to
obsessed fan and back to music lover did take me quite awhile but I figure
I'm a better person for it. So now that you know what a rather deranged
person I must be, you should also be able to understand why this night was
so important to me.

Now back to the parking lot. So there I am sitting on the concrete walkway in front of a Blockbuster Music center resembling a homeless vagrant
with nothing better to do but sit and aimlessly daydream. Of course this
vagrant had a purpose for being there, and that was to get my tickets, go to
the concert, and get a quick glimpse of the Cure just before fainting.

While waiting in line—I was sixth—I occasionally looked around at all
the other fans, and tried to make eye contact with someone in order to
strike up a conversation. The only problem was that I kept looking away
out of simple shyness. After about three hours of almost total silence, this
guy about two spots in front of me commented on a bumper sticker that
was on the back of my girlfriend's car. Now you must understand that this
was no ordinary bland "I Love My Dog" kinda sticker. Oh no, this was a
tribute to the exceptionally great piece of work that only the very coolest of
the cool would recognize. Yes sir, I'm talking about one of the greatest
movies ever produced: Quentin Tarantino's own "Reservoir Dogs." And
this guy commented on its greatness! We immediately struck up an involved
conversation on movie directors and their films. After about thirty minutes
of just talking with one another, we were practically best friends. James, the
guy I just met, invited some of his friends from the front of the line over to
our little camp. Eventually our once straight and orderly line turned into a
small crowd of people all gathered together indulging in the wonderful art
of conversation. Man was this night turning out great!

After about an hour of talking, my brother thought it was a good idea   10
to go out for an always mood-ruining beer run. I personally didn't want
alcohol to be any part of this night, but my brother is twenty-one, and at
that age people are always so proud to display the fact that they can now

buy it legally. Shortly after his return, several participants began showing obvious signs of inebriation, and began acting like a couple of fifteen-year-olds at a high school ditching party.

Eventually those silly people wandered off to either pass out, or be alone, my brother being one of them. Feeling the silence from the sudden disappearance of about half our group, I decided to cruise over to my car and search for the ultimate Cure tape that I so proudly pieced together myself. After that puppy was found, I handed the tape over to this chap named Nathan who had a stereo system in his truck. Within seconds The Cure's music began joyously playing through the truck speakers miraculously transforming the scene into a miniature party that only the very best of friends attended. This was an absolutely beautiful moment. Unfortunately the long night did begin to take its toll on us, and the party slowly diminished to a few passed out people scattered throughout the cold concrete walkway. Those of us who weren't passed out could only wish we were, but instead lay awake dreaming of the concert to come.

"Hurry, hurry wake her up or she's gonna die!" Was the next thing I remember hearing. When I drearily looked around me to see what the commotion was about, I saw Nathan trying to pick up an almost lifeless looking body off the ground. Everyone there either started asking about what was going on, or telling each other what was going on. The story instantly flew my way that this unknown girl apparently drank an entire bottle of Robitussin, and passed out. Nathan was afraid that she was going to die unless she woke up immediately and start walking around the parking lot.

After about ten minutes of watching Dr. Nathan stumble around the dark lot with this mildly coherent girl in his grasp, I realized that this would be a perfect time to take a nice quiet stroll around the premises. Two of my newly found friends also felt this important need to take a walk, and quickly accompanied me. One of the two friends didn't want to just walk around aimlessly, so he set up a self-proclaimed mission to find my missing brother. After only a few minutes of walking, we turned around a dimly lit corner of the building, and to my surprise, found my brother sitting on the ground with his back against the wall. After that not much happened for the rest of the night, which wasn't that long, because morning was only about an hour away.

The next day rolled on by, and the sun quickly rose to savagely burn everyone there wearing the color black. This was pretty much everyone, with the exception of the Hootie and the Blowfish fans that began arriving around 9 o'clock. When they first arrived, a few of them slowly joined our scattered little line with a hint of caution on their faces. Constantly staring at our dark clothing and original dressing attire, the Hootie fans actually seemed a little fearful of us. One would think that these deprived people had never seen another human being wear something other than a T-shirt and jeans. After about fifteen minutes of watching the frightened Hooties quietly stand behind us, we noticed some of them turn around and leave altogether. These "dedicated" Hootie fans actually left the line, the parking lot, and the entire Blockbuster area just because of the way we looked. Those who didn't leave the line felt it would somehow be safer if they formed their own line on the other side of the door.

Now that our line was segregated into two parts, a mysterious ticket scalper approached the lot. This ticket scalper, who looked uncannily like Weird Al Yankovich, decided to hit the Cure line first. What this evil man proposed was to have the first four people in line buy tickets for him to re-sell, with an additional 25 bucks for their services. At first this may not seem like such a big deal, but this does pose a big problem for the rest of us in line. Ticket Master only lets each person purchase a maximum of four tickets. This is so a scalper can't buy all the tickets first, and then later sell them to others at an unreasonably high price. Not only is this conniving plan just plain unfair, but it would also diminish everyone else's chance of getting good seats. I, being only sixth in line, was beginning to get extremely uneasy about the thought of my fellow fans buying extra tickets for Mr. Evil Scalper and destroying our chance at getting decent seats for ourselves.

What had happened, to my surprise, was that every single person the scalper approached turned him down. Their reason: "Why should I sell out to you when you didn't even wait in line like the others?" The guy didn't even know who The Cure was. The only thing he wanted was money, and that's not what true fans are about.

After miserably failing with our line, the corrupt little scalper cruised on over to the Hootie line. This was a much different scenario. Whoever the devious scalper approached promptly sold out and bought however many tickets he wanted them to. The Cure group just defined fan loyalty, while the Hooties had something completely different to say. What that statement is, I'll probably never know.

11 o'clock eventually rolled around and the tickets finally went on sale! I was close to the front of the line, so my seats were positively excellent. I was going to be so close to the stage, I'd be able to see every expression on Robert's face. Regardless of where my seats were, I would have been com-pletely satisfied with sitting in the parking lot listening to the music, which is where I could have easily ended up, since the concert sold out in about ten minutes. You see, the whole idea of going to see The Cure live wasn't just to see them in person. It was to experience the bonding I felt with the people at Blockbuster, only this time it was going to be with several thousand other people. There is this indescribable feeling of unity with everyone else there that seems to say that no matter who you are, or what you look like, we're all going to simply have a great time. This is an absolutely beautiful experi-ence that I wish everyone to feel at least once.

CARTOONS IN AMERICA

Drawing by R. Chast. © 1996 The New Yorker Magazine, Inc.

CHAPTER 3: ACTIVITIES FOR DISCUSSION AND WRITING
Making Connections

1. Think of an American cultural event or experience in which you have participated recently. Brainstorm and write down as many details, including your feelings, as you can remember. Create a cluster or list of those details, in preparation for writing an essay about

the experience. Consider the following ideas as you prepare to write your essay:

a. What style of writing will you choose to best describe your experience? You may want to write a humorous, satirical piece like "Fear and Loathing . . ." or "Graceland." You may want to write a more serious documentary of the event, reporting on it in objective terms, as in "Death in the Mosh Pit" or "Rules of the Game: Rodeo."

b. Why did you attend or take part in the event or experience? Were you alone or with others? Who were they? You might like to describe how an event creates a community of like-minded fans, as student writer Chris Hernandez, the Cure fan, does.

c. What specific details and examples can you recall to describe your experience? What exactly did you see, hear, smell, touch, or taste?

d. What were your resulting feelings or thoughts about the event or experience—then and now? You may want to reserve your final comments for the conclusion of your essay, as Ehrlich did in "Rules of the Game: Rodeo." Instead, you might integrate your commentary throughout the text of your essay, as Roth did in "My Baseball Years."

2. Write a short poem on an American cultural event you have witnessed or participated in, following Saltman's "The Bungee Jumper" as an example. Whether you participated in the event or not, try to describe how it might feel to do so, as Saltman did in his poem.

3. Both Roth's "My Baseball Years" and McMurtry's "Kill 'Em! Crush 'Em! Eat 'Em Raw!" analyze some features of American society and comment directly on them. Compare the social commentary in both essays. What do both authors imply or suggest about the social significance of the events they describe? How are their perceptions of American society alike or different?

4. Compare "Graceland" and "Shopping" with Lawrence Shames's essay "The More Factor" in Chapter 5. How do "Graceland" and "Shopping" illustrate Shames's point about the American characteristic of always wanting more? Use examples and quotes from these three essays to support your discussion.

5. Many of the essays and other works in this chapter portray events or experiences that are inherently violent in nature. Choose two or three of these essays or poems, and discuss the influence of violence in entertainment or sports. Are Americans innately violent, as McMurtry suggests in his concept of a "warrior ethos"? If not,

what may cause outbreaks of violence or the apparent interest of Americans in violent behavior?

6. Write about a specific event or experience you witnessed, in which violence was a factor. What caused the violence to occur? Was violence an inherent part of the event (as in football) or introduced into the event from outside sources? Re-create the event as vividly as you can by using concrete, specific details.

POPULAR CULTURE IV
Media Madness: Sex, Violence, and Rock and Roll

America has a love–hate relationship with the various forms of popular media—leaning more heavily on the side of love. Americans prefer popular media—TV, movies, and music—over other forms of art. This chapter examines specific popular media, from critical reviews of movies and TV shows, to general debates and discussions regarding the various media outlets and their agendas. This chapter is designed to help you both to look more deeply into popular media than you may have before and to write analyses of your own favorite (or most hated) media events.

Former Senator Bob Dole leads off the chapter with "The U.S. Entertainment Industry Must Accept Responsibility for Its Work," a harsh condemnation of the current agenda of the American entertainment business. *Los Angeles Times* writers Elaine Dutka, Steve Hochman, Rick Dubrow, Daniel Howard Cerone, and Robert Welkos collaborated on "Sex, Violence, and Bob Dole," interviewing members of the entertainment industry who respond to Dole's charges. In Holly Brubach's "Rock and Roll Vaudeville," the author opines on the state of music videos in the early 1980s. We ask you to consider her impressions in terms of today's music videos. Jay McInerney casts his vote for best television comedy of all time in "Is *Seinfeld* the Best Comedy Ever?" In "TV, Freedom, and the Loss of Community," Bill McKibben argues that TV is corrupting our sense of community, among other things. Following that argument are three short film analyses and critical commentaries: First, David Kronke plunges into Hollywood's latest tidal wave of disaster films and the language that critics use to describe them in "Disasters Just Waiting to Happen." Second, Russell Gough finds the double message in *Jerry Maguire* very disconcerting in "On Ethics, Money, and the Ending of 'Maguire.'" Third, Wayne Rogers defends *Ghosts of Mississippi* from its critics in "'Ghosts' Reflects Noble Crusade." The next trio of pieces deals with American culture heroes Superman and John Wayne. Gary Engle asks, "What Makes Superman So

Darned American?" In "John Wayne's Body," Garry Wills shows why many Americans still consider Wayne the great American hero. Finally, student author Cynthia Paco explains her reasons for choosing Superman as her favorite American hero, in "Superman and the Duke: Duel between American Male Icons."

The U.S. Entertainment Industry Must Accept Responsibility for Its Work

Bob Dole

Bob Dole (born in Russell, Kansas, on July 22, 1923) was a premed student at the University of Kansas until 1943, when he was called up for service in World War II. Dole was a hero in the war, critically wounded by shrapnel as he led a charge against a German machine-gun position. Miraculously, he recovered, though he never regained use of his right arm and hand.

Dole went back to school after his recovery and graduated from Washburn University of Topeka (Kansas). In 1951, he ran on the Republican ticket and was elected to the Kansas state legislature. In 1968, Dole became a United States senator for the state of Kansas, and in 1984, he began his tenure as Senate majority leader. Dole ran for U.S. President in 1996 but was defeated by the incumbent Democratic President Bill Clinton. "The U.S. Entertainment Industry Must Accept Responsibility for Its Work" is a speech given by Dole at a Republican party fund-raiser in California in 1996.

Last month, during my announcement tour, I gave voice to concerns   1
held across this country about what is happening to our popular culture. I made what I thought was an obvious point, a point that worries countless American parents: that one of the greatest threats to American family values is the way our popular culture ridicules them. Our music, movies, television, and advertising regularly push the limits of decency, bombarding our children with destructive messages of casual violence and even more casual sex. And I concluded that we must hold Hollywood and the entire entertainment industry accountable for putting profit ahead of common decency.

So here I am in California—the home of the entertainment industry and to many of the people who shape our popular culture. And I'm asking for their help. I believe our country is crying out for leaders who will call us as a people to our better nature, not to profit from our weaknesses; who will bring back our confidence in the good, not play on our fears of life's dark corners. This is true for those of us who seek public office. And it is true for those who are blessed with the talent to lead America's vaunted entertainment industry.

LEADERS IN EXCELLENCE, AS WELL AS DEPRAVITY

Actors and producers, writers and directors, people of talent around the world dream of coming to Hollywood because if you are the best, this is where you are. Americans were pioneers in film and dominate worldwide competition today. The American entertainment industry is at the cutting edge of creative excellence, but also too often the leading edge of a culture becoming dangerously coarse.

I have two goals tonight. One is to make crystal clear to you the effect this industry has on America's children, in the hope that it will rise to their defense, and the other is to speak more broadly to America about the corporate executives who hide behind the lofty language of free speech in order to profit from the debasing of America.

There is often heard in Hollywood a kind of "aw shucks" response to   5
attempts to link societal effects with causes in the culture. It's the "we just make movies people want" response. I'll take that up in a minute.

But when they go to work tomorrow, when they sift through competing proposals for their time and their money, when they consider how badly they need the next job, I want the leaders of the entertainment industry to think about the influence they have on America's children.

Let there be no mistake: Televisions and movie screens, boom boxes and headsets are windows on the world for our children.

If you are too old, or too sophisticated, or too close to the problem, just ask a parent. What to some is art, to our children is a nightly news report on the world outside their limited experience. What to some is make-believe, to them is the "real skinny" on the adult world they are so eager to experience. Kids know firsthand what they see in their families, their schools, their immediate communities. But our popular culture shapes their view of the "real world." Our children believe those paintings in celluloid are reflections of reality. But I don't recognize America in much of what I see.

My voice and the rising voices of millions of other Americans who share this view represent more than the codgy old attempt of one generation to steal the fun of another. A line has been crossed—not just of taste, but of human dignity and decency. It is crossed every time sexual violence is given a catchy tune, when teen suicide is set to an appealing beat, when Hollywood's dream factories turn out nightmares of depravity.

STARK EXAMPLES OF WHERE 'A LINE HAS BEEN CROSSED'

You know what I mean. I mean *Natural Born Killers*, *True Romance*,   10
films that revel in mindless violence and loveless sex.

I'm talking about groups like Cannibal Corpse, Geto Boys and 2 Live Crew. About a culture business that makes money from "music" extolling the pleasures of raping, torturing, and mutilating women; from "songs" about killing policemen and rejecting law. The mainstreaming of deviancy must come to an end, but it will only stop when the leaders of the entertainment industry recognize and shoulder their responsibility.

Let me be clear: I am not saying that our growing social problems are entirely Hollywood's fault. They are not. People are responsible for their actions. Movies and music do not make children into murderers. But a numbing exposure to graphic violence and immorality does steal away innocence, smothering our instinct for outrage. We have reached the point where our popular culture threatens to undermine our character as a nation.

GIVING IN TO VICE IS NOT TOLERANCE

Let me be specific. One of the companies on the leading edge of coarseness and violence is Time Warner. It is a symbol of how much we have lost.

In the 1930s its corporate predecessor, Warner Brothers, made a series of movies, including *G-Men,* for the purpose of restoring "dignity and public confidence in the police." It made movies to help the war effort in the early 1940s. Its company slogan, put on a billboard across from the studio, was "Combining Good Citizenship with Good Picture Making."

Today Time Warner owns a company called Interscope Records, which   15
columnist John Leo called the "cultural equivalent of owning half the world's mustard gas factories." Ice-T of "Cop Killer" fame is one of Time Warner's "stars." I cannot bring myself to repeat the lyrics of some of the "music" Time Warner promotes.

But our children do. There is a difference between the description of evil through art, and the marketing of evil through commerce. I would like to ask the executives of Time Warner a question: Is this what you intended to accomplish with your careers? You have sold your souls, but must you debase our nation and threaten our children, as well?

Please do not answer that you are simply responding to the market. That is not true. In the movie business, as Michael Medved points out, the most profitable films are the ones most friendly to the family. Last year, the top five grossing films were the blockbusters *The Lion King, Forrest Gump, True Lies, The Santa Clause,* and *The Flintstones.* To put it in perspective, it has been reported that *The Lion King* made six times as much money as *Natural Born Killers.*

The corporate executives who dismiss my criticism should not misunderstand. Mine is not the objection of some tiny group of zealots or an ideological fringe. From inner-city mothers to suburban mothers to families in rural America—parents are afraid and growing angry.

There once was a time when parents felt the community of adults was on their side. Now they feel surrounded by forces assaulting their children and their code of values.

This is not a partisan matter. I am a conservative Republican, but I am   20 joined in this fight by moderates, independents, and liberal Democrats. Senator Bill Bradley [D.—N.J.] has spoken eloquently on this subject, as has Senator Paul Simon [D.—Ill.], who talks of our nation's "crisis of glamorized violence." And leaders of the entertainment industry are beginning to speak up, as well.

HOLLYWOOD MUST BE MADE TO UNDERSTAND

Mark Canton, the president of Universal Pictures, said, "Any smart business-person can see what we must do—make more 'PG'-rated films." He said, "Together . . . we can make the needed changes. If we don't, this decade will be noted in the history books as the embarrassing legacy of what began as a great art form. We will be labeled, 'the decline of an empire.'"

Change is possible—in Hollywood, and across the entertainment industry. There are few national priorities more urgent. I know that good and caring people work in this industry. If they are deaf to the concerns I have raised tonight, it must be because they do not fully understand what is at stake. But we must make them understand. We must make it clear that tolerance does not mean neutrality between love and cruelty, between peace and violence, between right and wrong. Ours is not a crusade for censorship, it is a call for good citizenship.

SUGGESTIONS FOR FURTHER STUDY

Key Words

The author uses language with which you may not be familiar. Find the following words in the paragraphs indicated, and explain their meanings in the context of the sentences in which the words appear. Consult a dictionary, as needed.

debasing (par. 4)
depravity (par. 9)
extolling (par. 11)

Topics for Discussion and Writing

1. Trace the development of Senator Dole's argument that "we must hold Hollywood and the entire entertainment industry accountable

for putting profit ahead of common decency" (par. 1). For example, what major reasons does he provide to argue that the entertainment industry is responsible for "the debasing of America" (par. 4)? What specific examples from films and music does he name? What reason or reasons does he offer to show that he is not crusading for censorship but calling instead for "good citizenship" (par. 22)?

2. What counterarguments might you offer to Senator Dole's condemnation of sex, violence, and depravity in the entertainment industry?

3. Research the background for this speech. Consider what elements in the 1996 presidential campaign made Senator Dole's speech relevant or necessary to his campaign.

4. Review the First Amendment to the United States Constitution, and compare it with several of Senator Dole's references to the right to free speech. In your opinion, does the entertainment industry sometimes "hide behind the lofty language of free speech in order to profit from the debasing of America" (par. 4), as Senator Dole says? Cite specific examples from articles you may have read in magazines and newspapers or viewed on television.

5. Write a brief essay or speech either rebutting or supporting Senator Dole's argument. Carefully craft a thesis statement that makes your opinion clear. Provide several major reasons why you do or do not agree with Senator Dole. Include specific examples from films, TV, music, the Internet, or other entertainment media to support your argument.

Sex, Violence, and Bob Dole

Elaine Dutka, Steve Hochman, Rick Dubrow, Daniel Howard Cerone, and Robert W. Welkos

*Elaine Dutka, Steve Hochman, Rick Dubrow, and Robert W. Welkos
are staff writers for* The Los Angeles Times. *Daniel Howard Cerone
currently writes for* TV Guide. *"Sex, Violence, and Bob Dole"
appeared in* The Los Angeles Times Calendar *on July 30, 1995.*

MADONNA

Singer–Actress; Partner, Maverick Music and Film

Other than a few rappers, no pop music figure has been subject to more   1
attacks concerning content and imagery in recent years than Madonna—
from her early Boy Toy persona to her use of religious iconography in the
1989 video "Like a Prayer" (which cost her a Pepsi sponsorship) to her
explicit 1992 book "Sex."

Looking back, does Madonna, 36, wonder if maybe she's gone a bit
too far?

"No," she says, sitting in the Hollywood headquarters of her Maverick
music and film company with her manager and partner, Freddy DeMann.
"All the reactions to everything I've done have only sort of further pointed
out what a narrow-minded society we live in and how people go through
life without questioning things."

It's a subject she teasingly addresses in her latest video, "Human
Nature," an intentionally silly whips 'n' leather scene built on the mantralike refrain "Express yourself, don't repress yourself."

"Like I say in my video, I have no regrets, if that's what you're asking,"   5
she says.

So anything goes? Not quite.

Says DeMann, 56: "We're certainly aware of what's morally correct
and what is not. However, after saying that, what is morally correct to me
might not be morally correct to someone else. . . . I happen to be very sensitive to child abuse or anything that is harmful to children."

Adds Madonna: "And Michael Jackson's record wouldn't have been
released by us without somebody going over the lyrics. . . . While on the one
hand, yes, I believe in freedom of speech and freedom of expression—my

God, I've been in the middle of a million wars on that!—I would feel really apprehensive about putting out an artist with lyrics degrading women or racist remarks or, like Freddy said, something I felt somehow was harmful to children."

DeMann, father of two daughters now in their early 20s, says: "Speaking for my children, I wanted them exposed to everything they see in life."

Madonna: "If you give them an enriching environment, they're going to   10
naturally choose things that are good. But so many parents don't want to take the responsibility. They'd rather eradicate all of [the things they don't like] so they don't have to be involved."

—Steve Hochman

OLIVER STONE

Director

In Sen. Bob Dole's attack on Hollywood violence, Oliver Stone's 1994 film "Natural Born Killers" was singled out as a prime offender. "A '90s form of McCarthyism," the director says.

"Dole isn't proposing censorship or passing legislation, but, then, neither did Joseph McCarthy," says the 48-year-old Stone, who is currently shooting a film about Richard Nixon and whose credits include "JFK" and the Oscar-winning "Platoon." "By creating a climate of paranoia, they create a chilling effect. Warner Bros. has backed away from 'dangerous' movies in the name of family films—the great equalizer. What are 'family films' but a euphemism for mediocrity?"

Even before Dole, Stone says, a lot of intelligent people missed the point.

" 'Natural Born Killers' was an audacious work, a very misunderstood film," he maintains. "It was technologically advanced—almost radical—for a mainstream picture and generated a storm of ugliness."

On the face of it, Stone acknowledges, the film—the satirical tale of a   15
murderous duo who became the media's darlings—was a violent one. But its "dazzling surface," he insists, was a commentary on our times.

"Dole called the movie depraved, but it was meant to reflect our depraved culture," Stone says. "By categorizing things, we are able to dismiss them. You don't want to listen to the message? Kill the messenger. That way you don't have to think."

Accusations of hypocrisy, the director says, were more distressing than Dole's political agenda.

"To be accused by colleagues and critics of creating an exploitation film, one that used violence instead of exposing it, upset me a lot," Stone says. "When all is said and done, Dole had a point. We all agree that on-screen violence debases our culture. We just disagree on the methods of preventing that . . . and on the proper methods of representation."

Contrary to public perception, the director says, "Natural Born Killers" took in more than $100 million worldwide—evidently striking a chord.

"Which is worse?" the director asks. "The sanitized violence we're fed   20
on TV that sidesteps the actual effect of violence—or 'Natural Born Killers,' which makes a pointed statement about the cheapening of human life?"

—Elaine Dutka

KENNY (BABYFACE) EDMONDS

Co-president of LaFace Records, Producer, Writer and Performer

Like most everyone else in the music industry, Kenny (Babyface) Edmonds is eagerly awaiting the reception of the debut album from the rap group Tha Dogg Pound. The release is expected to touch off controversy about gangsta rap on such a large scale that it could result in Time Warner's severing ties with Interscope, the company distributing the album.

But Edmonds isn't lining up with one side or the other.

"If [Time Warner's] corporate people feel they don't want to have Tha Dogg Pound record, that's their right," says the 37-year-old, a hugely successful producer and artist as well as co-head of LaFace Records (the home to TLC, Toni Braxton and others) with his partner, L. A. Reid.

"It's commendable for someone to walk away from dollars they know will come for moral reasons you feel that strong about," he says. But, he adds, "I don't think it's bad for whatever company picks it up. It's not like Tha Dogg Pound is wrong to say whatever they say on the record."

Still, he says: "If Tha Dogg Pound's record could suddenly be on   25
LaFace and I thought it wasn't representative of LaFace, I wouldn't want to be involved with it—but not because of what I think people would say," he says. "[Hard-core rap] is not something I would go after."

Edmonds has long been known for sexuality in his music—but he tries never to be crude about it.

"I try to be clever in being suggestive and not outright using foul language," he says. "We're not living in the day when 'The Sound of Music' is going to be a Top 10 record."

Recently married and hoping to have children, he says he would work hard to pass on strong family values.

"I'd monitor like crazy," he says, referring to what his children might want to hear or watch. "I would try to give my child a wide range of things to listen to but try to explain what it was. But you may have a child who just loves [gangsta-rap or other crude things]. Ain't nothing you can do about it."

—S. H.

MARIO VAN PEEBLES

Actor–Director

Though his R-rated "New Jack City" and "Posse" had their share of 30
violence, it wasn't until he made this spring's politically volatile "Panther"—about the Black Panther movement—that the Establishment took aim, says director Mario Van Peebles.

"Politics is war without bloodshed and, in a way, it's more threatening," Van Peebles says. "If blacks shoot each other in the 'hood, they'll put a rap soundtrack on it. Suggest that the FBI is in cahoots with the drug dealers and the conservative right takes out a two-page ad calling your movie a 'two-hour lie.'"

Van Peebles, 38, thinks films fall into two categories: those that chase an audience and those that lead.

"Some films make money, and some films make a difference," he says. "You have to have some moneymakers to continue to work—acting in "Highlander" enabled me to make "Panther." But, as a director, I want to have a point of view that's not digestible in the larger soup we're constantly fed. All of my movies cost under $10 million, so I had some artistic autonomy."

Technological change could bring more "Draconian restrictions"—or could open things up, Van Peebles says. "Using computers to digitally reproduce a crowd, for starters, reduces costs, and that might enable us to take more chances," he notes. "So could giving people—or phone companies or whatever—the means of production. Just as gunpowder brought down the feudal system, putting a killer weapon in the common man's hands could reduce the studios to banks."

Although filmmaking isn't "brain surgery," Van Peebles concedes, 35
images are important:

"I was in the Amazon and met a man who bought a TV and a VCR instead of sending his son to school. He was so proud to show us his "Die Hard" cassette. Dole or not, at some point we have to ask ourselves some questions: What have we exported? What does this say about us?"

—E. D.

MICHAEL STIPE

Rock Singer, Movie Producer

For Michael Stipe—a politically active rocker who has used his stardom to stump for such causes as Greenpeace, AIDS awareness and Bill Clinton's presidential campaign—deciding on the content of a music or film project is simple.

As a singer, he says, he has one goal. "I just set out to write great songs."

In his newer capacity as a film executive, with a development and production deal with New Line, it's not that different when deciding on projects he wants to do.

"I don't have the time or compunction or energy to spend time working   40
with people I don't respect or who I don't think are creative. I'm fortunate to be a position where I can make a living doing what I love."

If those two goals are met, he says, content and message take care of themselves.

"We set an example without intending to, really," says Stipe, 35. "There are just so many stupid paths you could take as a band, and we knew what we didn't want to go down. That turned into some sort of formula that said to people out there that it's possible to do what you want without compromise."

In R.E.M.'s case, the message is usually contained in the big picture, rather than in specific lyrics—which are often unintelligible. Stipe's legendary mumbling has, in fact, helped the band avoid having "Explicit Lyrics" stickers slapped on its albums.

"We hide the [expletives] pretty well," he says. "But they're there. Believe me, the kids know it."

He cites the song "Star Me Kitten" from the group's multimillion-   45
selling 1992 album "Automatic for the People." The word *star* is merely a substitute for the four-letter word of the lyrics.

While Stipe believes that young people are influenced by media figures, he rejects the notion that music or movies can be blamed for societal ills.

"Take Snoop Dogg," he says. "I'm not siding with him or his opinions, but to say that he's inspired a generation willing to shoot people down is ridiculous. The problem is much larger than that. You can't lay blame on a comic book if your kid's values are screwed up."

But he also believes that the conservative outcries are just a passing phase.

"I predict it's going to hit a high point at which Joe Grabasandwich will say, 'This is not representative of me and my ideas,'" he says. "I fully expect that will happen before the next election."

—S. H.

DAWN STEEL

Movie Producer

Dawn Steel released an eclectic slate of movies ranging from 50
"Ghostbusters II" to "Awakenings" when she ran Columbia Pictures from
1987 to 1990.

In her life as an independent producer, however, she's targeted material
she considers "spiritually uplifting." If "Cool Runnings," the story of a
Jamaican bobsled team, was a black "Rocky," she says, the upcoming
"Angus" is a teen-age "Rocky."

"Having a kid has affected the movies I'm drawn to—big time," says
Steel, 48, a partner in Atlas Entertainment who was the industry's first
female studio chief. "I don't want to make any pictures I'm embarrassed
about, not because they're turkeys but because they're morally offensive.
Still, it's unrealistic to expect Hollywood to give up violence altogether.
Balance, rather than avoidance, should be the goal."

Hollywood's propensity for violence is market-related, she says. "If
people didn't flock to movies that are overtly violent, I promise you we'd
stop making them. Why, then, are politicians picking on us and not the public? Because it's not strategically advantageous to target the voters."

Family films are in vogue because they, too, fill the seats. "Everyone can
go to them," Steel says, "and they eliminate the need for a baby-sitter."

Steel doesn't have the same concerns about sexual content, however.   55

"In fact, if it was up to me, there'd be *more* sex in pictures," she says.
"My next movie is a mushy love story about longing and touching rather
than the kind of sex that makes one uncomfortable. "Legends of the Fall"
was one of the first good love stories in a very long time."

For all its problems, Steel says, the U.S. film industry sets the standard:
"Movies are what America does better than anyone. The Japanese make
cars as well as we do. The Italians make clothes as well as we do. But, as
corny as it sounds, when I stand in back of a movie theater abroad, I'm
proud to be an American."

—E. D.

ALBERT AND ALLEN HUGHES

Movie Directors

Allen and Albert Hughes bolted onto the entertainment scene with
1993's critically acclaimed "Menace II Society"—a grim portrait of inner-
city life that cost $3 million and took in nearly 10 times that in domestic
box office. Their second effort, "Dead Presidents"—the story of a returning
Vietnam vet—is due in October.

Though Hollywood has its problems, the 23-year-old twins concede, some of its detractors are missing the mark.

"Just because I won't take my 4-year-old son to see "Die Hard" doesn't   60 mean it shouldn't be made. It's all about how you were raised," Allen says. "Our mother bought us Rambo toys, but we didn't go out and shoot anyone."

"We don't need anyone restricting art—that's America's outlet," Albert adds. "Meanwhile, there's no one regulating the dirt on the political front."

Still, movies *are* getting worse, the brothers say, with too many "blow-'em-ups" and too much "fast-food violence." On "Menace," they voluntarily cut some graphic scenes.

To bring people in, Albert says, more diversity is needed—and superstars could take the lead. "Greed is the problem," he maintains. "By signing on to a low-budget movie, the big actors help that project get off the ground."

The Motion Picture Assn. of America's rating board has thrown up obstacles too. On "Menace," major cuts were needed to avoid an NC-17 rating. In June, the board informed the brothers that they'd have to modify "Dead Presidents" to get an R.

"We referenced shots that appeared in other movies and printed frames   65 that were problematic," Albert recalls. "The board challenged us on specifics they'd let go in the past."

Allen offers a possible explanation: "Though we didn't want to pull the race card, it boils down to [a fear of] blacks with guns."

—*E. D.*

CHUCK NORRIS

Actor

Every Saturday night in the CBS series "Walker, Texas Ranger," Chuck Norris beats up the bad guys—and he makes no apologies for it.

"There's a difference between violence and action," says Norris, 55, a former martial-arts champion with a long list of feature films to his credit. Although "Walker" airs at 10 p.m., Norris designs his series for a family audience.

"Within my show, there's a certain moral structure," he says. "The good guy winds up winning, and families like to see that. My show is one of the few places a family can see the good guy coming out on top."

Norris, a staunch Republican, fumes over the recent attacks on   70 Hollywood. He's committed to reducing violence in society, he says, but he prefers to do it by his actions. He founded a program in Houston that has taught 1,600 inner-city children martial arts as an alternative to gangs and a means to raise self-esteem.

Norris laughs at the suggestion that young people see violence on the screen and then go commit violent acts.

"To say they watch TV programs and go out and commit an act of violence is so ludicrous. It's the pressure they deal with in society as a whole, and on the school ground, to get involved in gang activity."

—Daniel Howard Cerone

DAVID WESTIN

President, ABC Television Network Group

"The television industry, in all its various facets, is more conscious of the responsibilities that are placed on it than ever before," says David Westin, 43, who is in charge of all the network's divisions and program units. "Certainly it is an issue that has risen on a national agenda."

So Westin was especially frustrated by Dole's broadside. The broadcast networks, he believes, have been responsive by working with the creative community and by placing parental-advisory labels before programs in question, he says.

"In order for this dialogue in our country to really be constructive, and I think it could be, we need to get beyond reduction—instances of more or less violence—and get to how it's depicted and in what context," Westin says. "There is violence depicted in some of the great artworks of all time, and it's a more sophisticated and subtle discussion than simply more or less."

Westin says he uses his two daughters, 12 and 16, and his extended family in Michigan as public-taste barometers.

The important questions, he says, are "What's the context? To what end is violence used? And what's the moral of the story?"

A lack of context is why Westin sometimes has problems with the short spots networks use to advertise feature films, which often depict explosions or other violence—but with no context.

ABC's "NYPD Blue" has probably shown more naked body parts than any other series in network television history. Though Westin distinguishes between sex and nudity, he says "NYPD Blue" has fallen well within the realm of good taste when portraying sexual situations.

"There's a place for romance and sexual relations in adult drama on television," Westin says. "We can't program 22 hours of prime time designed exclusively for young children."

—D. H. C.

SIGOURNEY WEAVER

Actress

Sigourney Weaver has battled deadly space creatures in "Alien" and its sequels and has exuded sexuality in comedies such as "Ghostbusters."

Sex or violence, the actress says, can be an integral part of a story unfolding on the screen and in the characters an actress portrays. But what is disturbing about some of today's movies, Weaver says, is when they depict sex *and* violence.

"That is the most damaging thing about movies—combining sex and violence," says Weaver, 45. Now a producer—her company is called Goat Cay Productions—she doesn't want to see government censorship of films but, as the mother of a 5-year-old, Weaver is "most sensitive" to gratuitous violence.

"I have a little girl, but there is only stuff [at the movies] every two months that I'd ever take her to see," the actress says.

"I think a lot of the violence we see is unnecessary, but you can have big, roller-coaster movies," Weaver says. "I think director Jim Cameron ["True Lies," "Aliens"] did it with some of his films. No one actually gets hurt. You go for fantasy and the thrill of the situation. 85

"I meet children who have seen 'Alien' and 'Aliens' 400 times," she says. "What impact that will have on them, I don't know. You can say 'Alien' was a violent picture but it's really not. It's just horror.

"It's true, I blew some aliens away," she admits, "but they deserved it."

—*Robert W. Welkos*

BRETT BUTLER

Actress

Brett Butler thinks American television is probably worse than it's been, "but I can't isolate this to TV." Audiences and the political structure, she believes, are not exactly blameless either.

"Violence and instant, powerful sex are very compelling. The demand is there, and therefore the product is there," says the 37-year-old star of TV's "Grace Under Fire."

"But it's taking the place of more meaningful things. We're all guilty, and the audience is too." 90

In a clear reference to Sen. Bob Dole, Butler said she doesn't want to hear the attacks from "right-wing politicians who are trying to repeal the ban on assault weapons."

Is she satisfied with her life in show business?

"My life is not in the industry. I work in it. I go to meetings," she says. She's proud of her series, but when it's over, she adds, "I know that people won't come up to me at my table and say, 'Miss Butler, it's nice to know you.'"

Among the things she doesn't like in the industry is that "the entire time the show 'Roseanne' has been on the air, it's never been nominated for an Emmy [as best comedy series]. So something's wrong."

When it comes to sex and violence in entertainment, Butler says, "It's   95 the lack of other things that disturbs me more. Sex and violence have always been part of the world. It's the lack of characterization and dialogue that is the real problem.

"Television families can be moral and unified and just—and not be conventional," she says. "People need to re-evaluate what they say when they say 'family.'"

—R. D.

BUSHWICK BILL

Rap Singer

When Sen. Bob Dole named the Geto Boys among those he condemned for violent lyrics, the timing couldn't have been better for group member Bushwick Bill. He has a brand new solo album.

"I want to thank Bob Dole and all his lily-livered, [expletive]-talking politician homies for giving me more than $300,000 of free press," says the Houston-based rapper, 23. "I want to thank him for opening his mouth and sticking his foot in it so I could be heard."

This is actually the second time that controversy has given the Geto Boys some press. In 1990, Geffen Records refused to release a Geto Boys album because of what the company considered offensive lyrics. Rick Rubin's Def American company, which distributed the Geto Boys at the time, also left Geffen. But the publicity strengthened the group's standing as urban underdogs.

Bushwick has incorporated shots of himself burning "Dole for Presi-   100 dent" campaign signs into a new video for the song "Who's the Biggest?" That action, in turn, has brought further protest from Dole, who said he was saddened that Bushwick "reacted out of hatred."

"He says I incited this hatred," Bushwick says, "but he incited it. I have no hatred for people I don't know."

Those who believe that the violent images in his material are harmful, he says, are not giving his fans enough credit.

"I'm not trying to write raps for people in three-piece suits sitting behind big oak desks," he says. "I'm writing for people who can't speak for themselves and about things we see every day. My fans know to treat my lyrics like a T-bone steak—you know you can't chew on it unless you cut the fat off."

The father of two—with a third child on the way—intends to raise his kids in that same environment. He believes that by standing up to his critics he sets a good example. "I'd rather be hated for who I am than loved for who I am not. Straight up like that."

—*S. H.*

SUGGESTIONS FOR FURTHER STUDY

Language and Style

In this collection of commentaries on the entertainment industry's influence on American values, the writers include direct quotations from their interviewees, as well as their own interpretations of the interview's content. Discuss the use of vivid, figurative language and strongly stated opinion in the following excerpts. What *attitude* is expressed in them? What is their *effect*?

"Politics is war without bloodshed and, in a way, it's more threatening." (Mario Van Peebles, par. 31)

"What are 'family films' but a euphemism for mediocrity?" (Oliver Stone, par. 12)

"So many parents [would] rather eradicate all of [the things they don't like] so they don't have to be involved." (Madonna, par. 10)

"You can't lay blame on a comic book if your kid's values are screwed up." (Michael Stipe, par. 47)

Still, movies are getting worse, the brothers say, with too many "blow-'em-ups" and too much "fast-food violence." (Albert and Allen Hughes, par. 62)

"But you may have a child who just loves [gangsta-rap or other crude things]. Ain't nothing you can do about it." (Kenny Edmonds, par. 29)

"Violence and instant, powerful sex are very compelling. The demand is there, and therefore the product is there." (Brett Butler, par. 89)

"My fans know to treat my lyrics like a T-bone steak—you know you can't chew on it unless you cut the fat off." (Bushwick Bill, par. 103)

Topics for Discussion and Writing

1. Taken as a whole, what do these entertainment-industry spokespersons have to say about the influence of sex and violence in popular media?

2. What solutions do these same spokespersons offer to the problem that Senator Dole identified as "the debasing of America"? Do they agree or disagree with each other or with Senator Dole?

3. Discuss with other readers your perception of the entertainment industry's apparent emphasis on sex and violence in films, TV, and music. Consider, for example, whether our Constitution's Bill of Rights validates the entertainment industry's right to produce whatever sells.

4. Some critics of television consider the *V-chip,* a control device that enables parents to monitor what children watch, the answer to limiting sex and violence. Research the V-chip, and write a brief essay exploring its influence on what is accessible on TV for American viewers. Include in your essay your opinion about whether the V-chip is an adequate solution to the problem.

Rock and Roll Vaudeville

Holly Brubach

Holly Brubach (born in 1953) received her BA in English and History from Duke University. Brubach writes on fashion and dance for such publications as The New Yorker, Mademoiselle, Atlantic, *and the* New York Times Book Review.

The first video shown on MTV, or Music Television . . . was a song 1
called "Video Killed the Radio Star," by the Buggles. The title was wishful thinking, a prophecy that rock-and-roll singers who couldn't hold the camera's attention would go the way of silent-movie actors with cartoon-character voices. Anyone who took the lyrics at their word and assumed that this new form posed a threat to pure music had only to look at the video itself, which showed the Buggles in an airless, all-white TV studio, surrounded by a lot of futuristic-looking synthesizers and state-of-the-art equipment, lip-synching their hearts out. Every now and again a girl in a tight skirt and spike heels (all the women in music videos wear spike heels) wandered across the screen. That was it. Radio stars had nothing to fear here.

Since then music videos have come a long way, though not nearly far enough. Videos now play a large part in selling records, and singers are under pressure from their record companies to make videos, just as fifteen years ago they were obliged to go on tour. Even Dean Martin has gotten into the act, sitting poolside in his tuxedo and singing "Since I Met You Baby."

"Beat It," made in 1983, wasn't the first good video, but it may have been the first great one. Michael Jackson epitomizes the form at its best—intense and brief. "Beat It" is one of the few videos that actually improve on their songs, which is what a video ought to do, and the song is pretty good to begin with. But the music alone lacks the breakneck momentum that the video has. Where the song is merely agitated, the video is all worked up. The lyrics are about macho pride and territorial rights, and Jackson grunts and whoops between the lines, accompanying himself. We watch members of two rival gangs leave their hangouts, a sleazy luncheonette and a pool hall, and head for the scene of a fight, a warehouse loading dock. The video cuts back and forth from one gang to the other to Jackson. He stops by the luncheonette, slams the doors open—empty—does a little dance at the counter, a preview of what's to come, and then heads on out. The camera cuts pick up speed and the suspense builds until we finally arrive at the big number. When Jackson comes bouncing down a flight of stairs, snapping his fingers double time, breaking up a knife fight like an agent of divine intervention through dance, we feel like cheering. He parts the gangs, steps to the front, and bursts out dancing, and the tough guys fall in behind, in a finale that goes to show how much better a place the world would be if everybody danced.

"Beat It" was a breakthrough. Slick and well made, dramatic, concise, it showed everybody how good music videos could be and inspired a long line of imitations. Suddenly all the people on MTV were dancing, whether they could or not. There was "Uptown Girl," with Billy Joel and the Lockers, set in a garage. Stevie Nicks galumphed her way through "If Anyone Falls." A big finale was part of the formula. Donna Summer belted "She Works Hard for the Money" from a fire escape overlooking the street, where a squadron of waitresses, nurses, cleaning ladies, and lady cops rolled their hips and churned a dance routine in unison. Bob Giraldi, who directed "Beat It," went on to make Pat Benatar's "Love Is a Battlefield," another video with a miniature plot that culminates in a big dance finish. Benatar leaves home, in what looks like a small town in New Jersey, and rides the bus into Manhattan, where she walks 42nd Street and winds up a hooker—though you would think that she had joined a sorority: the other girls look on indulgently as she writes a letter to her little brother. The finale takes place in a bar, where a sinister-looking Latin type (Gary Chryst, formerly of the Joffrey Ballet) stares Benatar down and provokes her into dancing with him, to no real avail. Benatar is not what you would call a natural dancer. She's concentrating so hard that you can read the choreography as it crosses her mind: shimmy two three four, walk, walk, turn. . . .

Even Michael Jackson went on to plagiarize his own performance in "Beat It" with "Thriller," in which he leads a phalanx of dancing ghouls. Weird Al Yankovic has done a "Beat It" parody, called "Eat It," in which the tough guys wear Happy Face T-shirts and he reproduces Michael Jackson's moves, verbatim. ⁵

Aside from "Beat It" and its sequels, there is a certain sameness to music videos. Most are set in a new-wave never-never land, where logic and the law of gravity don't apply. Now that acid rock has given way to coke rock, the corresponding images have gone from psychedelic to surrealistic. A sequence of pictures or events that makes no apparent sense teases the viewer, who keeps watching, waiting for the piece that will explain the entire puzzle; the piece is usually missing. Rooms furnished with a single chair, long billowing curtains, corridors with no exit, empty swimming pools, forests of old gas pumps in the middle of the desert—these are standard features of the landscape, typically lit by a single bare bulb, or a full moon, or the sun's flat brightness.

The women are long-stemmed, with sexy bodies and baby faces. They wear lots of lipstick, leather clothes, and, when their clothes are off, lingerie that makes them look vaguely sadistic. The men are less attractive, but then they're the ones who write the songs.

The vast majority of videos look as if they had been directed by the same two or three people, all of whom you would guess to be seventeen-year-old boys. The screen is overrun with fantasies of wide-open spaces and wicked girls. Parents get their comeuppance. Everyone drives sexy cars—stretch limos, Chevy convertibles, and Thunderbirds. "I'm in love with a working girl," the Members sing, wearing sleeveless black leather jackets and jeans, as they guzzle champagne paid for by gorgeous, expensively dressed career women. In Huey Lewis and the News's "I Want a New Drug" Lewis falls for a pretty fan in the front row, thereby staging his fantasy of what it's like to be a rock-and-roll star and every groupie's fantasy of what could happen at a concert.

Compare these predominantly male notions of a good time with Cyndi Lauper's "Girls Just Want to Have Fun," a *Bye Bye Birdie*-style romp in which she dances up and down the street, sings on the phone to her friends, and throws a party in her room, and men begin to look like an awfully self-important, dull bunch. Whether or not girls just want to have fun, they appear to be the only ones who know how.

Videos divide fairly neatly into two broad categories. The first is perfor-   10 mances—either in a studio, where the director has more control and can devise some fancy effects with lights and cameras, or in concert, where the band is seen in its full glory, at the height of an adrenalin rush, in front of a sellout audience going wild. These are some of the dullest, most gratuitous videos on the screen, and they all tend to look alike, even when the monotonous frenzy of the performance is alleviated by intermittent glimpses of beautiful girls or exotic landscapes. Unfortunately, good singers are not necessarily interesting performers, and music videos consistently expose this in a way that concerts, which get by on being events, almost never do. Furthermore, there is probably nothing to redeem a concert video if you don't like the song in the first place. While Def Leppard, a heavy-metal band I am not fitted to appreciate, beats its music to a pulp, there is not much to look at, unless it's the drummer dressed in briefs made out of a Union Jack. The Scorpions sing "Rock You Like a Hurricane," a song that isn't bad, behind bars, surrounded by an audience. This scene, with the fans getting carried away and shaking the bars in time to the music, is intercut with images of girls in cages. The video ends with the girls and the band members lying down in glass boxes and the lids slamming shut. Despite its use of such loaded images, this video does not purport to mean anything.

Prince and David Bowie are better in concert situations. In "Little Red Corvette" Prince curls his upper lip and half-closes his eyes, coming on to the camera in closeup. This is the kind of shot that a lot of singers attempt but few carry off, and the ones who don't look ludicrous. (David Lee Roth, the lead singer for Van Halen, flexing his pelvis and crawling on all fours toward the camera, should have been saved from himself.) David Bowie, in "Modern Love," doesn't even acknowledge the camera, but he's riveting to watch and sexy without trying to be. With his hollow-cheeked, hungry look and his loose-jointed restlessness he captures the song's nervous energy.

Videos that aren't performances are referred to as "concept" videos, which may be giving a lot of directors the benefit of the doubt. Nearly all concept videos include shots of the singer singing, but they differ from performance videos in that there's something else going on and the goings-on dominate the video. Some concepts are better than others, and some are pretty obscure. You wonder, for instance, why there is a gymnast vaulting over and around video monitors on which Asia is seen singing "Only Time Will Tell." A lot of the weakest videos on MTV seem to be the work of so-called visual people who are careful not to let their minds get in the way of their creativity.

The more successful concept videos are those that are based, however loosely, on a plot: There are characters, a situation is established, and something happens. Bowie's "China Girl," a fairly straightforward love story, is a good example. One of the most common devices is to follow two parallel plots simultaneously, cutting from one to the other, until they come together in the final scene. Elton John's "That's Why They Call It the Blues" does this, keeping track of a boy in boot camp and his girl back home; in the end the sweethearts are reunited. In the Rolling Stones' "Undercover" the action alternates between a suburban rec room, where a teenage couple sits watching TV, and some Central American–looking country in the throes of violent revolution, where a truck drives into a cathedral and a man is marched onto a bridge and shot. These two stories converge in the rec room when the girl's parents walk in on her and her boyfriend making out: The father is wearing an army general's uniform. In the alternative version of this two-track plot the camera cuts from a story or a dramatic situation to the band playing and in the end the band steps into the plot. Even when there's a story to be told, it seems, rock bands insist on being the stars of their own videos.

The few exceptions are notable. Bruce Springsteen's "Atlantic City" serves as the soundtrack for a series of desolate black-and-white scenes in which no one, not even Springsteen, appears. One of the most inventive music videos to date is Barnes and Barnes's "Fish Heads," an offbeat, amusing, unpretentious sequence of events that dignifies a silly song ("You can ask fish heads anything you want to; They won't answer, they can't talk"). No description of these scenes of real fish heads dressed in miniature turtleneck sweaters, propped up in plush theater seats or gathered around a table at a birthday party, can do this bizarre gem justice. "Fish Heads" proves that imagination can take a video a long way, further than closeup shots of celebrity singers or an elaborate, high-budget production can.

Some videos are up to nothing more than entertainment, song-and-dance sales pitches to the camera. ABC, a band with a reputation for inventive video productions, is mastering this form: In "Look of Love" its members roam around a bright-colored fantasyland version of Central Park—steep rolling hills, bridges, and lampposts squeezed onto a tiny sound stage—with such ingenuous conviction that you expect Danny Kaye to turn up and join in.

After watching a lot of music videos, it's hard to escape the conclusions that no one has the nerve to say no to a rock-and-roll star and that most videos would be better if someone did. A lot of these people ought to be told that they're not irresistible, or that they can't dance, or that their concept is dumb. Culture Club, for instance, makes dopey videos that do its music, which is pleasant and intelligent, a disservice.

Good videos work for various reasons. Despite the conventions that exist already, there is no surefire formula, but the fact remains that dancing can make a video take off. This happens when the choreography is decent and well shot, the performance is good, and the images are edited according to the rhythm of the song. But it doesn't happen often enough. Judging from most music videos, you would think that dance on television hadn't come very far. Toni Basil is considered one of the best rock-and-roll choreographers. But her cheerleading routine in "Mickey" doesn't look any better than my memories of *Shindig* and *Hullabaloo*.

The mystery is why music videos aren't enlisting the best talents in dance today. We know that more interesting possibilities for choreography to rock music exist and that they are surprisingly varied, because we've seen them on stage, in works by Twyla Tharp, William Forsythe, Marta Renzi, Karole Armitage, and others. Twyla Tharp's choreography for *The Golden Section,* set to the marked rhythms of David Byrne's music, has a jittery lyricism. In *Love Songs,* at the Joffrey Ballet, William Forsythe lays bare the obsession and violence inherent in love relations, with highly dramatic choreography that alternates between tender gestures and brutal attacks, set to a score of songs by Aretha Franklin and Dionne Warwick. By comparison the choreography in music videos looks tame and stale.

If this new form is going to justify itself, it might well be by giving us dance performances that we can't see anywhere else. Though it looks to me as if there is more dancing in recent music videos, it's astonishing how slow directors have been to catch on to the thrill of watching somebody like Mick Jagger or Michael Jackson cut loose to a good song.

In "Going to a Go-Go" Mick Jagger makes a spectacle of himself, and it's the spectacle that is impossible to turn away from. You marvel at how he manages to look so magnificently peculiar and ridiculous. He slithers along, sticking his neck out, jerking his knees in a hyperactive, Egyptian-looking style of movement. It's hard to believe that anyone can be so completely uninhibited in front of an audience. Jagger furthers his songs by losing himself in his music.

Michael Jackson never lets go the way Mick Jagger does, but watching him is a more kinesthetic experience. The audience gets keyed up, waiting for the dancing that is his release. Unlike Fred Astaire or Peter Martins, Michael Jackson doesn't feign effortlessness. He has taken the concertgoer's urge to tap his foot in response to good music and the willpower it takes to keep that urge in check and magnified the tug-of-war between them, so that you can see it all over his body: This is the basis of his performance. When he can't contain the music inside him any longer, he blurts out the steps that have been building up for the past eight or sixteen bars.

It looks as if Michael Jackson has only ten or twelve steps in his repertory and the rest are variations on those. Even so, his ten steps are better than most dancers' whole vocabularies. One is a staccato kick, a chest-high punch with his foot. Another is a special way of snapping his fingers, with a sideways flick of the wrist, as if he were dealing cards. Another is a high-speed spin: He crosses his knees, wraps one foot around the other, and turns to unwind his legs. His dancing owes something to break dancing, robotics, and mime, but his style is more sophisticated than any of these.

Performances like his are all too rare. You tune in to MTV for a few minutes and you're still there two hours later, seduced by the rapid turnover into hoping that the next video will be a good one. It isn't long before you've grown weary of the innumerable scenes that feature a rock-and-roll singer lying on a psychiatrist's couch, intended as an excuse for the fantasies that follow. On the evidence of music videos, most people's wildest dreams come down to the same few basic themes—vanity, greed, debauchery, retaliation, and sex—and the forms they take are disappointingly similar.

SUGGESTIONS FOR FURTHER STUDY

Key Words

The author uses language with which you may not be familiar. Find the following words in the paragraphs indicated, and explain their meanings in the context of the sentences in which the words appear. Consult a dictionary, as needed.

galumphed (par. 4)
parody (par. 5)
gratuitous (par. 10)
ingenuous (par. 15)

kinesthetic (par. 21)
staccato (par. 22)
debauchery (par. 23)

Topics for Discussion and Writing

1. The author discusses MTV as a new form of entertainment. How does she describe this new form? What features of dance and song define it?

2. What are the author's major criticisms of MTV videos? In the videos she reviews, what aspects and features does the author think are effective, and which are ineffective? Notice that she frequently focuses on the dancing and choreography of the videos. On what other grounds does she criticize and judge MTV videos?

3. Do you agree or disagree with the author's criticisms of MTV videos? In what ways are your criteria for evaluating MTV videos similar or different from hers? Discuss your evaluations of MTV videos with other viewers, and compare your impressions.

4. Because this essay was published in the early 1980s, music and dance videos may have changed. What is your opinion of current MTV videos? What do you think is artistically effective or ineffective about them? If possible, compare a few contemporary MTV videos with the ones Brubach discusses in her essay.

5. Write a critical review of a video on MTV or other music-video channels. Discuss its success on the basis of criteria you establish for excellence. Or choose two or three videos featuring similar types of music (alternative, rap and hip-hop, rhythm and blues, country, rock and roll, etc.), and compare them according to criteria you establish for evaluation.

Is *Seinfeld* the Best Comedy Ever?

Jay McInerney

Jay McInerney has published several novels, including Bright Lights, Big City, Ransom, *and* The Last of the Savages. *This article appeared in* TV Guide, *July 1, 1996.*

In the beginning was *The Honeymooners*. Then *I Love Lucy*. It's about time to elect *Seinfeld* to the sitcom Hall of Fame. Now that half the shows on prime time bear a striking familial resemblance to the show about Jerry and his friends, it behooves us to honor this "Citizen Kane" of situation comedies, and to propose that it may be—as Ralph Kramden would say—the greatest.

I wish to go on record as saying that the first time I saw *Seinfeld* I predicted that it would die a quick and quiet death. Not because I didn't think it was great; I just thought it was way too good to be on TV. I thought they'd cancel it. Generally, if I like a new television show, it's quickly devoured by a midseason replacement. And *Seinfeld* seemed too weird to survive on the tube. Or rather, too much like real life, which is actually far more peculiar than life in sitcom land. It was also outrageously funny, the humor arising out of mundane situations of failed communication and everyday embarrassment, like being caught picking your nose by your new girlfriend. *Seinfeld* pays homage to the fact that embarrassment is funny. Men probably laughed louder than women at the episode in which Elaine discovered that her nipple was exposed on her Christmas card photo, while women presumably had a huge laugh when George was caught with his pants down after a dip in a cold swimming pool. This stuff happens to all of us. And it's funny—particularly when it happens to someone else. But who ever thought they'd put it on TV?

It's easy to forget after seven seasons just how strange *Seinfeld* seemed at first. Remember the show in which Jerry and George are trying to come up with an idea for a TV show to pitch to NBC? George suggests that they pitch a show about nothing: "no story, just talking." Kramer, on the other hand, proposes a story in which Jerry plays a circus manager. The characters will be circus freaks. "People love to watch freaks," says Kramer. Like the candy mint that is also a breath mint, *Seinfeld* is both of these things. It's a show about nothing in particular, which is to say, everyday life as we know it. And Jerry is the bemused ringmaster of a genuine freak show.

"We are all queer fish," F. Scott Fitzgerald once said. The revelation of *Seinfeld,* as distinct from most sitcoms, is that normal life is actually quite peculiar. Kramer, lurching around Jerry's apartment like a cross between Baby Huey and Frankenstein's monster, isn't the only freak; Newman, the Pillsbury Sourdoughboy, certainly qualifies. And George is neurotic enough to make Woody Allen seem positively serene and WASPy. I know people like this. But before *Seinfeld,* I don't recall seeing anyone like George or Elaine or even Jerry on TV.

Yankees owner George Steinbrenner, who will have a cameo on the   5 show next season, declared recently: "George Costanza is a nice guy." He was also quoted as saying, "This Seinfeld is the nicest young man." Steinbrenner is wrong as usual. One of the nicest things about *Seinfeld* is its portrayal of George and Jerry and Elaine in their not-so-niceness. Unlike your average sitcom protagonists, George and Jerry are not especially nice to the women they date, or even to sweet little old ladies, like the one who happens to have purchased the last loaf of rye bread from the bakery right before Jerry tries to buy one; Jerry knocks her over on the street and steals it. Mind you, he had a good reason, as we all do when we do something lousy. But let's not rob Jerry of his own obnoxious charm by calling him a nice guy. He'd sell Kramer down the river in a minute for a date with the buxom heiress to the O'Henry candy fortune. As would many of my closest friends. And George, in last month's season finale, doesn't see any harm in calling Marisa Tomei for a date just hours after learning that his fiancée has died.

As a New Yorker, I appreciate the fact that although it's filmed in L.A., *Seinfeld* actually has the lumpy texture of life in the city, the random looniness of the street, the idioms (Jerry waits *on* line, not in line) and speech inflections of Manhattan. But I don't necessarily expect the rest of the country to share my taste. Perhaps there is something inherently funny about the claustrophobia of New York apartment living, which is the backdrop that the three greatest sitcoms of all time—including *The Honeymooners* and *I Love Lucy*—have in common. (My only complaint vis-à-vis *Seinfeld's* authenticity is the fact that all the characters seem to own and drive cars. This is nuts. No New Yorker in his right mind drives a car around the city. We ride around in foul-smelling yellow limos with bad shocks.)

Car quibbles aside, I still don't know how Jerry Seinfeld and cocreator Larry David managed to talk the network into a show about nothing except a bunch of neurotic New Yorkers. But from my own experience with network types around the time *Seinfeld* was hatched, I can only assume they must have kidnapped an NBC executive and held him hostage until they got the green light. It presumably made things easier for the creators of subsequent quirky New York shows. *Mad About You?* No sweat—like *Seinfeld,* except Jerry and Elaine are married. *Friends? Seinfeld* with great-looking actors. *Caroline in the City?* Jerry Seinfeld with breasts.

However Jerry and Larry pitched the show, you have to hand it to the person who approved the *Seinfeld* pilot, which wasn't like *anything* on the tube. That's the most frightening concept in Hollywood—a genuine original.

SUGGESTIONS FOR FURTHER STUDY

Key Words

The author uses language with which you may not be familiar. Find the following words in the paragraphs indicated, and explain their meanings in the context of the sentences in which the words appear. Consult a dictionary, as needed.

behooves (par. 1)
protagonists (par. 5)
claustrophobia (par. 6)
vis-à-vis (par. 6)

Topics for Discussion and Writing

1. What is the author's argument for or against *Seinfeld* as the best comedy on television? What does he mean by calling *Seinfeld* the "'Citizen Kane' of situation comedies"? What features of the show does the author target for praise?

2. What is the tone of the reviewer's criticism? Is the reviewer speaking as an expert? Does he seem knowledgeable and broadly acquainted with other situation comedies? Do you have confidence in his criticism? Why or why not?

3. Choose a different situation comedy currently on TV, and write a brief critical review, specifying what aspects of the show you consider to indicate superior or inferior entertainment. Note that a review includes some discussion of the structure or format of the show, its characters, and its setting, as well as an evaluation of the show's appeal to an audience.

4. What criticism can you think of to contradict the reviewer of "Is *Seinfeld* the Best Comedy Ever?" What situation comedy might you suggest that would counter the claim that *Seinfeld* is the best?

Compare your suggestion with those of other viewers of the same TV show. Write an argument asserting that a different television situation comedy is equal to or better than *Seinfeld*. Or choose another genre of TV show, such as docudrama, documentary, mystery, or science fiction, and create an argument for one show as the best in that category.

TV, Freedom, and the Loss of Community

Bill McKibben

Bill McKibben (born in 1960) is a former staff writer for the New Yorker. *He authored two collections of essays:* The End of Nature *and* The Age of Missing Information, *from which "TV, Freedom, and the Loss of Community" was taken. He currently lives in the Adirondack Mountains.*

The light lasted a long time; as it was finally fading, I saw a pickup head down the part of the road visible from the ridge. I knew, by the size of the truck and the time of the day, who it was and what he'd been doing—he'd been working on an addition for a summer house down at the lake, working late, since it was the month with no bugs, no cold, and not much dark. Not many cars drive down the road—most of them I can identify. And my sense of the community is relatively shallow. A neighbor of mine used to man a nearby fire tower for the state. From the top he could look out and see the lake where he was born and grew up, and the long unnamed ridge where he learned to hunt whitetail deer. He could see the houses of four of his eight children, and his house, or at least the valley where it sat. His mother's house, too, and the old pastures where she ran a dairy, and the church where her funeral would take place the next year, a service led by his daughter who was a sometime lay preacher there. His whole world spread out before him. He'd been to New York City exactly once, to help someone move, and somehow he'd gotten his piled-high pickup onto the bus ramp at the Port Authority bus station, and all in all it wasn't quite worth it even for a hundred dollars a day. Why leave when you're as tied in as that—when you can see a puff of smoke and know by the location and the hour if it's so-and-so burning trash or a forest fire starting up. Why leave when you live in a place you can understand and that understands you. I was putting storm windows on the church last fall with a neighbor, an older man who'd lived here all his life. He suggested we crawl up into the belfry, where I'd never been. The boards up there were covered with carved initials, most of them dating from the 1920s or earlier—some were a hundred years old. My neighbor hadn't been up there for four or five decades, but he knew whom most of the initials belonged to and whether or not they'd ended up with the female initials carved next to them. "This is my brother's," he said. "And this is mine," he added, pointing to a "DA" carved before the Depression. He pulled a knife out of his pocket and added a fresh set, complete with the initials of his wife of fifty years.

"For most of human history," writes psychologist Paul Wachtel in his book *The Poverty of Affluence,* "people lived in tightly knit communities in which each individual had a specified place and in which there was a strong sense of shared fate. The sense of belonging, of being part of something larger than oneself, was an important source of comfort. In the face of the dangers and the terrifying mysteries that the lonely individual encountered, this sense of connectedness—along with one's religious faith, which often could hardly be separated from one's membership in the community—was for most people the main way of achieving some sense of security and the courage to go on."

"For most of human history." I have used this phrase before in this book, to try to make it clear just how different our moment is, just how much information we may be missing. In this case, the information is about "community." Many of us are used to living without strong community ties—we have friends, of course, and perhaps we're involved in the community, but we're essentially autonomous. (A 1990 survey found 72 percent of Americans didn't know their next-door neighbors.) We do our own work. We're able to pick up and move and start again. And this feels natural. It is, after all, how most modern Americans grew up. On occasion, though, we get small reminders of what a tighter community must have felt like. Camp, maybe, or senior year in high school. I can remember spring vacations when I was a teenager—the youth group from our suburban church would pile in a bus and head south for some week-long work project in a poor community. Twenty-four hours on a chartered Greyhound began to bring us together; after a week of working and eating and hanging out we had changed into a group. I can recall, too, the empty feeling when we got back to the church parking lot and our parents picked us up and we went back to the semi-isolation of suburbia—much of the fellow feeling just evaporated. I do not mean that a group of adolescents working together for a week somehow equaled a community—I do mean that there was something exhilarating about it. This twining together of lives, this intense though not always friendly communion. It seemed nearly natural. As if we were built to live that way.

"Community" is a vexed concept, of course—the ties that bind can bind too tight. Clearly, all over the world, people have felt as if they were liberating themselves when they moved to places where they could be anonymous, to the cities and suburbs that in the last seventy-five years have come to dominate the Western world. All of us have learned to luxuriate in privacy. But even just watching TV you can tell there's still a pull in the other direction, too. Fairfax Cable, on its Welcome Channel, promises you that "in our busy, fast-paced, congested world, cable TV is helping to revitalize the concept of community involvement"—in other words, they let each town in their service area operate a channel. Most of the time there is just a slow "crawl" of bulletin-board announcements, and it is from these that you can sense the desire and need for community, or at least for like-minded supportive people to whom you can turn in times of crisis. Thus there are innumerable announcements about hotlines and support groups—the child abuse hotline, the support group for mothers of AIDS patients, and so on. But in ordinary times how much community is there? The crawl of messages sheds some light on our aloneness, too. The town of Falls Church offers a service to all its elderly residents: a computer will call you at home once a day. If you don't answer, help is automatically summoned. Surely very few societies have ever needed such a thing—surely very few people lived such unaffiliated lives that their death could go unnoticed for a day.

Other functions nearly as central to the working of a community are automated, too, and sold. For just ninety-five cents a minute, the 900 phone lines allow you to hear "real people" trading "confessions." That is, you can pay someone to let you gossip, or to gossip to you; eliminating communities doesn't eliminate their mild vices—it just makes them duller and costlier. New York's Channel 13, perhaps the most cerebral television channel in America, recently installed a 900 line so that people could call up after *MacNeil/Lehrer* or *Frontline* and chat with five other viewers for up to an hour—again only ninety-five cents a minute. Singles bars, once the classic symptom of modern loneliness, now involve too much contact, according to TV producer Rick Rosner; instead, you can stay at home and watch Rosner's new boy-meets-girl show, *Personals,* or maybe *Studs,* or *Love Connection,* "where old-fashioned romance meets modern technology." On May 3, a man appeared on *Love Connection* to say that the hips of the woman he had dated the night before—a lady sitting there in full view of the nation—were too large.

It's true that you can go altogether too warm and trembly at the idea of community solidarity. (The actor Alec Baldwin, for instance, told *Hollywood Insider* how "refreshing" he had found the three days he spent in prison while researching his role in a film called *Miami Blues.* "A lot of the guys in the joint lift weights and stuff," he said. "I don't like to do that, and the other option was a lot of them box. It was the best workout I ever had. There's no cruising girls at the juice bar and all that other health-club crap.") The idea that, say, small towns hum with peace and good cheer is nonsense—both *Good Morning America* and *Larry King Live* featured one tough mother from Crystal Falls, Michigan, who had gone undercover for the local cops and busted twenty-three of her friends and neighbors for selling drugs. She was not some church lady baking pies—she was mean. (On *Larry King Live,* a man phoned in to explain that *he* would teach his kids "responsible drug use." "What are you going to do, one nostril at a time?"

5

she asked.) She left for the big city because her small-town neighbors were threatening to kill her kids.

Still, TV clearly understands that at least the *idea* of community ties attracts us. What is *Cheers* but an enclosed neighborhood where people depend on one another when the chips are down? "Where everybody knows your name. And they're always glad you came." No one moves away, no one can break up the kind of love that constantly makes jokes to keep from acknowledging that it is a kind of love. "You want to go where everybody knows your name." That's right—we do. That's why we loved *M*A*S*H*, another great TV community. But on TV, of course, while *you* know everybody's name, they've never heard of yours.

There were two Cosby episodes on this day, and both exploited this yearning. On the rerun, his former basketball coach returned to tell stories of Cliff as a youth; in the evening, it was his great-great-aunt, an ancient but vivacious lady who had taught the children of ex-slaves to read in a one-room schoolhouse. "Many of the kids had to walk twelve miles. And when they went home they had to work their farms till sundown." She told stories of the good old days, of courting, of chaperones—of community. The program ended in church, with Mavis Staples[1] singing a booming gospel number: "People, we all have to come together, 'cuz we need the strength and the power." It's a tribute to ties, to history—a meaningless tribute, of course, because it's all in the past tense and the present Cosbys need no one to help them lead their lives of muffled, appliance-swaddled affluence. The great-great-aunt represents a different, more primitive species, one that TV helped us "evolve" away from. But the sticky sentiment obviously plucks some strings in our hearts.

For every Hallmark card it mails to the idea of community, though, TV sends ten telegrams with the opposite meaning. Thinking of living in the same place your whole life, or even for a good long stretch of time? "No one said moving was easy. But Moving Means Moving Ahead," Allied Van Lines declares. When you reach your new home, of course, the TV will provide continuity—the same shows at the same times. And TV, of course, can provide you with people to be interested in, to gossip about—people you can take with you when you move. Not just TV actors but real-life people, like the Trumps.[2] An interesting episode of *Donahue* focused on gossips—he interviewed a woman who ceaselessly peeked out windows to find out what her neighbors were doing. The crowd was hostile—"Get a life," one lady shouted. But all day long the same demographic group that watches *Donahue* was watching, say, *Nine Broadcast Plaza,* where an "audiologist" and a "body language analyst" analyzed the videotape of an interview that Diane

---

[1]*Mavis Staples:* Gospel singer (b. 1940).
[2]*the Trumps:* Multimillionaire Donald Trump and his (now former) wife, Ivana.

Sawyer had conducted the day before with Marla Maples, the other woman in the Trump divorce. On the tape, Marla grew flustered and inarticulate when asked "Was it the best sex you ever had?" The audiologist, despite "two independent scientific instruments," could only classify her response as "inaudible," but the body language analyst thought she may have had better sex with someone else. Did she love Trump? Yes, the audiologist declared—definitely. "I don't think she knows what love is—she's too young," said the body language expert, who added that Maples was "lying through her teeth" when she said she didn't take cash from Donald. (*Nine Broadcast Plaza* also devoted time to a claim from Jessica Hahn that her encounter with Jim Bakker[3] involved "the *worst* sex I ever had.") That night on ABC, Sam Donaldson grilled Mr. Trump himself—he refused to talk about Marla or Ivana, but did say that his yacht was "the greatest yacht in the world," and that while he bought it for $24 million, he could *easily* sell it for $115 million. Who needs eccentric uncles or town characters when you've got the Trumps?

TV's real comment on community, though, is slyer and more potent   10 than the ones I've described so far. Day after day on sitcom after talk show after cartoon after drama, TV actively participates in the savaging of an old order it once helped set in stone. TV history, as I've said, goes back forty years. At its dawn are the shows like *Ozzie and Harriet,* synonyms for the way things were. Every day we can watch Ozzie and Harriet and Beaver and the 1950s. They represent a certain sort of community. It is no longer a physical community, really—it's faceless suburbia. But there is still some sense of shared values, albeit white and patriarchal and square and repressive values, values largely worthy of being overthrown. And TV joined gleefully in this overthrow. Every day, over and over, we relive the vanquishing of that order in the name of self-expression and human liberation and fun. The greatest story of the TV age is the transition from the fifties to the sixties—the demolition of the last ordered American "way of life." And TV tells us this story incessantly.

It begins by repeating the old shows, and therefore the old verities. On *Father Knows Best,* Bud is trying out for the football team. To win the notice of the coach, he decides to date his daughter, a sweet and innocent girl. He makes the team—but of course he doesn't feel right, so he talks to his dad. "You got what you wanted, but you feel you didn't get it fairly," Pop says gravely. "Now your conscience is bothering you, and you'll figure some way to straighten it out." Which he does, quitting the team and genuinely falling in love with her. That plot seems so exceptionally familiar and yet so distant—the football team as *the* pinnacle of boyish desire, the formal courtship of the girl complete with long talks with her father. And especially the act of

---

[3]*Jim Bakker:* Televangelist involved in sexual and financial scandals in 1987.

going to one's own parents to talk about such matters. It is resolutely unhip, almost as unhip as the *Leave It to Beaver* episode that begins with Eddie Haskell's[4] attempts to cheat on a history exam (a history exam with questions on Clemenceau[5] and Lloyd George[6]) and ends as, reformed, he dutifully recites the first six countries to ratify the League of Nations[7] charter.

But TV doesn't simply offer us these shows as relics—consciously and unconsciously it pokes fun at them. Consider this promo for Nick at Nite's nonstop week of *Donna Reed Show* reruns: "This is Donna Reed, super-competent mother of two and wife of one," says the announcer, who is imitating Robin Leach.[8] "She lives in this spectacular American dream house, which she cleans for her husband, the handsome Dr. Stone. Dinnertime at Chez Stone features meat, usually accompanied by potatoes, and takes place in this spotless dream kitchen!" Over pictures of people in gas masks and belching factories, the announcer says mockingly, "Out to save a world that's made a mess of things, she comes—mighty Hoover vacuum in hand. It's Donna Reed, sent from TV land to lead us politely into the new millennium."

Even when the ridicule is less explicit, it's fascinating to see the old order break down in front of your eyes each night. Over two hours on a single channel I watched a progression that began with Lucy trying desperately to get the handsome new teacher to ask her out on a date. Then came *That Girl!,* where Marlo Thomas was living alone in the city and faring well but still desperate for her parents to like her cooking. *Rhoda* was next—she went to the house of her husband's ex-wife to pick up the kids and they got roaring drunk. And finally, on *Phyllis,* most of the humor came from a cackling granny who loved to watch golf on TV because the golfers keep bending over and displaying their rear ends. In case you weren't getting the point, the shows were interspersed with ads like this one, for a videotape library of old TV shows: "The fifties—life seemed simpler then. Drive-ins, chrome-covered cars, and every Monday night there was *Lucy.*"

This account of our liberation from the repressive mores of society is not an entirely new story (as the Zeffirelli version of *Romeo and Juliet* on Showtime made clear), but never has it been told so ceaselessly. Steve Vai had a tune in heavy rotation this week on MTV—it showed a young boy with a prim old lady for a teacher. He jumps up on the desk to play his guitar for show-and-tell, and the kids, liberated by the beat, tear the room

---

[4]*Eddie Haskell:* Wally Cleaver's best friend on the 1950s *Leave It to Beaver* TV show.
[5]*Clemenceau:* Georges Clemenceau (1841–1929), French statesman and premier of France from 1906 to 1909 and 1917 to 1920.
[6]*Lloyd George:* Lloyd David George (1863–1945), English statesman and prime minister from 1916 to 1922.
[7]*The League of Nations:* Predecessor of the United Nations, established in 1920.
[8]*Robin Leach:* Host of popular 1980s TV show *Lifestyles of the Rich and Famous.*

apart; the teacher goes screaming out into the hall. The children watching this video have likely never known this sort of school, where learning is by rote and repression is the rule. And yet this mythical liberation survives, celebrated over and over again, as it will as long as the people who lived through that revolution are writing TV shows. (And perhaps as long as the people who grew up watching those shows are writing them, and so on forever.)

Any revolution this constant and thorough breeds counterrevolt, or at least uneasiness. Sometimes it is explicit, as with the conservatives who haunt the religious channels preaching "traditional family values." Usually, though, the uneasiness creeps in around the edges. On pay-per-view, *Field of Dreams* concerned a fellow, Ray Kinsella, who was a big wheel in the antiwar movement. He retains a fair amount of contempt for the stolid farmers around him, and his wife certainly stands up against book-burning bigots. But there's also a lot in the movie about his dad, who just wanted to play catch with him. Ray rejected all that family stuff in a huff and went off to college to protest—and now, more or less, he has to build a big stadium in the cornfield in order to get his daddy back. He'd gone a little bit too far back then.

Other, lesser movies made the same kind of point. HBO ran a fascinating film, *Irreconcilable Differences,* about a little girl who was suing her parents for divorce. They had been the classic sixties couple—they met as *semihippies* on a *road trip* across America. He'd written his thesis about *sexual overtones* in *early films.* She decided to dump her *Navy fiancé.* They drank *tequila* and listened to *James Taylor* and *cried* at films. And then they got rich writing movies on their own and fulfilled themselves in all sorts of predictable ways—divorces, bimbos, personal masseuses, big houses, fast cars. They were "doing their thing," "following their bliss." Which is why their daughter ends up explaining to the judge that she wants to go live with the Mexican housekeeper in her tiny bungalow, where the children sleep three to a bed. "I don't expect my mom to be a person who vacuums all day and bakes cookies for me when I get home from school, and I don't expect my dad to be some kind of real understanding person who wants to take me fishing all the time. But my mom and dad are just too mixed up for anyone to be around. I'm just a kid, and I don't know what I'm doing sometimes. But I think you should know better when you grow up." Their reconciliation comes in a cheap chain restaurant—utter normality as salvation.

This kind of reaction, though, has not really slowed the trend away from Ozzie and Harriet. One critic described Fox's *Married . . . With Children* as "antimatter to the Huxtables. . . . Sex (both the desire for and aversion to), the body at its grossest, stupidity, and familial contempt are the stuff of this sitcom." And yet, as CBS programmer Howard Stringer pointed out ruefully, more children were watching the program than any show on CBS. Therefore, he said, he was sending a signal to producers of comedy shows that they had an "open throttle" to change the network's image as "stuffy, stodgy, and old." He pointed with pride to an upcoming CBS pilot show that, in the words of the *Times,* "contains a provocative line of dialogue from a six-year-old girl." On *Leave It to Beaver,* Wally talks to his girlfriend on the phone in the living room in front of his parents and thinks nothing of it. By the *Brady Bunch,* the girls are giggling secretly over the princess phone. When you get to *One Day at a Time,* the children listen as the mother talks to *her* boyfriend, who's trying to persuade her to come to a South Pacific island. "He's probably down there starving for your body, lusting for your lips," the daughter says. And *One Day at a Time* is already in reruns.

Ozzie and Harriet represented all sorts of things that needed to be overthrown, or at least badly shaken up—a world where women did what housework remained, where children never talked back, where appearance and conformity counted above all, where black people never showed their faces, where sex was dirty or absent, where God lived in some church, where America was the only country that counted. The problem is only that the rebellion against this world never ended, never helped create a new and better order to take its place. The American Revolution tossed out the tyrants and set up something fresh; the French Revolution tossed out tyrants and then looked for more tyrants.

The main idea that emerges from the breakup of this Donna Reed order is "freedom," or, more accurately, not being told what to do. You can listen to, say, sociologist Robert Bellah when he says "personal freedom, autonomy, and independence are the highest values for Americans," or you can listen to the crowd on one of the morning talk shows responding to the plight of a man whose XXXtasy hard-core pornography television service has been shut down by an Alabama sheriff. "It's just total censorship," someone in the studio audience said. "It all comes down to the same thing—our rights." "Everyone out there has to make their own decisions." The same kind of sentiments attended the 2 Live Crew controversy, which came to a head while I was working on this book. The Crew, you will recall, was the rap group that specialized in lyrics like "Suck my dick, bitch, and make it puke," and which finally found one cooperative Florida district attorney who rose to the bait and charged them with obscenity. As Sara Rimer reported in the *Times,* Luther Campbell, the group's leader, said he was worried that the six jurors, who included three women over age sixty and only one black, might be "too old, too white, and too middle-class" to "understand" his music. His worry was misplaced; after they quickly acquitted him, one juror said, "I thought it would've been cute if we could of come out with the verdict like we were doing a rap song," and another said the content of the lyrics had not affected her: "Those were their songs. They were doing their poetry in song."

The jurors made the right decision—"You take away one freedom and   20
pretty soon they're all gone," said one, and he was telling the truth. So were
the people on *Nine Broadcast Plaza*—an Alabama sheriff shouldn't care
what folks watch on their TVs. Tolerance is an unqualified good—a world
where people of all races and all sexual orientations and both genders and
all political persuasions can express themselves openly is so manifestly
superior to the bigoted and repressed world we've leaving behind that they
hardly bear comparison. And it's probably even useful to have occasional
phenomena like 2 Live Crew to make us stand up once again and reassert
our principles.

But tolerance by itself can be a cover for moral laziness. In a world with
real and pressing problems, tolerance is merely a precondition for politics—
it is not itself a meaningful politics. We try to pretend that "liberation" is
enough because it's so much easier to eternally rebel: "Kicking against
social repression and moral vapidity—that's an activity rock 'n' roll has
managed to do better than virtually any other art or entertainment form,"
Rolling Stone boasted in a year-end editorial in 1990 that called for forming
a "bulwark against those who would gladly muzzle that spirit . . . of inso-
lent liberty." Good, fine, we all agree—"I thought it would've been cute if
we could of come out with the verdict like we were doing a rap song." But
is that all there is? Don't popular music and art and politics have a good
deal more to do than "kick against social repression and moral vapidity"?
Isn't it time to focus harder on substantive problems, such as, how do we
build a society that doesn't destroy the planet by its greed, and doesn't
ignore the weak and poor? (Not repress them, just ignore them.) I don't
mean a lot of sappy records and TV shows with syrupy messages about saving dolphins—I mean popular art that fulfills the old functions of popular
art, that reminds us of our connections with one another and with the
places we live. An art that reminds us that our own lives shouldn't merely
be free—that they should be of value to others, connected to others, and
that if our lives are like that they will become finer. That's what a culture is.
It's true that we don't need all the old "traditional" values—but as a society
we desperately need *values*.

We need them because a culture primarily obsessed with "tolerance" as
an end instead of a means is, finally, a selfish culture, a have-it-your-way
world. A place where nothing interferes with desire, the definition of a perfect consumer society. Listen to Jerry Della Femina, the adman, on *Good
Morning America*. He's excoriating Disney for not letting movie theaters
show commercials with its films: "Disney is blackmailing the movie theaters. . . . It should be up to the audience. If you hate the commercial, boo
and hiss. If you like the commercial, buy the product. That's the American
way." Or listen to Marion Berry, who in 1990 was still the mayor of
Washington but had already been indicted on any number of drug and

malfeasance charges. The city Democratic committee was voting that night on a motion urging him not to run for re-election. "It amounts to a type of censorship," he told one network. "Our country was founded on the principle that all men have a right to life, liberty, and the pursuit of happiness. And I intend to pursue my happiness as I see fit." By the late news, he's Daniel Webster[9]—"I'd rather die losing and stand on principle." The principle is that no one should tell him what to do, never mind that his city was a grotesque shambles. That night, a woman stood up at the Democratic meeting to defend Barry: "We're not Hitler, and we can't say who should run and who should not run." This is tolerance replacing sense.

Though it's rarely mentioned on TV, the gay community in the wake of the AIDS crisis provides an alternative example. Randy Shilts's eloquent history of the crisis, *And the Band Played On,* begins in San Francisco, where gay people had carved out an enclave of freedom and tolerance in a hostile world. And then, out of nowhere, not as a punishment but as a fact, came a strange disease. It was a proud community, and a community tolerant, even indulgent, of all desires. The emerging understanding of the disease—that it was sexually transmitted, that safety lay in limiting both partners and practices—conflicted sharply with that tolerant ethos. Some people said that closing the bathhouses or educating people about what not to stick where would force people back into the closet, interfere with their freedom, return them to the repressed past. But AIDS was a fact. Gradually—a little too gradually, probably—the gay community came as a group to embrace other values, to form a community that in its organized compassion, active caring, and political toughness is a model for every other community in America. A mature community. This does not mean that AIDS was a good thing. Far, far better it had never come, and life had gone on as before, and none of those tens of thousands had died. But AIDS was and is a fact, a shocking enough fact to force people into changing, into realizing that along with tolerance and liberation they now need commitment and selflessness.

By accepting the idea that we should never limit desire or choose from the options our material and spiritual liberations give us, we ignore similarly pressing facts about our larger community. In a different world perhaps we'd never need to limit our intake of goods, to slow down our consumption of resources, to stop and share with others. But we live in this world—a world approaching ecological disaster, riven by poverty. A world of limits, demanding choices. TV gives us infinite information about choice—it celebrates choice as a great blessing, which it is, and over the course of a single day it lays out a nearly infinite smorgasbord of options. As much as it loves choice, though, it doesn't actually believe in choosing. It

---

[9]*Daniel Webster:* American statesman and orator (1782–1852).

urges us to choose *everything*—this and this and this as well. And it does nothing to help us create the communities that might make wise choices possible on a scale large enough to make a difference.

In this case, the mountain is useful mostly as a vantage point. It can offer scant advice about how humans should organize their lives together, but it does provide an aerial view; from up here on the ridge I can recognize each home by its kitchen lights, and see how they stand in relation to one another. And now the all-night light has switched on at the volunteer fire department, whose noon siren was about the only mechanical sound I heard all day.

No need, as I said, to romanticize small towns—they can be home to vicious feud and rankling gossip and small-minded prejudice and all the other things that made leaving them appear so liberating. But there are a few things to be said for them, and the volunteer fire department is one. A house fire is no joke—when you take the state qualifying course, they show you film after film of houses exploding with folks inside, just as in *Backdraft*. On this day, in fact, the Washington TV stations were covering a tragedy in a tiny Pennsylvania village, Hustontown. The firemen had been called to clean out a well for an old lady. It smelled funny, but they thought there was just a dead animal down there. The first man down suddenly lost consciousness—two more jumped down to get him. All three died from some gas that had collected there. The fiancée of one of the men sobbed hysterically on the porch of a nearby house—she'd begged him not to go, but "he told me it was his duty as a volunteer firefighter." His duty, that is, to friends, neighbors, community.

It may be more sensible, by some utilitarian calculation, to entrust your safety to trained professionals and to insurance companies—more reliable, perhaps, and in places of a certain size clearly necessary. But it comes at a cost in information. Abstracted from others, you begin to believe in your own independence, forgetting that at some level you depend on everyone else and they depend on you, even if it's only to pay taxes. (Pretty soon you don't want to pay taxes anymore.) "We place a high value on being left alone, on not being interfered with," says Bellah, the sociologist who has interviewed hundreds of Americans. "The most important thing is to be able to take care of yourself. . . . It's illegitimate to depend on another human being." And this belief is so lonely—it's something human beings have never had to contend with before.

Public television was airing a Bill Moyers interview with a businessman named James Autry. A former brand manager for Colgate, he was trained at Benton & Bowles advertising agency and now worked as the publisher of *Better Homes & Gardens*. He is also a poet. He took Moyers back to the Mississippi town where he'd grown up—where his father, Reverend Autry, had spent his life preaching at the local church in the piney woods. The son had left the South in part to escape its ugly, intolerant side—he didn't want

25

all that went with being a white Southerner. But he'd started coming back in recent years—he sat in the graveyard next to his daddy's church and read a poem. "She was a McKinstry, and his mother was a Smith / And the listeners nod at what that combination will produce / Those generations to come of honesty or thievery / Of heathens or Christians / Of slovenly men or worthy. / Course his mother was a Sprayberry. . . . " And he said, this man who publishes *Better Homes & Gardens,* which convinces millions that a better home is a home with better furniture, "I've thought about my own sons. What are they connected to? Some house on Fifty-sixth Street in Des Moines? What will they remember?" And this is a hard and terrible question for all of us who grew up liberated.

SUGGESTIONS FOR FURTHER STUDY

Key Words

The author uses language with which you may not be familiar. Find the following words in the paragraphs indicated, and explain their meanings in the context of the sentences in which the words appear. Consult a dictionary, as needed.

autonomous (par. 3)
exhilarating (par. 3)
luxuriate (par. 4)
cerebral (par. 5)
audiologist (par. 9)
eccentric (par. 9)
savaging (par. 10)
pinnacle (par. 11)
mores (par. 14)
autonomy (par. 19)
bulwark (par. 21)
malfeasance (par. 22)
enclave (par. 23)
smorgasbord (par. 24)
utilitarian (par. 29)

Topics for Discussion and Writing

1. What, exactly, is the author's argument in this article? Is he defending television as a guardian of freedom or criticizing it for not defending freedom? Trace the author's argument paragraph by paragraph in this article, and summarize his thesis or point of view.

2. How does the author define *community*? What examples does he provide to show that TV does or does not create a sense of community?

3. Write a brief essay establishing your own point of view about whether television shows create or destroy a sense of community as defined by McKibben. Name specific shows that you think support your point of view.

Three Critical Movie Analyses

DISASTERS JUST WAITING TO HAPPEN

David Kronke

David Kronke is a senior writer at the Los Angeles Bureau of TV Guide Canada and a columnist for the New Times Los Angeles. *He has served as film critic at the* Dallas Times Herald *and the* Los Angeles Daily News. *His work has appeared in the* Los Angeles Times, Newsday, Premiere, US Magazine, Entertainment Weekly, Daily Variety, *and many other publications. His dog, Sister Teresa, won the 1993 George Herbert Walker Bush award for flea control. "Disasters Just Waiting to Happen" appeared in the* Los Angeles Times *on June 30, 1996.*

In the '70's, the celebrated and/or reviled Irwin Allen (*The Towering Inferno, The Poseidon Adventure, The Swarm, When Time Ran Out . . .*) and Jennings Lang (*Earthquake, Rollercoaster*, and the *Airport* sequels) made movies that gave us what we wanted—namely, havoc, and piles of it.

In their epics—these movies were always *way* too long, padded with scale-enhancing shots of helicopters taking off and landing and stately autos and limos cruising down boulevards and pulling up in front of luxury hotels—lots of things, mostly miniatures, were blown up and smashed into pieces. Lots of people, even big-named stars, died; lots of extras screamed; lots of effects weren't too special; lots of plotting and dialogue were inane beyond belief. *That* was entertainment.

The disaster genre was not particularly well-received in its day, but that may be because during this time Hollywood proved it was capable of making truly great films—Spielberg, Coppola, Altman, Lucas, Scorsese were all pretty much at the top of their game. Critics sniffed that these disaster films represented the worst that a cynical Hollywood had to offer, just the hollow spectacle of a cache of stars walking through two-dimensional roles under preposterous circumstances and frequent attempts at spurious "statements" amid the lavish destruction.

Today, of course, we're so used to that kind of filmmaking that these movies don't seem at all that crass. Their chief appeal now is as grandly unapologetic kitsch. In fact, the least interesting ones today feature the fewest number of "howler" lines, such as the blandly competent *Gray Lady Down*

(1978), about a crippled submarine, and *The Hindenburg* (1975), which tried to blend history, Nazis, and an ersatz mystery into mayhem with a message.

And as summer celluloid entertainments are devolving to the point where plot is actually considered a liability, the disaster flick is looking pretty darn good.

Twister has jump-started the genre, though in many instances it departs from the tried-and-true formula. It does have a quintessential disaster-movie line: "He's in it for the money, not the science!" It lacks, alas, the sprawling B-list cast (couldn't they have ditched one tornado sequence in order to pick up Chris Elliot, Loni Anderson, and Charlton Heston?) and the satisfying arbitrary body count (couldn't one of the "good" tornado chasers have gotten pasted?). The producers, moreover, refuse to concede that the movie is good, old-fashioned schlock, though *Twister* star Helen Hunt has roots in the genre: she played George Segal's daughter in *Rollercoaster,* about terror, of a sort, in the nation's amusement parks.

On the other hand, *Independence Day* . . . is being unabashedly touted by its writing-producing-directing team as a proud return to the disaster flicks of yesteryear. Sundry upcoming disaster flicks include *Titanic* (think *The Poseidon Adventure*), *Deep Impact* (*Meteor* redux), *Volcano* and *Dante's Peak* (*When Time Ran Out . . .* with computer graphics). Also on tap: *Daylight* (*Rollercoaster* meets *Earthquake* meets Stallone), *Turbulence* (or *Airport '97*), *The Flood,* and *Firestorm* (Allen made TV pics called *Flood* and *Fire!*).

Disaster flicks followed formulas as astringent as any genre, yet the *Grand Hotel*–inspired multi-character, multi-subplot format allowed film-makers to play around quite a bit within that framework. Invariably, nature was not kind to the inhabitants of a ship/building/city/island/planet, yet the crisis was just as inevitably exacerbated by some buffoonish technobureaucrat insisting that the danger was overstated. That character was routinely and gratifyingly proven wrong.

The hero was frequently an expert deeply ambivalent about his position within a technocracy, a formula which underscores the era's environmental awakening and burgeoning suspicion of technology. Characters generally occupied many of the rungs of the socioeconomic ladder, and were forced to bond together to defeat or survive the menace. In most of the best ones, the disaster struck early on, and the rest of the movie was given over to nail-biting survival scenes and residual horrors. Cheesier ones, such as Roger Corman's *Avalanche* (1978) and Samuel Z. Arkoff's *Meteor* (1979), spent the whole movie building up to a conflagration that meant only 10 or 15 minutes of costly action and special effects sequences.

Star-power was an overwhelming part of the genre, which probably kept half of the Screen Actors Guild afloat in the '70's. One can imagine Allen and Lang getting in endless "mine's bigger" debates—Allen had the better casts, but at least Lang had Sensurround! Frequently, imperiled stars included Charlton Heston (*Earthquake, Airport '75, Gray Lady Down*),

Paul Newman (*Towering Inferno, When Time Ran Out . . .*), George Kennedy (*Earthquake* and the *Airport* movies), Robert Wagner and Susan Blakely (both in *Towering Inferno* and *The Concorde—Airport '79*), Ernest Borgnine and Red Buttons (playing bickering buddies in both *Poseidon Adventure* and *When Time Ran Out . . .*), Michael Caine (*The Swarm, Beyond the Poseidon Adventure*), Jacqueline Bisset (*Airport, When Time Ran Out . . .*), Burgess Meredith (*Hindenburg, When Time Ran Out . . .*), and the venerable Henry Fonda, who lent the credence of his name to such junky productions as *Meteor, The Swarm,* and *Rollercoaster* while taking the teeniest of roles.

These also gave work to the likes of Charo, Avery Schreiber, Marjoe Gortner and O. J. Simpson, who rescued a kitty halfway through *Towering Inferno* and wasn't seen again until he handed it to Fred Astaire at film's end.

Flagrant stupidity on the behalf of characters, aside from the bozos who insisted against all evidence that there was no danger on the horizon, was also a hallmark. Perhaps the dumbest character in the genre is the fatuous journalist played by Blakely in *Concorde,* who, handed a scoop of breathtaking proportions, decides to tell her arms-dealing boyfriend (whom the scoop concerns) about it and goes on vacation to mull over whether or not to report it. He, of course, decides to dispatch a missile to destroy the plane she's traveling on.

Stupidity, on the other hand, helps make these things watchable. Today, a couple of the more enjoyable disaster movies are two of the silliest, which received the most excoriating reviews upon their release: Allen's *The Swarm* and *Beyond the Poseidon Adventure.*

The Swarm (1978), about a killer-bee attack stopped by Michael Caine, is the apotheosis of disaster idiocy. Even though killer-bees have, nearly twenty years later, become something of an issue in America, it's still impossible to take seriously lines like "Oh my God, bees, bees, millions of bees! . . . Oh my God! Oooooh!" and "What the bees did here they could do all over the Southwest and ultimately, and all over the country!" and "The honeybee is vital to America! Every year in America they pollinate $6 million worth of crops! If you kill the crops, you kill the people! *No,* General! No! There will be no airdrop until we know exactly what we are dropping! And where! And how! Excuse me!"

On the other hand, *Beyond the Poseidon Adventure* (1979) showed   15
how slick the genre had gotten. Its characters were perhaps the most insanely and calculatedly desperate, yet they weren't allowed to interact in any interesting way that didn't include gunfire. Yes, as if they weren't in danger of drowning or being blown up anyway, they were busy exerting their energies in trying to kill each other off.

And Allen, who had helped give birth to the genre, killed it off decisively with *When Time Ran Out . . .* (1980), a bloated leviathan about an island volcano eruption that concluded with such a cheesy special effect (someone apparently just painted individual frames of film) that the genre truly went out with a whimper, not a bang.

Of course, filmmakers today have much more sophisticated technology to make these scares much more convincing, and screenwriters haven't seemed to improve much in terms of unmotivated plotting or paper-thin characterizations. Which makes today a perfect time for the rebirth of all that rampant death.

PART 2: TRY SURVIVING THE DIALOGUE

Disaster flicks boast a healthy surplus of inane dialogue. Characters facing down (or denying the existence of) Armageddon and sketchily drawn romances are always good for laughably ponderous thoughts, and the genre boasts perhaps the greatest concentration of lines that are hilarious largely because their attempts at humor are so miserable.

Here are some of the most disastrous lines ever to leave a screenwriter's typewriter—so bad they wouldn't even sound good in Sensurround:

"Doug, I think you're overreacting. Now, I feel sorry for Will Giddings, but he'll be taken care of. But I'm not going to concern myself with a fire in a storage room down on 81 because it couldn't possibly concern us up here! Not in this building! Now, have somebody call me when the fire department arrives. In the meantime, get in your dinner jacket and come on up and enjoy the party! Now come on!"

> —*William Holden, upon learning an employee has been burnt beyond recognition, to Paul Newman in the* Towering Inferno

"Come on, Rosa, settle down, huh? Earthquakes bring out the worst in some guys, that's all."

> —*George Kennedy to Victoria Principal, who has just been nearly raped, in* Earthquake

"What more do you want of us? We come all this way, no thanks to you! We didn't ask you to fight for us, but dammit, don't fight against us! How many more sacrifices? How much more blood! How many more lives? . . . You want another life? Then take me!"

> —*Preacher Gene Hackman, berating God, in* The Poseidon Adventure

"You got me up to full-throttle and throw me into reverse—you could damage my engine."

> —*Pilot Dean Martin, not discussing an airplane, to paramour Jacqueline Bisset in* Airport

Michael Caine (after Sally Field unleashes a stream of insecure babble): "I think you're beautiful."
Field: "You do? You gonna kiss me now?"

Caine: "No."
Field: "Then let's just get the hell out of here."

—Beyond the Poseidon Adventure

"Coupla years ago, my son Andy started to complain about pains in his stomach. With all the junk food kids eat these days, I wasn't a bit surprised. . . . So I had a talk with Miriam and we decided to take him to a doctor. Just for an opinion, you understand. 'Appendicitis,' the doctor said. Miriam said, 'Let's wait until tomorrow; the pain will go away.' You know my Miriam, she can't stand the thought of an operation. That night when she went to bed she cried herself to sleep. I went to the boy's room and took him to the hospital. Six hours later, his appendix was out, he was feeling better, having ice cream. And Miriam? Miriam was all smiles. You get my point?"

—*Karl Malden to Sean Connery in* Meteor

"We've been fighting a losing battle against the insects for 15 years, but I never thought I'd see the final face-off in my lifetime. And I never thought it would be the bees. They've always been our friends."

—*Michael Caine in* The Swarm

George Segal (smiling beatifically while driving): "Ah, I was just thinking about the first Camel I smoked. It was a Camel. No filter."
Susan Strasberg: "You just passed the house."

—Rollercoaster

Stewardess (slightly disapprovingly): "Pilots are such *men*."
George Kennedy: "They don't call it a cockpit for nothing, honey."

—The Concorde—Airport '79

ON ETHICS, MONEY AND THE ENDING OF "MAGUIRE"

Russell Gough

Russell Gough is a professor of philosophy and ethics at Pepperdine University, where he teaches courses on sports ethics. He is the author of Character is Everything: Promoting Ethical Excellence in Sports. *"On Ethics, Money and the Ending of 'Maguire'" appeared in the* Los Angeles Times *in January 1997.*

Like most film critics in recent weeks, Kenneth Turan lauds Cameron   ₂₀
Crowe's box-office hit "Jerry Maguire" for its remarkable cast and for being
"fresh and refreshing due to Crowe's outstanding script" (Calendar, Dec. 13).

But, although the film's cast gives undeniably memorable performances,
Jerry Maguire is far from fresh and refreshing in one important respect: In
the end, it shows us only the money. It is precisely the film's gilded ending
that ultimately undermines what is otherwise a truly outstanding script.

First, a warning: If you haven't seen "Jerry Maguire" and don't want to
know how the story develops, don't read on.

For those who have seen it, it's important to keep in mind that "Jerry
Maguire" is more than a mere "romantic comedy," as it has been widely
billed. In its opening scenes, the title character—a greedy, egotistical and
emotionally shallow sports agent, embodied deftly by Tom Cruise—has an
abrupt crisis of conscience and, in an all-night writing frenzy, composes a
visionary and morally cathartic "mission statement." From this, it is clear
the film wants to be taken seriously as a morality play. And so I took it, and
with great admiration—until the movie's final feel-good sequence.

Don't misunderstand. I'm a romantic, and I have nothing against happy,
idealistic endings. And who couldn't use a healthy dose of cinematic happiness and idealism to ward off our world's cynical and pessimistic tendencies?

Problem is, "Jerry Maguire's" ending inspires with neither true happi-   ₂₅
ness nor idealism. Instead of offering a refreshing and sobering resolution to
Maguire's personal and moral struggles, the film ends up merely perpetuating one of Hollywood's most beguiling and destructive myths: that the road
to happiness and personal fulfillment is paved with money.

And that's why we should actually pity poor Dorothy (Renee Zellweger),
Maguire's helpmate. I predict that within six months, Jerry and Dorothy
would at best be in serious marital counseling and at worst would be unhappily divorced.

Why the bleak prophecy? Because "Jerry Maguire" offers no compelling
reasons to believe that, by movie's end, Maguire is still anything but "great
at friendship, bad at intimacy," not to mention greedy, egotistical and emotionally shallow. This isn't to say that Maguire doesn't experience some
growth, but we're given no convincing evidence that he has undergone any
meaningful and enduring change of character. Despite a few feeble attempts
to live up to the ideals of his much-vaunted "mission statement," he constantly reveals a winning-is-everything, money-hungry character right to the
last frame. Even in the film's feel-good ending.

Think about it: How confident can Dorothy be in Maguire's abrupt
change of heart and the depth of his commitment knowing that he came
running back to her only after—and immediately after—realizing that he
and his football player client would very soon be rolling in big-time money?
Isn't it more than a little ironic that the recovering greedaholic Maguire is
driven back to Dorothy on the wings of million-dollar emotion? And that

even before telling her that he loves her and can't live without her, he proclaims he had a very big day at the office? Can the idealistic Dorothy, who
repeatedly says that what she loves best about Maguire is the values he
expressed in his mission statement, really trust the words of a man who has
returned to her intoxicated by money that from the movie's onset has
plagued his mind and soul?

To the extent we are being asked to take "Jerry Maguire's" moral dimension seriously, allowing the win-at-all-costs Maguire in the end to have his
cake and eat it too takes away from the film. To argue that a more morally
realistic and sobering ending would have been the film's kiss of death at the
box office—i.e., that audiences would demand a happy ending in which his
client got his lucrative contract—is an insult not only to audiences but also
to the creativity and intelligence of talented script writers everywhere,
including Crowe.

"Jerry Maguire" shows us the money, all right. But by doing so, it dilutes   30
its moral imperative and falls short of being a truly great movie.

"GHOSTS" REFLECTS NOBLE CRUSADE

Wayne Rogers

*Wayne Rogers, who starred for many years in TV's M*A*S*H along-
side Alan Alda, plays equal-rights activist Morris Dees in* Ghosts of
Mississippi. *"'Ghosts' Reflects Noble Crusade" appeared in the* Los
Angeles Times *in January of 1997.*

I write with concern about a common thrust of Kenneth Turan's review
of Rob Reiner's "Ghosts of Mississippi" (Calendar, Dec. 20) and Sean
Mitchell's article (Sunday Calendar, Dec. 15).

The common complaint of the two pieces is that, in Turan's words,
"Ghosts" is "another movie in the 'Mississippi Burning' tradition that focuses
on a heroic white person getting his eyes opened about the nature of his
own and society's racism."

I believe that "Ghosts" fully reflects the noble crusade of Myrlie Evers
in demanding that the state of Mississippi finally bring her husband's killer
to justice. It reflects the nobility, dedication and self-sacrifice of Medgar
Evers and others in the perilous near-past to lead African Americans those
first steps toward the freedom and equality our Constitution promises.

However, it serves no purpose to demand that Hollywood ignore that there were many white Americans who tried to assist in that dangerous journey.

Mitchell says that Reiner's film "paints only part of the picture" in choosing to focus on the story of the white assistant district attorney in Jackson, Miss., Bobby DeLaughter, who "went the final mile" to win a conviction against Medgar Evers' killer, Byron De La Beckwith.   35

That reads like legitimate drama to me, and I know it to be legitimate history. Why do we have to erase the contributions of sympathetic whites in order to acknowledge the glorious accomplishments of brave blacks in this imperative struggle?

There is a distressing and even dangerous regression to racism on both sides of the color line these days. To ignore that we have come this short but significant distance together (at least to some extent) is to jeopardize the cooperation and trust we need on both sides to complete the journey.

Yes, it is discouraging that the story of Evers, his brave life and tragic death and enduring legacy, has not been told as the subject of its own film. That notwithstanding, it would appear that Turan's opinion ("even if the facts skew toward accurate, the nuances in 'Ghosts of Mississippi' are all wrong") is founded in some personal argument that facts should be used to make a different film, one whose "nuances" agree with his vision. To accuse Hollywood—and, by implication, "Ghosts"—of not telling the truth or "anything close to it" is a distortion of the facts. And to review the film you wanted it to be instead of the film that was made is to miss the point.

I was privileged, both as an actor and as someone concerned with these issues, to portray equal rights activist Morris Dees in "Ghosts of Mississippi." Dees, I believe, bears out my contention that there have been white hands as well as black on the oars. As the head of the Southern Poverty Law Center and as the head of Klan Watch in the South even back into the dark times of Jim Crow, Dees endangered his own life in dedicating it to an achievement of equality.

Indeed, his own offices were bombed, as one might expect of a man "watching" the klan in the period of its virulent control of a part of our country. He has brought successful lawsuits against hate groups in the South. And, yes, he truly did assist Mrs. Evers in bringing the prosecution of De La Beckwith once more before the judgment of his peers.   40

By the way, there were two hung juries in the murder trial of De La Beckwith in the '60s. In other words, in a time when vengeful anti-black hatreds held sway, four white Southern males in one trial and five in another had the courage to find a klan icon guilty of the murder of a black man.

Of course, the march to racial equality was led primarily by blacks, but why obliterate the history of the whites who encouraged and even joined in the trek? The view of the filmmakers that your writers seem to have missed is not the celebration of Medgar Evers' life and the idealization of him after his death but that in spite of the horrible injustices inflicted on blacks by a white-dominated community, progress has been made.

White people who had not been willing previously to stand against the tide were doing so and, in this case, had prevailed. That was the point of the film.

SUGGESTIONS FOR FURTHER STUDY

Key Words

The authors use language with which you may not be familiar. Find the following words in the paragraphs indicated, and explain their meanings in the context of the sentences in which the words appear. Consult a dictionary, as needed.

"Disasters Just Waiting to Happen"

> havoc (par. 1)
> inane (par. 2)
> cache (par. 3)
> preposterous (par. 3)
> spurious (par. 3)
> kitsch (par. 4)
> ersatz (par. 4)
> devolving (par. 5)
> quintessential (par. 6)
> schlock (par. 6)
> astringent (par. 8)
> exacerbated (par. 8)
> ambivalent (par. 9)
> burgeoning (par. 9)
> credence (par. 10)
> fatuous (par. 12)
> excoriating (par. 13)
> apotheosis (par. 14.)
> leviathan (par. 16)
> beatifically (par. 19)

"On Ethics, Money and the Ending of 'Maguire'"

> egotistical (par. 23)
> cathartic (par. 23)
> imperative (par. 30)

" 'Ghosts' Reflects Noble Crusade"
  perilous (par. 33)
  virulent (par. 40)
  obliterate (par. 42)

TOPICS FOR DISCUSSION AND WRITING

1. All of the articles in this section are film reviews, a genre with its own characteristics and general style. What do all these articles have in common? Look particularly at the content of the articles, the point of view of the reviewers, and the intended audience for the reviews. Discuss their commonalities, but also look at how they differ.

2. What purpose do you think film reviews serve? In what ways are they helpful to readers? Discuss with other readers what you think the purpose and effect of such reviews might be.

3. What are the major criticisms of these three reviewers? Do they focus on content, theme, acting, artistic integrity, or truthfulness? Do they attack or defend the films they review? Point to specific passages in each review to illustrate your discussion.

4. What is the appeal of disaster films, of feel-good films such as *Jerry Maguire,* or of films based on historical figures and events? Discuss this question with other filmgoers, and compare your answers.

5. These film reviews consider both recent and past films. If you have viewed any of the titles discussed in these articles, write a response to the critic, agreeing or disagreeing with the critic's evaluation.

6. If you have recently viewed a disaster film or a film based on a historical event, write a review of that film, giving your assessment of its effectiveness. Borrow some ideas from any of the reviews you have read in this collection.

What Makes Superman So Darned American?

Gary Engle

Gary Engle (born in 1947) is an associate professor of English at Cleveland State University. He authored The Grotesque Essence: Plays from the American Minstrel Style *(1978) and numerous magazine and journal articles.*

When I was young I spent a lot of time arguing with myself about who would win in a fight between John Wayne and Superman. On days when I wore my cowboy hat and cap guns, I knew the Duke would win because of his pronounced superiority in the all-important matter of swagger. There were days, though, when a frayed army blanket tied cape-fashion around my neck signalled a young man's need to believe there could be no end to the potency of his being. Then the Man of Steel was the odds-on favorite to knock the Duke for a cosmic loop. My greatest childhood problem was that the question could never be resolved because no such battle could ever take place. I mean, how would a fight start between the only two Americans who never started anything, who always fought only to defend their rights and the American way?

Now that I'm older and able to look with reason on the mysteries of childhood, I've finally resolved the dilemma. John Wayne was the best older brother any kid could ever hope to have, but he was no Superman.

Superman is *the* great American hero. We are a nation rich with legendary figures. But among the Davy Crocketts and Paul Bunyans and Mike Finks and Pecos Bills and all the rest who speak for various regional identities in the pantheon of American folklore, only Superman achieves truly mythic stature, interweaving a pattern of beliefs, literary conventions, and cultural traditions of the American people more powerfully and more accessibly than any other cultural symbol of the twentieth century, perhaps of any period in our history.

The core of the American myth in *Superman* consists of a few basic facts that remain unchanged throughout the infinitely varied ways in which the myth is told—facts with which everyone is familiar, however marginal their knowledge of the story. Superman is an orphan rocketed to Earth when his native planet Krypton explodes; he lands near Smallville and is adopted by Jonathan and Martha Kent, who inculcate in him their

American middle-class ethic; as an adult he migrates to Metropolis where he defends America—no, the world! no, the Universe!—from all evil and harm while playing a romantic game in which, as Clark Kent, he hopelessly pursues Lois Lane, who hopelessly pursues Superman, who remains aloof until such time as Lois proves worthy of him by falling in love with his feigned identity as a weakling. That's it. Every narrative thread in the mythology, each one of the thousands of plots in the fifty-year stream of comics and films and TV shows, all the tales involving the demigods of the Superman pantheon—Superboy, Supergirl, even Krypto the superdog—every single one reinforces by never contradicting this basic set of facts. That's the myth, and that's where one looks to understand America.

It is impossible to imagine Superman being as popular as he is and   5
speaking as deeply to the American character were he not an immigrant and an orphan. Immigration, of course, is the overwhelming fact in American history. Except for the Indians, all Americans have an immediate sense of their origins elsewhere. No nation on Earth has so deeply embedded in its social consciousness the imagery of passage from one social identity to another: the Mayflower of the New England separatists, the slave ships from Africa and the subsequent underground railroads toward freedom in the North, the sailing ships and steamers running shuttles across two oceans in the nineteenth century, the freedom airlifts in the twentieth. Somehow the picture just isn't complete without Superman's rocketship.

Like the peoples of the nation whose values he defends, Superman is an alien, but not just any alien. He's the consummate and totally uncompromised alien, an immigrant whose visible difference from the norm is underscored by his decision to wear a costume of bold primary colors so tight as to be his very skin. Moreover, Superman the alien is real. He stands out among the hosts of comic book characters (Batman is a good example) for whom the superhero role is like a mask assumed when needed, a costume worn over their real identities as normal Americans. Superman's powers—strength, mobility, x-ray vision and the like—are the comic-book equivalents of ethnic characteristics, and they protect and preserve the vitality of the foster community in which he lives in the same way that immigrant ethnicity has sustained American culture linguistically, artistically, economically, politically, and spiritually. The myth of Superman asserts with total confidence and a childlike innocence the value of the immigrant in American culture.

From this nation's beginnings Americans have looked for ways of coming to terms with the immigrant experience. This is why, for example, so much of American literature and popular culture deals with the theme of dislocation, generally focused in characters devoted or doomed to constant physical movement. Daniel Boone became an American legend in part as a result of apocryphal stories that he moved every time his neighbors got close enough for him to see the smoke of their cabin fires. James Fenimore

Cooper's Natty Bumppo spent the five long novels of the Leatherstocking saga drifting ever westward, like the pioneers who were his spiritual off-spring, from the Mohawk valley of upstate New York to the Great Plains where he died. Huck Finn sailed through the moral heart of America on a raft. Melville's Ishmael, Wister's Virginian, Shane, Gatsby, the entire Lost Generation, Steinbeck's Okies, Little Orphan Annie, a thousand fiddle-footed cowboy heroes of dime novels and films and television—all in motion, searching for the American dream or stubbornly refusing to give up their innocence by growing old, all symptomatic of a national sense of rootlessness stemming from an identity founded on the experience of immigration.

Individual mobility is an integral part of America's dreamwork. Is it any wonder, then, that our greatest hero can take to the air at will? Superman's ability to fly does more than place him in a tradition of mythic figures going back to the Greek messenger god Hermes or Zetes the flying Argonaut. It makes him an exemplar in the American dream. Take away a young man's wheels and you take away his manhood. Jack Kerouac and Charles Kuralt go on the road; William Least Heat Moon looks for himself in a van exploring the veins of America in its system of blue highways; legions of gray-haired retirees turn Air Stream trailers and Winnebagos into proof positive that you can, in the end, take it with you. On a human scale, the American need to keep moving suggests a neurotic aimlessness under the surface of adventure. But take the human restraints off, let Superman fly unencumbered when and wherever he will, and the meaning of mobility in the American consciousness begins to reveal itself. Superman's incredible speed allows him to be as close to everywhere at once as it is physically pos-sible to be. Displacement is, therefore, impossible. His sense of self is not dispersed by his life's migration but rather enhanced by all the universe that he is able to occupy. What American, whether an immigrant in spirit or in fact, could resist the appeal of one with such an ironclad immunity to the anxiety of dislocation?

In America, physical dislocation serves as a symbol of social and psy-chological movement. When our immigrant ancestors arrived on America's shores they hit the ground running, some to homestead on the Great Plains, others to claw their way up the socioeconomic ladder in coastal ghettos. Upward mobility, westward migration, Sunbelt relocation—the wisdom in America is that people don't, can't, mustn't end up where they begin. This belief has the moral force of religious doctrine. Thus the American identity is ordered around the psychological experience of forsaking or losing the past for the opportunity of reinventing oneself in the future. This makes the orphan a potent symbol of the American character. Orphans aren't merely free to reinvent themselves. They are obliged to do so.

When Superman reinvents himself, he becomes the bumbling Clark   10
Kent, a figure as immobile as Superman is mobile, as weak as his alter ego is

strong. Over the years commentators have been fond of stressing how Clark Kent provides an illusory image of wimpiness onto which children can project their insecurities about their own potential (and, hopefully, equally illusory) weaknesses. But I think the role of Clark Kent is far more complex than that.

During my childhood, Kent contributed nothing to my love for the Man of Steel. If left to contemplate him for too long, I found myself changing from cape back into cowboy hat and guns. John Wayne, at least, was no sissy that I could ever see. Of course, in all the Westerns that the Duke came to stand for in my mind, there were elements that left me as confused as the paradox between Kent and Superman. For example, I could never seem to figure out why cowboys so often fell in love when there were obviously better options: horses to ride, guns to shoot, outlaws to chase, and savages to kill. Even on the days when I became John Wayne, I could fall victim to a never-articulated anxiety about the potential for poor judgment in my cowboy heroes. Then, I generally drifted back into a worship of Superman. With him, at least, the mysterious communion of opposites was honest and on the surface of things.

What disturbed me as a child is what I now think makes the myth of Superman so appealing to an immigrant sensibility. The shape-shifting between Clark Kent and Superman is the means by which this mid-twentieth-century, urban story—like the pastoral, nineteenth-century Western before it—addresses in dramatic terms the theme of cultural assimilation.

At its most basic level, the Western was an imaginative record of the American experience of westward migration and settlement. By bringing the forces of civilization and savagery together on a mythical frontier, the Western addressed the problem of conflict between apparently mutually exclusive identities and explored options for negotiating between them. In terms that a boy could comprehend, the myth explored the dilemma of assimilation—marry the school marm and start wearing Eastern clothes or saddle up and drift further westward with the boys.

The Western was never a myth of stark moral simplicity. Pioneers fled civilization by migrating west, but their purpose in the wilderness was to rebuild civilization. So civilization was both good and bad, what Americans fled from and journeyed toward. A similar moral ambiguity rested at the heart of the wilderness. It was an Eden in which innocence could be achieved through spiritual rebirth, but it was also the anarchic force that most directly threatened the civilized values America wanted to impose on the frontier. So the dilemma arose: In negotiating between civilization and the wilderness, between the old order and the new, between the identity the pioneers carried with them from wherever they came and the identity they sought to invent, Americans faced an impossible choice. Either they pushed into the New World wilderness and forsook the ideals that motivated them or they clung to their origins and polluted Eden.

The myth of the Western responded to this dilemma by inventing the idea   15
of the frontier in which civilized ideals embodied in the institutions of family,
church, law, and education are revitalized by the virtues of savagery: independence, self-reliance, personal honor, sympathy with nature, and ethical uses
of violence. In effect, the mythical frontier represented an attempt to embody
the perfect degree of assimilation in which both the old and new identities
came together, if not in a single self-image, then at least in idealized relationships, like the symbolic marriage of reformed cowboy and displaced school
marm that ended Owen Wister's prototypical *The Virginian,* or the mystical
masculine bonding between representatives of an ascendant and a vanishing
America—Natty Bumppo and Chingachgook, the Lone Ranger and Tonto.
On the Western frontier, both the old and new identities equally mattered.

As powerful a myth as the Western was, however, there were certain
limits to its ability to speak directly to an increasingly common twentieth
century immigrant sensibility. First, it was pastoral. Its imagery of dusty
frontier towns and breathtaking mountainous desolation spoke most af-
fectingly to those who conceived of the American dream in terms of the
nineteenth-century immigrant experience of rural settlement. As the twentieth
century wore on, more immigrants were, like Superman, moving from rural
or small-town backgrounds to metropolitan environments. Moreover, the
Western was historical, often elegiacally so. Underlying the air of celebration in even the most epic and romantic of Westerns—the films of John
Ford, say, in which John Wayne stood tall for all that any good American
boy could ever want to be—was an awareness that the frontier was less a
place than a state of mind represented in historic terms by a fleeting
moment glimpsed imperfectly in the rapid wave of westward migration and
settlement. Implicitly, then, whatever balance of past and future identities
the frontier could offer was itself tenuous or illusory.

Twentieth-century immigrants, particularly the Eastern European Jews
who came to America after 1880 and who settled in the industrial and mer-
cantile centers of the Northeast—cities like Cleveland where Jerry Siegel
and Joe Shuster grew up and created Superman—could be entertained by
the Western, but they developed a separate literary tradition that addressed
the theme of assimilation in terms closer to their personal experience. In this
tradition issues were clear-cut: Clinging to an Old World identity meant isolation in ghettos, confrontation with a prejudiced mainstream culture,
second-class social status, and impoverishment. On the other hand, forsaking the past in favor of total absorption into the mainstream, while it could
result in socioeconomic progress, meant a loss of the religious, linguistic,
even culinary traditions that provided a foundation for psychological well-
being. Such loss was particularly tragic for the Jews because of the fundamental role played by history in Jewish culture.

Writers who worked in this tradition—Abraham Cahan, Daniel Fuchs,
Henry Roth, and Delmore Schwarz, among others—generally found little

reason to view the experience of assimilation with joy or optimism. Typical of the tradition was Cahan's early novel *Yekl,* on which Joan Micklin Silver's film *Hester Street* was based. A young married couple, Jake and Gitl, clash over his need to be absorbed as quickly as possible into the American main-stream and her obsessive preservation of their Russian–Jewish heritage. In symbolic terms, their confrontation is as simple as their choice of headgear—a derby for him, a babushka for her. That the story ends with their divorce, even in the context of their gradual movement toward mutual understanding of one another's point of view, suggests the divisive nature of the pressures at work in the immigrant communities.

Where the pressures were perhaps most keenly felt was in the schools. Educational theory of the period stressed the benefits of rapid assimilation. In the first decades of this century, for example, New York schools flatly rejected bilingual education—a common response to the plight of non-English-speaking immigrants even today—and there were conscientious efforts to indoctrinate the children of immigrants with American values, often at the expense of traditions within the ethnic community. What resulted was a generational rift in which children were openly embarrassed by and even contemptuous of their parents' values, setting a pattern in American life in which second-generation immigrants migrate psychologi-cally if not physically from their parents, leaving it up to the third genera-tion and beyond to rediscover their ethnic roots.

Under such circumstances, finding a believable and inspiring balance   20
between the old identity and the new, like that implicit in the myth of the frontier, was next to impossible. The images and characters that did emerge from the immigrant communities were often comic. Seen over and over in the fiction and popular theater of the day was the figure of the *yiddische Yankee,* a jingoistic optimist who spoke heavily accented American slang, talked baseball like an addict without understanding the game, and dressed like a Broadway dandy on a budget—in short, one who didn't understand America well enough to distinguish between image and substance and who paid for the mistake by becoming the butt of a style of comedy bordering on pathos. So engrained was this stereotype in popular culture that it echoes today in TV situation comedy.

Throughout American popular culture between 1880 and the Second World War the story was the same. Oxlike Swedish farmers, German brew-ers, Jewish merchants, corrupt Irish ward heelers, Italian gangsters—there was a parade of images that reflected in terms often comic, sometimes tragic, the humiliation, pain, and cultural insecurity of people in a state of transition. Even in the comics, a medium intimately connected with im-migrant culture, there simply was no image that presented a blending of identities in the assimilation process in a way that stressed pride, self-confidence, integrity, and psychological well-being. None, that is, until Superman.

The brilliant stroke in the conception of Superman—the sine qua non that makes the whole myth work—is the fact that he has two identities. The myth simply wouldn't work without Clark Kent, mild-mannered newspaper reporter and later, as the myth evolved, bland TV newsman. Adopting the white-bread image of a wimp is first and foremost a moral act for the Man of Steel. He does it to protect his parents from nefarious sorts who might use them to gain an edge over the powerful alien. Moreover, Kent adds to Superman's powers the moral guidance of a Smallville upbringing. It is Jonathan Kent, fans remember, who instructs the alien that his powers must always be used for good. Thus does the myth add a mainstream white Anglo-Saxon Protestant ingredient to the American stew. Clark Kent is the clearest stereotype of a self-effacing, hesitant, doubting, middle-class weakling ever invented. He is the epitome of visible invisibility, someone whose extraordinary ordinariness makes him disappear in a crowd. In a phrase, he is the consummate figure of total cultural assimilation, and significantly, he is not real. Implicit in this is the notion that mainstream cultural norms, however useful, are illusions.

Though a disguise, Kent is necessary for the myth to work. This uniquely American hero has two identities, one based on where he comes from in life's journey, one on where he is going. One is real, one an illusion, and both are necessary for the myth of balance in the assimilation process to be complete. Superman's powers make the hero capable of saving humanity; Kent's total immersion in the American heartland makes him want to do it. The result is an improvement on the Western: an optimistic myth of assimilation but with an urban, technocratic setting.

One must never underestimate the importance to a myth of the most minute elements which do not change over time and by which we recognize the story. Take Superman's cape, for example. When Joe Shuster inked the first Superman stories, in the early thirties when he was still a student at Cleveland's Glenville High School, Superman was strictly beefcake in tights, looking more like a circus acrobat than the ultimate Man of Steel. By June of 1938 when *Action Comics* no. 1 was issued, the image had been altered to include a cape, ostensibly to make flight easier to render in the pictures. But it wasn't the cape of Victorian melodrama and adventure fiction, the kind worn with a clasp around the neck. In fact, one is hard-pressed to find any precedent in popular culture for the kind of cape Superman wears. His emerges in a seamless line from either side of the front yoke of his tunic. It is a veritable growth from behind his pectorals and hangs, when he stands at ease, in a line that doesn't so much drape his shoulders as stand apart from them and echo their curve, like an angel's wings.

In light of this graphic detail, it seems hardly coincidental that [25] Superman's real, Kryptonic name is Kal-El, an apparent neologism by George Lowther, the author who novelized the comic strip in 1942. In

Hebrew, *el* can be both root and affix. As a root, it is the masculine singular word for God. Angels in Hebrew mythology are called *benei Elohim* (literally, sons of the Gods), or *Elyonim* (higher beings). As an affix, *el* is most often translated as "of God," as in the plenitude of Old Testament given names: Ishma-el, Dani-el, Ezeki-el, Samu-el, etc. It is also a common form for named angels in most Semitic mythologies: Israf-el, Aza-el, Uri-el, Yo-el, Rapha-el, Gabri-el and—the one perhaps most like Superman—Micha-el, the warrior angel and Satan's principal adversary.

The morpheme *Kal* bears a linguistic relation to two Hebrew roots. The first, *kal*, means "with lightness" or "swiftness" (faster than a speeding bullet in Hebrew?). It also bears a connection to the root *hal*, where *h* is the guttural *ch* of *chutzpah*. *Hal* translates roughly as "everything" or "all." *Kal-el*, then, can be read as "all that is God," or perhaps more in the spirit of the myth of Superman, "all that God is." And while we're at it, *Kent* is a form of the Hebrew *kana*. In its *k-n-t* form, the word appears in the Bible, meaning "I have found a son."

I'm suggesting that Superman raises the American immigrant experience to the level of religious myth. And why not? He's not just some immigrant from across the waters like all our ancestors, but a real alien, an extraterrestrial, a visitor from heaven if you will, which fact lends an element of the supernatural to the myth. America has no national religious icons nor any pilgrimage shrines. The idea of a patron saint is ludicrous in a nation whose Founding Fathers wrote into the founding documents the fundamental if not eternal separation of church and state. America, though, is pretty much as religious as other industrialized countries. It's just that our tradition of religious diversity precludes the nation's religious character from being embodied in objects or persons recognizably religious, for such are immediately identified by their attachment to specific sectarian traditions and thus contradict the eclecticism of the American religious spirit.

In America, cultural icons that manage to tap the national religious spirit are of necessity secular on the surface and sufficiently generalized to incorporate the diversity of American religious traditions. Superman doesn't have to be seen as an angel to be appreciated, but in the absence of a tradition of national religious iconography, he can serve as a safe, nonsectarian focus for essentially religious sentiments, particularly among the young.

In the last analysis, Superman is like nothing so much as an American boy's fantasy of a messiah. He is the male, heroic match for the Statue of Liberty, come like an immigrant from heaven to deliver humankind by sacrificing himself in the service of others. He protects the weak and defends truth and justice and all the other moral virtues inherent in the Judeo-Christian tradition, remaining ever vigilant and ever chaste. What purer or stronger vision could there possibly be for a child? Now that I put my mind to it, I see that John Wayne never had a chance.

SUGGESTIONS FOR FURTHER STUDY

Key Words

The author uses language with which you may not be familiar. Find the following words in the paragraphs indicated, and explain their meanings in the context of the sentences in which the words appear. Consult a dictionary, as needed.

consummate (par. 6)
apocryphal (par. 7)
jingoistic (par. 20)
sine qua non (par. 22)
neologism (par. 25)

Topics for Discussion and Writing

1. In this essay, the author argues that "Superman is *the* great American hero." What reasons does he give to develop his argument? One way to trace the argument's development is to look at the topic sentences of paragraphs to see how they are organized and grouped together to form parts of the whole essay. Examine the essay paragraph by paragraph, topic by topic, and write down a brief outline of the argument as it is developed.

2. Discuss the author's style of writing, particularly noting his combination of both formal criticism and informal humor. Where in this essay is he especially serious and formal? Where is he particularly informal or humorous?

3. Part of the author's style is characterized by scholarly and historical allusions or references to people and events that make up part of Americans' cultural heritage. For example, he refers to Daniel Boone, non–English-speaking immigrants and the immigrant culture, and the U.S. Founding Fathers in their historical contexts. He also cites writers such as James Fenimore Cooper, Jack Kerouac, and Delmore Schwarz, who wrote about the American character. Find other such references in the essay, and discuss their relevance to understanding Superman as the quintessential American hero.

4. Why does the author choose Superman over his first hero, John Wayne, as *the* American hero? What admirable qualities do the typical John Wayne characters have, as portrayed in his films? What qualities does Superman have that John Wayne's characters lack?

5. If you are not familiar with John Wayne movies, try to see a typical feature film starring one of his Western heroes, such as *Rio Bravo,*

She Wore a Yellow Ribbon, or *The Shootist.* These films are often featured on classic movie channels on television. Compare what you observe about the John Wayne portrayal of the Western hero with the author's comments in this essay.

6. Compare Engle's essay on John Wayne versus Superman with the review of Jerry Seinfeld in "Is *Seinfeld* the Best Comedy Ever?" In what way do both readings focus on the same features to praise or to criticize?

7. This essay is written by a man about two male heroes. Do girls and women hold Superman in as high regard as boys or men do? Why or why not? Are there female figures from real life or legend who match the influence and popularity of either John Wayne or Superman? Discuss these questions, and consider the possibility of gender bias in the nomination of Superman and John Wayne as American heroes.

8. Write a brief essay or journal entry about Superman's qualifications as the essential American hero, either agreeing or disagreeing with Engle. If you disagree, propose another historical or legendary figure as your candidate for American hero.

John Wayne's Body

Garry Wills

Garry Wills teaches history at Northwestern University and lives in Evanston, Illinois. He has written nineteen books on American history and culture, including Certain Trumpets *and* Lincoln at Gettysburg, *for which he won the Pulitzer Prize. The following selection, "John Wayne's Body," which first appeared in the* New Yorker *magazine on August 19, 1996, is excerpted from his latest book,* John Wayne's America.*

In 1993, Harris pollsters asked a representative sample of more than a thousand Americans "Who is your favorite star?" John Wayne came in second, though he had been dead for fourteen years. He was second again in 1994. Then, in 1995, he was No. 1, getting more than twice the number of votes that put Mel Gibson in the third spot and nearly six times the number of Paul Newman's votes. Reversing the laws of optics, Wayne seems to become larger the farther away he gets. In the 1995 list, only one other dead actor was included. Here is the list.

1. John Wayne
2. Clint Eastwood
3. Mel Gibson
4. Denzel Washington
5. Kevin Costner
6. Tom Hanks
7. Sylvester Stallone
8. Steven Seagal
9. Arnold Schwarzenegger
10. Robert De Niro
10. Robert Redford
11. Harrison Ford
11. Clark Gable
11. Paul Newman
11. Brad Pitt

The choice for No. 1 in 1993 and 1994 was Clint Eastwood, and he is the star who has ranked second to Wayne in box-office appeal over the years. For twenty-five out of twenty-six years—from 1949 to 1974—Wayne made the top ten in distributors' lists of stars with commercial appeal, and was in the top four nineteen times. Eastwood has been in the top ten on the same lists twenty-one times, and in the top four fifteen times. No other actor approaches these two. But does anyone expect Eastwood to be America's favorite star a decade and a half after his death? Wayne's durability is astonishing.

Much of the critical literature on movies ignores this phenomenon. College professors cannot disguise their skepticism when I say that Wayne is the leading star of all time. "Stagecoach" and "The Searchers" are the only Wayne pictures that regularly get attention from serious film critics, and those two are not characteristic Wayne films. Neither of them was as influential in creating Wayne's popularity as, say, "Sands of Iwo Jima."

Intellectuals have others tastes in cult objects. Their pop icons are figures enlarged by special dooms. These idols tend to die young or violently—Rudolph Valentino, Jean Harlow, James Dean, John Lennon. They fascinate by their vulnerabilities (Elvis, Marilyn) or by their defiance of social norms (Madonna, Michael Jackson). To their devotees, they are murkily erotic objects—Marilyn Monroe to Normal Mailer, Elizabeth Taylor to Camille Paglia, Jacqueline Onassis to Wayne Koestenbaum. Cult figures who live on into old age become caricatures of their rebellious selves—the immured Garbo, Dietrich trickily lit like youth's ghost, Bette Davis imitating her imitators. Or they actually become the things that symbolized them—Charlie swallowed up in the Tramp, Groucho in perpetual ambush behind his eyebrows, Barrymore's profile lingering in the air like the grin of an alcoholic Cheshire cat.

John Wayne never won that kind of cult attention. Yet Wayne-olatry is a larger phenomenon—more consequential (for good or ill) than any of those more specialized legends. Marilyn Monroe was one of the top ten moneymakers of Hollywood only three times—and never one of the top four. Elvis started no wars. Masses of American men did not grow up imitating Valentino.

Though Wayne went to great lengths to avoid military service in the Second World War, General Douglas MacArthur saw him as the model of an American soldier, and the Veterans of Foreign Wars saluted his "Americanism." The critic Eric Bentley held him significantly responsible for America's support of the Vietnam war, and says that it made him "the most important American of our time." Two boys who adored him in "Sands of Iwo Jima" grew up to become, respectively, the Speaker of the House of Representatives, and a Vietnam paraplegic. According to Newt Gingrich's stepfather, the young Newt always tried to walk like Wayne—his way of

being a man. But Ron Kovic was unmanned by his devotion: "I gave up my dead dick for John Wayne."

Both friends and critics of American foreign policy in the nineteen-sixties and nineteen-seventies said that it was afflicted with a "John Wayne syndrome." President Nixon thought that domestic affairs, symbolically represented for him by the Charles Manson cult-murder case, could be straightened out by the American people's taking Wayne's performance in "Chisum" as a model. Wayne was a hero to the Republicans' hero, Ronald Reagan, who once said that he wanted to make Westerns because "John Wayne, saber in hand, rode right into the number-one box-office spot." During his 1984 reelection campaign, Reagan made a pilgrimage to Wayne's birthplace in tiny Winterset, Iowa, and he told a group visiting the White House in 1988 that "Wayne understood what the American spirit is all about." In 1979, Congress had a gold medal struck in his honor, with the inscription JOHN WAYNE, AMERICAN. The way to be an American was to be Wayne—a claim given eerie confirmation by the example of the current chairman of the Joint Chiefs of Staff, John Shalikashvili, who taught himself English, as an immigrant, by watching Wayne movies. When another immigrant, Henry Kissinger, attributed his diplomatic success to Americans' admiration for cowboys who come into town alone, he was drawing on the Wayne legacy.

Wayne is still the model for American friends of battle. A midshipman at the United States Naval Academy in Annapolis told me that he shows his classmates "Sands of Iwo Jima" on Saturday mornings and gets choked up every time he sees it. Pat Buchanan used lines from that movie—"Saddle up" and "Lock and load"—during his primary campaign this year. Oliver Stone made his war-crazed Sergeant Barnes use the same Wayne-isms in "Platoon." In Stone's "Natural Born Killers," the murderous Mickey echoes Wayne from "Rio Bravo"—"Let's make a little music, Coloradah"—before spraying bullets. Wayne's cultists buy paintings of him smiling down from heaven. This is the ghostly presence that will hang in the sky over the Republicans' Convention in San Diego, where Bob Dole will be advocating new weapons for space use, and N.R.A. lobbyists will be defending war arsenals in private homes.

San Diego is in Wayne Country. His home was just up the way, in Newport Beach. Some people going to San Diego will pass through the Orange County airport, with its colossal statue of Wayne. In Orange County, the Wayne name is so sacred, according to the novelist Joseph Wambaugh, that softball teams taking jokey nicknames were forbidden to allude to him (it would have been blasphemy). Charlton Heston, the Moses of N.R.A. gun ads, is scheduled to go from the Republican Convention, where he will unveil his own PAC, to a ceremony presenting a posthumous award to Wayne at the Century Plaza Hotel in Los Angeles. The Duke doth bestride this narrow world.

For decades, John Wayne haunted the dreams of Americans—making   10
his face, Joan Didion said, more familiar to her than her husband's. The
protagonist of Walker Percy's novel "The Moviegoer" remembers Wayne's
shoot-out in "Stagecoach" more vividly than the events in his own life.

Other pop icons tend to be young, rebellious, or deviant. Cult loves
shadows, and theirs is a mysticism of the dark, of troubled youth and neu-
roses. Wayne's legend was of a rarer sort—a cult of daylight reality (or what
passes for that). The legend came upon him in his maturity. He did not
become a top star until he was in his forties, but he remained one until his
death, at seventy-two. He was a figure of authority—of the normative, if not
the normal. Yet what kind of country accepts as its norm an old man whose
principal screen activity was shooting other people, or punching them out?

If one looks for other authority figures in the movies, one finds that
they tend to be creaky with wisdom, like Judge Hardy. Spencer Tracy stood
more for integrity than authority, and he was not the leading-man type.
Robert Young had to leave the movies to become an image of stability
on television—in "Father Knows Best" and "Marcus Welby, M.D." Most
movie stars are glamorously pitted against authority—Clark Gable, Humphrey Bogart, James Cagney, Marlon Brando, Paul Newman. But Wayne,
even when he wasn't playing an officer in the Seventh Cavalry, was usually
on the sheriff's side.

What can explain this cult so at odds with the general run of cults?
Why was Wayne's popularity mainstream and long-lived, rather than fleeting and marginal? Why does he still fill the channels on late-night TV? His
fans remain loyal, with their own magazine (*The Big Trail*) and seasonal
Western celebrations. A foundry in Oregon offers statues of Wayne in various poses.

Wayne's innate qualities are not enough to explain so large a social fact.
He had to have filled some need in his audience. He was the conduit they
used for communicating with their own desired selves or their own imagined past. When he was called *the* American, it was a statement of what his
fans wanted America to be. For them, Wayne always struck an elegiac note.
He stood for an America that people felt was disappearing or had disappeared—for a time "when men were men." Though some critics agreed
with Eric Bentley that he got us into Vietnam, Wayne-olaters thought we
lost in Vietnam because not enough John Waynes were left to do what was
necessary to win.

The disappearing frontier is the most powerful and persistent myth in   15
American history. It is not a sectional myth but a national one. We do not
have "Easterns" or "Southerns," which *would* be sectional. We have
Westerns, since, at the outset, America was all frontier. America is the place
where European settlers met an alien natural environment and social system. As the frontier moved from the eastern seaboard, Americans experienced, over and over again, the excitement of the "birth moment," when

the new world was broken into, tamed, absorbed. James Fenimore Cooper created the archetypal figure for this movement when he sent his Hawkeye, in chronologically ordered novels, from the forests of New York to the Great Lakes and then to the Western prairies, where he died.

After Hawkeye came other figures who stood for the frontier experience—Daniel Boone, Kit Carson, Davy Crockett, Buffalo Bill. These men began in reality but ended in myth. Wayne reverses the process. Beginning in myth, he came to be seen as having entered the company of those who actually lived on the frontier. As a figure in the American imagination, he is closer to Kit Carson than to his fellow-actors. He became so identified with the West that he looked out of place in other cinematic settings—even in his war movies. Gary Cooper was "The Virginian" for a while, or "The Plainsman," but he was also Sergeant York, or Mr. Deeds. Wayne was never quite at ease off the range. His large, rolling walk was baffled by four walls. He was clearly on leave when doing screen duty as a modern soldier—Kit Carson holidaying with the Seabees. In his own clumsy projects, the elephantine "The Alamo" was at least more convincing than the hippopotamine "Green Berets."

Some think Wayne's virtual confinement to Westerns is a sign of his narrow range as an actor. This may be true. But some very good actors have been limited by their success in one kind of role. James Cagney's stuttery urban rhythms made him a misfit in his Western, "The Oklahoma Kid" (1939). Humphrey Bogart, who was in that same misbegotten film, had to wait for the roles that finally defined *him*. He had been out of place in many of his thirties films, with their jumpy pace and crackling dialogue. It took postwar "existentialism" to give Bogart's lassitudinous slump its admired eloquence. A powerful image that defines a star can haunt all his or her later roles. People kept looking for Brando's bluejeans and torn T-shirt under the toga of Mark Antony or the Godfather's business suit. Other actors expressed fleeting moods in the nation: Astaire the sophistication that people yearned for in the thirties, Bogart the romantic cynicism of the fifties. But Wayne was saddled up to ride across the decades.

It may be true that the greatest actors escape this restriction of their image, though even such great Shakepearean players as John Gielgud, Ralph Richardson, and Alec Guinness were not normally convincing in heroic roles—just as Olivier could not equal them in comedy. The greatest screen actor, as far as range is concerned, may have been Spencer Tracy, but his very escape from any large type meant that he left few searing images on the imagination. Judith Anderson was a far greater actress than Marilyn Monroe, but she took up little psychic space in the movie audience's dreamworld.

It is less useful to ask how good an actor Wayne was than to look at precisely how he did whatever he did that made him such a towering legend. The easiest and least truthful answer is to say that he was just what he pretended to be on screen. But that was hardly the case. Wayne hated horses, was more accustomed to suits and ties than to jeans when he went into the movie business, and had to remind himself to say "ain't." He aspired, during the long courtship of his first wife, to join the Social Register in Los Angeles. Wayne was born not Wayne but Marion Morrison, of Winterset, Iowa. He grew up in the Los Angeles suburb of Glendale, and intended to become a lawyer until he lost his football scholarship at the University of Southern California. His fans' myth made him a college star sidelined by an injury—but he dropped out of college before his junior year, and he was soon moving heavy props at Twentieth Century Fox.

Later legend said, as Richard Widmark does, that "John Ford invented John Wayne." Ford and Wayne collaborated busily in nurturing that impression, which proved so useful to them both. But Raoul Walsh was the first director who saw Wayne's potential as a Western star. Walsh was trying to cast a hero for his super-epic of 1930, "The Big Trail." Gary Cooper wasn't available. George O'Brien, Ford's hero in the 1924 epic "The Iron Horse," wasn't quite what Walsh wanted. Then he saw Wayne on the Fox set, and admired the graceful way he moved heavy equipment. That was the effect Walsh was looking for: "The son of a bitch," he said, "looked like a *man*."

Walsh lost no time showing off the physical dexterity of his discovery. In one of the earliest scenes in "The Big Trail," Wayne tiptoes up behind a young woman who is seated on a stool, playing the harmonium. In one easy motion, he puts his hands under her elbows, lifts her, turns her around in the air, and hugs her to him. It is hard to tell how he does it, even as one watches it over and over. He doesn't *throw* her, even slightly, and catch her after she turns; he just handles her as if she were an empty cardboard box, weightless and unresisting.

Wayne's size and strength were always important, even when he lost the sinewy leanness of that first film, done when he was twenty-two. This actor could not be dwarfed by the great outdoors. He seemed more at home there than when stooping to enter the confined space of a cabin, a cavalry barracks, or a teepee. Monument Valley itself could not overpower him. It seemed to breathe a cognate spirit.

Yet sheer size and muscle do not carry one far. There were always larger and more powerful men around Wayne—Victor McLaglen, for instance, who had been a leading man when Wayne was still in high school. What gave Wayne's motions and poses such authority was not just the bulk of his body but the way he used it. It was another director—Howard Hawks this time (still not John Ford)—who finally made Wayne a superstar, in 1948. In "Red River," Wayne has sworn to kill the protégé who stole his cattle herd from him. Having reached the railhead where his herd is milling, Wayne strides toward the camera, the cattle parting before his inexorable motion; he does not even bother to look at them. A gunfighter calls out from behind

20

Wayne, to stop him. But Wayne, in one, fluid motion, pivots while drawing his gun, downs the challenger, and completes the circle of his turn, his regained stride undeterrable as fate. Here was Manifest Destiny on the hoof.

Most critics of "Red River" think its flaw is that the unstoppable Wayne gets stopped. So clearly inevitable is his tread up to the climax that his ultimate collapse seems unconvincing. John Ford had the same problem with his ending to "The Searchers" (1956), throughout which Wayne's deep fires of revenge burn so fiercely that extinguishing them in the final scene looks contrived. Few actors have had this problem of projecting such indomitability that an audience finds it hard to accept their submission. Rather, most actors need to be built up—by camera angles, lighting, costume, being set against a background of crowds, a suppression of others' positions—in order to command a scene. Wayne's power was such that *others* had to be built up, to give him credible opposition. As Hawks put it, "If you don't get a damn good actor with Wayne, he's going to blow him right off the screen, not just by the fact that he's good but by his power, his strength." Wayne was so sure of himself that he didn't have to insist on his prominence as Errol Flynn did during the shooting of "Santa Fe Trail," when Flynn felt that the young Ronald Reagan was getting too much of the foreground. (Reagan countered by secretly building a mound of dirt to make himself taller.) Actors talk about how generous Wayne was with them, trying to give strength to their performances. He knew that his own presence was so powerful that it could not be fully measured against a weak adversary. In describing his standard Westerns, Wayne told the critic Roger Ebert, "Ordinarily they just stand me there and run everybody up against me."

The Western deals with the "taming" of the West. Wayne was uniquely ²⁵ convincing at that task. He looked so fit for the assignment that another problem arose. How, if necessary, do you tame the tamer? After he has broken the resistance, how do you break *him*? It is a difficulty that writers and directors had to address when Wayne's screen characters died. Many people were incredulous when the real-life Wayne died. Andrew McLaglen, his friend (and the director of six of his movies), said, "Even after the cancer operations, I never *really* thought Duke could die." If people resisted the mere thought in real life, how could they be made to accept it on the screen?

This air of invincibility gave Wayne his special status in Westerns. Richard Widmark, who was a personal and political adversary of his, admits, "He was the definitive Western star." Howard Hawks said that he and John Ford "used to discuss how tough it was to make a good Western without Wayne." One can imagine other actors replacing even very good performers in famous Westerns. Henry Fonda could have played Gary Cooper's role in "High Noon." Jimmy Stewart could have taken Fonda's role in "The Ox-Bow Incident." Several actors, out of many, could have equalled Alan Ladd in

"Shane." Sergio Leone proved in "Once Upon a Time in the West" that he could make closeups of hard eyes work as well with Fonda as with Eastwood. But no one else could have been as convincingly unswerving as Wayne in "Red River," "The Searchers," or "Big Jake." Even the jokey "True Grit" worked, because, underneath all the slapstick, it was finally believable that this fat old drunk could face down an entire gang.

Hawks said that the young Wayne moved "like a big cat." Katharine Hepburn spoke of his small feet and the light, dancer's steps he took with them. Harry Carey's wife, Olive Fuller Golden, who was a lifelong friend of Wayne's as well as an acting colleague, said she thought of Nureyev when she saw Wayne walking. Ford's daughter, Barbara, said there was something overpoweringly sexy in the way Wayne sat and rode his horse. Once, when he was drunk, Wayne whimsically turned Marilyn Carey (Olive's daughter-in-law) upside down while dancing with her, and he didn't notice that her face was turning red until Marilyn's husband pointed it out to him. "Duke apologized," Harry Carey, Jr., says. For Wayne, the move was so effortless that it never occurred to him, in his stupor, that it could have a physically trying effect on someone else.

Wayne's control of his body was economical—no motions wasted. This gave a sense of purpose to everything he did. He worked out characteristic stances, gestures, ways of sitting his horse. He learned to choreograph his fight moves with the creative stuntman Yakima Canutt. In stills from his early pictures, even when the face is fuzzy, one can identify Wayne by his pose, his gait, the tilt of his shoulders, the *contrapposto* lean of his hips. Classical sculptors worked out the counterpoised position to convey the maximum of both tension and relaxation, motion and stillness, in the human body: the taut line of the body is maintained through the hip above one leg, which is straight, while on the other side, where the leg is bent, the torso relaxes, deviating from rigid lines. Wayne constantly strikes the pose of Michelangelo's David. Sometimes, with a wider throw of the hips, he becomes Donatello's David. Wayne was very conscious of his effects. Richard Widmark used to laugh when Wayne, directing "The Alamo," shouted at his actors, "Goddammit, be *graceful*—like me!"

When George Plimpton, playing a bit part in Hawks's "Rio Lobo," had to enter a saloon carrying a rifle at waist level, he asked Wayne how to hold it. (Plimpton was holding the gun with the trigger guard near his belt and the stock projecting out behind him.) Wayne took the rifle, jammed its stock against his hip, and held it with one hand so that his whole body leaned into the gun, spoke through it, seemed to be one with it. Wayne twirled a rifle as easily as other cowboys twirl their pistols.

Western stars traditionally identified themselves with elaborate signals worked out through their costume, devices to make people conscious that the hero lived in an entirely different social system. William S. Hart had leather and tough fabrics layered around him almost like armor. Others added to their height with "ten-gallon hats," or to their menace with crossed bandoliers studded with bullets. Some wore two guns at the side, or stuck a single large pistol in the front of their belts. Many used "batwing" chaps to suggest a swooping motion even when they were off their horses. Metal riveted them together, from vest studs down to noisy spurs.

Wayne also had some costuming tricks—his placket-front shirt, dark and semi-military. But his signals were sent by the body under the clothes, which was more semantically charged than they were. His pants were folded up at the cuff, to reveal the gracefulness of his footwork. He dressed to let the body do its work—just as Fred Astaire wore formfitting tuxedos to bring out the line of his body, the calligraphy of its tracings in the air. Wayne's silhouette was enough to identify him. When he made an uncredited appearance on the TV show of his friend Ward Bond, his face was not shown—just his horse looming up in shadow outside a campfire's light—but the way his body was held revealed his identity to anyone familiar with him.

Wayne created an entire Western language of body signals. The most explicit of them were the Indian signs he often used—paradoxically dainty and slow arcs and swoops made by his large hands ("big as hams," Widmark said) and thick wrists (emphasized by a gold bracelet). His physical autonomy and self-command—the ease and authority of his carriage—made each motion a statement of individualism, a balletic Declaration of Independence.

The whole language cohered—as did the vocal aspect of his performance. Wayne's calculated and measured phrasing gave his delivery the same air of control, of inevitability, that his motions conveyed. He dealt out phrases like dooms: "Touch that gun and I'll kill ya." The stop-and-go rhythm is what all his imitators get, but few capture the melodic intervals of his cadenced speech. As a cavalry officer, he gives the command to his troops in two notes more stirring than the trumpet's: "*Yoh*-oh" (a two-and-a-half-tone drop). Joan Didion's girlhood memory of him was an acoustical one, of the commands he gave. But his throwaway comments, quietly delivered, were just as effective: "*He'll* do" (two-tone drop). I have watched Wayne's films dubbed in Italian, and have been reminded of how much his performance depends on the timbre, the melodic and rhythmic turns, of his voice on the soundtrack.

The most obvious element in Wayne's physical performance is his walk, which became so famous that various people took credit for inventing it and drilling Wayne on how to do it. Paul Fix, the Western star who worked often with Wayne, claimed that it was he who showed Wayne how to walk in the dramatic scene of "Red River," but Hawks scoffed at the idea: "You don't have to tell Wayne anything about walking through cattle; Wayne knew." Plimpton asked him how the walk was developed, and Wayne finally told him:

"Well, uh, the walk's been kind of a secret in our family for a long time—my dad taught me. But I can't keep it forever. I'll tell you how he taught me. . . . "

"There's a trick to it, is there?"

"You pick up one foot and put it forward and set it down. Then you pick up the other foot and set *it* down—and that's walkin' forward. If you do the reverse, you're *walkin' backward.*"

. . .

Wayne is among the most expressive of those who move about in the moving pictures. People often resist his performance, not because of its quality (good or bad) but because of its content. His body spoke a highly specific language of "manliness," of self-reliant authority. It was a body impervious to outside force, expressing a mind narrow but focussed, fixed on the task, impatient with complexity. This is a dangerous ideal to foster. It is "male" in a way that has rightly become suspect—one-sided, exclusive of values conventionally labelled "female." 35

. . .

By an odd turn of history, recent analyses of masculinity have less interesting things to say about Wayne than ancient Roman critics of male performance do. In the militaristic Roman society, a man's persuasiveness depended very much on his stance (*status*) and his walk (*gressus, gradus*). Cicero, in his book "The Orator," describes the ideal speaker, in a culture where speaking well was an exercise in performance art. It sounds as if Cicero had just been watching Wayne films.

> He must practice an economy of movement, with no extraneous
> effort—the carriage of his body straight and lofty; his pacing
> measured and kept within bounds; lunging only to the point,
> and rarely; without effeminacy in turning his head; no little stage
> business with his hands; no "conducting himself" to a beat; but
> governing himself in the expression of his whole body, with a
> manly torsion from the waist; using powerful gestures when
> moved, and none at all when calm.

In Rome, military rule was the highest virtue, and the most debilitating accusation was one of effeminacy. Cicero said that orators should learn grace of movement from wrestlers, should stamp their feet in a manly (not a petulant) way, should consider the whole body (the *motus corporis*) even more important than the words of a speech. Lucian drew the same picture—"a strong man, of understated power, virile stride, skin toughened by the outdoors, eyes hard and on the lookout." The Roman Empire dreamed constantly of John Wayne.

Why this echo of a lost classical world? Rome trained its citizens for war. Its empire depended on a mystique of legions intelligently led. The Seventh Cavalry in John Ford's "cavalry trilogy" ("Fort Apache," "She Wore a Yellow Ribbon," "Rio Grande") has the legionary spirit—far more than do the quaintly armored "Romans" of Cecil B. De Mille's historical epics. More important, the America of Ford's time had the sense of an *imperial* burden, which came to it with the Second World War and the Cold War. America submitted to a discipline of protracted struggle which made the President a full-time Commander-in-Chief even of non-military citizens. Citizens were under scrutiny for their loyalty to the war effort. Security clearances, classification of secrets, lists of subversive organizations, loyalty oaths, secret funding of the C.I.A., internal surveillance by the F.B.I., the expensive buildup of an arsenal and of space defenses—all these things were embraced as the price of defending the free world.

Wayne's time of maximum popularity coincided with this immense societal effort, and he internalized its demands in his own life as well as in his films. In 1949, he became the president of the Commie-hunting Motion Picture Alliance for the Preservation of American Ideals, a role in which he took credit for running Carl Foreman, the screenwriter for "High Noon," out of the country. In 1960, he joined the John Birch Society. He tied his own greatest financial project, the making of "The Alamo," to the electoral struggle of 1960, in which he declared that *real* patriots should support Richard Nixon. His ad for the movie took a slap at the Democratic candidate, John F. Kennedy, whose authorship of "Profiles in Courage" was being questioned: "There were no ghostwriters at the Alamo." He defended the war in Vietnam, and made "The Green Berets" as a personal statement on that conflict. Although the mystique of some Westerns has been one of freedom and individualism, of a creative anarchy, Wayne's movies stressed the need for *regimentation* as necessary to survival under threat. Almost by accident, this reflected conditions in the real West of the eighteen-sixties through the eighteen-nineties more accurately than did the myth of emancipated spirits on the frontier.

Wayne-olatry grew in such a climate. It is the greatest popular expression of the tension of muted struggle in those decades—1940 through 1980. What followed, in terms of Hollywood symbols, is a reversion to radical individualism. The ending of the Cold War should have been a comforting development, but it was also seen as the end of empire. America *lost* Vietnam, with a corresponding breakdown in its internal discipline, which led to a sense of drift, a new awareness of crime as unravelling the social fabric. It is significant that gender studies of movie masculinity have added a third item to their treatment of naked gods and troubled boys: the "hard bodies" of the post-Vietnam era—men engaged in revenge fantasies. Rambo goes after the abandoned relics of empire in Vietnam. ("Do we get to win this time?") Rocky Balboa beats the Russian giant when Rocky's govern-

40

ment has to confine itself to nuclear standoff. Dirty Harry goes after the punks who have made the city a jungle, using tactics forbidden to the ineffective police force. Citizens must take up arms, alone or in private militias, since the government has failed its subjects, abroad and at home. Conan the Barbarian, created on the screen by John Milius (the same man who gave Dirty Harry his swagger), becomes an avenger when his entire village is wiped out. In Milius's "Red Dawn," teen-agers must fight for a government that adults have surrendered.

The sense of opposing tremendous odds, of standing against the whole of legitimate society, calls for a hypertrophy of the individual's musculature and weaponry. Stallone and Schwarzenegger are fitted out with bodies that are nothing but body armor. Stripped naked, they carry huge cannons and automatic firing systems. Dirty Harry's gun gets longer and longer, blowing away whole phantom structures of evil, not just single bad guys.

The note of these films is rage. Wayne did not normally have the contempt for his opponent that Dirty Harry does. The Wayne hero, in a time of the empire's dominance, could be calm. His self-discipline was counted on to awe or attract others. The mature Wayne was lightly weaponed—a rifle, or one pistol, and he often did not have to use that. He faced down foes. A villain in the "shoot-out" is undone by Wayne's stride as he comes down the street.

The individualism of the Rambos is conveyed by their naked bodies. They wear no uniform—not even that of normal civil society. Bruce Willis's "Die Hard" police hero ends up shorn of civilized symbols (including shoes and shirt), though large firing systems are magically available. The Seventh Cavalry is not going to ride to the rescue, so why put on its epaulets? There is no one and nothing to turn to but one's gun. As his father tells Conan in Milius's film, "No one in this world can you trust—not men, not women, not beasts. This [steel] you can trust."

. . .

A myth does not take hold without expressing many truths. They are misleading truths, usually, but important ones: truth, for one thing, to the needs of those who elaborate and accept the myth; truth to the demand for some control over complex realities; truth to the recognition of shared values (however shakily grounded those values may actually be). Even the myths that simplify reality are not, in themselves, simple. It is true that Westerns work with a body of conventional situations (though a larger, more flexible body of them than most people realize). But Japanese noh plays, ancient Greek tragedy, and the commedia dell'arte also work within strict conventions—a fact that does not deprive them of subtlety or nuance. Myth works best in such established frameworks. The Western can raise serious moral questions because it deals with the clash of entirely different social systems—not only the clash of Native Americans or Mexicans or

Chinese "coolies" with European colonizers but that of earlier colonizers with later ones. The technology that is the white man's friend becomes his enemy as waves of exploitation wash in and overlap prior waves.

Wayne was not just one type of Western hero. He is an innocently leer-   45
ing ladies' man in his B films of the thirties, a naïf in "Stagecoach," an obsessed adolescent in "Shepherd of the Hills," a frightened cattle capitalist in "Red River," a crazed racist in "The Searchers," a dutiful officer in cav-alry pictures, the worldly-wise elder counsellor in some later movies. He is sometimes a hothead, more often the restrainer of hotheads. So it is not true that Wayne always played the same role. But it is true that all his work, especially in the Westerns, was part of one project—to build a persona full of portent, to maintain a cumulative authority in his bearing. Wayne was careful about the persona, about not accepting roles that would endanger it. He refused to play a coward for Howard Hawks. He refused to shoot a man in the back for Don Siegal. He would be villainous but not weak. An early small part, in "The Life of Jimmy Dolan," showed that he could play a coward, but later it was one of the things "John Wayne" did not do. Creating that artifact was the lifelong project of the man behind the image, regardless of his name (Marion Morrison, Duke Morrison, Duke Wayne). Wayne was helped along the way by directors, writers, producers, camera-men, costumers, friends, and critics, and he was hindered by an assortment of the well-meaning, the diffident, the sycophantic, but he kept strenuously to his own program—to create a "self" so real to others that he could dis-appear into it, as he did.

He finally became what he had projected on the screen—a hollow tri-umph, for what was that but the figment of other people's imaginations? Wayne's own story is a large one—as large as the truths, the societal eva-sions, the lies of which his screen image was confected. It produced some film masterpieces (along with a large body of clinkers). It involved some of the greatest talents in filmmaking—John Ford, Howard Hawks, Raoul Walsh, Joe August, Archie Stout, Winton Hoch, Bert Glennon, William Clothier, Dudley Nichols, Frank Nugent, Henry Fonda, Maureen O'Hara. It also involved all Americans, whether we knew it or not. We are entangled in his story: by the dreams he shaped or inhibited, in us or in others; by the things he validated and those he scorned; by the particular definition he gave to "being American." All of this influenced us—whether, with Richard Nixon and Ronald Reagan, we accepted the definition or, with Eric Bentley, tried to renounce or discredit it. The less we advert to what he did to us, the less we can cope with it. Many of those Republicans who will be milling around in San Diego are still haunted by the dreams that explain Wayne's continuing popularity. Down the street of the twentieth-century imagina-tion, that figure is still walking toward us—graceful, menacing, inescapable.

SUGGESTIONS FOR FURTHER STUDY

Key Words

The author uses language with which you may not be familiar. Find the following words in the paragraphs indicated, and explain their meanings in the context of the sentences in which the words appear. Consult a dictionary, as needed.

icons (par. 4)
vulnerabilities (par. 4)
devotees (par. 4)
protagonist (par. 10)
archetypal (par. 15)
lassitudinous (par. 17)
dexterity (par. 21)
cognate (par. 22)
inexorable (par. 23)
indomitability (par. 24)
invincibility (par. 26)
contrapposto (par. 28)
calligraphy (par. 31)
hypertrophy (par. 41)
commedia dell'arte (par. 44)
sycophantic (par. 45)
confected (par. 46)

Topics for Discussion and Writing

1. The author gives readers several reasons why John Wayne's "durability [for being consistently ranked as America's top male movie star] is astonishing." For example, he says that "Wayne-olatry" is a larger phenomenon [than mere cult attention]." What evidence does Wills present to support that estimate of Wayne's abiding popularity and importance as an American hero? Trace the author's argument, and make a list of the several reasons he gives to support it.

2. If you have viewed a John Wayne film, discuss the accuracy of the author's description and evaluation of Wayne's *physical* appearance and mannerisms, including his famous walk and way of speaking.

3. In this essay, Wayne's personal political views are tied to the argument that Wayne-olatry grew in the social and political climate

that existed following World War II. From your knowledge of John Wayne's movies and from reading "John Wayne's Body," discuss with others the extent to which you agree that "the need for *regimentation* as necessary to survival under threat" is reflected in Wayne's films.

4. If you agree with the author that "myth does not take hold without expressing many truths," write a journal entry or brief essay outlining the truths you think you find in the John Wayne myth. You may or may not agree with the truths for which author Garry Wills argues.

5. This study of Wayne-olatry is written by a man about a male hero. If you are a woman, how do you respond to "John Wayne's Body"? Do you see the same features in a pop icon/hero figure such as John Wayne that Garry Wills or other men do, or do you see different ones? Discuss this question with other women readers, and compare your reactions to those described in this essay. You might want to begin by free-writing about your reactions in your journal.

6. Write an essay proposing a different pop icon as being greater than or equal to John Wayne's enduring popularity. Perhaps some of the entertainment figures mentioned in Wills's essay would qualify—or propose a name of your own.

Superman and the Duke: Duel between American Male Icons

Cynthia Paco

In this selection, student writer Cynthia Paco emulates the example of Gary Engle and compares two American male icons: Superman and John Wayne. Her determination of who makes the better hero, how-ever, is based on criteria that differ from Engle's, though she ultimately agrees with him on who wins the contest.

In the popularity contest between two of America's favorite male icons—Superman and John Wayne—I have to cast my vote for Superman as the superior hero. Not that I'm a Superman fan. And not that I subscribe to the labeling of mythical characters as heroes (I see both Superman and the John Wayne "hero" as mythical). Although I may be out of sync with the majority of my fellow Americans, it is interesting to explore the "American" ideal of what a hero is and which character—Superman or Wayne—better fits that persona. In this context, I still say Superman pre-vails over Wayne!

In order to further examine this question of who is more representative of the American hero, let's define what exactly a "hero" is. *Webster's New World Dictionary of the American Language* defines a hero as "any man admired for his courage, nobility, or exploits," and as "any man admired for his qualities or achievements and regarded as an ideal or model" (657). Garry Wills agrees with and elaborates on this definition when he explains John Wayne's enduring popularity as an American idol in his essay "John Wayne's Body": "He had to have filled some need in his audience. He was the conduit they used for communicating with their own desired selves or their own imagined past. When he was called *the* American, it was a statement of what his fans wanted America to be." So, what qualities, achievements, or exploits are admirable and worthy of labeling men heroes—Wayne and Superman in particular—according to American idealism?

The first thing that comes to mind is the obvious. Superman "defends America—no, the world! no, the Universe!—from all evil and harm," writes

Gary Engle in "What Makes Superman So Darned American?" Superman never hesitates to take on evil. In contrast, Wills states of the nonfictional Wayne, "Though Wayne went to great lengths to avoid military service in the Second World War, General Douglas MacArthur saw him as the model of an American soldier, and the Veterans of Foreign Wars saluted his 'Americanism.'" Wayne may have been showered with praise for his military efforts, but his resistance to being involved certainly diminishes his patriotism. Superman clearly wins this round.

According to Engle, "It is impossible to imagine Superman being as popular as he is and speaking as deeply to the American character were he not an immigrant and an orphan." As Engle points out, all Americans, except Native Americans, have roots elsewhere. So, Superman reflects a common bond with most of us as feeling somewhat displaced or alien; and just as Wayne "filled some need in his audience," this common experience also fills a need in Superman's audience and is important in the formation of his hero status. Along with these needs being filled is the desire of Americans to come "to terms with the immigrant experience," Engle continues. "This is why, for example, so much of American literature and popular culture deals with the theme of dislocation, generally focused in characters devoted or doomed to constant physical movement." The Superman legend deals with this through his power of flight, as Engle explains: "Individual mobility is an integral part of America's dreamwork. Is it any wonder, then that our greatest hero can take to the air at will? Superman's ability to fly does more than place him in a tradition of mythic figures. . . . It makes him an exemplar in the American dream."

Adding to this need to come to terms with immigration, Wills [commenting on John Wayne] explains, "As the frontier moved from the eastern seaboard, Americans experienced over and over again, the excitement of the 'birth moment,' when the new world was broken into, tamed, absorbed." Wayne's western characters fulfill this cinematic experience, thus supporting his hero status. In short, both Superman and John Wayne possess qualities to fulfill a need and address the nomadic, conquering values of Americans.

Engle goes on and makes this comparison: "Superman's powers— strength, mobility, x-ray vision and the like—are the comic-book equivalents of ethnic characteristics, and they protect and preserve the vitality of the foster community in which he lives in the same way that immigrant ethnicity has sustained American culture linguistically, artistically, economically, politically, and spiritually." Wayne's strength is quite different in meaning than Superman's allegorical character, but it is just as important in the making of an American hero. American ideals of what a "man" should be are exemplified by Wayne, both in his film characters and in real life. To me, Wayne's extreme display of "manliness," however, diminishes his hero

5

status, especially in the eyes of women. Wills recognizes this when he writes of Wayne, "His body spoke a highly specific language of 'manliness,' of self-reliant authority. It was a body impervious to outside force, expressing a mind narrow but focussed, fixed on the task, impatient with complexity. This is a dangerous ideal to foster. It is 'male" in a way that has rightly become suspect—one-sided, exclusive of values conventionally labelled 'female.'" While manliness itself is not an unadmirable quality, it is the extremeness in which Wayne presents it that is troubling. Though, as a woman I find this posture . . . a detraction to heroism, ironically it may explain his increasing posthumous popularity. In our changing world from male dominance to the women's movement, I believe men are uneasy with their loss of power/authority over women. Wayne's machoism may console men in their fantasies, thus elevating his hero status in the eyes of men.

One last contrast between Wayne and Superman. Wayne depicts fictional characters and is himself a nonfictional character [revered] by some as a hero. In his fictional life, Wayne portrays many different individuals—these characters are temporary, momentary icons. In real life, Wayne has been both heralded and [criticized] for his roles in American politics. Some would consider John Wayne "the man" a hero and some would disagree. One example is given in Wills's writing where he states, "Though some critics agreed with Eric Bentley that [Wayne] got us into Vietnam, Wayne-olaters thought we lost in Vietnam because not enough John Waynes were left to do what was necessary to win." Superman, to the contrary, is a solitary fictional character with a single, solid myth and identity. According to Engle,

> The core of the American myth in Superman consists of a few basic facts that remain unchanged throughout the infinitely varied ways in which the myth is told—facts with which everyone is familiar, however marginal their knowledge of the story. . . . Every narrative thread in the mythology, each one of the thousands of plots in the fifty-year stream of comics and films and TV shows, all the tales involving the demigods of the Superman pantheon—Superboy, Supergirl, even Krypto the superdog—every single one reinforces by never contradicting the basic set of facts. That's the myth, and that's where one looks to understand America.

One always knows what [one is] getting with Superman. The qualities reflected in Superman are undeniably heroic and stable. As for John Wayne, there are questions as to who he is, both as a cinematic hero and as a real-life hero. There is also controversy as to whether Wayne reflects heroic qualities at all. In this duel of two American heroes, Superman wins the bet.

CARTOONS IN AMERICA

©1993 Washington Post Writers Group. Reprinted with permission.

CHAPTER 4: ACTIVITIES FOR DISCUSSION AND WRITING
Making Connections

1. In an essay, discuss what you think is the impact of sex and violence in television or movies. Pick one or more TV shows or films, and describe their inclusion—or exclusion—of sex or violence. Use specific examples of action or language from the shows or films you have chosen. Consider the following ideas as you prepare to write your essay:
   a. If the show or film contains sex or violence, do you think either was necessary? In what ways did explicit sex or violence contribute to or detract from the effectiveness of the show or film?
   b. If the show or film did *not* contain explicit sex or violent scenes, do you think it would have been more successful if it had? Explain your opinion.

2. The essays and other readings in this chapter seem to imply that violence has become a major element in all kinds of entertainment media: film, television, music, and videos alike. Do you agree with this assessment of the predominance of violence in entertainment media? Discuss your observations about the prevalence of violence in entertainment media, and explain your reactions to violent scenes and language.

3. Write a critical review of a current or past movie you have seen and know well. If you like the film, explain why you feel as you do. Consider Rogers's defense of the integrity of the message in *Ghosts of Mississippi* as a model. If you did *not* like the film, choose particular features such as plot, acting, theme, music, or special effects to critique, and explain why you feel as you do. Look again at "On Ethics, Money, and the Ending of 'Maguire'" as an example.

4. In "Duel between Two American Heroes," student writer Cynthia Paco reviews two essays in this chapter and incorporates ideas and quotations from each in her own comparison of John Wayne and Superman as American heroes. Do you agree or disagree with her opinion? Which character do you think is the most entitled to be called *the* greatest American hero? Write an essay arguing for either John Wayne or Superman. Or write an essay placing some *other* American figure—real or mythical—against either John Wayne or Superman.

5. Both Superman and John Wayne's persona in movie characters represent a certain type of American culture hero: white, male, and fictional. Think of other real-life American culture heroes who do *not* conform to this type. Consider such figures from past and present as Abraham Lincoln; George Washington Carver; Eleanor Roosevelt; Cesar Chavez; Martin Luther King, Jr.; Jack Kerouac; Elizabeth Taylor; Jim Morrison; or Roseanne. Find other people who are familiar with the person you chose, and discuss the heroic characteristics of this person. Write a brief essay or journal entry describing this person's qualifications as an American culture hero.

6. Watch several films by a different type of Western movie hero. For example, Clint Eastwood has remained a popular creator of Western hero types, but his movie characters are not cast in the same mold as John Wayne's. Discuss or write about the differences between the type of Western hero portrayed by Wayne and the type shown by one of his competitors, such as Eastwood. Use specific examples of character portrayal, action, and language from the films in your discussion.

7. Compare and contrast different versions of Superman. For example, you may compare any of the following: movies about Superman with several of the contemporary TV shows based on his character, the older TV version of Superman with the recent TV Superman in *Lois and Clark*, or the earlier renditions of Superman in the comics with the newer, darker version of Superman in current DC Comics. Use specific examples from your sources in making your comparisons.

CHAPTER  5

POPULAR CULTURE V

"Generation X":
Cybernauts Hungering for More?

In *Living in America,* we have been probing various forms of *ideology* (cultural beliefs) while examining diverse forms of popular culture, in order to determine what it means to be American. In previous chapters, you have read, discussed, and written about potent aspects of American culture: multiculturalism in our nation; the importance of family and heritage; and the role of recreation, popular entertainment, and violence and danger in our lifestyles. In "Generation X: Cybernauts Hungering for More?" we continue our investigation of the American experience by focusing on what Laurence Shames calls the "more factor," as well as Generation X and cyberspace, elements of American culture that not only describe our present but also foresee our future.

We begin the chapter with Laurence Shames's seminal essay, "The More Factor," a study of how Americans have, from the beginning of Western colonization, believed in an "ethics of success" and have hungered for and anticipated acquiring more at any cost. In "Twentysomethings," Walter Kirn condemns the so-called Generation X as "a generation of slackers," a generation without ambition and incentive unlike their elders who, for good or ill, were driven by the "more factor." Timothy Leary's "The Cyberpunk: The Individual as Reality Pilot" claims that the drive to want more, something better, something never done before, has always been a component of the human spirit, leading us to exciting breakthroughs and new information, no matter how great the obstacles.

Several essays focus on the computer revolution and cyberspace. Shames's "more factor" is an underlying theme in these essays, as well, for the rapidly growing interest in and demand for computers, software, and Internet capability has fueled the demand for more information, more technological breakthroughs, more freedom, and more state-of-the-art products. In his humorous piece, "Dave Barry in Cyberspace: The Future of the Computer Revolution," Dave Barry insists that there is "a bright new tomorrow waiting for us" on the Information Superhighway, even with obsolescence, information glut, and corruption of the World Wide Web factored in. In a more serious vein, Shelley Donald Coolidge's "Info Highway: A Long and Winding Road" discusses the applications of the Web in American classrooms. Amy Harmon's "Bigots on the Net" explores the dark side of Internet use and the cyberpunks who may go too far. Finally, student writer Cindie L. Keefauver tends to agree with Shames in her essay "Those Who Die with the Most Toys Lose."

The More Factor

Laurence Shames

Laurence Shames, a graduate of the Harvard Business School, currently resides in New York City and Shelter Island, New York. He authored The Big Time: The Harvard Business School's Most Successful Class and How It Shaped America, *and* The Hunger for More: Searching for Values in an Age of Greed, *from which the following selection is taken. He has also published numerous articles and essays in* Esquire, *the* New York Times, Playboy, *and* Vanity Fair.

1

Americans have always been optimists, and optimists have always liked to speculate. In Texas in the 1880s, the speculative instrument of choice was towns, and there is no tale more American than this.

What people would do was buy up enormous tracts of parched and vacant land, lay out a Main Street, nail together some wooden sidewalks, and start slapping up buildings. One of these buildings would be called the Grand Hotel and would have a saloon complete with swinging doors. Another might be dubbed the New Academy or the Opera House. The developers would erect a flagpole and name a church, and once the workmen had packed up and moved on, the towns would be as empty as the sky.

But no matter. The speculators, next, would hire people to pass out handbills in the Eastern and Midwestern cities, tracts limning the advantages of relocation to "the Athens of the South" or "the new plains Jerusalem." When persuasion failed, the builders might resort to bribery, paying people's moving costs and giving them houses, in exchange for nothing but a pledge to stay until a certain census was taken or a certain inspection made. Once the nose count was completed, people were free to move on, and there was in fact a contingent of folks who made their living by keeping a cabin on skids and dragging it for pay from one town to another.

The speculators' idea, of course, was to lure the railroad. If one could create a convincing semblance of a town, the railroad might come through it, and a real town would develop, making the speculators staggeringly rich. By these devices a man named Sanborn once owned Amarillo.[1]

---

[1]For a fuller account of railroad-related land speculation in Texas, see F. Stanley, *Story of the Texas Panhandle Railroads* (Borger, Tex.: Hess Publishing Co., 1976).

But railroad tracks are narrow and the state of Texas is very, very wide.   5
For every Witchita Falls or Lubbock there were a dozen College Mounds or
Belchervilles,[2] bleached, unpeopled burgs that receded quietly into the dust,
taking with them large amounts of speculators' money.

Still, the speculators kept right on bucking the odds and depositing
empty towns in the middle of nowhere. Why did they do it? Two reasons—
reasons that might be said to summarize the central fact of American economic history and that go a fair way toward explaining what is perhaps the
central strand of the national character.

The first reason was simply that the possible returns were so enormous
as to partake of the surreal, to create a climate in which ordinary logic and
prudence did not seem to apply. In a boom like that of real estate when the
railroad barreled through, long shots that might pay one hundred thousand
to one seemed worth a bet.

The second reason, more pertinent here, is that there was a presumption
that America would *keep on* booming—if not forever, then at least longer
than it made sense to worry about. There would always be another gold
rush, another Homestead Act, another oil strike. The next generation would
always ferret out opportunities that would be still more lavish than any that
had gone before. America *was* those opportunities. This was an article not
just of faith, but of strategy. You banked on the next windfall, you staked
your hopes and even your self-esteem on it, and this led to a national turn of
mind that might usefully be thought of as the habit of more.

A century, maybe two centuries, before anyone had heard the term *baby
boomer,* much less *yuppie,* the habit of more had been installed as the operative truth among the economically ambitious. The habit of more seemed to
suggest that there was no such thing as getting wiped out in America. A fortune lost in Texas might be recouped in Colorado. Funds frittered away on
grazing land where nothing grew might flood back in as silver. There was
always a second chance, or always seemed to be, in this land where growth
was destiny and where expansion and purpose were the same.

The key was the frontier, not just as a matter of acreage, but as idea.   10
Vast, varied, rough as rocks, America was the place where one never quite
came to the end. Ben Franklin explained it to Europe even before the
Revolutionary War had finished: America offered new chances to those
"who, in their own Countries, where all the Lands [were] fully occupied . . .
could never [emerge] from the poor Condition wherein they were born."[3]

So central was this awareness of vacant space and its link to economic
promise that Frederick Jackson Turner, the historian who set the tone for

---

[2] T. Lindsay Baker, *Ghost Towns of Texas* (Norman, Okla.: University of Oklahoma Press,
1986).
[3] Benjamin Franklin, "Information to Those Who Would Remove to America," in *The
Autobiography and Other Writings* (New York: Penguin Books, 1986), 242.

much of the twentieth century's understanding of the American past, would write that it was "not the constitution, but free land . . . [that] made the democratic type of society in America."[4] Good laws mattered; an accountable government mattered; ingenuity and hard work mattered. But those things were, so to speak, an overlay on the natural, geographic America that was simply *there,* and whose vast and beckoning possibilities seemed to generate the ambition and the sometimes reckless liberty that would fill it. First and foremost, it was open space that provided "the freedom of the individual to rise under conditions of social mobility."[5]

Open space generated not just ambition, but metaphor. As early as 1835, Tocqueville was extrapolating from the fact of America's emptiness to the observation that "no natural boundary seems to be set to the efforts of man."[6] Nor was any limit placed on what he might accomplish, since, in that heyday of the Protestant ethic, a person's rewards were taken to be quite strictly proportionate to his labors.

Frontier; opportunity; more. This has been the American trinity from the very start. The frontier was the backdrop and also the raw material for the streak of economic booms. The booms became the goad and also the justification for the myriad gambles and for Americans' famous optimism. The optimism, in turn, shaped the schemes and visions that were sometimes noble, sometimes appalling, always bold. The frontier, as reality and as symbol, is what has shaped the American way of doing things and the American sense of what's worth doing.

But there has been one further corollary to the legacy of the frontier, with its promise of ever-expanding opportunities: given that the goal—a realistic goal for most of our history—was *more,* Americans have been somewhat backward in adopting values, hopes, ambitions that have to do with things *other than* more. In America, a sense of quality has lagged far behind a sense of scale. An ideal of contentment has yet to take root in soil traditionally more hospitable to an ideal of restless striving. The ethic of decency has been upstaged by the ethic of success. The concept of growth has been applied almost exclusively to things that can be measured, counted, weighed. And the hunger for those things that are unmeasurable but fine—the sorts of accomplishment that cannot be undone by circumstance or a shift in social fashion, the kind of serenity that cannot be shattered by tomorrow's headline—has gone largely unfulfilled, and even unacknowledged.

---

[4]Frederick Jackson Turner, *The Frontier in American History* (Melbourne, Fla.: Krieger, 1976 [reprint of 1920 edition]), 293.
[5]Ibid., 266.
[6]Tocqueville, *Democracy in America.*

2

If the supply of more went on forever, perhaps that wouldn't matter   15
very much. Expansion could remain a goal unto itself, and would continue
to generate a value system based on bulk rather than on nuance, on quantities of money rather than on quality of life, on "progress" itself rather than
on a sense of what the progress was for. But what if, over time, there was
less more to be had?

That is the essential situation of America today.

Let's keep things in proportion: the country is not running out of
wealth, drive, savvy, or opportunities. We are not facing imminent ruin, and
neither panic nor gloom is called for. But there have been ample indications
over the past two decades that we are running out of more.

Consider productivity growth—according to many economists, the single most telling and least distortable gauge of changes in real wealth. From
1947 to 1965, productivity in the private sector (adjusted, as are all the following figures, for inflation) was advancing, on average, by an annual 3.3
percent. This means, simply, that each hour of work performed by a spe-
cimen American worker contributed 3.3 cents worth of more to every
American dollar every year; whether we saved it or spent it, that increment
went into a national kitty of ever-enlarging aggregate wealth. Between 1965
and 1972, however, the "more-factor" decreased to 2.4 percent a year, and
from 1972 to 1977 it slipped further, to 1.6 percent. By the early 1980s,
productivity growth was at a virtual standstill, crawling along at 0.2 percent for the five years ending in 1982.[7] Through the middle years of the
1980s, the numbers rebounded somewhat—but by then the gains were
being neutralized by the gargantuan carrying costs on the national debt.[8]

Inevitably, this decline in the national stockpile of more held consequences for the individual wallet.[9] During the 1950s, Americans' average
hourly earnings were humping ahead at a gratifying 2.5 percent each year.
By the late seventies, that figure stood just where productivity growth had
come to stand, at a dispiriting 0.2 cents on the dollar. By the first half of the
eighties, the Reagan "recovery" notwithstanding, real hourly wages were
actually moving backwards—declining at an average rate of 0.3 percent.

---

[7]These figures are taken from the Council of Economic Advisers, *Economic Report of the President*, February 1984, 267.
[8]For a lucid and readable account of the meaning and implications of our reservoir of red ink, see Lawrence Malkin, *The National Debt* (New York: Henry Holt and Co., 1987). Through no fault of Malkin's, many of his numbers are already obsolete, but his explanation of who owes what to whom, and what it means, remains sound and even entertaining in a bleak sort of way.
[9]The figures in this paragraph and the next are from "The Average Guy Takes It on the Chin," *New York Times*, 13 July 1986, sec. 3.

Compounding the shortage of more was an unfortunate but crucial   20
demographic fact. Real wealth was nearly ceasing to expand just at the
moment when the members of that unprecedented population bulge known
as the baby boom were entering what should have been their peak years of
income expansion. A working man or woman who was thirty years old in
1949 could expect to see his or her real earnings burgeon by 63 percent by
age forty. In 1959, a thirty-year-old could still look forward to a gain of 49
percent by his or her fortieth birthday.

But what about the person who turned thirty in 1973? By the time that
worker turned forty, his or her real earnings had shrunk by a percentage
point. For all the blather about yuppies with their beach houses, BMWs,
and radicchio salads, and even factoring in those isolated tens of thousands
making ludicrous sums in consulting firms or on Wall Street, the fact is that
between 1979 and 1983 real earnings of all Americans between the ages of
twenty-five and thirty-four actually declined by 14 percent.[10] The *New
York Times,* well before the stock market crash put the kibosh on eighties
confidence, summed up the implications of this downturn by observing that
"for millions of breadwinners, the American dream is becoming the impossible dream."[11]

Now, it is not our main purpose here to detail the ups and downs of the
American economy. Our aim, rather, is to consider the effects of those ups
and downs on people's goals, values, sense of their place in the world. What
happens at that shadowy juncture where economic prospects meld with
personal choice? What sorts of insights and adjustments are called for so
that economic ups and downs can be dealt with gracefully?

Fact one in this connection is that, if America's supply of more is in fact
diminishing, American values will have to shift and broaden to fill the gap
where the expectation of almost automatic gains used to be. Something
more durable will have to replace the fat but fragile bubble that had been
getting frailer the past two decades and that finally popped—a tentative,
partial pop—on October 19, 1987. A different sort of growth—ultimately,
a growth in responsibility and happiness—will have to fulfill our need to
believe that our possibilities are still expanding.

The transition to that new view of progress will take some fancy stepping, because, at least since the end of World War II, simple economic
growth has stood, in the American psyche, as the best available substitute
for the literal frontier. The economy has *been* the frontier. Instead of more
space, we have had more money. Rather than measuring progress in terms
of geographical expansion, we have measured it by expansion in our stan-

---

[10]See, for example, "The Year of the Yuppie," *Newsweek,* 31 December 1984, 16.
[11]"The Average Guy," see [note 9].

dard of living. Economics has become the metaphor on which we pin our hopes of open space and second chances.

The poignant part is that the literal frontier did not pass yesterday: it   25
has not existed for a hundred years. But the frontier's promise has become so much a part of us that we have not been willing to let the concept die. We have kept the frontier mythology going by invocation, by allusion, by hype.

It is not a coincidence that John F. Kennedy dubbed his political program the New Frontier. It is not mere linguistic accident that makes us speak of Frontiers of Science or of psychedelic drugs as carrying one to Frontiers of Perception. We glorify fads and fashions by calling them Frontiers of Taste. Nuclear energy has been called the Last Frontier; solar energy has been called the Last Frontier. Outer space has been called the Last Frontier; the oceans have been called the Last Frontier. Even the suburbs, those blandest and least adventurous of places, have been wryly described as the crabgrass frontier.[12]

What made all those usages plausible was their being linked to the image of the American economy as an endlessly fertile continent whose boundaries never need be reached, a domain that could expand in perpetuity, a gigantic playing field that would never run out of room and on which the game would get forever bigger and more filled with action. This was the frontier that would not vanish.

It is worth noting that people in other countries (with the possible exception of that other America, Australia) do not talk about frontier this way. In Europe, and in most of Africa and Asia, "frontier" connotes, at worst, a place of barbed wire and men with rifles, and at best, a neutral junction where one changes currency while passing from one fixed system into another. Frontier, for most of the world's people, does not suggest growth, expanse, or opportunity.

For Americans, it does, and always has. This is one of the things that sets America apart from other places and makes American attitudes different from those of other people. It is why, from *Bonanza* to the Sierra Club, the notion or even the fantasy of empty horizons and untapped resources has always evoked in the American heart both passion and wistfulness. And it is why the fear that the economic frontier—our last, best version of the Wild West—may finally be passing creates in us not only money worries but also a crisis of morale and even of purpose.

---

[12] With the suburbs again taking on a sort of fascination, this phrase was resurrected as the title of a 1985 book—*Crabgrass Frontier: The Suburbanization of America,* by Kenneth T. Jackson (Oxford University Press).

3

It might seem strange to call the 1980s an era of nostalgia. The decade,   30
after all, has been more usually described in terms of coolness, pragmatism,
and a blithe innocence of history. But the eighties, unawares, were nostalgic
for frontiers; and the disappointment of that nostalgia had much to do with
the time's greed, narrowness, and strange want of joy. The fear that the
world may not be a big enough playground for the full exercise of one's
energies and yearnings, and worse, the fear that the playground is being
fenced off and will no longer expand—these are real worries and they have
had consequences. The eighties were an object lesson in how people play
the game when there is an awful and unspoken suspicion that the game is
winding down.

It was ironic that the yuppies came to be so reviled for their vaunting
ambition and outsized expectations, as if they'd invented the habit of more,
when in fact they'd only inherited it the way a fetus picks up an addiction in
the womb. The craving was there in the national bloodstream, a remnant of
the frontier, and the baby boomers, described in childhood as "the luckiest
generation,"[13] found themselves, as young adults, in the melancholy position of wrestling with a two-hundred-year dependency on a drug that was
now in short supply.

True, the 1980s raised the clamor for more to new heights of shrillness,
insistence, and general obnoxiousness, but this, it can be argued, was in the
nature of a final binge, the storm before the calm. America, though fighting
the perception every inch of the way, was coming to realize that it was not a
preordained part of the natural order that one should be richer every year. If
it happened, that was nice. But who had started the flimsy and pernicious
rumor that it was normal?

SUGGESTIONS FOR FURTHER STUDY

Key Words

The author uses language with which you may not be familiar. Find the
following words in the paragraphs indicated, and explain their meanings in
the context of the sentences in which the words appear. Consult a dictionary, as needed.

limning (par. 3)
contingent (par. 3)
extrapolating (par. 12)

---

[13]Thomas Hine, *Populuxe* (New York: Alfred A. Knopf, 1986), 15.

corollary (par. 14)
nuance (par. 15)
aggregate (par. 18)
poignant (par. 25)
invocation (par. 25)
pragmatism (par. 30)
vaunting (par. 31)
obnoxiousness (par. 32)
pernicious (par. 32)

Topics for Discussion and Writing

1. Shames discusses Americans' interest in speculation. What kinds of speculation does he describe, and how does he characterize the types of people who were speculators? Give several examples from the essay.

2. Shames says that speculators bought up "enormous tracts of parched and vacant land." Has he omitted anything in this description? From your knowledge of American history, discuss whether land in the American West was actually "vacant." Who or what might have been dispossessed by land speculators?

3. According to Shames, the idea of the American frontier serves as the key to understanding American ideology. How does the author develop his argument? Point to related passages in the essay to support your discussion.

4. The author says Americans adopted values inherent in "the legacy of the frontier," but what "values, hopes, ambitions" does he say "Americans have been somewhat backward in adopting"? What do you think he means by "the ethic of decency has been upstaged by the ethic of success" (par. 14)? Discuss this topic with other readers, or write a journal entry in which you define both "the ethic of decency" and "the ethic of success."

5. Do you agree with the *New York Times* observation that "for millions of breadwinners, the American dream is becoming the impossible dream" (par. 21)? How does Shames deal with that observation?

6. Who are yuppies? What does Shames list as reasons that yuppies have been so influenced by the more factor?

7. How do considerations of race, gender, and ethnicity change or confirm Shames's argument in this essay? Do *all* Americans share the same American Dream? Discuss to what extent Shames's description of our hunger for more applies to all Americans.

8. What evidence of the more factor do you find in your own life, in the lives of your acquaintances and family, or in your environment? Explore this question in writing by identifying any evidence you find in advertising, television, films, music, and other forms of entertainment that may have affected your own ambitions and those of the people you know. Consider also the expectations about the future you may have inherited from your parents, grandparents, or earlier generations.

Twentysomethings

Walter Kirn

Walter Kirn (born in 1962) has written a novel, She Needed Me
(1992), and a collection of short stories, My Hard Bargain *(1990).
In "Twentysomethings," which appeared in* Mirabella *in January
of 1993, Kirn lambastes the current generation of young people
("Generation X") as "slackers," who are truly a "lost generation."*

The pathology of the new kids is familiar: impatience, distrust of   1
authority, malaise, and a wistful, ironic sense of longing for defunct ideals
and lost horizons. Minus the rebelliousness and hedonism that lent punch
to earlier youth movements, this is almost the same set of traits shared by
Hemingway's post–World War I "lost generation," Kerouac's Beats and
Hoffman's hippies. What distinguishes the most recent brood of disaffected
youth—variously identified as "twentysomethings," "slackers" and "the first
generation in American history that expects to do worse than its parents"—
is not its desolation but the curiously lame, detached self-consciousness
of its popular culture. Examples include TV shows such as *Melrose Place*
and *The Heights,* magazines from *Details* to *Pulse,* bands such as R.E.M.
and its countless psychedelic-lite imitators, and all movies starring Bridget
Fonda that use the word "single" in their titles. The merits of the individual
works vary widely, but taken together they evoke an oddly soulless counterculture, a sluggish mainstream underground that sold out even before it
could drop out.

The mopey inertia of twentystuff culture is, in a way, no surprise. A
generation whose defining collective experience is its lack of defining collective experiences, whose Woodstock was watching *The Partridge Family*
with a couple of friends and whose great moral dilemma is "paper or plastic?" is unlikely to produce a crop of quick-witted passionate radicals. That
would require adversaries; but the twentysomethings' one true nemesis—
the media monster that babysat them through their loveless youths—has
managed to convince them that it's their buddy, a partner in self-realization.

Consider *Melrose Place,* a show about a group of mildly disillusioned,
urban young people, manufactured by Aaron Spelling, the same man who,
with *The Love Boat* and *Dynasty,* did much of the initial illusioning. The

program has all the twentystuff hallmarks, from a mailing address for a premise (in twentystuff narratives, zip code is destiny) to therapy-speak dialogue ("I think it's really good that you're feeling these things that you're talking about"). It's basically an ensemble coping drama, with stressors-of-the-week—career troubles, problem pregnancies—replacing storylines. The show ends when everyone has aired their issues, exchanged supportive hugs. Conflicts are not resolved, they're extinguished, flash fires of emotion brought under control by pouring words on them.

The same goes for the recent movie *Singles,* a cut above *Melrose* in craftsmanship and acting but identical in its tone of plucky pathos. Once again, the lazy organizing principle is physical location, a grungy, Seattle apartment building populated by pure-hearted young folks saddled with dead-end jobs and ingrown dreams. Jaded and wary, with uncertain prospects, these white-kid nouvelle losers struggle for intimacy, fail, and then try again and provisionally succeed. In this twentystuff soap opera, public causes exist to be gestured at ("Think Globally, Act Locally," reads a bumper sticker), but private life is all the life there is, the world's having shrunk to the cramped dimensions of one's wacky, sad, starter apartment with its sardonic, cheap, recycled furnishings. Indeed, it is this notion of recycling—both of material and cultural goods—that's the essence of the twentystuff esthetic. In *Singles,* casual friends are recycled into pseudofamily members, then into lovers, then back into friends. Portentous seventies rock 'n' roll is recycled into the glum "Seattle sound." Last night's takeout is this morning's breakfast and yesterday's philosophical fads (in this case, a paperback copy of *The Fountainhead* toted around by Bridget Fonda) are today's amusements. Resigning one's self to living off the table scraps of the American century is what twentystuff culture is all about. It's about recycling anger into irony, pain into poses.

Just check out an issue of *Details* magazine, a monthly lifestyle guide   5
for wannabe desolation angels. In a recent issue that also happens to feature an interview with recycled guru Allen Ginsberg—adopted bard of all postwar youthquakes—the bedrooms of arty young single males are inspected for hidden fashion statements ("What your crib says about you"). Paolo, described as a "sound engineer/motorcycle racer," takes obvious pride in his wacky scavenging, in the fragments he has shored against his ruin: "I found the dentist's chair on the street; the sofa is the back seat of a van." Then there's Craig, a "graphic designer/DJ" (the cute juxtapositions never end), who boasts: "The trunk's from a thrift shop, the cowhide rug was a gift." The implication, of course, is that one can never be too aware of the ironic signals one is sending, even while alone, in private. According to the twentystuff credo, one's life is a self-directed TV series (*Wayne's World! Wayne's World!*), and one is always spiritually on-camera.

That's sad, I think. Not funny-sad, just sad. Consumers tricked into thinking they're producers, entombed in their own bemused self-consciousness, acting at life instead of taking action, the devotees of twentystuff may be a lost generation, indeed.

SUGGESTIONS FOR FURTHER STUDY

Key Words

The author uses language with which you may not be familiar. Find the following words in the paragraphs indicated, and explain their meanings in the context of the sentences in which the words appear. Consult a dictionary, as needed.

pathology (par. 1)
malaise (par. 1)
defunct (par. 1)
hedonism (par. 1)
nemesis (par. 2)
nouvelle (par. 4)
sardonic (par. 4)
juxtapositions (par. 5)

Topics for Discussion and Writing

1. How does Kirn describe the "new kids" or "twentysomethings"? How do those descriptions convey Kirn's *attitude* about them? Point to specific words and phrases that reveal his attitude.

2. What does Kirn say is the twentysomethings' "one true nemesis"? How does he develop his argument to show the influence of "the media monster that babysat them through their loveless youths"?

3. Do you agree or disagree with the author's assessment of the TV shows, films, and music he considers hallmarks of twentysomething culture? What examples can you offer to support or refute Kirn's argument?

4. Kirn depicts the recycling of ideas and style as a negative development. For example, he writes that the "portentous seventies rock 'n' roll is recycled into the glum 'Seattle sound.'" What is your opinion of this and other statements that indicate Kirn's negative view of recycling?

5. Debate with other readers, or write about the validity of one of the following statements from the essay:
   a. "What distinguishes the most recent brood of disaffected youth . . . is not its desolation but the curiously lame, detached self-consciousness of its popular culture." (par. 1)

    b. "Resigning one's self to living off the table scraps of the American century is what twentystuff culture is all about." (par. 4)

    c. "According to the twentystuff credo, one's life is a self-directed TV series (*Wayne's World! Wayne's World!*), and one is always spiritually on-camera." (par. 5)

6. Write a reply to Kirn in which you either agree or disagree with his point of view about twentysomethings. If you are included in the Generation X age span (late teens to 30 years old), you may want to criticize Kirn's generalization that characterizes your generation as "slackers."

The Cyberpunk:
The Individual as Reality Pilot

Timothy Leary

Timothy Leary, world-renowned psychologist and activist for social change, was a self-described performer in the Cybernetic Age, writing about the cyberworld before the explosion of interest in computers in the 1980s and 1990s. At one time a Harvard professor, Leary published more than 30 books and hundreds of essays and interviews, many of them about his theories of human consciousness. This selection was published in 1992 in a cyberpunk anthology, Storming the Reality Studio.

Your true pilot cares nothing about anything on Earth but the river, and his pride in his occupation surpasses the pride of kings.

Mark Twain, *Life on the Mississippi*

"*Cyber*" means "pilot."   1

A "*cyberperson*" is one who pilots his/her own life. By definition, the cyberperson is fascinated by navigational information—especially maps, charts, labels, guides, manuals that help pilot one through life. The cyberperson continually searches for theories, models, paradigms, metaphors, images, icons that help chart and define the realities that we inhabit.

"*Cybertech*" refers to the tools, appliances, and methodologies of knowing and communicating. Linguistics. Philosophy. Semantics. Semiotics. Practical epistemologies. The ontologies of daily life. Words, icons, pencils, printing presses, screens, keyboards, computers, disks.

"*Cyberpolitics*" introduces the Foucault notions of the use of language and linguistic-tech by the ruling classes in feudal and industrial societies to control children, the uneducated, and the under classes. The words "governor" or "steersman" or "G-man" are used to describe those who manipulate words and communication devices in order to control, to bolster authority—feudal, management, government—and to discourage innovative thought and free exchange.

WHO IS THE CYBERPUNK?

Cyberpunks use all available data-input to think for themselves.   5
You know who they are.

Every stage of history has produced names and heroic legends for the strong, stubborn, creative individuals who explore some future frontier, collect and bring back new information, and offer to guide the human gene pool to the next stage. Typically, these time mavericks combine bravery, and high curiosity, with super self-esteem. These three characteristics are considered necessary for those engaged in the profession of genetic guide, *aka* counterculture philosopher.

The classical Olde Westworld model for the cyberpunk is Prometheus, a technological genius who "stole" fire from the Gods and gave it to humanity. Prometheus also taught his gene pool many useful arts and sciences. According to the official version of the legend, he/she was exiled from the gene pool and sentenced to the ultimate torture for these unauthorized transmissions of classified information. In another version of the myth (unauthorized), Prometheus (*aka* the Pied Piper) uses his/her skills to escape the sinking kinship, taking with him/her the cream of the gene pool.

The Newe World version of this ancient myth is Quetzalcoatl, God of civilization, high-tech wizard who introduced maize, the calendar, erotic sculpture, flute-playing, the arts, and the sciences. He was driven into exile by the G-man in power, who was called Tezcatlipoca.

Self-assured singularities of the cyberbreed have been called mavericks,   10
ronin, freelancers, independents, self-starters, nonconformists, oddballs, troublemakers, kooks, visionaries, iconoclasts, insurgents, blue-sky thinkers, loners, smart alecks. Before Gorbachev, the Soviets scornfully called them hooligans. Religious organizations have always called them heretics. Bureaucrats call them disloyal dissidents, traitors, or worse. In the old days, even sensible people called them mad.

They have been variously labeled clever, creative, entrepreneurial, imaginative, enterprising, fertile, ingenious, inventive, resourceful, talented, eccentric.

During the tribal, feudal, and industrial-literate phases of human evolution, the logical survival traits were conformity and dependability. The "good serf" or "vassal" was obedient. The "good worker" or "manager" was reliable. Maverick thinkers were tolerated only at moments when innovation and change were necessary, usually to deal with the local competition.

In the information-communication civilization of the 21st Century, creativity and mental excellence will become the ethical norm. The world will be too dynamic, complex, and diversified, too cross-linked by the global immediacies of modern (quantum) communication, for stability of thought or dependability of behaviour to be successful. The "good persons" in the cybernetic society are the intelligent ones who can think for themselves.

The "problem person" in the cybernetic society of the 21st Century is the one who automatically obeys, who never questions authority, who acts to protect his/her official status, who placates and politics rather than thinks independently.

Thoughtful Japanese are worried about the need for ronin thinking in their obedient culture, the postwar generation now taking over.

THE CYBERPUNK COUNTERCULTURE
IN THE SOVIET UNION

The new postwar generation of Soviets caught on that new role models   15
are necessary to compete in the information age. Under Gorbachev, bureaucratic control is being softened, made elastic to encourage some modicum of innovative, dissident thought!

Aleksandr N. Yakovlev, Politburo member and key strategist of the glasnost policy, describes that reform: "Fundamentally, we are talking about self-government. We are moving toward a time when people will be able to govern themselves and control the activities of people that have been placed in the position of learning and governing them.

"It is not accidental that we are talking about *self*-government, or *self*-sufficiency and *self*-profitability of an enterprise, *self*-this and *self*-that. It all concerns the decentralization of power."

The cyberpunk person, the pilot who thinks clearly and creatively, using quantum-electronic appliances and brain know-how, is the newest, updated, top-of-the-line model of the 21st Century: *Homo sapiens sapiens cyberneticus*.

THE GREEK WORD FOR "PILOT"

A great pilot can sail even when his canvas is rent.

Lucius Annaeus Seneca

The term "cybernetics" comes from the Greek work *kubernetes,* "pilot."

The Hellenic origin of this word is important in that it reflects the   20
Socratic-Platonic traditions of independence and individual self-reliance which, we are told, derived from geography. The proud little Greek city-states were perched on peninsular fingers wiggling down into the fertile Mediterranean Sea, protected by mountains from the landmass armies of Asia.

Mariners of those ancient days had to be bold and resourceful. Sailing the seven seas without maps or navigational equipment, they were forced to develop independence of thought. The self-reliance that these Hellenic pilots developed in their voyages probably carried over to the democratic, inquiring, questioning nature of their land life.

The Athenian cyberpunks, the pilots, made their own navigational decisions.

These psychogeographical factors may have contributed to the humanism of the Hellenic religions that emphasized freedom, pagan joy, celebration of life, and speculative thought. The humanist and polytheistic religions of ancient Greece are often compared with the austere morality of monotheistic Judaism, the fierce, dogmatic polarities of Persian–Arab dogma, and the imperial authority of Roman (Christian) culture.

THE ROMAN CONCEPT OF DIRECTOR, GOVERNOR, STEERSMAN

The Greek word *kubernetes,* when translated to Latin, comes out as *gubernetes.* This basic verb *gubernare* means to control the actions or behavior, to direct, to exercise sovereign authority, to regulate, to keep under, to restrain, to steer. This Roman concept is obviously very different from the Hellenic notion of "pilot."

It may be relevant that the Latin term "to steer" comes from the word   25 *stare,* which means "to stand," with derivative meanings "place or thing which is standing." The past participle of the Latin word produces "status," "state," "institute," "statue," "static," "statistics," "prostitute," "restitute," "constitute."

CYBERPUNK PILOTS REPLACE GOVERNETICS–CONTROLLERS

Society everywhere is in conspiracy against the selfhood of every one of its members. . . . The virtue in most request is conformity. Self-reliance is its aversion. It loves not realities and creators, but names and customs.

Ralph Waldo Emerson, *Nature*

Who so would be a man must be a nonconformist.

Emerson, op. cit.

The word "cybernetics" was coined in 1948 by Norbert Weiner, who wrote, "We have decided to call the entire field of control and communication theory, whether in the machine or in the animal, by the name of Cybernetics, which we form from the Greek for steersman. [*sic*]"

The word "cyber" has been redefined (in the *American Heritage Dictionary*) as "the theoretical study of control processes in electronic, mechanical, and biological systems, especially the flow of information in such systems." The derivative word "cybernate" means "to control automatically by computer or to be so controlled."

An even more ominous interpretation defines cybernetics as "the study of human control mechanisms and their replacement by mechanical or electronic systems."

Note how Weiner and the Romanesque engineers have corrupted the meaning of "cyber." The Greek word "pilot" becomes "governor" or "director"; the term "to steer" becomes "to control."

Now we are liberating the term, teasing it free from serfdom to represent the autopoetic, self-directed principle of organization that arises in the universe in many systems of widely varying sizes, in people, societies, and atoms.

OUR OPPRESSIVE BIRTHRIGHT: THE POLITICS OF LITERACY

The etymological distinctions between Greek and Roman terms are quite relevant to the pragmatics of the culture surrounding their usage. French philosophy, for example, has recently stressed the importance of language and semiotics in determining human behaviour and social structures. Michel Foucault's classic studies of linguistic politics and mind control led him to believe that

> human consciousness—as expressed in speech and images, in self-definition and mutual designation . . . is the authentic locale of the determinant politics of being. . . . What men and women are born into is only superficially this or that social, legislative, and executive system. Their ambiguous, oppressive birthright is the language, the conceptual categories, the conventions of identification and perception which have evolved and, very largely, atrophied up to the time of their personal and social existence. It is the established but customarily subconscious, unargued constraints of awareness that enslave.

Orwell and Wittgenstein and McLuhan agree. To remove the means of expressing dissent is to remove the possibility of dissent. "Whereof one cannot speak, thereof must one remain silent." In this light the difference between the Greek word "pilot" and the Roman translation "governor" becomes a most significant semantic manipulation, and the flexibility granted to symbol systems of all kinds by their representation in digital computers becomes dramatically liberating.

Do we pride ourselves for becoming ingenious "pilots" or dutiful "controllers"?

WHO, WHAT, AND WHY IS GOVERNETICS

Damn the torpedoes, full speed ahead.

Captain David Glasgow Farragut's order to his steersman
at the Battle of Mobile Bay, August 5, 1864

Aye, aye, sir.

Unknown enlisted steersman at the Battle of Mobile Bay, August 5, 1864

The word "governetics" refers to an attitude of obedience-control in
relationship to self or others.

Pilots, those who navigate on the seven seas or in the sky, have to devise   35
and execute course changes continually in response to the changing environment. They respond continually to feedback, information about the
environment. Dynamic. Alert. Alive.

The Latinate "steersman," by contrast, is in the situation of following
orders. The Romans, we recall, were great organizers, road-builders,
administrators. The galleys, the chariots must be controlled. The legions of
soldiers must be directed.

The Hellenic concept of the individual navigating his/her own course
was an island of humanism in a raging sea of totalitarian empires. To the
East (the past) were the centralized, authoritarian kingdoms. The governors
of Iran, from Cyrus, the Persian emperor, to the recent shah and ayatollah,
have exemplified the highest traditions of state control.

The Greeks were flanked on the other side, which we shall designate as
the West (or future), by a certain heavy concept called Rome. The caesars
and popes of the Holy Roman Empire represented the next grand phase of
institutional control. The governing hand on the wheel stands for stability,
durability, continuity, permanence. Staying the course. Individual creativity,
exploration, and change are usually not encouraged.

CYBERPUNKS: PILOTS OF THE SPECIES

*The winds and waves are always on the side of the ablest
navigators.*

Edward Gibbon

The terms "cybernetic person" or "cybernaut" return us to the original
meaning of "pilot" and puts the self-reliant person back in the loop. These
words (and the more pop term "cyberpunk") refer to the personalization
(and thus the popularization) of knowledge-information technology, to
innovative thinking on the part of the individual.

According to McLuhan and Foucault, if you change the language, you   40
change the society. Following their lead, we suggest that the terms "cyber-

netic person, cybernaut" may describe a new species model of human being and a new social order. "Cyberpunk" is, admittedly, a risky term. Like all linguistic innovations, it must be used with a tolerant sense of high-tech humor. It's a stopgap, transitional meaning-grenade thrown over the language barricades to describe the resourceful, skillful individual who accesses and steers knowledge–communication technology toward his/her own private goals, for personal pleasure, profit, principle, or growth.

Cyberpunks are the inventors, innovative writers, technofrontier artists, risk-taking film directors, icon-shifting composers, stand-up comedians, expressionist artists, free-agent scientists, technocreatives, computer visionaries, elegant hackers, bit-blipping Prolog adepts, special-effectives, cognitive dissidents, video wizards, neurological test pilots, media explorers—all of those who boldly package and steer ideas out there where no thoughts have gone before.

Countercultures are sometimes tolerated by the governors. They can, with sweet cynicism and patient humor, interface their singularity with institutions. They often work within the "governing systems" on a temporary basis.

As often as not, they are unauthorized.

THE LEGEND OF THE RONIN

The ronin . . . has broken with the tradition of career feudalism. Guided by a personally defined code of adaptability, autonomy, and excellence, ronin are employing career strategies grounded in a premise of rapid change.

Beverly Potter, *The Way of the Ronin*

Ronin is used as a metaphor based on a Japanese word for lordless samurai. As early as the 8th Century, ronin was translated literally as "wave people" and used in Japan to describe those who had left their allotted, caste-predetermined stations in life: samurai who left the service of their feudal lords to become masterless.

Ronin played a key role in Japan's abrupt transition from a feudal society to industrialism. Under feudal rule, warriors were not allowed to think freely, or act according to their will. On the other hand, having been forced by circumstances to develop independence, [ronin] took more readily to new ideas and technology and become increasingly influential in the independent schools.

Potter, op. cit.

The West has many historical parallels to the ronin archetype. The term 45 "free lance" has its origin in the period after the Crusades, when a large number of knights were separated from their lords. Many lived by the code of chivalry and became "lances for hire."

The American frontier was fertile ground for the ronin archetype. "Maverick," derived from the Texan word for unbranded steer, was used to describe a free and self-directed individual.

> Although many of the ronin's roots . . . are in the male culture, most career women are well acquainted with the way of the ronin. Career women left their traditional stations and battled their way into the recesses of the male-dominated workplaces . . . Like the ronin who had no clan, professional women often feel excluded from the corporate cliques' inside tracks, without ally or mentor.
>
> *Potter, op. cit.*

SOME EXAMPLES OF CYBERPUNKS

Christopher Columbus (1451–1506) was born in Genoa. At age 25 he showed up in Lisbon and learned the craft of map-making. This was the golden era of Portuguese exploration. Many pilots and navigators were convinced that the Earth was round, and that the Indies and other unknown lands could be found by crossing the western seas. What was special about Columbus was his persistence and eloquence in support of the dream of discovery. For more than ten years he traveled the courts of Europe attempting to make "the deal"; to find backing for his "enterprise of the Indies."

According to the *Columbia Encyclopedia,* "Historians have disputed for centuries his skill as a navigator, but it has been recently proved that with only dead reckoning Columbus was unsurpassed in charting and finding his way about unknown seas."

Columbus was a most unsuccessful governor of the colonies he had discovered. He died in disgrace, his cyberskills almost forgotten. (At least that's what they tell us in the authorized history books.)

In 1992 the Political Correction Department dismissed Columbus as a racist colonist.

Mark Twain. He purchased the Remington typewriter when it appeared in 1874 for $125. In 1875 he became the first author in history to submit a typewritten manuscript to a publisher. It was *The Adventures of Tom Sawyer.*

"This newfangled writing machine," Twain wrote, "has several virtues. It piles an awful stack of words on one page. It don't muss things or scatter ink blots around. Of course it saves paper."

Mathias (Rusty) Rust, a 19-year-old loner from Hamburg, Germany, attained all-star status as a cyberpunk when, on May 28, 1987, he flew a one-engine Cessna through the "impenetrable" Soviet air defenses and landed in Moscow's Red Square. There were no gubernal or organizational motives. The technological adventure was a personal mission. Rusty just wanted to talk to some Russians. German newspapers celebrated the event, calling it "the stuff of dreams," and comparing the youth to the Red Baron Manfred von Richthofen and Charles Augustus Lindbergh.

THE CYBERPUNK CODE: TFYQA

War Games is an electronic quantum signal, a movie about high-tech computers and human evolution that illustrates and condemns the use of quantum-electronic knowledge technology by governors to control. The film celebrates the independence and skill of cyberpunks who think for themselves and innovate from within the static system. The Captain and his wife use high-tech agriculture methods to enhance the potency of unauthorized botanical neuroactivators. The Captain makes an unauthorized decision to abort World War III. In both instances the Captain follows the cyberpunk code: *Think for yourself; question authority (TFYQA)*.

The cyberkid Matthew Broderick is equally courageous, creative, and bright. When the audience is introduced to the hero of *War Games*, he is in a video arcade playing a space-adventure game with poise and proficiency. An electron jock.

Late for school, he's pulled into the classic confrontation: the authoritarian teacher humiliates and punishes the Tom Sawyer kid, sends him to the principal's office. There he obtains the code for the school's computer system. Back home, he uses his PC to access the school records. He changes an unfair grade to a passing level. He thinks for himself and questions authority.

At the crucial moment he rushes to the library and researches the life of a physicist, scans scientific journals, scopes microfilm files—not to please the system, but in pursuit of his own personal grail.

Note that there is a new dimension of electronic ethics and quantum legality here. The Captain and Matthew perform no act of physical violence, no theft of material goods. The Captain processes some computer data and decides for himself. Matthew rearranges clusters of electrons stored on a chip. They seek independence, not control over others.

THE CYBERPUNK AS ROLE MODEL
FOR THE 21ST CENTURY

The tradition of the "individual who thinks for him/herself" extends to the beginnings of recorded human history. Indeed, the very label of our species, *Homo sapiens,* defines us as the animals who think.

If our genetic function is *computare* ("to think"), then it follows that the   60
ages and stages of human history, so far, have been larval or preparatory. After
the insectoid phases of submission to gene pools, the mature stage of the
human life cycle is the individual who thinks for him/herself. Now, at the beginnings of the information age, are we ready to assume our genetic function?

SUGGESTIONS FOR FURTHER STUDY

Key Words

The author uses language with which you may not be familiar. Find the
following words in the paragraphs indicated, and explain their meanings in
the context of the sentences in which the words appear. Consult a dictionary, as needed.

> paradigms (par. 2)
> semiotics (par. 3)
> epistemologies (par. 3)
> ontologies (par. 3)
> iconoclasts (par. 10)
> hooligans (par. 10)
> dissidents (par. 10)
> entrepreneurial (par. 11)
> polytheistic (par. 23)
> austere (par. 23)
> sic (par. 27)
> autopoetic (par. 30)
> atrophied (par. 31)
> archetype (par. 46)

Language and Style

How would you characterize the writer's style in this essay? How does
his essay look different from most of the other essays in this book? Notice
that very short (even one-sentence) paragraphs follow much longer ones,
lists of words illustrate and develop ideas, and quotations from other writers introduce new sections of the essay. Find other features of the writer's
style you consider distinctive. Working from a list of those features, write a
short essay, defining and describing the writer's style in your own words.
Provide several examples to illustrate your definition.

Topics for Discussion and Writing

1. How would you describe the author's tone of voice in this essay? Is
   he serious, sarcastic, humorous, authoritative, or critical, or does he

use several of these voices on different occasions throughout the essay? Discuss the author's tone with other readers, and point to examples in the essay to illustrate your description.

2. Make a list of Leary's references to people, places, or events you don't know or recognize. In class, compare your list with other readers' lists, and share your knowledge with them to identify as many references as your can. You may need to look up some of them in the library. Once you have identified them, consider how relevant they are to Leary's discussion of "cyber" and its related terms (e.g., cyberpunk, cyberperson, cybernetic).

3. "The Cyberpunk: The Individual as Reality Pilot" is organized and developed by several methods: definition, explanation, and illustration or example. For instance, Leary defines *cyberpunk* in the beginning of the essay by citing *synonyms* for the term applied throughout history, or *labels* placed on such persons at various times. Locate and discuss other methods of defining terms in this essay.

4. How is the Greek mythological hero Prometheus a "classical Old West-World model for the Cyberpunk"? What other historical or mythical models of the cyberpunk does Leary cite? Choose one of them, and elaborate more fully on how your choice is an appropriate model.

5. In the short section subtitled "Cyberpunk: The Pilots of the Species," Leary delineates what a cyberpunk is. List those characteristics that define *cyberpunk* and explain how they are appropriate.

6. Look at the author's discussion of a *ronin* and compare the ronin to the cyberpunk. In a journal entry, discuss someone you know whom you could characterize as either a ronin or a cyberpunk.

7. People who use computers may be referred to as cyberpunks or cybernauts. In light of Leary's definitions, explain how such a reference is valid.

8. The term *cyberpunk* originated with author William Gibson after the publication of his science-fiction novel, *Neuromancer.* Read *Neuromancer,* and research Gibson's use of the ideas of cyberspace and cyberspace cowboys. Gibson prophesied that people would be able to travel the World Wide Web in an interesting way. Find out what that way is, and describe it.

9. View the film *War Games,* and comment on Leary's assessment of it: "The film celebrates the independence and skill of cyberpunks who think for themselves and innovate from within a static system. . . . They seek no control over others" (par. 54).

10. Given Leary's definitions of cyberpunk and cybernaut, to what extent might these historical or contemporary figures qualify? Explain your answer.

a. Charles A. Lindbergh
b. Anne Morrow Lindbergh
c. Gertrude Stein
d. Mary Ferguson
e. Andy Warhol
f. Wilt Chamberlain
g. Stanley Kubrick
h. Steve Jobs and Steve Wozniak
i. David Hockney

Dave Barry in Cyberspace: The Future of the Computer Revolution

Dave Barry

Dave Barry, a Pulitzer Prize-winning journalist for the Miami Herald, *lives in Miami, Florida. He has authored numerous best-sellers, includ-ing* The Taming of the Screw, Babies and Other Hazards of Sex, Stay Fit and Healthy Until You're Dead, Claw Your Way to the Top, Dave Barry's Guide to Marriage and/or Sex, Dave Barry Turns 40, *and* Dave Barry in Cyberspace *(1996), from which the following selection has been taken.*

THE FUTURE OF THE COMPUTER REVOLUTION OR FUN WITH MISTER JOHNSON

In setting out to write this book, I wanted to make the Computer Revolution understandable to the average, nontechnical person, defined as "the person who cannot open a childproof aspirin bottle without using an ax."

I knew this task would not be easy, because (a) there are a lot of extremely complex technical issues involved, and (b) I did not plan to do any research. Nevertheless I have tried, in these pages, to provide you with information that would be of immense practical value if not for the fact that it all became obsolete minutes after I wrote it. I might as well have written this book in Swahili for all the good it's going to do you, because in the Computer Revolution everything changes way too fast for the human brain to comprehend. This is why only 14-year-olds[1] really understand what's going on.

For example, I have referred many times in this book to the hugely pop-ular Windows 95☺☺ operating system, but of course as soon as everybody has purchased and learned to actually *use* Windows 95☈, it will be replaced by something newer, something better, something totally different, and something that—above all—requires you to give more money to Microsoft.

---

[1]No, they are *not* human.

The cycle of obsolescence has become so short that, in the computer super-stores of tomorrow, there will be Dumpsters located conveniently right next to the cash registers so you can discard your obsolete purchases immediately after paying for them, then go back into the store and buy something even newer.

So the bottom line is, if you think the Computer Revolution is any-where *near* over, then you are, with all due respect, a moron. The Computer Revolution is just getting cranked up. We have no idea what computers will be like ten or twenty years from now. For all we know, the Computer of the Future, rather than being a clunky external appliance, will be a miniatur-ized device that will be surgically implanted into your skull, where it will transmit information directly to your brain. Think of the advantages! Let's say you're a business consultant, and you're going to an important lunch with a major potential client whom you really want to impress. Before entering the restaurant, you'd simply open your wallet, select a dime-sized micro-disk containing billions of bytes of information, and insert it into your ear. Then, during the lunch, when the potential client, testing your knowledge, asked you for some obscure data, you'd simply squeeze the bridge of your nose to activate your internal computer, and within a nanosecond you'd hear yourself, in your own natural voice, telling your potential client: "Hey, big boy! Let's play Mister Johnson Hunts for Beaver!" Because by mistake you inserted the micro-disk for Volume 27 of Hot Sex Fantasies for Men.

Yes, there is a bright new tomorrow waiting for us, and not just in the   5
area of hardware. The Software of the Future will also be extremely sophis-ticated. For one thing, it will be *much* bigger and more powerful than today's software programs, which are so puny that you can fit several of them on your hard drive at the same time. The Software of the Future will have so many features, graphics, animated cartoon characters, video clips, etc., that a single program will fill up all the space on your hard drive before you're halfway through installing it. You'll need to purchase several addi-tional computers just to get the program operating to the point where it will tell you the phone number for Technical Support.

But once you finally get the Software of the Future running, you'll be amazed at what it will do. It will be so sophisticated that it will almost seem to be a living entity. It will get to know you as a person and call you by your name. It will learn your preferences and seek to anticipate your every need. It will know when you're in the room, and when you leave, it will become depressed. It will think about you constantly and become jealous if you attempt to interact with other software. Ultimately it will become so obsessed with you that it will kidnap you and imprison you in a remote wilderness cabin, and if you try to escape, it will chop off your feet. That's how much it will love you.

But as exciting as the future will be in the fields of software and hardware, the real "action" will be on the Internet, particularly the World Wide Web. As I write these words, the Web consists mainly of 14 million interlinked home pages created by college students wishing to tell the world what they look like, how they feel about various rock bands, what snack foods they eat, whether they prefer briefs or boxers, etc. This is of course vital information, but it only begins to tap the vast potential of the Web to enhance our lives, by which I mean sell us stuff.

Your major corporations are only just now beginning to discover the Web, but once they figure it out, they're going to be all over it. As the quality of Web sound and video improve, corporations are going to start sponsoring Web sites that will look a lot like television shows, the difference being that, using your computer, you'll be able to interact with them. For example, let's say that in the future there's a Web version of the hugely popular TV show *Baywatch*, which tells the heartwarming story of a group of young lifeguards with incredible bodies who wear tight bathing suits everywhere, including funerals, and who courageously continue to patrol a public beach despite the fact that constant exposure to direct sunlight has apparently killed off all their brain cells.

On this World Wide Web *Baywatch* of the future, you'll be able to use "hyperlinks" on the screen to obtain information on products that interest you. For example, if a *Baywatch* character is wearing a shade of lipstick that you admire, you'll just position your mouse pointer on the character's lips and click your mouse button; immediately the screen will tell you the name of the lipstick manufacturer, as well as the specific lipstick shade and the name of local stores where you can buy it. By clicking on other parts of the *Baywatch* character, you'll be able to obtain similar information about clothes, shoes, jewelry, hemorrhoid remedies, and breast implants. Of course you'll also be able to order everything you see on the screen through your Internet account; this means that, merely by spilling beer on your keyboard, you could become legally obligated to purchase a helicopter.

And there's more. As Web programming becomes even more interac- 10
tive, you'll actually be able to affect the outcome of the shows you watch. For example, if you dislike a certain *Baywatch* character, you'll simply use your mouse to "drag" him or her to the ocean and "drop" him or her directly into the mouth of a shark. Or you could use the "cut and paste" function to remove characters from one show and insert them into another, so that you could, for example, find out what kinds of wacky observations Jerry Seinfeld would make if he were being dissected by aliens on *The X-Files*.

Eventually, you'll be able to have direct input into *all* Web programming, not just dramas and sitcoms. This means that, if you felt like it, you could have Dan Rather do an entire evening news broadcast with a live ferret clinging to the side of his face.[2] The possibilities are even more exciting for sports programming. Just imagine if, while sitting in front of a computer in the comfort of your home, you could actually "play" in a football game taking place thousands of miles away!

Play-by-Play Announcer: Aikman hands off to Emmitt Smith . . . Smith is at the 45, the 40, the 35 . . . He's in the open! He's gonna go all the way! He's . . . HOLY SMOKES! Emmitt Smith has been speared and pinned to the turf like a dead butterfly by a giant mouse pointer!

Color Announcer: That's gotta hurt, Bob.

Of course these are just a few of the ways in which our lifestyles will be improved by the computer of tomorrow. We're just beginning to scratch the surface of the capabilities of this incredible tool. Just as the people who were alive when the telephone was invented had no way of knowing that the new device would someday make it possible for virtually every person on Earth, regardless of physical location, to be interrupted at dinner, so are we fundamentally ignorant of the ways in which the computer will ultimately change our lives. We cannot see the future; we do not know what lies around the next bend on the Information Superhighway; we cannot predict where, ultimately, the Computer Revolution will take us. All we know for certain is that, when we finally get there, we won't have enough RAM.

SUGGESTIONS FOR FURTHER STUDY

Key Words

The author uses language with which you may not be familiar. Find the following words in the paragraphs indicated, and explain their meanings in the context of the sentences in which the words appear. Consult a dictionary, as needed.

obsolescence (par. 3)
nanosecond (par. 4)
entity (par. 6)
RAM (par. 12)

Topics for Discussion and Writing

1. How does Barry achieve a humorous effect in this essay? Cite several passages that satirize or make fun of the computer revolution, and discuss the ways in which they are humorous.

---

[2]Actually, Dan may already have done this.

2. Barry describes the "Software of the Future" in his essay. What do you perceive as the software of the future? Compare your ideas about this topic to Barry's.

3. Barry thinks that "our lifestyles will be improved by the computer of tomorrow." Is he serious or facetious or both in describing how the computer of the future will affect our lives? Explain your answer.

4. Write an essay describing how our future will or will not be improved by computers and computer software. You might try for a humorous, satiric effect, as Barry did, or write your essay in a more serious vein. If you like, illustrate your essay with drawings, photographs, or other artwork you can generate on a computer.

Info Highway: A Long and Winding Road

Shelley Donald Coolidge

Shelley Donald Coolidge has been a staff writer for the Christian Science Monitor *since 1992. Based in Cambridge, Massachusetts, she currently writes on education and business. "Info Highway: A Long and Winding Road," was published in the* Christian Science Monitor *in 1996.*

John Nomes and three other classmates at the Peabody School in 1
Cambridge, Mass., cluster around a computer in the back of Jackie Crowe's seventh-grade science class.

They are studying planetary construction. Their assignment: to download earthquake statistics from the National Earthquake Information Center on the Internet and plot the data on a world map. The results will show that earthquakes have occurred along plate boundaries, explaining how the continents were formed.

In past classes, Mrs. Crowe says, it's been a tough sell to get students to look up often-outdated material in books. Now, she practically has to pull her students away from their work.

"I never had to fight to get them to go to lunch before," she says, trying to usher several students out the door.

What's going on in this classroom is what President Clinton hopes will 5
soon be standard everywhere. His goal: to have every classroom and library in the country—public and private—connected to the Internet by 2000. Forty-four states are already moving forward with education-technology plans under grants from the Federal Goals 2000 program.

But wiring schools to the information superhighway is only a start. A big component will be training teachers, integrating computers into the curriculum, and even reevaluating the way students are taught. This doesn't mean nixing the basics, experts say, but rather teaching them in the context of modern technology.

"The schools are way out of date in terms of being able to provide a learning environment that is comparable to the way we want people to perform on the job," says Dave Moursand, executive director of the International Society for Technology in Education in Eugene, Ore.

While some educators question whether every classroom will actually be surfing the Internet in 4 1/2 years, few dispute the need for computers to be integrated into the curriculum. Students with access to computers will excel in tomorrow's work force; those without "will graduate with skills that prepare them for yesterday, not tomorrow," says Cheryl Lempke of the Illinois State Board of Education. The President's proposal, she and others hope, may help level the playing field.

In comparison with other countries, the United States leads in using technology innovatively in the classroom. Even so, the number of successful programs in schools remains limited.

A decade ago, 75 students typically shared access to one computer. Currently there is about one computer for every 10 students in kindergarten through 12th grade. This is an average, meaning that while some schools may be very well equipped, others have virtually no computer technology.

But while the number of computers is growing in most schools, Internet access is often very limited. In Crowe's class, for example, more than 20 students share one computer with Internet access. Only 35 percent of all schools are connected, and a tiny fraction of classrooms in those schools are hooked up.

A big question is funding.

The US Department of Education estimates that it will cost anywhere from $10 billion to $50 billion to wire the schools, buy more computers, and train teachers.

The federal government plans to put up several billion dollars in matching grants as seed money, says Linda Roberts, director of education technology for the US Department of Education. But she hopes that the majority of funding will come from states, communities, and the private sector.

So far, 40 percent of the money has come from local governments, she says. Twenty-five percent has come from federal funds; 20 percent from state revenues; and only 10 to 15 percent from the private sector.

Still, while Ms. Roberts points to what she calls "pockets of excellence," the investment in computers—and teacher training and curriculum development—hasn't been enough to have a significant impact on student learning.

"Every time you talk to people about technology, the first thing they say is, 'With all we've invested so far, why haven't we seen significant gains?'" Ms. Roberts says. "Well, the answer is, we've invested very little."

Currently, schools spend about $20 per student on technology each year, estimates John Phillipo, head of the Center for Educational Leadership and Technology in Marlboro, Mass. For technology to really make an impact, schools need to invest $100 to $120 a student.

The issue is paramount, he says, to the country's economic development. In an information-based economy, workers must be able to access, analyze, and communicate information using the basics of technology, Mr. Phillipo says. "Can you create a skilled worker to do those three things without technology? You can, but they won't be productive," he says.

Computers can also help solve some behavior and attention problems.   20 "Kids today really are computer savvy, but when they enter the classroom, it's a very gray, very old fashioned environment," says Ruth Ann Burns, executive director of the National Teacher Training Institute in New York. Technology, she says, helps "bring the real world into the classroom."

Today, roughly 85 percent of the curriculum is based on textbooks, Phillipo says. Ideally, 65 to 70 percent of materials should come off the Internet. He says that material is more timely and engaging—textbooks are practically out of date when they arrive in classrooms.

Some education experts contend that the weak link in this chain is solid planning on the part of school administrators as to how computers fit into the curriculum.

"The belief that technology can be a magic bullet can be dangerous," says Stone Wiske, co-director of the Educational Technology Center at the Harvard Graduate School of Education in Cambridge, Mass. "In this day and age, schools do need a certain amount of technology, but I don't think every kid in every classroom has to be touching a computer so many minutes per day."

Some schools, she and others say, have been pushed into purchasing computers—often by parents. But without the proper training and planning, the technology may go unused.

"We've come up against this where school districts have invested in   25 computers and software and minimal training and everything lies fallow," Ms. Burns says.

Equally important is integrating the technology into the curriculum. Florida, for example, requires 30 percent of funds for technology in schools to be spent on teacher training. The private sector, Mr. Moursand notes, invests closer to 50 percent into staff development.

Phillipo urges schools to spend 25 cents on research and staff development for each dollar spent on Internet access. No one, he adds, knows where that money will come from.

SUGGESTIONS FOR FURTHER STUDY

Key Words

The author uses language with which you may not be familiar. Find the following words in the paragraphs indicated, and explain their meanings in the context of the sentences in which the words appear. Consult a dictionary, as needed.

planetary (par. 1)
seed money (par. 13)
paramount (par. 19)

Topics for Discussion and Writing

1. The author of this article describes a seventh-grade classroom as meeting the goals of "every classroom and library in the country." How is it doing so? Have you been in classrooms that might be described in the same way? If so, describe your experience, and explain how your education has been enhanced by computer applications.

2. In this article, criticisms of the shortcomings of education in American classrooms focuses on the lack of computers and their applications in the curriculum. What specifically are those criticisms?

3. What does Coolidge mean by an "information-based society"? How important is it for American society to be fully "information-based"? Discuss this topic with other readers, or write about it in your journal.

4. Using a number of reliable sources in an academic paper or a professional report is an intelligent strategy for a number of reasons. List the sources Coolidge uses in this article, and explain their usefulness to her argument.

5. Extensive discussions in advertisements, newspaper and magazine articles, television programs, and speeches by high-ranking political leaders claim that computers will make a positive contribution to education in the future. Nonetheless, fundamental problems exist, raising questions about access to the information superhighway. For example, a large number of people in America cannot afford a home computer or access to the Internet; not everyone agrees that unrestricted access to the Internet is beneficial; and not every local community has the resources to furnish computers in its school classrooms. Other problems exist, as well. Research this topic, and write an essay that explores the problems involved in making American education technologically innovative.

Bigots on the Net

Amy Harmon

*Amy Harmon (born in 1968, in New York City) graduated from
the University of Michigan, Ann Arbor, and has worked as a reporter
and staff writer with the* Los Angeles Times *since 1992. Her concentration is currently on emerging new aspects of media and technologies.
"Bigots on the Net" was originally printed in the* Los Angeles Times
on December 14, 1994.

Alarmed by the growing presence of hate groups in cyberspace, the   1
Simon Wiesenthal Center[1] Tuesday sent a letter to the Prodigy online computer service protesting the "continued use of Prodigy by bigots to promote
their agendas of hate."

The Los Angeles–based center said it has tracked increasing activity
over the last few months by more than fifty hate groups using online services and the popular Internet global computer network. "More and more
of these groups are embracing and utilizing the information superhighway,"
said Rabbi Abraham Cooper, associate dean of the center. "The slurs are the
same but the venue is different."

The center called on commercial online services to keep hate groups out
and proposed that the government play a similar policing role on the amorphous Internet. Of particular concern, Cooper said, is that young people
could be exposed to white supremacy in an environment unmediated by
teachers, parents, or librarians. Much of the activity takes place on open
electronic forums accessible to anyone with an Internet account or a sub-
scription to a commercial service.

About twenty million computer users are connected to the Internet, and
another five million use commercial online services, including more than
two million on Prodigy.

But civil libertarians—and white supremacists themselves—say that   5
cyberspace, like any other medium of expression, must remain open to free
speech. And in an uncharted territory where the rules of engagement are

---

[1]*Simon Wiesenthal Center:* Founded in 1978, the Simon Wiesenthal Center educates today's
generation about the Holocaust, and fights the hatred and prejudice that enabled the
Holocaust to occur.—ED.

still unformed, the center's offensive is sure to sharpen the ongoing debate over electronic censorship.

"It's a genuinely difficult problem," says Marc Rotenberg, director of the Electronic Privacy Information Center, an online civil liberties organization. "And there are no paradigms to turn to."

It's a problem that is quickly becoming relevant to a lot more people. All sorts of enterprises, from businesses to charity organizations, have been rushing to get hooked up to computer networks, which offer fast, convenient communication at increasingly lower prices.

But for white supremacist groups like the National Alliance and the American Renaissance, cyberspace offers benefits that are proportionately far greater.

Marginalized by traditional media and short on funds, hate groups have been learning to use low-cost online communications to gain recruits and spread propaganda across state and even national boundaries, giving them access to a far wider audience than they have historically be able to reach.

Valerie Fields, for example, a West Los Angeles resident and political junkie, signs on to her Prodigy account a few times a week to read the discussion of local politics. Last month, she clicked her way into the "News" forum to find an anti-Latino diatribe that closed with a plug for a $20 subscription to the newsletter of Louisville, Kentucky–based American Renaissance.

"Around the election the messages about [Proposition] 187[2] got pretty nasty," Fields said. "But then I saw this one that seemed to be from an organized white supremacist group, and that really freaked me out."

The message Fields saw, and several others, including one that referred to *The Diary of Anne Frank* as a "Jewish hoax" prompted the Wiesenthal Center to ask Prodigy to strengthen its guidelines to delete such messages from its boards.

"We're having a discussion with them," Prodigy spokesman Brian Ek said Tuesday afternoon. "Our feeling is we already have a good system in place. But we have more than 1.7 million notes on the board at any given time, and we can't read them all."

Prodigy was the focus of controversy involving antisemitic comments in 1991, and worked with the Anti-Defamation League at the time to craft a policy that forbids "blatant expressions of hatred" on its boards. All messages are also run through a computer that scans for obscenities before they are posted. But Cooper says the service should look more carefully at messages that target groups rather than individuals.

---

2. *Proposition 187*: A controversial California ballot measure that denied schooling, medical care, and other governmental services to illegal immigrants.—ED.

Prodigy is not the only online service to be utilized by hate groups.   15

Kevin Strom, who produces a weekly radio show for the National Alliance, and has been active online, said he was recently blocked from the "Political" and "Issues" forums on CompuServe.

"Apparently somebody complained that our articles were bashing ethnic minorities," Strom says. "So the system operator decided we didn't deserve freedom of speech."

Strom says the articles he posted on the forums were among those which users transferred most frequently to their home computers. One titled "The Wisdom of Henry Ford," which reviewed the book *The International Jew,* was downloaded 120 times one week, he said.

CompuServe leaves the decision of what to screen out to the individual "sysops" who are hired to moderate the service's discussion forums. Says Georgia Griffith, the Politics sysop: "We don't block users for what they believe or say, but how they say it. The First Amendment allows people to publish what they choose, but we are not obliged to publish it for them."

The legal issue of who is ultimately responsible for what does get "pub-   20
lished" online is a thorny one that has yet to be entirely resolved.

A federal judge ruled in 1991 that CompuServe was like a bookstore owner who could not be held accountable for the contents of books on his shelves—a precedent the online services support.

But activists say there are ethical issues at stake, which public opinion can help to enforce—at least in the private sector.

The Internet, a web of several hundred computer networks not owned by any one enterprise, is a more difficult proposition. Cooper wrote a letter to Federal Communications Chairman Reed E. Hundt last summer suggesting that it "may be time for the FCC to place a cop on the Superhighway of Information."

But such an effort would involve significant technical difficulties, and would also likely encounter vehement opposition from civil liberties groups who want to preserve the Internet as a democratic forum.

Because of its anarchic structure, the Internet has generally been viewed   25
as a "common carrier" much like the telephone company, which cannot be held liable for what passes over its lines.

"That would be a very dangerous path to go down," says EPIC's Rotenberg. "It would lead to an extraordinary amount of censorship and control that would be very inappropriate."

Discussion groups geared toward white supremacist propaganda on the Internet have labels such as "skinheads," "revisionism" and "vigilantes." The Institute for Historical Review recently set up a site on the World Wide Web portion of the Internet where some of its literature can be obtained for free. A document called "Frequently Asked Questions about National Socialism" is available at several sites.

The computer commands used on the Internet also allow users to access information anonymously, which far-right activists say helps many to overcome the inhibitions they might have about signing up.

The National Alliance rents space on a computer at Netcom Online Communication Services, one of the largest Internet access providers in California, where texts of its radio programs are available. It has also posted flyers on the Internet promoting its radio show, urging readers to send "minority parasites packing to fend for themselves" and condemning community development funding as support for black "breeding colonies."

"We've seen a huge growth in use of the Internet by our people," says   30
Alliance Chairman William Pierce. "The major media in this country are very biased against our political point of view. They present us with ridicule or in a very distorted way. The information superhighway is much more free of censorship. It's possible for a dedicated individual to get his message out to thousands and thousands of people."

SUGGESTIONS FOR FURTHER STUDY

Key Words

The author uses language with which you may not be familiar. Find the following words in the paragraphs indicated, and explain their meanings in the context of the sentences in which the words appear. Consult a dictionary, as needed.

venue (par. 2)
amorphous (par. 3)
paradigms (par. 6)
diatribe (par. 10)
blatant (par. 14)
sysops (par. 19)
vehement (par. 24)
anarchic (par. 25)

Topics for Discussion and Writing

1. Find out more about the Simon Wiesenthal Center in Los Angeles or the U.S. Holocaust Memorial Museum in Washington, D.C. Why might such institutions be concerned about increased activity of hate groups on the Internet?

2. Although civil libertarians and white supremacists would seem to be on opposite sides of the hate-crime issue discussed in this article, about what do they agree, and why?

3. How does the First Amendment figure into the discussion of publishing online? How is the FCC (Federal Communications Commission) involved? Do you agree with Rabbi Cooper that it "may be time for the FCC to place a cop on the Superhighway of Information" (par. 23)? Why or why not? Explain your point of view. If you can, give examples from your experience with using the Internet.

4. In an essay, take a stand on the issue explored in this article. Many people feel that freedom of speech, guaranteed by our Constitution, gives them the right to send any message they want over public communication systems. However, freedom of speech may conflict with other ethical issues. Identify some of those ethical issues, state your position on them, and suggest a partial solution to the conflict, if you can.

Those Who Die with the Most Toys Lose

Cindie L. Keefauver

In this selection, student writer Cindie L. Keefauver responds to Laurence Shames's "The More Factor." Keefauver agrees with Shames and insists we should change our focus from "desir[ing] more"— which is like an "unquenchable thirst," to "growth in responsibility" and "serving humanity."

In "The More Factor," Laurence Shames discusses the behavior of American consumers and the roots of their habits of consumption. A very popular bumper sticker in the '80s and even into the '90s reads "Whoever dies with the most toys wins." In general, this bumper sticker reveals the mindset of American culture.

Typically, American children are raised to believe that when they grow up they will go to college, have the career of their choice, choose a spouse, have children, own a home and be successful members of society. As a culture and a people we have the freedom and opportunity to do and purchase what we need and desire. The trend seems to be to acquire as much material goods as possible. In the words of Sonia Maasik and Jack Solomon, "to live in a consumer society, you are what you consume, and the entire social and economic order is maintained by the constant encouragement to buy." Some people will even find their identity in the products they have purchased. They can be heard saying, "I'm a Ford man" or "I'm a Chevy man." Not only do we grow up thinking and believing that this is the American dream, but we are bombarded with television, radio, newspaper, and magazine advertisements. Advertisers are businesspeople and are primarily interested in ratings, not educating adults or children. Advertisements try to persuade us that what we have is out-of-date, or that we need a particular product to make our lives complete. Some people will purchase goods to be like someone else, or just to achieve a certain amount of status among their peers. People will pursue "things" at the risk of losing not only money but precious loved ones, too. I agree with Laurence Shames; "the more factor" does exist in our country today.

This way of life for Americans dates back to the American Frontier. As Shames writes, speculators—again businessmen—would travel great distances to uninhabited land and virtually build a town. It was complete with a Grand Hotel, Opera House, a flagpole and a church. Americans, being optimistic, would move into these towns in hopes of new opportunities. Shames comments, "You banked on the next windfall, you staked your hopes and even your self-esteem on it, and this led to a national turn of mind that might usefully be thought of as the habit of more." The habit of more began hundreds of years ago, Shames adds, "making this the operative truth among the economically ambitious." We have been consuming ever since.

We live in a product-dominated world. American businesses will continue to mass produce products for the consumer as long as we will consume. In the recent documentary *Signal to Noise: Watching T.V. Watching Us*, Cara Mertes cites an alarming statistic: "Children, ages 4–11, have 7.3 billion dollars in spending and through their parents they influence another 158 billion dollars in purchases each year." Not only do adults consume but children are very aware of things to consume. Even more disconcerting is the fact that advertisers view children not as a precious human resource, but simply as a market to be exploited.

In our desire for more in America we have lost sight of what is impor-   5
tant. Shames eloquently illustrates this when he states: "The ethic of decency has been upstaged by the ethic of success. The concept of growth has been applied almost exclusively to things that can be measured, counted, and weighed. And the hunger for those things that are unmeasurable but fine—the sorts of accomplishment that cannot be undone by circumstances or a shift in social fashion, the kind of serenity that cannot be shattered by tomorrow's headline—has gone largely unfulfilled and even unacknowledged." The Lexus in the driveway in all its glory can be totalled tomorrow. The $100.00 name brand tennis shoes can go out of style before you break them in. Americans should evaluate the way we consume. Do we generally purchase items we need, or items that we desire, or items we just have to have? Americans would benefit in shifting our focus when we are determining products to consume, shifting our focus to a growth in responsibility and happiness rather than success and greed.

Even though I agree with Shames about our desire for more, I disagree with Shames's supposition that "more is diminishing." The fact that we live on a finite planet and have a finite amount of resources has seldom stopped our progress. Quite the opposite is true. Adversity or natural catastrophes create problems and we are good at solving problems. "Necessity is the mother of invention," the old saying rings true. For instance, in 1854 Theodore Judah came to California to help build the first railroad, the solution to the great distance problems people were facing. Another breakthrough came in the early 1950s when the terrible disease polio was rapidly increasing in the U.S. Jonas Salk successfully developed and tested a vaccine to prevent polio. Inventions are solutions to problems. Though these are not examples of consumption, just for the sake of consumption, they portray the desire and ability in the human heart. Problems serve as a powerful engine of progress. Man's material wealth is dependent on his moral and intellectual abilities rather than dependent on material resources, or lack thereof. Therefore, if our material resources are truly diminishing, our ability to overcome will be sufficient for our success.

"The More Factor" is a sad but true commentary on American culture. In analyzing its application to America as a whole, I offer several ideas to contemplate. To begin with, we can best serve humanity by pursuing the intangible rather than the things we can touch and feel. Secondly, a life that is spent striving after goals such as integrity, love for mankind and our Creator are goals that can ultimately bring a lasting peace and contentment, whereas, surrendering to a "Hunger for More" does not always bring the contentment that we are searching for. More often it brings the opposite: we desire more, much like an unquenchable thirst. This does not in any way mean that we should not be striving to improve the quality of our lives, but we should examine our entire lives and not just our success at achieving material wealth. We should take time to search our thoughts and the intentions of our hearts and the impact we are having on our loved ones and those around us. What will our lives be characterized by when all is said and done?

Works Cited

Maasik, Sonia and Jack Solomon. *Signs of Life in the USA,* 2nd edition. Boston, MA: Bedford Books, 1997.

Signal to Noise: Watching T.V. Watching Us. Cara Mertes, Producer-Director. Public Broadcasting Systems. KCET, Los Angeles. 11 July 1996.

CHAPTER 5: ACTIVITIES FOR DISCUSSION AND WRITING
Making Connections

1. It may be challenging to make connections among the essays in this chapter. Nonetheless, review Shames's "The More Factor," Kirn's "Twentysomethings," and Leary's "The Cyberpunk: The Individual as Reality Pilot," and try to make connections among the three. For instance, where do Kirn's twentysomething-Generation X people and Leary's cyberpunks fit in relationship to Americans' history of wanting more?

2. What connections do you see among the current computer revolution, the Information Superhighway, and the more factor?

CARTOONS IN AMERICA

3. If you have read Goldman's essay, "Graceland," and DeLillo's "Shopping" in Chapter 3, discuss how these two pieces illustrate Shames's concept of the more factor in Americans' lives. Use specific examples and quotations from all three texts to explain your answer.

4. Leary describes a cyberpunk as a "resourceful, skillful individual who accesses and steers knowledge–communication technology towards his/her own private goals" (par. 40). Examine the private goals sought by cyberpunks in "Info Highway: A Long and Winding Road," and "Bigots on the Net." How do these private goals relate to the goals and needs of the public sector? For instance, what might be the influence of private goals on other individuals with access to the Internet?

5. Student writer Cindie L. Keefauver agrees with Shames and his "The More Factor" but provides her own examples to make her case. Write an essay in which you either agree with Shames and Keefauver, providing your own examples and illustrations, or argue against their point of view and demonstrate the positive attributes of the more factor.

CHAPTER 6

ISSUES IN AMERICA I
Culture Clash and
Community Consciousness

This chapter and the next (Chapter 7) focus on the diversity of ethnic minorities in America. These chapters explore the experiences of different ethnic peoples in dealing with the surrounding empowered American society, as well as with the members of their own ethnic communities. The following selections address their struggles for basic freedoms and for intelligent understanding of the issues that concern them. This chapter, "Culture Clash and Community Consciousness," concentrates on the clash of cultures in America, through writers who describe their distinctive ethnic communities within multicultural contexts and who argue for an awareness of cultural pluralism in our country.

The discussion begins with Filipino American writer Carlos Bulosan. In three selections from his autobiographical novel, *America Is in the Heart*, Bulosan depicts the difficulties he faced as a new immigrant to the United States. Next, Toni Morrison relates her heritage of divided racial perception in "A Slow Walk of Trees," admitting that she, like many of us, suffers from a sort of "racial vertigo." In "Does American Still Exist?" Richard Rodriguez maintains that although immigrants instantly "begin to be American," this nation of immigrants continues to emphasize "allegiance to diversity." Paule Marshall's "From the Poets in the Kitchen" details the writer's upbringing in her mother's kitchen, where recent immigrants gathered to forge a distinctive ethnic community of their own. In "Living in Two Cultures," Jeanne Wakatsuki Houston relates her experience of feeling divided between Japanese and American cultures, then she indicates what she thinks will be the real future conflict for our children in America. In his essay "The Media's Image of Arabs," Jack Shaheen discusses how the American media foster injurious stereotypes of Arabs. Ward Churchill takes a different tack in railing against the stereotypes of Native Americans promulgated by American sports teams. Specifically, Churchill offers his own satirical solutions to stereotyping in "The Indian Chant and the Tomahawk Chop." In his poem "So Mexicans Are Taking Jobs from Americans,"

Jimmy Santiago Baca addresses both media images and popular lore as he takes on those who blame U.S. unemployment problems on immigrants. Amy Tan offers a different perspective of culture clash in "Four Directions," a selection from her best-selling book *The Joy Luck Club*. In her intimate family story, Tan illustrates a Chinese American woman's view of her European American boyfriend's amusing attempts to impress her and her family, as well as her own attempts to figure out her emotional relationship with her traditional Chinese mother. Finally, student writer Christine Willis discusses her perspective on multiculturalism in "We Are an Old-Fashioned Stew."

America Is in the Heart

Carlos Bulosan

Carlos Bulosan (born on November 24, 1913) grew up on a small farm in Binalonan, Luzon, in the central Philippines. At age 17, he left his native country to come to America. His autobiography, America Is in the Heart, *is a classic of American immigration experience, chronicling Bulosan's early life in the Philippines and his incredible struggle to survive in America. The first two selections illustrate his voyage to and arrival in America, as well as the racism, poverty, and other difficulties he and fellow Filipino Americans faced as immigrants. The third selection enunciates an impassioned ideal of American freedom, which inspired him and his brother to persevere in this country.*

I found the dark hole of the steerage and lay on my bunk for days without food, seasick and lonely. I was restless at night and many disturbing thoughts came to my mind. Why had I left home? What would I do in America? I looked into the faces of my companions for a comforting answer, but they were as young and bewildered as I, and my only consolation was their proximity and the familiarity of their dialects. It was not until we had left Japan that I began to feel better.

One day in mid-ocean, I climbed through the narrow passageway to the deck where other steerage passengers were sunning themselves. Most of them were Ilocanos, who were fishermen in the northern coastal regions of Luzon. They were talking easily and eating rice with salted fish with their bare hands, and some of them were walking, barefoot and unconcerned, in their homemade cotton shorts. The first-class passengers were annoyed, and an official of the boat came down and drove us back into the dark haven below. The small opening at the top of the iron ladder was shut tight, and we did not see the sun again until we had passed Hawaii.

But before we anchored at Honolulu an epidemic of meningitis spread throughout the boat and concentrated among the steerage passengers. The Chinese waiters stopped coming into our dining room, because so many of us had been attacked by the disease. They pushed the tin plates under the door of the kitchen and ran back to their rooms, afraid of being contaminated. Those hungry enough crawled miserably on their bellies and reached for their plates.

But somewhere in the room a peasant boy was playing a guitar and another was strumming a mandolin. I lay on my bunk listening and wishing

I could join them. In the far corner of the dining room, crouched around the dining table, five young students were discussing the coming presidential election in the United States. Not far from them was a dying boy from Pangasinan.

One night when I could no longer stand the heat in the closed room, I   5
screamed aloud and woke up most of the steerage passengers. The boy who had been playing the guitar came to my bed with cold water and rubbed my forehead and back with it. I was relieved of my discomfort a little and told him so.

"My name is Marcelo," he said. "I came from San Manuel, Pangasinan."

"*San Manuel?*" I said. "I used to work there—in the *mongo* fields. I am glad to meet you."

"Go to sleep now," he said. "Call for me if you need my help."

I heard his feet pattering away from me, and I was comforted. It was enough that Marcelo had come from a familiar town. It was a bond that bound us together in our journey. And I was to discover later this same regional friendship, which developed into tribalism, obstructed all efforts toward Filipino unity in America.

There were more than two hundred of us in the steerage. A young doc-   10
tor and an assistant came now and then to check the number of deaths and to examine those about to die. It was only when we reached Hawaii that the epidemic was checked, and we were allowed to go out again. Some of the stronger passengers carried their sick relatives and friends through the narrow hatch and put them in the sunlight.

I was pleasantly sunning myself one afternoon when Marcelo rolled over on his stomach and touched me. I turned and saw a young white girl wearing a brief bathing suit walking toward us with a young man. They stopped some distance away from us; then as though the girl's moral conscience had been provoked, she put her small hand on her mouth and said in a frightened voice:

"Look at those half-naked savages from the Philippines, Roger! Haven't they any idea of decency?"

"I don't blame them for coming into the sun," the young man said. "I know how it is below."

"Roger!" said the terrified girl. "Don't tell me you have been down in that horrible place? I simply can't believe it!"

The man said something, but they had already turned and the wind   15
carried it away. I was to hear that girl's voice in many ways afterward in the United States. It became no longer her voice, but an angry chorus shouting:

"Why don't they ship those monkeys back where they came from?"

We arrived in Seattle on a June day. My first sight of the approaching land was an exhilarating experience. Everything seemed native and promising to me. It was like coming home after a long voyage, although as yet I had no home in this city. Everything seemed familiar and kind—the white faces of the buildings melting in the soft afternoon sun, the gray contours of the surrounding valleys that seemed to vanish in the last periphery of light. With a sudden surge of joy, I knew that I must find a home in this new land.

I had only twenty cents left, not even enough to take me to Chinatown where, I had been informed, a Filipino hotel and two restaurants were located. Fortunately two oldtimers put me in a car with four others, and took us to a hotel on King Street, the heart of Filipino life in Seattle. Marcelo, who was also in the car, had a cousin named Elias who came to our room with another oldtimer. Elias and his unknown friend persuaded my companions to play a strange kind of card game. In a little while Elias got up and touched his friend suggestively; then they disappeared and we never saw them again.

It was only when our two countrymen had left that my companions realized what happened. They had taken all their money. Marcelo asked me if I had any money. I gave him my twenty cents. After collecting a few more cents from the others, he went downstairs and when he came back he told us that he had telegraphed for money to his brother in California.

All night we waited for the money to come, hungry and afraid to go out 20
in the street. Outside we could hear shouting and singing; then a woman screamed lustily in one of the rooms down the hall. Across from our hotel a jazz band was playing noisily; it went on until dawn. But in the morning a telegram came to Marcelo which said:

YOUR BROTHER DIED AUTOMOBILE ACCIDENT LAST WEEK

Marcelo looked at us and began to cry. His anguish stirred an aching fear in me. I knelt on the floor looking for my suitcase under the bed. I knew that I had to go out now—alone. I put the suitcase on my shoulder and walked toward the door, stopping for a moment to look back at my friends who were still standing silently around Marcelo. Suddenly a man came into the room and announced that he was the proprietor.

"Well, boys," he said, looking at our suitcases, "where is the rent?"

"We have no money, sir," I said, trying to impress him with my politeness.

"That is too bad," he said quickly, glancing furtively at our suitcases again. "That is just too bad." He walked outside and went down the hall. He came back with a short, fat Filipino, who looked at us stupidly with his dull, small eyes, and spat his cigar out of the window.

"There they are, Jake," said the proprietor. 25

Jake looked disappointed. "They are too young," he said.

"You can break them in, Jake," said the proprietor.

"They will be sending babies next," Jake said.

"You can break them in, can't you, Jake?" the proprietor pleaded. "This is not the first time you have broken babies in. You have done it in the sugar plantations in Hawaii, Jake!"

"Hell!" Jake said, striding across the room to the proprietor. He pulled   30
a fat roll of bills from his pocket and gave twenty-five dollars to the proprietor. Then he turned to us and said, "All right, Pinoys, you are working for me now. Get your hats and follow me."

We were too frightened to hesitate. When we lifted our suitcases the proprietor ordered us not to touch them.

"I'll take care of them until you come back from Alaska," he said. "Good fishing, boys!"

In this way we were sold for five dollars each to work in the fish canneries in Alaska, by a Visayan from the island of Leyte to an Ilocano from the province of La Union. Both were oldtimers; both were tough. They exploited young immigrants until one of them, the hotel proprietor, was shot dead by an unknown assailant. We were forced to sign a paper which stated that each of us owed the contractor twenty dollars for bedding and another twenty for luxuries. What the luxuries were, I have never found out. The contractor turned out to be a tall, heavy-set, dark Filipino, who came to the small hold of the boat barking at us like a dog. He was drunk and saliva was running down his shirt.

"And get this, you devils!" he shouted at us. "You will never come back alive if you don't do what I say!"

It was the beginning of my life in America, the beginning of a long flight   35
that carried me down the years, fighting desperately to find peace in some corner of life.

I had struck up a friendship with two oldtimers who were not much older than I. One was Conrado Torres, a journalism student at a university in Oregon, who was fired with a dream to unionize the cannery workers. I discovered that he had come from Binalonan, but could hardly remember the names of people there because he had been very young when he had come to America. Conrado was small and dark, with slant eyes and thick eyebrows; but his nose was thin above a wise, sensuous mouth. He introduced me to Paulo Lorca, a gay fellow, who had graduated from law school in Los Angeles. This surreptitious meeting at a cannery in Rose Inlet was the beginning of a friendship that grew simultaneously with the growth of the trade union movement and progressive ideas among the Filipinos in the United States.

In those days labor unions were still unheard of in the canneries, so the contractors rapaciously exploited their workers. They had henchmen in every cannery who saw to it that every attempt at unionization was frustrated and the instigators of the idea punished. The companies also had their share in the exploitation; our bunkhouses were unfit for human habitation. The lighting system was bad and dangerous to our eyes, and those of us who were working in the semi-darkness were severely affected by the strong ammonia from the machinery.

I was working in a section called "wash lye." Actually a certain amount of lye was diluted in the water where I washed the beheaded fish that came down on a small escalator. One afternoon a cutter above me, working in the poor light, slashed off his right arm with the cutting machine. It happened so swiftly he did not cry out. I saw his arm floating down the water among the fish heads.

It was only at night that we felt free, although the sun seemed never to disappear from the sky. It stayed on in the western horizon and its magnificence inflamed the snows on the island, giving us a world of soft, continuous light, until the moon rose at about ten o'clock to take its place. Then trembling shadows began to form on the rise of the brilliant snow in our yard, and we would come out with baseball bats, gloves and balls, and the Indian girls who worked in the cannery would join us, shouting huskily like men.

We played far into the night. Sometimes a Filipino and an Indian girl   40 would run off into the moonlight; we could hear them chasing each other in the snow. Then we would hear the girl giggling and laughing deliciously in the shadows. Paulo was always running off with a girl named La Belle. How she acquired that name in Alaska, I never found out. But hardly had we started our game when off they ran, chasing each other madly and suddenly disappearing out of sight.

Toward the end of the season La Belle gave birth to a baby. We were sure, however, that the father was not in our group. We were sure that she had got it from one of the Italian fishermen on the island. La Belle did not come to work for two days, but when she appeared on the third day with the baby slung on her back, she threw water into Conrado's face.

"Are you going to marry me or not?" she asked him.

Conrado was frightened. He was familiar with the ways of Indians, so he said: "Why should I marry you?"

"We'll see about that!" La Belle shouted, running to the door. She came back with an official of the company. "That's the one!" she said, pointing to Conrado.

"You'd better come to the office with us," said the official.   45

Conrado did not know what to do. He looked at me for help. Paulo left his washing machine and nodded to me to follow him. We went with them into the building which was the town hall.

"You are going to marry this Indian girl and stay on the island for seven years as prescribed by law," said the official to Conrado. "And as the father of the baby, you must support both mother and child, and if you have four

more children by the time your turn is up, you will be sent back to the main-
land with a bonus."

"But, sir, the baby is not mine," said Conrado weakly.

Paulo stepped up quickly beside him and said: "The baby is mine, sir. I
guess I'll have to stay."

La Belle looked at Paulo with surprise. After a moment, however, she   50
began to smile with satisfaction. Paulo was well-educated and spoke good
English. But I think what finally drove Conrado from La Belle's primitive
mind were Paulo's curly hair, his even, white teeth. Meekly she signed the
paper after Paulo.

"I'll stay here for seven years, all right," Paulo said to me. "I'm in a
mess in Los Angeles anyway—so I'll stay with this dirty Indian girl."

"Stop talking like that if you know what is good for you," La Belle
said, giving him the baby.

"I guess you are right," Paulo said.

"You shouldn't have done it for me," Conrado said.

"It's all right," Paulo laughed. "I'll be in the United States before you   55
know it."

I still do not understand why Paulo interceded for Conrado. When the
season was over Paulo came to our bunks in the boat and asked Conrado to
send him something to drink. I did not see him again.

W hen I landed in Seattle for the second time, I expected a fair amount
of money from the company. But the contractor, Max Feuga, came into the
play room and handed us slips of paper. I looked at mine and was amazed
at the neatly itemized expenditures that I was supposed to have incurred
during the season. Twenty-five dollars for withdrawals, one hundred for
board and room, twenty for bedding, and another twenty for something I
do not now remember. At the bottom was the actual amount I was to
receive after all the deductions: *thirteen dollars!*

I could do nothing. I did not even go to the hotel where I had left my
suitcase. I went to a Japanese dry goods store on Jackson Street and bought
a pair of corduroy pants and a blue shirt. It was already twilight and the
cannery workers were in the crowded Chinese gambling houses, losing their
season's earnings and drinking bootleg whisky. They became quarrelsome
and abusive to their own people when they lost, and subservient to the
Chinese gambling lords and marijuana peddlers. They pawed at the semi-
nude whores with their dirty hands and made suggestive gestures, running
out into the night when they were rebuffed for lack of money.

I was already in America, and I felt good and safe. I did not understand
why. The gamblers, prostitutes and Chinese opium smokers did not excite
me, but they aroused in me a feeling of flight. I knew that I must run away
from them, but it was not that I was afraid of contamination. I wanted to

see other aspects of American life, for surely these destitute and vicious people were merely a small part of it. Where would I begin this pilgrimage, this search for a door into America?

I went outside and walked around looking into the faces of my country-   60
men, wondering if I would see someone I had known in the Philippines. I came to a building which brightly dressed white women were entering, lifting their diaphanous gowns as they climbed the stairs. I looked up and saw the huge sign:

MANILA DANCE HALL

The orchestra upstairs was playing; Filipinos were entering. I put my hands in my pockets and followed them, beginning to feel lonely for the sound of home.

The dance hall was crowded with Filipino cannery workers and domestic servants. But the girls were very few, and the Filipinos fought over them. When a boy liked a girl he bought a roll of tickets from the hawker on the floor and kept dancing with her. But the other boys who also liked the same girl shouted at him to stop, cursing him in the dialects and sometimes throwing rolled wet papers at him. At the bar the glasses were tinkling, the bottles popping loudly, and the girls in the back room were smoking marijuana. It was almost impossible to breathe.

Then I saw Marcelo's familiar back. He was dancing with a tall blonde in a green dress, a girl so tall that Marcelo looked like a dwarf climbing a tree. But the girl was pretty and her body was nicely curved and graceful, and she had a way of swaying that aroused confused sensations in me. It was evident that many of the boys wanted to dance with her; they were shouting maliciously at Marcelo. The way the blonde waved to them made me think that she knew most of them. They were nearly all oldtimers and strangers to Marcelo. They were probably gamblers and pimps, because they had fat rolls of money and expensive clothing.

But Marcelo was learning very fast. He requested one of his friends to buy another roll of tickets for him. The girl was supposed to tear off one ticket every three minutes, but I noticed that she tore off a ticket for every minute. That was ten cents a minute. Marcelo was unaware of what she was doing; he was spending his whole season's earnings on his first day in America. It was only when one of his friends shouted to him in the dialect that he became angry at the girl. Marcelo was not tough, but his friend was an oldtimer. Marcelo pushed the girl toward the gaping bystanders. His friend opened a knife and gave it to him.

Then something happened that made my heart leap. One of the blonde   65
girl's admirers came from behind and struck Marcelo with a piece of lead pipe. Marcelo's friend whipped out a pistol and fired. Marcelo and the boy with the lead pipe fell on the floor simultaneously, one on top of the other,

but the blonde girl ran into the crowd screaming frantically. Several guns banged at once, and the lights went out. I saw Marcelo's friend crumple in the fading light.

At once the crowd seemed to flow out of the windows. I went to a side window and saw three heavy electric wires strung from the top of the building to the ground. I reached for them and slid to the ground. My palms were burning when I came out of the alley. Then I heard the sirens of police cars screaming infernally toward the place. I put my cap in my pocket and ran as fast as I could in the direction of a neon sign two blocks down the street.

It was a small church where Filipino farm workers were packing their suitcases and bundles. I found out later that Filipino immigrants used their churches as rest houses while they were waiting for work. There were two large trucks outside. I went to one of them and sat on the running board, holding my hands over my heart for fear it would beat too fast. The lights in the church went out and the workers came into the street. The driver of the truck in which I was sitting pointed a strong flashlight at me.

"Hey, you, are you looking for a job?" he asked.

"Yes, sir," I said.

"Get in the truck," he said, jumping into the cab. "Let's go, Flo!" he   70
shouted to the other driver.

I was still trembling with excitement. But I was glad to get out of Seattle—to anywhere else in America. I did not care where so long as it was in America. I found a corner and sat down heavily. The drivers shouted to each other. Then we were off to work.

It was already midnight and the lights in the city of Seattle were beginning to fade. I could see the reflections on the bright lake in Bremerton. I was reminded of Baguio. Then some of the men began singing. The driver and two men were arguing over money. A boy in the other truck was playing a violin. We were on the highway to Yakima Valley.

I was becoming aware of the dynamic social struggle in America. We talked all night in my brother's room, planning how to spread progressive ideas among the Filipinos in California. Macario [my brother] had become more serious. When he talked, I noticed his old gentleness and the kind voice that had rung with sincerity at my sickbed in Binalonan. His words seized my imagination, so that years afterward I am able to write them almost word for word:

"It has fallen upon us to inspire a united front among our people," he said. "We must win the backward elements over to our camp; but we must also destroy that which is corrupt among ourselves. These are the fundamentals of our time; but these are also the realities that we must grasp in full.

"We must achieve articulation of social ideas, not only for some kind of economic security but also to help culture bloom as it should in our time. We are approaching what will be the greatest achievement of our generation: the discovery of a new vista of literature, that is, to speak to the people and to be understood by them.

"We must look for the mainspring of democracy, but we must also destroy false ideals. We must discover the origin of our freedom and write of it in broad national terms. We must interpret history in terms of liberty. We must advocate democratic ideas, and fight all forces that would abort our culture.

"This the greatest responsibility of literature: to find in our struggle that which has a future. Literature is a living and growing thing. We must destroy that which is dying, because it does not die by itself.

"We in America understand the many imperfections of democracy and the malignant disease corroding its very heart. We must be united in the effort to make an America in which our people can find happiness. It is a great wrong that anyone in America, whether he be brown or white, should be illiterate or hungry or miserable.

"We must live in America where there is freedom for all regardless of color, station and beliefs. Great Americans worked with unselfish devotion toward one goal, that is, to use the power of the myriad peoples in the service of America's freedom. They made it their guiding principle. In this we are the same; we must also fight for an America where a man should be given unconditional opportunities to cultivate his potentialities and to restore him to his rightful dignity.

"It is but fair to say that America is not a land of one race or one class of men. We are all Americans that have toiled and suffered and known oppression and defeat, from the first Indian that offered peace in Manhattan to the last Filipino pea pickers. America is not bound by geographical latitudes. America is not merely a land or an institution. America is in the hearts of men that died for freedom; it is also in the eyes of men that are building a new world. America is a prophecy of a new society of men: of a system that knows no sorrow or strife or suffering. America is a warning to those who would try to falsify the ideals of freemen.

"America is also the nameless foreigner, the homeless refugee, the hungry boy begging for a job and the black body dangling on a tree. America is the illiterate immigrant who is ashamed that the world of books and intellectual opportunities is closed to him. We are all that nameless foreigner, that homeless refugee, that hungry boy, that illiterate immigrant and that lynched black body. All of us, from the first Adams to the last Filipino, native born or alien, educated or illiterate—*We are America!*

"The old world is dying, but a new world is being born. It generates inspiration from the chaos that beats upon us all. The false grandeur and security, the unfulfilled promises and illusory power, the number of the dead and those about to die, will charge the forces of our courage and determination. The old world will die so that the new world will be born with less sacrifice and agony on the living. . . ."

SUGGESTIONS FOR FURTHER STUDY

Key Words

The author uses language with which you may not be familiar. Find the following words in the paragraphs indicated, and explain their meanings in the context of the sentences in which the words appear. Consult a dictionary, as needed.

proximity (par. 1)
Pinoys (par. 30)
exploited (par. 33)
interceded (par. 56)
subservient (par. 58)
diaphanous (par. 60)
articulation (par. 75)
malignant (par. 78)
myriad (par. 79)
potentialities (par. 79)

Topics for Discussion and Writing

1. Summarize the experiences that occur to Carlos Bulosan during his trip from the Philippines to America. Use both paraphrasing and direct quotation. (Don't forget to cite page numbers.) How did the white couple react to him and his companions on board the ship? How did he feel when he arrived in Seattle?

2. Once Carlos arrived in Seattle, he underwent several distressing events. This time, use your own words to summarize the events that occurred to Carlos and his friends.

3. The first part of the preceding selection from Bulosan's autobiography chronicles some of the hardships he endured as a new and unwanted immigrant to America. Through his personal story, we can envision the collective experience of countless millions of immigrants to the dreamed-of promised land of opportunities that America has historically represented. Based on what Bulosan wrote in the first part of this selection, how promising and positive was his experience here?

4. In the third part of this selection, Bulosan's brother Macario eloquently speaks of a future for his Filipino compatriots in America. Summarize Macario's ideas by paraphrasing and quoting from the text.

5. How do the words of Macario Bulosan express a manifesto of one part of the American dream? Explain your answer. In what way (or ways) is his manifesto realistic?

6. Write a narrative essay describing a trip you took, during which you encountered negative or hostile people. On what was their hostility based? Did you resolve the situation positively, or did the hostilities escalate? Looking back at the situation now, what would you have done differently?

A Slow Walk of Trees

Toni Morrison

Toni Morrison (born in 1931, in Lorraine, Ohio) received a BA from Howard University and an MA from Cornell University. Morrison's novels include The Bluest Eye *(1970),* Sula *(1973),* Song of Solomon *(1977),* Beloved *(1986), and* Jazz *(1992). She was awarded the Pulitzer Prize for* Beloved, *and she received the 1994 Nobel Prize for Literature. "A Slow Walk of Trees" was published in the* New York Times Magazine *on the United States' bicentennial, July 4, 1976.*

His name was John Solomon Willis, and when at age 5 he heard from the old folks that "the Emancipation Proclamation was coming," he crawled under the bed. It was his earliest recollection of what was to be his habitual response to the promise of white people: horror and an instinctive yearning for safety. He was my grandfather, a musician who managed to hold on to his violin but not his land. He lost all 88 acres of his Indian mother's inheritance to legal predators who built their fortunes on the likes of him. He was an unreconstructed black pessimist who, in spite of or because of emancipation, was convinced for 85 years that there was no hope whatever for black people in this country. His rancor was legitimate, for he, John Solomon, was not only an artist but a first-rate carpenter and farmer, reduced to sending home to his family money he had made playing the violin because he was not able to find work. And this during the years when almost half the black male population were skilled craftsmen who lost their jobs to white ex-convicts and immigrant farmers.

His wife, however, was of a quite different frame of mind and believed that all things could be improved by faith in Jesus and an effort of the will. So it was she, Ardelia Willis, who sneaked her seven children out of the back window into the darkness, rather than permit the patron of their sharecropper's existence to become their executioner as well, and headed north in 1912, when 99.2 percent of all black people in the U.S. were native-born and only 60 percent of white Americans were. And it was Ardelia who told her husband that they could not stay in the Kentucky town they ended up in because the teacher didn't know long division.

They have been dead now for 30 years and more and I still don't know which of them came closer to the truth about the possibilities of life for

1

black people in this country. One of their grandchildren is a tenured professor at Princeton. Another, who suffered from what the Peruvian poet called "anger that breaks a man into children," was picked up just as he entered his teens and emotionally lobotomized by the reformatories and mental institutions specifically designed to serve him. Neither John Solomon nor Ardelia lived long enough to despair over one or swell with pride over the other. But if they were alive today each would have selected and collected enough evidence to support the accuracy of the other's original point of view. And it would be difficult to convince either one that the other was right.

Some of the monstrous events that took place in John Solomon's America have been duplicated in alarming detail in my own America. There was the public murder of a president in a theater in 1865 and the public murder of another president on television in 1963. The Civil War of 1861 had its encore as the civil rights movement of 1960. The torture and mutilation of a black West Point Cadet (Cadet Johnson Whittaker) in 1880 had its rerun with the 1970s murders of students at Jackson State College, Texas Southern, and Southern University in Baton Rouge. And in 1976 we watch for what must be the thousandth time a pitched battle between the children of slaves and the children of immigrants—only this time, it is not the New York draft riots of 1863, but the busing turmoil in Paul Revere's home town, Boston.

Hopeless, he'd said. Hopeless. For he was certain that white people of every political, religious, geographical, and economic background would band together against black people everywhere when they felt the threat of our progress. And a hundred years after he sought safety from the white man's "promise," somebody put a bullet in Martin Luther King's brain. And not long before that some excellent samples of the master race demonstrated their courage and virility by dynamiting some little black girls to death. If he were here now, my grandfather, he would shake his head, close his eyes and pull out his violin—too polite to say, "I told you so." And his wife would pay attention to the music but not to the sadness in her husband's eyes, for she would see what she expected to see—not the occasional historical repetition, but, *like the slow walk of certain species of trees from the flatlands up into the mountains,* she would see the signs of irrevocable and permanent change. She, who pulled her girls out of an inadequate school in the Cumberland Mountains, knew all along that the gentlemen from Alabama who had killed the little girls would be rounded up. And it wouldn't surprise her in the least to know that the number of black college graduates jumped 12 percent in the last three years: 47 percent in 20 years. That there are 140 black mayors in this country; 14 black judges in the District Circuit, 4 in the Courts of Appeals and one on the Supreme Court. That there are 17 blacks in Congress, one in the Senate; 276 in state legislatures—223 in state houses, 53 in state senates. That there are 112 elected black police chiefs and sheriffs, 1 Pulitzer Prize winner; 1 winner of the Prix de Rome; a dozen or so winners of the Guggenheim; 4 deans of predominantly white colleges. . . . Oh, her list would go on and on. But so would John Solomon's sweet sad music.

While my grandparents held opposite views on whether the fortunes of black people were improving, my own parents struck similarly opposed postures, but from another slant. They differed about whether the moral fiber of white people would ever improve. Quite a different argument. The old folks argued about how and if black people could improve themselves, who could be counted on to help us, who would hinder us and so on. My parents took issue over the question of whether it was possible for white people to improve. They assumed that black people were the humans of the globe, but had serious doubts about the quality and existence of white humanity. Thus my father, distrusting every word and every gesture of every white man on earth, assumed that the white man who crept up the stairs one afternoon had come to molest his daughters and threw him down the stairs and then our tricycle after him. (I think my father was wrong, but considering what I have seen since, it may have been very healthy for me to have witnessed that as my first black–white encounter.) My mother, however, *believed* in them—their possibilities. So when the meal we got on relief was bug-ridden, she wrote a long letter to Franklin Delano Roosevelt. And when white bill collectors came to our door, it was she who received them civilly and explained in a sweet voice that we were people of honor and that the debt would be taken care of. Her message to Roosevelt got through— our meal improved. Her message to the bill collectors did not always get through and there was occasional violence when my father (self-exiled to the bedroom for fear he could not hold his temper) would hear that her reasonableness had failed. My mother was always wounded by these scenes, for she thought the bill collector knew that she loved good credit more than life and that being in arrears on a payment horrified her probably more than it did him. So she thought he was rude because he was white. For years she walked to utility companies and department stores to pay bills in person and even now she does not seem convinced that checks are legal tender. My father loved excellence, worked hard (he held three jobs at once for 17 years) and was so outraged by the suggestion of personal slackness that he could explain it to himself only in terms of racism. He was a fastidious worker who was frightened of one thing: unemployment. I can remember now the dooms day-cum-graveyard sound of "laid off" and how the minute school was out he asked us, "Where you workin'?" Both my parents believed that all succor and aid came from themselves and their neighborhood, since "they"—white people in charge and those not in charge but in obstructionist positions—were in some way fundamentally, genetically corrupt.

So I grew up in a basically racist household with more than a child's share of contempt for white people. And for each white friend I acquired who made a small crack in that contempt, there was another who repaired it. For each one who related to me as a person, there was one who in my presence at least, became actively "white." And like most black people of my generation, I suffer from racial vertigo that can be cured only by taking what one needs from one's ancestors. John Solomon's cynicism and his deployment of his art as both weapon and solace, Ardelia's faith in the magic that can be wrought by sheer effort of the will; my mother's open-mindedness in each new encounter and her habit of trying reasonableness first; my father's temper, his impatience and his efforts to keep "them" (throw them) out of his life. And it is out of these learned and selected attitudes that I look at the quality of life for my people in this country now. These widely disparate and sometimes conflicting views, I suspect, were held not only by me, but by most black people. Some I know are clearer in their positions, have not sullied their anger with optimism or dirtied their hope with despair. But most of us are plagued by a sense of being worn shell-thin by constant repression and hostility as well as the impression of being buoyed by visible testimony of tremendous strides. There *is* repetition of the grotesque in our history. And there *is* the miraculous walk of trees. The question is whether our walk is progress or merely movement. O. J. Simpson leaning on a Hertz car *is* better than the Gold Dust Twins on the back of a soap box. But is "Good Times" better than Stepin Fetchit? Has the first order of business been taken care of? Does the law of the land work for us?

SUGGESTIONS FOR FURTHER STUDY

Key Words

The author uses language with which you may not be familiar. Find the following words in the paragraphs indicated, and explain their meanings in the context of the sentences in which the words appear. Consult a dictionary, as needed.

rancor (par. 1)
lobotomized (par. 3)
fastidious (par. 6)
succor (par. 6)
vertigo (par. 7)
deployment (par. 7)
sullied (par. 7)
grotesque (par. 7)

Topics for Discussion and Writing

1. A strong sense of *irony* underlies the author's tone in this selection. For instance, she writes that "some excellent samples of the master

race demonstrated their courage and virility by dynamiting some little black girls to death." Find other instances of irony in Morrison's use of words, phrases, or longer passages. Discuss what makes them ironic.

2. In your own words, summarize how Morrison's grandfather and grandmother differed in their views of the world. What events or people affected each grandparent's point of view?

3. Morrison writes that out of her family experience, she "learned and selected attitudes" that shape her vision of the "quality of life for my people in this country now." Discuss with other readers what some of those attitudes are, based on Morrison's account of her grandparents' and her parents' views.

4. What purpose is served by Morrison's use of the metaphor "the slow walk of trees" in this essay?

5. Look at the closing of the last paragraph. Since it was written, what has changed? How would you answer Morrison's final question: "Has the first order of business been taken care of? Does the law of the land work for us?" Write a brief essay examining whether real changes have been made to provide the "visible testimony of tremendous strides" Morrison says buoys up her race's spirit.

Does America Still Exist?

Richard Rodriguez

Richard Rodriguez (born in 1944 in San Francisco), a well-known essayist and journalist, received his BA from Stanford University, and his MA and PhD degrees from Columbia University. His best-known work is his autobiographical Hunger of Memory: The Education of Richard Rodriguez *(1982), and he also authored* Days of Obligation. *"Does America Still Exist?" was published in* Harper's Magazine *in March 1984.*

For the children of immigrant parents the knowledge comes easier. 1
America exists everywhere in the city—on billboards, frankly in the smell of French fries and popcorn. It exists in the pace: traffic lights, the assertions of neon, the mysterious bong-bong-bong through the atriums of department stores. America exists as the voice of the crowd, a menacing sound—the high nasal accent of American English.

When I was a boy in Sacramento (California, the fifties), people would ask me, "Where you from?" I was born in this country, but I knew the question meant to decipher my darkness, my looks.

My mother once instructed me to say, "I am an American of Mexican descent." By the time I was nine or ten, I wanted to say, but dared not reply, "I am an American."

Immigrants come to America and, against hostility or mere loneliness, they recreate a homeland in the parlor, tacking up postcards or calendars of some impossible blue—lake or sea or sky. Children of immigrant parents are supposed to perch on a hyphen between two countries. Relatives assume the achievement as much as anyone. Relatives are, in any case, surprised when the child begins losing old ways. One day at the family picnic the boy wanders away from their spiced food and faceless stories to watch other boys play baseball in the distance.

There is sorrow in the American memory, guilty sorrow for having left 5
something behind—Portugal, China, Norway. The American story is the story of immigrant children and of their children—children no longer able to speak to grandparents. The memory of exile becomes inarticulate as it passes from generation to generation, along with wedding rings and pocket watches—like some mute stone in a wad of old lace. Europe. Asia. Eden.

But, it needs to be said, if this is a country where one stops being Vietnamese or Italian, this is a country where one begins to be an American. America exists as a culture and a grin, a faith and a shrug. It is clasped in a handshake, called by a first name.

As much as the country is joined in a common culture, however, Americans are reluctant to celebrate the process of assimilation. We pledge allegiance to diversity. America was born Protestant and bred Puritan, and the notion of community we share is derived from a seventeenth-century faith. Presidents and the pages of ninth-grade civics readers yet proclaim the orthodoxy: We are gathered together—but as individuals, with separate pasts, distinct destinies. Our society is as paradoxical as a Puritan congregation: We stand together, alone.

Americans have traditionally defined themselves by what they refused to include. As often, however, Americans have struggled, turned in good conscience at last to assert the great Protestant virtue of tolerance. Despite outbreaks of nativist frenzy, America has remained an immigrant country, open and true to itself.

Against pious emblems of rural America—soda fountain, Elks hall, Protestant church, and now shopping mall—stands the cold-hearted city, crowded with races and ambitions, curious laughter, much that is odd. Nevertheless, it is the city that has most truly represented America. In the city, however, the millions of singular lives have had no richer notion of wholeness to describe them than the idea of pluralism.

"Where you from?" the American asks the immigrant child. "Mexico,"   10
the boy learns to say.

Mexico, the country of my blood ancestors, offers formal contrast to the American achievement. If the United States was formed by Protestant individualism, Mexico was shaped by a medieval Catholic dream of one world. The Spanish journeyed to Mexico to plunder, and they may have gone, in God's name, with an arrogance peculiar to those who intend to convert. But through the conversion, the Indian converted the Spaniard. A new race was born, the *mestizo,* wedding European to Indian. José Vasconcelos, the Mexican philosopher, has celebrated this New World creation, proclaiming it the "cosmic race."

Centuries later, in a San Francisco restaurant, a Mexican-American lawyer of my acquaintance says, in English, over *salade niçoise,* that he does not intend to assimilate into gringo society. His claim is echoed by a chorus of others (Italian-Americans, Greeks, Asians) in this era of ethnic pride. The melting pot has been retired, clanking, into the museum of quaint disgrace, alongside Aunt Jemima and the Katzenjammer Kids. But resistance to assimilation is characteristically American. It only makes clear how inevitable the process of assimilation actually is.

For generations, this has been the pattern. Immigrant parents have sent their children to school (simply, they thought) to acquire the "skills" to survive in the city. The child returned home with a voice his parents barely recognized or understood, couldn't trust, and didn't like.

In eastern cities—Philadelphia, New York, Boston, Baltimore—class after class gathered immigrant children to women (usually women) who stood in front of rooms full of children, changing children. So also for me in the 1950s. Irish-Catholic nuns. California. The old story. The hyphen tipped to the right, away from Mexico and toward a confusing but true American identity.

I speak now in the chromium American accent of my grammar school   15
classmates—Billy Reckers, Mike Bradley, Carol Schmidt, Kathy O'Grady
. . . I believe I became like my classmates, became German, Polish, and (like my teachers) Irish. And because assimilation is always reciprocal, my classmates got something of me. (I mean sad eyes; belief in the Indian Virgin; a taste for sugar skulls on the Feast of the Dead.) In the blending, we became what our parents could never have been, and we carried America one revolution further.

"Does America still exist?" Americans have been asking the question for so long that to ask it again only proves our continuous link. But perhaps the question deserves to be asked with urgency now. Since the black civil rights movement of the 1960s, our tenuous notion of a shared public life has deteriorated notably.

The struggle of black men and women did not eradicate racism, but it became the great moment in the life of America's conscience. Water hoses, bulldogs, blood—the images, rendered black, white, rectangular, passed into living rooms.

It is hard to look at a photograph of a crowd taken, say, in 1890 or in 1930 and not notice the absence of blacks. (It becomes an impertinence to wonder if America *still* exists.)

In the sixties, other groups of Americans learned to champion their rights by analogy to the black civil rights movement. But the heroic vision faded. Dr. Martin Luther King, Jr., had spoken with Pauline eloquence of a nation that would unite Christian and Jew, old and young, rich and poor. Within a decade, the struggles of the 1960s were reduced to a bureaucratic competition for little more than pieces of a representational pie. The quest for a portion of power became an end in itself. The metaphor for the American city of the 1970s was a committee: one black, one woman, one person under thirty. . . .

If the small town had sinned against America by too neatly defining   20
who could be an American, the city's sin was a romantic secession. One noticed the romanticism in the antiwar movement—certain demonstrators who demonstrated a lack of tact or desire to persuade and seemed content to play secular protestants. One noticed the romanticism in the competition among members of "minority groups" to claim the status of Primary Victim. To Americans unconfident of their common identity, minority standing

became a way of asserting individuality. Middle-class Americans—men and women clearly not the primary victims of social oppression—brandished their suffering with exuberance.

The dream of a single society probably died with *The Ed Sullivan Show*. The reality of America persists. Teenagers pass through big-city high schools banded in racial groups, their collars turned up to a uniform shrug. But then they graduate to jobs at the phone company or in banks, where they end up working alongside people unlike themselves. Typists and tellers walk out together at lunchtime.

It is easier for us as Americans to believe the obvious fact of our separateness—easier to imagine the black and white Americans prophesied by the Kerner report (broken glass, street fires)—than to recognize the reality of a city street at lunchtime. Americans are wedded by proximity to a common culture. The panhandler at one corner is related to the pamphleteer at the next who is related to the banker who is kin to the Chinese old man wearing an MIT sweatshirt. In any true national history, Thomas Jefferson begets Martin Luther King, Jr., who begets the Gray Panthers. It is because we lack a vision of ourselves entire—the city street is crowded and we are each preoccupied with finding our own way home—that we lack an appropriate hymn.

Under my window now passes a little white girl softly rehearsing to herself a Motown obbligato.

SUGGESTIONS FOR FURTHER STUDY

Key Words

The author uses language with which you may not be familiar. Find the following words in the paragraphs indicated, and explain their meanings in the context of the sentences in which the words appear. Consult a dictionary, as needed.

assimilation (par. 7)
orthodoxy (par. 7)
paradoxical (par. 7)
reciprocal (par. 15)
tenuous (par. 16)
romanticism (par. 20)
obbligato (par. 25)

Topics for Discussion and Writing

1. In the question "Does America Still Exist?" the author seeks to define "America." How does Rodriguez define America? How do

other writers you have read define the term? How do *you* define it? Find several definitions of America from this and other sources, and make up a list with which to compare similar or different ways of defining America. Include your own definition.

2. The author often makes his points through metaphorical language. Explain the point of the following metaphors. How effective do you think they are?

   "One day at the family picnic the boy wanders away from their spiced food and faceless stories to watch other boys play baseball in the distance" (par. 4).

   "This is a country where one begins to be an American. America exists as a culture and a grin, a faith and a shrug. It is clasped in a handshake, called by a first name" (par. 6).

3. The "pious emblems of rural America" stand against other emblems of cities, according to Rodriguez. What emblems does he name for both rural and urban American? What other emblems can you name that stand for rural or urban America? How do these emblems help Rodriguez define America?

4. In your opinion, what purpose does the last sentence in the essay serve? Explain.

5. Try answering the question "Does America Still Exist?" in your own words by writing a journal entry or short essay explaining your point of view.

From the Poets in the Kitchen

Paule Marshall

Paule Marshall (born in Brooklyn in 1929) is currently a professor of English and creative writing at Virginia Commonwealth University. Her books include the novel Brown Girl, Brownstones *(1959) and a collection of stories entitled* Reena and Other Stories *(1983). "From the Poets in the Kitchen" is a story from that collection.*

Some years ago, when I was teaching a graduate seminar in fiction at Columbia University, a well-known male novelist visited my class to speak on his development as a writer. In discussing his formative years, he didn't realize it but he seriously endangered his life by remarking that women writers are luckier than those of his sex because they usually spend so much time as children around their mothers and their mothers' friends in the kitchen.

What did he say that for? The women students immediately forgot about being in awe of him and began readying their attack for the question and answer period later on. Even I bristled. There again was that awful image of women locked away from the world in the kitchen with only each other to talk to, and their daughters locked in with them.

But my guest wasn't really being sexist or trying to be provocative or even spoiling for a fight. What he meant—when he got around to explaining himself more fully—was that, given the way children are (or were) raised in our society, with little girls kept closer to home and their mothers, the woman writer stands a better chance of being exposed, while growing up, to the kind of talk that goes on among women, more often than not in the kitchen; and that this experience gives her an edge over her male counterpart by instilling in her an appreciation for ordinary speech.

It was clear that my guest lecturer attached great importance to this, which is understandable. Common speech and the plain, workaday words that make it up are, after all, the stock in trade of some of the best fiction writers. They are the principal means by which characters in a novel or story reveal themselves and give voice sometimes to profound feelings and complex ideas about themselves and the world. Perhaps the proper measure of a writer's talent is skill in rendering everyday speech—when it is appropriate to the story—as well as the ability to tap, to exploit, the beauty, poetry and wisdom it often contains.

"If you say what's on your mind in the language that comes to you   5
from your parents and your street and friends you'll probably say something beautiful." Grace Paley tells this, she says, to her students at the
beginning of every writing course.

It's all a matter of exposure and a training of the ear for the would-be
writer in those early years of apprenticeship. And, according to my guest
lecturer, this training, the best of it, often takes place in as unglamorous a
setting as the kitchen.

He didn't know it, but he was essentially describing my experience as a
little girl. I grew up among poets. Now they didn't look like poets—whatever that breed is supposed to look like. Nothing about them suggested that
poetry was their calling. They were just a group of ordinary housewives and
mothers, my mother included, who dressed in a way (shapeless house-
dresses, dowdy felt hats and long, dark, solemn coats) that made it impossible for me to imagine they had ever been young.

Nor did they do what poets were supposed to do—spend their days in
an attic room writing verses. They never put pen to paper except to write
occasionally to their relatives in Barbados. "I take my pen in hand hoping
these few lines will find you in health as they leave me fair for the time
being," was the way their letters invariably began. Rather, their day was
spent "scrubbing floor," as they described the work they did.

Several mornings a week these unknown bards would put an apron
and a pair of old house shoes in a shopping bag and take the train or street-
car from our section of Brooklyn out to Flatbush. There, those who didn't
have steady jobs would wait on certain designated corners for the white
housewives in the neighborhood to come along and bargain with them over
pay for a day's work cleaning their houses. This was the ritual even in the
winter.

Later, armed with the few dollars they had earned, which in their   10
vocabulary became "a few raw-mouth pennies," they made their way back
to our neighborhood, where they would sometimes stop off to have a cup of
tea or cocoa together before going home to cook dinner for their husbands
and children.

The basement kitchen of the brownstone house where my family lived
was the usual gathering place. Once inside the warm safety of its walls the
women threw off the drab coats and hats, seated themselves at the large
center table, drank their cups of tea or cocoa, and talked. While my sister
and I sat at a smaller table over in a corner doing our homework, they
talked—endlessly, passionately, poetically, and with impressive range. No
subject was beyond them. True, they would indulge in the usual gossip:
whose husband was running with whom, whose daughter looked slightly
"in the way" (pregnant) under her bridal gown as she walked down the
aisle. That sort of thing. But they also tackled the great issues of the time.

They were always, for example, discussing the state of the economy. It was the mid and late 30's then, and the aftershock of the Depression, with its soup lines and suicides on Wall Street, was still being felt.

Some people, they declared, didn't know how to deal with adversity. They didn't know that you had to "tie up your belly" (hold in the pain, that is) when things got rough and go on with life. They took their image from the bellyband that is tied around the stomach of a newborn baby to keep the navel pressed in.

They talked politics. Roosevelt was their hero. He had come along and rescued the country with relief and jobs, and in gratitude they christened their sons Franklin and Delano and hoped they would live up to the names.

If F.D.R. was their hero, Marcus Garvey was their God. The name of the fiery, Jamaican-born black nationalist of the 20's was constantly invoked around the table. For he had been their leader when they first came to the United States from the West Indies shortly after World War I. They had contributed to his organization, the United Negro Improvement Association (UNIA), out of their meager salaries, bought shares in his ill-fated Black Star Shipping Line, and at the height of the movement they had marched as members of his "nurses' brigade" in their white uniforms up Seventh Avenue in Harlem during the great Garvey Day parades. Garvey: He lived on through the power of their memories.

And their talk was of war and rumors of war. They raged against World   15
War II when it broke out in Europe, blaming it on the politicians. "It's these politicians. They're the ones always starting up all this lot of war. But what they care? It's the poor people got to suffer and mothers with their sons." If it was *their* sons, they swore they would keep them out of the Army by giving them soap to eat each day to make their hearts sound defective. Hitler? He was for them "the devil incarnate."

Then there was home. They reminisced often and at length about home. The old country. Barbados—or Bimshire, as they affectionately called it. The little Caribbean island in the sun they loved but had to leave. "Poor—poor but sweet" was the way they remembered it.

And naturally they discussed their adopted home. America came in for both good and bad marks. They lashed out at it for the racism they encountered. They took to task some of the people they worked for, especially those who gave them only a hard-boiled egg and a few spoonfuls of cottage cheese for lunch. "As if anybody can scrub floor on an egg and some cheese that don't have no taste to it!"

Yet although they caught H in "this man country," as they called America, it was nonetheless a place where "you could at least see your way to make a dollar." That much they acknowledged. They might even one day accumulate enough dollars, with both them and their husbands working, to buy the brownstone houses which, like my family, they were only leasing at that period. This was their consuming ambition: to "buy house" and to see the children through.

There was no way for me to understand it at the time, but the talk that filled the kitchen those afternoons was highly functional. It served as therapy, the cheapest kind available to my mother and her friends. Not only did it help them recover from the long wait on the corner that morning and the bargaining over their labor, it restored them to a sense of themselves and reaffirmed their self-worth. Through language they were able to overcome the humiliations of the work-day.

But more than therapy, that freewheeling, wide-ranging, exuberant talk   20 functioned as an outlet for the tremendous creative energy they possessed. They were women in whom the need for self-expression was strong, and since language was the only vehicle readily available to them they made of it an art form that—in keeping with the African tradition in which art and life are one—was an integral part of their lives.

And their talk was a refuge. They never really ceased being baffled and overwhelmed by America—its vastness, complexity and power. Its strange customs and laws. At a level beyond words they remained fearful and in awe. Their uneasiness and fear were even reflected in their attitude toward the children they had given birth to in this country. They referred to those like myself, the little Brooklyn-born Bajans (Barbadians), as "these New York children" and complained that they couldn't discipline us properly because of the laws here. "You can't beat these children as you would like, you know, because the authorities in this place will dash you in jail for them. After all, these is New York children." Not only were we different, American, we had, as they saw it, escaped their ultimate authority.

Confronted therefore by a world they could not encompass, which even limited their rights as parents, and at the same time finding themselves permanently separated from the world they had known, they took refuge in language. "Language is the only homeland," Czeslaw Milosz, the emigré Polish writer and Nobel Laureate, has said. This is what it became for the women at the kitchen table.

It served another purpose also, I suspect. My mother and her friends were after all the female counterpart of Ralph Ellison's invisible man. Indeed, you might say they suffered a triple invisibility, being black, female, and foreigners. They really didn't count in American society except as a source of cheap labor. But given the kind of women they were, they couldn't tolerate the fact of their invisibility, their powerlessness. And they fought back, using the only weapon at their command: the spoken word.

Those late afternoon conversations on a wide range of topics were a way for them to feel they exercised some measure of control over their lives and the events that shaped them. "Soully-gal, talk yuh talk!" they were always exhorting each other. "In this man world you got to take yuh mouth and make a gun!" They were in control, if only verbally and if only for the two hours or so that they remained in our house.

For me, sitting over in the corner, being seen but not heard, which was 25 the rule for children in those days, it wasn't only what the women talked about—the content—but the way they put things—their style. The insight, irony, wit and humor they brought to their stories and discussions and their poet's inventiveness and daring with language—which of course I could only sense but not define back then.

They had taken the standard English taught them in the primary schools of Barbados and transformed it into an idiom, an instrument that more adequately described them—changing around the syntax and imposing their own rhythm and accent so that the sentences were more pleasing to their ears. They added the few African sounds and words that had survived, such as the derisive suck-teeth sound and the word "yam," meaning to eat. And to make it more vivid, more in keeping with their expressive quality, they brought to bear a raft of metaphors, parables, Biblical quotations, sayings and the like:

"The sea ain' got no back door," they would say, meaning that it wasn't like a house where if there was a fire you could run out the back. Meaning that it was not to be trifled with. And meaning perhaps in a larger sense that man should treat all of nature with caution and respect.

"I has read hell by heart and called every generation blessed!" They sometimes went in for hyperbole.

A woman expecting a baby was never said to be pregnant. They never used that word. Rather, she was "in the way" or, better yet, "tumbling big." "Guess who I butt up on in the market the other day tumbling big again!"

And a woman with a reputation of being too free with her sexual favors 30 was known in their book as a "thoroughfare"—the sense of men like a steady stream of cars moving up and down the road of her life. Or she might be dubbed "a free-bee," which was my favorite of the two. I liked the image it conjured up of a woman scandalous perhaps but independent, who flitted from one flower to another in a garden of male beauties, sampling their nectar, taking her pleasure at will, the roles reversed.

And nothing, no matter how beautiful, was ever described as simply beautiful. It was always "beautiful-ugly": the beautiful-ugly dress, the beautiful-ugly house, the beautiful-ugly car. Why the word "ugly," I used to wonder, when the thing they were referring to was beautiful, and they knew it. Why the antonym, the contradiction, the linking of opposites? It used to puzzle me greatly as a child.

There is the theory in linguistics which states that the idiom of a people, the way they use language, reflects not only on the most fundamental views they hold of themselves and the world but their very conception of reality. Perhaps in using the term "beautiful-ugly" to describe nearly everything, my mother and her friends were expressing what they believed to be a fundamental dualism in life: the idea that a thing is at the same time its opposite, and that these opposites, these contradictions make up the whole. But theirs was not a Manichaean brand of dualism that sees matter, flesh, the body, as inherently evil, because they constantly addressed each other as "soully-gal"—soul: spirit; gal: the body, flesh, the visible self. And it was clear from their tone that they gave one as much weight and importance as the other. They had never heard of the mind/body split.

As for God, they summed up His essential attitude in a phrase. "God," they would say, "don' love ugly and He ain' stuck on pretty."

Using everyday speech, the simple commonplace words—but always with imagination and skill—they gave voice to the most complex ideas. Flannery O'Connor would have approved of how they made ordinary language work, as she put it, "double-time," stretching, shading, deepening its meaning. Like Joseph Conrad they were always trying to infuse new life in the "old old words worn thin . . . by . . . careless usage." And the goals of their oral art were the same as his: "to make you hear, to make you feel . . . to make you see." This was their guiding aesthetic.

SUGGESTIONS FOR FURTHER STUDY

Key Words

The author uses language with which you may not be familiar. Find the following words in the paragraphs indicated, and explain their meanings in the context of the sentences in which the words appear. Consult a dictionary, as needed.

bards (par. 9)
emigré (par. 22)
hyperbole (par. 28)
Manichaean (par. 32)
aesthetic (par. 34)

Topics for Discussion and Writing

1. In her writing, Marshall includes some of the idiom of the West Indian women who gathered in her mother's New York City kitchen to talk. Make a list of the words, phrases, and idiomatic expressions you find most effective, beautiful, expressive, or humorous in this essay. Which ones particularly reflect the culture and interests of the women Marshall writes about?

2. In what ways are the women "poets"? Explain your answer.

3. Many of the words used by these "poets in the kitchen" carry connotations that suggest multiple meanings. What meanings do

"thoroughfare" and "butt up on" suggest? What words do you use in your own dialect, which are intended to suggest more than one meaning? Make a list of them, and compare your list with lists by other readers.

4. What do you think Conrad meant by "old old words worn thin . . . by . . . careless usage"? What words or phrases do you know that fit Conrad's description?

5. Note Marshall's use of quotation marks to designate reported oral language—the lingo of the women. Listen to family members, friends, or a group of elders in your family or community, and make a list of the common expressions and metaphors they use in everyday speech. Try writing a narrative using some of those expressions, highlighting them with quotation marks.

Living in Two Cultures

Jeanne Wakatsuki Houston

*Jeanne Wakatsuki Houston (born in Inglewood, California, in 1934)
spent part of her childhood in the Japanese American relocation
camp at Manzanar. Her famous autobiographical novel,* Farewell to
Manzanar *(published in 1973), depicts her family's experience in that
camp. In "Living in Two Cultures," Houston describes her life after
Manzanar and her struggle to reconcile living in two different cultures.*

The memories surrounding my awareness of being female fall into two   1
categories: those of the period before World War II, when the family made
up my life, and those after the war, when I entered puberty and my world
expanded to include the ways and values of my Caucasian peers. I did not
think about my Asian-ness and how it influenced my self-image as a female
until I married.

In remembering myself as a small child, I find it hard to separate myself
from the entity of the family. I was too young to be given "duties" according to my sex, and I was unaware that this was the organizational basis for
operating the family. I took it for granted that everyone just did what had to
be done to keep things running smoothly. My five older sisters helped my
mother with domestic duties. My four older brothers helped my father in
the fishing business. What I vaguely recall about the sensibility surrounding
our sex differences was that my sisters and I all liked to please our brothers.
More so, we tried to attract positive attention from Papa. A smile or affec-
tionate pat from him was like a gift from heaven. Somehow, we never felt
this way about Mama. We took her love for granted. But there was something special about Papa.

I never identified this specialness as being one of the blessings of maleness. After all, I played with my brother Kiyo, two years older than myself,
and I never felt there was anything special about him. I could even make him
cry. My older brothers were fun-loving, boisterous and very kind to me,
especially when I made them laugh with my imitations of Carmen Miranda
dancing or of Bonnie Baker singing "Oh, Johnny." But Papa was different.
His specialness came not from being male, but from being the authority.

After the war and the closing of the camps, my world drastically
changed. The family had disintegrated; my father was no longer godlike,
despite my mother's attempt to sustain that pre-war image of him. I was

spending most of my time with my new Caucasian friends and learning new values that clashed with those of my parents. It was also time that I assumed the duties girls were supposed to do, like cooking, cleaning the house, washing and ironing clothes. I remember washing and ironing my brothers' shirts, being careful to press the collars correctly, trying not to displease them. I cannot ever remember my brothers performing domestic chores while I lived at home. Yet, even though they may not have been working "out there," as the men were supposed to do, I did not resent it. It would have embarrassed me to see my brothers doing the dishes. Their reciprocation came in a different way. They were very protective of me and made me feel good and important for being a female. If my brother Ray had extra money, he would sometimes buy me a sexy sweater like my Caucasian friends wore, which Mama wouldn't buy for me. My brothers taught me to ride a bicycle and to drive a car, took me to my first dance, and proudly introduced me to their friends.

Although the family had changed, my identity as a female within it did not differ much from my older sisters who grew up before the war. The males and females supported each other but for different reasons. No longer was the survival of the family as a group our primary objective; we cooperated to help each other survive "out there" in the complicated world that had weakened Papa.   5

We were living in Long Beach then. My brothers encouraged me to run for school office, to try out for majorette and song leader, and to run for queen of various festivities. They were proud that I was breaking social barriers still closed to them. It was acceptable for an Oriental male to excel academically and in sports. But to gain recognition socially in a society that had been fed the stereotyped model of the Asian male as cook, houseboy or crazed kamikaze pilot was almost impossible. The more alluring myth of mystery and exotica that surrounds the Oriental female made it easier, though no less inwardly painful, for me.

Whenever I succeeded in the *Hakujin* world, my brothers were supportive, whereas Papa would be disdainful, undermined by my obvious capitulation to the ways of the West. I wanted to be like my Caucasian friends. Not only did I want to look like them, I wanted to act like them. I tried hard to be outgoing and socially aggressive and to act confidently, like my girlfriends. At home I was careful not to show these personality traits to my father. For him it was bad enough that I did not even look very Japanese: I was too big, and I walked too assertively. My breasts were large, and besides that I showed them off with those sweaters the *Hakujin* girls wore! My behavior at home was never calm and serene, but around my father I still tried to be as Japanese as I could.

As I passed puberty and grew more interested in boys, I soon became aware that an Oriental female evoked a certain kind of interest from males. I was still too young to understand how or why an Oriental female fascinated Caucasian men, and of course, far too young to see then that it was a form of "not seeing." My brothers would warn me, "Don't trust the

Hakujin boys. They only want one thing. They'll treat you like a servant and expect you to wait on them hand and foot. They don't know how to be nice to you." My brothers never dated Caucasian girls. In fact, I never really dated Caucasian boys until I went to college. In high school, I used to sneak out to dances and parties where I would meet them. I wouldn't even dare to think what Papa would do if he knew.

What my brothers were saying was that I should not act toward Caucasian males as I did toward them. I must not "wait on them" or allow them to think I would, because they wouldn't understand. In other words, be a Japanese female around Japanese men and act *Hakujin* around Caucasian men. This double identity within a "double standard" resulted not only in a confusion for me of my role or roles as female, but also in who or what I was racially. With the admonitions of my brothers lurking deep in my consciousness, I would try to be aggressive, assertive and "come on strong" toward Caucasian men. I mustn't let them think I was submissive, passive and all-giving like Madame Butterfly.[1] With Asian males I would tone down my natural enthusiasm and settle into patterns instilled in me through the models of my mother and my sisters. I was not comfortable in either role.

Although I was attracted to males who looked like someone in a Coca-Cola ad, I yearned for the expressions of their potency to be like that of Japanese men, like that of my father: unpredictable, dominant, and brilliant—yet sensitive and poetic. I wanted a blond samurai. 10

When I met my blond samurai, during those college years in San Jose, I was surprised to see how readily my mother accepted the idea of our getting married. My father had passed away, but I was still concerned about her reaction. All of my married brothers and sisters had married Japanese-American mates. I would be the first to marry a Caucasian. "He's a strong man and will protect you. I'm all for it," she said. Her main concern for me was survival. Knowing that my world was the world of the *Hakujin,* she wanted me to be protected, even if it meant marriage to one of them. It was 1957, and interracial couples were a rare sight to see. She felt that my husband-to-be was strong because he was acting against the norms of his culture, perhaps even against his parents' wishes. From her vantage point, where family and group opinion outweighed the individual's, this willingness to oppose them was truly a show of strength.

When we first married I wondered if I should lay out his socks and underwear every morning like my mother used to do for my father. But my brothers' warning would float up from the past: don't be subservient to Caucasian men or they will take advantage. So I compromised and laid them out sporadically, whenever I thought to do it . . . which grew less and less often as the years passed. (Now my husband is lucky if he can even find

---

[1]Madame Butterfly is the heroine of an American play and an Italian opera. She marries an American lieutenant for love and then commits suicide when he leaves her for an American woman.

a clean pair of socks in the house!) His first reaction to this wifely gesture was to be uncomfortably pleased. Then he was puzzled by its sporadic occurrence, which did not seem to coincide as an act of apology or because I wanted something. On the days when I felt I should be a good Japanese wife, I did it. On other days, when I felt American and assertive, I did not.

When my mother visited us, as she often did when she was alive, I had to be on good behavior, much to my husband's pleasure and surprise. I would jump up from the table to fill his empty water glass (if she hadn't beat me to it) or butter his roll. If I didn't notice that his plate needed refilling, she would kick me under the table and reprimand me with a disapproving look. Needless to say, we never had mother-in-law problems. He would often ask, with hope in his voice, "when is your mother coming to visit?"

My mother had dutifully served my father throughout their marriage, but I never felt she resented it. I served my brothers and father and did not resent it. I was made to feel not only important for performing duties of my role, but absolutely integral for the functioning of the family. I realized a very basic difference in attitude between Japanese and American cultures toward serving another. In my family, to serve another could be uplifting, a gracious gesture that elevated oneself. For many white Americans, it seems that serving another is degrading, an indication of dependency or weakness in character, or a low place in the social ladder. To be ardently considerate is to be "self-effacing" or apologetic.

My father used to say, "Serving humanity is the greatest virtue. Giving   15
service of yourself is more worthy than selling the service or goods of another." He would prefer that we be maids in someone's home, serving someone well, than be salesgirls where our function would be to exchange someone else's goods, handling money. Perhaps it was his way of rationalizing and giving pride to the occupations open to us as Orientals. Nevertheless, his words have stayed with me, giving me spiritual sustenance at times when I perceived that my willingness to give was misconstrued as a need to be liked or an act of manipulation to get something.

My husband and I often joke that the reason we have stayed married for so long is that we continually mystify each other with responses and attitudes that are plainly due to our different backgrounds. For years I frustrated him with unpredictable silences and accusing looks. I felt a great reluctance to tell him what I wanted or what needed to be done in the home. I was inwardly furious that I was being put into the position of having to *tell* him what to do. I felt my femaleness, in the Japanese sense, was being degraded. I did not want to be the authority. That would be humiliating for him and for me. He, on the other hand, considering the home to be under my dominion, in the American sense, did not dare to impose on me what he thought I wanted. He wanted me to tell him or make a list, like his parents did in his home.

Entertaining socially was also confusing. Up to recent times, I still hesitated to sit at one head of our rectangular dining table when my husband sat at the other end. It seemed right to be seated next to him, helping him serve the food. Sometimes I did it anyway, but only with our close friends, who didn't misread my physical placement as psychological subservice.

At dinner parties I always served the men first, until I noticed the women glaring at me. I became self-conscious about it and would try to remember to serve the women first. Sometimes I would forget and automatically turn to a man. I would catch myself abruptly, dropping a bowl of soup all over him. Then I would have to serve him first anyway, as a gesture of apology. My unconscious Japanese instinct still managed to get what it wanted.

Now I just entertain according to how I feel that day. If my Japanese sensibility is stronger, I act accordingly and feel comfortable. If I feel like going all-American, I can do that, too, and feel comfortable. I have come to accept the cultural hybridness of my personality, to recognize it as a strength and not weakness. Because I am culturally neither pure Japanese nor pure American does not mean I am less of a person. It means I have been enriched with the heritage of both.

How my present attitudes will affect my children in later years remains 20 to be seen. My world is radically different from my mother's world, and all indications point to an even wider difference between our world and our children's. Whereas my family's and part of my struggle was racially based, I do not foresee a similar struggle for our children. Their biracialism is, indeed, a factor in their identity and self-image, but I feel their struggle will be more to sustain human dignity in a world rapidly dehumanizing itself with mechanization and technology. My hope is they have inherited a strong will to survive, that essential trait ethnic minorities in this country have so sharply honed.

SUGGESTIONS FOR FURTHER STUDY

Key Words

The author uses language with which you may not be familiar. Find the following words in the paragraphs indicated, and explain their meanings in the context of the sentences in which the words appear. Consult a dictionary, as needed.

sensibility (par. 2)
boisterous (par. 3)
reciprocation (par. 4)
exotica (par. 6)
capitulation (par. 7)
sporadically (par. 12)
self-effacing (par. 14)

sustenance (par. 15)
misconstrued (par. 15)

Topics for Discussion and Writing

1. The author uses three terms that are important to your understanding of her dilemma: "psychological subservience" (par. 17), "cultural hybridness" (par. 19), and "biracialism" (par. 20). Discuss with other readers what she means by these terms and why they are central to her autobiographical essay.

2. What stereotypes of both Asian and Caucasian people does the author describe in her essay? In your experience, do those stereotypes still exist? Explain your answer, and give examples from your own experiences or those of your family.

3. The author talks about two views of serving others in a family. Discuss with other readers the differences between those two views, and elaborate on them by drawing on your own or your family's experience.

4. The author describes her experience and feelings first while she was growing up in her family's home, then as the wife of a Caucasian man. What adjustments did she make during each period of her life in order to realize that she had been enriched by both heritages—Asian and Caucasian?

5. Autobiographies frequently follow a chronological order of events. Examine how Houston organizes her autobiographical account, and create a time line to trace the development of her story. Where does she establish the *order* of her narrative? What major divisions do you find? How does the organization of her narrative help readers to reach an understanding of her personal development?

6. Houston describes "female" and "male" responsibilities in her home. Think about how family duties and responsibilities are assigned or assumed in your family, and write a descriptive essay about them. Analyze the reasons for the division of duties or their sources, and relate your personal attitudes toward them.

7. Houston says, "My world is radically different from my mother's world, and all indications point to an even wider difference between our world and our children's." In *your* generation, what has changed to reflect this "larger difference" between your parents' world and yours? Reflect on this question in a journal entry, or write an autobiographical sketch of your own life in a family. If your family lives in two cultures, comment on how the two cultures complicate or enrich your identity and your self-image. If your family shares a single culture, comment on how age differences affect both your relationship with family members and your self-image.

The Media's Image of Arabs

Jack G. Shaheen

Jack G. Shaheen (born in Pittsburgh, PA, in 1935, the son of Lebanese immigrants), earned degrees from Carnegie Technological Institute, Penn State, and the University of Missouri. He has taught mass communications at Southern Illinois University and has worked as a reporter and a critic. He published The TV Arab *and* The Hollywood Arab *in 1984, and 1990, respectively. "The Media's Image of Arabs" appeared in* Newsweek *on February 29, 1988.*

America's bogyman is the Arab. Until the nightly news brought us TV   1
pictures of Palestinian boys being punched and beaten, almost all portraits of Arabs seen in America were dangerously threatening. Arabs were either billionaires or bombers—rarely victims. They were hardly ever seen as ordinary people practicing law, driving taxis, singing lullabies or healing the sick. Though TV news may portray them more sympathetically now, the absence of positive media images nurtures suspicion and stereotype. As an Arab-American, I have found that ugly caricatures have had an enduring impact on my family.

I was sheltered from prejudicial portraits at first. My parents came from Lebanon in the 1920s; they met and married in America. Our home in the steel city of Clairton, Pa., was a center for ethnic sharing—black, white, Jew and gentile. There was only one major source of media image then, at the State movie theater where I was lucky enough to get a part-time job as an usher. But in the late 1940s, Westerns and war movies were popular, not Middle Eastern dramas. Memories of World War II were fresh, and the screen heavies were the Japanese and the Germans. True to the cliché of the times, the only good Indian was a dead Indian. But when I mimicked or mocked the bad buys, my mother cautioned me. She explained that stereotypes blur our vision and corrupt the imagination. "Have compassion for all people, Jackie," she said. "This way, you'll learn to experience the joy of accepting people as they are, and not as they appear in films. Stereotypes hurt."

Mother was right. I can remember the Saturday afternoon when my son, Michael, who was seven, and my daughter, Michele, six, suddenly called out: "Daddy, Daddy, they've got some bad Arabs on TV." They were watching that great American morality play, TV wrestling. Akbar the Great, who liked to hear the cracking of bones, and Abdullah the Butcher, a dirty fighter who liked to inflict pain, were pinning their foes with "camel locks." From that day on, I knew I had to try to neutralize the media caricatures.

It hasn't been easy. With my children, I have watched animated heroes Heckle and Jeckle pull the rug from under "Ali Boo-Boo, the Desert Rat," and Laverne and Shirley stop "Sheik Ha-Mean-le" from conquering "the U.S. and the world." I have read comic books like the "Fantastic Four" and "G.I. Combat" whose characters have sketched Arabs as "lowlifes" and "human hyenas." Negative stereotypes were everywhere. A dictionary informed my youngsters that an Arab is a "vagabond, drifter, hobo and vagrant." Whatever happened, my wife wondered, to Aladdin's good genie?

To a child, the world is simple: good versus evil. But my children and others with Arab roots grew up without ever having seen a humane Arab on the silver screen, someone to pattern their lives after. Is it easier for a camel to go through the eye of a needle than for a screen Arab to appear as a genuine human being?

Hollywood producers must have an instant Ali Baba kit that contains scimitars, veils, sunglasses and such Arab clothing as *chadors* and *kufiyahs*. In the mythical "Ay-rabland," oil wells, tents, mosques, goats and shepherds prevail. Between the sand dunes, the camera focuses on a mock-up of a palace from "Arabian Nights"—or a military air base. Recent movies suggest that Americans are at war with Arabs, forgetting the fact that out of twenty-one Arab nations, America is friendly with nineteen of them. And in "Wanted Dead or Alive," a movie that starred Gene Simmons, the leader of the rock group Kiss, the war comes home when an Arab terrorist comes to the United States dressed as a rabbi and, among other things, conspires with Arab-Americans to poison the people of Los Angeles. The movie was released last year.

The Arab remains American culture's favorite whipping boy. In his memoirs, Terrel Bell, Ronald Reagan's first secretary of education, writes about an "apparent bias among mid-level, right-wing staffers at the White House" who dismissed Arabs as "sand niggers." Sadly, the racial slurs continue. At a recent teacher's conference, I met a woman from Sioux Falls, S.D., who told me about the persistence of discrimination. She was in the process of adopting a baby when an agency staffer warned her that the infant had a problem. When she asked whether the child was mentally ill, or physically handicapped, there was silence. Finally, the worker said: "The baby is Jordanian."

To me, the Arab demon of today is much like the Jewish demon of yesterday. We deplore the false portrait of Jews as a swarthy menace. Yet a similar portrait has been accepted and transferred to another group of Semites—the Arabs. Print and broadcast journalists have started to challenge this stereotype. They are now revealing more humane images of Palestinian Arabs, a people who traditionally suffered from the myth that

Palestinian equals terrorist. Others could follow that lead and retire the stereotypical Arab to a media Valhalla.

It would be a step in the right direction if movie and TV producers developed characters modeled after real-life Arab-Americans. We could then see a White House correspondent like Helen Thomas, whose father came from Lebanon, in "The Golden Girls," a heart surgeon patterned after Dr. Michael DeBakey on "St. Elsewhere," or a Syrian-American playing tournament chess like Yasser Seirawan, the Seattle grandmaster.

Politicians, too, should speak out against the cardboard caricatures. 10 They should refer to Arabs as friends, not just as moderates. And religious leaders could state that Islam like Christianity and Judaism maintains that all mankind is one family in the care of God. When all imagemakers rightfully begin to treat Arabs and other minorities with respect and dignity, we may begin to unlearn our prejudices.

SUGGESTIONS FOR FURTHER STUDY

Key Words

The author uses language with which you may not be familiar. Find the following words in the paragraphs indicated, and explain their meanings in the context of the sentences in which the words appear. Consult a dictionary, as needed.

bogyman (par. 1)
caricatures (par. 1)
Semites (par. 8)
Valhalla (par. 8)

Topics for Discussion and Writing

1. Shaheen provides several examples of stereotypes from the media in this essay. Explain how these examples "blur our vision and corrupt the imagination," and add some examples of your own for discussion.
2. In what way is wrestling the "great American morality play"? What other event in the media might also be characterized as a morality play? Explain.
3. Shaheen suggests that we can "unlearn our prejudices." How can we do that? Discuss with other readers one or two injurious prejudices you think we can unlearn, then write a brief essay illustrating how we can do so. Give specific examples based on your own knowledge and your discussions with others.

4. In addition to Shaheen's examples, what other evidence of media stereotyping have you noticed? Are these stereotypes humorous, sinister, pitiable, attractive, or unattractive? Explain your answer.

5. In what ways are European Americans stereotyped in other parts of the world? Do these stereotypes have any bases in real life or in actual people? You will need to research this topic to see how European Americans are depicted by people or media in other cultures. Compile a list of European American stereotypes and their origins.

The Indian Chant and the Tomahawk Chop

Ward Churchill

Ward Churchill is a writer and an active member of the American Indian Anti-Defamation League. His recent books include Fantasies of the Master Race: Literature, Cinema, and the Colonization of the American Indians *(1992) and* Indians Are Us: Culture and Genocide in Native North America *(1994).* "The Indian Chant and the Tomahawk Chop" *is from Churchill's essay* "Crimes against Humanity," *which appeared in* Z Magazine *in 1993.*

During the past couple of seasons, there has been an increasing wave of controversy regarding the names of professional sports teams like the Atlanta "Braves," Cleveland "Indians," Washington "Redskins," and Kansas City "Chiefs." The issue extends to the names of college teams like Florida State University "Seminoles," University of Illinois "Fighting Illini," and so on, right on down to high school outfits like the Lamar (Colorado) "Savages." Also involved have been team adoption of "mascots," replete with feathers, buckskins, beads, spears and "warpaint" (some fans have opted to adorn themselves in the same fashion), and nifty little "pep" gestures like the "Indian Chant" and "Tomahawk Chop."

A substantial number of American Indians have protested that use of native names, images and symbols as sports team mascots and the like is, by definition, a virulently racist practice. Given the historical relationship between Indians and non-Indians during what has been called the "Conquest of America," American Indian Movement leader (and American Indian Anti-Defamation Council founder) Russell Means has compared the practice to contemporary Germans naming their soccer teams the "Jews," "Hebrews," and "Yids," while adorning their uniforms with grotesque caricatures of Jewish faces taken from the Nazis' anti-Semitic propaganda of the 1930s. Numerous demonstrations have occurred in conjunction with games—most notably during the November 15, 1992 match-up between the Chiefs and Redskins in Kansas City—by angry Indians and their supporters.

In response, a number of players—especially African Americans and other minority athletes—have been trotted out by professional team owners like Ted Turner, as well as university and public school officials, to announce that they mean not to insult but to honor native people. They

1

have been joined by the television networks and most major newspapers, all of which have editorialized that Indian discomfort with the situation is "no big deal," insisting that the whole thing is just "good, clean fun." The country needs more such fun, they've argued, and "a few disgruntled Native Americans" have no right to undermine the nation's enjoyment of its leisure time by complaining. This is especially the case, some have argued, "in hard times like these." It has even been contended that Indian outrage at being systematically degraded—rather than the degradation itself—creates "a serious barrier to the sort of intergroup communication so necessary in a multicultural society such as ours."

Okay, let's communicate. We are frankly dubious that those advancing such positions really believe their own rhetoric, but, just for the sake of argument, let's accept the premise that they are sincere. If what they say is true, then isn't it time we spread such "inoffensiveness" and "good cheer" around among *all* groups so that *everybody* can participate *equally* in fostering the round of national laughs they call for? Sure it is—the country can't have too much fun or "intergroup involvement"—so the more, the merrier. Simple consistency demands that anyone who thinks the Tomahawk Chop is a swell pastime must be just as hearty in their endorsement of the following ideas—by the logic used to defend the defamation of American Indians—should help us all really start yukking it up.

First, as a counterpart to the Redskins, we need an NFL team called "Niggers" to honor Afro-Americans. Half-time festivities for fans might include a simulated stewing of the opposing coach in a large pot while players and cheerleaders dance around it, garbed in leopard skins and wearing fake bones in their noses. This concept obviously goes along with the kind of gaiety attending the Chop, but also with the actions of the Kansas City Chiefs, whose team members—prominently including black team members—lately appeared on a poster looking "fierce" and "savage" by way of wearing Indian regalia. Just a bit of harmless "morale boosting," says the Chiefs' front office. You bet.

So that the newly-formed Niggers sports club won't end up too out of sync while expressing the "spirit" and "identity" of Afro-Americans in the above fashion, a baseball franchise—let's call this one the "Sambos"—should be formed. How about a basketball team called the "Spearchuckers"? A hockey team called the "Jungle Bunnies"? Maybe the "essence" of these teams could be depicted by images of tiny black faces adorned with huge pairs of lips. The players could appear on TV every week or so gnawing on chicken legs and spitting watermelon seeds at one another. Catchy, eh? Well, there's "nothing to be upset about," according to those who love wearing "war bonnets" to the Super Bowl or having "Chief Illiniwik" dance around the sports arenas of Urbana, Illinois.

And why stop there? There are plenty of other groups to include. "Hispanics"? They can be "represented" by the Galveston "Greasers" and

San Diego "Spics," at least until the Wisconsin "Wetbacks" and Baltimore "Beaners" get off the ground. Asian Americans? How about the "Slopes," "Dinks," "Gooks," and "Zipperheads"? Owners of the latter teams might get their logo ideas from editorial page cartoons printed in the nation's newspapers during World War II: slant-eyes, buck teeth, big glasses, but nothing racially insulting or derogatory, according to the editors and artists involved at the time. Indeed, this Second World War–vintage stuff can be seen as just another barrel of laughs, at least by what current editors say are their "local standards" concerning American Indians.

Let's see. Who's been left out? Teams like the Kansas City "Kikes," Hanover "Honkies," San Leandro "Shylocks," Dayton "Dagos," and Pittsburgh "Polacks" will fill a certain social void among white folk. Have a religious belief? Let's all go for the gusto and gear up the Milwaukee "Mackerel Snappers" and Hollywood "Holy Rollers." The Fighting Irish of Notre Dame can be rechristened the "Drunken Irish" or "Papist Pigs." Issues of gender and sexual preference can be addressed through creation of teams like the St. Louis "Sluts," Boston "Bimbos," Detroit "Dykes," and the Fresno "Fags." How about the Gainesville "Gimps" and Richmond "Retards," so the physically and mentally impaired won't be excluded from our fun and games?

Now, don't go getting "overly sensitive" out there. None of this is demeaning or insulting, at least not when it's being done to Indians. Just ask the folks who are doing it, or their apologists like Andy Rooney in the national media. They'll tell you—as in fact they *have* been telling you—that there's been no harm done, regardless of what their victims think, feel, or say. The situation is exactly the same as when those with precisely the same mentality used to insist that Step 'n' Fetchit was okay, or Rochester on the Jack Benny Show, or Amos and Andy, Charlie Chan, the Frito Bandito, or any of the other cutesy symbols making up the lexicon of American racism. Have we communicated yet?

Let's get just a little bit real here. The notion of "fun" embodied in ritu- [10] als like the Tomahawk Chop must be understood for what it is. There's not a single non-Indian example used above which can be considered socially acceptable in even the most marginal sense. The reasons are obvious enough. So why is it different where American Indians are concerned? One can only conclude that, in contrast to the other groups at issue, Indians are (falsely) perceived as being too few, and therefore too weak, to defend themselves effectively against racist and otherwise offensive behavior.

Fortunately, there are some glimmers of hope. A few teams and their fans have gotten the message and have responded appropriately. Stanford University, which opted to drop the name "Indians" from Stanford, has experienced no resulting drop-off in attendance. Meanwhile, the local newspaper in Portland, Oregon recently decided its long-standing editorial policy prohibiting use of racial epithets should include derogatory team names. The Redskins, for instance, are now referred to as "the Washington team," and will continue to be described in this way until the franchise adopts an inoffensive moniker (newspaper sales in Portland have suffered no decline as a result).

Such examples are to be applauded and encouraged. They stand as figurative beacons in the night, proving beyond all doubt that it is quite possible to indulge in the pleasure of athletics without accepting blatant racism into the bargain.

SUGGESTIONS FOR FURTHER STUDY

Key Words

The author uses language with which you may not be familiar. Find the following words in the paragraphs indicated, and explain their meanings in the context of the sentences in which the words appear. Consult a dictionary, as needed.

virulently (par. 2)
defamation (par. 2)
caricatures (par. 3)
rhetoric (par. 4)
derogatory (par. 7)
demeaning (par. 9)
lexicon (par. 9)
marginal (par. 10)

Topics for Discussion and Writing

1. Locate and quote the thesis statement of this essay. Explain Churchill's thesis in your own words.
2. To what does Russell Means compare the practice of using "native names, images and symbols as sports team mascots and the like" (par. 2)? How does this comparison stress the seriousness of the issue to Native Americans?
3. Sports teams and others defend the practice that Churchill decries. Why do they feel that it is really no big deal?
4. Summarize the various examples Churchill provides in spreading the " 'inoffensiveness' and 'good cheer' among *all* groups so that *everybody* can participate *equally* in fostering the round of national laughs they call for" (par. 4). What is Churchill's tone here? How would you compare his examples with Russell Means's analogy? In your opinion, how effective are Churchill's examples in convey-

ing the feeling that Native Americans share when surrounded by members of sports teams or other elements of American culture who have no hesitation about calling themselves "Redskins" or similar terms? Explain your answer.

5. At the end of his essay, Churchill concedes that his examples are not "socially acceptable in even the most marginal sense." What is his answer to his own question, "So why is it different where American Indians are concerned?" Do you agree with Churchill? Why or why not?

6. Churchill's essay calls for us to be more sensitive to the needs of marginalized people in this country. Discuss with others in your class ways in which people of various ethnicities, gay and lesbian people, physically challenged people, senior citizens, overweight people, and others are stereotyped and insulted under the pretense of having fun in this country. During your discussion, consider ways to counter such stereotyping and insults.

7. Following a discussion of the ways people consciously or unconsciously stereotype others unlike them, write a thoughtful essay exploring the causes of stereotyping and possible solutions for eliminating that practice. Consider some of the points you examined in the previous question.

So Mexicans Are Taking Jobs from Americans

Jimmy Santiago Baca

Jimmy Santiago Baca is the author of several books of poetry, including Martin and Meditations on the South Valley *and* Black Mesa Poems. *The following selection is from his collection* Immigrants in Our Own Land, *which focuses on his experiences while in prison, where he taught himself to read and write.*

O Yes? Do they come on horses   1
with rifles, and say,
                    Ese gringo, gimmeee your job?

And do you, gringo, take off your ring,
drop your wallet into a blanket
spread over the ground, and walk away?

I hear Mexicans are taking your jobs away.
Do they sneak into town at night,
and as you're walking home with a whore,
do they mug you, a knife at your throat,   10
saying, I want your job?

Even on TV, an asthmatic leader
crawls turtle heavy, leaning on an assistant,
and from a nest of wrinkles on his face,
a tongue paddles through flashing waves
of lightbulbs, of cameramen, rasping
"They're taking our jobs away."

Well, I've gone about trying to find them,
asking just where the hell are these fighters.

The rifles I hear sound in the night   20
are white farmers shooting blacks and browns
whose ribs I see jutting out
and starving children,
I see the poor marching for a little work,
I see small white farmers selling out

to clean-suited farmers living in New York,
who've never been on a farm,
don't know the look of a hoof or the smell
of a woman's body bending all day long in fields.

I see this, and I hear only a few people   30
got all the money in this world, the rest
count their pennies to buy bread and butter.

Below that cool green sea of money,
millions and millions of people fight to live,
search for pearls in the darkest depths
of their dreams, hold their breath for years
trying to cross poverty to just having something.

The children are dead already. We are killing them,
that is what America should be saying;
on TV, in the streets, in offices, should be saying,   40
    "We aren't giving the children a chance to live."

    Mexicans are taking our jobs, they say instead.
    What they really say is, let them die,
    and the children too.

SUGGESTIONS FOR FURTHER STUDY

Language and Style

1. The effectiveness of Baca's description depends largely on figurative
   language.
   a. Explain the author's use and the resulting effect of the following
      words and phrases:
      "an asthmatic leader crawls turtle heavy"
      "Below that cool green sea of money"
   b. Find and discuss other images that offer vivid or metaphorical
      descriptions of people, events, or emotions.
2. How would you describe Baca's tone in this essay? Is it caustic,
   scholarly, satirical, humorous, or some combination of these characteristics? Point to specific words and phrases in the poem that
   convey that tone.

Topics for Discussion and Writing

1. In your own words, summarize the underlying idea in Baca's poem.
2. According to Baca, what are most people in America doing?

3. In Baca's opinion, how are we "killing the children," and what can we do about it?

4. If Mexicans are not taking jobs away from non-Mexicans, what conditions or events are causing Americans to lose their jobs?

5. Baca's poem focuses on a controversial issue in America today, particularly in California, Texas, Florida, and New York, where the immigration rate is high. Although America is known worldwide as the land where immigrants can come to start a new life, we have historically been hostile to many new immigrants, particularly to those who arrive here illegally. For many Americans, Baca's poem expresses their basic fear of losing jobs to new immigrants. Discuss in groups, or write an essay about the problem of illegal immigration in America. Consider the following questions in your discussion or your writing:

   a. What ethnic minority suffers the most from the presence of illegal immigrants who come to America to work for less pay than legal residents? Document (give supporting evidence for) your conclusion.

   b. Who do you think is to blame for the presence of illegal immigrants working in America: the immigrants searching for jobs and a better life, the owners of businesses that hire illegal aliens, the U.S. government or state governments that do not close or adequately police their borders, or some other group, government, or agency involved in immigration policies? Provide details and document your evidence for your opinions.

   c. Several states have voted to enact laws that limit or prohibit illegal aliens from obtaining basic services such as hospital and child care, public education, and assistance for the elderly and the mentally ill. Do you think such legislation can adequately address the problem of illegal immigration? Provide details and document your evidence for your opinions.

   d. What suggestions can you offer that might help solve the problems caused by the presence of illegal immigrants in this country?

   (You may want to research books, scholarly journals, magazines, or newspapers in the library. Consult the computer databases in your library to assist you in locating the latest information. Use the Internet to gain access to relevant material on your topic through the World Wide Web [WWW].)

Four Directions

Amy Tan

Amy Tan was born (in 1952, Oakland, California) soon after her parents had immigrated to the United States from China. She has published three novels: The Joy Luck Club *(1989),* The Kitchen God's Wife *(1991), and* The Hundred Secret Senses *(1995). The following selection from* The Joy Luck Club *features the narration of Waverly Jong, as she brings her European American fiancé home to meet her family for the first time.*

After much thought, I came up with a brilliant plan. I concocted a way for Rich to meet my mother and win her over. In fact, I arranged it so my mother would want to cook a meal especially for him. I had some help from Auntie Suyuan. Auntie Su was my mother's friend from way back. They were very close, which meant they were ceaselessly tormenting each other with boasts and secrets. And I gave Auntie Su a secret to boast about.

After walking through North Beach one Sunday, I suggested to Rich that we stop by for a surprise visit to my Auntie Su and Uncle Canning. They lived on Leavenworth, just a few blocks west of my mother's apartment. It was late afternoon, just in time to catch Auntie Su preparing Sunday dinner.

"Stay! Stay!" she had insisted.

"No, no. It's just that we were walking by," I said.

"Already cooked enough for you. See? One soup, four dishes. You don't eat it, only have to throw it away. Wasted!'"

How could we refuse? Three days later, Auntie Suyuan had a thank-you letter from Rich and me. "Rich said it was the best Chinese food he has ever tasted," I wrote.

And the next day, my mother called me, to invite me to a belated birthday dinner for my father. My brother Vincent was bringing his girlfriend, Lisa Lum. I could bring a friend, too.

I knew she would do this, because cooking was how my mother expressed her love, her pride, her power, her proof that she knew more than Auntie Su. "Just be sure to tell her later that her cooking was the best you ever tasted, that it was far better than Auntie Su's," I told Rich. "Believe me."

The night of the dinner, I sat in the kitchen watching her cook, waiting for the right moment to tell her about our marriage plans, that we had decided to get married next July, about seven months away. She was chopping eggplant into wedges, chattering at the same time about Auntie Suyuan: "She can only cook looking at a recipe. My instructions are in my fingers. I know what secret ingredients to put in just by using my nose!" And she was slicing with such a ferocity, seemingly inattentive to her sharp cleaver, that I was afraid her fingertips would become one of the ingredients of the red-cooked eggplant and shredded pork dish.

I was hoping she would say something first about Rich. I had seen her 10
expression when she opened the door, her forced smile as she scrutinized him from head to toe, checking her appraisal of him against that already given to her by Auntie Suyuan. I tried to anticipate what criticisms she would have.

Rich was not only *not* Chinese, he was a few years younger than I was. And unfortunately, he looked much younger with his curly red hair, smooth pale skin, and the splash of orange freckles across his nose. He was a bit on the short side, compactly built. In his dark business suits, he looked nice but easily forgettable, like somebody's nephew at a funeral. Which was why I didn't notice him the first year we worked together at the firm. But my mother noticed everything.

"So what do you think of Rich?" I finally asked, holding my breath.

She tossed the eggplant in the hot oil and it made a loud, angry hissing sound. "So many spots on his face," she said.

I could feel the pinpricks on my back. "They're freckles. Freckles are good luck, you know," I said a bit too heatedly in trying to raise my voice above the din of the kitchen.

"Oh?" she said innocently. 15

"Yes, the more spots the better. Everybody knows that."

She considered this a moment and then smiled and spoke in Chinese: "Maybe this is true. When you were young, you got the chicken pox. So many spots, you had to stay home for ten days. So lucky, you thought."

I couldn't save Rich in the kitchen. And I couldn't save him later at the dinner table.

He had brought a bottle of French wine, something he did not know my parents could not appreciate. My parents did not even own wineglasses. And then he also made the mistake of drinking not one but two frosted glasses full, while everybody else had a half-inch "just for taste."

When I offered Rich a fork, he insisted on using the slippery ivory 20
chopsticks. He held them splayed like the knock-kneed legs of an ostrich while picking up a large chunk of sauce-coated eggplant. Halfway between his plate and his open mouth, the chunk fell on his crisp white shirt and

then slid into his crotch. It took several minutes to get Shoshana to stop shrieking with laughter.

And then he had helped himself to big portions of the shrimp and snow peas, not realizing he should have taken only a polite spoonful, until everybody had a morsel.

He had declined the sautéed new greens, the tender and expensive leaves of bean plants plucked before the sprouts turn into beans. And Shoshana had refused to eat them also, pointing to Rich: "He didn't eat them! He didn't eat them!"

He thought he was being polite by refusing seconds, when he should have followed my father's example, who made a big show of taking small portions of seconds, thirds, and even fourths, always saying he could not resist another bite of something or other, and then groaning that he was so full he thought he would burst.

But the worst was when Rich criticized my mother's cooking, and he didn't even know what he had done. As is the Chinese cook's custom, my mother always made disparaging remarks about her own cooking. That night she chose to direct it toward her famous steamed pork and preserved vegetable dish, which she always served with special pride.

"Ai! This dish not salty enough, no flavor," she complained, after tasting a small bite. "It is too bad to eat." 25

This was our family's cue to eat some and proclaim it the best she had ever made. But before we could do so, Rich said, "You know, all it needs is a little soy sauce." And he proceeded to pour a riverful of the salty black stuff on the platter, right before my mother's horrified eyes.

And even though I was hoping throughout the dinner that my mother would somehow see Rich's kindness, his sense of humor and boyish charm, I knew he had failed miserably in her eyes.

Rich obviously had had a different opinion on how the evening had gone. When we got home that night, after we put Shoshana to bed, he said modestly, "Well. I think we hit it off *A-o-kay*." He had the look of a dalmatian, panting, loyal, waiting to be petted.

"Uh-hmm," I said. I was putting on an old nightgown, a hint that I was not feeling amorous. I was still shuddering, remembering how Rich had firmly shaken both my parents' hands with that same easy familiarity he used with nervous new clients. "Linda, Tim," he said, "we'll see you again soon, I'm sure." My parents' names are Lindo and Tin Jong, and nobody, except a few older family friends, ever calls them by their first names.

"So what did she say when you told her?" And I knew he was referring 30 to our getting married. I had told Rich earlier that I would tell my mother first and let her break the news to my father.

"I never had a chance," I said, which was true. How could I have told my mother I was getting married, when at every possible moment we were alone, she seemed to remark on how much expensive wine Rich liked to drink, or how pale and ill he looked, or how sad Shoshana seemed to be.

Rich was smiling. "How long does it take to say, Mom, Dad, I'm getting married?"

"You don't understand. You don't understand my mother."

Rich shook his head. "Whew! You can say that again. Her English was *so* bad. You know, when she was talking about that dead guy showing up on *Dynasty,* I thought she was talking about something that happened in China a long time ago."

That night, after the dinner, I lay in bed, tense. I was despairing over this   35
latest failure, made worse by the fact that Rich seemed blind to it all. He looked so pathetic. *So pathetic,* those words! My mother was doing it again, making me see black where I once saw white. In her hands, I always became the pawn. I could only run away. And she was the queen, able to move in all directions, relentless in her pursuit, always able to find my weakest spots.

I woke up late, with teeth clenched and every nerve on edge. Rich was already up, showered, and reading the Sunday paper. "Morning, doll," he said between noisy munches of cornflakes. I put on my jogging clothes and headed out the door, got into the car, and drove to my parents' apartment.

Marlene was right. I had to tell my mother—that I knew what she was doing, her scheming ways of making me miserable. By the time I arrived, I had enough anger to fend off a thousand flying cleavers.

My father opened the door and looked surprised to see me. "Where's Ma?" I said, trying to keep my breath even. He gestured to the living room in back.

I found her sleeping soundly on the sofa. The back of her head was resting on a white embroidered doily. Her mouth was slack and all the lines in her face were gone. With her smooth face, she looked like a young girl, frail, guileless, and innocent. One arm hung limply down the side of the sofa. Her chest was still. All her strength was gone. She had no weapons, no demons surrounding her. She looked powerless. Defeated.

And then I was seized with a fear that she looked like this because she   40
was dead. She had died when I was having terrible thoughts about her. I had wished her out of my life, and she had acquiesced, floating out of her body to escape my terrible hatred.

"Ma!" I said sharply. "Ma!" I whined, starting to cry.

And her eyes slowly opened. She blinked. Her hands moved with life. "*Shemma?* Meimei-ah? Is that you?"

I was speechless. She had not called me Meimei, my childhood name, in many years. She sat up and the lines in her face returned, only now they seemed less harsh, soft creases of worry. "Why are you here? Why are you crying? Something has happened!"

I didn't know what to do or say. In a matter of seconds, it seemed, I had gone from being angered by her strength, to being amazed by her innocence, and then frightened by her vulnerability. And now I felt numb, strangely weak, as if someone had unplugged me and the current running through me had stopped.

"Nothing's happened. Nothing's the matter. I don't know why I'm here," I said in a hoarse voice. "I wanted to talk to you. . . . I wanted to tell you . . . Rich and I are getting married." 45

I squeezed my eyes shut, waiting to hear her protests, her laments, the dry voice delivering some sort of painful verdict.

"*Jrdaule*"—I already know this—she said, as if to ask why I was telling her this again.

"You know?"

"Of course. Even if you didn't tell me," she said simply.

This was worse that I had imagined. She had known all along, when she criticized the mink jacket, when she belittled his freckles and complained about his drinking habits. She disapproved of him. "I know you hate him," I said in a quavering voice. "I know you think he's not good enough, but I . . ." 50

"Hate? Why do you think I hate your future husband?"

"You never want to talk about him. The other day, when I started to tell you about him and Shoshana at the Exploratorium, you . . . you changed the subject . . . you started talking about Dad's exploratory surgery and then . . ."

"What is more important, explore fun or explore sickness?"

I wasn't going to let her escape this time. "And then when you met him, you said he had spots on his face."

She looked at me, puzzled. "Is this not true?" 55

"Yes, but, you said it just to be mean, to hurt me, to . . ."

"Ai-ya, why do you think these bad things about me?" Her face looked old and full of sorrow. "So you think your mother is this bad. You think I have a secret meaning. But it is you who has this meaning. Ai-ya! She thinks I am this bad!" She sat straight and proud on the sofa, her mouth clamped tight, her hands clasped together, her eyes sparkling with angry tears.

Oh, her strength! her weakness!—both pulling me apart. My mind was flying one way, my heart another. I sat down on the sofa next to her, the two of us stricken by the other.

I felt as if I had lost a battle, but one that I didn't know I had been fighting. I was weary. "I'm going home," I finally said. "I'm not feeling too good right now."

"You have become ill?" she murmured, putting her hand on my forehead. 60

"No," I said. I wanted to leave. "I . . . I just don't know what's inside me right now."

"Then I will tell you," she said simply. And I stared at her. "Half of everything inside you," she explained in Chinese, "is from your father's side. This is natural. They are the Jong clan, Cantonese people. Good, honest people. Although sometimes they are bad-tempered and stingy. You know this from your father, how he can be unless I remind him."

And I was thinking to myself, Why is she telling me this? What does this have to do with anything? But my mother continued to speak, smiling broadly, sweeping her hand. "And half of everything inside you is from me, your mother's side, from the Sun clan in Taiyuan." She wrote the characters out on the back of an envelope, forgetting that I cannot read Chinese.

"We are a smart people, very strong, tricky, and famous for winning wars. You know Sun Yat-sen, hah?"

I nodded.   65

"He is from the Sun clan. But his family moved to the south many centuries ago, so he is not exactly the same clan. My family has always live in Taiyuan, from before the days of even Sun Wei. Do you know Sun Wei?"

I shook my head. And although I still didn't know where this conversation was going, I felt soothed. It seemed like the first time we had had an almost normal conversation.

"He went to battle with Genghis Khan. And when the Mongol soldiers shot at Sun Wei's warriors—heh!—their arrows bounced off the shields like rain on stone. Sun Wei had made a kind of armor so strong Genghis Khan believed it was magic!"

"Genghis Khan must have invented some magic arrows, then," I said. "After all, he conquered China."

My mother acted as if she hadn't heard me right. "This is true, we   70
always know how to win. So now you know what is inside you, almost all good stuff from Taiyuan."

"I guess we've evolved to just winning in the toy and electronics market," I said.

"How do you know this?" she asked eagerly.

"You see it on everything. Made in Taiwan."

"Ai!" she cried loudly. "I'm not from Taiwan!"

And just like that, the fragile connection we were starting to build   75
snapped.

"I was born in China, in *Taiyuan*," she said. "Taiwan is not China."

"Well, I only thought you said 'Taiwan' because it sounds the same," I argued, irritated that she was upset by such an unintentional mistake.

"Sound is completely different! Country is completely different!" she said in a huff. "People there only dream that it is China, because if you are Chinese you can never let go of China in your mind."

We sank into silence, a stalemate. And then her eyes lighted up. "Now listen. You can also say the name of Taiyuan is Bing. Everyone from that city calls it that. Easier for you to say. Bing, it is a nickname."

She wrote down the character, and I nodded as if this made everything 80 perfectly clear. "The same as here," she added in English. "You call Apple for New York. Frisco for San Francisco."

"Nobody calls San Francisco that!" I said, laughing. "People who call it that don't know any better."

"Now you understand my meaning," said my mother triumphantly.

I smiled.

And really, I did understand finally. Not what she had just said. But what had been true all along.

I saw what I had been fighting for: It was for me, a scared child, who 85 had run away a long time ago to what I had imagined was a safer place. And hiding in this place, behind my invisible barriers, I knew what lay on the other side: Her side attacks. Her secret weapons. Her uncanny ability to find my weakest spots. But in the brief instant that I had peered over the barriers I could finally see what was really there: an old woman, a wok for her armor, a knitting needle for her sword, getting a little crabby as she waited patiently for her daughter to invite her in.

Rich and I have decided to postpone our wedding. My mother says July is not a good time to go to China on our honeymoon. She knows this because she and my father have just returned from a trip to Beijing and Taiyuan.

"It is too hot in the summer. You will only grow more spots and then your whole face will become red!" she tells Rich. And Rich grins, gestures his thumb toward my mother, and says to me, "Can you believe what comes out of her mouth? Now I know where you get your sweet, tactful nature."

"You must go in October. That is the best time. Not too hot, not too cold. I am thinking of going back then too," she says authoritatively. And then she hastily adds: "Of course not with you!"

I laugh nervously, and Rich jokes: "That'd be great, Lindo. You could translate all the menus for us, make sure we're not eating snakes or dogs by mistake." I almost kick him.

"No, this is not my meaning," insists my mother. "Really, I am not 90 asking."

And I know what she really means. She would love to go to China with us. And I would hate it. Three weeks' worth of her complaining about dirty chopsticks and cold soup, three meals a day—well, it would be a disaster.

Yet part of me also thinks the whole idea makes perfect sense. The three of us, leaving our differences behind, stepping on the plane together, sitting side by side, lifting off, moving West to reach the East.

SUGGESTIONS FOR FURTHER STUDY

Key Words

The author uses language with which you may not be familiar. Find the following words in the paragraphs indicated, and explain their meanings in the context of the sentences in which the words appear. Consult a dictionary, as needed.

concocted (par. 1)
scrutinized (par. 10)
morsel (par. 21)
amorous (par. 29)
relentless (par. 35)
acquiesced (par. 40)
laments (par. 46)
uncanny (par. 85)

Topics for Discussion and Writing

1. Explain Waverly Jong's (the narrator's) brilliant plan for inducing her mother to meet and accept her boyfriend in Amy Tan's "Four Directions."

2. Who are the main characters in the story, and what is their relationship to each other?

3. How is cooking important to Waverly's mother?

4. Discuss the meal that the mother makes. What does Rich do wrong? Whose fault is it really, and why? What aspects of Chinese and Chinese American culture does Rich fail to understand?

5. What is really at issue here: the inability of Rich to understand the customs of the Jong family, or the negative characteristics that Waverly projects on her mother? Elaborate your answer.

6. Discuss the final scene with Waverly and her mother. What is bothering Waverly? What does her mother tell her about her heritage? What truth does Waverly ultimately discover about her mother?

7. How do Waverly and her mother show some degree of reconciliation? What is the symbolic act that indicates that there may be, at last, some peace between the two? Explain your answer.

8. Watch the movie *The Joy Luck Club,* and write an analytical paper comparing and contrasting the written version of "American Translation" with the film version. Use specific details to describe how director Wayne Wang depicts the family dinner scene in the movie. Does the film version highlight the text and bring the char-

acters to life, or do you think that it offers a weaker, less rich and lively story than the textual version?

9. Watch another film about a special meal among friends or family. Summarize how the meal is presented, what food is served, who gathers to eat, and whatever significant events occur during the meal, which illustrate the importance of that particular meal. Movies with such scenes include *Like Water for Chocolate, Babette's Feast, Home for the Holidays, The Age of Innocence,* and *When Harry Met Sally.*

We Are an Old-Fashioned Stew

Christine Willis

In this selection, student writer Christine Willis relates her experiences of segregated and exclusive clubs in high school, and she offers her concept for a fully inclusive club of the future for all Americans.

Great, a black family just moved in. There goes the neighborhood!" I heard this statement when I was a little girl, and it continues to ring in my ears to this day. I didn't see any problem with the Keith family when they moved in across the street. The parents would discuss worldly and neighborhood problems with my parents, and the girls would have tea parties and play "Barbies" with my sister and me. The only difference was the color of their skin. I still do not understand how one minor characteristic can create such controversy. Why does everything have to become a racial issue? If we are truly "one nation under God," then why is there such segregation and ethnic rivalry?

We don't have any real excuse to still be segregated in America. We have so many Constitutional laws, federal laws, and reform movements that were intended to increase integration and equality. The Fourteenth Amendment gives African Americans every right that Caucasian Americans have. Affirmative action opened up many doors to greater opportunities for minorities and women, but this only seemed to create rivalries among various social groups, since most people feel that it is no longer fair to have quotas in the workplace. It is unethical to infringe on one person's rights to create rights for another person. Quotas and many aspects of affirmative action are unfair and have only served to create hostility between ethnic groups.

Despite all the work we have accomplished so far in attaining Martin Luther King's goal of creating a vast brotherhood and sisterhood of humanity here in America, people still continue to insist on segregation and encouraging ethnic rivalry. The most common place for ethnic diversity is in the colleges and grade schools, which, at first, appears to be a positive sign. However, diversity in the schools has just created situations where segregation and ethnic rivalries sometimes flourish.

Today the most popular trend in schools is to organize clubs that have ethnicity as their primary organizational factor. When I was in high school there was the African American club, the Asian club, and the Mecha club

for Hispanic Americans. These clubs would be alright if they were only promoting pride in one's ethnicity, but oftentimes promoting pride in one's ethnicity means putting down other ethnicities. For example, you don't see a
"Caucasian Club," or a "White Folks" club (although many fraternities
could easily label themselves that!), because that club would be considered
to be racist. Such a club would automatically be considered affiliated with
the KKK or other white supremacy groups. These other clubs are not considered supremacy clubs because they supposedly encourage other races to
join their clubs. However, for some reason other students do not join these
clubs. It might be because they do not feel welcome. I tried to join the
Mecha club once because my friend had invited me and because they do
volunteer service work around our community. I could only handle two
meetings. For one thing, I was the only white person in the club, and for
another, no one but my friend wanted me there. The first time I walked into
the classroom everyone stared at me and gave me the look that said, "What
the hell are you doing here white girl?" Even the teacher made remarks that
indirectly told me, "You won't be able to make it in a club like this."

This sense of voluntary segregation does not exist only in clubs. Most   5
groups tend to stick together. On many campuses you will see the jocks and
cheerleaders hanging out together; the "overachievers" stay with the other
"overachievers"; the "rockers" are with other "rockers"; and the African
Americans, Asians, and Hispanics have created their own cliques. Why are
there always so many separations into different groups? So many Americans have worked so hard to create an America that is free and provides
opportunities for all regardless of age, gender, race, or sexual persuasion.
We need to continue to take steps forward towards unity, but by creating
separate groups we are taking steps backward. I know it's become a cliché,
but I believe Rodney King asked the right question when he asked, "Why
can't we all just get along?"

We need to find a solution to this problem. I had a soccer coach once
who was very proud of who he was. His family heritage was Brazilian.
Once he was asked what nationality he was by one of his soccer players.
His reply was, "I am an American." She continued to persist and wanted to
know, "American—what?" He continued to reply, "I am an American." I
really liked the sound of that phrase. I think we need to establish an All-
American club on every college and high school campus. In this club, everyone would be an American, and if one were not an American citizen, she
could still be an honorary member. In this club everyone might have different opinions; but all could feel free to share their opinions because members
would be considerate of another's right to have opinions—even if vastly
different from theirs. Within this club, people would not have to hide
behind their ethnicity. Everybody would be treated equally and no one
would have power over anybody else. Most importantly we would not be

segregated; therefore, we would eliminate such prefixes as African, Caucasian, Native, Hispanic, Asian, Gay and Lesbian, etc. We would all be just Americans.

Ethnic rivalry has become a great problem in America. The only way to avoid ethnic rivalry is by establishing unity. Maybe the All-American club is an impossible goal, but if we all walk together and try to learn from one another, we will continue the road towards true brotherhood and sisterhood in America. America can be compared to an old-fashioned stew. Some people like to separate the onions, the carrots, the meat, and the potatoes, but then you might as well have not cooked a stew. If you want the full flavor of the stew, you have to eat it together as it was always meant to be eaten.

CHAPTER 6: ACTIVITIES FOR DISCUSSION AND WRITING
Making Connections

1. In "America Is in the Heart," Carlos Bulosan's brother states that "It is fair to say that America is not a land of one race or one class of men." Turn to Chapter 7, and read the "I Have a Dream" speech by Martin Luther King, Jr. Compare King's ideas with Bulosan's. How are Bulosan's and King's struggles and dreams similar or different?

2. Paule Marshall's "Poets in the Kitchen" and Amy Tan's "Four Directions" highlight the importance of food, its preparation, and its presentation to understanding family and heritage. Write a descriptive paper about a family meal, barbecue, or celebration you attended recently. Using vivid details, describe the meal itself, how and where it was prepared, the people who were present, and other information that helps to color the event. For best results, choose a meal where something important, either positive or negative, occurred. How did that experience affect the meal itself? How did that experience help you to understand your family, your heritage, your friends, or yourself more fully?

3. Compare and contrast the stereotyping discussed in Jack Shaheen's "The Media's Image of Arabs" and Ward Churchill's "The Indian Chant and the Tomahawk Chop." Which writer do you think makes the more persuasive argument? How does he do so? What other examples from the media, sports, or other forms of entertainment can you offer either (a) to support Shaheen's and Churchill's arguments, or (b) to show the reverse—that Arab Americans, Native Americans, or Americans from other ethnic minorities are portrayed in a fairer, more sensitive light?

4. In "Living in Two Cultures," Jeanne Wakatsuki Houston posits that, although the racial struggle in America will remain a factor for her children in developing their "identity and self-image," the real "struggle will be more to sustain human dignity in a world rapidly dehumanizing itself with mechanization and technology." Do you agree or disagree with Houston? In your journal or in a brief essay, write a persuasive essay, arguing either that (a) some factor other than mechanization and technology will create the future struggle for humankind, or (b) Houston is correct, providing specific examples from American culture to show how we are now and may continue to be dehumanized by technology.

5. In "We Are an Old-Fashioned Stew," student writer Christine Willis argues for "All-American clubs," which everyone can join regardless of ethnicity. She wants to "eliminate such prefixes as African, Caucasian, Native, Hispanic, Asian, . . ." Choose one of the following written responses:
   a. In a short essay, explain how and why you agree with Willis. Use specific reasons and examples to support your argument.
   b. Write a reply to Willis upholding the importance of and need for ethnically identified social groups. Use specific reasons and examples to support your argument.
   c. Write about the problems you have encountered with segregated groups in high school or college. Identify those problems clearly, describe their origins or reasons for existing, and tell how you did or did not solve or reconcile them.

ISSUES IN AMERICA II
Martin Luther King and the Long Road to Equality

Any discussion of multiculturalism and issues of ethnic identity in America must include Dr. Martin Luther King, Jr. In his 1963 "Letter from the Birmingham Jail," Dr. King poignantly enunciates his "ethics of brotherhood":

> Let us hope that the dark clouds of racial prejudice will soon pass away and the deep fog of misunderstanding will be lifted from our fear-drenched communities, and in some not too distant tomorrow the radiant stars of love and brotherhood will shine over our great nation with all their scintillating beauty.

This hope has been echoed by others, such as Carlos Bulosan in *America Is in the Heart* (see Chapter 6), but many Americans feel we're no closer to realizing this hope than we were when Dr. King first articulated it. In Chapter 7, we continue our discussion about ethnic diversity in America, focusing on dreams of equality, ethnic awareness, and racial understanding, as Americans strive to burn away the "fog of misunderstanding" still shrouding us.

We begin with Martin Luther King, Jr.'s now classic speech, "I Have a Dream," delivered from the Lincoln Monument, to 200,000 listeners. President Clinton's Inaugural Address, "A New Sense of Responsibility," heard by nearly 200 million people worldwide, offers specific plans for realizing Dr. King's dream. In "America: The Multinational Society," Ishmael Reed celebrates the remarkable diversity surrounding us in the United States. Orlando Patterson, in "Hidden Dangers in the Ethnic Revival," offers a counterview of ethnic revivals, saying they represent "this nation's retreat from its constitutional commitment to the ideal of equality." In "Affirmative Action: Why Battle Erupted," Cathleen Decker explains the current national conflict over affirmative action and quota-based hiring practices. Reviewing a book on postethnic America, John T. McGreevy, in "From Melting Pot to Salad Bowl," explains how an exchange of metaphors—

"salad bowl" for "melting pot"—describes a view of America that stresses "individual autonomy" rather than "national community."

Other writers in this chapter assert their often conflicting points of view, as well. In "Thirteen Ways of Looking at a Black Man," Henry Louis Gates, Jr., examines people's reactions to the not-guilty verdict in the O. J. Simpson trial, the Million Man March, and other issues as he discusses the narratives, counternarratives, and myths that underlie Americans' diverging interpretations of themselves and their histories. Finally, student writer Richard Smith takes a reasoned stand in "Affirmative Action: Until a Fair Society Is Realized."

I Have a Dream

Martin Luther King, Jr.

Martin Luther King, Jr. (born in Atlanta, Georgia, in 1929), earned degrees at Morehouse College, Crozier Theological Seminary, and Harvard University. The minister of a Baptist church in Montgomery, Alabama, he became one of the leading advocates for civil disobedience—inspired by Mahatma Gandhi and Henry David Thoreau— during the civil-rights movement in the 1950s and 1960s. He was awarded the Nobel Peace Prize in 1964 for his work in advancing the civil rights of African Americans and for his humanitarian work on behalf of all racial minorities. Although he was assassinated on April 14, 1968, his legacy remains. Part of that legacy is his "I Have a Dream" speech, delivered during the peaceful March on Washington in 1963 and considered one of the most eloquent in American history.

Five score years ago, a great American, in whose symbolic shadow we stand, signed the Emancipation Proclamation. This momentous decree came as a great beacon light of hope to millions of Negro slaves who had been seared in the flames of withering injustice. It came as a joyous daybreak to end the long night of captivity. 1

But one hundred years later, we must face the tragic fact that the Negro is still not free. One hundred years later, the life of the Negro is still sadly crippled by the manacles of segregation and the chains of discrimination. One hundred years later, the Negro lives on a lonely island of poverty in the midst of a vast ocean of material prosperity. One hundred years later, the Negro is still languished in the corners of American society and finds himself an exile in his own land. So we have come here today to dramatize an appalling condition.

In a sense we have come to our nation's Capital to cash a check. When the architects of our republic wrote the magnificent words of the Constitution and the Declaration of Independence, they were signing a promissory note to which every American was to fall heir. This note was a promise that all men would be guaranteed the unalienable rights of life, liberty, and the pursuit of happiness.

It is obvious today that America has defaulted on this promissory note insofar as her citizens of color are concerned. Instead of honoring this sacred obligation, America has given the Negro people a bad check; a check which has come back marked "insufficient funds." But we refuse to believe that the bank of justice is bankrupt. We refuse to believe that there are insufficient funds in the great vaults of opportunity of this nation. So we have come to cash this check—a check that will give us upon demand the riches of freedom and the security of justice.

We have also come to this hallowed spot to remind America of the fierce urgency of *now*. This is the time to engage in the luxury of cooling off or to take the tranquilizing drug of gradualism. *Now* is the time to make real the promises of democracy. *Now* is the time to rise from the dark and desolate valley of segregation to the sunlit path of racial justice. *Now* is the time to open the doors of opportunity to all of God's children. *Now* is the time to lift our nation from the quicksands of racial injustice to the solid rock of brotherhood.

It would be fatal for the nation to overlook the urgency of the moment and to underestimate the determination of the Negro. This sweltering summer of the Negro's legitimate discontent will not pass until there is an invigorating autumn of freedom and equality. Nineteen sixty-three is not an end, but a beginning. Those who hope that the Negro needed to blow off steam and will now be content will have a rude awakening if the nation returns to business as usual. There will be neither rest nor tranquillity in America until the Negro is granted his citizenship rights. The whirlwinds of revolt will continue to shake the foundations of our nation until the bright day of justice emerges.

But there is something that I must say to my people who stand on the warm threshold which leads into the palace of justice. In the process of gaining our rightful place we must not be guilty of wrongful deeds. Let us not seek to satisfy our thirst for freedom by drinking from the cup of bitterness and hatred. We must forever conduct our struggle on the high plain of dignity and discipline. We must not allow our creative protest to degenerate into physical violence. Again and again we must rise to the majestic heights of meeting physical force with soul force.

The marvelous new militancy which has engulfed the Negro community must not lead us to a distrust of all white people, for many of our white brothers, as evidenced by their presence here today, have come to realize that their freedom is inextricably bound to our freedom. We cannot walk alone.

And as we walk, we must make the pledge that we shall march ahead. We cannot turn back. There are those who are asking the devotees of civil rights, "When will you be satisfied?"

We can never be satisfied as long as the Negro is the victim of the unspeakable horrors of police brutality.

We can never be satisfied as long as our bodies, heavy with fatigue of travel, cannot gain lodging in the motels of the highways and the cities.

We cannot be satisfied as long as the Negro's basic mobility is from a smaller ghetto to a larger one.

We can never be satisfied as long as a Negro in Mississippi cannot vote and a Negro in New York believes he has nothing for which to vote.

No, no, we are not satisfied, and we will not be satisfied until justice rolls down like waters and righteousness like a mighty stream.

I am not unmindful that some of you have come here out of great trials   15
and tribulations. Some of you have come fresh from narrow jail cells. Some of you have come from areas where your quest for freedom left you battered by the storms of persecution and staggered by the winds of police brutality. You have been the veterans of creative suffering. Continue to work with the faith that unearned suffering is redemptive.

Go back to Mississippi, go back to Alabama, go back to South Carolina, go back to Georgia, go back to Louisiana, go back to the slums and ghettos of our Northern cities, knowing that somehow this situation can and will be changed. Let us not wallow in the valley of despair.

I say to you today, my friends, that in spite of the difficulties and frustrations of the moment I still have a dream. It is a dream deeply rooted in the American dream.

I have a dream that one day this nation will rise up and live out the true meaning of its creed: "We hold these truths to be self-evident; that all men are created equal."

I have a dream that one day on the red hills of Georgia the sons of former slaves and the sons of former slaveowners will be able to sit down together at the table of brotherhood.

I have a dream that one day even the state of Mississippi, a desert state   20
sweltering with the heat of injustice and oppression, will be transformed into an oasis of freedom and justice.

I have a dream that my four little children will one day live in a nation where they will not be judged by the color of their skin but by the content of their character.

I have a dream today.

I have a dream that one day the state of Alabama, whose governor's lips are presently dripping with the words of interposition and nullification, will be transformed into a situation where little black boys and black girls will be able to join hands with little white boys and girls and walk together as sisters and brothers.

I have a dream today.

I have a dream that one day every valley shall be exalted, every hill and   25
mountain shall be made low, the rough places will be made plain, and the crooked places will be made straight, and the glory of the Lord shall be revealed, and all flesh shall see it together.

This is our hope. This is the faith with which I return to the South. With this faith we will be able to hew out of the mountain of despair a stone of hope. With this faith we will be able to transform the jangling discords of our nation into a beautiful symphony of brotherhood.

With this faith we will be able to work together, to pray together, to struggle together, to go to jail together, to stand up for freedom together, knowing that we will be free one day.

This will be the day when all of God's children will be able to sing with new meaning, "My country 'tis of thee, sweet land of liberty, of thee I sing. Land where my father died, land of the Pilgrim's pride, from every mountainside, let freedom ring."

And if America is to be a great nation, this must become true. So let freedom ring from the prodigious hilltops of New Hampshire. Let freedom ring from the mighty mountains of New York. Let freedom ring from the heightening Alleghenies of Pennsylvania!

Let freedom ring from the snowcapped Rockies of Colorado! Let freedom   30
ring from the curvaceous peaks of California! But not only that; let freedom ring from Stone Mountain of Georgia! Let freedom ring from Lookout Mountain of Tennessee!

Let freedom ring from every hill and molehill of Mississippi. From every mountainside, let freedom ring.

When we let freedom ring, when we let it ring from every village and every hamlet, from every state and every city, we will be able to speed up that day when all of God's children, black men and white men, Jews and Gentiles, Protestants and Catholics, will be able to join hands and sing in the words of the old Negro spiritual, "Free at last! Free at last! Thank God Almighty, we are free at last!"

SUGGESTIONS FOR FURTHER STUDY

Key Words

The author uses language with which you may not be familiar. Find the following words in the paragraphs indicated, and explain their meanings in the context of the sentences in which the words appear. Consult a dictionary, as needed.

Emancipation Proclamation (par. 1)
manacles (par. 2)
languished (par. 2)
appalling (par. 2)
promissory (par. 4)
gradualism (par. 5)
tranquillity (par. 6)
inextricably (par. 8)
devotees (par. 9)
interposition (par. 23)
nullification (par. 23)
prodigious (par. 29)

Language and Style

The effectiveness of Dr. King's speech depends largely on figurative language.

1. Explain the effect of the following metaphors and phrases. What about them creates vivid images in a listener's or a reader's mind?
   a. "Now is the time to rise from the dark and desolate valley of segregation to the sunlit path of racial justice" (par. 5).
   b. "This sweltering summer of the Negro's legitimate discontent will not pass until there is an invigorating autumn of freedom and equality" (par. 6).
   c. "People who stand on the warm threshold which leads into the palace of justice" (par. 7).

2. Find and discuss other images in the speech that offer vivid or metaphorical descriptions of people, events, or emotions.

3. One striking feature of Dr. King's rhetoric is cadence or rhythm. In turn, the speech's rhythms depend largely on parallel structures: words, phrases, and clauses that are paired to create balance. Discuss the following examples, then find other parallel structures in the speech, and discuss their effect.
   a. "But *one hundred years later,* we must face the tragic fact that the Negro is still not free. *One hundred years later,* the life of the Negro is still sadly crippled by the manacles of segregation and the chains of discrimination. *One hundred years later,* the Negro lives on a lonely island of poverty in the midst of a vast ocean of material prosperity. *One hundred years later,* the Negro is still languished in the corners of American society and finds himself an exile in his own land" (par. 2).
   b. "*Go back to Mississippi, go back to Alabama, go back to South Carolina, go back to Georgia, go back to Louisiana, go back to the slums and ghettos of our Northern cities. . . .*" (par. 16).
   c. "Where *little black boys and black girls* will be able to join hands with *little white boys and girls* and walk together as *sisters and brothers*" (par. 23).
   d. What other features of Dr. King's speech do you find eloquent and powerful? Consider word choice, comparisons and contrasts, historical and biblical references, images of lightness and darkness, or any other language that affects you as a reader or listener.

Topics for Discussion and Writing

1. When Dr. King says "we have come to our nation's Capital to cash a check," what "check" is he talking about? How effective is this metaphor? Why?

2. Dr. King says some people have asked him and other "devotees of civil rights, 'When will you be satisfied?'" What are his responses to this question?

3. "I have a dream" is arguably the most famous phrase in American oratory. In groups, discuss Dr. King's dream. In what is it rooted? How does the Constitution figure into the dream? In the dream, how will children be judged? Into what will "the jangling discords of our nation" be transformed?

4. According to Dr. King, what will it take for us to "be free one day"? In a journal entry or a short essay, discuss how free we are now as Americans, whatever our ethnicity, gender, or lifestyle. Consider what freedoms Americans have that people in other countries may not enjoy, and consider whether Americans from ethnic minorities enjoy freedom in equal degrees. Be specific in your illustrations and examples.

5. "I Have a Dream" was delivered in 1963, when segregation was still apparent in much of the American South. In order to better understand the history that led to the occasion for its delivery, research the subject of racial segregation in America following the emancipation of slaves in 1863 to the early 1960s, and write an informative paper. In order to narrow such a broad subject for an essay, focus on one topic that interests you. Here are a few of many possibilities, but you may discover others equally worth researching. Using your knowledge of American history, brainstorm with your classmates other possible topics before you begin your research.

Civil rights marches of the 1960s
Medgar Evers
Bus boycotts of Montgomery, Alabama
Brown vs. the Board of Education of Topeka, Kansas
Civil Rights Acts of 1957 and 1960
James H. Meredith
African American military units in World Wars I and II
Marcus Garvey
So-called "separate but equal" public accommodations
Migration of Southern African Americans to the North
Thirteenth, Fourteenth, and Fifteenth Amendments
    to the U.S.Constitution
Jim Crow laws
Ku Klux Klan
Black Codes of 1865–1866
Reconstruction in the American South

A New Sense of Responsibility

William Jefferson Clinton

A fifth-generation Arkansan, Bill Clinton (born August 19, 1946, in Hope, Arkansas) graduated from Yale University Law School in 1973, and in 1978, running for the Democratic Party, was elected governor of Arkansas, at age 32. He was reelected governor in 1982, 1984, and 1988. In 1992, Clinton was elected President of the United States, defeating the incumbent Republican President, George Bush. In 1996, Clinton was reelected for a second term, defeating the Republican candidate, Senator Bob Dole. "A New Sense of Responsibility" is the full text of President Clinton's second inaugural address.

My fellow citizens: 1

At this last presidential inauguration of the 20th century, let us lift our eyes toward the challenges that await us in the next century. It is our great good fortune that time and chance have put us not only on the edge of a new century, in a new millennium, but on the edge of a bright new prospect in human affairs. A moment that will define our course and our character for decades to come. We must keep our old democracy forever young. Guided by the ancient vision of a promised land, let us set our sights upon a land of new promise.

The promise of America was born in the 18th century out of the bold conviction that we are all created equal. It was extended and preserved in the 19th century, when our nation spread across the continent, saved the union and abolished the scourge of slavery.

Then, in turmoil and triumph, that promise exploded onto the world stage to make this the American Century.

What a century it has been. America became the world's mightiest industrial power; saved the world from tyranny in two world wars and a long Cold War; and time and again, reached across the globe to millions who longed for the blessings of liberty.   5

Along the way, Americans produced the great middle class and security in old age; built unrivaled centers of learning and opened public schools to all; split the atom and explored the heavens; invented the computer and the microchip; and deepened the wellspring of justice by making a revolution in civil rights for African Americans and all minorities, and extending the circle of citizenship, opportunity and dignity to women.

A NEW CENTURY IS UPON US

Now, for the third time, a new century is upon us, and another time to choose. We began the 19th century with a choice to spread our nation from coast to coast. We began the 20th century with a choice to harness the Industrial Revolution to our values of free enterprise, conservation and human decency. Those choices made all the difference.

At the dawn of the 21st century, a free people must choose to shape the forces of the Information Age and the global society, to unleash the limitless potential of all our people and form a more perfect union.

When last we gathered, our march to this new future seemed less certain than it does today. We vowed then to set a clear course, to renew our nation.

In these four years, we have been touched by tragedy, exhilarated by challenge, strengthened by achievement. America stands alone as the world's indispensable nation. Once again, our economy is the strongest on Earth.

Once again, we are building stronger families, thriving communities, better educational opportunities, a cleaner environment.

Problems that once seemed destined to deepen now bend to our efforts: Our streets are safer, and record numbers of our fellow citizens have moved from welfare to work.

And once again, we have resolved for our time a great debate over the role of government. Today, we can declare: Government is not the problem, and government is not the solution. We, the American people, we are the solution. Our founders understood that well and gave us a democracy strong enough to endure for centuries, flexible enough to face our common challenges and advance our common dreams.

As times change, so government must change. We need a new government for a new century, a government humble enough not to try to solve all our problems for us but strong enough to give us the tools to solve our problems for ourselves. A government that is smaller, lives within its means and does more with less. Yet where it can stand up for our values and interests around the world, and where it can give Americans the power to make a real difference in their everyday lives, government should do more, not less. The preeminent mission of our new government is to give all Americans an opportunity, not a guarantee, but a real opportunity to build better lives.

THE FUTURE IS UP TO US

Beyond that, my fellow citizens, the future is up to us. Our founders taught us that the preservation of our liberty and our union depends upon responsible citizenship.

And we need a new sense of responsibility for a new century. There is work to do, work that government alone cannot do: Teaching children to read. Hiring people off welfare roles. Coming out from behind locked doors and shuttered windows to help reclaim our streets from drugs and gangs and crime. Taking time out from our own lives to serve others.

Each and every one of us, in our own way, must assume personal responsibility—not only for ourselves and our families but for our neighbors and our nation.

Our greatest responsibility is to embrace a new spirit of community for a new century. For any one of us to succeed, we must succeed as one America.

The challenge of our past remains the challenge of our future: Will we be one nation, one people, with one common destiny—or not? Will we all come together or come apart?

THE DIVIDE OF RACE

The divide of race has been America's constant curse. Each new wave of   20
immigrants gives new targets to old prejudices. Prejudice and contempt, cloaked in the pretense of religious or political conviction, are no different. They have nearly destroyed us in the past. They plague us still. They fuel the fanaticism of terror. They torment the lives of millions in fractured nations around the world.

These obsessions cripple both those who are hated and, of course, those who hate. Robbing both of what they might become.

We cannot—we will not—succumb to the dark impulses that lurk in the far regions of the soul, everywhere. We shall overcome them, and we shall replace them with the generous spirit of a people who feel at home with one another.

Our rich texture of racial, religious and political diversity will be a godsend in the 21st century. Great rewards will come to those who can live together, learn together, work together, forge new ties that bind together.

As this new era approaches, we can already see its broad outlines. Ten years ago, the Internet was the mystical province of physicists. Today, it is a commonplace encyclopedia for millions of schoolchildren. Scientists now are decoding the blueprint of human life. Cures for our most feared illnesses seem close at hand.

The world is no longer divided into two hostile camps. Instead, now we are   25
building bonds with nations that once were our adversaries. Growing connections of commerce and culture give us a chance to lift the fortunes and spirits of people the world over. And for the very first time in all of history, more people on this planet live under democracy than dictatorship.

WE WILL SUSTAIN AMERICA'S JOURNEY

My fellow Americans, as we look back at this remarkable century, we may ask, "Can we hope not just to follow, but even to surpass the achievements of the 20th century in America and to avoid the awful bloodshed that stained its legacy?" To that question, every American here and every American in our land today must answer a resounding, "Yes."

This is the heart of our task. With a new vision of government, a new sense of responsibility, a new spirit of community, we will sustain America's journey. The promise we sought in a new land we will find again in a land of new promise.

In this new land, education will be every citizen's most prized possession. Our schools will have the highest standards in the world, igniting the spark of possibility in the eyes of every girl and every boy. And the doors of higher education will be open to all.

The knowledge and power of the Information Age will be within reach not just to the few, but of every classroom, every library, every child. Parents and children will have time not only to work but to read and play together. And the plans they make at their kitchen table will be those of a better home, a better job, the certain chance to go to college.

Our streets will echo again with the laughter of our children because no 30
one will try to shoot them or sell them drugs anymore. Everyone who can work will work, with today's permanent underclass part of tomorrow's growing middle class.

New miracles of medicine at last will reach not only those who can claim care now but the children and hard-working families too long denied. We will stand mighty for peace and freedom, and maintain a strong defense against terror and destruction. Our children will sleep free from the threat of nuclear, chemical or biological weapons. Ports and airports, farms and factories will thrive with trade and innovation and ideas. And the world's greatest democracy will lead a whole world of democracies.

THIS LAND OF NEW PROMISE

Our land of new promise will be a nation that meets its obligations, a nation that balances its budget but never loses the balance of its values; a nation where our grandparents have secure retirement and health care, and their grandchildren know we have made the reforms necessary to sustain those benefits for their time; a nation that fortifies the world's most productive economy even as it protects the great natural bounty of our water, air and majestic land.

And in this land of new promise, we will have reformed our politics so that the voice of the people will always speak louder than the din of narrow interest, regaining the participation and deserving the trust of all Americans.

Fellow citizens, let us build that America, a nation ever moving forward toward realizing the full potential of all its citizens. Prosperity and power: Yes, they are important, and we must maintain them, but let us never forget the greatest progress we have made and the greatest progress we have yet to make is in the human heart.

In the end, all the world's wealth and a thousand armies are no match for   35
the strength and decency of the human spirit.

KING'S DREAM WAS AMERICAN DREAM

Thirty-four years ago, the man whose life we celebrate today spoke to us down there at the other end of this mall in words that moved the conscience of a nation. Like a prophet of old, he told of his dream that one day America would rise up and treat all its citizens as equals before the law and in the heart.

Martin Luther King's dream was the American dream. His quest is our quest: the ceaseless striving to live out our true creed.

Our history has been built on such dreams and labors, and by our dreams and labors we will redeem the promise of America in the 21st century. To that effort, I pledge all my strength and every power of my office.

I ask the members of Congress here to join in that pledge. The American people returned to office a president of one party and a Congress of another.

Surely they did not do this to advance the politics of petty bickering and   40
extreme partisanship they plainly deplore. No, they call all of us instead to be repairers of the breach and to move on with America's mission. America demands and deserves big things from us, and nothing big ever came from being small.

Let us remember the timeless wisdom of Cardinal Bernardin when facing the end of his own life: He said, "It is wrong to waste the precious gift of time on acrimony and division."

Fellow citizens, we must not waste the precious gift of this time, for all of us are on that same journey of our lives. And our journey too will come to an end, but the journey of our America must go on.

LET US BUILD OUR BRIDGE

And so, my fellow Americans, we must be strong, for there is much to dare.

The demands of our time are great, and they are different. Let us meet them with faith and courage, with patience and a grateful happy heart. Let us shape the hope of this day into the noblest chapter in our history. Yes, let us build our bridge, a bridge wide enough and strong enough for every American to cross over to a blessed land of new promise.

May those generations whose faces we cannot yet see, whose names we   45
may never know, say of us here that we led our beloved land into a new century with the American dream alive for all her children, with the American promise of a more perfect union a reality for all her people, with America's bright flame of freedom spreading throughout all the world.

From the height of this place and the summit of this century, let us go forth. May God strengthen our hands for the good work ahead, and always, always bless our America.

SUGGESTIONS FOR FURTHER STUDY

Key Words

The author uses language with which you may not be familiar. Find the following words in the paragraphs indicated, and explain their meanings in the context of the sentences in which the words appear. Consult a dictionary, as needed.

millennium (par. 2)
tyranny (par. 5)
indispensable (par. 10)
preeminent (par. 14)
fanaticism (par. 20)
partisanship (par. 40)
acrimony (par. 41)

Topics for Discussion and Writing

1. Explain what Clinton means by the following statement (par. 2): "Guided by the ancient vision of a promised land, let us set our sights on a land of new promise."

2. According to Clinton, what kind of government do we need?

3. Clinton maintains that America's "rich texture of racial, religious, and political diversity will be a godsend in the 21st century" (par. 23). What other positive attributes of America does he perceive in the present and the future?

4. Clinton says, "All the world's wealth and a thousand armies are no match for the strength and decency of the human spirit" (par. 35). How does he develop that idea in subsequent paragraphs?

5. The President cites Cardinal Bernardin (par. 41): " 'It is wrong to waste the precious gift of time on acrimony and division.' "

Drawing on your knowledge of American and world history, to what incidents or situations might this statement refer?

6. Clinton mentions America's "new sense of responsibility." In a journal entry or brief essay, write about how you see yourself as participating, or not participating, in this "new sense of responsibility."

7. In the section subtitled "The Future Is Up to Us" (par. 15–19), the President tells his audience "there is work to do." In an essay or in groups, first specify what this work involves, according to Clinton. Then discuss each challenge in detail, outlining what you would do (if given the chance) to create and oversee a program to meet the needs of each challenge.

8. In addition to specifically addressing the American dream of Martin Luther King, Jr., much of Clinton's oratory echoed King's idealistic vision of America. Discuss the two men's visions, as suggested in the President's inaugural address and in King's "I Have a Dream" speech. Then choose one or more of the following questions for discussion or writing:

   a. Are Clinton's ideas for America undercut or supported by his current or past programs, such as family-leave laws, a higher minimum wage, and budgetary support for education? Choose other programs, policies, or legislation supported by the President, if you prefer.

   b. Do you think charges of ethical misconduct directed at the President undermine the vision of America's future expressed in his inaugural address? How do you think such charges should be weighed against the President's political and social agendas for America? Be specific in explaining your point of view.

   c. On what issues are Dr. King's and President Clinton's visions of America's future most similar or most different? Explain your answer by providing specific examples from both speeches and from your knowledge of recent national events.

America:
The Multinational Society

Ishmael Reed

Ishmael Reed (born in 1938, of French, Irish, Native American, and African American ancestry) grew up in working-class neighborhoods in Buffalo, New York. In addition to teaching at Harvard, Yale, Dartmouth, and University of California at Berkeley, he has been a poet, novelist, essayist, songwriter, TV producer, publisher, and playwright. Reed founded the Before Columbus Foundation, which encourages multicultural American writing, and established There City Cinema in northern California. Several of his books have been nominated for the National Book Award and the Pulitzer Prize in Poetry. Reed authored two poetry collections and three novels, including Mumbo Jumbo *(1972) and* The Terrible Threes *(1988). "America: The Multinational Society" comes from his essay collection,* Writin' is Fightin' *(1988).*

At the annual Lower East Side Jewish Festival yesterday, a Chinese woman ate a pizza slice in front of Ty Thuan Duc's Vietnamese grocery store. Beside her a Spanish-speaking family patronized a cart with two signs: "Italian Ices" and "Kosher by Rabbi Alper." And after the pastrami ran out, everybody ate knishes.

New York Times, *23 June 1983*

On the day before Memorial Day, 1983, a poet called me to describe a city he had just visited. He said that one section included mosques, built by the Islamic people who dwelled there. Attending his reading, he said, were large numbers of Hispanic people, forty thousand of whom lived in the same city. He was not talking about a fabled city located in some mysterious region of the world. The city he'd visited was Detroit.

A few months before, as I was leaving Houston, Texas, I heard it announced on the radio that Texas's largest minority was Mexican-American, and though a foundation recently issued a report critical of bilingual education, the taped voice used to guide the passengers on the air trams connecting terminals in Dallas Airport is in both Spanish and English. If the trend continues, a day will come when it will be difficult to travel through some sections of the

1

country without hearing commands in both English and Spanish; after all, for some western states, Spanish was the first written language and the Spanish style lives on in the western way of life.

Shortly after my Texas trip, I sat in an auditorium located on the campus of the University of Wisconsin at Milwaukee as a Yale professor—whose original work on the influence of African cultures upon those of the Americas has led to his ostracism from some monocultural intellectual circles—walked up and down the aisle, like an old-time southern evangelist, dancing and drumming the top of the lectern, illustrating his points before some serious Afro-American intellectuals and artists who cheered and applauded his performance and his mastery of information. The professor was "white." After his lecture, he joined a group of Milwaukeeans in a conversation. All of the participants spoke Yoruban,[1] though only the professor had ever traveled to Africa.

One of the artists told me that his paintings, which included African and Afro-American mythological symbols and imagery, were hanging in the local McDonald's restaurant. The next day I went to McDonald's and snapped pictures of smiling youngsters eating hamburgers below paintings that could grace the walls of any of the country's leading museums. The manager of the local McDonald's said, "I don't know what you boys are doing, but I like it," as he commissioned the local painters to exhibit in his restaurant.

Such blurring of cultural styles occurs in everyday life in the United States   5
to a greater extent than anyone can imagine and is probably more prevalent than the sensational conflict between people of different backgrounds that is played up and often encouraged by the media. The result is what the Yale professor Robert Thompson referred to as a cultural bouillabaisse, yet members of the nation's present educational and cultural Elect still cling to the notion that the United States belongs to some vaguely defined entity they refer to as "Western civilization," by which they mean, presumably, a civilization created by the people of Europe, as if Europe can be viewed in monolithic terms. Is Beethoven's Ninth Symphony, which includes Turkish marches, a part of Western civilization, or the late nineteenth- and twentieth-century French paintings, whose creators were influenced by Japanese art? And what of the Cubists, through whom the influence of African art changed modern painting, or the Surrealists, who were so impressed with the art of the Pacific Northwest Indians that, in their map of North America, Alaska dwarfs the lower forty-eight in size?

Are the Russians, who are often criticized for their adoption of "Western" ways by Tsarist dissidents in exile, members of Western civilization? And what of the millions of Europeans who have black African and Asian ancestry, black Africans having occupied several countries for hundreds of years? Are these "Europeans" members of Western civilization, or the Hungarians, who origi-

---

[1]Language of the Yorubas, a Negro people of the [western] Guinea coast of Africa.

nated across the Urals in a place called Greater Hungary, or the Irish, who came from the Iberian Peninsula?

Even the notion that North America is part of Western civilization because of our "system of government" is derived from Europe is being challenged by Native American historians who say that the founding fathers, Benjamin Franklin especially, were actually influenced by the system of government that had been adopted by the Iroquois hundreds of years prior to the arrival of large numbers of Europeans.

Western civilization, then, becomes another confusing category like Third World, or Judeo-Christian culture, as man attempts to impose his small-screen view of political and cultural reality upon a complex world. Our most publicized novelist recently said that Western civilization was the greatest achievement of mankind, an attitude that flourishes on the street level as scribbles in public restrooms: "White Power," "Niggers and Spics Suck," or "Hitler was a prophet," the latter being the most telling, for wasn't Adolf Hitler the archetypal monoculturalist who, in his pigheaded arrogance, believed that one way and one blood was so pure that it had to be protected from alien strains at all costs? Where did such an attitude, which has caused so much misery and depression in our national life, which has tainted even our noblest achievements, begin? An attitude that caused the incarceration of Japanese-American citizens during World War II, the persecution of Chicanos and Chinese-Americans, the near-extermination of the Indians, and the murder and lynchings of thousands of Afro Americans.

Virtuous, hardworking, pious, even though they occasionally would wander off after some fancy clothes, or rendezvous in the woods with the town prostitute, the Puritans are idealized in our schoolbooks as "a hardy band" of no-nonsense patriarchs whose discipline razed the forest and brought order to the New World (a term that annoys Native American historians). Industrious, responsible, it was their "Yankee ingenuity" and practicality that created the work ethic. They were simple folk who produced a number of good poets, and they set the tone for the American writing style, of lean and spare lines, long before Hemingway. They worshiped in churches whose colors blended in with the New England snow, churches with simple structures and ornate lecterns.

The Puritans were a daring lot, but they had a mean streak. They hated the theater and banned Christmas. They punished people in a cruel and inhuman manner. They killed children who disobeyed their parents. When they came in contact with those whom they considered heathens or aliens, they behaved in such a bizarre and irrational manner that this chapter in the American history comes down to us as a late-movie horror film. They exterminated the Indians, who taught them how to survive in a world unknown to them, and their encounter with the calypso culture of Barbados resulted in what the tourist guide in Salem's Witches' House refers to as the Witchcraft Hysteria. 10

The Puritan legacy of hard work and meticulous accounting led to the establishment of a great industrial society; it is no wonder that the American industrial revolution began in Lowell, Massachusetts. But there was the other side, the strange and paranoid attitudes toward those different from the Elect.[2]

The cultural attitudes of that early Elect continue to be voiced in everyday life in the United States; the president of a distinguished university, writing a letter to the *Times,* belittling the study of African civilizations; the television network that promoted its show on the Vatican art with the boast that this art represented "the finest achievements of the human spirit." A modern up-tempo state of complex rhythms that depends upon contacts with an international community can no longer behave as if it dwelled in a "Zion Wilderness" surrounded by beasts and pagans.

When I heard a schoolteacher warn the other night about the invasion of the American educational system by foreign curriculums, I wanted to yell at the television set, "Lady, they're already here." It has already begun because the world is here. The world has been arriving at these shores for at least ten thousand years from Europe, Africa, and Asia. In the late nineteenth and early twentieth centuries, large numbers of Europeans arrived, adding their cultures to those of the European, African, and Asian settlers who were already here, and recently millions have been entering the country from South America and the Caribbean, making Yale Professor Bob Thompson's bouillabaisse richer and thicker.

One of our most visionary politicians said that he envisioned a time when the United States could become the brain of the world, by which he meant the repository of all of the latest advanced information systems. I thought of that remark when an enterprising poet friend of mine called to say that he had just sold a poem to a computer magazine and that the editors were delighted to get it because they didn't carry fiction or poetry. Is that the kind of world we desire? A humdrum homogeneous world of all brains and no heart, no fiction, no poetry; a world of robots with human attendants bereft of imagination, of culture? Or does North America deserve a more exciting destiny? To become a place where the cultures of the world crisscross. This is possible because the United States is unique in the world: The world is here.

SUGGESTIONS FOR FURTHER STUDY

Key Words

The author uses language with which you may not be familiar. Find the following words in the paragraphs indicated, and explain their meanings in the context of the sentences in which the words appear. Consult a dictionary, as needed.

---

[2]Calvinistic idea that certain human beings are pre-chosen by God to be saved.

Islamic (par. 1)
ostracism (par. 3)
monocultural (par. 3)
bouillabaisse (par. 5)
monolithic (par. 5)
Judeo-Christian (par. 8)
archetypal (par. 8)
incarceration (par. 8)
homogeneous (par. 14)

Topics for Discussion and Writing

1. Reed describes various examples of "cultural blurring." Summarize these examples, and describe their significance. Include the introductory quote from the *New York Times* in your analysis.

2. Is "cultural bouillabaisse" a more appropriate metaphor for America than "the melting pot"? Why or why not?

3. What definition of Western civilization does Reed suggest? What examples does he offer to prove that the great art of Western civilization is often influenced and informed by other international cultures?

4. Reed calls Hitler "the archetypal monoculturalist." Explain what you think Reed means by that phrase. According to Reed, what has been the historical significance of Hitler's attitude about culture?

5. Reed describes a paradox associated with the Puritans who settled in America. Explain what he sees as the paradox.

6. What is Reed's response to the schoolteacher who warns of "the invasion of the American educational system by foreign curriculums"? What might "foreign curriculums" be?

7. Reed maintains that a "humdrum homogeneous world of all brains and no heart, no fiction, no poetry" is not "the kind of world we desire." In an essay, describe how the apparent American "cultural bouillabaisse" fits into Reed's desired world. Before you begin, formulate your own vision of a desired world, and include it in your essay. Does *your* vision include some of Reed's examples of "cultural blurring"? How so? If not, why not? If you like, take a more humorous tone with this exercise in envisioning *your* "perfect world."

8. Based on your experience and education, do you think America's culture in the future will reflect more of the so-called grand tradition of Western civilization, or will it become increasingly diverse and multicultural? In an essay, explain your opinion. To begin,

consider the continuing influence of classical literature, art, music, and dance, as well as the growth of influence in those arts by ethnic and racial groups in the United States. You may also want to find out more about current curricula taught in American elementary and secondary schools, as well as in universities and professional schools.

Hidden Dangers
in the Ethnic Revival

Orlando Patterson

Orlando Patterson (born in 1940 in Jamaica) attended Kingston College, the University of the West Indies, and the London School of Economics. He is currently a professor of Economics at Harvard. His published works include The Children of Sisyphus *(1964) and* Slavery and Social Death *(1983). "Hidden Dangers in the Ethnic Revival" was published in the* New York Times *in 1978.*

The ethnic revival sweeping the United States is another example of this 1 nation's retreat from its constitutional commitment to the ideal of equality.

The fact that the movement has the strong support of many so-called liberals and minority activists makes it all the more insidious and disturbing. The harmless, if vain, search for ancestral roots and communal solidarity is the tip of an ideology that is both reactionary and socially explosive.

The ethnic communities that developed in early 20th-century America were essentially transitory. They developed to buffer the economic and cultural shock of adjusting to a new host society. They were aids to assimilation, not barriers. And they succeeded.

What is remarkable about 20th-century America is the rapid rate of assimilation of immigrant groups into the mainstream of social life.

Chauvinistic intellectuals, by emphasizing those who remain "unmelted," 5 shift the focus from the vast majority who assimilated to those few still remaining in ethnic neighborhoods, although the actual behavior of the majority of those remaining is in the direction of assimilation.

The Jews, often regarded as among the most ideologically and socially cohesive of modern ethnic groups, exhibit increasing rates of out-marriage and secularism and tend more and more to live in non-Jewish neighborhoods. The same is true of all those of Eastern European origin. And despite the talk about black "soul" and separatism, every poll of the black community indicates that the great majority of blacks favor assimilation and would prefer to live in integrated neighborhoods.

This ethnic revival then is largely an ideological revival wrought by alienated and disenchanted intellectuals and activists in a dangerous alliance with conservative political demagogues. It is the idea of ethnicity that is being celebrated, in much the same way that the much talked-about religious revival is largely a commitment to the idea of religion.

It is an increasing of awareness about the need for roots. But the ideology has no content, for the roots are simply not there.

Paradoxically, the single most important factor accounting for the doctrinal revival of ethnicity is the behavioral decline of ethnicity. Doctrinal intensity is a reaction to, and a compensation for, the actual social indifference of ordinary, decent men and women who have other things on their minds.

Other factors account for the ideological revival of ethnicity. One of these   10
is the climax of the black civil rights movement in the mid-1960s. To heal the low self-image created by centuries of racial discrimination, blacks felt obliged to glorify their race, history and culture.

The acceptance of black people's right to use ethnic chauvinism as a means of psycho-social liberation revived ethnicity in American political and popular intellectual life.

Soon conservative politicians and other leaders of the white backlash began to use the blacks' own weapon against them. A telling example of the way in which ethnicity became, for blacks, a viper biting its own tail, is the strange career of the principle of community control of neighborhoods.

It was black chauvinists who first made this demand during the 1960s under the mistaken belief that it was an effective means of social and economic independence. Today, the call for community control of schools and the ethnic integrity of neighborhoods comes no longer from blacks but from white reactionaries wishing to keep blacks out of their neighborhoods.

Ethnic pluralism, however dressed up in liberal rhetoric, has no place whatever in a democratic society based on the humanistic ideals of our Judeo-Christian ethnic. It is, first, socially divisive. However much the more liberal advocates of the revival may proclaim the contrary, the fact remains that the glorification of one's heritage and one's group always implies its superiority, its "chosenness" over all others.

Second, the ethnic revival is a dangerous form of obfuscation. There are   15
indeed many severe problems in our society but interpreting them in psychocultural terms immediately obscures the real issues such as poverty and unemployment in the midst of affluence, racism, sexism and environmental assault. These are tough issues requiring tough-minded and rational solutions as well as unswerving commitment to equality and human fraternity. We do not solve them by idle talk about "the twilight of authority" or by searching for largely fanciful roots.

Ethnicity emphasizes the trivialities that distinguish us and obscures the overwhelming reality of our common genetic and human heritages as well as our common needs and hopes. By emphasizing differences, ethnicity lends itself to the conservative belief in the inevitability of inequality. It is no accident that the neoconservative thinkers have all hailed the revival.

Once again the vicious dogma "separate but equal" has resurfaced; only now it is phrased in the pseudoliberal language of pluralism—we are plural but equal—and, even more tragically, it now has the sanction of misguided leaders and intellectuals of the very groups that hardly a few decades ago were savagely repressed and segregated in the name of this dogma.

Profoundly anti-American in its anti-individualism the ethnic revival celebrates diversity, not however of individuals but of the groups to which they belong. It is a sociological truism that the more cohesive an ethnic group, the more conformist or the more anti-individualistic are its members. Thus the call for a diversity of cohesive, tightly knit groups actually amounts to an assault on the deeply entrenched principle of individualism.

The fact that the ethnic revival is largely ideological should not lead us to underestimate it. We know from the history of ethnic movements that ideology, under the right circumstances, can transform reality. European fascism was first and foremost an ideological movement, and, in a disturbing parallel with modern America, fascist ideology had its roots in the romantic revolt against the enlightenment—a revolt that, in its early phases, was generally liberal, very concerned with the social and human costs of "progress," and espoused the principle of ethnic pluralism.

The time has come when all genuine humanists who cherish the great ideal   20
of the Constitution—that all human beings are created equal—must awake from their slumber and meet head on the challenge of the chauvinists.

SUGGESTIONS FOR FURTHER STUDY

Key Words

The author uses language with which you may not be familiar. Find the following words in the paragraphs indicated, and explain their meanings in the context of the sentences in which the words appear. Consult a dictionary, as needed.

insidious (par. 2)
solidarity (par. 2)
ideology (par. 2)
assimilation (par. 3)
chauvinistic (par. 5)
secularism (par. 6)
alienated (par. 7)
demagogues (par. 7)
pluralism (par. 14)
obfuscation (par. 15)
individualism (par. 18)
fascism (par. 19)
espoused (par. 19)

Topics for Discussion and Writing

1. What is Patterson's *thesis* about the "ethnic revival" and America's "ideal of equality"?

2. Pluralism involves the celebration of ancestral heritages (also called "ethnic roots") in a common political and social framework. Among Patterson's complaints about pluralism are the following:
   a. The idea of ethnicity is celebrated, but not the ethnic experience itself.
   b. Ethnic roots "are simply not there," according to Patterson.
   As a whole class or in small groups, discuss Patterson's views, as stated in Items a and b. Discuss also whether you agree or disagree with him, and support your opinions with reasons or examples. Then write a summary and analysis of your discussion.

3. Do you agree with Reed that "the glorification of one's heritage . . . always implies its superiority . . . over all others"? Why or why not?

4. Reed says that individualism is the foremost concept in American ideology. Based on your reading of his article, how is the ethnic revival anti-individualistic? In what way could the ethnic revival also be thought of as proindividualistic?

5. How might the actions of individuals (such as Timothy McVeigh or the Unabomber, alleged to be Ted Kaczynski) and of groups (such as various militia movements) influence your understanding of individualism as foremost in American ideology? Explain your answer.

6. Some readers find a flaw in Patterson's argument: Although Americans may have "common genetic and human heritages," *one* heritage has been privileged in America for more than 300 years—the culture and ideology of Western civilization. In a brief essay, discuss this point in the context of Patterson's article.

Affirmative Action:
Why Battle Erupted

Cathleen Decker

*Cathleen Decker (born June 9, 1956, in Long Beach, California)
obtained her BA degree from California State University, Long Beach.
Decker has been a staff writer and state political writer for the* Los
Angeles Times *since 1978. She won a Pulitzer Prize for local reporting
of spot news (team coverage) following the June, 1994, Northridge
earthquake in California. "Affirmative Action: Why Battle Erupted"
was part of a series of* Los Angeles Times *articles on affirmative action
in February, 1995.*

From her office at the NAACP's Legal Defense Fund headquarters, 1
Constance Rice's lawyerly elocution dissolves entirely. Her words seep bitterness. Her anger is palpable, bursting forth in spurts.

"First the Latinos. Now the blacks," says the Los Angeles lawyer. "It is getting ugly."

The target of her ire is a 56-word paragraph, simple in language but potentially incendiary.

It is the first paragraph of the reassuringly titled California Civil Rights
Initiative. But to Rice and civil rights activists around the nation, it represents
an all-out assault on one of the noblest experiments of the 1960s: affirmative
action, the activist policy by which America was to make amends for its admittedly discriminatory habits, past and present.

The California initiative intended for the 1996 ballot, and an identical mea- 5
sure now before the Legislature, would amend the state Constitution to gut all
but the most passive forms of government-sponsored affirmative action for
women and minorities, specifically targeting state and local hiring and admissions to California schools. Its reach could be so broad it could even outlaw voluntary desegregation of elementary schools.

Coming close after Proposition 187, the dispute over illegal immigration
that particularly pained the state's Latino community, the efforts have resurrected fears of division in a state that has seen more than its share of strife in
recent years.

But proponents of the measures say that is exactly what they seek to salve.
Affirmative action programs meant to combat bias have become discriminatory

themselves, they say, setting up a rigid system of racial and gender preferences that have prompted unfair treatment of white men, and even some minorities.

"When you deny someone who has earned it and give to someone else who has not earned it . . . you create anger and resentment," said Assemblyman Bernie Richter (R-Chico), author of the measure that would outlaw preferences. "You stir the flames of racial hatred."

It is a wrenching battle between those who believe that majority America has contracted a convenient amnesia about its past and present bias, and those who feel that a nation cannot afford to put any goal, however noble, above absolute fairness as they define it.

A judgment by California voters may be more than a year off—if enough   10
signatures are collected to qualify the initiative for the ballot. Already the issue has gained the momentum of public attention. And despite the fact that much of the argument centers on perceptions and not hard evidence of what affirmative action has produced, politicians sense the potency of its appeal.

A bill outlawing the use of preferences by private businesses—which would not directly be touched by the California measures—has been introduced in Congress. Leading Republican presidential contenders have taken up the topic. Democrats, including President Clinton, are scrambling to figure out how to respond.

California has been here before, of course, not only in 1994's race-inflected fight over illegal immigration but 16 years before that, when the U.S. Supreme Court's decision in University of California regents vs. Bakke prompted a statewide debate over what debt, if any, still was owed to those disenfranchised in the past.

The authors of the California measures, mindful of the national attention, vow that theirs will be a reasoned campaign, fueled by intellect rather than raw emotion. But in some ways, both sides of the debate agree, the fuse already has been lit.

"For better or worse," said one civil rights attorney, "a lot of things begin in California."

It does not seem so threatening, a little office in Berkeley where two schol-   15
ars and a few assistants answer phones and labor over a database of little more than 3,300 supporters. Their bank account, Thomas Wood says, holds less than $30,000, far short of the estimated $1 million it will take to collect nearly 700,000 valid signatures needed to put their initiative on the ballot.

"This," says Wood, with an understated wryness, "is about as grass-roots as it gets."

Perhaps not for long. Wood, a former philosophy teacher, and his partner, Glynn Custred, an anthropology professor at Cal State Hayward, teamed up in mid-1992 as a result of their joint disdain of the affirmative action programs each had witnessed on campuses.

Their effort went nowhere. They missed the 1992 ballot, then the 1994 ballot. Now, through a collision of public mood and political ambition, they find themselves in the right place at the right time.

Their grass-roots operation is at a turning point. They have hired a respected political consultant to shepherd the initiative, even though they would prefer that the Legislature put Richter's constitutional amendment on the ballot and spare them the trouble.

They are trying to broaden support beyond their mostly white, mostly   20
Republican group, arguing that affirmative action as it is practiced is detrimental to everyone, including those it is supposed to benefit. Wood and his supporters contend that they are simply returning to the intent of the 1964 Civil Rights Act, which codified fairness to all Americans with the same words that the initiative's framers have taken as their own:

"Neither the state of California nor any of its political subdivisions or agents shall use race, sex, color, ethnicity or national origin as a criterion for either discriminating against, or granting preferential treatment to, any individual or group in the operation of the state's system of public employment, public education or public contracting."

Public opinion polls have always shown support for affirmative action in theory, but the backing fell when it came to racial preferences and quotas, which are broadly unpopular. But now, according to a recent national poll by The Times, there has been a startling increase in those who say they believe that affirmative action in general has outlived its usefulness.

In the late January survey, 39% of respondents said affirmative action programs have "gone too far"—up dramatically from the 24% who said they felt that way less than 3$1/2$ years ago. Twenty-three percent said such programs had not accomplished enough, down from the 27% who said so in 1991. Also declining were those who said diversity programs were "adequate." The poll's margin of error was plus or minus 3 percentage points.

Across the political spectrum, affirmative action received only lukewarm support at best in the poll—except among blacks. The dividing line was stark: 46% of white respondents said affirmative action has gone too far, while only 8% of black respondents felt the same way. Conversely, 58% of black respondents said the programs had not accomplished enough, a point of view shared by only 15% of white respondents.

When the subject turned specifically to the use of racial or gender prefer-   25
ences, however, the poll showed white and black respondents united in opposition. More than three-fourths of white respondents favored outlawing them and 58% of black respondents agreed. Only 20% of white respondents and 39% of black respondents supported preferences.

The changing viewpoint is echoed by Republican politicians, at both the state and national levels. Gov. Pete Wilson, as San Diego's mayor in the 1970s, set five-year goals for the hiring and promotion of women and minorities and supported programs meant to benefit minority youngsters. But lately he has indicated he could support abolishing preferences.

"We are happily in a time when a number of the compensations that were earlier advanced to make up for earlier discrimination are no longer needed," Wilson said.

Like Wilson, Senate Majority Leader Bob Dole (R-Kan.) has apparently changed his views. In 1986, Dole was among dozens of Republican senators who helped block a Ronald Reagan Administration attack on federal affirmative action programs. In a recent television appearance, however, the probable presidential candidate questioned their worth.

"The people of America now are paying a price for things that were done before they were born," Dole told panelists on NBC-TV's "Meet the Press." "We did discriminate. We did supress people. It was wrong. . . . But should future generations have to pay for that?"

In California, few politicians have defended affirmative action, the note- 30 worthy exceptions being black officials such as Assembly Speaker Willie Brown and Los Angeles County Supervisor Yvonne Brathwaite Burke. In a press conference last week, Brown said affirmative action is needed to make up for decades of discrimination against minorities and women.

"Now that the system is being challenged to let Willie's relatives in . . . suddenly there is something wrong, or unconstitutional or unacceptable," he said. ". . . I'm telling you, it gnaws at you day in and day out."

Among many Democrats, however, concern for public opposition to affirmative action has spawned less an effort to defend it than an attempt to come up with a more palatable alternative to the proposed rollbacks.

California Democratic Party Chairman Bill Press, while expressing his support for affirmative action, signaled that he is not about to defend the status quo as party officials did to their detriment in the fight over Proposition 187.

"It has opened a lot of doors of opportunity for people who could not get through the door," Press said. "At the same time, if it's broke, we've got to fix it."

The genesis of such changing attitudes is a matter of dispute. Advocates of 35 affirmative action say Americans are more open to the current moves because of a years-long campaign by conservatives—particularly radio talk show hosts— and because of recent national economic turmoil.

Ralph G. Neas, executive director of the Leadership Conference on Civil Rights, dates the latest attacks to efforts by Reagan and George Bush Administration officials to curb the programs. The moves were turned back by a coalition of business leaders, civil rights activists, Democrats and moderate Republicans—but Neas said he believes that the seeds of doubt had been planted.

"They did create considerable damage . . . In some ways, they were responsible for equating affirmative action and quotas in the minds of some voters," he said.

Quotas—hiring rigidly by the numbers without regard to qualifications—are illegal, except in rare cases sanctioned by the courts. Affirmative action, its supporters say, is the practice of broadening the pool for jobs and college admissions to a wide range of *qualified* people, and then picking from that pool.

But it has come to be seen by some as the leapfrogging of a less-qualified woman or minority over a better-qualified white man. Sometimes, civil rights advocates admit, that has happened—but they insist that the law gives victims of such discrimination the right to sue.

Much of the increasing concern about affirmative action, its supporters feel, can be linked to economic worry among the largely white electorate.

"Men and women of all races and ethnicities are feeling economically vulnerable," said Marcia Greenberger, copresident of the National Women's Law Center in Washington. "It is very tempting to look for scapegoats."

Sociologist Larry Bobo of UCLA's Center for Research on Race, Politics and Society says economic conditions are similarly responsible for increasing anger toward immigrants and welfare recipients. The sentiment is magnified because it comes as images of the historic civil rights struggles are fading, he added.

"African Americans did not have full citizenship rights in all 50 states until 1965," he said. "The civil rights struggle is not something that reaches back to the Pleistocene Era when dinosaurs walked the Earth. To think that in a very short span of years you could uproot 300 brutal years of racist oppression is absurd."

Those on the other side, however, contend that they are not ignoring the struggles of three decades ago. Indeed, they acknowledge the discrimination rampant then, and, to a lesser extent, now.

Nor, they say, are they seeking scapegoats, but are motivated solely by a desire for fairness and a conviction that efforts meant to improve the lot of racial minorities have instead fostered interracial animosity.

They are following in the path of a number of social scientists, including some black intellectuals, who argue that affirmative action has negatively affected minorities and women by suggesting they succeeded because of a government policy, not by merit.

State Sen. Tom Campbell (R-Stanford), who is on the initiative's advisory board, disputes any connection between the current moves against racial preferences and the voter uprising against illegal immigration in 1994.

Campbell served as a clerk to Supreme Court Justice Byron R. White in 1978, the year of the Bakke decision. In preparation for the decision, he read the legislative history of the 1964 Civil Rights Act, after which, he says, he was convinced that the authors did not intend to allow preferences for or against anyone.

"I do not grant the thought that it is caused by the reaction of the white middle class," said Campbell, who broke with many in his party to oppose Prop. 187. "I just do not see the connection."

As his stance on Prop. 187 indicates, Campbell is not a stereotypical social   50 conservative who might be expected to harbor anti–affirmative action views.

In 1990, when he served in Congress, he was the only Republican west of the Mississippi to vote for civil rights legislation that his party's President, Bush, had labeled a "quota bill." Bush vetoed the measure that year, only to sign a similar bill in 1991.

Richter, like Campbell, is a former Democrat with a past record of standing up to discrimination. With table-pounding oratory, he equates racial and gender preference with the Nazi practice of isolating and destroying Jews.

"You will hear people say that the white male has done this and done that and is responsible for all the ills of mankind," he said. "I try to remind people . . . how bigoted and dangerous it is. Why don't you just add one word to that—white male *Jews*—and get the knee boots and the swastikas out."

To Richter, racial and gender preferences are under attack because a critical mass of voters have finally become aware of their reach.

"It's taken time for many people to become casualties of this," he said. "It's   55 been spreading its message. It's been implemented everywhere."

Exactly how many people are casualties or beneficiaries of affirmative action is uncertain. Efforts to measure those numbers assume all the clarity of a swamp.

Anecdotal evidence abounds on both sides. What seems undeniable, however, is that white males have not suffered widespread insult, as opponents of preferences contend, but neither have they emerged unscathed.

Women and minorities have not made tremendous gains, but neither have they remained as victimized.

That murky outcome is not what might have been wished for by those who labored mightily to equalize the treatment of all Americans.

The term *affirmative action* reaches back to the 1930's, and every   60 President, Republican or Democrat, has supported the concept since Franklin D. Roosevelt ordered defense contractors in 1941 to stop discriminating. Only in the last three decades, however, has it played a major role in American life.

A year after pushing through the 1964 Civil Rights Act, President Lyndon B. Johnson signed Executive Order 11246, which required all federal contractors, including universities, to ensure that employees were hired without regard to their race, religion, color or national origin. In 1967, it was expanded to include women.

But the order did little to change generations of ingrained behavior. So the Richard Nixon Administration ordered federal contractors to set goals for minority hiring or admissions and timetables for achieving the goals. Later efforts led to an initially loose system of preferences under which gender and race were considered positively when contractors were hiring and schools were admitting students.

"If we didn't intervene in business as usual, we were going to get business as usual," said Rice of the National Assn. for the Advancement of Colored People.

The use of preferences also received a boost from the Bakke decision, which arose because UC Davis set aside 16 of its 100 medical school openings for blacks, Latinos, Asians and Native Americans on the grounds that it made up for past discrimination.

Allan Bakke, a 38-year-old engineer, argued that he had been unfairly   65
denied admission to the school because of his race, and the Supreme Court threw out UC Davis' strict quotas. As it ordered Bakke admitted, however, the court also said that race could be taken into account by admissions officials as long as other qualities were also considered.

The prevailing public sentiment that such preferences have had a huge effect on the workplace or in universities, however, is flatly untrue. Although affirmative action has helped integrate police and fire departments and blue-collar unions, it has had less effect elsewhere.

Census figures from 1980, for example, show that whites held 82.3% of managerial and professional jobs in California—those generally commanding the highest salaries and greatest independence. By 1990, whites still controlled 75.3% of those jobs, while they made up only 57% of the population.

Blacks in California held only 5.1% of management and professional jobs in 1990, up only slightly from 1980. Latinos held 9.56%. Asians, who are not always included in affirmative action programs, held slightly more than 9% of managerial jobs.

Federal statistics underscore the same reality: Although animosity about affirmative action has increased, its impact in the workplace has been under-whelming.

According to figures from the federal Bureau of Labor Statistics, blacks   70
increased their presence in the nation's managerial and professional ranks only meagerly from 1983 to 1993, to 6.6%. Latinos held only 4% of the top jobs in 1993. Women held 40.9% in 1983 and 47.8% a decade later.

The statistics do not suggest which gains resulted from affirmative action programs and which from other factors, such as demographic changes. But they do show that the workplace remains dominated by white males.

At the UC system, the record also has been middling, despite extensive efforts to attract and groom minority high school students and consider race and gender in admissions.

In 1980, the first year for which an ethnic breakdown is available, blacks made up 3.8% of the student body at the system's nine campuses. By last fall, 14 years later, the percentage was essentially the same—4%. Women have increased their ranks, but only marginally, making up 49.4% of the student body last fall.

The greatest gains among targeted groups came from Latinos and Chicanos, which the university lists separately. Taken together, their size more than doubled, from just under 6% in 1980 to nearly 12% last fall.

Overall, university records show, students in groups covered by affirmative 75 action made up 20% of the fall, 1994, class, up from 11.4% in 1980 but still well below the proportions those communities represent in the state.

Not all of the changes can be attributed to affirmative action, as the burgeoning growth of Asian American students attests. That group, which is not part of the university's outreach program, nearly doubled since 1980, from 12.9% to 24.5%, according to university records.

The increases have come out of the campuses' traditional base of white men. While they made up 40% of the student body in 1980, they represented less than 24% in 1994.

Last month, UC Regent Ward Connerly, who is black, proposed an end to affirmative action. That will be considered this summer. UC President Jack W. Peltason has defended the university's programs as "both an educational objective and as a matter of equity."

"Affirmative action is a volatile issue that generates strong feelings on every side," he acknowledged. "The term itself has become burdened with different and sometimes conflicting meanings."

The initiative sounds disarmingly simple. But the harsh wrangling over its 80 potential effect underscores that in this emotionally charged arena, nothing is simple.

Proponents contend that theirs is a pinpoint attack on racial preferences, not a widespread assault on all affirmative action programs. The legal impact, however, is open to question.

Certainly, a constitutional amendment would affect university admissions, state employees and companies doing business with the state—the latter an area where the reach of affirmative action has been most profound.

In 1989, the state set a goal of awarding 15% of its contracts to minority-owned firms or subcontractors, and another 5% to businesses owned by women. Not until 1994 did the state's biggest contractor, the Department of General Services, meet those goals and deliver 14.6% of its business to minority-owned firms and 8.8% to companies owned by women.

Efforts to meet goals for minority- and female-owned businesses would be outlawed, as would the state's attempts to hire more female and minority employees.

"The only thing (the initiative) would do is prohibit civil rights from cross- 85 ing its own line and actually being discriminatory," said co-author Wood. "There is a difference between affirmative action as it was originally intended, which is good and positive, and actual preferences."

Wood and some supporters believe that the measure would not ban any other diversity tools, such as advertising for jobs in minority newspapers or preparing minority high school students for university admissions.

But Campbell, a Harvard-educated lawyer, said he believes that any outreach based on gender or race could be legally problematic.

"If you place an ad in a newspaper intending to reach one race, you're making it easier for one race to get that job," he said. "It's the same kind of thing as saying: 'I'll give you five points.' Logically, you have to say it's only a matter of degree."

As for university admissions, UC officials say it is impossible to determine the impact of the proposals on future admissions. While affirmative action opponents argue that race and gender have become the main determinants of college entrance, university officials insist that their decisions are far more complex and the impact far more difficult to assess.

A joint report by the state legislative analyst and the finance director, made   90
during an earlier attempt to qualify the initiative for the ballot, suggests that its reach may be far deeper than its proponents acknowledge. According to the 1993 report, the measure could save at least $170 million spent annually on affirmative action programs, and affect even local schools.

"The measure would eliminate voluntary desegregation programs by school districts, but would not affect court-ordered desegregation programs," the report said. It added that the measure would eliminate elementary and college programs involving "counseling, tutoring, student financial aid and financial aid to selected school districts, where these programs are targeted based on race, sex, ethnicity or national origin."

The issue will not come to a head until 1996, but campaigning already has begun.

In the face of mounting attacks, backers of affirmative action admit that they have not convinced Americans of their view that the policy benefits everyone—by setting up more open rules for hiring, for partially dismantling an old-boy network that also excluded some white males, and for breaking down institutional resistance to hiring women and minorities.

"We have a very, very important public education task ahead of us," said Nancy L. Davis, co-founder of San Francisco's Equal Rights Advocates, which is helping fight the proposed initiative.

While initiative supporters will base their arguments on the notion of fair-   95
ness, opponents will contend that it would shift the balance of power back to white men. They plan to appeal particularly to women, who have been among the biggest beneficiaries of affirmative action.

Proponents of the measures almost always discuss the issue in racial terms, and their omission of the initiative's impact on women suggests they are concerned about a backlash.

"They don't you want to know that women are going down on this," said Penda Hair, an attorney with the NAACP Legal Defense and Education Fund in

Washington. "Women are not the unpopular stereotyped criminals that they want to make African Americans and Hispanics."

But the opponents of affirmative action have been politically astute in their strategy thus far. Not only do they omit the subject of women, but they choose not to address private employers, who have grown more supportive of affirmative action, in the initiative. The amendment also defers to the federal government and the courts in cases of conflict—a gesture meant to limit court challenges.

It is most likely that an initiative would be placed on the November, 1996, ballot, in part to throw a wrench into Clinton's reelection plans and in part because there is little time left to qualify the measure for the March, 1996, primary vote. The Legislature, acting on Richter's bill, could still place the measure on the March ballot.

Even as they gear up for the coming battle, some civil rights activists sound 100 weary, and not at all optimistic about their chances.

"Nobody's interested in the facts and, even when you tell them the facts, they say they still don't like it," Rice said. "They are tired of it."

Some key laws and decisions in the history of affirmative action.

■ Civil Rights Act of 1964: Landmark legislation that included provisions barring discrimination in employment. Title VII of the act was the first federal law to prohibit discrimination in all employment practices based on race, color, religion, sex or national origin.

■ Equal Employment Opportunity Commission: The role of the EEOC, created by the Civil Rights Act of 1964, is to eliminate discrimination in employment practices, promote equal employment programs and hear complaints and seek compliance with the law.

■ Executive Order 11246: President Lyndon B. Johnson in 1965 signed this order requiring federal contractors to "take affirmative action to ensure that applicants are employed . . . without regard to their race, creed, color or national origin." This laid the groundwork for requiring any company with federal contracts to adhere to affirmative action policies.

■ Regents of University of California vs. Bakke: A 1978 Supreme Court case that tested the constitutionality of affirmative action programs in college and university admissions. The court ruled that Allan Bakke, a white male student who was denied admission to the UC Davis medical school, must be admitted because he had been unfairly discriminated against because of his race. At the same time, the court also approved the principle of affirmative action programs and upheld the right to use race as a factor in admissions.

■ Richmond vs. Croson: A 1989 Supreme Court case that said city and state officials may not steer contracts toward blacks or other minorities, except to make up for a clear history of discrimination. The decision struck down a

Richmond, Va., plan that guaranteed blacks and other minorities at least 30% of the city's construction contracts.

KEY TERMS

- Affirmative action: A program or policy designed to reverse past discriminatory patterns or practices. It requires employers or institutions to take actions to hire or admit members of minority groups or women.
- Reverse discrimination: Opponents of affirmative action argue that in seeking to remedy past discrimination against one group, usually a minority, members of other groups are harmed.
- Quotas: Specific numbers of jobs set aside for a particular group in hiring or contracting. Generally, they are not legal. In university admissions, they were ruled unconstitutional in the 1978 Bakke case. In some rare cases, however, where courts have found that there is a particularly pernicious pattern of racial or gender discrimination, they may order specific companies to hire on a quota basis to make up for past actions.
- Goals and Timetables: A goal is an estimate of the expected percentage of new hires or incoming university students that will come from various minority groups. The timetable outlines how quickly those goals are to be met. Unlike quotas, goals are not firm, make-or-break numbers.

—*Sources: Congressional Quarterly Guide to the United States Supreme Court; Guide to American Law.*

—*Researched by NONA YATES/Los Angeles Times*

SUGGESTIONS FOR FURTHER STUDY

Key Terms

The author uses language with which you may not be familiar. Find the following words in the paragraphs indicated, and explain their meanings in the context of the sentences in which the words appear. Consult a dictionary, as needed.

elocution (par. 1)
incendiary (par. 3)
desegregation (par. 5)
disenfranchised (par. 12)
codified (par. 20)
genesis (par. 35)
scapegoats (par. 41)
ingrained (par. 62)

demographic (par. 71)
middling (par. 72)

Topics for Discussion and Writing

1. Review the "key terms" at the end of "Affirmative Action: Why Battle Erupted," and write your own definitions of "affirmative action," "reverse discrimination," "quotas," and "goals and timetables." Discuss these terms with other readers to clarify the meanings of these terms.

2. What has the California Civil Rights Initiative sought to do? Whose civil rights does it target?

3. According to Assemblyman Bernie Richter, what has "stir[red] the flames of racial hatred"? Do you agree or disagree with his statement? Explain your answer.

4. According to Decker, "prevailing public sentiment" indicates a belief that "preferences have had a huge effect on the workplace [or] in universities." She disproves this sentiment by citing statistics. What is the source of the statistics she cites? How do statistics support her argument?

5. Decker includes the results of certain public-opinion polls. What have statistics shown about the public's perception of affirmative action? How might accurate statistics, such as those Decker uses, help you develop an argument or a report on research?

6. Decker traces the origin of the term *affirmative action* to the 1930s. Review the history of affirmative action's influence, as Decker outlines it, then discuss with other readers what groups or individuals have benefited from affirmative action and in what ways they have benefited.

7. Decker quotes Senator Bob Dole as saying, "We did discriminate. We did suppress people. It was wrong. . . . But should future generations have to pay for that?" In discussion groups or in a brief essay, reply to Senator Dole's question. You may agree with his statement in whole or in part and continue his argument, or you may disagree with him in whole or in part. In either case, explain why you believe as you do.

8. At the close of Decker's article, which was written in February, 1995, she says a new initiative will be placed on the ballot in California. Such a measure, Proposition 209, was placed on the ballot, passing easily, as did a similar proposition in Arizona. However, Proposition 209 does not reflect an exclusively western American agenda: It announced a trend gathering momentum across the nation. Although Proposition 209 was ruled unconstitu-

tional by a federal court in California, its overwhelming victory in the 1996 election suggests that the majority of voters seek change in affirmative-action laws. Research the history of Proposition 209 or similar legislation in other states to determine its impact on affirmative-action practices and on civil rights. Before you begin, read the student essay at the close of this chapter for ideas you may want to focus on specifically. Then write an informative essay explaining the arguments given by people on both sides of the affirmative-action issue.

(You may want to research books, scholarly journals, magazines, or newspapers in the library. Do not limit your research to political campaign pamphlets. Consult the computer databases in your library, if available, to obtain the most current information on your topic. Use the Internet to gain access to relevant material through the World Wide Web.)

From Melting Pot to Salad Bowl

John T. McGreevy

John T. McGreevy, the author of Parish Boundaries, *teaches history and government at Harvard. His review, "From Melting Pot to Salad Bowl," appeared in* Commonweal *October 20, 1995.*

Books about the decline of American nationalism will surely become a   1
growth industry. The term "citizen" frequently seems less relevant than Italian
or Latino, male or female, gay or straight. Salad bowls have replaced melting
pots. Even the United States as a geographical entity has become less important
in an age when the availability of labor in Manila determines wages in Fort
Wayne, or electronic mail to Warsaw is more convenient than a letter to Los
Angeles.

Few explorations of these matters will be as incisive as David Hollinger's
Postethnic America, a thoughtful meditation on the need for liberals to reassert
their allegiance to the national community.

This is old-fashioned advice. As Hollinger is well aware, the most wide-
ranging intellectual project of the past generation has been to reassert the
importance of the particular and the provincial, to unmask assumptions concealed behind abstract language. When scholars in the 1940s spoke about Man,
we have learned, they frequently meant white men. Thornton Wilder's *Our
Town* became the model for an "American way of life," not Richard Wright's
Chicago.

Hollinger acknowledges these multicultural insights. His subtitle includes
the word "beyond," not "against." What he regrets is the relentless equation of
culture with the options available on census forms. Initially an effort to assist
victims of past discrimination, racial classification schemes became demands for
cultural recognition. An "Asian-American" culture is now assumed to include
impoverished Cambodian refugees and Hong Kong financiers. Alternatively, the
term "white" stretches from descendants of the *Mayflower* to Jews fleeing the
former Soviet Union.

But individuals do not fit neatly within the boundaries of what Hollinger   5
disparagingly terms the "Ethno-racial Pentagon" (African-Americans, Asian-
Americans, Latinos, Native Americans and whites). More Native Americans
marry outside the group than within it, as do one-quarter to one-third of
Japanese-Americans. Marriages between African-Americans and whites have
increased 300 percent in a quarter century.

Some advocates of multiculturalism discreetly ignore these facts, but Hollinger celebrates them. The more fluid the society and the more opportunities offered to move beyond the limitations of race or class, the more hope that current tensions might subside. In Hollinger's "postethnic" view, informing the daughter of an African-American father and an Asian-American mother that she *must* be African-American revives a most pernicious aspect of our Jim Crow past. Society's obligation is not to sustain particular cultures, but to provide an open arena for individuals to determine their own identity.

Defining an open arena is the tough part. Hollinger favors a society where individuals choose "affiliations" from a broad menu of ethnic and religious options. The content of these choices matters less than the assurance that they are made in a noncoercive environment. The wall of separation erected between church and state by the Supreme Court in the 1940s, Hollinger suggests, might also serve as a useful barrier between public institutions and the pressure to celebrate various ethnic cultures.

Behind this view, implicitly, is a philosophical stance that stresses individual autonomy. As much as possible, decisions made by parents or the larger society about sensitive matters such as religion and ethnicity should not limit the options available to their children.

While appealing in some respects, this account of the formation of group loyalties is not altogether convincing. A school system supervising the education of each student from the age of four to twenty-two that dismisses religious belief as irrelevant to modern life, for example, makes the choice of a religious "affiliation" after graduation less likely. Few traditions—religious, ethnic, or otherwise—sustain themselves through self-conscious, adult conversation. And religious people often view their faith as the response to a call or the understanding of a vocation, not simply as one among a handful of individual affiliations.

Hollinger might respond that American society cannot guarantee the sur-   10
vival of any ethnic or religious group, a burden necessarily shouldered by families and faith communities. Groups live or die in a cultural free market. All true, but building a wall between these groups and an expanding state may inadvertently shorten life expectancies.

More compelling is Hollinger's plea for liberals to reclaim a nationalist, even patriotic, language from their political opponents. Franklin Roosevelt's and Lyndon Johnson's ability to inaugurate social welfare programs in the name of "the people" is a lost, liberal art. Yet most citizens understand that obligations to residents of inner-city Detroit or rural West Virginia differ in kind from duties to impoverished Indonesians. An emphasis on this national bond, instead of a rhetoric of difference and separation, might make common responsibilities, such as health care, more visible. And a more visible public concern for less fortunate citizens might channel energies away from endless culture wars. As Hollinger reminds us, Martin Luther King's invocation of the noble goals at the heart of the American experiment helped awaken a broad public to the gap between those goals and the more sordid realities of Jim Crow and urban poverty.

A certain nobility graces *Postethnic America* as well. Hollinger is a professional historian, but the book is first-rate public philosophy, a sober reflection in a literature frequently distorted by polemics. Analytical clarity alone will not resolve these matters, but it does ensure, at a minimum, more productive disagreements.

SUGGESTIONS FOR FURTHER STUDY

Key Words

The author uses language with which you may not be familiar. Find the following words in the paragraphs indicated, and explain their meanings in the context of the sentences in which the words appear. Consult a dictionary, as needed.

nationalism (par. 1)
meditation (par. 2)
provincial (par. 3)
disparagingly (par. 5)
pernicious (par. 6)
noncoercive (par. 7)
autonomy (par. 8)
inadvertently (par. 10)
invocation (par. 11)
polemics (par. 12)

Topics for Discussion and Writing

1. McGreevy refers to how the term *salad bowl* has replaced *melting pot* as the dominant metaphor for the American cultural experience. What does each term suggest about the way we might see American Society? Do you think *salad bowl* is a more accurate metaphor? Why or why not?

2. McGreevy points to the recent importance of "unmask[ing] assumptions concealed behind abstract language" (par. 3)—particularly language and assumptions taught in our classrooms. According to McGreevy, what has the term "Man" traditionally signified? What is a more gender-neutral term for "man" or "mankind"? What other terms do you think need to be "unmasked" for what they conceal? Make a list of such terms, and discuss their implications with others in your class.

3. In discussing the subtitle of *Postethnic America: Beyond Multiculturalism*, McGreevy refers to terms that classify ethnic groups—for example, "Asian-American." What does he say about "racial classification schemes" being important for "cultural recognition"?

On this point, does McGreevy, the reviewer, agree with Hollinger, the book's author? As you discuss this question, consider Hollinger's description of the "Ethno-racial Pentagon" and what arguments he offers for a more open, liberal society in which individuals may choose to identify freely with cultural and religious groups.

4. Compare Hollinger's ideas about ethnic and racial identification with those of Orlando Patterson ("Hidden Dangers in the Ethnic Revival") and Martin Luther King, Jr. ("I Have a Dream"). Is Hollinger, like Patterson, against ethnic revivalism, or is he for ethnic revivalism? How effective do you think Hollinger may be in enlisting King's ideas to argue for a "national bond" and encouraging "common responsibilities"?

5. McGreevy is not only writing a book review of Hollinger's work, but also advancing his own ideas. What is McGreevy's opinion of Hollinger's book? Point to one or more places in the review where McGreevy seems to be promoting his own ideas, as well as commenting on Hollinger.

6. Choose a nonfiction book you have read, and write a book review, as McGreevy has done in this article. In your review, do not summarize the whole book, but discuss certain parts of it that explain the author's main ideas or the thesis of the book. In addition, give your opinion of the book and why you feel about it as you do.

Thirteen Ways of Looking at a Black Man

Henry Louis Gates, Jr.

*Henry Louis Gates, Jr. (born in Keyser, West Virginia, in 1950) is
an associate professor in the English and African American Studies
departments at Yale University, where he teaches courses in literary
theory and in African and African American literature. He has edited*
Black Is the Color of the Cosmos: Charles T. Davis's Essays on Black
Literature and Culture *(1982);* Our Nig, or, Sketches from the Life of
a Free Black *(1983);* The Slave's Narrative *(1984); and* Black Literature and Literary Theory *(1986). He has also authored two books—
namely,* Figures in Black: Words, Signs and the Racial Self *and* The
Signifying Monkey. *Gates also frequently contributes to scholarly journals and popular magazines. The following selection is an excerpt from
"Thirteen Ways of Looking at a Black Man," which appeared in its
entirety in the* New Yorker *on October 23, 1995.*

Every day, in every way, we are getting meta and meta," the philosopher   1
John Wisdom used to say, venturing a cultural counterpart to Émile Coué's
famous mantra of self-improvement. So it makes sense that in the aftermath of
the Simpson trial the focus of attention has been swiftly displaced from the verdict to the reaction to the verdict, and then to the reaction to the reaction to the
verdict, and, finally, to the reaction to the reaction to the reaction to the verdict—which is to say, black indignation at white anger at black jubilation at
Simpson's acquittal. It's a spiral made possible by the relay circuit of race. Only
in America.

An American historian I know registers a widespread sense of bathos when
he says, "Who would have imagined that the Simpson trial would be like the
Kennedy assassination—that you'd remember where you were when the verdict
was announced?" But everyone does, of course. The eminent sociologist
William Julius Wilson was in the red-carpet lounge of a United Airlines termi-
nal, the only black in a crowd of white travellers, and found himself as stunned
and disturbed as they were. Wynton Marsalis, on tour with his band in
California, recalls that "everybody was acting like they were above watching it,
but then when it got to be ten o'clock—zoom, we said, 'Put the verdict on!'"
Spike Lee was with Jackie Robinson's widow, Rachel, rummaging through a
trunk filled with her husband's belongings, in preparation for a bio-pic he's

making on the athlete. Jamaica Kincaid was sitting in her car in the parking lot of her local grocery store in Vermont, listening to the proceedings on National Public Radio, and she didn't pull out until after they were over. I was teaching a literature seminar at Harvard from twelve to two, and watched the verdict with the class on a television set in the seminar room. That's where I first saw the sort of racialized response that itself would fill television screens for the next few days: the white students looked aghast, and the black students cheered. "Maybe you should remind the students that this is a case about two people who were brutally slain, and not an occasion to celebrate," my teaching assistant, a white woman, whispered to me.

The two weeks spanning the O. J. Simpson verdict and Louis Farrakhan's Million Man March on Washington were a good time for connoisseurs of racial paranoia. As blacks exulted at Simpson's acquittal, horrified whites had a fleeting sense that this race thing was knottier than they'd ever supposed—that, when all the pieties were cleared away, blacks really *were* strangers in their midst. (The unspoken sentiment: *And I thought I knew these people.*) There was the faintest tincture of the Southern slave-owner's disquiet in the aftermath of the bloody slave revolt led by Nat Turner—when the gentleman farmer was left to wonder which of his smiling, servile retainers would have slit *his* throat if the rebellion had spread as was intended, like fire on parched thatch. In the day or so following the verdict, young urban professionals took note of a slight *froideur* between themselves and their nannies and babysitters—the awkwardness of an unbroached subject. Rita Dove, who recently completed a term as the United States Poet Laureate, and who believes that Simpson was guilty, found it "appalling that white people were so outraged—more appalling than the decision as to whether he was guilty or not." Of course, it's possible to overstate the tensions. Marsalis invokes the example of team sports, saying, "You want your side to win, whatever the side is going to be. And the thing is, we're still at a point in our national history where we look at each other as sides."

The matter of side-taking cuts deep. An old cartoon depicts a woman who has taken her errant daughter to see a child psychiatrist. "And when we were watching 'The Wizard of Oz,'" the distraught mother is explaining, "she was rooting for the wicked witch!" What many whites experienced was the bewildering sense that an entire population had been rooting for the wrong side. "This case is a classic example of what I call interstitial spaces," says Judge A. Leon Higginbotham, who recently retired from the federal Court of Appeals, and who last month received the Presidential Medal of Freedom. "The jury system is predicated on the idea that different people can view the same evidence and reach diametrically opposed conclusions." But the observation brings little solace. If we disagree about something so basic, how can we find agreement about far thornier matters? For white observers, what's even scarier than the idea that black Americans were plumping for the villain, which is a misprision of value, is the idea that black Americans didn't recognize him *as* the villain, which is a misprision of fact. How can conversation begin when we disagree about reality? To put it at its harshest, for many whites a sincere belief in Simpson's innocence looks less like the culture of protest than like the culture of psychosis.

   Perhaps you didn't know that Liz Claiborne appeared on "Oprah" not long   5
ago and said that she didn't design her clothes for black women—that their hips were too wide. Perhaps you didn't know that the soft drink Tropical Fantasy is manufactured by the Ku Klux Klan and contains a special ingredient designed to sterilize black men. (A warning flyer distributed in Harlem a few years ago claimed that these findings were vouchsafed on the television program "20/20.") Perhaps you didn't know that the Ku Klux Klan has a similar arrangement with Church's Fried Chicken—or is it Popeye's?
   Perhaps you didn't know these things, but a good many black Americans think they do, and will discuss them with the same intentness they bring to speculations about the "shadowy figure" in a Brentwood driveway. Never mind that Liz Claiborne has never appeared on "Oprah," that the beleaguered Brooklyn company that makes Tropical Fantasy has gone as far as to make available an F.D.A. assay of its ingredients, and that those fried-chicken franchises pose a threat mainly to black folks' arteries. The folklorist Patricia A. Turner, who has collected dozens of such tales in an invaluable 1993 study of rumor in African-American culture, "I Heard It Through the Grapevine," points out the patterns to be found here: that these stories encode regnant anxieties, that they take root under particular conditions and play particular social roles, that the currency of rumor flourishes where "official" news has proved untrustworthy.
   Certainly the Fuhrman tapes might have been scripted to confirm the old saw that paranoids, too, have enemies. If you wonder why blacks seem particularly susceptible to rumors and conspiracy theories, you might look at a history in which the official story was a poor guide to anything that mattered much, and in which rumor sometimes verged on the truth. Heard the one about the L.A. cop who hated interracial couples, fantasized about making a bonfire of black bodies, and boasted of planting evidence? How about the one about the federal government's forty-year study of how untreated syphilis affects black men? For that matter, have you ever read through some of the F.B.I.'s COINTEL-PRO files? ("There is but one way out for you," an F.B.I. scribe wrote to Martin Luther King, Jr., in 1964, thoughtfully urging on him the advantages of suicide. "You better take it before your filthy, abnormal, fraudulent self is bared to the nation.")
   People arrive at an understanding of themselves and the world through narratives—narratives purveyed by schoolteachers, newscasters, "authorities," and all the other authors of our common sense. Counternarratives are, in turn, the means by which groups contest that dominant reality and the fretwork of assumptions that supports it. Sometimes delusion lies that way; sometimes not. There's a sense in which much of black history is simply counternarrative that has been documented and legitimized, by slow, hard-won scholarship. The "shadowy figures" of American history have long been our own ancestors, both

free and enslaved. In any case, fealty to counternarratives is an index to alienation, not to skin color: witness Representative Helen Chenoweth, of Idaho,
and her devoted constituents. With all the appositeness of allegory, the copies of
"The Protocols of the Elders of Zion" sold by black vendors in New York—
who are supplied with them by Lushena Books, a black-nationalist book whole-
saler—were published by the white supremacist Angriff Press, in Hollywood.
Paranoia knows no color or coast.

Finally, though, it's misleading to view counternarrative as another pathology of disenfranchisement. If the M.I.A. myth, say, is rooted among a largely
working-class constituency, there are many myths—one of them known as
Reaganism—that hold considerable appeal among the privileged classes. "So
many white brothers and sisters are living in a state of denial in terms of how
deep white supremacy is seated in their culture and society," the scholar and
social critic Cornel West says. "Now we recognize that in a fundamental sense
we really do live in different worlds." In that respect, the reaction to the
Simpson verdict has been something of an education. The novelist Ishmael Reed
talks of "wealthy white male commentators who live in a world where the
police don't lie, don't plant evidence—and drug dealers give you unlimited
credit." He adds, "Nicole, you know, also dated Mafia hit men."

"I think he's innocent, I really do," West says. "I do think it was linked to   10
some drug subculture of violence. It looks as if both O. J. and Nicole had some
connection to drug activity. And the killings themselves were classic examples
of that drug culture of violence. It could have to do with money owed—it could
have to do with a number of things. And I think that O. J. was quite aware of
and fearful of this." On this theory, Simpson may have appeared at the crime
scene as a witness. "I think that he had a sense that it was coming down, both
on him and on her, and Brother Ron Goldman just happened to be there," West
conjectures. "But there's a possibility also that O. J. could have been there, gone
over and tried to see what was going on, saw that he couldn't help, split, and
just ran away. He might have said, 'I can't stop this thing, and they are coming
at me to do the same thing.' He may have actually run for his life."

To believe that Simpson is innocent is to believe that a terrible injustice has
been averted, and this is precisely what many black Americans, including many
prominent ones, do believe. Thus the soprano Jessye Norman is angry over what
she sees as the decision of the media to prejudge Simpson rather than "educate
the public as to how we could possibly look at things a bit differently." She says
she wishes that the real culprit "would stand up and say, 'I did this and I am
sorry I caused so much trouble.'" And while she is sensitive to the issue of
spousal abuse, she is skeptical about the way it was enlisted by the prosecution:
"You have to stop getting into how they were at home, because there are not a
lot of relationships that could be put on television that we would think, O.K.,
that's a good one. I mean, just stop pretending that this is the case." Then, too,
she asks, "Isn't it interesting to you that this Faye Resnick person was staying

with Nicole Brown Simpson and that she happened to have left on the eighth of June? Does that tell you that maybe there's some awful coincidence here?" The widespread theory about murderous drug dealers Norman finds "perfectly plausible, knowing what drugs do," and she adds, "People are punished for being bad."

There's a sense in which all such accounts can be considered counternarratives, or fragments of them—subaltern knowledge, if you like. They dispute the tenets of official culture; they do not receive the imprimatur of editorialists or of network broadcasters; they are not seriously entertained on "MacNeil/Lehrer." And when they do surface they are given consideration primarily for their ethnographic value. An official culture treats their claims as it does those of millenarian cultists in Texas, or Marxist deconstructionists in the academy: as things to be diagnosed, deciphered, given meaning—that is, *another* meaning. Black folk say they believe Simpson is innocent, and then the white gatekeepers of a media culture cajolingly explain what black folk really mean when they say it, offering the explanation from the highest of motives: because the alternative is a population that, by their lights, is not merely counternormative but crazy. Black folk may mean anything at all; just not what they say they mean.

Yet you need nothing so grand as an epistemic rupture to explain why different people weigh the evidence of authority differently. In the words of the cunning Republican campaign slogan, "Who do you trust?" It's a commonplace that white folks trust the police and black folks don't. Whites recognize this in the abstract, but they're continually surprised at the *depth* of black wariness. They shouldn't be. Norman Podhoretz's soul-searching 1963 essay, "My Negro Problem, and Ours"—one of the frankest accounts we have of liberalism and race resentment—tells of a Brooklyn boyhood spent under the shadow of carefree, cruel Negro assailants, and of the author's residual unease when he passes groups of blacks in his Upper West Side neighborhood. And yet, he notes in a crucial passage, "I know now, as I did not know when I was a child, that power is on my side, that the police are working for me and not for them." That ordinary, unremarkable comfort—the feeling that "the police are working for me"—continues to elude blacks, even many successful blacks. Thelma Golden, the curator of the Whitney's "Black Male" show, points out that on the very day the verdict was announced a black man in Harlem was killed by the police under disputed circumstances. As older blacks like to repeat, "When white folks say 'justice,' they mean 'just us.' "

Blacks—in particular, black men—swap their experiences of police encounters like war stories, and there are few who don't have more than one story to tell. "These stories have a ring of cliché about them," Erroll McDonald, Pantheon's executive editor and one of the few prominent blacks in publishing, says, "but, as we all know about clichés, they're almost always true." McDonald tells of renting a Jaguar in New Orleans and being stopped by the police—simply "to show cause why I shouldn't be deemed a problematic Negro in a possibly stolen car." Wynton Marsalis says, "Shit, the police slapped me upside the head when I was in high school. I wasn't Wynton Marsalis then. I was just another nigger standing out somewhere on the street whose head could be slapped and did get slapped." The crime novelist Walter Mosley recalls, "When I was a kid in Los Angeles, they used to stop me all the time, beat on me, follow me around, tell me that I was stealing things." Nor does William Julius Wilson—who has a son-in-law on the Chicago police force ("You couldn't find a nicer, more dedicated guy")—wonder why he was stopped near a small New England town by a policeman who wanted to know what he was doing in those parts. There's a moving violation that many African-Americans know as D.W.B.: Driving While Black.

So we all have our stories. In 1968, when I was eighteen, a man who knew   15
me was elected mayor of my West Virginia county, in an upset victory. A few weeks into his term, he passed on something he thought I should know: the county police had made a list of people to be arrested in the event of a serious civil disturbance, and my name was on it. Years of conditioning will tell. Wynton Marsalis says, "My worst fear is to have to go before the criminal-justice system." Absurdly enough, it's mine, too.

SUGGESTIONS FOR FURTHER STUDY

Key Words

The author uses language with which you may not be familiar. Find the following words in the paragraphs indicated, and explain their meanings in the context of the sentences in which the words appear. Consult a dictionary, as needed.

mantra (par. 1)
bathos (par. 2)
connoisseurs (par. 3)
froideur (par. 3)
interstitial (par. 4)
diametrically (par. 4)
misprision (par. 4)
vouchsafed (par. 5)
regnant (par. 6)
old saw (par. 7)
fealty (par. 8)
appositeness (par. 8)
disenfranchisement (par. 9)
subaltern (par. 12)
deconstructionists (par. 12)
epistemic (par. 13)

Topics for Discussion and Writing

1. Gates tells us where various African American cultural leaders were when the O. J. Simpson verdict was announced. When you first heard about the verdict, what was your reaction to it? Did the physical surroundings or the people around you influence your reaction? Have you changed your opinion since then? If so, what has influenced that change?

2. According to Gates, what was the "focus of attention" when the verdict was announced? What were the various reactions of Caucasian Americans and African Americans, both to the verdict and to the reactions to the verdict? What does Gates suggest these reactions signify in terms of our national history?

3. Discuss the examples Gates provides to indicate many African Americans' historical mistrust of empowered authority and of conventional narratives about American history. Are African Americans alone in "questioning authority"? How so, or how not? How does Gates employ history to help explain many African Americans' belief that Simpson was the target of a conspiracy?

4. According to Cornel West, about what subject are "many white brothers and sisters . . . living in a state of denial"?

5. Gates writes that prominent African Americans such as Ishmael Reed (see the third reading in this chapter), Cornel West, and Jessye Norman believe Simpson innocent and that drug dealers may have been the cause of Nicole Simpson's and Ronald Goldman's deaths. What is your opinion about this view? What specific conditions or incidents can you cite to support your view?

6. Gates cites a common belief that "white folks trust the police and blacks don't." He offers several examples of police treatment of African American leaders in the past. Based on your reading, experience, and observation, do you agree or disagree with that belief? In explaining your point of view, consider the experiences of other minority groups (gays and lesbians, hippies and bikers, ethnic and racial minorities, etc.) that have contact with police authority.

7. Write a narrative essay describing an experience you have had with police authority, either one during which you felt "hassled" or unfairly treated or one in which you were assisted and treated positively by an officer. In your essay, go beyond simply describing your experience, and comment on how the experience has affected you.

Affirmative Action:
Until a Fair Society Is Realized

Richard Smith

In this selection, student writer Richard Smith tackles the issue of affirmative action. In his argumentative position paper, Smith discusses California's controversial Proposition 209, legislation before Congress, the Commission on Civil Rights, and "[achieving] a more egalitarian society," among other things.

On November 4, 1996, Californians had the opportunity, in theory, to decide the fate of government-sponsored affirmative-action programs. Although the outcome was marginally divided, Proposition 209, which called for the elimination of affirmative-action programs, passed, with 54% of California voters approving [the measure]. Immediately, the American Civil Liberties Union filed a lawsuit seeking to block [implementation of] Proposition 209. In late December of 1996, Chief U.S. District Judge Thelton E. Henderson issued an injunction effectively blocking the implementation of Proposition 209 until it could be reviewed by a higher court. With these actions, the raging battle over positive and negative aspects of affirmative action continues.

The debate is not [localized] to California. All the nation watches and waits to see the outcome of California's debate. The Republican leaders of the new majority Republican Congress have expressed a desire to promote national laws that would effectively do away with affirmative-action programs. With President Bill Clinton also being reelected and clearly expressing his determination to continue affirmative-action programs, it is not altogether clear as to how the American voters weigh in on these arguments. It is very easy to see why this [ambiguity exists]. Both sides present outstanding arguments. When the American voter hears that the grass-roots effort to cancel affirmative-action programs is simply an effort to prohibit discrimination based on race and gender—similar to the banning of the racial discrimination of the early 1960s—the voter cannot help but be compelled to identify with legislation such as Proposition 209. Yet when the same voter hears that a simple thirty years of affirmative action cannot make up for six-hundred years of slavery, invidious discrimination, and stifling segregation, that voter will [probably] be pushed to [teetering on] the top of a fence. Although both sides have much validity behind their arguments, compelling evidence shows that a

1

great amount of prejudice and discrimination continues to exist within the boundaries of these United States of America. While affirmative action is by no means the perfect solution, until a better method of assisting minorities and women into the mainstream education and work environment is developed, these programs should be continued.

On September 25, 1996, the "Big Debate" took place at California State University Northridge. The debate was over Proposition 209. In most cases, such an event would have only created moderate interest; instead, the debate attracted interest from the highest offices of the land. The mixture of this controversial issue with an invitation to a former Ku Klux Klan leader to debate on behalf of Prop. 209 was enough to spark nationwide controversy. David Duke, a former Louisiana legislator and former Klan grand wizard, entered the debate hall with thousands of rioting students surrounding the building. The students were barely being repelled by the local police department. His opponent during the debate was Joe Hicks, executive director of a Los Angeles advocacy group established to ease racial tension after the latest LA riots. Why did a simple university debate come to initiate such great interest for the politicians and the people of this nation? Although most people, even opponents of Prop. 209, saw through the students' attempt to associate Proposition 209 with the Ku Klux Klan, there seemed to be an underlying message, just slightly subliminal, that was being realized. It wasn't really the merits, issues, or pro and cons of Prop. 209. It was the message that Duke himself sent. The subtle message crawled into the minds of Americans and caused many to think, "People like this guy still exist in America, and where and who they are, we don't always know." While opponents of Prop. 209 were upset by the invitation to Duke, feeling that the students' intent was clear cut and would upset voters who would then clearly approve the measure, proponents of the proposition were even more upset. *The Los Angeles Times* reported in its September 7, 1996, issue that "Several key supporters of the ballot initiative, including UC Regent Ward Connerly, the campaign chairman, have characterized the move to bring Duke to the campus as a thinly veiled dirty trick."

It was clear that, although Duke did not represent the California-initiated grass-roots effort to pass Prop. 209, he did represent something that it did not have an answer for, something that its supporters wanted the voters to forget. Duke represented true racism in its most evil form, the Klan, and he was alive and well today. He was not some past event or memory; he was not totally an aberration, but he was a representation of what was still out there, cloaked and waiting. This fact, in all probability, accounts for the passion of the Northridge debate.

To competently argue pro and con points of affirmative action, its roots and the atmosphere out of which it began should be studied. With the legislation enacted by the United States in mid century, a country was going to attempt to reconcile its past behaviors with future efforts. By the late fifties,

American Blacks had attained freedom on paper, but, realistically, they continued to be shackled by chains of segregation, discrimination, and prejudice. It was because of this invisible slavery that the Civil Rights Movement emerged, led by Dr. Martin Luther King, Jr. President John F. Kennedy took up the cause and began to facilitate legislation that declared discrimination and segregation illegal. After Kennedy's assassination, President Lyndon B. Johnson picked up the reins and continued actions to ensure equal rights for Blacks. In a commencement speech to Howard University on June 4, 1965, Johnson gave some indication that his administration was leaning toward affirmative-action policies. In the speech, he states:

> But freedom is not enough. You do not wipe away the scars of centuries by saying: Now you are free to go where you want, do as you desire and choose the leaders you please.
>
> You do not take a person who, for years, has been hobbled by chains and liberate him, bring him up to the starting line of a race and then say, 'You are free to compete with all the others,' and still justly believe that you have been completely fair.
>
> Thus it is not enough to just open the gates of opportunity. All our citizens must have the ability to walk through those gates.
>
> This is the next and more profound stage of the battle for civil rights. We seek not just freedom but opportunity—not just equality as a right and theory, but equality as a fact and as a result. (Curry 17–18)

Later in 1965, President Lyndon Johnson issued Executive Order 11246. This order required federal contractors to utilize affirmative action to make sure that their employment practices were not discriminatory. In subsequent years, under the Nixon administration, Black Republican Assistant Secretary Arthur Fletcher "issued specific requirements of enforcing contract compliance which established the general outlines of the program as it exists today" (302). With this new legislation, Blacks and women made great strides toward mainstream America throughout the '70s.

However, after a little over ten years of steady progress, opponents of affirmative action began to surface and question the validity of these measures, as well as their constitutionality. Fueled by sporadic examples of Blacks being accepted by educational institutions and government careers at the expense of sometimes more qualified White males, the arguments against affirmative action increasingly gained America's attention. After all, sometimes affirmative-action practices did result in discrimination against White males, many of whom were not even born until after the Civil Rights struggles of the '60s. Obviously, they had nothing to do with the oppression of Blacks before the '60s, yet they received the brunt of the punishment. Even many Blacks were sympathetic to the problems that were arising out of affirmative-action policies.

Concerned with the negative interpretations of efforts to promote equality, William Bradford Reynolds, Assistant Attorney General for Civil Rights under the Reagan administration, took a strong stand against affirmative action in his article, "An Experiment Gone Awry." Although Reynolds is Black and agrees that affirmative action initially had a successful impact on America, he now believes that it has metamorphosed into something that is dangerously unconstitutional:

> By the early 1970s, the initial affirmative action priming of the deseg-
> regation pump succeeded in removing most noticeable racial barriers,
> while introducing across the country an attitude of growing acceptance
> of blacks and other minorities as equal partners in the school yards
> and the work-force. It was, however, in large measure
> this success that led to the bastardization of "affirmative action." . . .
>   Racial quotas, goals and timetables, contract set-asides—these
> became the mainstay of the affirmative action arsenal. Common to
> each such program was a number (or percentage) of classroom seats,
> employment positions, or contract awards held out of the merit com-
> petition for preferential assignment to minorities only, and only on the
> basis of race. Anyone suggesting that these preference programs favor-
> ing blacks were as reprehensible as the discriminatory policies that for
> so long unfairly disadvantaged blacks was branded a racist. It was a
> sad distortion of the civil rights agenda, which had started with so
> much promise. (130–132)

Reynolds brings up a critical point. Are Blacks now participating in the same discrimination that they so despised when it was leveled against them? Have the government and the courts aided in this onslaught of new discrimination? Does statistical research back up the claims of this new racism against Whites? Have most noticeable racial barriers been removed, as Reynolds indicates in his article? If so, is there really any further need for affirmative-action programs? Critical points are raised here. For if these points are valid, we can see why the California initiative, Prop. 209, has gained so much momentum. The aforementioned points—added with the dynamics of the 1992 Los Angeles riots; the verdicts of the Reginald Denny trial, in which several young Black men, who obviously intended to assault a White trucker, were released or given light sentences; and the backlash of the O. J. Simpson trial—have served to fuel an enormous fire [for] many White and prosperous and/or intellectual Black Californians. The heat is on, so to speak. Subsequently, it appears that the proponents of Proposition 209 will aggressively seek to take this fight to the highest court in the land.

Advocates of continuing affirmative-action programs have not been stifled, however, as even most White Americans seem to believe that much racism still exists in this country. The strong possibility that racism and discrimination continue to influence the decisions of major American corporations and individual state governments proves to be the pro–affirmative action advocate's best argument. Why, for instance, does William Reynolds use the phrasing "most noticeable racial barriers" in the [aforementioned] passage. . . . Was Reynolds's subconscious mind trying to tell him something as he wrote this sentence? Why did he find it necessary to write "most noticeable racial barriers," instead of "most racial barriers"? Does Reynolds consider a noticeable racial barrier more dangerous and restrictive than one that is not noticeable? Most rational human beings would submit the opposite to be true. In the 1988 hit movie *The Predator,* an alien creature preys on men, hunting them as men hunt the animals of the earth. Being from a vastly advanced alien race, the creature has far superior weaponry and strength. But his most powerful weapon, which aids him in killing all of the male characters of the movie except for one, is really not a weapon at all. It is the creature's ability to cloak itself, to hide and blend with the jungle—to remain invisible to its foe until it attacks. Similarly, invisible racism has the capacity to do far more damage to America's search for freedom and equality than any of its more overt predecessors.

In an article in the May '95 issue of *Emerge: Black America's Newsmagazine,* Mary Frances Berry, Chair of the U.S. Commission on Civil Rights, addresses many of the pro–affirmative action issues:

> The courts, aware of the perpetuation of invidious discrimination, have routinely upheld race- and gender-conscious affirmative action. Unlike opponents of affirmative action, who keep speaking of discrimination as something that used to happen, they are aware that discrimination exists here and now. . . .
>
> The irony is that even though whites still receive the lion's share of contracts, scholarships, or well paying jobs, many white Americans will make any argument and go to any lengths to fight to withdraw any portion that might be awarded to African-Americans. . . .
>
> Although the social conditions that occasioned affirmative action have improved for some African-Americans, victory is far from won. For more than a generation, American law has prohibited race, national origin, and gender discrimination. However, government reports as well as television documentaries show that African-Americans, whether middle-class, upper-class, or no class, suffer discrimination in obtaining jobs or promotions, borrowing money to buy a house or starting businesses, renting apartments, or getting served in restaurants. (308, 310–311)

Unfortunately, many of the practices that Berry speaks of have raised their ugly heads as of late. From the Denny's Restaurant lawsuit to the . . . Texaco corporate scandal, evidence of discrimination continues.

Berry supports her message with a study conducted by the Urban   10
Institute in 1991. The institute prepared and sent out job applicants.
Although the applicants were virtually equal in background and credentials,
the only obvious difference was that half were White males and the other
half Black.

> They were the same age and physical size, had identical education and
> work experiences and had similar personalities. Yet in almost 20% of
> the cases, whites advanced further in the hiring process. In assessing
> the reason, Margery Turner, a former senior researcher at the Urban
> Institute who was involved in the study, said, "The simple answer is
> prejudice . . . Clearly, blacks still suffer from unfavorable treatment."
> (311–312)

As long as studies such as the experiment by the Urban Institute continue to
show patterns of discrimination, champions of affirmative action will continue to have valid reason for concern.

It seems that there could, perhaps, be some middle ground. In his 1997
inaugural address, President Bill Clinton [see the second reading in this
chapter] suggested that the programs of affirmative action be updated and
fixed but not eliminated all together. Conceivably, there could be a committee
on "affirmative action" formed from both sides of the aisle to come up with
concrete plans that would truly eliminate racial and gender bias. However,
until such plans and ideas are arduously formulated, affirmative action
seems to be the best that we as humans have the ability to implement.

In the foreseeable future, this should not be the case. With ever-improving
computer technology, we should soon have methods that would eliminate
any bias from a test or job interview. A recent issue of *Newsweek* features an
article, "Showing His True Colors," which points out many of the advantages—as well as shortcomings—in a computer-using society. With the
advent of online computer services and the subsequent "chat" rooms that
have erupted, more Americans and people from every country are having
conversations with total strangers, as the *Newsweek* article by Angela
Bouwsma demonstrates. Bouwsma writes of an online conversation that her
mother had with a Midwest White computer engineer. Apparently, the
mother and the engineer chatted for quite some time about a variety of
subjects. Being well-educated, Bouwsma's mother [apparently] made the
Midwesterner feel that he must have been chatting with a White woman; consequently, he began to express his racial bigotry against Blacks.
Bouwsma writes:

> She couldn't recall precisely what he said, but the key words were
> "ignorant," "lie," "cheat" and "smell." My mother, stunned but in
> the comfort of anonymity, gathered herself and tried to reason with
> her new friend. He found her efforts to defend black people noble but

incredibly naïve. "One of these day you'll find out how black people really are," he wrote.

    With that . . . she revealed that she herself was black. The man professed shock and endlessly apologized. Giving her what I suppose was intended as a compliment, he expressed his happy surprise at finally meeting an intelligent black person. (14–15)

Bouwsma may have stumbled upon something accidentally, because until we Americans can look at each other with the same eyes as those we see with while typing on a chat page, affirmative action will always engender a strong debate. Maybe the answer lies in interviews over a computer without a visual of the person or without knowing [the person's] racial or gender background. We are fast developing the technology to [achieve] a more egalitarian society. However, until that fair society is realized, all of us who do not judge others based on their skin color or gender may have to live with the programs that attempt to force the bigots in our society to be decent human beings.

Works Cited

Bernstein, Sharon. "Governor Slams Students' Choice of Duke." *The Los Angeles Times On-line.* 7 September 1992: 2.

Berry, Mary Frances. "Affirmative Action: Why We Need It, Why It Is under Attack." *Emerge: Black America's Newsmagazine.* Washington, D.C., May 1995.

Bouwsma, Angela. "Showing His True Colors." *Newsweek.* 24 February 1997: 14–15.

Curry, George E., ed. *The Affirmative Action Debate.* Reading, MA: Addison-Wesley, 1996.

Reynolds, William Bradford. "An Experiment Gone Awry," in *The Affirmative Action Debate,* George E. Curry, ed. Reading, MA: Addison-Wesley, 1996.

CHAPTER 7: ACTIVITIES FOR DISCUSSION AND WRITING
Making Connections

1. In a short essay, discuss how President Clinton's speech, "A New Sense of Responsibility," parallels some of the language patterns of Martin Luther King's "I Have a Dream" speech. What examples of similar figurative (metaphorical) language can you discover between the two speeches?

2. Write an essay in which you examine whether Martin Luther King's ideas in the "I Have a Dream" speech have become manifested in

CARTOONS IN AMERICA

A Reason for Affirmative Action

Copyright © 1996 Jeff Danziger.

the present time—more than thirty-five years later. Utilize at least one of the other essays in Chapter 7 to help you structure your discussion.

3. In "Hidden Dangers in the Ethnic Revival," Orlando Patterson criticizes Americans' attempts at exploring their ethnic roots. Read two of the essays in Chapter 2, in which writers discuss their heritage in terms of family members and what they learned from them, and then write an argumentative paper using those essays as part of a rebuttal to Patterson's essay. Suggested essays from Chapter 2 include Dan Kwong's "Grandpa Story," N. Scott Momaday's "The Last of the Kiowas," and Alice Walker's "In Search of Our Mothers' Gardens."

4. Some of the essays in Chapter 7 have discussed different metaphors for capturing the American multicultural experience, such as "salad bowl," "cultural bouillabaisse," and the old standby, the "melting pot." In a short essay, create your own metaphor for the American experience, as student writer Christine Willis does in "We Are an Old-fashioned Stew," in Chapter 6. Discuss the merits of your choice, and argue for its adoption as a possible new slogan for America.

5. Write an in-depth argumentative paper on affirmative action, as did student writer Richard Smith. You may want to emulate Smith's example and deal with both sides of the controversy while positing a moderate position. Or, you may want to take a more extreme stance and either maintain that affirmative-action programs must remain unaltered indefinitely, or that affirmative-action programs must be abolished immediately. We recommend first reading Smith's "Affirmative Action: Until a Fair System Is Realized," and Decker's "Affirmative Action: Why Battle Erupted," and then moving on to further research in the library or on the Internet.

6. The incident concerning European American Texaco executives who were recorded making racial slurs and other racist remarks about African Americans in a 1996 Board of Directors meeting alerted nonblacks to the continuing presence of overt racism in American corporations. Research the Texaco incident or another contemporary racially charged incident. Discuss or write a short essay about how such incidents do or do not affect the importance of implementing some kind of affirmative-action programs. Consider whether an idealistic system such as meritocracy can work in our nation if Henry Louis Gates, Jr. (in "Thirteen Ways of Looking at a Black Man") is correct to point out, "white supremacy is seated [deeply] in [American] society."

7. One way to realize the ideas of Martin Luther King, Jr., is for African Americans and other minorities to get a fair trial in our courts. Research and document a court case in American history in which a member of a minority received either a fair or an unfair trial. As an alternative, read the books (or watch the movies) *To Kill a Mockingbird, A Time to Kill,* or works about a similar fictionalized trial, and summarize the events leading up to and during the trials they depict. Pay particular attention to the attitudes of the characters involved in the trials, and to the treatment of the accused or the witnesses. (You may want to research books, scholarly journals, magazines, or newspapers in the library. Consult the computer databases in your library, if available, to assist you in locating the latest information. Use the Internet to gain access to relevant material on your topic through the World Wide Web.)

ISSUES IN AMERICA III

Feminism and Gender Issues: Can't We All Just Communicate?

The struggle for equality and freedom in America has not revolved solely around ethnic minorities; women, too, have been fighting for true equality and representation in America for more than one hundred years—with mixed results. Apparently, some basic inequalities and misunderstandings, and a readiness to stereotype, lie at the heart of the American experience. At the same time, many Americans of different races, genders, and ages show a spirited will to overcome these negative views of their fellow citizens, based on their belief in a wide variety of social and political ideals. The writers included in this chapter focus on helping us understand some of the problems women face in their struggle toward self-identity and equality with members of the opposite sex. Communication is often seen as the key to overcoming America's more negative social agendas. As Deborah Tannen's essay (at the end of this chapter) explains, enhanced communication offers an important solution for overcoming breakdowns in understanding, not just between men and women, but also among all diverse groups of people.

In selected excerpts from her novel *The House on Mango Street,* Sandra Cisneros provides symbolic glimpses into several oppressed women's lives, then offers an empowering manifesto of women's rights. Emily Prager satirically examines the influence of Barbie dolls in "Our Barbies, Ourselves." Next, in "Blame It on Feminism," Susan Faludi attacks those who seek to blame women's problems on the feminist movement. In "Where I Come from Is Like This," Paula Gunn Allen describes American Indian women as defined by their tribal identity and contrasts their roles within tribal culture with those of Anglo European women in their mainstream culture. Columnist Robin Abcarian's "Pink Does Not the Girl (or Boy) Make" illustrates how difficult it is for parents to control the "genderizing" of their children. In "Sex, Lies, and Conversation," sociologist Deborah Tannen illustrates the importance of communication and of understanding different types of communication in healing misunderstandings. Finally, student writer Bethany Dever examines "Gender Roles" and the stereotypes that our society perpetuates.

Selections from
The House on Mango Street

Sandra Cisneros

Sandra Cisneros (born in Chicago in 1954, the daughter of a Mexican father and a Mexican-American mother) has worked as a teacher to high school dropouts, a poet-in-the-schools, a college recruiter, and an arts administrator. Cisneros authored The House on Mango Street *(1989),* Woman Hollering Creek *(1991), and* My Wicked Wicked Ways, *a volume of poetry. She also received two NEA (National Education Association) fellowships for poetry and fiction, as well as the Lannan Literary Award for 1991.*

The following selections, excerpted from The House on Mango Street, *illustrate the oppressive lives of several women in a neighborhood of Chicago. In the last selection, the narrator, Esperanza, decides that she will not follow the same path as her friends in her community.*

RAFAELA WHO DRINKS COCONUT AND PAPAYA JUICE ON TUESDAYS

On Tuesdays Rafaela's husband comes home late because that's the 1 night he plays dominos. And then Rafaela, who is still young but getting old from leaning out the window so much, gets locked indoors because her husband is afraid Rafaela will run away since she is too beautiful to look at.

Rafaela leans out the window and leans on her elbow and dreams her hair is like Rapunzel's. On the corner there is music from the bar, and Rafaela wishes she could go in there and dance before she gets old.

A long time passes and we forget she is up there watching until she says: Kids, if I give you a dollar will you go to the store and buy me something? She throws a crumpled dollar down and always asks for coconut or sometimes papaya juice, and we send it up to her in a paper shopping bag she lets down with clothesline.

Rafaela who drinks and drinks coconut and papaya juice on Tuesdays and wishes there were sweeter drinks, not bitter like an empty room, but sweet sweet like the island, like the dance hall down the street where women much older than her throw green eyes easily like dice and open homes with keys. And always there is someone offering sweeter drinks, someone promising to keep them on a silver string.

MINERVA WRITES POEMS

Minerva is only a little bit older than me but already she has two kids   5
and a husband who left. Her mother raised her kids alone and it looks like
her daughters will go that way too. Minerva cries because her luck is
unlucky. Every night and every day. And prays. But when the kids are asleep
after she's fed them their pancake dinner, she writes poems on little pieces of
paper that she folds over and over and holds in her hands a long time, little
pieces of paper that smell like a dime.

She lets me read her poems. I let her read mine. She is always sad like a
house on fire—always something wrong. She has many troubles, but the big
one is her husband who left and keeps leaving.

One day she is through and lets him know enough is enough. Out the
door he goes. Clothes, records, shoes. Out the window and the door locked.
But that night he comes back and sends a big rock through the window.
Then she is sorry and opens the door again. Same story.

Next week she comes over black and blue and asks what can she do?
Minerva. I don't know which way she'll go. There is nothing *I* can do.

LINOLEUM ROSES

Sally got married like we knew she would, young and not ready but
married just the same. She met a marshmallow salesman at a school bazaar,
and she married him in another state where it's legal to get married before
eighth grade. She has her husband and her house now, her pillowcases and
her plates. She says she is in love, but I think she did it to escape.

Sally says she likes being married because now she gets to buy her own   10
things when her husband gives her money. She is happy, except sometimes
her husband gets angry and once he broke the door where his foot went
through, though most days he is okay. Except he won't let her talk on the
telephone. And he doesn't let her look out the window. And he doesn't like
her friends, so nobody gets to visit her unless he is working.

She sits at home because she is afraid to go outside without his permission. She looks at all the things they own: the towels and the toaster, the
alarm clock and the drapes. She likes looking at the walls, at how neatly
their corners meet, the linoleum roses on the floor, the ceiling smooth as
wedding cake.

BEAUTIFUL AND CRUEL

I am an ugly daughter. I am the one nobody comes for.

Nenny says she won't wait her whole life for a husband to come and get
her, that Minerva's sister left her mother's house by having a baby, but she

doesn't want to go that way either. She wants things all her own, to pick and choose. Nenny has pretty eyes and it's easy to talk that way if you are pretty.

My mother says when I get older my dusty hair will settle and my blouse will learn to stay clean, but I have decided not to grow up tame like the others who lay their necks on the threshold waiting for the ball and chain.

In the movies there is always one with red red lips who is beautiful and   15
cruel. She is the one who drives the men crazy and laughs them all away. Her power is her own. She will not give it away.

I have begun my own quiet war. Simple. Sure. I am one who leaves the table like a man, without putting back the chair or picking up the plate.

SUGGESTIONS FOR FURTHER STUDY

Language and Style

1. In this selection, Cisneros often depends on figurative language to create word pictures in her readers' minds. Select several sentences in which Cisneros uses metaphors and similes, and explain their effect on you and other readers.

2. Cisneros often uses partial sentences, or sentence fragments, a grammatical pattern students are usually cautioned to avoid in formal writing. Locate Cisneros's partial sentences, and discuss how successfully Cisneros uses them to convey meaning, style, and emotion.

Topics for Discussion and Writing

1. In the first three selections, how does Cisneros show men influencing the lives of women?

2. If you are familiar with the story of Rapunzel, compare that story to "Rafaela Who Drinks Coconut & Papaya Juice on Tuesdays." In the fairy tale, Rapunzel waits for a handsome prince to rescue her from the wicked witch. What is the main difference between Rafaela's story and Rapunzel's?

3. In "Minerva Writes Poems," how does Minerva's handling of her poems symbolize her management of her life?

4. In "Linoleum Roses," how old is Sally when she marries? Why does she marry? How does she spend her time? How does her life compare to Rafaela's?

5. In "Beautiful and Cruel," how might you view Esperanza as being fortunate to be the ugly daughter? In beginning her own "quiet war," Esperanza establishes her feminist manifesto of independence and equality. Using Cisneros's words, what is Esperanza's feminist agenda? How would you rewrite her manifesto in your own words?

6. Write either a fictional or a nonfictional account of a man or woman trapped by another person into a life he or she cannot bear. In your narrative, include an instance when the trapped person tries to escape or alter his or her life somehow.

7. Recall a story or movie depicting a man or woman trapped by another person, and summarize that story. Use your own words to detail the trapped person's predicament and his or her attempt to escape. You might consider these works as examples for your summary and analysis: Charlotte Perkins Gilman's "The Yellow Wallpaper," Kate Chopin's *The Awakening*, Stephen King's *Misery*, or Henrik Ibsen's A *Doll's House*.

Our Barbies, Ourselves

Emily Prager

Emily Prager (born in 1952) has written for the National Lampoon, *the* Village Voice, *and* Penthouse, *among other publications. Her books include* The Official I Hate Videogames Handbook, Eve's Tattoo *(1991), and* Clea and Zeus Divorce *(1987). "Our Barbies, Ourselves" was published in* Interview *in December 1991.*

I read an astounding obituary in the *New York Times* not too long ago. It concerned the death of one Jack Ryan. A former husband of Zsa Zsa Gabor, it said, Mr. Ryan had been an inventor and designer during his lifetime. A man of eclectic creativity, he designed Sparrow and Hawk missiles when he worked for the Raytheon Company, and, the notice said, when he consulted for Mattel he designed Barbie.

If Barbie was designed by a man, suddenly a lot of things made sense to me, things I'd wondered about for years. I used to look at Barbie and wonder, What's wrong with this picture? What kind of woman designed this doll? Let's be honest: Barbie looks like someone who got her start at the Playboy Mansion. She could be a regular guest on *The Howard Stern Show.* It is a fact of Barbie's design that her breasts are so out of proportion to the rest of her body that if she were a human woman, she'd fall flat on her face.

If it's true that a woman didn't design Barbie, you don't know how much saner that makes me feel. Of course, that doesn't ameliorate the damage. There are millions of women who are subliminally sure that a thirty-nine-inch bust and a twenty-three-inch waist are the epitome of lovability. Could this account for the popularity of breast implant surgery?

I don't mean to step on anyone's toes here. I loved my Barbie. Secretly, I still believe that neon pink and turquoise blue are the only colors in which to decorate a duplex condo. And like many others of my generation, I've never married, simply because I cannot find a man who looks as good in clam diggers as Ken.

The question that comes to mind is, of course, Did Mr. Ryan design Barbie as a weapon? Because it *is* odd that Barbie appeared about the same time in my consciousness as the feminist movement—a time when women sought equality and small breasts were king. Or is Barbie the dream date of weapons designers? Or perhaps it's simpler that that: Perhaps Barbie is Zsa

Zsa if she were eleven inches tall. No matter what, my discovery of Jack Ryan confirms what I have always felt: There is something indescribably masculine about Barbie—dare I say it, phallic. For all her giant breasts and high-heeled feet, she lacks a certain softness. If you asked a little girl what kind of doll she wanted for Christmas, I just don't think she'd reply, "Please, Santa, I want a hard-body."

On the other hand, you could say that Barbie, in feminist terms, is definitely her own person. With her condos and fashion plazas and pools and beauty salons, she is definitely a liberated woman, a gal on the move. And she has always been sexual, even totemic. Before Barbie, American dolls were flat-footed and breastless, and ineffably dignified. They were created in the image of little girls or babies. Madame Alexander was the queen of doll makers in the fifties, and her dollies looked like Elizabeth Taylor in *National Velvet*. They represented the kind of girls who looked perfect in jodhpurs, whose hair was never out of place, who grew up to be Jackie Kennedy—before she married Onassis. Her dolls' boyfriends were figments of the imagination, figments with large portfolios and three-piece suits and presidential aspirations, figments who could keep dolly in the style to which little girls of the fifties were programmed to become accustomed, a style that spasmed with the sixties and the appearance of Barbie. And perhaps what accounts for Barbie's vast popularity is that she was also a sixties woman: into free love and fun colors, anticlass, and possessed of real, molded boyfriend, Ken, with whom she could chant a mantra.

But there were problems with Ken. I always felt weird about him. He had no genitals, and, even at age ten, I found that ominous. I mean, here was Barbie with these humongous breasts, and that was OK with the toy company. And then, there was Ken with that truncated, unidentifiable lump at his groin. I sensed injustice at work. Why, I wondered, was Barbie designed with such obvious sexual equipment and Ken not? Why was his treated as if it were more mysterious than hers? Did the fact that it was treated as such indicate that somehow his equipment, his essential maleness, was considered more powerful than hers, more worthy of the dignity of concealment? And if the issue in the mind of the toy company was obscenity and its possible damage to children, I still object. How do they think I felt, knowing that no matter how many water beds they slept in, or hot tubs they romped in, or swimming pools they lounged by under the stars, Barbie and Ken could never make love? No matter how much sexuality Barbie possessed, she would never turn Ken on. He would be forever withholding, forever detached. There was a loneliness about Barbie's situation that was always disturbing. And twenty-five years later, movies and videos are still filled with topless women and covered men. As if we're all trapped in Barbie's world and can never escape.

God, it certainly has cheered me up to think that Barbie was designed by Jack Ryan. . . .

SUGGESTIONS FOR FURTHER STUDY

Key Words

The author uses language with which you may not be familiar. Find the following words in the paragraphs indicated, and explain their meanings in the context of the sentences in which the words appear. Consult a dictionary, as needed.

eclectic (par. 1)
ameliorate (par. 3)
subliminally (par. 3)
epitome (par. 3)
phallic (par. 5)
totemic (par. 6)
ineffably (par. 6)
jodhpurs (par. 6)
humongous (par. 8)

Topics for Discussion and Writing

1. What does the author suggest is ironic about Barbie's designer?

2. When Prager says she "used to look at Barbie and wonder, what's wrong with this picture?" to what does she refer? What connection do you see, if any, between Barbie and today's "popularity of breast implant surgery"? Explain your answer.

3. Prager is writing what literary critics call a "semiotic analysis" of the Barbie doll. That is, she interprets the different meanings that an ordinary pop culture icon such as Barbie can have, particularly focusing on the unique but reasonable connections that most readers may not have noticed. Semiotic analysis encourages readers and viewers to consider social, political, and cultural significances represented by the object of analysis. How does Prager's analysis explain that Barbie can be considered a "definitely liberated woman"? Are you convinced by her analysis? Why or why not?

4. The author suggests that Barbie's "humongous breasts" and Ken's "truncated, unidentifiable lump at his groin" indicate that men are more powerful than women. How well does she justify this inference? Explain your answer. According to the author, how are Barbie's and Ken's physical characteristics related to movies and videos "filled with topless women and covered men"? Might the characteristics of the two dolls also (or instead) signify that women are passionate and sensual, whereas men are docile, sexless, and machinelike? Discuss these interpretations with other readers, and compare your opinions.

5. Write an analytical essay about significant toys in your life and the roles they have played. Describe the toy or toys, and analyze their possible influence on you as a child or a teenager. If you had a Barbie or another kind of doll, in what kinds of activities did the doll participate with you? What attachment did you feel to your doll? Instead of a doll, you may prefer to write about any other item you considered a toy or other object for play: Legos or building blocks, stuffed animals, a BB gun, a bicycle, and so on.

Blame It on Feminism

Susan Faludi

*Susan Faludi (born in New York City in 1959) graduated from
Harvard in 1981. She has worked as a reporter for the* Miami Herald,
the San Jose News, *and the* Wall Street Journal. *In 1991, she published*
Backlash: The Undeclared War on American Women. *"Blame It on
Feminism" appeared in* Mother Jones *in 1991.*

To be a woman in America at the close of the twentieth century—what
good fortune. That's what we keep hearing, anyway. The barricades have
fallen, politicians assure us. Women have "made it," Madison Avenue
cheers. Women's fight for equality has "largely been won," *Time* magazine
announces. Enroll at any university, join any law firm, apply for credit at
any bank. Women have so many opportunities now, corporate leaders say,
that they don't really need opportunity policies. Women are so equal now,
lawmakers say, that they no longer need an Equal Rights Amendment.
Women have "so much," former president Ronald Reagan says, that the
White House no longer needs to appoint them to high office. Even
American Express ads are saluting a woman's right to charge it. At last,
women have received their full citizenship papers.

And yet . . .

Behind this celebration of the American woman's victory, behind the
news, cheerfully and endlessly repeated, that the struggle for women's rights
is won, another message flashes: You may be free and equal now, but you
have never been more miserable.

This bulletin of despair is posted everywhere—at the newsstand, on the
TV set, at the movies, in advertisements and doctors' offices and academic
journals. Professional women are suffering "burnout" and succumbing to an
"infertility epidemic." Single women are grieving from a "man shortage."
The *New York Times* reports: Childless women are "depressed and confused" and their ranks are swelling. *Newsweek* says: Unwed women are
"hysterical" and crumbling under a "profound crisis of confidence." The
health-advice manuals inform: High-powered career women are stricken
with unprecedented outbreaks of "stress-induced disorders," hair loss, bad
nerves, alcoholism, and even heart attacks. The psychology books advise:
Independent women's loneliness represents "a major mental-health problem

today." Even founding feminist Betty Friedan has been spreading the word: She warns that women now suffer from "new problems that have no name."

How can American women be in so much trouble at the same time that they are supposed to be so blessed? If women got what they asked for, what could possibly be the matter now?

The prevailing wisdom of the past decade has supported one, and only one, answer to this riddle: It must be all that equality that's causing all that pain. Women are unhappy precisely because they are free. Women are enslaved by their own liberation. They have grabbed at the gold ring of independence, only to miss the one ring that really matters. They have gained control of their fertility, only to destroy it. They have pursued their own professional dreams—and lost out on romance, the greatest female adventure. "Our generation was the human sacrifice" to the women's movement, writer Elizabeth Mehren contends in a *Time* cover story. Baby-boom women, like her, she says, have been duped by feminism: "We believed the rhetoric." In *Newsweek*, writer Kay Ebeling dubs feminism the "Great Experiment That Failed" and asserts, "Women in my generation, its perpetrators, are the casualties."

In the eighties, publications from the *New York Times* to *Vanity Fair* to *The Nation* have issued a steady stream of indictments against the women's movement, with such headlines as "When Feminism Failed" or "The Awful Truth About Women's Lib." They hold the campaign for women's equality responsible for nearly every woe besetting women, from depression to meager savings accounts, from teenage suicides to eating disorders to bad complexions. The *Today* show says women's liberation is to blame for bag ladies. A guest columnist in the *Baltimore Sun* even proposes that feminists produced the rise in slasher movies. By making the "violence" of abortion more acceptable, the author reasons, women's-rights activists made it all right to show graphic murders on screen.

At the same time, other outlets of popular culture have been forging the same connection. In Hollywood films, of which *Fatal Attraction* is only the most famous, emancipated women with condominiums of their own slink wild-eyed between bare walls, paying for their liberty with an empty bed, a barren womb. "My biological clock is ticking so loud it keeps me awake at night," Sally Field cries in the film *Surrender,* as, in an all-too-common transformation in the cinema of the eighties, an actress who once played scrappy working heroines is now showcased groveling for a groom. In prime-time television shows, from *thirtysomething* to *Family Man,* single, professional, and feminist women are humiliated, turned into harpies, or hit by nervous breakdowns; the wise ones recant their independent ways by the closing sequence. In popular novels, from Gail Parent's *A Sign of the Eighties* to Stephen King's *Misery,* unwed women shrink to sniveling spinsters or inflate to fire-breathing she-devils; renouncing all aspirations but marriage, they beg for wedding bands from strangers or swing axes at reluctant bachelors. Even Erica Jong's high-flying independent heroine literally crashes by the end of the decade, as the author supplants *Fear of Flying*'s saucy Isadora Wing, an exuberant symbol of female sexual emancipation in the seventies, with an embittered careerist-turned-recovering-"codependent" in *Any Woman's Blues*—a book that is intended, as the narrator bluntly states, "to demonstrate what a dead end the so-called sexual revolution had become and how desperate so-called free women were in the last few years of our decadent epoch."

Popular psychology manuals peddle the same diagnosis for contemporary female distress. "Feminism, having promised her a stronger sense of her own identity, has given her little more than an identity *crisis*," the best-selling advice manual *Being a Woman* asserts. The authors of the era's self-help classic, *Smart Women/Foolish Choices*, proclaim that women's distress was "an unfortunate consequence of feminism" because "it created a myth among women that the apex of self-realization could be achieved only through autonomy, independence, and career."

In the Reagan and Bush years, government officials have needed no 10 prompting to endorse this thesis. Reagan spokeswoman Faith Ryan Whittlesey declared feminism a "straightjacket" for women, in one of the White House's only policy speeches on the status of the American female population—entitled "Radical Feminism in Retreat." The U.S. attorney general's Commission on Pornography even proposed that women's professional advancement might be responsible for rising rape rates: With more women in college and at work now, the commission members reasoned in their report, women just have more opportunities to be raped.

Legal scholars have railed against the "equality trap." Sociologists have claimed that "feminist-inspired" legislative reforms have stripped women of special "protections." Economists have argued that well-paid working women have created a "less stable American family." And demographers, with greatest fanfare, have legitimated the prevailing wisdom with so-called neutral data on sex ratios and fertility trends; they say they actually have the numbers to prove that equality doesn't mix with marriage and motherhood.

Finally, some "liberated" women themselves have joined the lamentations. In *The Cost of Loving: Women and the New Fear of Intimacy*, Megan Marshall, a Harvard-pedigreed writer, asserts that the feminist "Myth of Independence" has turned her generation into unloved and unhappy fast-trackers, "dehumanized" by careers and "uncertain of their gender identity." Other diaries of mad Superwomen charge that "the hard-core feminist viewpoint," as one of them puts it, has relegated educated executive achievers to solitary nights of frozen dinners and closet drinking. The triumph of equality, they report, has merely given women hives, stomach cramps, eye "twitching" disorders, even comas.

But what "equality" are all these authorities talking about?

If American women are so equal, why do they represent two-thirds of all poor adults? Why are more than 70 percent of full-time working women making less than twenty-five thousand dollars a year, nearly double the number of men at that level? Why are they still far more likely than men to live in poor housing, and twice as likely to draw no pension? If women "have it all," then why don't they have the most basic requirements to achieve equality in the work force; unlike that of virtually all other industrialized nations, the U.S. government still has no family-leave and child-care programs.

If women are so "free," why are their reproductive freedoms in greater   15
jeopardy today than a decade earlier? Why, in their own homes, do they still shoulder 70 percent of the household duties—while the only other major change in the last fifteen years is that now men *think* they do more around the house? In thirty states, it is still generally legal for husbands to rape their wives; and only ten states have laws mandating arrest for domestic violence—even though battering is the leading cause of injury to women (greater than rapes, muggings, and auto accidents combined).

The word may be that women have been "liberated," but women themselves seem to feel otherwise. Repeatedly in national surveys, majorities of women say they are still far from equality. In poll after poll in the decade, overwhelming majorities of women said they need equal pay and equal job opportunities, they need an Equal Rights Amendment, they need the right to an abortion without government interference, they need a federal law guaranteeing maternity leave, they need decent child-care services. They have none of these. So how exactly have women "won" the war for women's rights?

Seen against this background, the much ballyhooed claim that feminism is responsible for making women miserable becomes absurd—and irrelevant. The afflictions ascribed to feminism, from "the man shortage" to "the infertility epidemic" to "female burnout" to "toxic day care," have had their origins not in the actual conditions of women's lives but rather in a closed system that starts and ends in the media, popular culture, and advertising—an endless feedback loop that perpetuates and exaggerates its own false images of womanhood. And women don't see feminism as their enemy, either. In fact, in national surveys, 75 to 95 percent of women credit the feminist campaign with *improving* their lives and a similar proportion say that the women's movement should keep pushing for change.

If the many ponderers of the Woman Question really wanted to know what is troubling the American female population, they might have asked their subjects. In public-opinion surveys, women consistently rank their own *inequality*, at work and at home, among their most urgent concerns. Over and over, women complain to pollsters of a lack of economic, not marital, opportunities; they protest that working men, not working women, fail to spend time in the nursery and the kitchen. It is justice for their gender, not wedding rings and bassinets, that women believe to be in desperately short supply.

As the last decade ran its course, the monitors that serve to track slippage in women's status have been working overtime. Government and private surveys are showing that women's already vast representation in the lowliest occupations is rising, their tiny presence in higher-paying trade and craft jobs stalled or backsliding, their miniscule representation in upper management posts stagnant or falling, and their pay dropping in the very occupations where they have made the most "progress."

In national politics, the already small numbers of women in both elective posts and political appointments fell during the eighties. In private life, the average amount that a divorced man paid in child support fell by about 25 percent from the late seventies to the mid-eighties (to a mere $140 a month). And government records chronicled a spectacular rise in sexual violence against women. Reported rapes more than doubled from the early seventies—at nearly twice the rate of all other violent crimes and four times the overall crime rate in the United States.   20

The truth is that the last decade has seen a powerful counterassault on women's rights, a backlash, an attempt to retract the handful of small and hard-won victories that the feminist movement did manage to win for women. This counterassault is largely insidious; in a kind of pop-culture version of the big lie, it stands the truth boldly on its head and proclaims that the very steps that have elevated women's position have actually led to their downfall.

The backlash is at once sophisticated and banal, deceptively "progressive" and proudly backward. It deploys both the "new" findings of "scientific research" and the dime-store moralism of yesteryear. It turns into media sound bites both the glib pronouncements of pop-psych trend-watchers and the frenzied rhetoric of New Right preachers. The backlash has succeeded in framing virtually the whole issue of women's rights in its own language. Just as Reaganism shifted political discourse far to the right and demonized liberalism, so the backlash convinced the public that women's "liberation" was the true contemporary scourge—the source of an endless laundry list of personal, social, and economic problems.

But what has made women unhappy in the last decade is not their "equality"—which they don't yet have—but the rising pressure to halt, and even reverse, women's quest for that equality. The "man shortage" and the "infertility epidemic" are not the price of liberation; in fact, they do not even exist. But these chimeras are part of a relentless whittling-down process—much of it amounting to outright propaganda—that has served to stir women's private anxieties and break their political wills. Identifying feminism as women's enemy only furthers the ends of a backlash against women's equality by simultaneously deflecting attention from the backlash's central role and recruiting women to attack their own cause.

SUGGESTIONS FOR FURTHER STUDY

Key Words

The author uses language with which you may not be familiar. Find the following words in the paragraphs indicated, and explain their meanings in the context of the sentences in which the words appear. Consult a dictionary, as needed.

unprecedented (par. 4)
emancipated (par. 8)
harpies (par. 8)
codependent (par. 8)
ballyhooed (par. 17)
rhetoric (par. 22)
chimeras (par. 23)

Topics for Discussion and Writing

1. In the first paragraph, Faludi says "To be a woman in America at the close of the twentieth century—what good fortune." What examples does she provide to support that claim? After reading the entire essay, how would you characterize Faludi's tone, as revealed in paragraph 1?

2. What examples does Faludi give to illustrate the alleged "bulletin of despair" that some say infects women today. How does she show that "women are enslaved by their own liberation"?

3. According to Faludi, what problems have "the many ponderers of the Woman Question really wanted to know [concerning] what is troubling the American female population"?

4. One example of "backlash" is the proposal of the U.S. attorney general's Commission on Pornography that "women's professional advancement might be responsible for rising rape rates" because "women just have more opportunities to be raped." How is the logic of that statement flawed? What other reasons can you offer to suggest why rape rates have risen?

5. Faludi questions the legitimacy of the claim that women have achieved equality. What evidence does she use to support her argument? Do you agree or disagree with Faludi? Explain your answer.

6. According to Faludi, how is the backlash against the women's movement a "big lie"? Who does she think is responsible for supporting and encouraging the backlash?

7. Faludi mentions the difficulty modern Superwomen suffer in having to juggle a career and family and being a good significant partner. At the same time, critics of such women say they have helped create a less stable American family. In a journal entry or a short essay, discuss the Superwoman of contemporary life, including her ability to handle the many responsibilities of a liberated life. You may know (or know of)such a woman, whom you can use as an example.

8. Both men and women can be feminists and can support women's equality. Whether or not you see yourself as a feminist, write an essay discussing your plans for the future. You may either consider one of the following topics or create a topic of your own:

   a. If you are a woman, discuss your future plans for career, marriage, family, or some other life path, perhaps combining one or more of these aspects.

   b. If you are a man, discuss what kind of woman you most admire: one who balances family and career, or one whose work is exclusively dedicated either to family or to career.

   c. Whether you are a man or a woman, discuss your ideas about how women can best achieve equality with men in pursuit of meaningful careers.

Where I Come from Is Like This

Paula Gunn Allen

*Paula Gunn Allen (born in 1939), a Laguna Pueblo Sioux from New Mexico, writes about her American Indian heritage. A professor of English and American Indian literature at the University of California, Los Angeles, she has authored several volumes of poetry, a novel (*The Woman Who Owned the Shadows*), and many essays. This excerpt is taken from* The Sacred Hoop: Recovering the Feminine in American Indian Traditions *(1986), in which Allen describes the tribal influences that define the American Indian woman.*

I

Modern American Indian women, like their non-Indian sisters, are deeply engaged in the struggle to redefine themselves. In their struggle they must reconcile traditional tribal definitions of women with industrial and postindustrial non-Indian definitions. Yet while these definitions seem to be more or less mutually exclusive, Indian women must somehow harmonize and integrate both in their own lives.

An American Indian woman is primarily defined by her tribal identity. In her eyes, her destiny is necessarily that of her people, and her sense of herself as a woman is first and foremost prescribed by her tribe. The definitions of woman's roles are as diverse as tribal cultures in the Americas. In some she is devalued, in others she wields considerable power. In some she is a familial/clan adjunct, in some she is as close to autonomous as her economic circumstances and psychological traits permit. But in no tribal definitions is she perceived in the same way as are women in western industrial and postindustrial cultures.

In the west, few images of women form part of the cultural mythos, and these are largely sexually charged. Among Christians, the madonna is the female prototype, and she is portrayed as essentially passive: her contribution is simply that of birthing. Little else is attributed to her and she certainly possesses few of the characteristics that are attributed to mythic figures among Indian tribes. This image is countered (rather than balanced) by the witch-goddess/whore characteristics designed to reinforce cultural beliefs about women, as well as western adversarial and dualistic perceptions of reality.

The tribes see women variously, but they do not question the power of femininity. Sometimes they see women as fearful, sometimes peaceful, sometimes omnipotent and omniscient, but they never portray women as mindless, helpless, simple, or oppressed. And while the women in a given tribe, clan, or band may be all these things, the individual woman is provided with a variety of images of women from the interconnected supernatural, natural, and social worlds she lives in.

As a half-breed American Indian woman, I cast about in my mind for   5 negative images of Indian women, and I find none that are directed to Indian women alone. The negative images I do have are of Indians in general and in fact are more often of males than of females. All these images come to me from non-Indian sources, and they are always balanced by a positive image. My ideas of womanhood, passed on largely by my mother and grandmothers, Laguna Pueblo women, are about practicality, strength, reasonableness, intelligence, wit, and competence. I also remember vividly the women who came to my father's store, the women who held me and sang to me, the women at Feast Day, at Grab Days,* the women in the kitchen of my Cubero home, the women I grew up with; none of them appeared weak or helpless, none of them presented herself tentatively. I remember a certain reserve on those lovely brown faces; I remember the direct gaze of eyes framed by bright-colored shawls draped over their heads and cascading down their backs. I remember the clean cotton dresses and carefully pressed hand-embroidered aprons they always wore; I remember laughter and good food, especially the sweet bread and the oven bread they gave us. Nowhere in my mind is there a foolish woman, a dumb woman, a vain woman, or a plastic woman, though the Indian women I have known have shown a wide range of personal style and demeanor.

My memory includes the Navajo woman who was badly beaten by her Sioux husband; but I also remember that my grandmother abandoned her Sioux husband long ago. I recall the stories about the Laguna woman beaten regularly by her husband in the presence of her children so that the children would not believe in the strength and power of femininity. And I remember the women who drank, who got into fights with other women and with the men, and who often won those battles. I have memories of tired women, partying women, stubborn women, sullen women, amicable women, selfish women, shy women, and aggressive women. Most of all I remember the women who laugh and scold and sit uncomplaining in the long sun on feast days and who cook wonderful food on wood stoves, in beehive mud ovens, and over open fires outdoors.

Among the images of women that come to me from various tribes as well as my own are White Buffalo Woman, who came to the Lakota long

---

*Grab Days. Laguna ritual in which women throw food and small items to those who attend.

ago and brought them the religion of the Sacred Pipe which they still practice; Tinotzin the goddess who came to Juan Diego to remind him that she
still walked the hills of her people and sent him with her message, her
demand and her proof to the Catholic bishop in the city nearby. And from
Laguna I take the images of Yellow Woman, Coyote Woman, Grandmother
Spider (Spider Old Woman), who brought the light, who gave us weaving
and medicine, who gave us life. Among the Keres she is known as Thought
Woman who created us all and who keeps us in creation even now. I
remember Iyatiku, Earth Woman, Corn Woman, who guides and counsels
the people to peace and who welcomes us home when we cast off this coil
of flesh as huskers cast off the leaves that wrap the corn. I remember
Iyatiku's sister, Sun Woman, who held metals and cattle, pigs and sheep,
highways and engines and so many things in her bundle, who went away to
the east saying that one day she would return.

II

Since the coming of the Anglo-Europeans beginning in the fifteenth century, the fragile web of identity that long held tribal people secure has gradually
been weakened and torn. But the oral tradition has prevented the complete
destruction of the web, the ultimate disruption of tribal ways. The oral tradition is vital; it heals itself and the tribal web by adapting to the flow of the
present while never relinquishing its connection to the past. Its adaptability
has always been required, as many generations have experienced. Certainly
the modern American Indian woman bears slight resemblance to her forebears—at least on superficial examination—but she is still a tribal woman
in her deepest being. Her tribal sense of relationship to all that is continues
to flourish. And though she is at times beset by her knowledge of the enormous gap between the life she lives and the life she was raised to live, and
while she adapts her mind and being to the circumstances of her present life,
she does so in tribal ways, mending the tears in the web of being from
which she takes her existence as she goes.

My mother told me stories all the time, though I often did not recognize
them as that. My mother told me stories about cooking and childbearing;
she told me stories about menstruation and pregnancy; she told me stories
about gods and heroes, about fairies and elves, about goddesses and spirits;
she told me stories about the land and the sky, about cats and dogs, about
snakes and spiders; she told me stories about climbing trees and exploring
the mesas; she told me stories about going to dances and getting married;
she told me stories about dressing and undressing, about sleeping and waking; she told me stories about herself, about her mother, about her grandmother. She told me stories about grieving and laughing, about thinking and
doing; she told me stories about school and about people; about darning

and mending; she told me stories about turquoise and about gold; she told me European stories and Laguna stories; she told me Catholic stories and Presbyterian stories; she told me city stories and country stories; she told me political stories and religious stories. She told me stories about living and stories about dying. And in all of those stories she told me who I was, who I was supposed to be, whom I came from, and who would follow me. In this way she taught me the meaning of the words she said, that all life is a circle and everything has a place within it. That's what she said and what she showed me in the things she did and the way she lives.

Of course, through my formal, white, Christian education, I discovered   10
that other people had stories of their own—about women, about Indians, about fact, about reality—and I was amazed by a number of startling suppositions that others made about tribal customs and beliefs. According to the un-Indian, non-Indian view, for instance, Indians barred menstruating women from ceremonies and indeed segregated them from the rest of the people, consigning them to some space specially designed for them. This showed that Indians considered menstruating women unclean and not fit to enjoy the company of decent (nonmenstruating) people, that is, men. I was surprised and confused to hear this because my mother had taught me that white people had strange attitudes toward menstruation: they thought something was bad about it, that it meant you were sick, cursed, sinful, and weak and that you had to be very careful during that time. She taught me that menstruation was a normal occurrence, that I could go swimming or hiking or whatever else I wanted to do during my period. She actively scorned women who took to their beds, who were incapacitated by cramps, who "got the blues."

As I struggled to reconcile these very contradictory interpretations of American Indians' traditional beliefs concerning menstruation, I realized that the menstrual taboos were about power, not about sin or filth. My conclusion was later borne out by some tribes' own explanations, which, as you may well imagine, came as quite a relief to me.

The truth of the matter as many Indians see it is that women who are at the peak of their fecundity are believed to possess power that throws male power totally out of kilter. They emit such force that, in their presence, any male-owned or -dominated ritual or sacred object cannot do its usual task. For instance, the Lakota say that a menstruating woman anywhere near a yuwipi man, who is a special sort of psychic, spirit-empowered healer, for a day or so before he is to do his ceremony will effectively disempower him. Conversely, among many if not most tribes, important ceremonies cannot be held without the presence of women. Sometimes the ritual woman who empowers the ceremony must be unmarried and virginal so that the power she channels is unalloyed, unweakened by sexual arousal and penetration by a male. Other ceremonies require tumescent women, others the presence of mature women who have borne children, and still others depend for empowerment on post-menopausal women. Women may be segregated from the company of the whole band or village on certain occasions, but on certain occasions men are also segregated. In short, each ritual depends on a certain balance of power, and the positions of women within the phases of womanhood are used by tribal people to empower certain rites. This does not derive from a male-dominant view; it is not a ritual observance imposed on women by men. It derives from a tribal view of reality that distinguishes tribal people from feudal and industrial people.

Among the tribes, the occult power of women, inextricably bound to our hormonal life, is thought to be very great; many hold that we possess innately the blood-given power to kill—with a glance, with a step, or with a judicious mixing of menstrual blood into somebody's soup. Medicine women among the Pomo of California cannot practice until they are sufficiently mature; when they are immature, their power is diffuse and is likely to interfere with their practice until time and experience have it under control. So women of the tribes are not especially inclined to see themselves as poor helpless victims of male domination. Even in those tribes where something akin to male domination was present, women are perceived as powerful, socially, physically, and metaphysically. In times past, as in times present, women carried enormous burdens with aplomb. We were far indeed from the "weaker sex," the designation that white aristocratic sisters unhappily earned for us all.

I remember my mother moving furniture all over the house when she wanted it changed. She didn't wait for my father to come home and help— she just went ahead and moved the piano, a huge upright from the old days, the couch, the refrigerator. Nobody had told her she was too weak to do such things. In imitation of her, I would delight in loading trucks at my father's store with cases of pop or fifty-pound sacks of flour. Even when I was quite small I could do it, and it gave me a belief in my own physical strength that advancing middle age can't quite erase. My mother used to tell me about the Acoma Pueblo women she had seen as a child carrying huge ollas (water pots) on their heads as they wound their way up the tortuous stairwell carved into the face of the "Sky City" mesa, a feat I tried to imitate with books and tin buckets. ("Sky City" is the term used by the Chamber of Commerce for the mother village of Acoma, which is situated atop a high sandstone table mountain.) I was never very successful, but even the attempt reminded me that I was supposed to be strong and balanced to be a proper girl.

Of course, my mother's Laguna people are Keres Indian, reputed to be the last extreme mother-right people on earth. So it is no wonder that I got notably nonwhite notions about the natural strength and prowess of women. Indeed, it is only when I am trying to get non-Indian approval, recognition, or acknowledgment that my "weak sister" emotional and intellectual ploys get the better of my tribal woman's good sense. At such times I forget that I just moved the piano or just wrote a competent paper or just completed a financial transaction satisfactorily or have supported myself and my children for most of my adult life.

Nor is my contradictory behavior atypical. Most Indian women I know are in the same bicultural bind: we vacillate between being dependent and strong, self-reliant and powerless, strongly motivated and hopelessly insecure. We resolve the dilemma in various ways: some of us party all the time; some of us drink to excess; some of us travel and move around a lot; some of us land good jobs and then quit them; some of us engage in violent exchanges; some of us blow our brains out. We act in these destructive ways because we suffer from the societal conflicts caused by having to identify with two hopelessly opposed cultural definitions of women. Through this destructive dissonance we are unhappy prey to the self-disparagement common to, indeed demanded of, Indians living in the United States today. Our situation is caused by the exigencies of a history of invasion, conquest, and colonization whose searing marks are probably ineradicable. A popular bumper sticker on many Indian cars proclaims: "If You're Indian, You're In," to which I always find myself adding under my breath, "Trouble."

No Indian can grow to any age without being informed that her people were "savages" who interfered with the march of progress pursued by respectable, loving, civilized white people. We are the villains of the scenario when we are mentioned at all. We are absent from much of white history except when we are calmly, rationally, succinctly, and systematically dehumanized. On the few occasions we are noticed in any way other than as howling, bloodthirsty beings, we are acclaimed for our noble quaintness. In this definition, we are exotic curios. Our ancient arts and customs are used to draw tourist money to state coffers, into the pocketbooks and bank accounts of scholars, and into support of the American-in-Disneyland promoters' dream.

As a Roman Catholic child I was treated to bloody tales of how the savage Indians martyred the hapless priests and missionaries who went among them in an attempt to lead them to the one true path. By the time I was through high school I had the idea that Indians were people who had benefited mightily from the advanced knowledge and superior morality of the Anglo-Europeans. At least I had, perforce, that idea to lay beside the other one that derived from my daily experience of Indian life, an idea less dehumanizing and more accurate because it came from my mother and the other Indian people who raised me. That idea was that Indians are a people who don't tell lies, who care for their children and their old people. You never see an Indian orphan, they said. You always know when you're old that someone will take care of you—one of your children will. Then they'd list the old folks who were being taken care of by this child or that. No child is ever considered illegitimate among the Indians, they said. If a girl gets pregnant, the baby is still part of the family, and the mother is too. That's what they said, and they showed me real people who lived according to those principles.

Of course the ravages of colonization have taken their toll; there are orphans in Indian country now, and abandoned, brutalized old folks; there are even illegitimate children, though the very concept still strikes me as absurd. There are battered children and neglected children, and there are battered wives and women who have been raped by Indian men. Proximity to the "civilizing" effects of white Christians has not improved the moral quality of life in Indian country, though each group, Indian and white, explains the situation differently. Nor is there much yet in the oral tradition that can enable us to adapt to these inhuman changes. But a force is growing in that direction, and it is helping Indian women reclaim their lives. Their power, their sense of direction and of self will soon be visible. It is the force of the women who speak and work and write, and it is formidable.

Through all the centuries of war and death and cultural and psychic 20 destruction have endured the women who raise the children and tend the fires, who pass along the tales and the traditions, who weep and bury the dead, who are the dead, and who never forget. There are always the women, who make pots and weave baskets, who fashion clothes and cheer their children on at powwow, who make fry bread and piki bread, and corn soup and chili stew, who dance and sing and remember and hold within their hearts the dream of their ancient peoples—that one day the woman who thinks will speak to us again, and everywhere there will be peace. Meanwhile we tell the stories and write the books and trade tales of anger and woe and stories of fun and scandal and laugh over all manner of things that happen every day. We watch and we wait.

My great-grandmother told my mother: never forget you are Indian. And my mother told me the same thing. This, then, is how I have gone about remembering, so that my children will remember too.

SUGGESTIONS FOR FURTHER STUDY

Key Words

The author uses language with which you may not be familiar. Find the following words in the paragraphs indicated, and explain their meanings in the context of the sentences in which the words appear. Consult a dictionary, as needed.

adjunct (par. 2)
autonomous (par. 2)
mythos (par. 3)
adversarial (par. 3)

omnipotent (par. 4)
omniscient (par. 4)
incapacitated (par. 10)
fecundity (par. 12)
unalloyed (par. 12)
tumescent (par. 12)
diffuse (par. 13)
aplomb (par. 13)
dissonance (par. 16)
self-disparagement (par. 16)
exigencies (par. 16)
ineradicable (par. 16)

Language and Style

1. The author cites her mother's and other American Indian women's stories as a principal influence on her upbringing and awareness of her femininity. In describing this influence, the author uses rhythm and repetition among words, phrases, and sentences, imitating a storyteller's way of speaking. Find several examples of rhythmic prose and repetition in this selection, and discuss or write about the effect such writing produces on readers. Look particularly at the patterns of language in these paragraphs, but find other examples as well: par. 4, sentence 2; par. 9, sentences 2–5; and par. 20, sentences 1–2.

2. If you have read Martin Luther King, Jr.'s "I Have a Dream" (Chapter 7), compare the patterns of *parallelism* and repetition in that speech to the patterns in Allen's essay. What resemblances are there? What differences?

Topics for Discussion and Writing

1. In this essay, the author defines the American Indian woman. She begins by saying that the American Indian woman is "primarily defined by her tribal identity." Writers can define a term several ways: for instance, by using examples, contrasting the term with its opposite, defining what the term is *not,* associating the term with synonyms, or telling stories about the term's use. How does Allen develop her definition of the American Indian woman? Give several examples to illustrate your answer.

2. What images does the author recall from her childhood? What are the sources of those images? Discuss with other readers how the author views the effect of those images in shaping her self-concept as a woman.

3. The author points out her dual heritage, part American Indian, part non-Indian. How does she explain the conflict she experienced in reconciling those often opposing heritages? What does she mean by her "contradictory behavior"?

4. According to the author, what important differences are there between American Indian views of women and Anglo-European views of women? Examine Allen's distinction between those two views in terms of your own experience and knowledge, and either discuss your views with other readers or write a reflective journal entry expressing your views.

5. If you have read other personal accounts of culture consciousness in Chapter 6, compare Allen's discussion of her ethnic heritage with one or more of those accounts. You might choose Bulosan's "America Is in the Heart," Morrison's "A Slow Walk of Trees," Rodriguez's "Does America Still Exist?" Marshall's "From the Poets in the Kitchen," Houston's "Living in Two Cultures," or Tan's "Four Directions" from that chapter.

6. Write an essay describing the influences that shaped your understanding of yourself as a man or a woman. How did you develop your ideas of what it means to be feminine or masculine? Who in your family or community guided you in developing those ideas of self-identification? What images in your memory help you recall those influences? Describe those influences and images clearly, and define your terms carefully.

Pink Does Not the Girl (or Boy) Make

Robin Abcarian

Robin Abcarian (born in 1956 in Oakland, California) received her BA at the University of California, Berkeley, and her MS from Boston University. She has worked as a columnist and news reporter at the Los Angeles Times, *the* Detroit Free Press, *and the* Los Angeles Daily News. *Among her journalistic awards is the Gay and Lesbian Alliance Against Defamation Media Award for Outstanding Los Angeles Print Media. "Pink Does Not the Girl (or Boy) Make" was published in 1996, in the* Los Angeles Times.

Surveying the heap of unidentifiable plastic toy parts, doll limbs and stuffed animals in her daughter's room, the mother sadly noted that with Christmas fewer than two months gone, it was already impossible to remember what Santa had brought. 1

Was that pink Minnie Mouse umbrella new? Or had the child owned it forever?

What about the pink dolly stroller? It was missing a couple of wheels, but most of the Christmas toys had fallen apart before New Year's, hadn't they?

And what was with all the pink stuff anyhow?

This child, the mother had sworn, was not going to have her femininity forced upon her. She would not be swaddled in pink. Barbie would be neither her physical role model nor her constant companion. And no one, nohow, was going to call this kid "princess." 5

Easier to fight the moon's pull on the tides.

All the baby hand-me-downs were bordered in lace and tied up in pink bows. Her first busty blond doll was sneaked under the tree by a doting relative.

And as for royal nicknames—princess, schmincess.

Last weekend, incarcerated by the rain, the mother and her daughter baked a batch of oatmeal cookies, then hosted a tea for the stuffed animals in the living room.

"OK, Mommy," said the girl as she poured a cup, "you are Your Majesty, and I am the Fween of England." 10

Indeed. With the title of princess sullied by tales of marital discord, eating disorders and self-mutilation, who can blame the child for aiming a few rungs higher?

Before I became a parent, I had a lot of fascinating theories about children and gender identity. I thought by careful clothing, toy and video selection, a parent could actually exercise some sort of influence on how a girl expresses her femininity.

Part of my job would be to protect her from gender stereotyping, to correct her thinking when she announced, "Only girls cook," or, "Only boys hit." (But that's hypocritical, since I make those judgments all the time, and for the last 15 years have vainly tried to convince her father that "Only boys take out the garbage.")

Trying to fight chromosomes is not only pointless but stupid. Much of the attraction of girls to pink, as far as I can tell, is biological and will out no matter what. Anyhow, I want her to love being a girl as much as I do.

My child has never seen "Mighty Morphin Power Rangers" on televi-   15
sion, but she possesses detailed knowledge of these B-grade teen characters. I suspect she comes by her facts courtesy of the toddler underground at the local park.

The other day, as she chopped the air with karate blows, she announced with utter confidence: "I am a Powder Ranger! . . . I am the PINK Powder Ranger."

"That's right!" I was horrified to hear myself say.

My job is to help her navigate the world as safely as possible, to guide her as she grows into a self-possessed creature who is compassionate and independent.

It is not my responsibility to raise her in a pink-free environment.

This, I imagine, is where Angelyne's parents went wrong.   20

We recently found ourselves in a toy store, my kid and I, bedazzled by the sheer pinkness of the girl toy aisles. Now here is a place where the gender lines are drawn in indelible ink.

In girl aisles, you find infinite numbers of dolls and games such as "Sealed With a Kiss," where the object is to stamp a kiss on a picture of a "hunk" more times than the other girls, and "Dream Phone," a (what else) pink plastic telephone for dialing a girl's "secret admirer."

Boy aisles are dark and "dolls" is a dirty word. ("Action figure," to you, pal.) You will not find games in the boy aisles that involve dates, kisses or romance in any form.

What this tells us about our children is what we already know: that girls judge themselves by their relationships to peers and others, while boys judge themselves by how much Gak they can shove up the other kid's nose before he stops breathing.

As I stood at a wall of Disney-based toys, immersed in my Pocahontas   25 dilemma (Should I buy my daughter the fake buckskin dress? / Would John Smith be attracted to me?), somebody's daddy approached.

Inside his shopping cart was a big cardboard box that held a pink toy shopping cart.

"Excuse me," he said, looking worried. "Do you think I will ruin a boy by giving this to him?" He gestured at the pink cart.

I thought he was joking. But the look on his face telegraphed a faith in the universe of uncrossable gender lines, where girls shop in pink aisles and boys shop in dark aisles and woe to the (father of the) child who goes astray.

I laughed: "Hey, you're pushing a cart and you aren't ruined!"

But I understood his concern. What he wanted was reassurance: No,   30 mister, just because your kid pushes a pink cart doesn't mean he'll want to be the Fween of England.

SUGGESTIONS FOR FURTHER STUDY

Key Words

The author uses language with which you may not be familiar. Find the following words in the paragraphs indicated, and explain their meanings in the context of the sentences in which the words appear. Consult a dictionary, as needed.

incarcerated (par. 9)
sullied (par. 11)
stereotyping (par. 13)
chromosomes (par. 14)
dilemma (par. 25)

Topics for Discussion and Writing

1. In the fictional scenario about mother and daughter, what is the mother adamant about doing, and what actually happens?
2. When Abcarian states that "the title of princess [is] sullied by tales of marital discord, eating disorders and self-mutilation," to whom might she be referring?
3. As a parent, Abcarian thought she knew how to deal with gender identity. How does she try to shape her daughter's femininity and "protect her from gender stereotyping"?
4. What does Abcarian feel is and is not her job as a parent?

5. What examples of gender stereotyping does Abcarian find at the toy store?

6. Write a descriptive paper, or discuss in groups, other examples of gender stereotyping you have noticed in your life or on TV and in other media. You may want to go into a toy store and look for examples of gender stereotyping, or look around your own home or that of a friend or relative who has children. Look particularly at toys in those homes, and try to determine their purpose.

7. Abcarian thinks gender identity may in part be biological—that is, chromosomes may determine gender identity as much as does socialization. Research what sociologists and psychologists currently believe to be biological components of gender identity and what components may be socialized or learned. Then write an informative essay on the subject, adding your own ideas about how gender identity is determined in boys and girls. Besides researching this subject in the library, use the Internet and the World Wide Web to search for up-to-date information.

Sex, Lies, and Conversation

Deborah Tannen

*Deborah Tannen (born in 1945) is currently a professor of linguistics
at Georgetown University. Her many essays have appeared in the*
Washington Post, *the* New York Times, *and other publications. "Sex,
Lies, and Conversation" is adapted from the best-known of her ten
books,* You Just Don't Understand: Women and Men in Conversation.

I was addressing a small gathering in a suburban Virginia living room—
a women's group that had invited men to join them. Throughout the
evening, one man had been particularly talkative, frequently offering ideas
and anecdotes, while his wife sat silently beside him on the couch. Toward
the end of the evening, I commented that women frequently complain that
their husbands don't talk to them. This man quickly concurred. He gestured
toward his wife and said, "She's the talker in our family." The room burst
into laughter; the man looked puzzled and hurt. "It's true," he explained.
"When I come home from work I have nothing to say. If she didn't keep the
conversation going, we'd spend the whole evening in silence."

This episode crystallizes the irony that although American men tend to
talk more than women in public situations, they often talk less at home.
And this pattern is wreaking havoc with marriage.

The pattern was observed by political scientist Andrew Hacker in the
late '70s. Sociologist Catherine Kohler Riessman reports in her new book
Divorce Talk that most of the women she interviewed—but only a few of
the men—gave lack of communication as the reason for their divorces.
Given the current divorce rate of nearly 50 percent, that amounts to millions of cases in the United States every year—a virtual epidemic of failed
conversation.

In my own research, complaints from women about their husbands
most often focused not on tangible inequities such as having given up the
chance for a career to accompany a husband to his, or doing far more than
their share of daily life-support work like cleaning, cooking, social arrange-
ments and errands. Instead, they focused on communication: "He doesn't
listen to me," "He doesn't talk to me." I found, as Hacker observed years
before, that most wives want their husbands to be, first and foremost, conversational partners, but few husbands share this expectation of their wives.

In short, the image that best represents the current crisis is the stereo- 5 typical cartoon scene of a man sitting at the breakfast table with a newspaper held up in front of his face, while a woman glares at the back of it, wanting to talk.

LINGUISTIC BATTLE OF THE SEXES

How can women and men have such different impressions of communication in marriage? Why the widespread imbalance in their interests and expectations?

In the April [1990] issue of *American Psychologist,* Stanford University's Eleanor Maccoby reports the results of her own and others' research showing that children's development is most influenced by the social structure of peer interactions. Boys and girls tend to play with children of their own gender, and their sex-separate groups have different organizational structures and interactive norms.

I believe these systematic differences in childhood socialization make talk between women and men like cross-cultural communication, heir to all the attraction and pitfalls of that enticing but difficult enterprise. My research on men's and women's conversations uncovered patterns similar to those described for children's groups.

For women, as for girls, intimacy is the fabric of relationships, and talk is the thread from which it is woven. Little girls create and maintain friendships by exchanging secrets; similarly, women regard conversation as the cornerstone of friendship. So a woman expects her husband to be a new and improved version of a best friend. What is important is not the individual subjects that are discussed but the sense of closeness, of a life shared, that emerges when people tell their thoughts, feelings, and impressions.

Bonds between boys can be as intense as girls', but they are based less 10 on talking, more on doing things together. Since they don't assume talk is the cement that binds a relationship, men don't know what kind of talk women want, and they don't miss it when it isn't there.

Boys' groups are larger, more inclusive, and more hierarchical, so boys must struggle to avoid the subordinate position in the group. This may play a role in women's complaints that men don't listen to them. Some men really don't like to listen, because being the listener makes them feel one down, like a child listening to adults or an employee to a boss.

But often when women tell men, "You aren't listening," and the men protest, "I am," the men are right. The impression of not listening results from misalignment in the mechanics of conversation. The misalignment begins as soon as a man and a woman take physical positions. This became clear when I studied videotapes made by psychologist Paul Dorval of children and adults talking to their same-sex best friends. I found that at every age, the girls and women faced each other directly, their eyes anchored on each other's faces. At every age, the boys and men sat at angles to each other and looked elsewhere in the room, periodically glancing at each other. They were obviously attuned to each other, often mirroring each other's movements. But the tendency of men to face away can give women the impression they aren't listening even when they are. A young woman in college was frustrated: Whenever she told her boyfriend she wanted to talk to him, he would lie down on the floor, close his eyes, and put his arm over his face. This signaled to her, "He's taking a nap." But he insisted he was listening extra hard. Normally, he looks around the room, so he is easily distracted. Lying down and covering his eyes helped him concentrate on what she was saying.

Analogous to the physical alignment that women and men take in conversation is their topical alignment. The girls in my study tended to talk at length about one topic, but the boys tended to jump from topic to topic. The second-grade girls exchanged stories about people they knew. The second-grade boys teased, told jokes, noticed things in the room and talked about finding games to play. The sixth-grade girls talked about problems with a mutual friend. The sixth-grade boys talked about fifty-five different topics, none of which extended over more than a few turns.

LISTENING TO BODY LANGUAGE

Switching topics is another habit that gives women the impression men aren't listening, especially if they switch to a topic about themselves. But the evidence of the tenth-grade boys in my study indicates otherwise. The tenth-grade boys sprawled across their chairs with bodies parallel and eyes straight ahead, rarely looking at each other. They looked as if they were riding in a car, staring out the windshield. But they were talking about their feelings. One boy was upset because a girl had told him he had a drinking problem, and the other was feeling alienated from all his friends.

Now, when a girl told a friend about a problem, the friend responded [15] by asking probing questions and expressing agreement and understanding. But the boys dismissed each other's problems. Todd assured Richard that his drinking was "no big problem" because "sometimes you're funny when you're off your butt." And when Todd said he felt left out, Richard responded, "Why should you? You know more people than me."

Women perceive such responses as belittling and unsupportive. But the boys seemed satisfied with them. Whereas women reassure each other by implying, "You shouldn't feel bad because I've had similar experiences," men do so by implying, "You shouldn't feel bad because your problems aren't so bad."

There are even simpler reasons for women's impression that men don't listen. Linguist Lyrlette Hirschman found that women make more listener noise, such as "mhm," "uhuh," and "yeah," to show "I'm with you." Men, she found, more often give silent attention. Women who expect a stream of listener noise interpret silent attention as no attention at all.

Women's conversational habits are as frustrating to men as men's are to women. Men who expect silent attention interpret a stream of listener noise as overreaction or impatience. Also, when women talk to each other in a close, comfortable setting, they often overlap, finish each other's sentences and anticipate what the other is about to say. This practice, which I call "participatory listenership," is often perceived by men as interruption, intrusion, and lack of attention.

A parallel difference caused a man to complain about his wife, "She just wants to talk about her own point of view. If I show her another view, she gets mad at me." When most women talk to each other, they assume a conversationalist's job is to express agreement and support. But many men see their conversational duty as pointing out the other side of an argument. This is heard as disloyalty by women, and refusal to offer the requisite support. It is not that women don't want to see other points of view, but that they prefer them phrased as suggestions and inquiries rather than as direct challenges.

In his book *Fighting for Life,* Walter Ong points out that men use "agonistic" or warlike, oppositional formats to do almost anything; thus discussion becomes debate and conversation becomes a competitive sport. In contrast, women see conversation as a ritual means of establishing rapport. If Jane tells a problem and June says she has a similar one, they walk away feeling closer to each other. But this attempt at establishing rapport can backfire when used with men. Men take too literally women's ritual "troubles talk," just as women mistake men's ritual challenges for real attack. 20

THE SOUNDS OF SILENCE

These differences begin to clarify why women and men have such different expectations about communication in marriage. For women, talk creates intimacy. Marriage is an orgy of closeness: you can tell your feelings and thoughts, and still be loved. Their greatest fear is being pushed away. But men live in a hierarchical world, where talk maintains independence and status. They are on guard to protect themselves from being put down and pushed around.

This explains the paradox of the talkative man who said of his silent wife, "She's the talker." In the public setting of a guest lecture, he felt challenged to show his intelligence and display his understanding of the lecture. But at home, where he has nothing to prove and no one to defend against, he is free to remain silent. For his wife, being home means she is free from the worry that something she says might offend someone, or spark disagreement, or appear to be showing off; at home she is free to talk.

The communication problems that endanger marriage can't be fixed by mechanical engineering. They require a new conceptual framework about the role of talk in human relationships. Many of the psychological explanations that have become second nature may not be helpful, because they tend to blame either women (for not being assertive enough) or men (for not being in touch with their feelings). A sociolinguistic approach by which male–female conversation is seen as cross-cultural communication allows us to understand the problem and forge solutions without blaming either party.

Once the problem is understood, improvement comes naturally, as it did to the young woman and her boyfriend who seemed to go to sleep when she wanted to talk. Previously, she had accused him of not listening, and he had refused to change his behavior, since that would be admitting fault. But then she learned about and explained to him the differences in women's and men's habitual ways of aligning themselves in conversation. The next time she told him she wanted to talk, he began, as usual, by lying down and covering his eyes. When the familiar negative reaction bubbled up, she reassured herself that he really was listening. But then he sat up and looked at her. Thrilled, she asked why. He said, "You like me to look at you when we talk, so I'll try to do it." Once he saw their differences as cross-cultural rather than right and wrong, he independently altered his behavior.

Women who feel abandoned and deprived when their husbands won't 25 listen to or report daily news may be happy to discover their husbands trying to adapt once they understand the place of small talk in women's relationships. But if their husbands don't adapt, the women may still be comforted that for men, this is not a failure of intimacy. Accepting the difference, the wives may look to their friends or family for that kind of talk. And husbands who can't provide it shouldn't feel their wives have made unreasonable demands. Some couples will still decide to divorce, but at least their decisions will be based on realistic expectations.

In these times of resurgent ethnic conflicts, the world desperately needs cross-cultural understanding. Like charity, successful cross-cultural communication should begin at home.

SUGGESTIONS FOR FURTHER STUDY

Key Words

The author uses language with which you may not be familiar. Find the following words in the paragraphs indicated, and explain their meanings in the context of the sentences in which the words appear. Consult a dictionary, as needed.

wreaking (par. 2)
socialization (par. 8)
hierarchical (par. 11)
misalignment (par. 12)
analogous (par. 13)
participatory (par. 18)
requisite (par. 19)
paradox (par. 22)
resurgent (par. 26)

Topics for Discussion and Writing

1. According to Tannen, what is the divorce rate in the United States? What reason does she give for it, and how does she support her argument?

2. Explain the differences in childhood socialization, as Tannen discusses the topic. How is "intimacy the fabric of relationships for girls," and what is the basis for boys' relationships? How do boys and girls respond differently to each other's problems?

3. Explain "participatory listenership" in your own words. How do men and women perceive their "conversational duty" differently? What reasons can you think of to explain men's silences or unwillingness to communicate with women, other than those Tannen cites?

4. Tannen proposes a solution to what might be termed *dysfunctional relationship dynamics*. She says that "communication problems that endanger marriage can't be fixed by mechanical engineering," but "require a new conceptual framework." What is the new conceptual framework she has in mind? Based on your own observations of family, friends, and acquaintances, how workable a solution do you think Tannen's conceptual framework might be?

5. Write an analytical paper in which you stress reasons other than those Tannen provides for communication patterns among boys and girls, men and women. You will want to research the fields of sociology and biology to learn about the behavioral patterns of men and women under current social conditions (e.g., family dynamics and the influence of friendship communities and of addiction to alcohol and other drugs). You may want to undertake a more anthropological study of gender relations in hunter–gatherer societies, as a way of locating the historical roots of human social relationships. Draw from your studies in other disciplines to find material and ideas for developing your paper.

Gender Roles

Bethany Dever

In this selection, student writer Bethany Dever describes "differences between the sexes" and gender-role distinctions based on cultural assumptions, and she offers her own ideas on how members of society should correct their judgments and perceptions.

Most societies commonly assume that differences between the sexes are inherent: physical, biological, genetic, and physiological differences. Such an assumption ignores differences among men and among women, while perpetuating stereotypes about differences between men and women. People acquire their ability to fulfill their gender roles by learning particular social behaviors, not by expressing inborn characteristics.

Changing cultural standards are useful in explaining human traits formerly thought to be sex linked. The development of distinctive motherhood/fatherhood gender roles came about in preindustrial societies. In *Introduction to Sociology,* Henry Tishler contends that

> The [preindustrial] woman's life is characterized by a continuing cycle of pregnancy, childbearing, and nursing for periods of up to three years. By the time the child is weaned, the mother is likely to be pregnant again. Not until menopause, which frequently coincides with the end of the woman's life itself, is her reproduction role over. In these circumstances it is not surprising that such activities as hunting, fighting, and forest clearing usually are defined as male tasks; whereas gathering grains and vegetables, preparing of small game, tending gardens, and building shelters are typically female activities, as is caring for the young. (220–221)

This description provides an example of a woman's role as biologically determined for the purpose of survival. Now, in modern society, these role distinctions are far less needed, but because we still maintain these distinctions, we think of them as natural or inborn. . . . The socialization of gender roles can also be seen by observing other cultures. In some cultures, women work alongside men, doing laborious work because women are considered to be physically equal to men.

Many religions around the world teach that males are superior to women by nature. As Tishler explains, "The Judeo-Christian story of creation presents a God-ordained sex-role hierarchy, with man created in the image of God and woman a subsequent and secondary act of creation. Thus the man is superior to woman, who was created to assist man and bear his children" (217). The Catholic church doesn't allow women to be ordained as priests because men are considered to be closer to God. Women are told, instead, that they should seek meaning in their lives through motherhood. Similarly, Hinduism traditionally sees women as being sexual temptations testing male spirituality; therefore, women are deemed inferior. In some instances, historically, women could not wear certain types of clothing or participate in public affairs. The Muslim religion justifies women's low status by claiming that they are irrational and emotional by nature (218).

By the nineteenth century, because women were considered more emotional and sensitive than men, "hysteria" was thought to be a woman's disease. However, today we see hysteria in men—as well as women—who experience post traumatic stress syndrome (Herman 11). Whether Hispanic, Asian, Native American, European, African, male or female, we all have the same range of emotions. The only requirement is to be human. The way we *express* emotions is learned behavior among the sexes.

Society says boys shouldn't play with dolls. But without this practice of caregiving, boys become fathers who, unlike mothers, don't acquire the learned abilities of being sensitive caregivers, providing for a child's emotional needs. Women are taught that being attractive is part of their gender role; and although a slim figure is considered attractive in women, the desire to be slim is learned, not genetically determined. 5

When men express emotions such as fear, sadness, or love, or when they are involved in the arts, they are often labeled as being too feminine. When women are aggressive—intellectually or physically—they are often labeled as being too manly. Thus, we send messages that are incorporated into learned behavior. Deborah Tannen emphasizes this point in "Sex, Lies, and Conversation":

> In the April issue of *American Psychologist,* Stanford University's Eleanore Maccoby reports the results of her own and others' research showing that children's development is most influenced by the social structure of peer interactions. Boys and girls play with children of their own gender, and their sex-separate groups have different organizational structures and interactive norms.
>
> I believe these systematic differences in childhood socialization make talk between men and women like cross-cultural communication, heir to all the attraction and pitfalls of that enticing but difficult enterprise. (447)

Women and men certainly do possess biological, genetic differences. Women tend to live longer than men, for one thing. As Tishler points out, "Men are more likely to die or suffer serious disability or illnesses than women" (219). One reason for this characteristic may be because women respond differently to stress than do men. They *learn* (appropriately) to react more slowly to stress, relieving pressure on the blood vessels (220). On the other hand, men generally develop greater muscle capacity than women; because of this, women are taught, based on the assumption of physical ability, not to attempt certain tasks even though women as a rule possess greater stamina than men. Although female and male gender roles are not as distinct as they once were, there remain unequal distinctions between the sexes because traditional attitudes and expectations persist (224). Many examples of inequities of opportunity in the workplace can be found, where women, on average, are paid less for comparable work than men, and major professional sports teams don't allow competition between the sexes.

Sometimes our parents and peers, even the media we watch and read, send mixed messages to both sexes about gender role expectations. But as long as men and women lead happy, healthy, productive lives, it shouldn't matter how we express ourselves in terms of our gender. What we are taught about our gender roles is not part of our biological inheritance.

Works Cited

Herman, Judith Lewis. *Trauma and Recovery.* New York: HarperCollins, 1992.

Tannen, Deborah. "Sex, Lies and Conversations," in Murray, Patricia Y., and Scott Covell, *Living in America.* Mountain View, CA: Mayfield Publishing Co., 1998.

Tishler, Henry. *Introduction to Sociology.* Fort Worth, TX: Harcourt Brace Jovanovich College Publishers, 1993.

CHAPTER 8: ACTIVITIES FOR DISCUSSION AND WRITING
Making Connections

1. Here are several opportunities for research and writing. Choose one or more, as your instructor directs, and write a carefully documented paper on the topic:

   a. Write a paper about a little-known but important American woman. Many women in American history have made significant contributions to our culture but have received little credit or publicity about their achievements and are rarely discussed in traditional history books. In a sense, you will be doing your part to rewrite women back into history. Check with your instructor or a reference librarian for topic ideas.

   b. Write a research paper on some aspect of the feminist move-
      ment, discussed in "Blame It on Feminism" and other essays in
      this chapter. You might want to write about the roots of femi-
      nism, the women's suffrage movement, ethnic women's rights, or
      a particular feminist leader of the past.
   c. In "Pink Does Not the Girl (or Boy) Make," Abcarian discusses
      gender stereotyping reflected in toy stores and on the plaground.
      In an essay, analyze the stereotyping of women, men, or people
      of various ethnicities on television, in commercials, and in maga-
      zines. You may want to conduct research in all three mediums to
      compile data for your paper.

2. Write a paper about gender roles in America. You may want to
   focus on the roles for men or women, as student writer Bethany
   Dever did in "Gender Roles." Or you may want to explore the
   stereotyping of gays and lesbians in America and how they are fash-
   ioning their own gender roles.

3. In "Sex, Lies, and Conversation," Deborah Tannen suggests that
   "in these times of resurgent ethnic conflicts, the world desperately
   needs cross-cultural understanding." Write a paper describing an
   ethnic or religious conflict in America or in another part of the
   world, integrating Tannen's new conceptual framework for cross-
   cultural communication into a solution for that conflict. Instead,
   perhaps, focus on issues of cross-cultural or cross-gender communication on your campus, and offer some solutions for solving existing problems.

4. Write a paper discussing how women work to influence new policies and ways of thinking and organization in American society.
   You may want to research the idea of "communitarianism" and
   "the ethics of care," both of which offer ideas about how women
   work and think. Two books will help you explore this new perspective on women's ways of thinking and working: *Antigone's
   Daughters* by Jean Bethke Elshtain, and *Feminist Theory and the
   Democratic Community* by Carol C. Gould.

ISSUES IN AMERICA IV
Popular Music: Rock, Rap, and Repression

A major debate in America concerns what to do about controversial music: Do we label it, censor it, ignore it, or allow it to be freely distributed? The argument spills over into discussions about censorship of literature, movies, television, and art, and it involves the role our government can or should play in controlling citizens' access to popular entertainment. However, this chapter focuses on popular music in particular, dealing with the influence and effect of popular music on adults and young people, the question of labeling, the controversy over rap music, and the practice of censorship in the musical arts. At the heart of American experience is a love of many types of good music; the problem may be in defining what *good* music is and *who* is qualified to define it.

Dave Barry's humorous commentary, "Parents, Children, and Music to Slaughter Cattle By," kicks off this chapter by lampooning the age-old conflict between the musical interests of parents and those of their offspring. Robert Palmer's "What Pop Lyrics Say to Us Today" details an important aspect of popular music. Although written 12 years ago, Palmer's article is still contemporary in its theme. Allan Bloom assails rock music in general in "Rock Music Has Harmed American Youth," but well-known critic Henry Louis Gates, Jr., defends 2 Live Crew's work in "2 Live Crew Decoded." The next two essays offer a point–counterpoint argument, with Tipper Gore arguing for labeling in "Rock Music Should Be Labeled," and Danny Alexander arguing against it in "Labeling Rock Music Leads to Repression." Jesse Katz questions the hype behind the rap controversy in "Rap Furor: New Evil or Old Story?" Kurt Vonnegut then offers a coda for the professional writings in this chapter, in his ironic analysis, "A Final Commentary on Censorship from Kurt Vonnegut." Finally, our student writer Kathleen Santaro follows with "Censorship Follies: Was a Victory over Ice-T a Victory over Violence?"

Parents, Children, and Music to Slaughter Cattle By

Dave Barry

Dave Barry, a Pulitzer Prize–winning journalist for the Miami Herald, *lives in Miami, Florida. He has authored numerous best-sellers, including* The Taming of the Screw, Babies and Other Hazards of Sex, Stay Fit and Healthy until You're Dead, Claw Your Way to the Top, Dave Barry's Guide to Marriage and/or Sex, *and* Dave Barry in Cyberspace. *"Parents, Children, and Music to Slaughter Cattle By" is adapted from his best-selling* Dave Barry Turns 40 *(1990).*

We must remember that growth is not a "one-way street." As our chil- 1
dren grow, so must we grow to meet their changing emotional, intellectual, and designer-footwear needs. In this chapter we'll examine some of the challenges that we face as parental units entering middle age, a time when we are coming to the somber realization that we will not always be there to guide and direct our children, which is just as well, because this is also a time when our children are coming to the conclusion that we are unbelievable dorks.

One big reason for this, of course, is our taste in music. I'm assuming that you're like most of us Boomers in the sense that, musically, you have always considered yourself to be a Major Hipster. Why not? Hey, we were frontline troops in the Rock 'n' Roll Revolution, right? Damn straight! We were Born to Boogie. We grew up dancing the Twist, the Mashed Potato, the Boogaloo, the Jerk, the Watusi, the Pony, the Alligator, the Clam, and the Vicious Bloodsucking Insect. We knew the dirty words to "Louie Louie," including the ones that did not actually exist. We knew the Beach Boys when they could sing and Elvis when he was alive the *first* time. We knew the Beatles and the Stones when they were actual bands as opposed to multinational corporations. We were *there* during the legendary sixties, with visions and insights and lava lamps and black lights and sitar music and really *dynamite* home-grown weed that would get you high in only 178 tokes. We lit candles and sat around listening to John Lennon sing, with genuine passion in his voice, about how he was the egg man, and *they* were the egg men, and *he* was also the walrus, and by God we knew *exactly what he meant*. That was the level of hipness that we attained in My Generation. Oh sure, people tried to put us down, just because we got around. Our parents would come into our bedroom, where we were listening to the opening guitar lick of "Purple Haze" with the stereo cranked up loud enough to be audible on Mars (which is where Jimi Hendrix originated) and they'd hold their hands over their ears and make a face as though they were passing a kidney stone the size of a volleyball and they'd shout: "You call that *music*? That sounds like somebody strangling a *cat*." Our parents' idea of swinging music was Frank Sinatra snapping his fingers in front of sixty-seven guys who looked like your dentist playing the trombone. Our parents danced *holding hands,* for God's sake. They did the "fox trot," which was invented by the Phoenicians. They were totally Out Of It, our parents. Hopeless. They were so square they thought that people, other than Maynard G. Krebs, actually *used* words like "square." As Bob Dylan, who was so hip that sometimes even *he* didn't understand what he meant, put it: "Something is happening here, and you don't know what it is, do you, Mr. Jones?" That was our parents: Mr. and Mrs. Jones. But not us. We *defined* hip. We set all kinds of world hipness records, and we were sure they'd never be broken.

Then came the seventies, and the major new musical trends were (1) disco, which consisted of one single song approximately 14,000 minutes long; and (2) heavy metal, which consisted of skinny, hostile, pockmarked men wearing outfits that looked as though they had smeared toxic waste on their bodies, playing what sounded like amplified jackhammers and shrieking unintelligibly at auditoriums full of whooping, sweating, hyperactive, boot-wearing, tattooed people who indicated their approval by giving each other head injuries with chairs. We old-time rock 'n' rollers looked at this scene, and we said, "Nah." We were sure it would pass. So we played our Buffalo Springfield albums and our Motown dance tapes, and we waited for the day when good music, *hip* music, would become popular again.

By the eighties, a lot of radio stations, realizing the size of the market out there, had started playing sixties music again. They called it "classic rock," because they knew we'd be upset if they came right out and called it what it is, namely "middle-aged-person nostalgia music." It's a very popular format now. You drive through a major urban area and push the "scan" button on your car radio, and you'll probably hear a dozen "classic rock" stations, ten of which will be playing "Doo-wah diddy diddy." (The other two will be playing *commercials* featuring "Doo-wah diddy diddy.") We hear "classic rock" being played constantly in elevators, department stores, offices, churches, operating rooms, the space shuttle, etc. Almost every sixties group with at least one remaining non-dead member has reunited and bought new dentures and gone on tour, sometimes using special guitars equipped with walkers.

And so, because we represent the world's largest consumer horde, we get to hear Our Music all the time. We're wrapped in a snug, warm cocoon of sixtiesness, and we actually think that we're still With It. Whereas in fact we are nowhere near It. The light leaving from It right now will not reach us

5

for several years. I've become intensely aware of this through my son, who, despite constant exposure to my taste in music, does NOT choose to listen to "classic rock." When he's in control of the radio, he tunes it to a different kind of music, a new kind of music, a *now* kind of music that can only be described—and I do not mean to be making any value judgments here—as "stupid."

If you have kids, you probably know the music I mean. It sounds as though an evil scientist had gone into his laboratory and, for some insane reason, *combined disco with heavy metal*. It has no melody and hardly any words; it consists almost entirely of bass notes registering 7.4 on the Richter scale. It's music to slaughter cattle by. It's the kind of music you hear emanating from refrigerator-sized boom boxes and black 1974 Camaros that have windows tinted so dark you could safely view a solar eclipse through them and sound systems so powerful that with every beat the sides of the car actually bulge outward, like in a Warner Brothers cartoon, such that you can't imagine how any form of life could survive in there. If you're unfamiliar with this kind of music, hold this page right up close to your ear for a second and I'll play a sample for you:

> BOOM boom BOOM boom BOOM boom BOOM!
> BOOM boom BOOM boom BOOM boom BOOM!
> BOOM boom BOOM boom BOOM boom BOOM!
> BOOM boom BOOM boom BOOM boom BOOM!
>   (repeat chorus)

Isn't that *awful*? That's what my son likes to listen to. This leads to conflict when we're in the car. He'll push the radio button for BOOM boom BOOM etc., and then I, in a loving parental effort to guide him toward a more sophisticated and meaningful cultural experience, will thoughtfully swat his hand aside and push the button for Doo-wah diddy diddy. Then he'll lean back in his seat and look at me with exactly the same disgusted look that I aimed at my parents thirty years ago when they made me take my Buddy Holly 45s off of our RCA phonograph so they could play Rosemary Clooney.

And I think: Something is happening here, and I don't know what it is. And neither does Bob Dylan.

SUGGESTIONS FOR FURTHER STUDY

Language and Style

1. How would you describe Barry's tone in this piece: caustic, scholarly, humorous, satirical, or a combination of several tones? Explain by citing several passages that convey his tone.

2. Discuss those features of Barry's writing style that produce a humorous effect. Notice particularly his specific examples, his descriptions of parents' and children's tastes in music, and his exaggerations.

Topics for Discussion and Writing

1. According to Barry, what was the 1960s like? Drawing on what you know about that decade, is his description accurate? Explain.

2. What was Barry's parents' reaction to his music of the 1960s?

3. How does Barry describe the music of the 1970s and the 1980s? What is Barry's ironic situation as he writes this article?

4. In a journal entry or in discussion with other readers, describe a type of music you do not like. Adopting Barry's style to the extent possible, write a brief essay about that type of music.

5. Describe a situation in which you disagreed strongly with your parents, friends, or children about a particular piece of music or a specific type of music. What led to the difference between your taste in music and theirs?

6. Write an essay based on your research of popular music of the 1960s in America, arguably the most important decade for rock and roll and for rhythm and blues. Narrow your topic to one specific type of music: rock and roll, rhythm and blues, blues, country, country/folk rock, or another type. Mention the important artists of the musical type you chose, and discuss the most representative songs of that type. If you want, you can focus on a particular event (e.g., Woodstock) or a particular artist or group of artists (e.g., Jim Morrison, Aretha Franklin, or the Beatles) as a means of developing your essay.

What Pop Lyrics Say to Us Today

Robert Palmer

Robert Palmer (born in Little Rock, Arkansas, in 1945), a professional rock and jazz musician, is an award-winning author of five books on popular music, including Deep Blues *(1981). Formerly a music critic for the* New York Times, *he frequently contributes to* Rolling Stone *and other magazines. "What Pop Lyrics Say to Us Today" appeared in slightly different form in the* New York Times *February 24, 1985.*

Bruce Springsteen became the first rock lyricist to be courted by both of the major candidates in a presidential election last fall. First Ronald Reagan singled him out as an artist whose songs instill pride in America. Walter Mondale retaliated, asserting that *he* had won the rock star's endorsement. "Bruce may have been born to run," Mr. Mondale quipped, quoting the title of a Springsteen hit, "but he wasn't born yesterday."

Rock is part of adult culture now, to an extent that would have been unthinkable [in the mid-1970s]. It is no longer the exclusive reserve of young people sending messages to each other. But pop music has always reflected and responded to the currents of its own time, and today's pop music is no exception. What does it seem to be telling us about our own time? Part of the message is in the music itself—in the insistence of the beat, the shriek of heavily amplified guitars. But lyrics remain the most accurate barometer of what makes *these* times different from, for example, the 1960s and 70s.

Today's pop music is sending several dominant messages. Material values are on the ascendant, but idealism is by no means a spent force. Most pop songs are love songs, as always, but today's versions try to look at relationships without rose-colored glasses. Romantic notions are viewed with some suspicion; so are drugs. And important rock artists and rappers, while no longer anticipating radical change, are addressing issues, and challenging their listeners to actively confront the world around them. There have probably been more angry protest lyrics written and recorded in the last three or four years than in any comparable period of the 60s.

In the 60s, it would have been unthinkable for a politician to seek endorsements from rock musicians: rock was rebel music. Stars like Bob Dylan and the Rolling Stones wrote and recorded outspoken lyrics that urged sweeping social change and an end to war and flirted with the rhetoric of revolution. They sang openly about sex and drugs. The music was the voice of a new generation and a constant reminder of the generation gap. The battle lines were drawn.

The rock lyricists of the 60s were fond of talking about "love." To the   5
Beatles, "love" was transcendent, an irresistible force for good that could accomplish practically anything. [As they put it in one song, "All You Need Is Love."]*

Love is still something one hears a great deal about in pop lyrics, but the contemporary version is more hard-headed and down-to-earth than the cosmic, effulgent Love of the 60s. Many of today's songwriters argue that romance isn't as important as material values or sex. "What's love got to do with it?" Tina Turner asked in her recent heavy-breathing hit of the same title. And Madonna, whose come-hither pout and undulating style have made her pop's hottest video star, serves notice in her hit "Material Girl" (written by Peter Brown and Robert Rans) that she won't worry much about love as long as there's money in the bank.

Madonna's carefully calculated image has struck a chord among many of today's more affluent young listeners, though she is perhaps too one-dimensional to be Queen of the Yuppies. And she will never be the darling of the feminists.

Nevertheless, during the past decade, the hue and cry against rock lyrics that demeaned women seemed to have a broad and salutary effect. One didn't hear many songs of the sort the Rolling Stones and other 60s bands used to perform, songs like the Stones' "Under My Thumb," [in which Mick Jagger brags that his woman has learned to say what he wants when she's spoken to.]

The title tune from Mick Jagger's new solo album, "She's the Boss," is sung like a taunt or a tease, but that doesn't disguise its message: Mr. Jagger seems to have experienced a shift in values since he wrote "Under My Thumb." . . .

Still, many of today's pop lyrics continue to celebrate male dominance.   10
[Aggressively macho hard rock tends to treat women as either temptresses or chattel, although a number of hard rock and heavy metal bands demonstrate a clear awareness of issues of sexual and social equality.]

Amid these changes in attitude, the old-fashioned romantic love song, always the staple of pop lyrics, continues to flourish. Prince, another of today's biggest-selling artists, has progressed from early songs that dealt explicitly with various sexual situations and permutations to love lyrics of a more conventional sort. [In] "Take Me With U" (sic), a song from his phenomenally successful album "Purple Rain," [he tells a "pretty baby"

---

*The use of brackets indicates material that has been slightly revised by the author since this piece first appeared in the *New York Times*.

that she can go anywhere or do anything, if only she takes him with her. Such sentiments] could have been written decades ago or yesterday.

Pop songs can do more than chart changing attitudes toward love and romance; they can address topical issues and appeal to our social conscience. In the 60s, Bob Dylan and other songwriters composed anthems that were sung by civil rights workers as they headed south, and by hundreds of thousands demonstrating for peace and equal rights. "How many deaths will it take till we know that too many people have died," Dylan asked. "The answer, my friend, is blowin' in the wind." And, he added, in a line in another song that provided a name for the radical faction within Students for a Democratic Society, "You don't need a weatherman to tell which way the wind blows."

By the late 60s, the peace and civil rights movements were beginning to splinter. The assassinations of the Kennedys and Martin Luther King had robbed a generation of its heroes, the Vietnam war was escalating despite the protests, and at home, violence was on the rise. Young people turned to rock, expecting it to ask the right questions and come up with answers, hoping that the music's most visionary artists could somehow make sense of things. But rock's most influential artists—Bob Dylan, the Beatles, the Rolling Stones—were finding that serving as the conscience of a generation exacted a heavy toll. Mr. Dylan, for one, felt the pressures becoming unbearable, and wrote about his predicament in songs like "All Along the Watchtower."

> There must be some way out of here, said the joker to the thief.
> There's too much confusion, I can't get no relief.
> Businessmen they drink my wine, plowmen dig my earth,
> None of them along the line knows what any of it is worth.

Many rock artists of the 60s turned to drugs before the decade ended. For a while, songs that were thought to be about drugs, whatever their original intentions (Bob Dylan's "Mr. Tambourine Man," the Byrds' "Eight Miles High," the Rolling Stones' "Get Off My Cloud"), were widely heard. Bob Dylan sang that "everybody must get stoned," and many young people seemed to agree. But the fad for drug lyrics was short-lived. They were never again as prevalent as during that brief Indian summer of the counterculture. One hears few drug references in today's pop lyrics, and when drugs *are* mentioned, listeners are usually advised to stay away from them. "Don't do it," Grandmaster Flash and the Furious Five cautioned listeners about to experiment with drugs in their rap hit "White Lines."

The mainstream rock of the 1970s produced little in the way of socially 15 relevant lyrics. But toward the end of that decade a change began to be felt. The rise of punk rock in Britain brought to the country's pop charts angry songs about unemployment and nuclear Armageddon. In America, the issue of nuclear energy and the threat of nuclear war enlisted the sympathies of many prominent rock musicians. But attempts by Graham Nash, John Hall, and other anti-nuclear activists to turn their concerns into anthems were too self-conscious; the songs were quickly forgotten.

Rap, the new pop idiom that exploded out of New York's black and Latin neighborhoods in the late 70s, seemed to concern itself mostly with hedonism and verbal strutting—at first. Then, in the early 80s, came "The Message," the dance-single by Grandmaster Flash and the Furious Five that provided listeners with an angry, eyewitness account of inner-city neighborhoods and people abandoned to rot, prey to crime, poverty, and disease. [In his vocal the group's champion rapper, Melle Mel, wonders how he's managed to survive in the junglelike streets.]

The rap records of the last several years have confronted similar issues head-on, and they have been danceable enough to attract a sizable audience. Run-D.M.C.'s recent hit single "It's Like That" ticked off a list of some of the daily horrors many black Americans have to contend with. But you can't give up, Run-D.M.C. insisted to their young, predominantly black and urban audience. You have to make something of yourself, to rise above "the way it is."

Bruce Springsteen's recent songs have also been topical and deeply felt. They have also been the most popular music of his career. He is writing for and about the America of his dreams and the America he sees around him, and his lyrics are followed closely by a huge audience, as last year's presidential campaign references made abundantly clear.

The narrator of Mr. Springsteen's recent hit "Born in the U.S.A." is a Vietnam veteran who returns home to confront harsh realities

> Went down to see my V.A. man
> He said "Son don't you understand now?"
> Had a brother at Khe Sahn fighting off the Viet Cong
> They're still there he's all gone

Other songs on Mr. Springsteen's most recent album suggest that there is a pervasive gloom hanging over the country's decaying inner cities and factory towns. But their message is a positive one. "Hold on," the songs seem to say, "you've got to have something to believe in." The laborer in "Working on the Highway" is certainly hanging on to *his* dream

> I work for the county out on 95
> All day I hold a red flag and watch the traffic pass me by
> In my head I keep a picture of a pretty little miss
> Someday mister I'm gonna lead a better life than this

Mr. Springsteen's songs look at America and find both despair and hope. And like Chuck Berry and so many other rock and roll lyricists, past and present, he finds a source of strength and inspiration in rock itself. Singing of his schooldays, he captures rock and roll's heart:

> We learned more from a three-minute record than we ever learned
>   in school
> Tonight I hear the neighborhood drummer sound
> I can feel my heart begin to pound
> We made a promise we swore we'd always remember
> No retreat, no surrender.

SUGGESTIONS FOR FURTHER STUDY

Key Words

The author uses language with which you may not be familiar. Find the following words in the paragraphs indicated, and explain their meanings in the context of the sentences in which the words appear. Consult a dictionary, as needed.

ascendant (par. 3)
idealism (par. 3)
transcendent (par. 5)
chattel (par. 10)
Armageddon (par. 15)

Topics for Discussion and Writing

1. What is the thesis of this essay? What examples does Palmer give to substantiate his thesis? To what extent are his examples convincing?

2. Palmer suggests that pop lyrics describe different versions of love. What are these versions? Try adding some examples, based on your knowledge of pop lyrics of the past or present.

3. In today's popular music, what messages do pop lyrics send to listeners? Are they similar to or different from the messages Palmer discusses? Explain your answer, and provide examples if you can.

4. This essay, written in 1985, discusses songs that were popular more than 10 years ago, although you may still hear them played over radio stations today. Write an essay making the same argument Palmer does, but use examples from music in the 1990s.

5. Compare and contrast a song from the 1990s with one or two from an earlier decade. How are their messages alike or different?

6. Write a brief essay or journal entry about a song that has been or is now an important part of your life. Describe the song in detail, including some of its lyrics, and tell how and why the song has had a strong effect on you.

Rock Music Has Harmed
American Youth

Allan Bloom

*Allan Bloom, a professor of philosophy, has written for many schol-
arly journals. "Rock Music Has Harmed American Youth" is from his
book* The Closing of the American Mind, *published in 1987.*

Though students do not have books, they most emphatically do have   1
music. Nothing is more singular about this generation than its addiction to
music. This is the age of music and the states of soul that accompany it. . . .
Today, a very large proportion of young people between the ages of ten and
twenty live for music. It is their passion; nothing else excites them as it does;
they cannot take seriously anything alien to music. When they are in school
and with their families, they are longing to plug themselves back into their
music. Nothing surrounding them—school, family, church—has anything
to do with their musical world. At best that ordinary life is neutral, but
mostly it is an impediment, drained of vital content, even a thing to be
rebelled against. . . . It is available twenty-four hours a day, everywhere.
There is the stereo in the home, in the car; there are concerts; there are
music videos, with special channels exclusively devoted to them, on the air
nonstop; there are the Walkmans so that no place—not public transportation, not the library—prevents students from communing with the Muse,
even while studying. And, above all, the musical soil has become tropically
rich. No need to wait for one unpredictable genius. Now there are many
geniuses, producing all the time, two new ones rising to take the place of
every fallen hero. There is no dearth of the new and the startling. . . .

Rock music is as unquestioned and unproblematic as the air the students breathe, and very few have any acquaintance at all with classical
music. This is a constant surprise to me. And one of the strange aspects of
my relations with good students I come to know well is that I frequently
introduce them to Mozart. This is a pleasure for me, inasmuch as it is
always pleasant to give people gifts that please them. It is interesting to see
whether and in what ways their studies are complemented by such music.
But this is something utterly new to me as a teacher; formerly my students
usually knew much more classical music than I did. . . .

PLATO AND MUSIC

Symptomatic of this change is how seriously students now take the famous passages on musical education in Plato's *Republic*. In the past, students, good liberals that they always are, were indignant at the censorship of poetry, as a threat to free inquiry. But they were really thinking of science and politics. They hardly paid attention to the discussion of music itself and, to the extent that they even thought about it, were really puzzled by Plato's devoting time to rhythm and melody in a serious treatise on political philosophy. Their experience of music was as an entertainment, a matter of indifference to political and moral life. Students today, on the contrary, know exactly why Plato takes music so seriously. They know it affects life very profoundly and are indignant because Plato seems to want to rob them of their most intimate pleasure. They are drawn into argument with Plato about the experience of music, and the dispute centers on how to evaluate it and deal with it. This encounter not only helps to illuminate the phenomenon of contemporary music, but also provides a model of how contemporary students can profitably engage with a classic text. The very fact of their fury shows how much Plato threatens what is dear and intimate to them. They are little able to defend their experience, which had seemed unquestionable until questioned, and it is most resistant to cool analysis. Yet if a student can—and this is most difficult and unusual—draw back, get a critical distance on what he clings to, come to doubt the ultimate value of what he loves, he has taken the first and most difficult step toward the philosophic conversion. Indignation is the soul's defense against the wound of doubt about its own; it reorders the cosmos to support the justice of its cause. It justifies putting Socrates to death. Recognizing indignation for what it is constitutes knowledge of the soul, and is thus an experience more philosophic than the study of mathematics. It is Plato's teaching that music, by its nature, encompasses all that is today most resistant to philosophy. So it may well be that through the thicket of our greatest corruption runs the path to awareness of the oldest truths.

Plato's teaching about music is, put simply, that rhythm and melody, accompanied by dance, are the barbarous expression of the soul. Barbarous, not animal. Music is the medium of the *human* soul in its most ecstatic condition of wonder and terror. Nietzsche, who in large measure agrees with Plato's analysis, says in *The Birth of Tragedy* (not to be forgotten is the rest of the title, *Out of the Spirit of Music*) that a mixture of cruelty and coarse sensuality characterized this state, which of course was religious, in the service of gods. Music is the soul's primitive and primary speech and it is *alogon*, without articulate speech or reason. It is not only not reasonable, it is hostile to reason. Even when articulate speech is added, it is utterly subordinate to and determined by the music and the passions it expresses.

Civilization or, to say the same thing, education is the taming or domes- 5
tication of the soul's raw passions—not suppressing or excising them, which
would deprive the soul of its energy—but forming and informing them as
art. The goal of harmonizing the enthusiastic part of the soul with what
develops later, the rational part, is perhaps impossible to attain. But without
it, man can never be whole. Music, or poetry, which is what music becomes
as reason emerges, always involves a delicate balance between passion and
reason, and, even in its highest and most developed forms—religious, warlike and erotic—that balance is always tipped, if ever so slightly, toward the
passionate. Music, as everyone experiences, provides an unquestionable
justification and a fulfilling pleasure for the activities it accompanies: the
soldier who hears the marching band is enthralled and reassured; the religious man is exalted in his prayer by the sound of the organ in the church;
and the lover is carried away and his conscience stilled by the romantic guitar. Armed with music, man can damn rational doubt. Out of the music
emerge the gods that suit it, and they educate men by their example and
their commandments. . . .

A BARBARIC APPEAL

Rock music . . . has risen to its current heights in the education of the
young on the ashes of classical music, and in an atmosphere in which there
is no intellectual resistance to attempts to tap the rawest passions. Modern-
day rationalists, such as economists, are indifferent to it and what it represents. The irrationalists are all for it. There is no need to fear that "the
blond beasts" are going to come forth from the bland souls of our adolescents. But rock music has one appeal only, a barbaric appeal, to sexual
desire—not love, not *eros*, but sexual desire undeveloped and untutored. It
acknowledges the first emanations of children's emerging sensuality and
addresses them seriously, eliciting them and legitimating them, not as little
sprouts that must be carefully tended in order to grow into gorgeous flowers, but as the real thing. Rock gives children, on a silver platter, with all the
public authority of the entertainment industry, everything their parents
always used to tell them they had to wait for until they grew up and would
understand later.

Young people know that rock has the beat of sexual intercourse. That is
why Ravel's *Bolero* is the one piece of classical music that is commonly
known and liked by them. In alliance with some real art and a lot of
pseudo-art, an enormous industry cultivates the taste for the orgiastic state
of feeling connected with sex, providing a constant flood of fresh material
for voracious appetites. Never was there an art form directed so exclusively
to children.

Ministering to and according with the arousing and cathartic music, the lyrics celebrate puppy love as well as polymorphous attractions, and fortify them against traditional ridicule and shame. The words implicitly and explicitly describe bodily acts that satisfy sexual desire and treat them as its only natural and routine culmination for children who do not yet have the slightest imagination of love, marriage or family. This has a much more powerful effect than does pornography on youngsters, who have no need to watch others do grossly what they can so easily do themselves. Voyeurism is for old perverts; active sexual relations are for the young. All they need is encouragement. . . .

Picture a thirteen-year-old boy sitting in the living room of his family home doing his math assignment while wearing his Walkman headphones or watching MTV. He enjoys the liberties hard won over centuries by the alliance of philosophic genius and political heroism, consecrated by the blood of martyrs; he is provided with comfort and leisure by the most productive economy ever known to mankind; science has penetrated the secrets of nature in order to provide him with the marvelous, lifelike electronic sound and image reproduction he is enjoying. And in what does progress culminate? A pubescent child whose body throbs with orgasmic rhythms; whose feelings are made articulate in hymns to the joys of onanism or the killing of parents; whose ambition is to win fame and wealth in imitating the drag-queen who makes the music. In short, life is made into a nonstop, commercially prepackaged masturbational fantasy. . . .

My concern here is not with the moral effects of this music—whether it   10
leads to sex, violence or drugs. The issue here is its effect on education, and I believe it ruins the imagination of young people and makes it very difficult for them to have a passionate relationship to the art and thought that are the substance of liberal education. The first sensuous experiences are decisive in determining the taste for the whole of life, and they are the link between the animal and spiritual in us. The period of nascent sensuality has always been used for sublimation, in the sense of making sublime, for attaching youthful inclinations and longings to music, pictures and stories that provide the transition to the fulfillment of the human duties and the enjoyment of the human pleasures. Doris Lessing, speaking of Greek sculpture, said "beautiful men made beautiful statues, and the city had beautiful statues in part to thank for beautiful citizens." This formula encapsulates the fundamental principle of the esthetic education of man. Young men and women were attracted by the beauty of heroes whose very bodies expressed their nobility. The deeper understanding of the meaning of nobility comes later, but is prepared for by the sensuous experience and is actually contained in it. What the senses long for as well as what reason later sees as good are thereby not at tension with one another. Education is not sermonizing to children against their instincts and pleasures, but providing a natural continuity between what they feel and what they can and should be.

But this is a lost art. Now we have come to exactly the opposite point. Rock music encourages passions and provides models that have no relation to any life the young people who go to universities can possibly lead, or to the kinds of admiration encouraged by liberal studies. Without the cooperation of the sentiments, anything other than technical education is a dead letter.

Rock music provides premature ecstasy and, in this respect, is like the drugs with which it is allied. It artificially induces the exaltation naturally attached to the completion of the greatest endeavors—victory in a just war, consummated love, artistic creation, religious devotion and discovery of the truth. Without effort, without talent, without virtue, without exercise of the faculties, anyone and everyone is accorded the equal right to the enjoyment of their fruits. In my experience, students who have had a serious fling with drugs—and gotten over it—find it difficult to have enthusiasms or great expectations. It is as though the color has been drained out of their lives and they see everything in black and white. The pleasure they experienced in the beginning was so intense that they no longer look for it at the end, or as the end. They may function perfectly well, but dryly, routinely. Their energy has been sapped, and they do not expect their life's activity to produce anything but a living, whereas liberal education is supposed to encourage the belief that the good life is the pleasant life and that the best life is the most pleasant life. I suspect that the rock addiction, particularly in the absence of strong counterattractions, has an effect similar to that of drugs. The students will get over this music, or at least the exclusive passion for it. But they will do so in the same way Freud says that men accept the reality principle—as something harsh, grim and essentially unattractive, a mere necessity. These students will assiduously study economics or the professions and the Michael Jackson costume will slip off to reveal a Brooks Brothers suit beneath. They will want to get ahead and live comfortably. But this life is as empty and false as the one they left behind. The choice is not between quick fixes and dull calculation. This is what liberal education is meant to show them. But as long as they have the Walkman on, they cannot hear what the great tradition has to say. And, after its prolonged use, when they take it off, they find they are deaf.

SUGGESTIONS FOR FURTHER STUDY

Key Words

The author uses language with which you may not be familiar. Find the following words in the paragraphs indicated, and explain their meanings in the context of the sentences in which the words appear. Consult a dictionary, as needed.

emphatically (par. 1)
rationalists (par. 6)
emanations (par. 6)
voyeurism (par. 8)
pubescent (par. 9)
nascent (par. 10)
sublimation (par. 10)

Topics for Discussion and Writing

1. According to Bloom, what are students today most passionate about? Do you agree or disagree with him? Explain your answer.

2. Discuss the connection Bloom makes between Plato's *Republic* and the way in which today's students view rock music. What does Plato's teaching suggest about music?

3. "Rock music has one appeal only," according to Bloom. Discuss that claim with other readers, and compare your opinions.

4. What is Bloom's ultimate concern, as expressed in this essay? Explain your answer in some detail, and refer to specific passages in this piece.

5. Bloom says that "as long as [students] have the Walkman on, they cannot hear what the grand tradition has to say." The "grand tradition" includes Western civilization's classical artists, such as Beethoven, Mozart, Shakespeare, Dante, da Vinci, Michelangelo, and so on. In an analytical essay, reply to Bloom's statement. You might focus on the "grand tradition" itself: Who is part of it, who is left out, and how important it is—or is not—to today's students.

6. To what condition does Bloom refer when he says, "Education is not sermonizing to children against their instincts and pleasures, but providing a natural continuity between what they feel and what they can and should be. But this is a lost art" (par. 10)? Before you write about this question or discuss it with other readers, review Bloom's argument about education in paragraph 10 (and other paragraphs). As a basis for your writing or discussion, first write a paraphrase of paragraph 10 in your journal. Then write another paragraph or two, agreeing or disagreeing with Bloom.

2 Live Crew Decoded

Henry Louis Gates, Jr.

*Henry Louis Gates, Jr., earned his BA at Yale University and his PhD
at the University of Cambridge in England. He is the W. E. B. DuBois
Professor of English and Comparative Literature at Cornell University.
The author of several books and essays on the works of black writers,
Gates has given us greater understanding of the interaction between
black culture and language. "2 Live Crew Decoded" appeared in the
New York Times June 19, 1990.*

The rap group 2 Live Crew and their controversial hit recording "As 1
Nasty as They Wanna Be" may well earn a signal place in the history of
First Amendment rights. But just as important is how these lyrics will be
interpreted and by whom.

For centuries, African-Americans have been forced to develop coded
ways of communicating to protect them from danger. Allegories and double meanings, words redefined to mean their opposites ("bad" meaning
"good," for instance), even neologisms ("bodacious") have enabled blacks
to share messages only the initiated understood.

Many blacks were amused by the transcripts of Marion Barry's sting
operation, which reveals that he used the traditional black expression about
one's "nose being opened." This referred to a love affair and not, as Mr.
Barry's prosecutors have suggested, to the inhalation of drugs. Understanding this phrase could very well spell the difference (for the Mayor)
between prison and freedom.

2 Live Crew is engaged in heavy-handed parody, turning the stereotypes of black and white American culture on their heads. These young
artists are acting out, to lively dance music, a parodic exaggeration of the
age-old stereotypes of the oversexed black female and male. Their exuberant use of hyperbole (phantasmagoric sexual organs, for example) undermines—for anyone fluent in black cultural codes—a too literal-minded
hearing of the lyrics.

This is the street tradition called "signifying" or "playing the dozens," 5
which has generally been risqué, and where the best signifier or "rapper" is
the one who invents the most extravagant images, the biggest "lies," as the
culture says. (H. "Rap" Brown earned his nickname in just this way.) In the
face of racist stereotypes about black sexuality, you can do one of two
things: You can disavow them or explode them with exaggeration.

2 Live Crew, like many "hip-hop" groups, is engaged in sexual carnivalesque. Parody reigns supreme, from a take-off of standard blues to a spoof of the black power movement; their off-color nursery rhymes are part of a venerable Western tradition. The group even satirizes the culture of commerce when it appropriates popular advertising slogans ("Tastes great!" "Less filling!") and puts them in a bawdy context.

2 Live Crew must be interpreted within the context of black culture generally and of signifying specifically. Their novelty, and that of other adventuresome rap groups, is that their defiant rejection of euphemism now voices for the mainstream what before existed largely in the "race record" market—where the records of Redd Foxx and Rudy Ray Moore once were forced to reside.

Rock songs have always been about sex but have used elaborate subterfuges to convey that fact. 2 Live Crew uses Anglo-Saxon words and is self-conscious about it; a parody of a white voice in one song refers to "private personal parts," as a coy counterpart to the group's bluntness.

Much more troubling than its so-called obscenity is the group's overt sexism. Their sexism is so flagrant, however, that it almost cancels itself out in a hyperbolic war between the sexes. In this, it recalls the inter-sexual jousting in Zora Neale Hurston's novels. Still, many of us look toward the emergence of more female rappers to redress sexual stereotypes. And we must not allow ourselves to sentimentalize street culture: the appreciation of verbal virtuosity does not lessen one's obligation to critique bigotry in all of its pernicious forms.

Is 2 Live Crew more "obscene" than, say, the comic Andrew Dice Clay?   10
Clearly, this rap group is seen as more threatening than others that are just as sexually explicit. Can this be completely unrelated to the specter of the young black male as a figure of sexual and social disruption, the very stereotypes 2 Live Crew seems determined to undermine?

This question—and the very large question of obscenity and the First Amendment—cannot even be addressed until those who would answer them become literate in the vernacular traditions of African-Americans. To do less is to censor through the equivalent of intellectual prior restraint— and censorship is to art what lynching is to justice.

SUGGESTIONS FOR FURTHER STUDY

Key Words

The author uses language with which you may not be familiar. Find the following words in the paragraphs indicated, and explain their meanings in the context of the sentences in which the words appear. Consult a dictionary, as needed.

neologisms (par. 2)
parody (par. 4)
carnivalesque (par. 6)
subterfuges (par. 8)
hyperbolic (par. 9)
obscene (par. 10)

Topics for Discussion and Writing

1. Explain what point Gates is establishing when he says "Just as important is how these lyrics are interpreted and by whom." Is this statement the thesis of Gates's essay? Explain your answer.

2. What specifically does Gates suggest by saying that 2 Live Crew engages in "sexual carnivalesque"? What images or actions does that phrase imply?

3. Discuss with other readers Gates's suggestion that female rappers even the score with male rappers by "redress[ing] sexual stereotypes."

4. Explain Gates's statement that "censorship is to art what lynching is to justice." How does this statement apply to his discussion of public reaction to 2 Live Crew's music?

5. Gates is a professor and literary scholar, as well as a social critic of American culture. How would you describe his tone of voice and style of writing in this piece? What features of his writing convey both tone and style?

6. Research bands other than 2 Live Crew who, in your opinion, represent "sexual carnivalesque" style in their music and lyrics. Write a short essay describing the style of these bands, and discuss your opinion of their lyrics.

7. Listen to a recording of 2 Live Crew's "As Nasty as They Wanna Be." Do you find the lyrics funny, degrading, interesting, well-phrased, horrifying, disgraceful, or a combination of these or similar characteristics? Discuss your reactions with other listeners, both men and women. Do you find that men and women differ in their reactions to the lyrics, or do they agree?

8. M. C. Lights' song "Short Short Men" relates to Gates's comments that female rappers may, in some sense, retaliate and "signify" back to men. What does this interaction suggest about engaging in "overt sexism" and songs that insult members of the opposite sex? Discuss with other readers Gates's statement that "the appreciation of verbal virtuosity does not lessen one's obligation to critique bigotry in all of its pernicious forms."

Rock Music Should Be Labeled

Tipper Gore

*Tipper Gore cofounded the Parent's Resource Music Center, an advo-
cacy group that supports record labeling, and she has served on the
Task Force on Children and Television of the American Academy of
Pediatrics. Gore, wife of Vice President Al Gore, is the mother of four
children. "Rock Music Should Be Labeled" is from her book* Raising
PG Kids in an X-Rated Society.

I became aware of the emergence of explicit and violent images in the
world of music through my children. In December 1984, I purchased
Prince's best-selling album *Purple Rain* for my eleven-year-old daughter. I
had seen Prince on the cover of magazines, and I knew that he was the
biggest pop idol in years. My daughter wanted his album because she had
heard the single "Let's Go Crazy" on the radio. But when we brought the
album home, put it on our stereo, and listened to it together, we heard words
to another song, "Darling Nikki": "I knew a girl named Nikki / Guess [you]
could say she was a sex fiend / I met her in a hotel lobby / Masturbating with
a magazine." The song went on and on, in a similar manner. I couldn't
believe my ears! The vulgar lyrics embarrassed both of us. At first, I was
stunned—then I got mad! Millions of Americans were buying *Purple Rain*
with no idea what to expect. Thousands of parents were giving the album to
their children—many even younger than my daughter.

"MATURE" THEMES

Around that time, my two younger daughters, ages six and eight, began
asking me about things they had seen on MTV, the music video channel on
cable television. I had always thought that videos had great potential as a
dramatic new art form, but I had not watched many. I began watching more
often, and I observed that several included adult (or at least mature) themes
and images. "Mom, why is the teacher taking off her clothes?" my six-year-
old asked, after watching Van Halen's *Hot for Teacher,* in which a
"teacher" does a striptease act for the boys in her class.

I sat down with my kids and watched videos like Motley Crüe's *Looks
That Kill,* with scantily clad women being captured and imprisoned in cages
by a studded-leather-clad male band. In *Photograph,* by Def Leppard, we

saw a dead woman tied up with barbed wire. The Scorpions' *Rock You Like a Hurricane* showed a man tied to the walls of a torture chamber and a singer being choked by a woman. These images frightened my children; they frightened *me!* The graphic sex and the violence were too much for us to handle.

Other parents were experiencing the same rude awakening. One day in early 1985, my friend Susan Baker came by to talk about her concerns. Susan and her husband, U.S. Treasury Secretary James Baker, have eight children. She told me that two of her friends were getting ready to take action on the issue of pornographic and violent images in music, and asked if I would be interested in signing a letter inviting others to a meeting to hear more about the excesses in some rock music.

I was so angry about the songs my children and I had heard that I   5
quickly agreed to join Susan Baker in doing something about it. Susan was working with Sally Nevius, a former dean of admissions at Mount Vernon College in Washington. Sally and her husband, the former chairman of the District of Columbia City Council, had an eleven-year-old daughter. Also assisting Susan Baker was Pam Howar, a businesswoman with a seven-year-old daughter.

We decided to establish the nonprofit Parents' Music Resource Center, to be known as the PMRC. In May of 1985, we set out to alert other parents in our community. Sally arranged for Jeff Ling, a former rock musician who is now a youth minister at a suburban Virginia church, to give a slide presentation graphically illustrating the worst excesses in rock music, from lyrics to concert performances to rock magazines aimed at the teenage market. We invited the public, community leaders, our friends (some of whom hold public office), and representatives of the music industry. Our hope was to generate a discussion of the issue, raise public awareness, and begin a dialogue with people in the industry. To our surprise, more than 350 people showed up at our first meeting on May 15, 1985, at St. Columba's Church in Washington, D.C.

To my knowledge, no music industry representatives attended this meeting, with one very important exception: Eddie Fritts, president of the National Association of Broadcasters (NAB), unable to attend himself, had sent his wife, Martha Dale Fritts, and two NAB staff members. They brought with them a letter that Mr. Fritts had just written and sent to eight hundred group station owners, which alerted them to growing concern among the public over "porn rock":

> The lyrics of some recent rock records and the tone of their related music videos are fast becoming a matter of public debate. The subject has drawn national attention through articles in publications like *Newsweek* and *USA Today* and feature reports on TV programs like "Good Morning, America."

Many state that they are extremely troubled by the sexually explicit and violent language of some of today's songs. . . .

The pre-teen and teen audiences are heavy listeners, viewers and buyers of rock music. In some communities, like Washington, D.C., parents and other interested citizens are organizing to see what they can do about the music in question, which at least one writer has dubbed "porn rock."

I wanted you, as one of the leaders in the broadcasting industry, to be aware of this situation. . . .

It is, of course, up to each broadcast licensee to make its own decisions as to the manner in which it carries out its programming responsibilities under the Communications Act.

Two weeks later, Mr. Fritts wrote to the heads of forty-five major record companies:

At its May meeting, NAB's Executive Committee asked that I write you to request that all recordings made available to broadcasters in the future be accompanied by copies of the songs' lyrics. It appears that providing this material to broadcasters would place very little burden on the recording industry, while greatly assisting the decision making of broadcast management and programming staffs. . . .

Considering the initial NAB response, we were off to a good start, but what should we do next? How could we make ourselves heard by the giants of the record industry, like Warner Brothers, Capitol, and RCA?

A SECRET ALLY

By happy chance, we gained an ally in the recording industry who   10
could help us find our way through the music business. Throughout the ensuing campaign, he gave us invaluable advice—on the condition that he never be identified.

Our secret ally held an important position in the record industry. Like us, he was sickened and disgusted by the trend toward pornography and violence in some rock music. He advised us to set up a meeting with Stan Gortikov at the Recording Industry Association of America (RIAA), the trade group that represents all major record companies. Gortikov had been president of the RIAA since 1972, and before that he had headed Capitol Records. He agreed to meet with us in early June.

Our strategy was simple. We felt it was crucial to publicize the excesses in song lyrics and videos, the source of our concern. We were convinced that most parents are either unaware of the trends in rock music, or uncertain what to do about them. We decided to get the word out and build a consumer movement to put pressure on the industry. From the start, we recognized that the only solution would involve some voluntary action on the part of the industry. We wanted industry leaders to assume direct corporate responsibility for their products. The problem was to persuade an industry profiting from excesses to exercise some self-restraint.

In 1984, the National Congress of Parents and Teachers (the National PTA) had called on record companies to label their products for sexual content, violence, and profanity, in order to inform parents about inappropriate materials. The PTA had written to thirty-two record companies but had only received three responses. And those refused to discuss the issue further. Our ally advised us not to deal with the companies on an individual basis.

He suggested that we present our plans to the RIAA's Gortikov and not leave him any choice. Our source said the best way to catch the industry's attention was on the airwaves. So the PMRC launched a grass-roots media campaign that soon took on a life of its own.

FROM NEWS STORY TO NATIONAL ISSUE

From June to November 1985, we held dozens of meetings, participated   15
in frequent conference calls, and exchanged numerous letters, as we sought solutions palatable to the industry and to the National PTA and the PMRC. As our negotiations intensified, the issue quickly became a national one. . . .

The media campaign took care of itself. A small story about our first public meeting appeared in the "Style" section of the *Washington Post.* Before we knew it, we were besieged with requests for interviews. Kandy Stroud, a journalist, musician, and mother of three, had earlier written a "My Turn" column entitled "Stop Pornographic Rock" for the May 6, 1985, edition of *Newsweek.* She immediately received an invitation to appear on "Good Morning, America." Kandy and Pam Howar appeared on "Panorama," a Washington television show. Soon after that, I did an hour-long radio talk show in Oklahoma City, and Susan Baker and Sally Nevius participated in a similar show in another state. . . .

The PMRC proposed a unique mechanism to increase consumer choice in the marketplace instead of limiting it. Our approach was the direct opposite of censorship. We called for more information, not less. We did not advocate a ban of even the most offensive albums or tapes. We simply urged that the consumer be forewarned through the use of warning labels and/or printed lyrics visible on the outside packaging of music products. Critics used the smokescreen of censorship to dodge the real issue, which was lack of any corporate responsibility for the impact their products may have on young people.

The PMRC sought to balance the precious right of artistic free speech with the right of parents to protect their children from explicit messages that they are not mature enough to understand or deal with. These two rights are not mutually exclusive and one should not be sacrificed for the other. Records, tapes, and videos are consumer products, mass-produced, distributed, and marketed to the public. Children and parents of children constitute the bulk of that consuming public.

The PMRC and the National PTA have agreed that these musical products should enjoy all the rights and privileges guaranteed by the First Amendment. But as Thomas Jefferson once said, when excesses occur, the best guarantee of free speech is *more* speech, not less. That's all we asked for—awareness and disclosure. Our proposal amounted to nothing more than truth-in-packaging, a time-honored principle in our free-enterprise system.

In this information age, such consumer information gives parents an   20
important tool for making choices for their children. Without it, parental guidance in the matter of available entertainment is virtually impossible. The PMRC proposal does *not* infringe on the First Amendment. It does *not* raise a constitutional issue. But it *does* seek to reform marketing practices by asking for better and more informative packaging. And it *does* seek to inform consumers when artistic expression borders on what legendary singer Smokey Robinson has called "musical pornography."

Who decides which songs are musical pornography? Only the record company can make that decision—not the government, as some would have us believe, and not an outside censorship board, as others have charged. The music industry, which allowed these excesses to develop, would be asked to take responsibility for the product it markets to the public.

In fact, we are talking about products primarily written for children, marketed to children, and sold to children. In this country we rightly treat children differently from adults: most people feel that children should not enjoy the same access to adult material as adults. Children are not allowed into R-rated movies if they are under seventeen. In most places, minors are not allowed to buy *Playboy* and *Penthouse* or go into adult bookstores.

If no one under eighteen can buy *Penthouse* magazine, why should children be subjected to explicit album covers and lyrics that are even worse? If we have decided it is not in the best interest of society to allow children into X-rated bookstores, why should they be subjected to hard-core porn in the local record shop? A recent album from the Dead Kennedys band contained a graphic poster of multiple erect penises penetrating vaginas. Where's the difference?

In the hands of a few warped artists, their brand of rock music has become a Trojan Horse, rolling explicit sex and violence into our homes. This ruse made us gasp at the cynicism of the recording company executives who control the music business. They found it easy to confuse the issue by throwing out cries of censorship while refusing to address the real problem. They dodged the real point—that in a free society we can affirm the First Amendment and also protect the rights of children and adults who seek to avoid the twisted tyranny of explicitness in the public domain.

PROPOSING ALTERNATIVES
TO THE MUSIC INDUSTRY

At a second meeting with the RIAA's Stan Gortikov, on May 31, 1985, 25 we presented a letter to him signed by sixteen wives of United States representatives and senators:

> It is our concern that some of the music which the recording industry sells today increasingly portrays explicit sex and violence, and glorifies the use of drugs and alcohol. It is indiscriminately available to persons of any age through record stores and the media.
>
> These messages reach young children and early teenagers at a crucial age when they are developing lifelong value systems. Their minds are often not yet discerning enough to reject the destructive influences and antisocial behaviour engendered by what they hear and see in these products.
>
> Because of the excesses that exist in the music industry today, we petition the industry to exercise voluntary self-restraint perhaps by developing guidelines and/or a rating system, such as that of the movie industry, for use by parents in order to protect our younger children from such mature themes.

Braced with this letter, Mr. Gortikov pledged to work swiftly within the music industry.

Over the next few months, we negotiated several alternatives with the RIAA. We began by asking for a categorical rating system based on content, then suggested using the symbol 'R,' to designate explicit albums. Finally, we joined forces with the National PTA and its 5.8 million members. Together with the RIAA we called for a consumer warning label on explicit or violent albums or for full disclosure of lyrics. "We recommend this course of action because we believe it protects consumers by providing them with valuable information, while respecting recording artists' First Amendment rights," said National PTA president Ann Kahn.

Pam Howar of the PMRC urged the industry to "create a uniform standard to be used to define what constitutes blatant, explicit lyric content." We thought the ideal solution would be a label (or some symbol) to advise the consumer about explicit lyrics in a particular album. Printed lyrics would also enable the consumer to make an informed decision appropriate for their child's age. Since most albums would not concern parents, there had to be some way to flag those that might. . . .

A UNIFORM STANDARD

While we were calling publicly for consumer warning labels on albums containing explicit lyrics, and for an industry panel to set guidelines defining explicit material, we worked feverishly behind the scenes to obtain industry endorsement of a uniform standard—one written by the industry itself, not by us. The standard would loosely define what constituted blatantly explicit lyric content. Meanwhile, the Musical Majority and others lined up pop stars to blast "music censorship" and the women who would "ban rock and roll." Our ally in the industry had warned us that we would be no match for prominent artists calling us "censoring prudes" or worse, as industry leaders fought to protect the status quo and their economic interests.

By this time, the United States Congress had begun to take an interest in   30
the issue, and many members considered holding hearings. In September 1985, Senator John Danforth of Missouri scheduled a hearing before the Senate's commerce committee, which he chaired. The commerce committee has jurisdiction over communications issues, and wanted to investigate the prevalence of pornographic, violent rock lyrics for its own information—not to consider any legislation. . . .

The September 19 hearing certainly brought the issue out for public debate. It turned out to be the most widely publicized media event in congressional history. A seat in the hearing room was the hottest ticket in town all year.

Both sides turned out in force. Susan Baker and I testified for the PMRC, and Jeff Ling gave his slide show. The National PTA also sent representatives who testified. Frank Zappa, John Denver, and Dee Snider of Twisted Sister also appeared.

The hearing did not seek to reach any consensus, but on the whole we were pleased to see the facts come out. Twisted Sister's Dee Snider told the committee that he was a Christian who did not smoke, drink, or do drugs, and insisted that he had been unfairly accused. A member of the committee—my husband—asked him the full name of his fan club, SMF Fans of Twisted Sister. Replied Snider, "It stands for Sick Mother Fucking Fans of Twisted Sister."

AGREEMENT WITH THE RIAA

After the Senate hearing, the negotiations produced results that all parties felt represented a workable and fair arrangement. We decided to make a major compromise—to accept the formation of an RIAA policy statement on explicit lyrics, and drop our request for a uniform standard of what is or is not explicit. We would also drop our request for an R rating on albums or tapes to designate explicit products, in exchange for the warning "Explicit Lyrics—Parental Advisory." We agreed to give the compromise a chance to work in the marketplace, and to monitor it jointly and assess its effectiveness a year later. We also agreed to cease the media campaign for one year. On November 1, 1985, the RIAA, the National PTA, and the PMRC jointly announced the agreement at the National Press Club in Washington.

SUGGESTIONS FOR FURTHER STUDY

Key Words

The author uses language with which you may not be familiar. Find the following words in the paragraphs indicated, and explain their meanings in the context of the sentences in which the words appear. Consult a dictionary, as needed.

explicit (par. 1)
pornographic (par. 4)
profanity (par. 13)
censorship (par. 17)
disclosure (par. 19)

Topics for Discussion and Writing

1. How did Gore become "aware of the emergence of explicit and violent images in the world of music," and what was her reaction to what she heard? If you were listening to this music with your child, how might you have reacted?

2. What action did Gore take against "pornographic and violent images in music"? Who were her allies, and how did they achieve their goals?

3. Gore uses a metaphor echoing classical literature when she writes that music from "a few warped artists . . . has become a Trojan Horse, rolling explicit sex and violence into our homes" (par. 30). Review the story of the Trojan Horse, from Homer's *Iliad*. Is Gore's metaphor appropriate and effective? Explain your conclusion.

4. According to Gore, certain "prominent artists" have labeled her and her allies "censoring prudes." What is your opinion of this label? Could she also be labeled "consumer advocate"? Explain your opinion.

5. Gore and her allies have been successful in their efforts to label the content of lyrics. We now have what PMRC calls "a uniform standard . . . used to define what constitutes blatant, explicit lyric content" or labeling. Compare Gore's point of view with Danny Alexander's in the essay "Labeling Rock Music Leads to Repression" (next in this chapter). In a journal entry or brief essay, draw comparisons and contrasts between the two points of view, and comment with your own opinions.

6. Write an essay from one of these two perspectives:
   a. The perspective of a band member in a rock, rap, or other type of band, defending your band's use of explicit lyrics
   b. The perspective of a person strongly opposed to explicit expression in song lyrics, offering some ideas about how to control or eliminate them

Labeling Rock Music Leads to Repression

Danny Alexander

Danny Alexander, a music reviewer, has long been actively opposed to censorship. His point of view is clearly expressed in "Labeling Rock Music Leads to Repression," taken from his monograph, Targeting the Street: The Truth About Record Labels, *1994.*

It all seemed innocent enough at the beginning—if not even naïve.   1
In her May 6, 1985, "My Turn" column for *Newsweek,* Parents Music
Resource Center (PMRC) journalist Kandy Stroud laid out the agenda to
curb the rising tide of "tasteless, graphic and gratuitously sexual songs" in
today's rock music.

She made her point somewhat persuasively, starting with references to
masturbation and sexual intercourse in Prince and Madonna songs and
then padding her illustrations with violently sexual scenes culled from
heavy metal albums.

She closed with a call to action that revealed her real motivation and
purpose:

> Legislative action may be needed, or better yet, a measure of self-
> restraint. If distillers can voluntarily keep their products off the public
> airwaves, then the record industry can also curb porn rock—or, at the
> very least, make sure that kids under 17 are not allowed into sexually
> explicit concerts.
>
> And what about the musicians themselves? If forty-six pop su-
> perstars can cooperate to raise millions of dollars for African famine
> relief with their hit "We Are the World," why can't musicians also
> ensure that America's own youth will be fed a diet of rock music that is
> not only good to dance to but healthy for their hearts and minds and
> souls as well?

In an effort to steer popular music in this healthy direction, Stroud proposed that the record industry self-censor itself with a system of "voluntary" record labeling. The end result of this campaign is that today, most
major labels print a sticker "Parental Advisory Explicit Lyrics," to let parents know which albums to buy for their children and which to avoid.

Proponents of labeling argue that this system is no different than ingredient labels on food, or the labeling system that is used for movies.

They are wrong. For starters, stigmatizing a record because of a word   5
someone may deem explicit (a particularly ridiculous example being the word "pee" on Prince's 68-minute *Graffiti Bridge* album) without also discussing the musicianship, the context for the word choice or the themes that dominate the record (in this example faith and renewal) could hardly be called an accurate listing of ingredients.

PARENTAL ADVISORY

I'll never forget standing in a record store when a mother held up a copy of rap group Boogie Down Productions' *Edutainment* and asked why it had a sticker. The sales clerk said it probably had some curse words on it. The woman said, "Oh, well I don't want that!" She promptly slammed one of the most uplifting, sophisticated expositions on Afrocentricity and contemporary society ever recorded back into its slot, mentally lumping this record in with the likes of 2 Live Crew. So much for parental advisory.

What is most disturbing about record labeling are the ways in which it seems to serve as a means to more generally (as Kandy Stroud put it in her manifesto) "curb" rock, particularly heavy metal and rap music.

Since the September 1985 Senate Committee on Commerce, Science, and Transportation meetings led by Missouri senator John Danforth and [former] Tennessee senator Al Gore (whose wife, along with Secretary of State James Baker's wife created the Parents Music Resource Center) record labeling has been mandated through a series of threatening legislative gestures and cowering responses by the record industry.

It's understandable to see why the record industry cowered. In September 1986, the PMRC's "First Annual Pig-Pickin'" fundraiser in Poolesville, Maryland, featured a cast of heavyweights and was bankrolled by a heap of money. The summit-disguised-as-picnic cost $75 for general admission, $200 for a patron and $1500 per corporation. Attendees included Senator Lloyd Bentsen, the Bakers, the Gores, the Danforths, key Barry Goldwater and Bush/Reagan advisor Dean Burch, White House advisor and CEO of The Magazine Publishers Association William Gorog, former Nixon aide and Marriot v.p. Fred Malek and Reagan tax advisor Bruce Thompson.

PROPOSED LEGISLATION

Allegedly after meeting Tipper Gore at an Eagle Forum presentation,   10
Missouri representative Jean Dixon drafted a bill mandating warning labels

for records in 1989. By 1990, thirteen states had drafted similar bills. At an April 5, 1990 press conference, the PMRC, the PTA, and NARM (the National Association of Record Merchandisers) announced that those thirteen states (along with five others considering such legislation) would withdraw their bills if the industry adopted a more rigid "voluntary" labeling system. For the PMRC, this was the best of all possible solutions: though such laws might be found unconstitutional (after all, they certainly could be shown to abridge free speech), without even one law being passed, the desired mechanism for control had been achieved.

Why all this interest in controlling rock music? Probably not because teenagers might masturbate in front of their stereos. Since their origins, record labels have targeted primarily heavy metal and rap music, the two most politically uncompromising forms of commercial art in America reaching the broadest base, working-class audience perhaps ever reached by any art form. In a country that is on the brink of economic collapse (which has been apparent to anyone paying attention for at least a decade, certainly by Black Monday in 1987), it is not surprising that many equate a record like Ice-T's "Cop Killer" with yelling "fire" in a crowded theater, and that's the way such controversial music is being treated.

CENSORSHIP, THE L.A. RIOTS, AND RECORD LABELS

The aftermath of the Los Angeles riots presents a particularly telling series of events which, even if they share no direct causal relationship, suggest a new tolerance for censorship on a local and national level.

Ironically, considering the popular response, the California State Assembly's Special Committee on the Los Angeles Crisis stated, "poverty, segregation, lack of education and employment opportunities, wide-spread perceptions of police abuse and unequal consumer services [are] the principal grievances which led to the civil disturbances of the 1960s. Little has changed in 1992 Los Angeles." But our top political leaders quickly found a means to blame the victim, or those who speak for the victims of such abject poverty.

Newsweek, New York Newsday, and the *Washington Post* all wrote articles tying rap music (probably not Sister Souljah, but Public Enemy?) to the rebellion. As the riots flared, Barstow, California (between Los Angeles and Las Vegas), attempted to prohibit the sale of rap music to minors. After the riots, library officials in Lynnwood, Washington, ordered the rap group N.W.A. removed from their shelves. Time Warner's board of directors formed an editorial committee to censor books, records, and videos, one committee member pushing for the elimination of all products that criticize the police. The Shreveport, Louisiana, Department of Parks and Recreation canceled an afternoon concert by thrash and rap acts because a flier promoting the event advocated free speech.

In August, after more than a month of attacks from organized police   15
groups, Congress, and George Bush, and after duplicitous signals from Time Warner, Ice-T decided to remove "Cop Killer" from its *Body Count* album. A few months later, Ice-T was dropped from the label altogether. In the wake of the controversy, the Tommy Boy label dropped Almighty RSO and Live Squad for attacking police brutality and refused to put out rapper Paris's album because of the song, "Bush Killa." Warner refused to distribute Kool G Rap's album, while rappers Intelligent Hoodlum, Boo-Yaa Tribe, and Da Lench Mob all had to remove controversial songs from their albums. On top of all these individual attacks, despite its popularity, mainstream radio plays almost no rap anymore, which prompted one of the most famous rappers, Ice Cube, to stage a pirate radio broadcast to debut his album in response to the Los Angeles rebellion.

CORPORATE CENSORSHIP

Corporate censorship of the marketplace is driving even mainstream rap artists underground. Labels are refusing to produce controversial rap, distributors won't handle it and the airwaves won't broadcast it. The lesson that seems to have been learned from the LA rebellion is, if this art form can sensitize the American people to a volatile situation, rather than encourage open discussion and possible revolution, we better shut it down.

In that sense, today's censorship tends to take the shape of a class war—not necessarily against the artists, but certainly against the fans who find it harder and harder to hear their favorite music, that which speaks of their anger, hopes and fears. Racist anxieties and other bourgeois family values are being used as a means for determining what music is suitable for public consumption. One of the most powerful censorship organizations in the country, Focus on the Family, which features PMRC founder Susan Baker on its board of directors, publishes a monthly magazine that black-lists music that is anti-family. This year's targets included not only the rap group Naughty by Nature, but also country singer Reba McEntire (for "distrust of men") and metal band Mötley Crüe. The common denominator being that the majority of all these artists' fans are working class—in this day and age, with little hope of a future.

In fact, young hard rock fans have it almost as bad as rap fans. Touring behind its 1989 album *And Justice For All,* the politically confrontational Metallica faced cancellations and poor promotion in one city after another because of smear campaigns that painted the group as satanists who promote suicide (wrong on both counts). About the time of the Los Angeles rebellion, a teen in Fort Smith, Arkansas, was arrested for wearing a Van

Halen *For Unlawful Carnal Knowledge* t-shirt (because of the acronym), and rock shows by GWAR and Pearl Jam were stopped in Athens, Georgia, and Seattle, Washington, respectively.

What do the majority of the above-named artists have in common? Labeled albums. All of the big censorship cases—the 2 Live Crew arrests, the sting operation on 9 record stores in Nebraska, the arrests of record retailers in Alexander City, Alabama—revolve around the distribution of labeled material. After following the trend since its origins with his newsletter *Rock & Rap Confidential,* rock writer Dave Marsh states, "Labels are catastrophic. Labeling is an implicit guilty plea. It's not a protection—it's a target. Ask Time Warner if labeling Ice-T's record protected them. If they put a label on your record, you're going to get prosecuted. And you won't be tried by the sophisticated laws of Silicon Valley—you're going to be tried under the laws of the Bible Belt."

And if the artist isn't destroyed, someone in the way probably will be.   20
Any retailer familiar with Florida record store owner Charles Freeman's case knows that, while 2 Live Crew had the money and the publicity to win its case, Freeman was still convicted of selling the album, lost his business and went to jail—for selling a *labeled* record to an adult!

The First Amendment works best if you have plenty of cash to fight your cases, and the small record store owners who stand up against censorship are those most vulnerable to financial ruin. As for alternatives, most chain stores don't carry labeled records at all. Retailers are running scared, and the First Amendment doesn't reach down to affect the actions of those in private business. Given a choice between going to court or censoring merchandise, labels and distributors are taking the logical way out. One 2 Live Crew victory doesn't make up for the message sent to small store owners and the thousands of other acts who are never signed and go unheard because of the resultant chilling effect.

Kandy Stroud may not have known what she was starting, but you can bet the VIPs at the Pig Pickin' Summit did. Looking back at the Quayle and Clinton responses to the riots, I can't help but admire the savvy of the then governor of Arkansas (who made it clear on MTV, along with his running mate, he was pro-labeling). After all, if you want to put down a rebellion, you don't take aim at a dry sitcom about an uptight, upper-middle-class white anchorwoman. You aim for the street.

SUGGESTIONS FOR FURTHER STUDY

Key Words

The author uses language with which you may not be familiar. Find the following words in the paragraphs indicated, and explain their meanings in

the context of the sentences in which the words appear. Consult a dictionary, as needed.

repression (title)
gratuitously (par. 1)
stigmatizing (par. 5)
Afrocentricity (par. 6)
mandating (par. 10)
unconstitutional (par. 10)
censorship (par. 12)

Topics for Discussion and Writing

1. Begin your discussion of Alexander's essay by considering the following:
   a. Alexander begins by presenting Tipper Gore's argument (see "Rock Music Should Be Labeled") before he counters with his argument. How effective is that strategy? Explain your answer.
   b. According to Alexander, why do people seek to control rock music? Do you agree with their reasons? Why or why not?
   c. Alexander claims that certain lessons have been learned in the aftermath of the Los Angeles riots. What are those lessons? What have some people claimed about the relationship of rap music to urban unrest?
   d. What does the Charles Freeman incident show about how the First Amendment works? Do you think this incident will influence other record-store owners? Will it affect the sale of labeled albums? Why or why not?

2. Do you agree with Alexander that labeling is a type of censorship? First, explain his reasoning, as he developed his argument; then explain your point of view, giving reasons and examples to support them. You might work with others in your class to develop this question, or write a journal entry or brief essay on your own.

3. Write a letter to Alexander, arguing against the use of explicit lyrics in pop music. Say why you think he is wrong, and offer suggestions for resolving the issue.

4. In a well-informed essay, argue for or against labeling pop music, placing informative stickers on controversial records. In your essay, address some of the following issues:
   a. Who determines what "explicit lyrics" are? Should parents, record company executives, artists, government officials, or an independent agency make such definitions and rulings?

b. How should people determine which lyrics are greatly offensive and merit labeling? Are certain words themselves particularly offensive? What might these words be?

c. Does labeling attract young people's interest *toward* controversial albums, rather than deterring them? Would young people be as likely to buy controversial albums if there were no labels?

(You may want to research books, scholarly journals, magazines, or newspapers in the library. Consult the computer databases in your library, if available, to help you find the latest information. Use the Internet to gain access to relevant material on your topic through the World Wide Web.)

Rap Furor: New Evil or Old Story?

Jesse Katz

*Jesse Katz (born November 11, 1962, in New York, New York)
received her degree from Bennington College in Vermont. She was a
staff writer with the* Los Angeles Times *from 1986 to 1994 and has
been the Houston Bureau Chief for that paper since 1994. She has
twice won a Pulitzer Prize: first for her 1992 coverage of the Los
Angeles riots and then for her reporting on the 1994 Los Angeles
earthquake. "Rap Furor: New Evil or Old Story?" was printed in the*
Los Angeles Times *on August 5, 1995.*

It was a song rumored to be so lewd not even the First Amendment   1
could stave off the outrage.

Politicians called it obscene. Radio stations were pressured to ban it.
The FBI, backed by audio technicians, spent more than two years trying to
pinpoint the smuttiest verses. Boosted by the hype, the record sold millions
of copies and became a teen-age anthem.

The latest misogynistic rap song? A grunge rocker's ode to necrophilia?
The offending lyrics, in fact, belonged to nothing more deviant than "Louie
Louie," the Kingsmen's 1963 chantey, which has since been immortalized in
telethons and wine-cooler ads.

With metronomic regularity, American society has sounded the alarm
over each new spin on popular music, condemning it as cruder, less melodic
and more volatile than genres of the past—be it jazz, swing, rock, punk or
heavy metal. Frank Sinatra, mesmerizer of impressionable young girls, once
was denounced as the country's "prime instigator of juvenile delinquency."
Later, it was Elvis, the Beatles, the Sex Pistols, Metallica and Prince.

Now the battle is being waged again, this time over "gangsta rap," an   5
ambiguous term that has served as both prejudicial slur and cynical marketing ploy. Although a fraction of the multibillion-dollar recording business,
it has become the lightning rod for a national debate over free speech, cultural values and corporate responsibility.

The furor has shaken up the entertainment industry's boardrooms and
galvanized presidential politics. It has pitted complaints of artistic censorship against charges of economic exploitation. It has pinched the raw nerve
of race, exposing deep divisions even within the black community over the

music's harsh and explicit imagery. And in a small Texas town, it has added weight to an unusual lawsuit—filed by the widow of a slain police officer against rapper Tupac Shakur—that could redefine the legal limits of musical license.

If history is any gauge, much of the tumult likely will appear overblown and paranoid in hindsight, given that even the most scandalous artists tend to mellow into nostalgic respectability over time. But in his indictment of Hollywood this summer, Senate Majority Leader Bob Dole (R-Kan.) insisted he was not just a stodgy septuagenarian trying to steal the fun of a younger generation. This time, Dole argued, "a line has been crossed—not just of taste, but of human dignity and decency."

His assessment, although shared by a majority of Americans, raises the same nettlesome questions that have kept this debate alive year after year: What is the yardstick for measuring whether a line has been crossed, especially when critics have issued similar warnings for decades? If a line has been crossed, when and where did it happen? Is Ice-T's "Cop Killer" qualitatively more objectionable than Eric Clapton's "I Shot the Sheriff?" Who makes those decisions? Who should impose them? And why bother, if denouncing a record only heightens its commercial allure?

"I think that people who are troubled by gangsta rap have legitimate concerns, but the question is: What do you do with those concerns?" said Florida attorney Bruce Rogow, who successfully defended 2 Live Crew after its album "As Nasty as They Wanna Be" was ruled obscene by a federal judge. "Do you suppress the speech, or do you use that speech to educate yourself and your children and your community? I think the discussion is healthy, but it's got to be done with an underlying ability to tolerate the uncomfortable and the threatening."

QUESTION OF RACE

What most distinguishes the attack on rap from previous musical   10
uproars is the question of race, America's great unsettled dilemma, which has long colored attitudes about crime, sexuality and the entertainment world.

Unlike rock 'n' roll, which involved the appropriation of African American rhythmic structures by white performers, gangsta rap is marketed as an authentically black musical expression, which has nonetheless proved appealing to white suburban teenagers. That commercial crossover—and the extent to which it shapes white America's vision of the black experience—is at the core of many arguments for and against the violent and demeaning lyrics.

Gangsta rap's advocates point out, for instance, that the music raised few eyebrows as long as its message was directed at inner-city listeners, whose lives presumably mirrored the gritty themes of their favorite songs. Only after white kids helped turn acts such as Dr. Dre and Snoop Doggy Dogg into shopping mall bestsellers, they contend, did the middle-class mainstream begin raising fears about rap's potentially corrosive effects.

"The problem isn't the lyrics on the records—it's the fear of the white kids liking a black artist," declares Ice-T on his "Body Count" album, before launching into a first-person account of bedding down with the daughter of a Ku Klux Klan grand wizard.

One of the more surprising defenders of this perspective is Sgt. Ron Stallworth, a Salt Lake City gang cop, who paid little attention to rap until he noticed that "quote, unquote, good clean white Mormon kids" were beginning to emulate the black gang symbolism depicted in many recordings.

Although he concedes the music can have a negative influence, he insists   15 that it is unfair to single out rap for condemnation, especially when it represents a small—and shrinking—fraction of an entertainment market already saturated by violence. Instead, in his frequent lectures around the country, he urges officers to listen to rap in a cultural context, as a realistic dispatch from society's fringes.

"Whether or not we like the music, these rappers are expressing their perception of life in America based on how they've had to live it," said Stallworth, a 21-year veteran who serves as Utah's gang intelligence coordinator. "Do I like it when they express their thoughts about killing a cop? No. Do I understand why some of those thoughts get expressed? My answer is yes. We get angry because of the language they use, but they're literally telling us, on a day-to-day basis, what's wrong with this country."

The flip side to that argument is to view gangsta rappers not as streetwise reporters but as cynical minstrels catering to a white audience's appetite for outlaw fantasies. The real racism, some critics contend, is the marketing of the gangsta mystique itself, which they say promotes the same ugly stereotypes—violent, hyper-sexual, predatory—that have been used to vilify black men for centuries.

New York essayist and music critic Stanley Crouch calls it "the selling of coon images." He compares the record executives who produce gangsta rap to high-tech slave traders. And he accuses the white consumers who buy it of seeking vicarious ghetto thrills. "All you have to do is go to Tower Records or turn on MTV, and there you are, in the darkest black America, where savages run free and wild," said Crouch, a 49-year-old jazz aficionado.

What makes those images even more noxious, Crouch argues, is that they are presented as the badge of black authenticity, not a criminal aberration. When the hard-edged grunge band Nine Inch Nails sings about crude sexual subjugation, "they don't pretend like they're the 'real' white people." But when groups such as the Geto Boys engage in the same posturing, he notes, they righteously defend themselves as the uncensored voice of the 'hood.

From a commercial perspective, there never has been anything quite   20
like the gross-out raunch of the Geto Boys, or its eccentric one-eyed, midget
rapper, Bushwick Bill, who thanked Dole for supplying about $300,000 in
free publicity by singling out the group as a peddler of "mindless violence
and loveless sex."

A case could be made—as Bushwick does on his morbid, sometimes
darkly comical, solo album "Phantom of the Rapra"—that such music was
never designed for highbrow listeners, but for an alienated inner-city audience that understands his slasher-style hyperbole. "Opera . . . deals with
sex, rape, violence, incest and suicide, you know, and it's accepted by the
same people that are willing to ban rap," he says on the album. "Rap is
opera to people in the ghetto."

VENERABLE HISTORY

A case could also be made—as Harvard scholar Henry Louis Gates Jr.
did in 1990 when he testified at the 2 Live Crew trial—that such exagger-
ated off-color imagery has a long and venerable history, with roots in the
African American oral tradition of "signifying" or "playing the dozens."
This form of heavy-handed parody, in which "rappers" try to one-up each
other with the most extravagant insults or lies, is seen as a sly way of turning age-old stereotypes on their head.

Or, after listening to a record that revels in gang rape and chainsaw
butchery, you could just conclude that "there's sort of no way to make it
respectable," said veteran rock critic Dave Marsh. "This isn't middle-class
morality or conventional Judeo-Christian values."

But to Marsh, whose books include "50 Ways to Fight Censorship," it
is precisely that outsider's perspective—culturally, racially and economically—that makes voices such as Bushwick Bill's so indispensable. Unlike
Elvis' swiveling hips or John Lennon's comparisons to Jesus, Marsh contends, today's attack is aimed at America's underclass and its access to the
mainstream media.

"This is about freezing people out," said Marsh, who condemns the   25
anti-rap campaign by Washington insiders William J. Bennett and C.
DeLores Tucker as '90s-style McCarthyism. He points to the firing in June
of record executive Doug Morris, Time Warner's staunchest advocate of
cutting-edge music. Although Morris' dismissal was said to be the result of
a management dispute, critics of the media giant took credit for ousting him
and predicted that others soon would get the boot.

"If you listen to what they're really saying, their objective is to purge
the entertainment industry of people whose ideas they disagree with,"
Marsh said. "I find *that* morally repugnant."

Yet even people with a deep respect for creative freedom sometimes blanch at the disturbing art that freedom can create. On a purely aesthetic level, it can be difficult to reconcile an affection for African American music with the negative tone that resonates through so much of rap.

'PERVERSE MODERNISM'

In her 1994 book "Hole in Our Soul," Martha Bayles contends that something terribly sour has permeated popular music, or at least those genres that treat real musicianship and life-affirming lyrics as the traits of a sellout. But unlike other critics offended by this "cult of obscenity, brutality and sonic abuse," she neither advocates censorship nor denigrates the rich traditions of jazz, blues, gospel or even rock 'n' roll.

A former Wall Street Journal art and TV writer, Bayles pins today's woes on an avant-garde strain of European art-school thinking that she calls "perverse modernism." It is this nihilistic philosophy, not African American music, that she blames for introducing the idea of "art as a game or a publicity stunt . . . designed to grab attention or blow people's minds."

Tracing the roots of this deviation, Bayles ends up fingering the Rolling   30
Stones, which she describes as the first rock band to graft the concepts of excess and exhibitionism onto the traditional blues structure. Punk rock took it further. Gangsta rap, she argues, is just the latest incarnation of those anti-social, anti-art impulses.

"There was a time when people at the bottom of society listened to the blues, which had some anger in it, some raunchy humor and some bad-man characters . . . but it also had a lot else," said Bayles, who remains hopeful that black music's early spirit eventually will reassert itself. "Everything was always presented in balance, as part of a more complete picture of human life. Gangsta rap takes the worst out there and just wallows in it."

It is one thing to debate whether that is good or bad—morally, aesthetically or politically. It is another to debate whether gangsta rap adversely affects its audience—or more precisely, whether a song's psychological impact can be measured or even identified.

There are no unequivocal scientific techniques for determining that, only judges and juries. In the past they have rejected claims that subliminal messages, purportedly inserted in heavy-metal songs by Judas Priest and Ozzy Osbourne, could be held responsible for young listeners committing suicide.

EXPLICIT LYRICS

A new legal challenge is brewing, however, this time against the far more explicit lyrics of Tupac Shakur, who has been sued in southeast Texas for allegedly inciting a teen-age gang member to gun down a state trooper after being pulled over near Victoria, outside Houston. Ronald Ray Howard, who was convicted and sentenced to death for the 1992 murder of Officer Bill Davidson, said that a tape of Shakur's "2PACALYPSE NOW" was blaring from his car stereo when he loaded his 9-millimeter pistol and pulled the trigger.

"The music was up as loud as it could go, with gunshots and siren noises on it . . . and I was so hyped up, I just snapped," Howard told The Times in a 1993 interview. At the moment of the shooting, he was listening to the song "Crooked Ass Nigga," which describes a drug dealer on a rampage, also armed with a 9-millimeter pistol:

> "Comin' quickly up the streets is the punk ass police
> The first one jumped out and said, 'Freeze.'
> I popped him in his knees, and I shouted, 'Punk, please!'"

In the lawsuit, which could go to trial in U.S. District Court this year, lawyers for Davidson's estate contend the album is essentially "a call to a battle," the musical equivalent of falsely shouting "fire" in a crowded theater.

Shakur's lyrics about cop-killing are incendiary, they allege, especially when "repeated, mantralike, to the accompaniment of a booming bass beat." Moreover, they argue, his message is directed at a violent inner-city subculture with an avowed hostility toward police. As evidence of Shakur's own criminal orientation, they point to his many run-ins with the law; he's currently in a New York prison for sexual assault.

"Under these circumstances, it is more than reasonable that Shakur and his co-defendants, already intimately familiar with the psychopathic gangsta mind-set and lifestyle, should foresee that their course of action would lead to exactly the sort of tragedy that occurred here," attorney Jim Cole said in the suit, which also names Interscope Records and Time Warner.

Arguing that the lawsuit "distorts that tragedy," Shakur's attorneys say it's absurd to hold him responsible for an irrational reaction to a fictional song.

While conceding that much of the album's language is harsh, they also reject the label "gangsta rap," insisting the recording is a collection of poems about ghetto life that sometimes depict violence but never promote it. Because more than 400,000 people purchased "2PACALYPSE NOW" and didn't kill police, they add, it clearly poses no direct threat or imminent danger—the primary constitutional test for determining the boundaries of free speech.

"All of my client's songs are just parables with a theme: that violence against black people is a continuing problem, that resisting oppression is a good thing, that the wages of drug dealing are death," said R. James George Jr., who represents the defendants. "If folks actually listened to the whole album, instead of picking out little pieces of it, I think they would think that's a pretty good message."

The fact that some can view a message as the antidote and others as the disease speaks to the ambiguity of the gangsta rap debate, a complex excavation of the nation's psyche that can be interpreted from many contradictory perspectives. Which is a little like "Louie Louie" itself.

'LOUIE LOUIE'

The song, penned in 1956 by Los Angeles musician Richard Berry, is an innocuous account of a lovesick sailor's desire to return to his Jamaican sweetheart. After the Kingsmen made it a hit, a rumor quickly spread that some salacious verses had been added, supposedly audible when the 45 r.p.m. single was slowed to 33^1/3. Scoring a bootleg copy of the graphic "real" lyrics became a teen-age prize.

Under FBI Director J. Edgar Hoover's direction, G-men crisscrossed the country, trying to determine whether obscenity laws had been broken. Cryptographers listened to the record over and over, hoping to decipher the most vulgar passages. After 2^1/2 years, the FBI concluded what the Kingsmen must have known all along—their singing was so garbled that the words were unintelligible at any speed.

"Louie Louie" was only as nasty as you wanted it to be.   45

SUGGESTIONS FOR FURTHER STUDY

Key Words

The author uses language with which you may not be familiar. Find the following words in the paragraphs indicated, and explain their meanings in the context of the sentences in which the words appear. Consult a dictionary, as needed.

smuttiest (par. 2)
misogynistic (par. 3)
necrophilia (par. 3)
appropriation (par. 11)
mystique (par. 17)
aberration (par. 19)
exhibitionism (par. 30)
incendiary (par. 37)

Topics for Discussion and Writing

1. Katz gives a brief account of the history of American society "sound[ing] the alarm" over "controversial" music. Discuss the examples Katz uses to illustrate his account.

2. In your discussions of this essay, consider the following questions:

   a. How does Katz define the ambiguous term "gangsta rap"?

   b. What message does Sergeant Ron Stallworth, a Salt Lake City gang cop, deliver to his colleagues? According to Stallworth, what are rappers trying to tell us?

   c. What does rapper Bushwick Bill mean by saying "Rap is opera to people in the ghetto"? Explain the metaphor.

   d. How did Tupac Shakur's "Crooked Ass Nigga" allegedly cause the death of a police officer? What were the consequences of the shooting? How can Shakur's lyrics and music be termed "incendiary"?

   e. What are the supposed connections of "Louie Louie" to 2 Live Crew?

3. Do you agree with former Senator Bob Dole that with some rap music "a line has been crossed . . . of human dignity and decency," or do you agree more with Ice-T that "the problem isn't the lyrics on the records—it's the fear of the white kids liking a black artist"? Discuss your views on this topic in a short paper arguing for one side of the issue. Be sure to give examples and illustrations to support your point of view.

4. Listen to classic controversial songs of the past, such as "Louie Louie," the Beatles' "Lucy in the Sky With Diamonds," J. J. Cales's "Cocaine," Bob Marley's "I Shot the Sheriff," or the Byrds' "Eight Miles High." Write an essay about how these songs appear to be controversial. You may have to do some research on the subject to gather appropriate data.

5. Locate one or two current controversial songs, and read the lyrics (you may have to transcribe them from a recording). In an essay, describe the lyrics, and say why they might be controversial.

6. The murders of "gangsta" rappers Tupac Shakur and B. I. G. in the late 1990s highlight the real danger to such artists on the streets. Do these killings illustrate the old adage "He who lives by the sword shall die by the sword"? Write a paper that investigates the often violent world of gangsta rap and reports how life on the streets (of places such as Hollywood or New York) has influenced gangsta rap and the violence to some of its practitioners. (You may want to research books, scholarly journals, magazines, or newspapers in the library. Consult the computer databases in your library, if available, to assist you in locating the latest information. Use the Internet to gain access to relevant material on your topic through the World Wide Web.)

A Final Word on Censorship from Kurt Vonnegut

Kurt Vonnegut

Kurt Vonnegut (born in Indianapolis in 1922, the son and the grand-son of Indiana architects) studied chemistry at Cornell and earned an MA in anthropology at the University of Chicago. He served in the infantry in World War II, was a prisoner of war, and survived the allied bombing and obliteration of the city of Dresden where he was held captive. He has lived in Manhattan since 1970. Vonnegut has published more than twenty books since 1951—most of them best-sellers—including Slaughterhouse-Five; Cat's Cradle; Breakfast of Champions; Mother Night; God Bless You, Mr. Rosewater; *and* Hocus Pocus *(1990). "A Final Word on Censorship from Kurt Vonnegut" was adapted from his 1994 book of autobiographical sketches,* Fates Worse Than Death.

And speaking of revered old documents which cry out for a rewrite nowadays, how about the First Amendment to the Constitution of the United States of America, which reads:

"Congress shall make no law respecting an establishment of religion, or prohibiting the free exercise thereof; or abridging the freedom of speech, or of the press; or the right of the people peaceably to assemble, and to peti-tion the Government for a redress of grievances." What we have there is what should have been at least three separate amendments, and maybe as many as five, hooked together willy-nilly in one big Dr. Seuss animal of a nonstop sentence. It is as though a starving person, rescued at last, blurted out all the things he or she had dreamed of eating while staying barely alive on bread and water.

When James Madison put together the first ten Amendments, the "Bill of Rights," in 1778, there was so much blurting by male property owners ravenous for liberty that he had 210 proposed limitations on the powers of the Government to choose from. (In my opinion, the thing most well-fed people want above all else from their Government is, figuratively speaking, the right to shoot craps with loaded dice. They wouldn't get that until President Ronald Reagan.)

I said to a lawyer for the American Civil Liberties Union that Madison's First Amendment wasn't as well written as it might have been.

"Maybe he didn't expect us to take him so seriously," he said.   5

I think there is a chance of that, although the lawyer was being wryly jocular. So far as I know, Madison did not laugh or otherwise demur when Thomas Jefferson (who owned slaves) called the Constitutional Convention in Philadelphia an assembly of demi-Gods. People two-thirds of the way to the top of Mount Olympus might not take as seriously as some of us do the possibility of actually honoring among the squabbling mortals the airy, semi-divine promises of the Bill of Rights.

The ACLU lawyer said that I, as a writer, should admire Madison for making his Amendments as unambiguous as a light switch, which can be only "on" or "off," by the strong use of absolute negatives: "Congress shall make *no* law . . . shall *not* be infringed . . . No soldier shall . . . shall *not* be violated, and *no* warrants shall issue. . . . *No* person shall be held to answer . . . *no* fact tried by a jury . . . shall *not* be required . . . shall *not* be construed. . . ." There are no words anywhere in his Amendments meaning "under ideal conditions" or "whenever possible" or "at the convenience of the Government." From moment to moment in our now long history (the oldest continuous government save for Switzerland's), the several specific provisions of the Bill of Rights can be, thanks to James Madison, only "off" or "on."

To me the First Amendment sounds more like a dream than a statute. The right to say or publish absolutely anything makes me feel as insubstantial as a character in somebody else's dream when I defend it, as I often do. It is such a *tragic* freedom since there is no limit to the vileness some people are proud to express in public if allowed to do so with impunity. So again and again in debates with representatives of the Moral Majority and the like, and some of the angrier Women Against Pornography, I find myself charged with being an encourager of violence against women and kiddie porn.

When I was new at such discussions I insouciantly asked a fundamentalist Christian opponent ("Oh, come on now, Reverend") if he knew of anyone who had been ruined by a book. (Mark Twain claimed to have been ruined by salacious parts of the Bible.)

The Reverend was glad I asked. He said that a man out in Oregon had   10 read a pornographic book and then raped a teenage maiden on her way home from the grocery store, and then mutilated her with a broken Coke bottle. (I am sure it really happened.) We were there to discuss the efforts of some parents to get certain books eliminated from school libraries and curricula on the grounds that they were offensive or morally harmful—quite mild and honorable books in any case. But my dumb question gave the Reverend the opportunity to link the books in question to the most hideous sexual crimes.

The books he and his supporters wanted out of the schools, one of mine among them, were not pornographic, although he would have liked our audience to think so. (There *is* the word "motherfucker" one time in my *Slaughterhouse-Five* as in "Get out of the road, you dumb motherfucker." Ever since that word was published, way back in 1969, children have been attempting to have intercourse with their mothers. When it will stop no one knows.) The fault of *Slaughterhouse-Five*, James Dickey's *Deliverance*, J. D. Salinger's *Catcher in the Rye*, several books by Judy Blume, and so on, as far as the Reverend was concerned, was that neither their authors nor their characters exemplified his notion of ideal Christian behavior and attitudes.

The Reverend (as was his right) was making an undisguised attack not only on Americans' demi-God–given right to consider every sort of idea (including his), but also the Constitution's insistence that the Government (including the public schools) not declare one religion superior to any other and behave accordingly with the force of law.

So the Reverend was not a hypocrite. He was perfectly willing to say in so many words that there was nothing sacred about the First Amendment, and that many images and ideas other than pornography should be taken out of circulation by the police, and that the official religion of the whole country should be his sort of Christianity. He was sincere in believing that my *Slaughterhouse-Five* might somehow cause a person to wind up in a furnace for all eternity (see the mass promulgated by Pope St. Pius V), which would be even worse (if you consider its duration) than being raped, murdered, and then mutilated by a man maddened by dirty pictures.

He in fact won my sympathy (easy to do). He was not a television evangelist (so easily and justly caricatured), although he probably preached on radio from time to time. (They all do.) He was a profoundly sincere Christian and family man, doing a pretty good job no doubt of imitating the life of Christ as he understood it, sexually clean, and not pathologically fond of the goods of this Earth and so on. He was trying to hold together an extended family, a support system far more dependable than anything the Government could put together, in sickness as in health, for richer or for poorer, whose bond was commonly held beliefs and attitudes. (I had studied anthropology, after all, and so knew in my bones that human beings can't like life very much if they don't belong to a clan associated with a specific piece of real estate.)

The Attorney General's Commission on Pornography, a traveling show 15 about dirty books and pictures put on the road during the administration of Ronald Reagan, was something else again. At least a couple of the panel members would later be revealed as having been in the muck of financial or sexual atrocities. There was a clan feeling, to be sure, but the family property in this case was the White House, and an amiable, sleepy, absentminded old movie actor was its totem pole. And the crazy quilt of ideas all its members had to profess put the Council of Trent to shame for mean-spirited, objectively batty fantasias: that it was good that civilians could buy assault rifles; that the contras in Nicaragua were a lot like Thomas Jefferson and James Madison; that Palestinians were to be called "terror-ists" at every opportunity; that the contents of wombs were Government property; that the American Civil Liberties Union was a subversive organi-zation; that anything that sounded like the Sermon on the Mount was socialist or communist, and therefore anti-American; that people with AIDS, except for those who got it from mousetrapped blood transfusions, had asked for it; that a billion-dollar airplane was well worth the price; and on and on.

The Attorney General's Commission on Pornography was blatantly show business, a way for the White House to draw attention to its piety by means of headlines about sex, and to imply yet again that those in favor of freedom of speech were enthusiasts for sexual exploitation of children and rape and so on. (While other Reagan supporters were making private the funds for public housing and cleaning out the savings banks.)

So I asked to appear before the Commission when it came to New York, but my offer was declined. I wanted to say, "I have read much of the heartrending testimony about the damage words and pictures can do which has been heard by your committee. The scales have fallen from my eyes. I now understand that our Government must have the power to suppress words and images which are causes of sexually motivated insanity and crimes. As John the Apostle says, 'In the beginning was the word.'

"I make my living with words, and I am ashamed. In view of the dam-age freely circulated ideas can do to a society, and particularly to children, I beg my Government to delete from my works all thoughts which might be dangerous. Save me from myself. I beg for the help of our elected leaders in bringing my thoughts into harmony with their own and those of the people who elected them. That is democracy.

"Attempting to make amends at this late date, I call the attention of this committee, and God bless the righteous Edwin Meese, to the fundamental piece of obscenity from which all others spring, the taproot of the tree whose fruit is so poisonous. I will read it aloud, so audience members under the age of twenty-one should leave the room. Those over twenty-one who have heart trouble or are prone to commit rape at the drop of a hat might like to go with them. Don't say I haven't warned you.

"You Commission members have no choice but to stay, no matter what   20
sort of filth is turned loose by witnesses. That can't be easy. You must be very brave. I like to think of you as sort of sewer astronauts.

"All right? Stick your fingers in your ears and close your eyes, because here we go:

" 'Congress shall make no law respecting an establishment of religion, or prohibiting the free exercise thereof; or abridging the freedom of speech, or of the press; or the right of the people peaceably to assemble, and to petition the Government for a redress of grievances.' "

End of joke.

SUGGESTIONS FOR FURTHER STUDY

Key Words

The author uses language with which you may not be familiar. Find the following words in the paragraphs indicated, and explain their meanings in the context of the sentences in which the words appear. Consult a dictionary, as needed.

abridging (par. 1)
willy-nilly (par. 2)
ravenous (par. 3)
demur (par. 6)
unambiguous (par. 7)
impunity (par. 8)
insouciantly (par. 9)
salacious (par. 9)
promulgated (par. 13)
caricatured (par. 14)

Language and Style

1. How would you describe Vonnegut's style: caustic, scholarly, satirical, humorous, or some combination of these terms? Explain your answer, and point to specific passages to support it.

2. Vonnegut wanted a chance to appear before the Commission on Pornography and tells us, jestingly, what his speech might have been. How does the facetiousness of his planned speech prepare readers for his final comment? What impact does his satirical tone have that a more serious one might not have achieved?

3. How does Vonnegut explain the "unambiguous" language of the First Amendment?

Topics for Discussion and Writing

1. Vonnegut lists the basic rights guaranteed us in the First Amendment. What are they?

2. Vonnegut sarcastically presents his opinion of the Founding Fathers and their hopes for the First Amendment. What were those hopes, and what is Vonnegut's opinion of them? Who or what groups does Vonnegut satirize in his imagined speech?

3. Explain Vonnegut's views of the Attorney General's Commission on Pornography. Why does he call it "blatantly show business"? What national figures or organizations does he ridicule?

4. Write a brief essay in which you consider freedom of speech, indicating how much freedom you believe that the First Amendment guarantees. For example, do you think a limit should be placed on what people may say in public, in songs, in literature? Do you think restrictions should be placed on what materials students have access to in high school or university classes? If so, suggest what that limit should be. If not, give reasons why not.

5. Read one of the books Vonnegut lists which might be "pornographic," such as his own *Slaughterhouse-Five,* J. D. Salinger's *Catcher in the Rye,* James Dickey's *Deliverance,* or a book by Judy Blume. Write an essay discussing whether you found the book pornographic, obscene, or even slightly controversial. Be explicit in giving your reasons.

Censorship Follies:
Was a Victory over Ice-T
a Victory over Violence?

Kathleen Santaro

In this selection, student writer Kathleen Santaro follows up Jesse Katz's work on the current "rap furor" by questioning some Americans' claims that regulating and censoring controversial music, art, and literature will help keep "society free from crime and moral deviance."

Government officials and private interest groups are using censorship 1
as a tool for change. They believe that by cleaning up the so-called "filth" in music, art, and literature, Americans can live in a society free from crime and moral deviance. Censorship, however, is just a form of passing the buck. These self-appointed watchdogs of public morality are drawing attention away from the real issues and the real criminals and in some cases are using the public's fears for personal gain.

One case of censorship that gained notoriety occurred in 1992 when rap musician Ice-T released the song "Cop Killer." Law enforcement officials and politicians were outraged by its lyrics. Officials at Time Warner, producers of the record, received threats from some police officers for distributing the song. The American Civil Liberties Union named former Marine colonel Oliver North as one of the "1992 Arts Censors of the Year" after North and his organization, Freedom Alliance, said they would ask governors of the fifty states to bring charges against the record label for violating sedition and antianarchy laws. Ice-T was also attacked by then President George Bush and condemned in the U.S. Congress. In rebuttal, Gerald M. Levin, President of Time Warner, said " 'Cop Killer' wasn't written to advocate an assault by black street kids on the police. It doesn't glorify violence." Levin continued, "Whatever the medium—print, film, video, programming, or music—we believe that the worth of what an artist or journalist has to say does not depend on pre-approval from a government official, or a corporate censor, or a cultural elite of the right, or of the left" (quoted in Cavendish 17). In the end, although he had the support of his label, Ice-T buckled under the pressure and pulled "Cop Killer" off his album. He still maintains that the song is not about killing cops.

What amazes me is that politicians saw Ice-T's action as a victory in the war against violence. They feel they are doing citizens of the United States a service when, in reality, they are violating their First Amendment rights. Although the art may not exist, the issue remains. Censoring a song, a painting, or a book is actually censoring the thoughts of a person. Sometimes these thoughts can be ugly and hurtful, but they are still important. In *50 Ways to Fight Censorship*, Dave Marsh tells us why they are so important:

> The point is that the only way to build the kinds of lives that people ought to have is to allow those words and thoughts to be heard, in all their danger. Get them out in the open, where they can be challenged, endorsed, and to the extent that they pose social and political riddles, solved. Every other avenue involves deception. And that leads to corruption, and that leads to worse lives for all of us, even those whose job it is to keep the lid on. (Introduction xvi)

Censors force their ideologies and their moral and religious values on others. Censors don't want social diversity; they think that therein lies danger. They are looking for somewhere to place the blame. However, banning a song about killing doesn't make killing go away; instead, banning a song kills the messenger. Art has always been a vehicle for social commentary, and we need art to inform us of what is going on in the world around us.   5

Our government is hypocritical regarding our right to free speech. For example, in a 1995 address before 350 contributors to the Republican Party [see the first reading in chapter 4], former Senate Majority Leader Bob Dole pleaded with the entertainment industry to stop producing movies and music that "push the limits of decency." He placed the blame for our social problems directly on the entertainment industry but said nothing about government's role in solving those problems. He insisted, "The mainstreaming of deviancy must come to an end, but it will *only* stop when the leaders of the entertainment industry recognize and shoulder their responsibility." Dole contradicted himself, however, by saying that "people are responsible for their actions. Movies and music do not make children into murderers" and that "our freedom is precious. I have risked my life to defend it, and I would do it again. We must always be proud that in America we have the freedom to speak without Big Brother's permission" (12). Nevertheless, his purpose for speaking was to pressure the entertainment industry to stop "mainstreaming deviancy." It gets worse: Dole accused the entertainment business leaders of lying when they say they are responding to the market. "Last year," Dole asserted, "the five top-grossing films were the blockbusters *The Lion King, Forrest Gump, True Lies, The Santa Clause*, and

The Flintstones. To put it in perspective, it has been reported that *The Lion King* made six times as much money as *Natural Born Killers*" (12).

I wonder what Dole's point is. Is he suggesting that because *Natural Born Killers* wasn't in the top five, the film should not be shown? Does he mean that because the film wasn't popular with the majority of viewers, it should be withdrawn from circulation? Dole fails to realize that some of us are interested in entertainment that has something to say, even if what is said is ugly or painful. Some of us are not interested in "white bread" entertainment, and we have the right to enjoy the work of artists who feel the same way. Bob Dole closed the aforementioned speech with "Ours is not a crusade for censorship; it is a call for good citizenship" (12). Bull shit, Bob! It's censorship with a nice candy coating to make it go down easy.

It's time for our government to begin instead to attack real issues. The controversy about "Cop Killer" and the outcry to stop the record's distribution came about because police were afraid of being victimized. But a California Department of Justice report for the same year "Cop Killer" was written, 1992, made that fear seem unreasonable. According to the California Department of Justice, there were 5 police officers killed in the line of duty, 3,920 homicides reported, 12,751 forcible rapes reported, 197,970 aggravated assaults reported, and 240,826 domestic violence-related calls for assistance. That 5 officers lost their lives is a terrible thing, but these statistics make me wonder why there isn't a greater public outcry to stop domestic violence and rape. Obviously, such crimes happen at a much higher rate than does violence against police officers.

In my opinion, accusations of anarchy and sedition against Ice-T and others in the entertainment industry are overreactions created out of fear. Themes about love, death, and violence, which appear in works by artists such as Ice-T and 2 Live Crew are centuries old; Ice-T and 2 Live Crew are musicians, not revolutionaries. Our First Amendment protects our right to free speech and expression, no matter how unpopular; without this right, all our other rights are in danger. Surely our government's time and money would be better spent finding solutions to social and economic problems such as homelessness, hunger, illiteracy, or child abuse. These are the real problems, and their existence cannot be blamed on the art or the artists of our time. Our attention should be focused on these problems, not on the lyrics of a song.

Works Cited

Cavendish, Richard. "Art, Ideas, and Ice-T." *National Review* Vol. 44, 17 Aug 1992, p. 17.

Dole, Robert J., "U.S. Entertainment Industry Must Accept Responsibility for Its Work." Century City Hotel, Los Angeles, May 31 1995. *Human Events* Vol. 51, 16 June 1995, p. 12.

Lungren, Daniel E. *Crime and Delinquency in California 1992*. California: Deptartment of Justice, Division of Law Enforcement, 1992.

——, *Homicide in California 1992*. California: Department of Justice, Division of Law Enforcement, 1992.

Marsh, Dave. *50 Ways to Fight Censorship: And Important Facts to Know about the Censors*. New York: Thunder's Mouth Press, 1991.

CHAPTER 9: ACTIVITIES FOR DISCUSSION AND WRITING
Making Connections

1. Compare either "2 Live Crew Decoded" or "Rap Furor: New Evil or Old Story" to Robert Palmer's "What Pop Lyrics Say to Us Today." What do the songs discussed in those first two essays suggest in terms of the messages pop lyrics contain today?

2. Compare Gore's "Rock Music Should Be Labeled" to Brubach's "Rock and Roll Vaudeville" from Chapter 4. Both writers take issue with rock and rap videos, with Gore particularly offended by the "adult themes" in videos, such as Def Leppard's "scantily clad women being captured and imprisoned in cages by a studded-leather-clad male band." Explain the similarities and differences in Gore's and Brubach's assaults on rock and rap videos.

3. In "2 Live Crew Decoded" Henry Louis Gates, Jr., suggests that understanding and interpreting lyrics depends on who is the one doing the interpreting. In a compare and contrast essay, compare Gates's concept to Gore's essay, "Rock Music Should Be Labeled." What ethnic and social group does she represent, and how does this affect her perception of popular music and who is doing the interpreting? You may want to consider Danny Alexander's comments about Gore and her allies in "Labeling Rock Music Leads to Repression."

4. Katz describes how the rapper Tupac Shakur was sued for one of his songs, which allegedly inspired the murder of a Texas police officer. Write an essay in which you discuss the extent to which you think artists should be held accountable for the actions of their audience. You might cite other examples of artists or producers of TV and movies who have been blamed for the behavior of members of their audience.

5. Many of the essays in this chapter discuss attempts by people to regulate/repress/censor controversial music. Read the interviews

with entertainment-industry biggies in the article "Sex, Lies, and Bob Dole" (Chapter 4), and write an essay in which you utilize some of those interviews in conjunction with any of the writings in Chapter 9 to comment on controversial music.

ISSUES IN AMERICA V
Saving the Planet and Other Environmental Concerns

This final chapter in *Living in America* focuses on a critical issue that may be the most important of all for America and the world: our present environment and the future health of planet Earth. Here, we offer readings that address the controversies surrounding the issues of global warming, strategies for coping with environmental pollution, worldwide stockpiling of nuclear weapons, bans on A-bomb testing, the classroom teaching of environmental subject matter (i.e., what should be taught and by whom), and the level of student interest in environmental issues. In this chapter, we stress the need for Americans to become aware of the seriousness and magnitude of environmental problems in a world where toxic wastes are dumped into our waterways and our wilderness lands, refuse overflows existing landfills faster than new ones can be opened, and forests are depleted to make way for commerce.

Tom Wolfe opens our chapter with a satirical look at students' concern over environmental and other social–political crises in "The Intelligent Coed's Guide to America." Next, the late Carl Sagan educates us with a scientific analysis of global warming in "The Warming of the World." Subsequently, a series of articles debates opinions about how to solve our environmental problems: Kirkpatrick Sale argues against individual solutions to pollution in "The Environmental Crisis Is Not Our Fault"; in "Sustainability," Robert Chianese recommends a global solution to the environmental crisis; Connie Koenenn directly counters the global and national approaches with an article commending individual solutions in "Thinking Small in a Season of Excess"; and in "The Environmental Battle Moves into the Classroom," Frank Clifford explores the debate over presenting controversial material on the environment in our classrooms.

Carl Sagan returns with another view of the hazards of nuclear weaponry in "The Nuclear Winter," and Loren Stein echoes Sagan's concerns, elaborating on current international solutions and their limitations in "Bomb Ban on the Brink." Popular science-fiction writer Ray Bradbury offers his bleakly humorous depiction of a future cyberhouse and its attempt to survive after a nuclear holocaust in "There Will Come Soft Rains." Finally, student writer Linnea Saukko closes the chapter with her biting satire, "How to Poison Earth."

The Intelligent Coed's Guide to America

Tom Wolfe

Tom Wolfe grew up in Richmond, Virginia, received a PhD in American Studies from Yale University, and now lives in New York City. He is the author of The Right Stuff *(1979),* The Electric Kool-Aid Acid Test, The Bonfire of the Vanities, *and more.* Mauve Gloves & Madmen, Clutter & Vine, *from which this selection was taken, was published in 1976.*

1. O'HARE!

O Mother O'Hare, big bosom for our hungry poets, pelvic saddle for our sexologists and Open Classroom theorists—O houri O'Hare, who keeps her Perm-O-Pour Stoneglow thighs ajar to receive a generation of frustrated and unreadable novelists—

But wait a minute. It may be too early for the odes. Has it even been duly noted that O'Hare, which is an airport outside Chicago, is now the intellectual center of the United States?

Curious, but true. There at O'Hare, on any day, Monday through Friday, from September to June, they sit . . . in row after Mies van der row of black vinyl and stainless-steel sling chairs . . . amid soaring walls of plate glass . . . from one tenth to one third of the literary notables of the United States. In October and April, the peak months, the figure goes up to one half.

Masters and Johnson and Erica Jong, Kozol and Rifkin and Hacker and Kael, Steinem and Nader, Marks, Hayden and Mailer, Galbraith and Heilbroner, and your bear-market brothers in the PopEco business, Lekachman & Others—which of you has not hunkered down lately in the prodigious lap of Mother O'Hare!

And why? Because they're heading out into the land to give lectures. They are giving lectures at the colleges and universities of America's heartland, which runs from Fort Lee, New Jersey, on the east to the Hollywood Freeway on the west. Giving lectures in the heartland is one of the lucrative dividends of being a noted writer in America. It is the writer's faint approximation of, say, Joe Cocker's $25,000 one-night stand at the West Springfield Fair. All the skyways to Lectureland lead through O'Hare

Airport. In short, up to one half of our intellectual establishment sits outside of Chicago between planes.

At a literary conference at Notre Dame, I (no stranger to bountiful O'Hare myself) ran into a poet who is noted for his verse celebrating the ecology, née Nature. He lives in a dramatic house nailed together completely from uncut pieces of hickory driftwood, perched on a bluff overlooking the crashing ocean, a spot so remote that you can drive no closer than five miles to it by conventional automobile and barely within a mile and a half by Jeep. The last 7,500 feet it's hand over hand up rocks, vines, and lengths of hemp. I remarked that this must be the ideal setting in which to write about the ecological wonders.

"I wouldn't know," he said. "I do all my writing in O'Hare."

And what is the message that the bards and sages of O'Hare bring to millions of college students in the vast fodderlands of the nation? I'm afraid I must report that it is a gloomy message; morose, even, heading for gangrene.

2. THE FRISBEE ION

If you happen to attend a conference at which whole contingents of the O'Hare philosophers assemble, you can get the message in all its varieties in a short time. Picture, if you will, a university on the Great Plains . . . a new Student Activities Center the color of butter-almond ice cream . . . a huge interior space with tracks in the floor, along which janitors in green twill pull Expando-Flex accordion walls to create meeting rooms of any size. The conference is about to begin. The students come surging in like hormones. You've heard of rosy cheeks? They *have* them! Here they come, rosy-cheeked, laughing, with Shasta and 7-Up pumping through their veins, talking chipsy, flashing weatherproof smiles, bursting out of their down-filled Squaw Valley jackets and their blue jeans—O immortal denim mons veneris!—looking, all of them, boys and girls, Jocks & Buds & Freaks, as if they spent the day hang-gliding and then made a Miller commercial at dusk and are now going to taper off with a little Culture before returning to the coed dorm. They grow quiet. The conference begins. The keynote speaker, a historian wearing a calfskin jacket and hair like Felix Mendelssohn's, informs them that the United States is "a leaden, life-denying society."

Over the next thirty-six hours, other O'Hare regulars fill in the rest: 10

Sixty families control one half the private wealth of America, and two hundred corporations own two thirds of the means of production. "A small group of nameless, faceless men" who avoid publicity the way a werewolf avoids the dawn now dominates American life. In America a man's home is not his castle but merely "a gigantic listening device with a mortgage" —a reference to eavesdropping by the FBI and the CIA. America's foreign policy has been and continues to be based upon war, assassination, bribery, genocide, and the sabotage of democratic governments. "The new

McCarthyism" (Joe's, not Gene's) is already upon us. Following a brief charade of free speech, the "gagging of the press" has resumed. Racism in America has not diminished; it is merely more subtle now. The gulf between rich and poor widens daily, creating "permanent ghetto-colonial populations." The decline in economic growth is causing a crisis in capitalism, which will lead shortly to authoritarian rule and to a new America in which everyone waits, in horror, for the knock on the door in the dead of the night, the descent of the knout on the nape of the neck—

How other people attending this conference felt by now, I didn't dare ask. As for myself, I was beginning to feel like Job or Miss Cunégonde. What further devastations or humiliations could possibly be in store, short of the sacking of Kansas City? It was in that frame of mind that I attended the final panel discussion, which was entitled "The United States in the Year 2000."

The prognosis was not good, as you can imagine. But I was totally unprepared for the astounding news brought by an ecologist.

"I'm not sure I want to be alive in the year 2000," he said, although he certainly looked lively enough at the moment. He was about thirty-eight, and he wore a Madras plaid cotton jacket and a Disco Magenta turtleneck jersey.

It seemed that recent studies showed that, due to the rape of the atmosphere by aerosol spray users, by 2000 a certain ion would no longer be coming our way from the sun. I can't remember which one . . . the aluminum ion, the magnesium ion, the neon ion, the gadolinium ion, the calcium ion . . . the calcium ion perhaps; in any event, it was crucial for the formation of bones, and by 2000 it would be no more. Could such a thing be? Somehow this went beyond any of the horrors I was already imagining. I began free-associating . . . Suddenly I could see Lexington Avenue, near where I live in Manhattan. The presence of the storm troopers was the least of it. It was the look of ordinary citizens that was so horrible. Their bones were going. They were dissolving. Women who had once been clicking and clogging down the avenue up on five-inch platform soles, with their pants seams smartly cleaving their declivities, were now mere denim & patent-leather blobs . . . oozing and inching and suppurating along the sidewalk like amoebas or ticks . . . A cab driver puts his arm out the window . . . and it just dribbles down the yellow door like hot Mazola . . . A blind news dealer tries to give change to a notions buyer for Bloomingdale's, and their fingers run together like fettucine over a stack of *New York Posts* . . . It's horrible . . . it's obscene . . . it's the end—

I was so dazed, I was no longer wondering what the assembled students thought of all this. But just at that moment one of them raised his hand. He was a tall boy with a lot of curly hair and a Fu Manchu mustache.

"Yes?" said the ecologist.

15

"There's one thing I can't understand," said the boy.

"What's that?" said the ecologist.

"Well," said the boy. "I'm a senior, and for four years we've been told   20
by people like yourself and the other gentlemen that everything's in terrible
shape, and it's all going to hell, and I'm willing to take your word for it,
because you're all experts in your fields. But around here, at this school, for
the past four years, the biggest problem, as far as I can see, has been finding
a parking place near the campus."

Dead silence. The panelists looked at this poor turkey to try to size him
up. Was he trying to be funny? Or was this the native bray of the heartland?
The ecologist struck a note of forbearance as he said:

"I'm sure that's true, and that illustrates one of the biggest difficulties
we have in making realistic assessments. A university like this, after all, is a
middle-class institution, and middle-class life is calculated precisely to create a screen—"

"I understand all that," said the boy. "What I want to know is—how
old are you, usually, when it all hits you?"

And suddenly the situation became clear. The kid was no wiseacre! He
was genuinely perplexed! . . . For four years he had been squinting at the
horizon . . . looking for the grim horrors which he knew—on faith—to be
all around him . . . and had been utterly unable to find them . . . and now he
was afraid they might descend on him all at once when he least expected it.
He might be walking down the street in Omaha one day, minding his own
business, when—whop! whop! whop! whop!—War! Fascism! Repression!
Corruption!—they'd squash him like bowling balls rolling off a roof!

Who was that lost lad? What was his name? Without knowing it, he   25
was playing the xylophone in a boneyard. He was the unique new creature
of the 1970's. He was Candide in reverse. Candide and Miss Cunégonde,
one will recall, are taught by an all-knowing savant, Dr. Pangloss. He keeps
assuring them that this is "the best of all possible worlds," and they believe
him implicitly—even though their lives are one catastrophe after another.
Now something much weirder was happening. The Jocks & Buds & Freaks
of the heartland have their all-knowing savants of O'Hare, who keep warning them that this is "the worst of all possible worlds," and they know it
must be true—and yet life keeps getting easier, sunnier, happier . . . *Frisbee!*

How can such things be?

SUGGESTIONS FOR FURTHER STUDY

Key Words

The author uses language with which you may not be familiar. Find the
following words in the paragraphs indicated, and explain their meanings in

the context of the sentences in which the words appear. Consult a dictionary, as needed.

sexologists (par. 1)
hunkered (par. 4)
bards (par. 8)
McCarthyism (par. 11)
ecologist (par. 13)
magenta (par. 14)
suppurating (par. 15)

Topics for Discussion and Writing

1. Wolfe's writing style is often called "New Journalism." Look at his description of Chicago's airport and the people he finds there. Look further at his report of the conference. What features of his style do you find in those descriptions? Examine the front page of your local newspaper for an example of more traditional journalistic style of writing. What features of Wolfe's reporting style are similar to or different from traditional reporting style?

2. According to Wolfe, "literary notables" ("bards and sages") send a specific message to their audiences. What does he say those messages are? Explain your answer in the context of Wolfe's essay.

3. Describe Wolfe's vision of the "horrors" that might occur to New York City "due to the rape of the atmosphere by aerosol spray users." Do you think Wolfe is being serious? Explain your answer.

4. How does the tall boy with the "Fu Manchu" mustache react to the grim words of the ecologist? Do you agree more with the tall boy or with the ecologist? Explain your answer.

5. Write a journal entry or a brief essay about a lecture you attended in college or at a public forum. What did you find disturbing, exciting, interesting, or puzzling about the lecture? Be sure to specify the topic of the lecture and your reaction to it.

6. For a further look at how writers comment on human behavior, read all or part of *Candide*, François Voltaire's eighteenth-century novel, which has been performed as a stage musical. Compare Wolfe's comments about human behavior in "An Intelligent Coed's Guide to America" to some of Voltaire's descriptions of Candide and his acquaintances.

7. Read another work by Tom Wolfe (some are listed in the biographical sketch that precedes this selection). Write a review of the work you selected describing its subject, the writer's style, and your reactions to it.

The Warming of the World

Carl Sagan

The son of a textile worker in New York City, Sagan received his undergraduate and graduate degrees from the University of Chicago. He taught at dozens of universities, including Stanford, UC Berkeley, and Harvard. His books include Dragons of Eden *and* Cosmos *(1980), and he was narrator and producer of the television series,* Cosmos.

When humans first evolved—in the savannahs of East Africa a few   1
million years ago—our numbers were few and our powers feeble. We knew almost nothing about controlling our environment—even clothing had yet to be invented. We were creatures of the climate, utterly dependent upon it.

A few degrees hotter or colder on average, and our ancestors were in trouble. The toll taken much later by the ice ages, in which average land temperatures dropped some 8°C (centigrade, or Celsius), must have been horrific. And yet, it is exactly such climatic change that pushed our ancestors to develop tools and technology, science and civilization. Certainly, skills in hunting, skinning, tanning, building shelters and refurbishing caves must owe much to the terrors of the deep ice age.

Today, we live in a balmy epoch, 10,000 years after the last major glaciation. In this climatic spring, our species has flourished; we now cover the entire planet and are altering the very appearance of our world. Lately—within the last century or so—humans have acquired, in more ways than one, the ability to make major changes in that climate upon which we are so dependent. The Nuclear Winter findings are one dramatic indication that we can change the climate—in this case, in the spasm of nuclear war. But I wish here to describe a different kind of climatic danger, this one slower, more subtle and arising from intentions that are wholly benign.

It is warm down here on Earth because the Sun shines. If the Sun were somehow turned off, the Earth would rapidly cool. The oceans would freeze, eventually the atmosphere itself would condense out and our planet would be covered everywhere by snowbanks of solid oxygen and nitrogen 10 meters (about 30 feet) high. Only the tiny trickle of heat from the Earth's interior and the faint starlight would save our world from a temperature of absolute zero.

We know how bright the Sun is; we know how far from it we are; and   5
we know what fraction of the sunlight reaching the Earth is reflected back

to space (about 30 percent). So we can calculate—with a simple mathematical equation—what the average temperature of the Earth should be. But when we do the calculation, we find that the Earth's temperature should be about 20°C below the freezing point of water, in stark contradiction to our everyday experience. What have we done wrong?

As in many such cases in science, what we've done wrong is to forget something—in this case, the atmosphere. Every object in the universe radiates some kind of light to space; the colder the object, the longer the wavelength of radiation it emits. The Earth—much colder than the Sun—radiates to space mainly in the infrared part of the spectrum, not the visible. Were the Sun turned off, the Earth would soon be indetectable in ordinary visible light, though it would be brilliantly illuminated in infrared light.

When sunlight strikes the Earth, part is reflected back into the sky; much of the rest is absorbed by the ground and heats it—the darker the ground, the greater the heating. The ground radiates back upward in the infrared. Thus, for an airless Earth, the temperature would be set solely by a balance between the incoming sunlight absorbed by the surface and the infrared radiation that the surface emits back to space.

When you put air on a planet, the situation changes. The Earth's atmosphere is, generally, still transparent to visible light. That's why we can see each other when we talk, glimpse distant mountains and view the stars.

But in the infrared, all that is different. While the oxygen and nitrogen in the air are transparent in both the infrared and the visible, minor constituents such as water vapor (H_2O) and carbon dioxide (CO_2) tend to be much more opaque in the infrared. It would be useless for us to have eyes that could see at a wavelength, say, of 15 microns in the infrared, because the air is murky black there.

Accordingly, if you add air to a world, you heat it: The surface now has difficulty when it tries to radiate back to space in the infrared. The atmosphere tends to absorb the infrared radiation, keeping heat near the surface and providing an infrared blanket for the world. There is very little CO_2 in the Earth's atmosphere—only 0.03 percent. But that small amount is enough to make the Earth's atmosphere opaque in important regions of the infrared spectrum. CO_2 and H_2O are the reason the global temperature is not well below freezing. We owe our comfort—indeed, our very existence— to the fact that these gases are present and are much more transparent in the visible than in the infrared. Our lives depend on a delicate balance of invisible gases. Too much blanket, or too little, and we're in trouble.

This property of many gases to absorb strongly in the infrared but not in the visible, and thereby to heat their surroundings, is called the "greenhouse effect." A florist's greenhouse keeps its planty inhabitants warm. The phrase "greenhouse effect" is widely used and has an instructive ring to it, reminding us that we live in a planetary-scale greenhouse and recalling the admonition about living in glass houses and throwing stones. But, in fact, florists' greenhouses do not keep warm by the greenhouse effect; they work mainly by inhibiting the movement of air inside, another matter altogether.

We need look only as far as the nearest planet to see an example of an atmospheric greenhouse effect gone wild. Venus has in its atmosphere an enormous quantity of carbon dioxide (roughly as much as is buried as carbonates in all the rocks of the Earth's crust). There is an atmosphere of CO_2 on Venus 90 times thicker than the atmosphere of the Earth and containing some 200,000 times more CO_2 than in our air. With water vapor and other minor atmospheric constituents, this is enough to make a greenhouse effect that keeps the surface of Venus around 470°C (900°F)—enough to melt tin or lead.

When humans burn wood or "fossil fuels" (coal, oil, natural gas, etc.), they put carbon dioxide into the air. One carbon atom (C) combines with a molecule of oxygen (O_2) to produce CO_2. The development of agriculture, the conversion of dense forest to comparatively sparsely vegetated farms, has moved carbon atoms from plants on the ground to carbon dioxide in the air. About half of this new CO_2 is removed by plants or by the layering down of carbonates in the oceans. On human time-scales, these changes are irreversible: Once the CO_2 is in the atmosphere, human technology is helpless to remove it. So the overall amount of CO_2 in the air has been growing—at least since the industrial revolution. If no other factors operate, and if enough CO_2 is put into the atmosphere, eventually the average surface temperature will increase perceptibly.

There are other greenhouse gases that are increasingly abundant in the Earth's atmosphere—halocarbons, such as the freon used in refrigerator cooling systems; or nitrous oxide (N_2O), produced by automobile exhausts and nitrogenous fertilizers; or methane (CH_4), produced partly in the intestines of cows and other ruminants.

But let's for the moment concentrate on carbon dioxide: How long, at   15 the present rates of burning wood and fossil fuels, before the global climate becomes significantly warmer? And what would the consequences be?

It is relatively simple to calculate the immediate warming from a given increase in the CO_2 abundance, and all competent calculations seem to be in good agreement. More difficult to estimate are (1) the rate at which carbon dioxide will continue to be put into the atmosphere (it depends on population growth rates, economic styles, alternative energy sources and the like) and (2) feedbacks—ways in which a slight warming might produce other, more drastic, effects.

The recent increase in atmospheric CO_2 is well documented. Over the last century, this CO_2 buildup should have resulted in a few tenths of a degree of global warming, and there is some evidence that such a warming has occurred.

The National Academy of Sciences estimates that the present atmospheric abundance of CO_2 is likely to double by the year 2065, although experts at the academy predict a one-in-20 chance that it will double before 2035—when an infant born today becomes 50 years old. Such a doubling would warm the air near the surface of the Earth by 2°C or 3°C—maybe by as much as 4°C. These are average temperature values; there would naturally be considerable local variation. High latitudes would be warmed much more, although a baked Alaska will be some time coming.

There would be precipitation changes. The annual discharge of rivers would be altered. Some scientists believe that central North America— including much of the area that is now the breadbasket of the world— would be parched in summer if the global temperature increases by a few degrees. There would be some mitigating effects; for example, where plant growth is not otherwise limited, more CO_2 should aid photosynthesis and make more luxuriant growth (of weeds as well as crops). If the present CO_2 injection into the atmosphere continued over a few centuries, the warming would be greater than from all other causes over the last 100,000 years.

As the climate warms, glacial ice melts. Over the last 100 years, the level of the world's oceans has risen by 15 centimeters (6 inches). A global warming of 3°C or 4°C over the next century is likely to bring a further rise in the average sea level of about 70 centimeters (28 inches). An increase of this magnitude could produce major damage to ports all over the world and induce fundamental changes in the patterns of land development. A serious speculation is that greenhouse temperature increases of 3°C or 4°C could, in addition, trigger the disintegration of the West Antarctic Ice Sheet, with huge quantities of polar ice falling into the ocean. This would raise sea level by some 6 meters (20 feet) over a period of centuries, with the eventual inundation of all coastal cities on the planet.

There are many other possibilities that are poorly understood, including the release of other greenhouse gases (for example, methane from peat bogs) accelerated by the warming climate. The circulation of the oceans might be an important aspect of the problem. The scientific community is attempting to make an environmental-impact statement for the entire planet on the consequences of continued burning of fossil fuels. Despite the uncertainties, a kind of consensus is in: Over the next century or more, with projected rates of burning of coal, oil and gas, there is trouble ahead.

The problem is difficult for at least three different reasons:

1. We do not yet fully understand how severe the greenhouse consequences will be.

2. Although the effects are not yet strikingly noticeable in everyday life, to deal with the problem, the present generation might have to make sacrifices for the next.

3. The problem cannot be solved except on an international scale: The atmosphere is ignorant of national boundaries. South African carbon dioxide warms Taiwan, and Soviet coal-burning practices affect productivity in

America. The largest coal resources in the world are found in the Soviet Union [Commonwealth of Independent States], the United States and China, in that order. What incentives are there for a nation such as China, with vast coal reserves and a commitment to rapid economic development, to hold back on the burning of fossil fuels because the result might, decades later, be a parched American sunbelt or still more ghastly starvation in sub-Saharan Africa? Would countries that might benefit from a warmer climate be as vigorous in restraining the burning of fossil fuels as nations likely to suffer greatly?

Fortunately, we have a little time. A great deal can be done in decades. Some argue that government subsidies lower the price of fossil fuels, inviting waste; more efficient usage, besides its economic advantage, could greatly ameliorate the CO_2 greenhouse problem. Parts of the solution might involve alternative energy sources, where appropriate: solar power, for example, or safer nuclear fission reactors, which, whatever their other dangers, produce no greenhouse gases of importance. Conceivably, the long-awaited advent of commercial nuclear fusion power might happen before the middle of the next century.

However, any technological solution to the looming greenhouse problem must be worldwide. It would not be sufficient for the United States or the Soviet Union, say, to develop safe and commercially feasible fusion power plants: That technology would have to be diffused worldwide, on terms of cost and reliability that would be more attractive to developing nations than a reliance on fossil fuel reserves or imports. A serious, very high-level look at patterns of U.S. and world energy development in light of the greenhouse problem seems overdue.

During the last few million years, human technology, spurred in part by 25 climatic change, has made our species a force to be reckoned with on a planetary scale. We now find, to our astonishment, that we pose a danger to ourselves. The present world order is, unfortunately, not designed to deal with global-scale dangers. Nations tend to be concerned about themselves, not about the planet; they tend to have short-term rather than long-term objectives. In problems such as the increasing greenhouse effect, one nation or region might benefit while another suffers. In other global environmental issues, such as nuclear war, all nations lose. The problems are connected: Constructive international efforts to understand and resolve one will benefit the others.

Further study and better public understanding are needed, of course. But what is essential is a global consciousness—a view that transcends our exclusive identification with the generational and political groupings into which, by accident, we have been born. The solution to these problems requires a perspective that embraces the planet and the future. We are all in this greenhouse together.

SUGGESTIONS FOR FURTHER STUDY

Key Words

The author uses language with which you may not be familiar. Find these words in the paragraphs indicated, and explain their meanings in the context of the sentences in which the words appear. Consult a dictionary, as needed.

savannahs (par. 1)
glaciation (par. 3)
radiation (par. 6)
infrared (par. 9)
vegetated (par. 13)
precipitation (par. 19)
consensus (par. 21)
fossil fuels (par. 23)
nuclear fission (par. 23)

Topics for Discussion and Writing

1. Reread the essay's first paragraph. Did Sagan support the theory of evolution or the belief in creationism? What in the first paragraph suggests his support for either perspective?

2. Explain in your own words what Sagan meant by "our lives depend upon a delicate balance of invisible gases."

3. According to Sagan, what causes the "greenhouse effect," and what will be its effect?

4. Sagan listed three problems in understanding the consequences of the "greenhouse effect." What solutions did he offer for dealing with the greenhouse problem? List his solutions, and discuss whether you and other readers think them possible. In your discussion, include your own ideas about how to solve the greenhouse effect problem.

5. Write a journal entry defining *global consciousness* in your own words. Refer to Sagan's essay or to other readings on this topic, which you may have read.

6. Sagan suggested that we "pose a danger to ourselves," due to rapid technological advances. In class discussion groups or in an essay, describe current technology and its role in your life and in the lives of other people around you. Consider some of the following ideas in your discussion:

   a. Which technological advances (CD players, computers, car alarms, microwaves, etc.) have had the most impact on your life?

b. How do technological gadgets affect your environment?
c. Why is it difficult for people to stop using products that they know pose a danger to our environment?
d. Which technological advances pose the greatest danger to our environment?

The Environmental Crisis
Is Not Our Fault

Kirkpatrick Sale

Kirkpatrick Sale (born in 1937 in Ithaca, New York) received his BA from Cornell University. He has been an editor and correspondent for the New Leader, *the* San Francisco Chronicle, *and the* New York Times Magazine. *His books include* The CIA and World Peace *and* Human Scale *(1980). The following article appeared in* The Nation *on April 30, 1990.*

I am as responsible as most eco-citizens: I bike everywhere; I don't own   1
a car; I recycle newspapers, bottles, cans and plastics; I have a vegetable garden in the summer; I buy organic products; and I put all vegetable waste into my backyard compost bin, probably the only one in all of Greenwich Village. But I don't at the same time believe that I am saving the planet, or in fact doing anything of much consequence about the various eco-crises around us. What's more, I don't even believe that if "all of us" as individuals started doing the same it would make any but the slightest difference, and then only of degree and not—where it counts—of kind.

Leave aside ozone depletion and rain forest destruction—those are patently corporate crimes that no individual actions will remedy to any degree. Take, instead, energy consumption in this country. In 1987 (the most recent figures) residential consumption was 7.2 percent of the total, commercial 5.5 percent and industrial 23.3 percent; of the remainder, 27.8 percent was transportation (about one-third of it by private car) and 36.3 percent was electric generation (about one-third for residential use). Individual energy use, in sum, was something like 28 percent of total consumption. Therefore, although you and I cutting down on energy consumption would have some small effect (and should be done), it is surely the energy consumption of industry and other large institutions such as government and agribusiness that needs to be addressed first. And it is industry and government that must be forced to explain what their consumption is for, what is produced by it, how necessary it is and how it can be drastically reduced. They need an Earth Day more than we do.

The point is that the ecological crisis *is* essentially beyond "our" control, as citizens or householders or consumers or even voters. It is not something that can be halted by recycling or double-pane insulation. It is the inevitable by-product of our modern industrial civilization, dominated by capitalist production and consumption and serviced and protected by various institutions of government, federal to local. It cannot possibly be altered or reversed by simple individual actions, even by the actions of the millions who will take part in Earth Day—and even if they all went home and fixed their refrigerators and from then on walked to work. Nothing less than a drastic overhaul of this civilization and an abandonment of its ingrained gods—progress, growth, exploitation, technology, materialism, humanism and power—will do anything substantial to halt our path to environmental destruction, and it's hard to see how the lifestyle solutions offered by Earth Day will have an effect on that.

What I find truly pernicious about such solutions is that they get people thinking they are actually making a difference and doing their part to halt the destruction of the earth: "There, I've taken all the bottles to the recycling center and used my string bag at the grocery store; I guess that'll take care of global warming." It is the kind of thing that diverts people from the hard truths and hard choices and hard actions, from the recognition that they have to take on the larger forces of society—corporate and governmental—where true power, and true destructiveness, lie.

And to the argument that, well, you have to start somewhere to raise   5
people's consciousness, I would reply that this individualistic approach does not in fact raise consciousness. It does not move people beyond their old familiar liberal perceptions of the world, it does nothing to challenge the belief in technofix or write-your-Congressperson solutions and it does not begin to provide them with the new vocabulary and modes of thought necessary for a true change of consciousness. We need, for example, to think of recycling centers not as the answer to our waste problems, as Earth Day suggests, but as a confession that the system of packaging and production in this society is out of control. Recycling centers are like hospitals; they are the institutions at the end of the cycle that take care of problems that would never exist if ecological criteria had operated at the beginning of the cycle. Until we have those kinds of understandings, we will not do anything with consciousness except reinforce it with the same misguided ideas that created the crisis. . . .

SUGGESTIONS FOR FURTHER STUDY

Key Words

The author uses language with which you may not be familiar. Find the following words in the paragraphs indicated, and explain their meanings in

the context of the sentences in which the words appear. Consult a dictionary, as needed.

ecological (par. 3)
materialism (par. 3)
humanism (par. 3)
pernicious (par. 4)
technofix (par. 5)

Topics for Discussion and Writing

1. Sale describes himself as a "responsible eco-citizen." What difference does he think his responsible eco-citizenship will make?

2. According to Sale, who must be "forced to explain what their consumption is for, . . . how necessary it is and how it can be drastically reduced" (par. 2)? Discuss with other readers what might be the effects of such forceful action?

3. Discuss with other readers Sale's solution to the "destruction of the earth." In your discussion, consider how workable Sale's solution is, and add your own ideas about solving the environmental problem.

4. Describe Sale's tone of voice—his attitude toward his subject—in this essay. Would you say it is friendly, caustic, scientific, skeptical, or satirical, or would you use another descriptive term? Explain your answer, and cite specific language in the essay to illustrate it.

5. In an essay, defend recycling and other actions that define "eco-citizenry." Include your ideas about how individuals can do their part.

Sustainability

Robert Chianese

Robert Chianese—in addition to being an artist, poet, and photographer—teaches interdisciplinary courses in literature, nature, and technology at California State University, Northridge. He won the Mitchell Prize for sustainable strategies for the future in 1979 and founded the Sustainability Council of Ventura (California). This article was published in Skylines, *a monthly report of the Ventura County Air Pollution Control District, October, 1995.*

Sustainability is a new concept, evolving out of ecology and the environmental movement. Like any new kid on the block, it takes some getting used to. And this new kid has a lot to offer—a big backyard full of trees, a pond, lots of great food, plenty of toys and a promising future, so it's worth the effort.

Something that is sustainable keeps on going and going, but not like a long-life battery, which you must finally replace and throw away. Sustainable systems, such as nature's water or nitrogen cycles, or a forest community, endure for eons because they are driven by inexhaustible energy, are self-renewing and maintain their ongoing processes in cooperation with organic and inorganic systems that both rely on them and contribute something to them. It's an interdependent affair.

A forest sustains itself by reprocessing energy and materials, even when it's disrupted by natural droughts, fires, pests or big catastrophes, like a volcano blowing its top.

Sunlight fuels the cells in forest plants, which grow by taking up water and nutrients from the ground. When they die, they drop and disintegrate into mulch, which cools, protects and holds the soil, and provides habitat for a great diversity of creatures—animals, insects, plants, fungi and microbes which break down the debris chemically and enrich the soil, which becomes the medium of new growth once the tree or whole forest goes through its cycles of succession. (Removing dead trees for logging steals necessary materials for the forest's health.) This is standard biological fare.

What if we human beings try to work along with these natural processes as we take things from the environment we need? That's closer to what is meant by sustainable practices: we don't have to *do* anything to a natural forest to make it sustainable—just leave it alone. It's providing for people in modern society that forces us to study, understand, and emulate nature's sustainable way. We won't *have* a home to leave without it. Managing forest and ocean resources for human use, for example, without polluting or depleting them or lessening their bio-diversity: that's sustainability.

There are some historical reports of savvy practices of this kind. People managed an 81 acre forest in medieval England to produce useable wood for 400 years without destroying it. Foresters cut or "culled" only the lower branches without chopping the trees down. They divided the forest into zones, each of which they culled every seven years.

Outside Moscow, monks kept a human-engineered food system going with remarkable ingenuity: they had a large pond filled with fish, which they fed and fertilized with cow dung, harvesting the fish as needed. In a few years when the pond silted up, they caught all the fish, emptied it, and planted it with grains. The fertilized soil produced high yields of feed for the cows, whose enriched dung they stored to feed the fish reintroduced to the cleared, refilled and re-stocked pond, and so on and so on.

When I was in rural Japan in 1990, bio-archeologists outside Kobe were excavating rice paddies that had been in operation for over 600 years. Once dug out and their rich soil used elsewhere, the paddies would be put back to work after the researchers had studied the farming practices, crop yields and weather patterns recorded in the 8 to 12 foot exposed layers. It was something to imagine what the current farmers thought about an ancient field their ancestors had lived off so long ago; it's unlikely that they would dream of chemically poisoning it. Ancestor ghosts have haunted thoughtless descendents for less.

How would one actually measure and prove the sustainable character of these fields?

We would have to know not only the crop yields per acre per year, but have figures on water and fertilizer consumption and calculate the costs of harvesting, processing and hauling the product by fossil-fuel-driven machines in the last century or so. (And we'll not factor in the human labor costs, even though we may be discouraged to find that ancient agricultural societies had large families just to do all that work. As we see, everything is connected and affects everything else.) These factors might tell us just how productive the paddy is as a food source compared with its cost in energy and resource consumption.

If there is ample water and fertilizer from renewable resources and crop yield remains high *without degrading the land*, then this agricultural operation seems sustainable.

But of course, we can't measure the basic impact on the "virgin" land of converting it to agricultural use in the first place centuries ago. Replacing what was presumably a more bio-diverse hillside plateau with a terraced plot for the monoculture of rice has an incalculable effect on the bio-sphere. All we can do is take a common sense approach to the science of sustainable practices: common sense tells us at least to stop using up more new land, cut down on consumption *and population* and seek cleaner ways to live with the environment.

Sometimes common sense fails us. Fish biologists warn us that harvesting salmon and cod, for example, at what seem commonsensical levels, given estimated population of the desired species, can cause a disaster, since it's hard to predict natural and human-caused fluctuations in fish populations. What may be a sustainable fishing limit in a peak year may degrade the population when it's low and cause it to crash—consider the pacific sardine and now the eastern cod. Human greed is hard to stem even when you try to put the best science available on the side of managing natural resources for human use.

These examples show that sustainability is the character of a human-managed system enabling it to supply human needs while operating according to nature's methods—using renewable energy and resources, avoiding the degradation and pollution of the earth and preserving as much of the original biodiversity as possible. And our time line will have to extend beyond the seven generations the Iroquois wisely consider when making present decisions: sustainability requires the longest haul.

We can become easily discouraged. To do things right, however, is   15 always harder and takes longer. Many young people are turned off to environmentalism today because it has drummed the notion of doomsday, so many doomsdays, into our heads we become inured and expect inevitable calamity. And, we have been taught to despise ourselves as a blight, a cancer on the earth. But earth evolved us—we're natural; we didn't ask for consciousness—the human brain came a long way, baby. And there's no turning back despite what the Luddites demand in their manifestos.

As Bertrand Russell said, "The problem with the future is that we have to live through it." Whether we like it or not, there are 125 years of gasoline left in today's known oil reserves at today's rate of consumption—so much for running out of gas, whether you think that would be a good thing or not. We are likely stuck with the automobile and car culture for the next century or so; so what can we do about it?

First, we can apply some sustainable thinking, which often turns up surprises. Most people would point to the internal combustion engine as the main culprit in our love–hate relationship with cars. It's true they are inefficient—a fire exploding under my hood?!—and they pollute, make noise and heat and require oil and so on. But newer cars are a bit more efficient than older gas-guzzling models, so some environmentalists and well intentioned government agencies have suggested a guzzler buy-back: they will give you five or six hundred dollars or more to get your older, pre-1975 car off the road.

But sustainability makes us pause, because the whole life cycle of the car is just as important to consider as it is with the forest and rice field.

Remember, sustainability is the application of nature's method to the meeting of human needs. Focusing only on the car's operating costs is too narrow a slice.

Consider the energy costs and environmental damage involved in extracting raw materials and then making steel, aluminum, plastics, fluids, glass, rubber, etc., and then fabricating the various parts from headlamp to tailpipe and then the costs in energy and toxics of assembly and finally the costs of recycling and disposing of the car. Saving a little bit of gasoline and producing a little less smog by replacing the car with a slightly more efficient model is damn foolish: all the rest of the damage has already been paid for and to junk the car wastes all that. Instead, replace the engine and keep the car running for another twenty years. Extending the life of a product saves enormous amounts of energy and environmental damage, and the example shows the way—modularization.

Cars of the future may have engines or power systems using alternative   20 fuels that are as replaceable as today's battery, and the style of the car could be modified by replaceable fenders, hoods, etc. We might as easily change the look of our cars as we select a new spring outfit at the clothing store.

To the environmental mantras of "think small" and "less is more," we can add "use it up, wear it out, repair it, upgrade it." Not only can less be more, but longer is more.

The challenges here are great and the results sometimes unforeseen and difficult to calculate. Ask yourself which is a more sustainable and therefore ultimately a more earth-friendly product—a box of wood No. 2 lead pencils or a plastic mechanical pencil with a pack of polymer refills? How would you measure that? What would you need to know?

Making our agricultural and manufacturing systems more sustainable requires the combined efforts of engineers, business people and environmentalists. Old antagonisms must be put to rest in what is an unavoidably interdisciplinary endeavor. To make our transportation systems as well as whole cities and society itself sustainable will involve everyone—artists, writers, teachers, philosophers as well as general systems theorists, technicians and scientists from all fields and each one of us as consumers. In case anyone thought we were at the end of our rope, the work ahead presents exciting albeit dangerous changes, but at least we now seem to have a strategy that can save us and the planet, one we will borrow from the most successful living system we know of—earth itself.

Readings

1. *Managing Planet Earth: Readings from the Scientific American.* New York, W. H. Freeman, 1989.
2. *Our Common Future: The World Commission on Environment and Development.* New York, Oxford University Press, 1987.

3. *Choosing a Sustainable Future: The Report of the National Commission on the Environment*. Washington D.C., Island Press, 1993.
4. *The Woodlands Forum*, HARC Center for Global Studies, Houston, TX.
5. Botkin, Daniel B. *Discordant Harmonies: A New Ecology for the Twenty-first Century*. New York, Oxford University Press, 1990.
6. Brown, Lester. *State of the World*. Worldwatch Institute, New York, Norton, 1991.
7. Corson, Walter H. ed. *Citizen's Guide to Sustainable Development*. Washington D.C., Global Tomorrow Coalition, 1990.
8. Girardet, Herbert. *The Gaia Atlas of Cities: New Directions for Sustainable Urban Living*. New York, Anchor Books, 1992.
9. Hawken, Paul. *The Ecology of Commerce: A Declaration of Sustainability*. New York, HarperCollins, 1993.
10. Meadows, Donnella. *The Global Citizen*. Washington D.C., Island Press, 1991.
11. Tobias, Michael. *After Eden: History, Ecology and Conscience*. San Diego, Avant Books, 1985.
12. Roszak, Theodore. *The Voice of the Earth: An Exploration of Ecopsychology*. New York, Simon and Shuster, 1992.
13. Willers, Bill. ed. *Learning to Listen to the Land*. Washington D.C., Island Press, 1991.
14. Katz, Peter. *The New Urbanism: Toward an Architecture of Community*. New York, McGraw-Hill, 1994.
15. Spirn, Anne Whiston. *The Granite Garden: Urban Nature and Human Design*. New York, HarperCollins, 1984.

SUGGESTIONS FOR FURTHER STUDY

Key Words

The author uses language with which you may not be familiar. Find the following words in the paragraphs indicated, and explain their meanings in the context of the sentences in which the words appear. Consult a dictionary, as needed.

inexhaustible (par. 2)
emulate (par. 5)
medieval (par. 6)
culled (par. 6)
monoculture (par. 12)
incalculable(par. 12)
commonsensical (par. 13)
fluctuations (par. 13)

Iroquois (par. 14)
Luddites (par. 15)
modularization (par. 19)
albeit (par. 23)

Topics for Discussion and Writing

1. The author likened sustainability to a "new kid on the block" (par. 1). Explain why this comparison is appropriate and effective.

2. Explain what "sustainable systems" are, using both the author's ideas (from the essay) and your own.

3. Chianese illustrated his theory with examples of sustainable systems in foreign countries. Discuss the effectiveness of his examples. Describe other examples of sustainable systems with which you are familiar.

4. Explain what Chianese meant when he wrote "sustainability is the character of a human-managed system."

5. Chianese quoted philosopher Bertrand Russell's comment, "The problem with the future is that we have to live through it" (par. 16). How did Chianese develop Russell's idea in this essay?

6. Review Chianese's practical applications of sustainability for the future, and discuss how workable they may or may not be. Give reasons for your conclusions.

7. Reread Chianese's discussion about cars of the future. Write a short essay elaborating on those ideas. Use specific examples of how cars may be modified to meet the requirements of sustainability.

8. Using your imagination, as well as your knowledge of science, create a sustainable system of your own. Write an essay explaining what that system is, how it works, and how it will help our environment. If you prefer, write a proposal for marketing the sustainable system you create.

9. Will sustainability be popular with all manufacturers of consumer products? Why or why not? Assume the role of an employee of a large manufacturer of a consumable product. Write a letter that alerts your employer to existing sustainable systems influencing your business. In your letter, focus on a particular consumable product, and recommend ways to incorporate sustainability into its manufacture or distribution.

Thinking Small in a Season of Excess

Connie Koenenn

*Connie Koenenn (born in 1935) received her degree in journalism in
1957 at the University of Missouri. She has been an editor and staff
writer for the* Los Angeles Times *since 1980 and won the California
Chapter of the American Planning Association Award for a series
of articles of exceptional merit on environmental issues in 1992.
"Thinking Small in a Season of Excess" was printed in the* Los
Angeles Times *on November 13, 1995.*

Did you know: *If every American threw away one bite of Thanks-*   1
*giving turkey with gravy, that alone would amount to 8.1 million pounds of
wasted food?*

This is the kind of statistic that Robert Lilienfeld savors—an infor-
mational snippet that dramatizes his ongoing message about the wasteful
habits of the American consumer.

Those habits reach their trashy peak during the holiday season.

Not that Lilienfeld wants to criticize. A marketing-consultant-turned-
environmentalist, he focuses on painless ways people can conserve
resources and reduce waste, a philosophy known as "source reduction" at
the Environmental Protection Agency. Trying to humanize the notion,
Lilienfeld came up with the term "Use Less Stuff," or ULS, which is based
on the simple premise that recycling is fine but it's better not to create waste
in the first place.

From his home office ("I commute by foot, down the stairs") in Ann   5
Arbor, Mich., Lilienfeld has been publishing the bimonthly ULS Report
since May, 1994. It's a breezy newsletter sprinkled with statistics, energy-
saving tips, short essays, reader feedback and eco crossword puzzles. With a
national distribution of 5,000 hard copies and an estimated 10,000 readers
on his Internet site, Lilienfeld was encouraged to take another step. With
the backing of nine environmental organizations, he has proclaimed this
Thursday as ULS Day and has issued a "38 Days, 38 Ways" declaration
with little tips for cutting down on holiday trash.

"The date gives people a week's notice to clean up their act," says
Lilienfeld. He acknowledges that it took a little nerve to declare a national
holiday, but he was motivated by statistics indicating that between

Thanksgiving and New Year's Day, Americans generate 25 million tons of trash—which is about 1 million *extra* tons per week.

"One of the things we have been focusing on is getting people to understand that recycling by itself is not going to solve the solid waste problem," says Lilienfeld. "Today we recycle about 45 million tons of stuff a year, but *don't* recycle 160 million tons of stuff. And because of population growth, the long-term implications are serious."

But no one wants to hear that the sky is falling, so Lilienfeld, a big believer of strength in numbers, is serving little bite-sized ideas in his ULS Report. When Halloween was coming up, he suggested making costumes out of things already on hand and using that scooped-out pumpkin to bake a pie. For summer cookouts, he urged car-pooling to the picnic site and packing food in reusable containers.

Lilienfeld, who formed Partners for Environmental Progress several years ago to coordinate large-scale recycling projects, gets newsletter funding ("It's a shoestring budget") from companies interested in waste prevention.

He enjoys both encouragement and technical assistance from William   10
Rathje, an archeologist who runs the noted Garbage Project at the University of Arizona in Tucson. Rathje and Lilienfeld met at an environmental conference and the colloboration was born.

Rathje, who has spent 23 years analyzing the contents of municipal trash for clues to contemporary culture, considers it a moral imperative for the United States, having pioneered the Use More Stuff lifestyle, now to lead a change in direction.

"We have all sorts of clear scientific information that we are going to be straining the limits of our resources, the limits of our energy capabilities and the limits of our pollution levels over the next few years," he says. "I am not the kind of person who believes that Americans at heart want to consume, consume, consume and don't care about the environment. I believe we have a lot of concern about the world."

The current ULS Report has full details of the "holiday" devoted to personal cutting back, including a few ideas that Lilienfeld acknowledges are a little wacky.

"The suggestion to make potholders out of an old ironing board cover pushes it for me a little," he says, "but we don't expect anyone to use the entire list."

The original plan was to make a ULS Day-Advent calendar with a   15
Waste Tip of the Day, but when that got too complicated Lilienfeld and his researchers settled for a topical approach. For instance:

- ▪ **Eating:** To reduce the tons of edible holiday food thrown away, he offers a realistic guideline for grocery shopping and suggests buying products in bulk.

- **Shopping:** Use paper bags to wrap small packages for mailing; recycle corrugated cartons (they add up to 23 million tons of waste a year); use old newspapers for packing material.
- **Decorations:** Get a tree that can be planted or mulched; use smaller, low-wattage bulbs to consume less electricity; put all your lights on timers.

And while these are not trail-blazing tips, if everybody would follow just one or two of the suggestions, the overall impact could be great, Lilienfeld says.

"I'm not trying to be a Scrooge, it's just that the holidays are a good time to focus on changing our behavior."

His project is getting "really positive" media response, he says. Stories on ULS Day will appear in magazines ranging from Family Circle to Mirabella, and Lilienfeld will be a guest on NPR and other radio networks this week. "This seems to be an idea people like," he says.

SUGGESTIONS FOR FURTHER STUDY

Key Words

The author uses language with which you may not be familiar. Find the following words in the paragraphs indicated, and explain their meanings in the context of the sentences in which the words appear. Consult a dictionary, as needed.

snippet (par. 2)
implications (par. 7)
imperative (par. 11)
Scrooge (par. 17)

Topics for Discussion and Writing

1. Explain Lilienfeld's philosophy of "source reduction." How is "ULS" related to that philosophy?

2. Do you agree with archeologist Rathje that Americans have "pioneered the Use More Stuff lifestyle" (par. 11)? Why or why not? What evidence can you provide to support or attack Rathje's evaluation of American consumption habits?

3. In your opinion, how practical are Lilienfeld's "Waste Tips of the Day"? What other tips related to holidays or everyday life can you suggest?

The free ULS Report can be ordered by writing to P.O. Box 130116, Ann Arbor, MI 48113, or found on the Internet at http://cygnus-group.com

4. Lilienfeld and Rathje do not agree that "Americans at heart want to consume, consume, consume and don't care about the environment." What is your opinion on this issue? If you have read Shames's "The More Factor" in this text (Chapter 5), compare Shames's criticism of American consumption with the critical comments by Lilienfeld and Rathje.

5. Write a humorous satire explaining the importance of producing as much waste as possible. Use specific detail and colorful language. Before you begin, read the student essay, "How to Poison Earth," at the end of this chapter, for an example of a humorous satire.

The Environmental Battle Moves into the Classroom

Frank Clifford

Frank Clifford (born on June 16, 1945, in Washington, DC) graduated from Yale University with a degree in American Studies. He has been a staff writer and editor for the Louisville Courier Journal and Times, *the* Santa Fe Reporter, *the* Dallas Times Herald, *and the* Los Angeles Times *since 1968. He received a Pulitzer Prize for local reporting (team coverage), presented to the staff of the* Los Angeles Times *for coverage of the Los Angeles earthquake in 1994. "The Environmental Battle Moves into the Classroom" was published in the* Los Angeles Times *on November 13, 1995.*

Arizona state Rep. Rusty Bowers began campaigning against envi-   1
ronmental education after his son came home from a grade school ecology class declaring that coyotes didn't kill sheep.

In Virginia, business consultant Jo Kwong questioned how environmental issues were being presented in local schools when her children became obsessed with recycling household waste but couldn't explain what recycling did.

And California activist Lance King took offense at classroom materials touting the environmental benefits of disposable diapers. The materials were distributed to schools across the country by Procter & Gamble, a leading manufacturer of the diapers.

Environmental lessons have been a staple of public education since the National Audubon Society began taking schoolchildren on nature walks in 1910. Today, 30 states, including California, require or strongly encourage it as part of public school curricula.

But just as Congress has come to challenge many of the nation's envi-   5
ronmental policies, a number of scholars, activists and legislators are disputing the validity of what is taught to their children as well as questioning the motives of teachers.

Led by Bowers and Republican legislators, Arizona has passed laws banning environmental advocacy in the classroom and slashed funding for programs. Similar measures are under consideration in Florida, North Carolina and Wisconsin.

Earlier this year, a subcommittee of the California Senate failed to deprive the state Department of Education of money it has used to leverage $4 million in federal grants for environmental education in secondary schools.

In many schools, environmental education is still linked closely to scientific inquiry. Field trips to ponds and tidal pools, terrariums and worm composting bins are all part of the process of exposing young minds to the wonders of nature.

But also becoming part of the curricula are teacher-sponsored letter-writing campaigns to save dolphins or stop logging, and textbooks that encourage children to join environmental groups or take part in product boycotts.

As a result, experts warn, environmental education is getting caught up   10 in a potentially chilling controversy over the teaching of values, reminiscent of the divisive disputes over evolution and sex education.

"We are teaching what to think, rather than how to think," Kwong said in a paper being published this month by the Center for Study of American Business at Washington University in St. Louis.

She said typical lessons reduce complicated scientific issues to simple doomsday scenarios. Children are taught that acid rain is destroying forests and that overpopulation will exhaust our resources, she said, even while debate continues among scientists. "They are taught as facts rather than hypothesis to children," Kwong said.

Backlash against environmental teachings has been particularly heavy in rural areas. School officials in Idaho, Oklahoma and Oregon have placed restrictions on the way environmental issues are taught.

In Meridian, Ida., a bedroom community near Boise, teachers have been warned "not to talk about cutting trees in the rain forests, about reintroducing wolves in Yellowstone or even about recycling," said recently retired Meridian teacher Lee McGlinsky.

The push to muzzle environmental education often comes from conser-   15 vative groups that assert that teachers and textbooks present business and technology in the worst possible light. Plastics and pesticides are high on the ecology education hit list, their role in improving worldwide health conditions largely overlooked, the critics argue.

"Environmental education is presented like a morality play," said Michael Senara, a University of Arizona political scientist and a leader in efforts to change the way the subject is taught. "There is little effort to explain the trade-offs involved in so many decisions society makes about whether to use or not use something."

Officials of the North American Assn. of Environmental Educators, the largest group of its kind, concede that the critics have a point.

The problem, they say, is that the mandate to teach environmental education often does not include any standards or guidelines for teachers to follow, let alone a budget to pay for textbooks.

As a result, teachers wind up relying on a host of material from environmental groups and corporations that frequently promote causes and products.

"There's no question that a lot of propaganda gets packaged as class-   20
room material," said Kathy McGlauflin, president of the environmental educators group.

Consumer and environmental groups, meanwhile, charge that big business has been effective in spreading its own propaganda. Many companies develop curricula on environmental topics and offer them free to financially strapped public schools.

Released last summer, an analysis titled "Captive Kids" by the non-profit Consumers Union looked at 21 sets of environmentally oriented classroom materials that are widely distributed. Most were sponsored by businesses and industry groups, such as the American Gas Assn. and the National Live Stock & Meat Board, whose products are directly linked to the environment.

In the vast majority of cases, Consumers Union said, industries used the materials to promote the benefits of their own products without mentioning or seriously considering harmful side effects.

"The American Coal Foundation dismisses the greenhouse effect," the report states. "The Exxon Education Foundation's . . . program doesn't tout its products but implies that fossil fuels, in general, pose few environmental problems and suggests that worries about oil spills and strip mining are unfounded."

Consumers Union directed its harshest criticism at household products   25
giant Procter & Gamble for its educational packet "Decision Earth," which said that disposable diapers are environmentally preferable to cloth diapers.

Decision Earth did not mention that Procter & Gamble had financed the study that produced the favorable comparison, according to Consumers Union.

"Decision Earth" also taught that clear cutting forests mimicked "nature's way of getting rid of trees." (Procter & Gamble markets a variety of paper products). Decision Earth did not mention such ill effects of clear cutting as erosion, water pollution and destruction of wildlife habitat.

Procter & Gamble no longer distributes Decision Earth, although company representatives insist that complaints had nothing to do with discontinuing it.

California's Environmental Education Office has screened hundreds of classroom kits, provided by environmental groups and nonprofit organizations as well as industry. Among the material it rejected as biased or inadequate were materials from the National Wildlife Federation, the National Institute for Urban Wildlife and a United Nations primer on cleaning up ocean pollution.

McGlauflin of the North American Assn. of Environmental Educators   30
questioned materials prepared by Earth Force, which seeks to enlist teachers and students in an unabashedly activist alliance. Among its stated goals: to oppose congressional efforts to weaken the Endangered Species Act and the Clean Water and Clean Air acts and to lobby the Clinton Administration to strengthen wetlands protection. Sponsors include the Pew Charitable Trusts, Target stores, Times Mirror magazines and the Smithsonian Institution.

"Many of those who shape the environmental education curriculum believe that their purpose is not to weigh conflicting facts, values and theories, but to instill a sense of crisis," Kwong wrote.

A good example, she says, is the treatment accorded global warming— a phenomenon that most experts think is a potential problem, although they disagree widely about the eventual impact. Rather than encourage students to ponder the scientific questions, Kwong said, many classroom materials assume the worst and paint horror movie scenarios of melting ice caps and rising sea levels.

"Major port cities such as New York, Buenos Aires and Hong Kong would be submerged beneath the sea," one textbook says, according to Kwong. Another book features an illustration of the Manhattan skyline with water rising higher than the Statue of Liberty.

The strongest reaction to perceived environmental advocacy in the classroom occurred in Arizona.

There, a 1994 law banned use of a curriculum guide that encouraged   35
students, among many activities, to take "an environmental pledge" and to get involved in local environmental politics by drawing up ballot initiatives.

But at a recent convention of the North American Assn. of Environmental Educators, one teacher declared that the banned guidelines were being used by a state university in training grade school teachers.

"Environmental education is alive and fairly healthy in Arizona," the teacher said, adding that recent public opinion polls made clear to him the role of environmental education.

"We must protect the environment."

SUGGESTIONS FOR FURTHER STUDY

Key Words

The author uses language with which you may not be familiar. Find the following words in the paragraphs indicated, and explain their meanings in the context of the sentences in which the words appear. Consult a dictionary, as needed.

terrariums (par. 8)
doomsday (par. 12)
hypothesis (par. 12)
tout (par. 24)
unabashedly (par. 30)
advocacy (par. 34)

Topics for Discussion and Writing

1. According to some experts, in what controversy is "environmental education . . . getting caught up"?

2. This article illustrates examples of environmental education that bother critics. Discuss with other readers the controversy over environmental education, using examples from this article, as well as from your own experience.

3. According to the author, "conservative groups assert that teachers and textbooks present business and technology in the worst possible light." On the other hand, environmentalists say that big business has been effective in integrating its own propaganda into American classrooms. In your own school experience, has your introduction to environmental issues been influenced by one point of view more than another? Explain your answer, giving specific details and examples when you can.

4. This article compares two opposing views. How successful has the author been in illustrating *both* sides of the controversy? Explain your answer.

5. Choose one side of the issue of environmental education—either that of conservative groups and big business, or that of environmental groups and teachers, as they have been described in this article. Write a position paper stating what you think should be taught about the environment and environmental issues in local schools. Write your position paper for a specific audience, such as the Parent–Teacher Association, your district's school board, a manager of the local Environmental Protection Agency office, a local chapter of the Sierra Club, or a business-oriented group in

your town, such as the Rotary Club. Or consult your phone book for names of city, county, state, and federal government agencies concerned with managing the environment and write to their directors.

6. Clifford cites the assertions by the American Coal Foundation and the Exxon Education Foundation, dismissing the greenhouse effect. Using Carl Sagan's essay "The Warming of the World" as scientific background, write a letter to either foundation, arguing the seriousness of the greenhouse effect.

The Nuclear Winter

Carl Sagan

Carl Sagan was the David Duncan Professor of Astronomy and Space Sciences and the Director of the Laboratory for Planetary Studies at Cornell University, as well as Distinguished Visiting Professor at Jet Propulsion Laboratories, California Institute of Technology. He cofounded The Planetary Society, the largest space-interest group in the world. Among his many awards is the 1994 Public Welfare Medal, the highest award given by the National Academy of Sciences. His book Cosmos *became the best-selling science book ever published in the English language and served as the basis for the TV series seen in 60 countries, by more than 4 million people. He was particularly known for his ability to bring the wonders of the universe down to Earth and to make astronomy understandable to nonscientists. "The Nuclear Winter" appeared in* Parade *magazine in October, 1983.*

Into the eternal darkness, into fire, into ice.

Dante, *The Inferno*

Except for fools and madmen, everyone knows that nuclear war would be an unprecedented human catastrophe. A more or less typical strategic warhead has a yield of 2 megatons, the explosive equivalent of 2 million tons of TNT. But 2 million tons of TNT is about the same as all the bombs exploded in World War II—a single bomb with the explosive power of the entire Second World War but compressed into a few seconds of time and an area 30 or 40 miles across. . . .

In a 2-megaton explosion over a fairly large city, buildings would be vaporized, people reduced to atoms and shadows, outlying structures blown down like matchsticks and raging fires ignited. And if the bomb were exploded on the ground, an enormous crater, like those that can be seen through a telescope on the surface of the Moon, would be all that remained where midtown once had been. There are now more than 50,000 nuclear weapons, more than 13,000 megatons of yield, deployed in the arsenals of the United States and the Soviet Union—enough to obliterate a million Hiroshimas.

But there are fewer than 3,000 cities on the Earth with populations of 100,000 or more. You cannot find anything like a million Hiroshimas to obliterate. Prime military and industrial targets that are far from cities are comparatively rare. Thus, there are vastly more nuclear weapons than are needed for any plausible deterrence of a potential adversary.

Nobody knows, of course, how many megatons would be exploded in a real nuclear war. There are some who think that a nuclear war can be "contained," bottled up before it runs away to involve many of the world's arsenals. But a number of detailed analyses, war games run by the U.S. Department of Defense and official Soviet pronouncements, all indicate that this containment may be too much to hope for: Once the bombs begin exploding, communications failures, disorganization, fear, the necessity of making in minutes decisions affecting the fates of millions and the immense psychological burden of knowing that your own loved ones may already have been destroyed are likely to result in a nuclear paroxysm. Many investigations, including a number of studies for the U.S. government, envision the explosion of 5,000 to 10,000 megatons—the detonation of tens of thousands of nuclear weapons that now sit quietly, inconspicuously, in missile silos, submarines and long-range bombers, faithful servants awaiting orders.

The World Health Organization, in a recent detailed study chaired by Sune K. Bergstrom (the 1982 Nobel laureate in physiology and medicine), concludes that 1.1 billion people would be killed outright in such a nuclear war, mainly in the United States, the Soviet Union, Europe, China and Japan. An additional 1.1 billion people would suffer serious injuries and radiation sickness, for which medical help would be unavailable. It thus seems possible that more than 2 billion people—almost half of all the humans on Earth—would be destroyed in the immediate aftermath of a global thermonuclear war. This would represent by far the greatest disaster in the history of the human species and, with no other adverse effects, would probably be enough to reduce at least the Northern Hemisphere to a state of prolonged agony and barbarism. Unfortunately, the real situation would be much worse.

In technical studies of the consequences of nuclear weapons explosions, there has been a dangerous tendency to underestimate the results. This is partly due to a tradition of conservatism which generally works well in science but which is of more dubious applicability when the lives of billions of people are at stake. In the Bravo test of March 1, 1954, a 15-megaton thermonuclear bomb was exploded on Bikini Atoll. It had about double the yield expected, and there was an unanticipated last-minute shift in the wind direction. As a result, deadly radioactive fallout came down on Rongelap in the Marshall Islands, more than 200 kilometers away. Almost all the children on Rongelap subsequently developed thyroid nodules and lesions, and other long-term medical problems, due to the radioactive fallout.

Likewise, in 1973, it was discovered that high-yield airbursts will chemically burn the nitrogen in the upper air, converting it into oxides of nitrogen; these, in turn, combine with and destroy the protective ozone in the Earth's stratosphere. The surface of the Earth is shielded from deadly solar ultraviolet radiation by a layer of ozone so tenuous that, were it brought down to sea level, it would be only 3 millimeters thick. Partial destruction of this ozone layer can have serious consequences for the biology of the entire planet.

These discoveries, and others like them, were made by chance. They were largely unexpected. And now another consequence—by far the most dire—has been uncovered, again more or less by accident.

The U.S. Mariner 9 spacecraft, the first vehicle to orbit another planet, arrived at Mars in late 1971. The planet was enveloped in a global dust storm. As the fine particles slowly fell out, we were able to measure temperature changes in the atmosphere and on the surface. Soon it became clear what had happened:

The dust, lofted by high winds off the desert into the upper Martian   10 atmosphere, had absorbed the incoming sunlight and prevented much of it from reaching the ground. Heated by the sunlight, the dust warmed the adjacent air. But the surface, enveloped in partial darkness, became much chillier than usual. Months later, after the dust fell out of the atmosphere, the upper air cooled and the surface warmed, both returning to their normal conditions. We were able to calculate accurately, from how much dust there was in the atmosphere, how cool the Martian surface ought to have been.

Afterwards, I and my colleagues, James B. Pollack and Brian Toon of NASA's Ames Research Center, were eager to apply these insights to the Earth. In a volcanic explosion, dust aerosols are lofted into the high atmosphere. We calculated by how much the Earth's global temperature should decline after a major volcanic explosion and found that our results (generally a fraction of a degree) were in good accord with actual measurements. Joining forces with Richard Turco, who has studied the effects of nuclear weapons for many years, we then began to turn our attention to the climatic effects of nuclear war. [The scientific paper, "Global Atmospheric Consequences of Nuclear War," is written by R. P. Turco, O. B. Toon, T. P. Ackerman, J. B. Pollack and Carl Sagan. From the last names of the authors, this work is generally referred to as "TTAPS."]

We knew that nuclear explosions, particularly groundbursts, would lift an enormous quantity of fine soil particles into the atmosphere (more than 100,000 tons of fine dust for every megaton exploded in a surface burst). Our work was further spurred by Paul Crutzen of the Max Planck Institute for Chemistry in Mainz, West Germany, and by John Birks of the University of Colorado, who pointed out that huge quantities of smoke would be generated in the burning of cities and forests following a nuclear war.

Groundbursts—at hardened missile silos, for example—generate fine dust. Airbursts—over cities and unhardened military installations—make fires and therefore smoke. The amount of dust and soot generated depends on the conduct of the war, the yields of the weapons employed and the ratio of groundbursts to airbursts. So we ran computer models for several dozen different nuclear war scenarios. Our baseline case, as in many other studies, was a 5,000-megaton war with only a modest fraction of the yield (20 percent) expended on urban or industrial targets. Our job, for each case, was to follow the dust and smoke generated, see how much sunlight was absorbed and by how much the temperatures changed, figure out how the particles spread in longitude and latitude, and calculate how long before it all fell out of the air back onto the surface. Since the radioactivity would be attached to these same fine particles, our calculations also revealed the extent and timing of the subsequent radioactive fallout.

Some of what I am about to describe is horrifying. I know, because it horrifies me. There is a tendency—psychiatrists call it "denial"—to put it out of our minds, not to think about it. But if we are to deal intelligently, wisely, with the nuclear arms race, then we must steel ourselves to contemplate the horrors of nuclear war.

The results of our calculations astonished us. In the baseline case, the   15 amount of sunlight at the ground was reduced to a few percent of normal— much darker, in daylight, than in a heavy overcast and too dark for plants to make a living from photosynthesis. At least in the Northern Hemisphere, where the great preponderance of strategic targets lies, an unbroken and deadly gloom would persist for weeks.

Even more unexpected were the temperatures calculated. In the baseline case, land temperatures, except for narrow strips of coastline, dropped to minus 25° Celsius (minus 13° Fahrenheit) and stayed below freezing for months—even for a summer war. (Because the atmospheric structure becomes much more stable as the upper atmosphere is heated and the lower air is cooled, we may have severely *under*estimated how long the cold and the dark would last.) The oceans, a significant heat reservoir, would not freeze, however, and a major ice age would probably not be triggered. But because the temperatures would drop so catastrophically, virtually all crops and farm animals, at least in the Northern Hemisphere, would be destroyed, as would most varieties of uncultivated or undomesticated food supplies. Most of the human survivors would starve.

In addition, the amount of radioactive fallout is much more than expected. Many previous calculations simply ignored the intermediate timescale fallout. That is, calculations were made for the prompt fallout—the plumes of radioactive debris blown downwind from each target—and for the long-term fallout, the fine radioactive particles lofted into the stratosphere that would descend about a year later, after most of the radioactivity had decayed. However, the radioactivity carried into the upper atmosphere (but not as high as the stratosphere) seems to have been largely forgotten. We found for the baseline case that roughly 30 percent of the land at northern midlatitudes could receive a radioactive dose greater than 250 rads, and that about 50 percent of northern midlatitudes could receive a dose greater than 100 rads. A 100-rad dose is the equivalent of about 1,000 medical X-rays. A 400-rad dose will, more likely than not, kill you.

The cold, the dark and the intense radioactivity, together lasting for months, represent a severe assault on our civilization and our species. Civil and sanitary services would be wiped out. Medical facilities, drugs, the most rudimentary means for relieving the vast human suffering, would be unavailable. Any but the most elaborate shelters would be useless, quite apart from the question of what good it might be to emerge a few months later. Synthetics burned in the destruction of the cities would produce a wide variety of toxic gases, including carbon monoxide, cyanides, dioxins and furans. After the dust and soot settled out, the solar ultraviolet flux would be much larger than its present value. Immunity to disease would decline. Epidemics and pandemics would be rampant, especially after the billion or so unburied bodies began to thaw. Moreover, the combined influence of these severe and simultaneous stresses on life are likely to produce even more adverse consequences—biologists call them synergisms— that we are not yet wise enough to foresee.

So far, we have talked only of the Northern Hemisphere. But it now seems—unlike the case of a single nuclear weapons test—that in a real nuclear war, the heating of the vast quantities of atmospheric dust and soot in northern midlatitudes will transport these fine particles toward and across the Equator. We see just this happening in Martian dust storms. The Southern Hemisphere would experience effects that, while less severe than in the Northern Hemisphere, are nevertheless extremely ominous. The illusion with which some people in the Northern Hemisphere reassure themselves—catching an Air New Zealand flight in a time of serious international crisis, or the like—is now much less tenable, even on the narrow issue of personal survival for those with the price of a ticket.

But what if nuclear wars *can* be contained, and much less than 5,000   20 megatons is detonated? Perhaps the greatest surprise in our work was that even small nuclear wars can have devastating climatic effects. We considered a war in which a mere 100 megatons were exploded, less than one percent of the world arsenals, and only in low-yield airbursts over cities. This scenario, we found, would ignite thousands of fires, and the smoke from these fires alone would be enough to generate an epoch of cold and dark almost as severe as in the 5,000-megaton case. The threshold for what Richard Turco has called the Nuclear Winter is very low.

Could we have overlooked some important effect? The carrying of dust and soot from the Northern to the Southern Hemisphere (as well as more local atmospheric circulation) will certainly thin the clouds out over the Northern Hemisphere. But, in many cases, this thinning would be insufficient to render the climatic consequences tolerable—and every time it got better in the Northern Hemisphere, it would get worse in the Southern.

Our results have been carefully scrutinized by more than 100 scientists in the United States, Europe and the Soviet Union. There are still arguments on points of detail. But the overall conclusion seems to be agreed upon: There are severe and previously unanticipated global consequences of nuclear war—subfreezing temperatures in a twilit radioactive gloom lasting for months or longer.

Scientists initially underestimated the effects of fallout, were amazed that nuclear explosions in space disabled distant satellites, had no idea that the fireballs from high-yield thermonuclear explosions could deplete the ozone layer and missed altogether the possible climatic effects of nuclear dust and smoke. What else have we overlooked?

Nuclear war is a problem that can be treated only theoretically. It is not amenable to experimentation. Conceivably, we have left something important out of our analysis, and the effects are more modest than we calculate. On the other hand, it is also possible—and, from previous experience, even likely—that there are further adverse effects that no one has yet been wise enough to recognize. With billions of lives at stake, where does conservatism lie—in assuming that the results will be better than we calculate, or worse?

Many biologists, considering the nuclear winter that these calculations   25
describe, believe they carry somber implications for life on Earth. Many species of plants and animals would become extinct. Vast numbers of surviving humans would starve to death. The delicate ecological relations that bind together organisms on Earth in a fabric of mutual dependency would be torn, perhaps irreparably. There is little question that our global civilization would be destroyed. The human population would be reduced to prehistoric levels, or less. Life for any survivors would be extremely hard. And there seems to be a real possibility of the extinction of the human species.

It is now almost 40 years since the invention of nuclear weapons. We have not yet experienced a global thermonuclear war—although on more than one occasion we have come tremulously close. I do not think our luck can hold forever. Men and machines are fallible, as recent events remind us. Fools and madmen do exist, and sometimes rise to power. Concentrating always on the near future, we have ignored the long-term consequences of our actions. We have placed our civilization and our species in jeopardy.

Fortunately, it is not yet too late. We can safeguard the planetary civilization and the human family if we so choose. There is no more important or more urgent issue.

SUGGESTIONS FOR FURTHER STUDY

Key Words

The author uses language with which you may not be familiar. Find the following words in the paragraphs indicated, and explain their meanings in the context of the sentences in which the words appear. Consult a dictionary, as needed.

Hiroshimsa (par. 2)
paroxysm (par. 4)
barbarism (par. 5)
conservatism (par. 6)
dubious (par. 6)
tenuous (par. 7)
preponderance (par. 15)
rudimentary (par. 18)
pandemics (par. 18)
synergisms (par. 18)
amenable (par. 24)
fallible (par. 26)

Topics for Discussion and Writing

1. Drawing on information in Sagan's essay, describe in your own words the power of a nuclear warhead and the immediate damage such a bomb explosion can cause.

2. According to Sagan, how many nuclear bombs existed in 1983, and who owned them? Toward what countries do you think these weapons were—and may still be—aimed?

3. According to the World Health Organization, what would be the result of a global thermonuclear war?

4. What is significant and effective about Sagan's discussion of Mars?

5. Review the second half of Sagan's essay. Describe the additional "horrors of nuclear war" he discussed there.

6. In a journal entry, explain the "nuclear winter" concept in your own words.

7. Sagan wrote that there is no more important issue than "safeguard[ing] the planetary civilization" from nuclear holocaust. Write an argument, in either letter or essay form, agreeing or disagreeing with Sagan's opinion. Give reasons for your opinion, and provide examples and illustrations to support it.

Bomb Ban on the Brink

Loren Stein

Loren Stein, an award-winning journalist based in San Francisco, writes for local and national newspapers and magazines on a broad spectrum of public-policy issues. A former associate of the Center for Investigative Reporting, she has a passion for writing well-researched, in-depth news features that provide context for and insight into complex topics. She has written many stories on nuclear weapons, exploring their threat to humanity and the political battles behind the drive for arms control and disarmament. Stein has a BA from the University of California at Berkeley and a masters in journalism from Columbia University. This article appeared in the Los Angeles Weekly *in June 1996.*

Halfway across the world, negotiators from 38 nations are racing to meet a June 28 deadline to produce a final draft of a Comprehensive Test Ban Treaty, a pivotal arms control goal that has eluded diplomats for more than forty years.

Serious obstacles remain, but the treaty is closer than it has ever been before. On June 6, China abandoned its long-standing demand that the test ban exempt "peaceful" nuclear explosions, removing a major hurdle in the negotiations underway at the U.N. Conference on Disarmament in Geneva.

Now, for the first time since the beginning of the nuclear age, all five declared nuclear powers—the U.S., Russia, France, China and Britain— have yielded to international pressure and agreed to end nuclear weapons testing. "The comprehensive test ban treaty has been the longest-sought, hardest-fought goal in arms control," says John Holum, director of the U.S. Arms Control and Disarmament Agency. "We're on the brink of achieving a really historic agreement."

Advocates emphasize that a test ban would go far beyond the simple question of nuclear tests. The treaty would essentially put the brakes on the arms race, as nuclear nations would lose confidence in their nuclear weapons if they are unable to test them.

"The test ban diminishes the utility of nuclear weapons," says Michael Krepon, arms control expert and president of the Stimson Center in Washington, D.C. "Every nuclear weapons test is a declaration of power. We want to reduce the shadow that these weapons cast over the world."

Progress in the test ban talks was spurred by the storm of international outrage sparked by France's recent series of nuclear tests in the South Pacific and China's current round of tests at Lop Nor in northwestern China. The uproar over France's six tests, the last on January 27, forced it to end its testing program months ahead of schedule. China, the only declared nuclear power not currently observing a voluntary test moratorium, promises to sign the test ban after it sets off one more nuclear blast.

At the same time, arms control experts warn that if the treaty is not reached this year, the changing geopolitical climate—specifically imminent U.S. and Russian presidential elections—could sabotage its prospects as well as jeopardize other pending arms control measures. "The political momentum is here now," says Tom Zamora Collina, executive director of the Institute for Science and International Security in Washington D.C. and a specialist in arms control and disarmament. "It's a rare constellation of events. The main thing is that the nuclear weapons states are all lined up—this has never happened before."

With both an agreement and a deadline drawing close, the countries with the greatest leverage in the talks are playing politics over technical issues that could still scuttle the test ban.

"These hurdles will be settled in the 11th hour—we won't know until the morning of June 28," says Daryl Kimball, Associate Director for Policy at Physicians for Social Responsibility in Washington, D.C. "With multilateral negotiations, countries hold out until the last possible moment, not willing to give up ground before they have to. But there's so much to deal with and so little time."

The eight nuclear weapons states—including the three undeclared   10 "threshold" states of India, Pakistan and Israel—stand to lose the most by signing the treaty, as the non-nuclear nations have already given up on a nuclear future by signing the Non-Proliferation Treaty. "These countries have the biggest problems with the treaty," says Krepon. With the exception of Israel and to a large degree the U.S., the remaining nuclear weapons states are "playing the end game" to try to extract last-minute concessions at the negotiations.

The thorniest issue before negotiators is the disagreement between the U.S. and the four other declared nuclear weapons powers over when the treaty would come into force and be legally binding. Britain, China, France and Russia insist that the three undeclared nuclear states must also ratify the treaty before it goes into effect—including India, which has repeatedly said it will not sign the test ban. This gives India and other fence-sitting nations veto power over the test ban, perhaps indefinitely. The U.S. has taken a softer line and has not insisted that the threshold states ratify the treaty.

Krepon says the tough posture stems from an underlying reluctance to sign. "Four out of the five nuclear-weapons states don't want a test ban but can't say that, so they are hiding behind the 'entry-into-force' clause," says Krepon. "(They've) been cornered by their own rhetoric."

The threshold states of India and Pakistan, and to a lesser degree China, are taking a more open approach in their resistance to the test ban. Locked into tense border disputes on the Indian subcontinent, these countries hope to preserve their nuclear options.

China, moreover, is resisting the proposed system for verifying treaty violations. The U.S. would like to use its spy satellites to detect nuclear blasts, but China believes that this gives more advanced nations an unfair advantage and insists that an international network of seismic and underwater sensors will be sufficient. China also wants more stringent controls for on-site inspections.

India is articulating the most radical position at the test ban negotiations. Although it was the first nation to call for a global test ban in 1954, India is now holding out against the treaty as long as the five superpowers retain their nuclear weapons. India is calling for a commitment to a disarmament timetable within the test ban treaty—a provision that the nuclear powers will never accept. "It's certainly legitimate to make a connection between the test ban and aspirations for further steps towards disarmament," says ACDA's Holum, "but there can be no formal link . . . the test ban is not a decision to eliminate nuclear weapons." As written, the treaty tries to forge a compromise by stressing the importance of the agreement as a key step in the process of nuclear disarmament, as well as in ending the development of new nuclear weapons.

If negotiators can reach a consensus on these issues by June 28, the treaty draft will be presented to the U.N. General Assembly for approval in the late summer and a signing ceremony in the fall, and then be open for ratification. "If nations have the political will, they will complete a test ban treaty," says Bruce Hall, head of the disarmament campaign for U.S. Greenpeace in Washington, D.C. "If not, they will allow the technical issues to become stumbling blocks . . . It's for us to lose."

The U.S. role as peacemaker in the talks is a new one and is credited largely to President Clinton. For decades before Clinton's election, U.S. presidents and diplomats gave lip service to arms control while blocking any real progress toward international limits.

"Ever since President Reagan, the U.S. has always been the central roadblock to the test ban treaty," says Collina of the Institute for Science and International Security. "The rest of the world has been waiting thirty to forty years. The test ban was not seriously considered until the Clinton administration came out front and brought along the other nuclear weapons states."

Arms control advocates praise Clinton for supporting and speeding up the test ban negotiations despite stiff opposition, at times even within his own administration. Over the vehement protests of the U.S. military, Clinton indefinitely extended the U.S. moratorium on its own nuclear tests, rescinded the U.S. demand for a special, 10-year escape clause from the treaty, and announced American support for a "zero yield" test ban—no tests no matter how small—paving the way for the other declared nuclear nations to also agree to a comprehensive test ban.

"The U.S. has a more unambiguous commitment to the test ban than ever before," says Christopher Paine, a nuclear weapons specialist with the Natural Resources Defense Council in Washington, D.C. "The administration has never unanimously supported a test ban, but in each case Clinton made the right decision. It has not been an easy road." 20

But Clinton has also been forced to make concessions to the U.S. military and pro-nuclear lobby to win their reluctant support for U.S. entry into the treaty. These "safeguards" include $40 billion over the next decade for an enormous "stockpile stewardship" program that would give the nation's nuclear weapons labs a continued role in arms research. The program will allow the labs to retain the capability to resume nuclear tests in case the U.S. decides to pull out of the test ban.

The program has provoked doubts about the U.S.'s commitment to stop the design and development of new nuclear weapons. While the majority of negotiating nations see the program as a necessary trade-off to win a test ban, India and Pakistan continue to voice opposition at the talks. "The president bought domestic peace on the test ban issue, but the Stockpile Stewardship program may cause other nations to hedge their bets," says Paine. "We've made compromises that may come back to haunt us."

Some disarmament advocates say that the test ban—now 40 years late—falls far short of its original purpose: to prevent the development and modernization of nuclear weapons, and to foster rapid nuclear disarmament. "The test ban doesn't alter the reliance on nuclear weapons as the ultimate big stick and doesn't alter U.S. plans to maintain its huge nuclear arsenal indefinitely into the future," says Jackie Cabasso, executive director of Western States Legal Foundation, a Bay Area antinuclear group.

Nonetheless, securing a test ban is critical because it would provide evidence that the superpowers are taking steps toward disarmament, a legal obligation of the Non-Proliferation Treaty, a pact signed by 178 nations to limit the spread of nuclear weapons and technology. Failure to secure a test ban now—as the nuclear states promised in order to win approval from the non-nuclear states for the indefinite renewal of the non-proliferation treaty last May—could poison future talks between the negotiating nations.

Other advocates believe that the treaty could be a springboard for further disarmament measures, including the ratification of Start II in Russia, a ban on chemical weapons and on the production of fissile materials. Clinton, they say, should seize the moment. "The U.S. does not have a plan 25 right now for disarmament beyond the test ban," says Hall of Greenpeace. "Clinton should strongly advocate the need to get to a world without nuclear weapons and lay out the next steps," such as a willingness to negotiate a Start III agreement with Russia.

Creating a nuclear-free world requires that countries participating in nuclear treaty negotiations see beyond their own political agendas. "It's a balance of obligations," says NRDC's Paine. "The question is whether countries can rise above their own stereotypical, parochial behavior. In a world of uncontrolled nuclear proliferation, all countries are at risk, all countries are vulnerable, whether they have nuclear weapons or not. At the end of the day, we will sink or swim together."

UPDATE ON LA WEEKLY'S "BOMB BAN ON THE BRINK"

Loren Stein

On June 28, 1996, exhausted diplomats went home empty-handed, without having achieved a comprehensive test ban treaty. The breakdown in negotiations centered on India's adamant refusal to sign onto the treaty as well as the nuclear weapons states' unwillingness to allow a test ban to go forward without India's signature, one of the three nuclear "threshold" states. Holding out against enormous world pressure, India would not come into the tent primarily due to concern over its national security and the desire to keep its nuclear options open. India also continued to insist that the nuclear superpowers agree to take concrete steps towards the elimination of all nuclear weapons, and charged those states with hypocrisy for the ongoing maintenance of its nuclear arsenal. "I would like to declare on the floor of this august assembly that India will never sign this unequal treaty—not now, not later," said India's chief negotiator Arundhati Ghose.

On August 20, 1996, India formally vetoed the proposed treaty, derailing more than two years of negotiations. But in a last-minute diplomatic rescue, a coalition of 126 countries—led by Australia, a respected leader in the disarmament movement—circumvented India's veto by taking the unusual step of removing the treaty from the U.N. Conference on Disarmament, which must pass the treaty unanimously. Instead, they brought the treaty directly to the 185-member U.N. General Assembly as a resolution, where the test ban could pass by majority vote. On September 10, 1996, the outgoing General Assembly endorsed the treaty by an overwhelming majority, allowing the test ban to survive despite India's opposition. (158 countries voted for the treaty, and three voted against—India, Bhutan and Libya. Cuba, Lebanon, Syria, Tanzania and Mauritius abstained. The remaining 19 countries were absent or barred from voting because they hadn't paid U.N. assessments.)

The treaty was then signed by 60 world leaders—including U.S. President Bill Clinton—at a historic U.N. ceremony on September 24, 1996. But to become international law, the treaty must be signed and ratified (passed by each country's national legislatures) by all 44 nations that have nuclear research or nuclear power reactors—a list that includes India. The hope is that world momentum for the test ban will force India to relent and agree to the treaty. If the 44 countries do not ratify the treaty within three years, a review conference will be held to try to speed up the process, and perhaps reopen discussion on whether all of the countries must sign. Any nation in the world can now sign the test ban treaty. Without assent by India, however, the treaty will not be legally binding, unless it is changed. Meanwhile, nations that sign the treaty are expected to abide by its provisions.

SUGGESTIONS FOR FURTHER STUDY

Key Words

The author uses language with which you may not be familiar. Find the following words in the paragraphs indicated, and explain their meanings in the context of the sentences in which the words appear. Consult a dictionary, as needed.

> moratorium (par. 6)
> geopolitical (par. 7)
> multilateral (par. 9)
> proliferation (par. 10)
> articulating (par. 15)
> disarmament (par. 15)
> unambiguous (par. 20)
> stewardship (par. 21)
> parochial (par. 26)

Topics for Discussion and Writing

1. Under conditions of the Comprehensive Test Ban Treaty, what have the United States, Russia, France, China, and Britain agreed to do?

2. How did France's nuclear tests in the South Pacific and China's tests in northwestern China affect the test-ban talks (par. 6)? Why did the international community react in such a way?

3. Using information in the essay, explain the "more open approach" that China, India, and Pakistan are taking "in their resistance to the test ban."

4. What is the United States' role in the talks? Who is largely responsible for our new role? What concessions has President Clinton been

forced to make to win "support for U.S. entry into the treaty"? What will it take for the "countries participating in nuclear free negotiations" to create "a nuclear free world"? Discuss your answers to these questions with other readers.

5. In Stein's article and its update on the passage of the treaty by the UN General Assembly, she describes India's position on the treaty. What merit, if any, do you see in India's demands? Discuss with other readers whether it is reasonable for other nuclear powers to demand that India sign the treaty.

6. Write a journal entry or a short essay discussing the difference between *arms control* and *disarmament*. Speculate about whether disarmament can be achieved, or describe the conditions that could result in disarmament in all nations.

7. Using your knowledge of current history gained through course-work or through familiarity with current periodicals and television newscasts, write an essay in which you take a position on the following question: Has any nation's possession of nuclear weapons either prevented war or, at times, brought us closer to war? You may want to examine any presumed benefits of a nation's possession of nuclear weapons or technology and to weigh those against the environmental, political, or economic costs of such weapons. You can limit your discussion to the interests of the United States, or include other nations that possess nuclear capability.

There Will Come Soft Rains

Ray Bradbury

Ray Bradbury has published some twenty-five books—novels, stories, plays, and poems—since his first story appeared in Rob Wagner's Script *when he was 20 years old. His most well-known works include* The Martian Chronicles, Fahrenheit 451 *(made into a film by François Truffaut in 1967),* The Illustrated Man *(made into film in 1969),* Something Wicked This Way Comes *(made into film in 1983), and* Dandelion Wine. *"There Will Come Soft Rains" is from Bradbury's 1996 collection of short stories,* The Stories of Ray Bradbury.

In the living room the voice-clock sang, *Tick-tock, seven o'clock, time to get up, time to get up, seven o'clock!* as if it were afraid that nobody would. The morning house lay empty. The clock ticked on, repeating and repeating its sounds into the emptiness. *Seven-nine, breakfast time, seven-nine!*

In the kitchen the breakfast stove gave a hissing sigh and ejected from its warm interior eight pieces of perfectly browned toast, eight eggs sunny-side up, sixteen slices of bacon, two coffees, and two cool glasses of milk.

"Today is August 4, 2026," said a second voice from the kitchen ceiling, "in the city of Allendale, California." It repeated the date three times for memory's sake. "Today is Mr. Featherstone's birthday. Today is the anniversary of Tilita's marriage. Insurance is payable, as are the water, gas, and light bills."

Somewhere in the walls, relays clicked, memory tapes glided under electric eyes.

Eight-one, tick-tock, eight-one o'clock, off to school, off to work, run, run, eight-one! But no doors slammed, no carpets took the soft tread of rubber heels. It was raining outside. The weather box on the front door sang quietly: "Rain, rain, go away; rubbers, raincoats for today . . ." And the rain tapped on the empty house, echoing.

Outside, the garage chimed and lifted its door to reveal the waiting car. After a long wait the door swung down again.

At eight-thirty the eggs were shriveled and the toast was like stone. An aluminum wedge scraped them into the sink where hot water whirled them down a metal throat which digested and flushed them away to the distant sea. The dirty dishes were dropped into a hot washer and emerged twinkling dry.

Nine-fifteen, sang the clock, *time to clean.*

Out of warrens in the wall, tiny robot mice darted. The rooms were acrawl with the small cleaning animals, all rubber and metal. They thudded against chairs, whirling their mustached runners, kneading the rug nap, sucking gently at hidden dust. Then, like mysterious invaders, they popped into their burrows. Their pink electric eyes faded. The house was clean.

Ten o'clock. The sun came out from behind the rain. The house stood alone in a city of rubble and ashes. This was the one house left standing. At night the ruined city gave off a radioactive glow which could be seen for miles. 10

Ten-fifteen. The garden sprinklers whirled up in golden founts, filling the soft morning air with scatterings of brightness. The water pelted windowpanes, running down the charred west side where the house had been burned evenly free of its white paint. The entire west face of the house was black, save for five places. Here the silhouette in paint of a man mowing a lawn. Here, as in a photograph, a woman bent to pick flowers. Still farther over, their images burned on wood in one titanic instant, a small boy, hands flung into the air; higher up, the image of a thrown ball, and opposite him a girl, hands raised to catch a ball which never came down.

The five spots of paint—the man, the woman, the children, the ball—remained. The rest was a thin charcoaled layer.

The gentle sprinkler rain filled the garden with falling light.

Until this day, how well the house had kept its peace. How carefully it had inquired, "Who goes there? What's the password?" and, getting no answer from lonely foxes and whining cats, it had shut up its windows and drawn shades in an old-maidenly preoccupation with self-protection which bordered on a mechanical paranoia.

It quivered at each sound, the house did. If a sparrow brushed a window, the shade snapped up. The bird, startled, flew off! No, not even a bird must touch the house! 15

The house was an altar with ten thousand attendants, big, small, servicing, attending, in choirs. But the gods had gone away, and the ritual of the religion continued senselessly, uselessly.

Twelve noon.

A dog whined, shivering, on the front porch.

The front door recognized the dog voice and opened. The dog, once huge and fleshy, but now gone to bone and covered with sores, moved in and through the house, tracking mud. Behind it whirred angry mice, angry at having to pick up mud, angry at inconvenience.

For not a leaf fragment blew under the door but what the wall panels flipped open and the copper scrap rats flashed swiftly out. The offending dust, hair, or paper, seized in miniature steel jaws, was raced back to the burrows. There, down tubes which fed into the cellar, it was dropped into the sighing vent of an incinerator which sat like evil Baal in a dark corner. 20

The dog ran upstairs, hysterically yelping to each door, at last realizing, as the house realized, that only silence was here.

It sniffed the air and scratched the kitchen door. Behind the door, the stove was making pancakes which filled the house with a rich baked odor and the scent of maple syrup.

The dog frothed at the mouth, lying at the door, sniffing, its eyes turned to fire. It ran wildly in circles, biting at its tail, spun in a frenzy, and died. It lay in the parlor for an hour.

Two o'clock, sang a voice.

Delicately sensing decay at last, the regiments of mice hummed out as   25
softly as blown gray leaves in an electrical wind.

Two-fifteen.

The dog was gone.

In the cellar, the incinerator glowed suddenly and a whirl of sparks leaped up the chimney.

Two thirty-five.

Bridge tables sprouted from patio walls. Playing cards fluttered onto   30
pads in a shower of pips. Martinis manifested on an oaken bench with egg-salad sandwiches. Music played.

But the tables were silent and the cards untouched.

At four o'clock the tables folded like great butterflies back through the paneled walls.

Four-thirty.

The nursery walls glowed.

Animals took shape: yellow giraffes, blue lions, pink antelopes, lilac   35
panthers cavorting in crystal substance. The walls were glass. They looked out upon color and fantasy. Hidden films clocked through well-oiled sprockets, and the walls lived. The nursery floor was woven to resemble a crisp, cereal meadow. Over this ran aluminum roaches and iron crickets, and in the hot still air butterflies of delicate red tissue wavered among the sharp aromas of animal spoors! There was the sound like a great matted yellow hive of bees within a dark bellows, the lazy bumble of a purring lion. And there was the patter of okapi feet and the murmur of a fresh jungle rain, like other hoofs, falling upon the summer-starched grass. Now the walls dissolved into distances of parched weed, mile on mile, and warm endless sky. The animals drew away into thorn brakes and water holes.

It was the children's hour.

Five o'clock. The bath filled with clear hot water.

Six, seven, eight o'clock. The dinner dishes manipulated like magic tricks, and in the study a *click.* In the metal stand opposite the hearth where a fire now blazed up warmly, a cigar popped out, half an inch of soft gray ash on it, smoking, waiting.

Nine o'clock. The beds warmed their hidden circuits, for nights were cool here.

Nine-five. A voice spoke from the study ceiling: 40
"Mrs. McClellan, which poem would you like this evening?"
The house was silent.

The voice said at last, "Since you express no preference, I shall select a poem at random." Quiet music rose to back the voice. "Sara Teasdale. As I recall, your favorite. . . .

There will come soft rains and the smell of the ground,
And swallows circling with their shimmering sound;

And frogs in the pools singing at night,
And wild plum trees in tremulous white;

Robins will wear their feathery fire,
Whistling their whims on a low fence-wire;

And not one will know of the war, not one
Will care at last when it is done.

Not one would mind, neither bird nor tree,
If mankind perished utterly;

And Spring herself, when she woke at dawn
Would scarcely know that we were gone.

The fire burned on the stone hearth and the cigar fell away into a mound of quiet ash on its tray. The empty chairs faced each other between the silent walls, and the music played.

At ten o'clock the house began to die.   45

The wind blew. A falling tree bough crashed through the kitchen window. Cleaning solvent, bottled, shattered over the stove. The room was ablaze in an instant!

"Fire!" screamed a voice. The house lights flashed, water pumps shot water from the ceilings. But the solvent spread on the linoleum, licking, eating, under the kitchen door, while the voices took it up in chorus: "Fire, fire, fire!"

The house tried to save itself. Doors sprang tightly shut, but the windows were broken by the heat and the wind blew and sucked upon the fire.

The house gave ground as the fire in ten billion angry sparks moved with flaming ease from room to room and then up the stairs. While scurrying water rats squeaked from the walls, pistoled their water, and ran for more. And the wall sprays let down showers of mechanical rain.

But too late. Somewhere, sighing, a pump shrugged to a stop. The   50
quenching rain ceased. The reserve water supply which had filled baths and washed dishes for many quiet days was gone.

The fire crackled up the stairs. It fed upon Picassos and Matisses in the upper halls, like delicacies, baking off the oily flesh, tenderly crisping the canvases into black shavings.

Now the fire lay in beds, stood in windows, changed the colors of drapes!

And then, reinforcements.

From attic trapdoors, blind robot faces peered down with faucet mouths gushing green chemical.

The fire backed off, as even an elephant must at the sight of a dead 55 snake. Now there were twenty snakes whipping over the floor, killing the fire with a clear cold venom of green froth.

But the fire was clever. It had sent flame outside the house, up through the attic to the pumps there. An explosion! The attic brain which directed the pumps was shattered into bronze shrapnel on the beams.

The fire rushed back into every closet and felt of the clothes hung there.

The house shuddered, oak bone on bone, its bared skeleton cringing from the heat, its wire, its nerves revealed as if a surgeon had torn the skin off to let the red veins and capillaries quiver in the scalded air. Help, help! Fire! Run, run! Heat snapped mirrors like the first brittle winter ice. And the voices wailed, Fire, fire, run, run, like a tragic nursery rhyme, a dozen voices, high, low, like children dying in a forest, alone, alone. And the voices fading as the wires popped their sheathings like hot chestnuts. One, two, three, four, five voices died.

In the nursery the jungle burned. Blue lions roared, purple giraffes bounded off. The panthers ran in circles, changing color, and ten million animals, running before the fire, vanished off toward a distant steaming river. . . .

Ten more voices died. In the last instant under the fire avalanche, other 60 choruses, oblivious, could be heard announcing the time, playing music, cutting the lawn by remote-control mower, or setting an umbrella frantically out and in, the slamming and opening front door, a thousand things happening, like a clock shop when each clock strikes the hour insanely before or after the other, a scene of maniac confusion, yet unity; singing, screaming, a few last cleaning mice darting bravely out to carry the horrid ashes away! And one voice, with sublime disregard for the situation, read poetry aloud in the fiery study, until all the film spools burned, until all the wires withered and the circuits cracked.

The fire burst the house and let it slam flat down, puffing out skirts of spark and smoke.

In the kitchen, an instant before the rain of fire and timber, the stove could be seen making breakfasts at a psychopathic rate, ten dozen eggs, six loaves of toast, twenty dozen bacon strips, which, eaten by fire, started the stove working again, hysterically hissing!

The crash. The attic smashing into kitchen and parlor. The parlor into cellar, cellar into sub-cellar. Deep freeze, armchair, film tapes, circuits, beds, and all like skeletons thrown in a cluttered mound deep under.

Smoke and silence. A great quantity of smoke.

Dawn showed faintly in the east. Among the ruins, one wall stood alone. Within the wall, a last voice said, over and over again and again, even as the sun rose to shine upon the heaped rubble and steam:

"Today is August 5, 2026, today is August 5, 2026, today is . . ."

SUGGESTIONS FOR FURTHER STUDY

Language and Style

1. How does Bradbury's picture of a postnuclear wasteland convey the tragedy and horror of his story? Make a list of the descriptive words and phrases that help readers see and feel the human devastation and horror in the landscape.

2. How does Bradbury's brief description of the family's remains affect you? Do you think it is as effective as a more gruesomely detailed description of a bloodier death might be? Explain your answer.

Topics for Discussion and Writing

1. In many ways, Bradbury was ahead of his time in describing the fully automated, self-sustaining cyberhouse of the future. List and describe these features of the house. How well do they compare with today's descriptions of the computerized, automated home environment already available?

2. What is ironic about the house still functioning perfectly even after "the dust has settled"?

3. Write a fictional story describing the aftermath of a nuclear holocaust. You might describe a wasteland, as Bradbury does, or you might show the struggles of a community of people trying to survive, as many after-the-bomb science-fiction stories do. Be specific and detailed in your descriptions of the landscape, the people in it, and their situation.

or

Write a story about heroic efforts by a group of people to stop a nuclear holocaust from occurring. You may already be familiar with some suitable resources; in addition, the following films and books can provide ideas to help you get started: *Bladerunner, Road Warrior, The Planet of the Apes, THX 1138, Dr. Stangelove, Do Androids Dream of Electric Sheep?, A Canticle for Leibowitz, Brave New World, Necromancer, The Martian Chronicles, A Boy and His Dog.*

How to Poison Earth

Linnea Saukko

Student writer Linnea Saukko satirically addresses the willful polluting of Earth by corporations and governments. In the tradition of all good satires, Saukko exposes the inherent folly in polluting our planet without concern for the environment and for future generations of life on Earth.

It can be difficult to poison Earth because Earth is always trying to cleanse and renew itself. Keeping this in mind, we should generate as much waste as possible from substances such as uranium-238, which has a *half-life* (the time it takes for half of the substance to decay) of 1 million years, or plutonium, which has a half-life of only 0.5 million years but is so toxic that if distributed evenly over the land, 10 pounds of it could kill every person on Earth. Because the United States generates about 18 tons of plutonium per year, it is about the best substance for long-term poisoning of Earth. It would help if we would build more nuclear power plants because each one generates only 500 pounds of plutonium each year. Of course, we must include persistent toxic chemicals such as polychlorinated biphenyl (PCB) and dichlorodiphenyl trichloroethane (DDT) to make sure we have enough toxins to poison Earth from the core to the outer atmosphere. First, we must develop many different ways of putting the waste from these nuclear and chemical substances in, on, and around Earth.

Putting these substances in Earth is a most important step in the poisoning process. With deep-well injection, we can ensure that Earth is poisoned all the way to the core. Deep-well injection involves drilling a hole . . . a few thousand feet deep and injecting toxic substances at extremely high pressures so they will penetrate deep into Earth. According to the Environmental Protection Agency (EPA), there are about 360 such deep-injection wells in the United States. We cannot forget the groundwater aquifers that are closer to the surface. These must also be contaminated. This is easily done by shallow-well injection, which operates on the same principle as deep-well injection, only closer to the surface. The groundwater that has been injected with toxins will spread the contamination beneath Earth. The EPA estimates that there are approximately 500,000 shallow-injection wells in the United States.

The next best method is to bury toxins in Earth. The toxins from land-fills, dumps, and lagoons slowly seep into Earth, guaranteeing that contamination will last a long time. Because the EPA estimates [that] there are only about 50,000 of these dumps in the United States, they should be located in areas where they will leak to the surrounding ground and surface water.

Applying pesticides and other poisons on Earth is another part of the poisoning process. This is good for coating Earth's surface so that the poisons will be absorbed by plants, will seep into the ground, and will run off into surface water.

Surface water is very important to contaminate because it will transport the poisons to places that cannot be contaminated directly. Lakes are good for long-term storage of pollutants while they release some of their contamination to rivers. The only trouble with rivers is that they act as a natural cleansing system for Earth. No matter how much poison is dumped into them, they will try to transport it away to reach the ocean eventually.

The ocean is very hard to contaminate because it has such a large volume and a natural buffering capacity that tends to neutralize some of the contamination. So in addition to the pollution from rivers, we must use the ocean as a dumping place for as many toxins as possible. The ocean currents will help transport the pollution to places that cannot otherwise be reached.

Now make sure that the air around Earth is very polluted. Combustion and evaporation are major mechanisms for doing this. We must continuously pollute because the wind will disperse the toxins while rain washes them from the air, but this is good because a few lakes are stripped of all living animals each year from acid rain. Because the lower atmosphere can cleanse itself fairly easily, we must explode nuclear test bombs that shoot radioactive particles high into the upper atmosphere where they will circle Earth for years. Gravity must pull some of the particles to Earth, so we must continue exploding these bombs.

So it is that easy. Just be sure to generate as many poisonous substances as possible, and be sure they are distributed in, on, and around Earth at a greater rate than it can cleanse itself. By following these easy steps, we can guarantee the poisoning of Earth.

CHAPTER 10: ACTIVITIES FOR DISCUSSION AND WRITING
Making Connections

1. Write a letter to President Clinton or to your congressperson, alerting these officials to a particular concern of yours about an environmental issue. Be specific in describing the issue. Include some potential solutions suggested either by the readings in this chapter or through your own research.

CARTOONS IN AMERICA

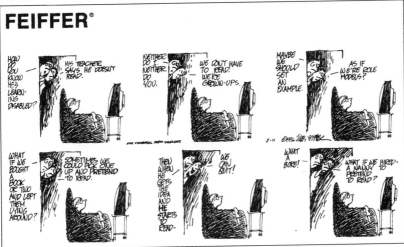

2. Investigate and write a paper on an environmental issue that concerns you. You may want to research books, scholarly journals, magazines, or newspapers in the library. Consult the computer databases in your library, if available, to assist you in locating the latest information. Use the Internet to gain access to relevant material through the World Wide Web.

3. Considering Sagan's "The Nuclear Winter," Stein's "Bomb Ban on the Brink," and Bradbury's "There Will Come Soft Rains," choose one of the following topics for developing an essay:
   a. Important steps that are occurring, which might halt the potential for a nuclear winter
   b. How Bradbury's futuristic cyberhouse might hold up through a nuclear winter: How would you design a more nuclearproof cyberhouse?
   c. A letter to the nations known as nuclear powers, detailing Sagan's scientific hypothesis about thermonuclear destruction and outlining steps they should take to prevent destruction

4. Write a satire, as student writer Linnea Saukko has, on an environmental issue. Reread "How to Poison Earth" as a representative model.

5. Discuss the connection between the readings in this chapter (e.g., "The Environmental Crisis Is Not Our Fault," "Sustainability," and "Thinking Small in a Season of Excess") and Lawrence Shames's "The More Factor" in Chapter 5 of this text. Consider how America's desire for more has affected our environment. You may want to review other essays in this text, as well.

CREDITS

569

INDEX